THE INTERNATIONAL DIRECTORY OF
MILITARY AIRCRAFT

1998/99

Gerard Frawley

CONTENTS

Published by Aerospace Publications Pty Ltd (ACN: 001 570 458) PO Box 1777, Fyshwick, ACT 2609, Australia.
Phone (02) 6280 0111 Fax (02) 6280 0007 – Publishers of monthly *Australian Aviation* magazine.
www.aviationbooks.com.au

ISBN 1 875671 32 3

Copyright © 1998 Aerospace Publications Pty Ltd
Proudly Printed in Australia by Pirie Printers Pty Ltd, 140 Gladstone St, Fyshwick, ACT 2609.
Distributed throughout Australia by Network Distribution Company, 54 Park St, Sydney, 2000. Fax (02) 9264 3278
Distribution in North America by Motorbooks International, 729 Prospect Ave, Osceola, Wisconsin, 54020, USA.
Fax (715) 294 4448. Co-produced and distributed throughout Europe and the UK by Airlife Publishing Ltd,
101 Longden Rd, Shrewsbury SY3 9EB, Shropshire, UK. Fax (743) 232944.

Front cover: (top left) The first F-22 Raptor in flight [Lockheed Martin]; (top right) the world's biggest bomber, the Tu-160 [Robert Meerding]; (bottom left) An Australian Army Black Hawk [ADF PR]; (bottom right) A New Zealand CT-4 Airtrainer [RNZAF]. Back cover: (clockwise from top left) Israeli C-130 [Paul Merritt], German F-4F Phantom [Gary Gentle], USAF B-52H [Paul Merritt], Saab Gripens [Saab], USMC AH-1W Super Cobra [Paul Sadler], Czech MiG-23 [Paul Merritt].

INTRODUCTION

Welcome to the second, thoroughly revised edition of the all colour *International Directory of Military Aircraft.*

This book aims to provide the aviation industry and aviation enthusiasts with the only regularly updated reference work on military aircraft at an affordable price. While in itself that statement does not sound shattering, what makes this book different is that it includes aircraft still in service rather than only those currently in production.

Therefore on the following pages you will find entries on such famous and long lived types as the MiG-15, Hawker Hunter, Douglas C-47, Alizé, Sioux and scores of others alongside the very latest in military aviation technology such as the F-22 Raptor, Sukhoi's S-37 technology demonstrator, Boeing's and Lockheed Martin's JSF contenders and Mitsubishi's F-2.

The International Directory of Military Aircraft is published every two years. It includes the latest aircraft types under development and updated entries on the more established types. The present pace of aircraft development does not warrant an annual publication and so biennial are a more economic and efficient answer to the problem of providing you with as much data as possible on a wide range of differing types at affordable cost. Consequently, this *Military Directory* supersedes the first edition (1996/97), and will itself be replaced by an updated edition in early 2000, and so on.

As you may be aware, this book is a companion to the successful *International Directory of Civil Aircraft*, first released early in 1995. Like the edition you hold before you, the *Civil Directory* is superseded by a new and updated edition every two years. Consequently, each year a new Directory is published, odd years Civil and even years Military. Together, these all colour volumes are to our knowledge the only source of data on just about all the aircraft of the world that are not just in production but also still in everyday use. We hope that they are of practical use to you and serve as valuable reference works in your aviation library.

To be eligible for coverage an aircraft must still be in operational service or currently under development. There are a very small number of aircraft currently in military service that are not covered in this volume – mainly civil based light aircraft, details of which can be found in the *International Directory of Civil Aircraft*. Other aircraft that are only in the initial stages of development are likely to appear in subsequent *Military Directory* editions when the designs of these aircraft firm and more information is made public.

While preparing this edition over the past two years a number of famous types, such as the Intruder, Sabre and F-4G Wild Weasel, have been retired and so sadly they no longer appear in this book.

For ease of reference aircraft are listed alphabetically by manufacturer. Where aircraft manufacturers have changed name, through mergers or acquisitions, aircraft currently in production are listed under their current manufacturer (ie Boeing F/A-18, rather than McDonnell Douglas), while aircraft out of production are listed under the manufacturer name they are most commonly known by (such as the English Electric Canberra).

Where a type has a long and distinguished history with numerous improved and much changed variants (the Hercules, Mirage and Phantom come to mind) some of the more important models have been split up into their own entries to give them fair and proper coverage. Hopefully this greatly enhances the overall value of this publication and makes referencing data on specific types much easier.

The format of the book is largely self explanatory and hopefully user friendly (an asterix in the operators column and in the World Air Power Guide indicates aircraft on order or currently being delivered).

Both metric and imperial measures are used. While much of the world has now adopted metric as its official system of measure, aviation continues to record its figures in knots, nautical miles and feet.

Finally thanks to those individuals and organisations (including manufacturers, embassies and defence department public relations sections) which have helped in the compilation of this book, whether through providing facts and figures or suggestions and encouragement. In particular thanks to Jim Thorn, Maria Davey, Ian Hewitt and Stewart Wilson of Aerospace Publications, Brian Pickering of Military Aircraft Photographs, and Paul Merritt, plus Al, Brad, Chris and Justin.

Gerard Frawley
Canberra, January 1998.

MILITARY AVIATION IN REVIEW

The rate of change in military aviation hasn't slowed down at all.

The last two years have witnessed corporate marriages, significant first flights and program milestones achieved, project delays and the inevitable continuing funding cuts with planned buys reduced and existing air arm fleets rationalised.

Preparing this second edition of the *International Directory of Military Aircraft* confirmed, if any confirmation was needed, that in today's post Cold War environment almost no military aircraft development/production programs can escape the evils of escalating costs, delayed schedules and reduced production runs, due not so much to technical development problems but the growing cost of developing high tech warplanes and reducing or static at best military spending budgets.

For example during 1997 the US Government completed another Quadrennial Defense Review which saw planned F-22 Raptor and F/A-18E Super Hornet buys reduced. At late 1997 the planned F-22A requirement stood at 339, about half the projected buy when the Advanced Tactical Fighter program was born in the 1980s. The USAF does however plan to boost F-22 production by buying up to 250 of a strike variant to replace the F-15E and F-117.

An earlier development with the F-22 program was the cancellation of the F-22B two seat operational conversion trainer in 1996 as an economy measure, making it the first significant USAF jet fighter since the F-86 Sabre not to be built in two seat trainer form, although with modern training aids and simulators prospective Raptor pilots would have little to fear when they fly the aircraft for the first time.

After some minor glitches the Raptor made its first flight in September 1997. An initial operating capability is planned for 2004.

The F/A-18E planned buy was reduced even further from 1000 to between 550 and 758. This aeroplane is very important to the USN as it will replace early F/A-18A/Cs and F-14s and the retired A-6 Intruder's long range strike capability but with three major tactical fighter programs now

being funded in the USA (F-22, JSF and F/A-18E) one of them had to give. However in contrast to other tactical fighter programs, development of the Super Hornet has been running smoothly and to schedule.

The JSF – Joint Strike Fighter – program has come some way since it was discussed in these pages in the inaugural *Military Directory* two years ago. JSF is on track to become the world's largest military development/production project, with an estimated price tag for development and production of \$US165bn. Initial buys for the US Air Force, Navy and Marines respectively are 2036, 642 and 300, while the UK's Royal Navy wants 60 to replace Sea Harriers.

The stealthy, multirole JSF will be unique in that it will be built in conventional land based, carrier capable and short takeoff and vertical landing (STOVL) variants and will form the core of the three services' tactical fighter fleets, replacing F-16s, F/A-18A/Cs and AV-8Bs, complementing USAF F-22s and USN F/A-18Es. In the past the separate US military services have developed and bought their own aircraft, with the only exceptions arising not through design but almost chance. (The most notable example is the USAF's adoption of the McDonnell F4H Phantom, an aircraft initially developed as a carrier based fleet air defence interceptor for the USN but adopted widely by the USAF for a variety of roles. Incidentally, the legendary Phantom celebrates the 40th anniversary of its first flight during the life of this edition.)

The last significant program to develop a common military aircraft for the USN and USAF was the TFX program which resulted in the F-111. After some initial teething problems the F-111 proved a very potent long range all weather fighter-bomber in USAF and Australian service (Australia intends to keep its updated F-111Cs and F-111Gs in service through to 2020 – remarkable for a fast jet which first flew in 1964). However the F-111B, the US Navy's interceptor version intended to replace F-4s, was too big and too heavy and doomed to failure.

So there is a lot at stake with the JSF program. Boeing and Lockheed Martin were both selected (ahead of McDonnell Douglas) to build two JSF evaluation aircraft each of their respective JSF designs to fly in 2000, and the prospect of building a minimum of 3000 fighters will no doubt sharpen their senses and motivate the two companies to ensure the concept can work. (Interestingly Boeing and General Dynamics Fort Worth, now Lockheed Martin Tactical Aircraft Systems, were the two finalists in the TFX program, with GD triumphant.)

That 3000 build figure too doesn't take into account potential export sales with just about every current F-16 and F/A-18 operator (more than two dozen nations) a potential future JSF customer. This could take the final total built out to 4000 or even 5000 (and rival the F-4's total).

Interestingly too, second generation JSFs could be built unmanned. The US military is now seriously studying unmanned combat aircraft for service some time next century, initially for high risk missions such as SEAD.

There are some doubts about the JSF program, with its high price tag making it an obvious target for defence budget cost cutters and questions about whether Boeing and Lockheed Martin can build the aircraft to the low unit costs demanded, but the US Air Force and Marines in

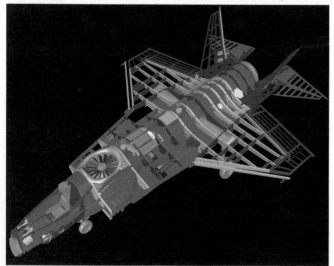

A computer generated modelling image of Lockheed Martin's Joint Strike Fighter contender, the X-35. This image shows to good effect the lift fan configuration of LM's STOVL variant. (Lockheed Martin)

Hopefully Europe's next major combat aircraft programs will not result in unneccessary duplication such as the concurrent development of the Eurofighter and Rafale (pictured). There's not enough difference in their intended roles to justify separate development of the two fighters in the new united Europe. Here the first naval configured Rafale is pictured over the French aircraft carrier Foch. (Francois Robineau, Dassault/Aviaplans)

particular are committed to the program's survival. Initial operating capability with the USAF is planned for 2007.

Across the Atlantic, Europe's biggest defence program, Eurofighter, looks to have seen off the biggest threats to its existence, with the governments of all four partner nations (UK, Germany, Italy and Spain) now having agreed in principle to the production phase of the program. The biggest hurdle the program had to jump was German parliamentary approval, which came through in late 1997, clearing the way for the four nations to sign firm production contracts.

The four Eurofighter partners signed a Memorandum of Understanding covering the full production go-ahead of the aircraft in late December 1997. Service entry won't be until 2003, around a decade later than first deliveries were originally planned when the concept was first conceived.

Another multinational European military aircraft program that has been heading down the same protracted development path is the FLA (Future Large Airlifter). However if the partner nations sign up and hand over money for development and let the Airbus Military Company get on with the job of designing and building the new transport, there is no reason why this relatively straightforward project can't progress smoothly and be developed on time and within budget.

Further east in Russia most major military aircraft programs have stalled, been cancelled or delayed due to funding shortfalls. The highest profile casualty of recent times has been MiG MAPO's 1.42, an F-22 rival designed to replace the Su-27, Russia's current premier air defence fighter. The 1.42 is understood to have undergone taxi tests but never flown, not because of technical issues but due to a lack of money. Another recent MiG MAPO casualty was the Russian air force's planned buy of improved multirole MiG-29M fighters.

Rival designer Sukhoi seems to have been travelling better in comparison, with some big export sales of its Su-27 'Flanker' series of aircraft – notably to India and China, but also Indonesia and Vietnam. Proceeds from these sales have also allowed Sukhoi to develop its S-37 technology demonstrator, which flew for the first time in September 1997. The S-37 is intended primarily to test the benefits of

forward swept wings but could also form the basis of a new generation fighter for the Russian air force.

Sukhoi has also been working hard on various developments of the very capable Flanker series, including the two seat side by side Su-34 strike fighter (designed to replace the Su-24 'Fencer') and the very impressive thrust vectored, canard and phased array radar equipped Su-37, which may also end up in Russian military service. This aircraft, like just about everything else in Russia, is being offered widely for export, and would prove more than a handful in combat against current western fighters.

In these pages in the inaugural *International Directory of Military Aircraft* we noted the opening rounds of the rationalisation of the aerospace industry, stating "foremost of the US consolidation has been the merger of Lockheed and Martin Marietta..." creating Lockheed Martin. Even this marriage of giants however has been overshadowed by the marriage of Boeing and McDonnell Douglas, which was consummated in August 1997 (on top of Boeing's December '96 acquisition of Rockwell's aircraft division, creating Boeing North American).

The new Boeing has over 200,000 employees and is now the undisputed largest aerospace company in the world, with an amazing corporate heritage (the P-51 Mustang, B-25 Mitchell, F-86 Sabre, A-5 Vigilante, C-47 Skytrain/ Dakota, A-4 Skyhawk, F-101 Voodoo, F-4 Phantom, B-17, B-29, B-47, B-52, KC-135 are all products of Boeing and its predecessors).

Also during 1997 Lockheed Martin and Northrop Grumman announced their intention to merge too, pending regulatory and shareholder approval. The new combine's current aircraft stable will range from the B-2 Spirit to the E-2C Hawkeye, E-8 Joint STARS, F-16, F-22 Raptor, C-130J Hercules and P-3 Orion. But just as important to the combined company will be its defence electronics, information systems, missiles, commercial aerostructures and space work.

In Europe the pace of change has been significantly slower. While there has been general agreement that Europe's aerospace industry needs to rationalise, there has been little action yet and moves to consolidate have been frustrated, most notably by France. Whereas the US is set to head into the next century with just two aerospace giants, Europe's inability to consolidate will leave it with several national based aerospace companies at a distinct long term competitive disadvantage. ✈

Boeing is no stranger to military transport production but the C-17 Globemaster has only been part of its stable since August 1997 when McDonnell Douglas was merged into Boeing. (Boeing)

ADA Light Combat Aircraft

Country of origin: India

Type: Light multirole fighter

Powerplant: Prototypes – One 80.5kN (18,100lb) with afterburning General Electric F404-GE-FJ23 turbofan. Production aircraft – One 83.4kN (18,740lb) with afterburning GTRE Kaveri turbofan.

Performance: Few details released other than an estimated top speed of Mach 1.8 at altitude and a service ceiling of over 50,000ft.

Weights: Empty approx 5500kg (12,125lb), clean takeoff approx 8500kg (18,740lb), max takeoff approx 12,500kg (27,530lb).

Dimensions: Wing span 8.20m (26ft 11in), length overall 13.20m (43ft 4in), height overall 4.40m (14ft 5in). Wing area approx 38.4m² (413sq ft).

Accommodation: Pilot only, but two seat conversion trainer planned.

Armament: One 23mm twin barrel GSh-23 gun. Six underwing and one centreline external stores stations will carry a variety of weaponry, ranging from conventional bombs and rockets to laser guided bombs, air-to-air and air-to-surface missiles

Operators: India requires up to 200 to replace MiG-21s, but none yet on firm order.

History: India's most ambitious aircraft program will result in a capable lightweight multirole fighter in the weight class of Saab's Gripen which will replace the Indian Air Force's substantial fleet of MiG-21s.

The Light Combat Aircraft, or LCA, is being developed by India's Aeronautical Development Agency (ADA) based in Bangalore. Development work on the new fighter has been underway since 1983 when Indian Government approval was given for the new project. The basic design of the LCA was finalised in 1990 and HAL (Hindustan Aeronautics Ltd) began construction of the first prototype in mid 1991.

This first prototype, TD1, was publicly rolled out on November 17 1995, about nine months behind schedule. TD1's first flight was planned for June 1996, but this event has been delayed several times and at late 1997 first flight was expected sometime during 1998. Although the LCA's maiden flight has been delayed, an initial operational capability (IOC) with the Indian Air Force is planned for 2002. The IAF requires around 200 to replace MiG-21s and possibly other similar types.

The LCA features a tailless delta configuration. The design includes extensive use of composite materials in its construction, including the wing and vertical tail, and has a fixed external refuelling probe. The cockpit features a HUD, HOTAS controls and two colour LCD multifunction displays, with all avionics built on dual MIL STD 1553B databuses. The radar will be a multimode unit with track while scan and ground mapping.

Perhaps the LCA's most important feature is its Kaveri engine. Except for the first two prototypes, all LCAs will be powered by the Indian developed engine. The Kaveria will be in the same size and thrust class as the GE F404 (which will power the first two prototypes) and is under development with India's Gas Turbine Research Establishment. The engine is being designed specifically to operate in India's hot weather and high altitude conditions.

An advanced development, the Medium Combat Aircraft, is being studied as a replacement for Indian Jaguars and Mirage 2000s.

Photo: The first prototype LCA, rolled out in November 1995.

Aermacchi MB-326

Country of origin: Italy

Type: Two seat basic and advanced trainer

Powerplant: MB-326G – One 15.3kN (3410lb) Rolls-Royce Viper 11 turbojet.

Performance: MB-326G – Max speed 867km/h (468kt), max cruising speed 797km/h (430kt). Max initial rate of climb 6050ft/min. Service ceiling 47,000ft. Range with internal and tip tanks 1850km (1000nm), range with underwing tanks 2445km (1320nm). Combat radius (hi-lo-hi) with 770kg (1695lb) payload 650km (350nm).

Weights: MB-326G – Basic operating empty 2685kg (6920lb), max takeoff clean 4577kg (10,090lb), max takeoff armed 5215kg (11,500lb).

Dimensions: Wing span over tip tanks 10.85m (35ft 7in), length 10.67m (35ft 0in), height 3.72m (12ft 3in). Wing area 19.4m² (208.3sq ft).

Accommodation: Seating for two in tandem.

Armament: MB-326G – Provision for up to 1815kg (4000lb) of armaments, including bombs, rockets and gun pods on six underwing pylons.

Operators: Argentina, Australia, Brazil, Ghana, Italy, Paraguay, South Africa, Togo, Tunisia, UAE (Dubai), Zaire, Zambia.

History: Macchi initiated design of this classic two seat jet trainer in 1954 against an Italian air force requirement.

The 326 was designed by Dr-Ing Ermano Bazzochi (responsible for the B in the MB prefix) and a prototype flew for the first time on December 10 1957. The prototype MB-326 was powered by a 7.8kN (1750lb) thrust Bristol-Siddeley (later Rolls-Royce) Viper 8 turbojet and the aircraft featured the same basic configuration of almost every two seat jet trainer to follow it, with a low, straight wing, a single jet engine and tandem seating, with benign handling characteristics.

Flight testing of the prototype revealed an aircraft that was highly suited to its intended role, displaying viceless flying characteristics and spritely performance. The aircraft impressed the Italian air force which ordered the type into production, with the first examples arriving on strength in 1962.

The Italian air force took delivery of 100 basic, 11.1kN (2500lb) Viper 11 powered MB-326s (including 15 preproduction aircraft), and was offered, but did not order, the armed MB-326A with six underwing hardpoints. Similar armed versions were built for other nations however, including Ghana (MB-326F) and Tunisia (MB-326B), while the Italian airline Alitalia took delivery of four unarmed MB-326Ds. Significant orders for the basic Viper 11 model meanwhile came from South Africa and Australia, the former taking delivery of 191, most of which were assembled locally by Atlas as Impala Mk 1s; the latter 97 MB-326Hs, the majority of which were built locally by CAC.

The successful MB-326G was a more powerful and strengthened development with improved weapons payload. Powered by a 15.2kN (3140lb) Viper 20 Mk.540 engine, examples were delivered to Argentina, Zaire and Zambia, while six similar but Viper 11 powered MB-326Es were delivered to Italy. Embraer licence built MB-326G versions as Xavantes. These were delivered to Brazil, Paraguay and Togo.

The final two seater was the MB-326L, which included features introduced on the single seat MB-326K (described separately). Total MB-326 production was 761.

Photo: Australia's MB-326Hs are used for lead-in fighter training.

Aermacchi MB-326K

Country of origin: Italy

Type: Single seat light attack aircraft

Powerplant: One 17.9kN (4000lb) Rolls-Royce Viper Mk 632-43 turbojet.

Performance: Max speed at 5000ft 890km/h (480kt), max speed with armament at 30,000ft 685km/h (370kt). Max initial rate of climb 6500ft/min. Time to 36,000ft 9min 30sec. Service ceiling 47,000ft. Ferry range with external fuel over 2130km (1150nm). Combat radius with 1280kg (2822lb) warload lo-lo-lo 268km (145nm), with a 1815kg (4000lb) payload on a lo-lo-lo mission 130km (70nm), radius on a hi-lo-hi photo reconnaissance mission with two external tanks and recce pod 1040km (560nm).

Weights: Empty equipped 2964kg (6534lb), normal takeoff 4210kg (9285lb), max takeoff 5900kg (13,000lb).

Dimensions: Wing span with tip tanks 10.85m (35ft 7in), without tip tanks 10.15m (33ft 4in), length 10.67m (35ft 0in), height 3.72m (12ft 2in). Wing area 19.4m² (208.3sq ft).

Accommodation: Pilot only.

Armament: Max payload of 1815kg (4000lb) on six hardpoints, comprising bombs, wire guided AS.12 ASMs, Matra R550 Magic AAMs, unguided rockets, cannon and reconnaissance pods. Fixed armament comprises two 30mm DEFA 553 cannon with 125 rounds per gun.

Operators: Ghana, Tunisia, Zaire, South Africa (Impala Mk 2), UAE (Dubai).

History: The MB-326K is one of the most successful single seat development of a two seat jet trainer, and has provided a number of nations with a useful light attack capability.

Right from the beginning of the MB-326 jet trainer program, its designer Dr-Ing Ermano Bazzochi intended that the aircraft also be an effective light attack platform, and this capability no doubt influenced a number of the two seat MB-326's customers to order it. The two seater proved to be a stable and effective weapons platform and so a single seater optimised for light attack was a logical development.

The single seat MB-326K was developed well into the 326's career, given that the prototype two seater flew in 1957 and the single seat prototype flew on August 22 in 1970. The K was based on the MB-326G, which compared to earlier Macchis featured a strengthened airframe and more powerful Viper 20 engine. The first K prototype featured the 15.2kN (3410lb) Viper 20, while the second had the more powerful 17.9kN (4000lb) Viper Mk 632-43 intended for production aircraft, allowing an increased armament capability compared with two seaters and the fitting of two internal 30mm DEFA cannon. The second seat gave way to avionics and fuel.

Despite a 1970 first flight, the first production machines were not built until 1974 because of a lack of orders. The first customer was Dubai, which eventually took delivery of six MB-326KDs, while others were delivered to Zaire (MB-326KB), Ghana (MB-326KG) and Tunisia (MB-326KT).

South Africa was the MB-326K's largest customer, taking delivery of seven Italian built MB-326KMs and 73 Atlas licence assembled 15.1kN (3360lb) Viper 540 powered Impala 2s.

Photo: Ghana operates four MB-326Ks. (MAP)

Aermacchi MB-339

Country of origin: Italy

Type: Advanced trainer, lead-in fighter trainer & light attack

Powerplant: MB-339A – One 17.9kN (4000lb) Rolls-Royce Viper Mk 632-43 turbojet (licence built in Italy). MB-339C – One 19.6kN (4400lb) Viper Mk 680-43.

Performance: MB-339A – Max speed at 30,000ft 817km/h (441kt), at sea level 898km/h (485kt). Max initial rate of climb 6595ft/min. Climb to 30,000ft 7min 6sec. Service ceiling 48,000ft. Ferry range with drop tanks 2110km (1140nm), range 1760km (950nm). Combat radius with four Mk 82 bombs and two drop tanks (hi-lo-hi) 393km (212nm). MB-339C – Max speed 902km/h (487kt). Max initial rate of climb 7085ft/min. Climb to 30,000ft 6min 40sec. Service ceiling 46,700ft. Ferry range with two drop tanks 2035km (1100nm). Combat radius with four Mk 82 bombs (hi-lo-hi) 500km (270nm).

Weights: MB-339A – Empty equipped 3125kg (6889lb), max takeoff 5895kg (13,000lb). MB-339C – Empty equipped 3310kg (7297lb), max takeoff 6350kg (14,000lb).

Dimensions: MB-339A – Wing span over tip tanks 10.86m (35ft 8in), length 10.97m (36ft 0in), height 3.99m (13ft 1in). Wing area 19.3m² (207.7sq ft). MB-339C – Same except wing span over tip tanks 11.22m (36ft 10in), length 11.24m (36ft 11in).

Accommodation: Seating for two in tandem.

Armament: MB-339A – Up to 2040kg (4500lb) of external stores on six hardpoints including bombs, rockets, cannon pods, Matre anti shipping missiles (MB-339AM) and Magic and Sidewinder AAMs. MB-339C – Up to 1815kg (4000lb) of external ordnance, as above, plus Maverick ASMs and Vinten recce pod.

Operators: Argentina, Eritrea, Ghana, Italy, Malaysia, New Zealand, Nigeria, Peru, UAE (Dubai).

History: The MB-326 was Aermacchi's most successful postwar design, and so an upgraded successor, the MB-339, was a logical development.

The main change to the airframe was the reprofiled forward fuselage with stepped tandem cockpits with greatly improved forward vision from the rear seat. Aermacchi also considered new powerplant options, including turbofans and a twin engine configuration, but settled upon the familiar Viper turbojet for its performance, ease of maintenance and lower acquisition cost.

The first of two prototypes flew on August 12 1976, since which time the basic aircraft has been developed into a small number of models. The base MB-339A has accounted for almost all sales and 101 were delivered to the Italian air force (some as MB-339PANS fitted with smoke generators for the Frecce Tricolori aerobatic team). The MB-339C meanwhile is optimised for lead-in fighter and light attack duties with advanced nav and attack systems, ability to carry missiles, a more powerful engine, lengthened nose and larger tip tanks. So far New Zealand is the only C customer.

The Italian air force's Viper 632 powered MB-339CD and the export Viper 680 powered MB-339FD (Viper 680) feature a digital cockpit, including three colour LCD displays and HOTAS controls, plus a removable inflight refuelling probe.

The single seat MB-339K Veltro 2 was built in prototype form only.

Photo: A New Zealand MB-339C. (RNZAF)

Aermacchi RediGO & Valmet Vinka

Countries of origin: Finland and Italy

Type: Two seat basic trainers

Powerplant: L-70 – One 150kW (200hp) Lycoming AEIO-360-A1B6 flat four piston engine, driving a two blade propeller. L-90TP – One 375kW (500shp) Allison 250-B17F turboprop driving a three blade prop.

Performance: L-70 – Max speed at sea level 235km/h (127kt), cruising speed at 5000ft 222km/h (120kt). Max initial rate of climb 1120ft/min. Service ceiling 16,405ft. Range 950km (512nm). L-90TP – Max speed 415km/h (224kt), max cruising speed 352km/h (190kt), economical cruising speed 312km/h (168kt). Max initial rate of climb 1170ft/min. Service ceiling 25,000ft. Range 1400km (755nm). Endurance 6hr 20min.

Weights: L-70 – Operating empty 767kg (1690lb), max takeoff 1250kg (2755lb). L-90TP – Empty equipped 950kg (2095lb), max takeoff 1900kg (4190lb).

Dimensions: L-70 – Wing span 9.63m (31ft 7in), length 7.50m (24ft 8in), height 3.31m (10ft 11in). Wing area 14.0m² (150.7sq ft). L-90TP – Wing span 10.60m (34ft 9in), length 8.53m (28ft 0in), height 3.20m (10ft 6in). Wing area 14.7m² (158.8sq ft).

Accommodation: Two side by side. Two extra seats can be installed in rear of cabin.

Armament: L-70 – Up to 300kg (660lb) on underwing hardpoints, including rockets, gun pods and light bombs. L-90TP – Up to 800kg (1765lb) of armament on six underwing hardpoints. Weapon options similar to L-70.

Operators: L-70 – Finland. L-90TP – Eritrea, Finland.

History: Valmet's L-70 is currently Finland's basic military trainer, while the turboprop powered L-90TP Redigo development is now part of the expanded Aermacchi trainer product line.

The L-70 Miltrainer flew for the first time on July 1 1975. The L-70 is of conventional configuration for a basic trainer, with seating for the student and instructor side by side, fixed tricycle undercarriage and a Lycoming AEIO-360 flat four piston engine driving a two blade prop. Hardpoints under the wings are designed for practice bombs or light armament including gun pods or rockets.

In 1978 the Finnish air force ordered 30 L-70 Miltrainers, which it named Vinka (Blast), to replace its Saab Safir basic trainers. They were delivered between 1980 and 1982. Apart from their basic training role one Vinka serves with each fighter squadron as a liaison aircraft.

The L-90TP Redigo is a turboprop powered development of the Miltrainer. Powered by an Allison 250 driving a three blade prop, other changes to the Redigo include retractable undercarriage, a slight fuselage stretch, lengthened wings and greater external weapons load. First flight was on July 1 1986. Ten were built for the Finnish air force and others went to the Mexican navy and Eritrea. A second prototype was flown in 1987 powered by a Turboméca TP 319, although no production aircraft were built to this standard.

The final Valmet built Redigo was delivered in 1995. In January 1996 Aermacchi purchased the rights to the Redigo and will build any new aircraft ordered in Italy, as M-290TP RediGOs.

Photo: A Finnish AF Vinka basic trainer.

Aermacchi SF.260

Country of origin: Italy

Type: Two seat trainer & light attack

Powerplant: SF.260TP – One 261kW (380hp) Allison 250-B17D turboprop driving a three blade propeller.

Performance: SF.260TP – Max speed at 10,000ft 426km/h (230kt), max cruising speed 400km/h (216kt), economical cruising speed 315km/h (170kt). Max initial rate of climb 2170ft/min. Service ceiling 24,600ft. Range with max fuel and reserves at 15,000ft 950km (512nm).

Weights: SF.260TP – Empty equipped 750kg (1654lb), max takeoff 1300kg (2866lb).

Dimensions: SF.260TP – Wing span 8.35m (27ft 5in), length 7.10m (23ft 4in), height 2.41m (7ft 11in). Wing area 10.1m² (108.7sq ft).

Accommodation: Seating for two side by side, with optional third seat behind.

Armament: SF.260TP – Four underwing hardpoints can carry a max ordnance load of 300kg (660lb) including gun pods, bombs, practice bombs and rockets.

Operators: Belgium, Bolivia, Brunei, Burundi, Chad, Ireland, Italy, Libya, Nicaragua, Philippines, Singapore, Sri Lanka, Thailand, Tunisia, Turkey, UAE (Dubai), Uganda, Zaire, Zambia, Zimbabwe.

History: The nimble SF.260 is one of the most successful piston engine powered military trainers of recent times.

The retractable undercarriage SF.260 was designed by respected Italian aircraft designer Stelio Frati in the early 1960s. It was originally flown in 185kW (250hp) Lycoming O-540 form by the Aviamilano company as the F.250. However SIAI-Marchetti undertook production of the new aircraft (initially under licence, it later assumed full responsibility for the program) as the 195kW (260hp) O-540 powered SF.260. The second aircraft to fly was the first built by SIAI-Marchetti and the first powered by the more powerful version of the O-540. This second prototype first flew in 1966.

Initial civil production was of the SF.260A and SF.260B. Improvements launched on the military SF.260M included a stronger undercarriage, a redesigned wing leading edge and a taller fin. It first flew on October 10 1970. The SF.260 has been further developed into E and F forms with minor mods, while the definitive SF.260 military piston powered variants are the SF.260E and F Warriors, with a further strengthened airframe and two or four underwing hardpoints for up to 300kg (660lb) of rockets and bombs for light ground attack, weapons training and forward air control. The Warrior's first flight was in May 1972.

The 260kW (350shp) Allison 250-B17D turboprop powered SF.260TP meanwhile has been built since the early 1980s. About 60 have been built for the air forces of Dubai, Ethiopia, the Philippines, Sri Lanka and Zimbabwe.

Production of piston powered SF.260s amounts to over 860, the vast majority of which have been for military customers. Aermacchi acquired SIAI-Marchetti in January 1997 and now builds SF.260s (both piston and turbine powered) at its Venegono plant.

Photo: Turkish SF.260s.

Aermacchi S.211

Country of origin: Italy

Type: Two seat jet trainer

Powerplant: S.211 – One 11.1kN (2500lb) Pratt & Whitney JT15D-4C turbofan. S.211A – One 14.2kN (3190lb) JT15D-5C.

Performance: S.211 – Max cruising speed at 25,000ft 667km/h (360kt). Max initial rate of climb 4200ft/min. Service ceiling 40,000ft. Combat radius with four rocket launchers hi-lo-hi 555km (300nm), or lo-lo-lo 230km (125nm). Ferry range with external fuel 2485km (1340nm), range with internal fuel 1665km (900nm). Endurance 3hr 50min. S.211A – Max cruising speed at 25,000ft 767km/h (414kt). Max initial rate of climb 5100ft/min. Service ceiling 42,000ft. Ferry range with external fuel 2685km (1450nm). Endurance 4hr 15min.

Weights: S.211 – Empty equipped 1850kg (4078lb), max takeoff 3150kg (6955lb). S.211A – Empty equipped 2030kg (4475lb), max takeoff 4000kg (8188lb).

Dimensions: Wing span 8.43m (27ft 8in), length 9.50m (31ft 2in), height 3.96m (13ft 0in). Wing area 12.6m² (135.6sq ft).

Accommodation: Two in tandem.

Armament: Four underwing hardpoints can carry a max external ordnance load of 660kg (1455lb) for bombs, practice bombs, rockets and machine gun pods.

Operators: Philippines, Singapore.

History: The S.211 was developed as a private venture to fulfil basic/intermediate and weapons training and light ground attack roles.

Models of SIAI-Marchetti's new basic jet trainer were first displayed at the 1977 Paris Airshow, although it was not until almost four years later that the first of two prototypes made the type's first flight on April 10 1981. Production deliveries began in November 1984.

Major customers/operators are Singapore (30) and the Philippines (24), with both countries assembling most of their S.211s under licence. The former's aircraft are based near Perth in Australia, where they are free to train without Singapore's airspace constraints. The Philippines uses its aircraft for both training and ground attack, but the fleet has suffered from high attrition. Haiti took delivery of four but subsequently sold them in the USA to civilian customers.

The S.211 is of conventional design and configuration. The shoulder mounted wing has four hardpoints for light weaponry. Power is from a single Pratt & Whitney JT15D turbofan, which is used in a number of light business jets (including the Raytheon Beech T-1 Jayhawk), while the crew sit on stepped tandem lightweight Martin-Baker ejection seats. The S.211's comparatively low airframe weight results from 61% of external surfaces being made from composite materials.

The uprated S.211A has yet to find a customer and was unsuccessfully offered by Northrop Grumman (originally Grumman) to meet the USAF/USN's JPATS trainer requirement.

Aermacchi acquired SIAI-Marchetti in January 1997 and any new S.211s ordered will be built at Aermacchi's Venegono plant.

Photo: Singapore's S.211s are based primarily at RAAF Base Pearce in Western Australia. (Les Bushell)

Aero L-29 Delfin

Country of origin: Czech Republic

Type: Two seat basic and advanced jet trainer

Powerplant: One 8.78kN (1960lb) Motorlet M 701c 500 turbojet.

Performance: Max speed at 16,400ft 655km/h (353kt), at sea level 620km/h (335kt), cruising speed at 16,400ft 545km/h (294kt). Max initial rate of climb 2755ft/min. Time to 16,400ft 8min, time to 36,100ft 25min. Service ceiling 36,100ft. Ferry range with drop tanks 895km (482nm), range with standard fuel 640km (345nm).

Weights: Empty equipped 2365kg (5212lb), normal takeoff 3280kg (7230lb), max takeoff 3540kg (7805lb).

Dimensions: Wing span 10.29m (33ft 9in), length 10.81m (35ft 6in), height 3.13m (10ft 3in). Wing area 19.9m² (213sq ft).

Accommodation: Seating for two in tandem.

Armament: Max warload of 200kg (441lb) on two underwing hardpoints (one per wing). Armament can include two 7.62mm gun pods, or two 100kg (220lb) bombs, eight light rockets, or two drop tanks.

Operators: Bulgaria, Czech Republic, Egypt, Iraq, Mali, Nigeria, Romania, Syria.

History: One of the Czech aircraft industry's most successful aircraft designs, the L-29 Delfin saw widespread use in the Soviet Union as that country's primary advanced jet trainer for more than a decade from the early 1960s.

Early designs studies for a two seat jet engined trainer were conducted by K Tomas and Z Rubic in 1955. A major feature of the resulting L-29 Delfin (Dolphin) is its design concept of simplicity. Evidence of this includes easy construction and maintenance and docile handling qualities. Other design features are typical of jet trainers of the era, such as a small turbojet engine, straight wing, tandem seating and lightweight ejection seats. Unlike many of its contemporaries and later jet trainers, the L-29 features a T-tail and can operate from grass, waterlogged and dirt strips.

The first XL-29 prototype was powered by a Bristol Siddeley Viper engine and flew for the first time on April 5 1959. A second prototype flew in July 1960, powered by the indigenously developed M 701 turbojet. The following year the Delfin was pitted against the Yak-30 and PZL Mielec TS-11 Iskra in a competitive fly-off. The result of that competition saw the Delfin equip the air forces of every Warsaw Pact nation except Poland. The Soviet Union alone took delivery of more than 2000 Delfins, while significant numbers also served with Czechoslovakia, East Germany and Hungary. In these countries the Delfin was used in all-through training from ab initio to advanced stages. The first Delfins were delivered in 1963, with the last of over 3600 built rolling off the production line in 1974.

Almost all production was of the basic trainer variant (which was given the NATO codename 'Maya'), although two other variants did appear. Small numbers of single seat L-29A Delfin Akrobats were built for aerobatics while a prototype L-29R dedicated attack aircraft was also built.

Photo: A Hungarian L-29 wearing old style Hungarian air force roundels. (MAP)

Aero Albatros

Country of origin: Czech Republic

Type: Two seat advanced trainer and light strike aircraft

Powerplant: L-39 C – One 16.9kN (3972lb) Progress (nee Ivchenko) AI-25 TL turbofan. L-59 – One 21.6kN (4850lb) Progress DV-2 turbofan.

Performance: L-39 C – Max speed at sea level 700km/h (378kt), at 16,400ft 750km/h (405kt). Max initial rate of climb 4130ft/min. Range with max internal fuel 1100km (595nm), with external fuel 1750km (945nm). Endurance with external fuel 3hr 50min. L-59 – Max speed at 16,400ft 876km/h (473kt). Max initial rate of climb 5120ft/min. Service ceiling 38,485ft. Ferry range with external fuel 1500km (810nm).

Weights: L-39 C – Empty equipped 3455kg (7617lb), max takeoff 4700kg (10,362lb). L-59 – Empty equipped 4150kg (9149lb), max takeoff 7000kg (15,432lb).

Dimensions: L-39 C – Wing span incl tip tanks 9.46m (31ft 0in), length 12.13m (39ft 10in), height 4.77m (15ft 8in). Wing area 18.8m² (202.4sq ft). L-59 – Same except wing span incl tip tanks 9.54m (31ft 4in) and length 12.20m (40ft 0in).

Accommodation: Seating for two in tandem.

Armament: L-39 C – Unarmed. L-39 ZA & L-59 – Max external warload of 1000kg (2205lb) comprising rockets and pods, plus a 23mm GSh-23 two barrel cannon on centreline station.

Operators: L-39 – Afghanistan, Algeria, Bulgaria, Congo, Cuba, Czech Republic, Egypt, Ethiopia, Hungary, Iraq, Libya, Nicaragua, Nigeria, North Korea, Russia, Slovakia, Syria, Thailand and various CIS republics. L-59 – Egypt, Tunisia.

History: Design work on the Albatros, under the leadership of Dipl Ing Jan Vicek, began in 1966, just three years after the aircraft it was designed to replace, the Delfin, had entered production.

First flight of the second prototype took place on November 4 1968. Two other initial prototypes were built, both for structural testing, while a further four flying prototypes later joined the original aircraft in flight test duties. After a production decision was finally made in 1972 the L-39 was adopted for widespread use by Warsaw Pact countries (including the Soviet Union) and USSR client states.

One notable feature of the L-39 is its modular construction, it being designed to be easily manufactured and maintained.

Variants of the basic L-39 are numerous. The L-39 C is the basic two seat, unarmed trainer, and accounts for the majority of L-39 production. The L-39 V is a target tug, the L-39 ZO is an armed weapons trainer with a reinforced wing and four underwing hardpoints, while the L-39 ZO is similar to the ZA, but has reinforced undercarriage and can carry a reconnaissance pod. The L-39 ZA/ART was built for Thailand and features Israeli Elbit electronics. The L-139 Albatros 2000 is powered by a 18.2kN (4080lb) AlliedSignal TFE731 turbofan, features Bendix/King avionics and Flight Vision HUD and is offered for export.

The L-59 development (and Czech AF L-39MS) is similar to the L-39 but has a more powerful engine, upgraded avionics and reinforced fuselage. The AlliedSignal/ITEC F124 powered L 159 single and two seat development is described separately.

Photo: Aero's TFE731 powered L-139 demonstrator. (Aero)

Aero L 159 ALCA

Country of origin: Czech Republic

Type: Light multirole fighter and lead-in fighter trainer

Powerplant: One 28kN (6000lb) AlliedSignal/ITEC F124-GA-100 non afterburning turbofan.

Performance: L 159 – Max speed at sea level 930km/h (502kt). Max initial rate of climb 9250ft/min. Service ceiling 43,300ft. Range with max internal fuel 1570km (850nm), max range with external fuel 2530km (1370nm).

Weights: Empty equipped 4160kg (9171lb), ramp weight 8000kg (17,637lb).

Dimensions: Wing span including tip tanks 9.54m (31ft 2in), length 12.73m (41ft 9in), height 4.77m (15ft 4in). Wing area 18.8m² (202.4sq ft).

Accommodation: Pilot only, or two in tandem in L 159T.

Armament: Seven external hardpoints can carry a total ordnance/fuel load of 2340kg (5159lb). Weapon options include AIM-9 Sidewinder AAMs, AGM-65 Maverick ASMs, gun pods, rockets and bombs.

Operators: Czech Republic*

History: The L 159 ALCA (Advanced Light Combat Aircraft) is the latest and most advanced development of the Aero L 39/L 139/L 59 family of advanced jet trainers and is being built in single seat light multirole fighter and two seat lead-in fighter trainer forms.

The L 159 takes the basic Albatros airframe and combines it with a new engine, modern avionics and a radar. The engine is AlliedSignal/ITEC's F124 (which in afterburning F125 form powers the Taiwanese AIDC Ching-Kuo fighter) a modern design turbofan equipped with FADEC. The Rockwell Collins integrated avionics suite is built around a MIL STD 1553B databus linking a head-up display, two colour multifunction LCDs, Flight Visions dual mission computers, ring laser gyro INS with GPS nav system, and the Italian FIAR Grifo L multimode radar (with look down/shoot down and ground mapping functions). Other features include HOTAS controls, plus a Sky Guardian radar warning receiver and Vinten countermeasures (chaff and flares) dispenser, and cockpit armour and a fuel tank inerting system in the single seater, enhancing combat survivability.

Apart from the cockpit armour and fuel inerting system, the single seater differs from the two seater in having an additional fuel tank in place of the second seat. Otherwise the two aircraft are similar, and there are no external differences.

The L 159 has been under development since late 1992 and is on order with the Czech air force. First flight, of a two seater, took place on August 4 1997, while the first single seater, built to full Czech air force standards, is due to fly during 1998. Deliveries are expected to begin in 1999.

The Czech air force ordered 72 L 159s (most are expected to be single seaters) in April 1995, while Aero, engine manufacturer AlliedSignal and Aero part owner Boeing have formed a joint marketing team to sell the aircraft on the world market. Developing countries and former Warsaw Pact nations in particular are seen as potential customers.

Photo: The first L 159 prototype, a two seater, flew for the first time on August 2 1997. (Jan Kouba, Aero)

Aerospatiale CM 170 Magister

Country of origin: France

Type: Two seat jet trainer

Powerplants: CM 170-1 – Two 3.94kN (880lb) Maborè IIA turbojets. CM 170-2 – Two 4.74kN (1058lb) Maborè VICs.

Performance: CM 170-1 – Max speed 715km/h (385kt) at 29,925ft, 650km/h (350kt) at sea level. Max initial rate of climb 3345ft/min. Service ceiling 36,090ft. Ferry range with auxiliary fuel 1200km (650nm), range with standard fuel 925km (500nm). CM 170-2 – Max speed clean at 30,000ft 745km/h (402kt), at sea level 700km/h (378kt). Max initial rate of climb 3540ft/min. Service ceiling 44,300ft. Range 1250km (675nm).

Weights: CM 170-1 – Empty equipped 2150kg (4740lb), max takeoff 3200kg (7055lb). CM 170-2 – Empty equipped 2310kg (5093lb), max takeoff 3200kg (7055lb).

Dimensions: Wing span over tip tanks 12.15m (39ft 10in), span without tip tanks 11.40m (37ft 5in), length 10.06m (33ft 0in), height 2.80m (9ft 2in). Wing area 17.3m² (186.1sq ft).

Accommodation: Standard seating for two in tandem.

Armament: Two 7.5mm or 7.62mm fixed machine guns mounted in the nose. Underwing hardpoints can carry bombs, rockets and Nord AS.12 air-to-ground missiles.

Operators: Bangladesh, Belgium, Cameroon, France, Gabon, Ireland, Israel, Libya, Morocco, El Salvador, Senegambia, Togo.

History: The Magister was the first aircraft in the world specifically designed as a jet trainer, and was arguably postwar France's first successful world class military aircraft.

The Magister resulted from a French Armée de l'Air requirement for a jet powered trainer. The basic aircraft was conceived by Fouga designers Castello and Mauboussin (hence the CM prefix in the designation) in 1950. The first of three prototypes flew for the first time on June 27 1951, the type's promising performance leading to an Armée de l'Air order for 10 pre production aircraft. Prolonged testing and development of the aircraft followed, with the first pre production aircraft not flying for the first time until June 1954 and the first production aircraft (for the French air force) flying on February 29 1956.

The Magister proved an ideal aircraft for its intended role as it was easy to fly with predictable flying characteristics, despite the uncommon two surface butterfly tail arrangement. Some 387 were eventually built for the French air force while several hundred others were built in France and under licence in Finland, Germany and Israel for a large number of export customers including West Germany, Austria, Belgium, Lebanon and Cambodia. Total French production amounted to 622 (built mainly by Fouga's successors Potez, Sud Aviation and Aerospatiale), while IAI built 36, Finland's Valmet 62 and Germany's Flugzeug Union Sud 188.

The Magister was built in three versions – the initial CM 170-1, the CM 170-2 Super Magister with more powerful engines and ejection seats, and the navalised, carrier capable CM 175 Zéphyr. The French navy took delivery of 30 arrester hook equipped Zéphyrs. The Magister remains in service in fairly large numbers, a number of nations having acquired examples second hand.

Photo: Belgium flies 10 Magisters. (Belgium SID)

Aerospatiale TB 30 Epsilon

Country of origin: France

Type: Two seat basic trainer

Powerplant: TB 30B – One 225kW (300hp) Textron Lycoming AEIO-540-L1B5D fuel injected flat six piston engine, driving a two blade constant speed Hartzell propeller.

Performance: TB 30B – Max speed at sea level 378km/h (204kt), cruising speed at 6000ft 358km/h (193kt). Max initial rate of climb 1850ft/min. Service ceiling 23,000ft. Range 1250km (675nm). Endurance at 60% power 3hr 45min.

Weights: TB 30B – Empty equipped 932kg (2055lb), max takeoff 1250kg (2755lb).

Dimensions: TB 30B – Wing span 7.92m (26ft 0in), length 7.59m (24ft 1in), height 2.66m (8ft 9in). Wing area 9.0m² (96.0sq ft).

Accommodation: Seating for two in tandem.

Armament: Togolese aircraft only – Maximum external ordnance of 300kg (660lb) with pilot only, comprising two twin 7.62mm machine gun pods, or four 68mm six rocket tubes or two 120kg (265lb) bombs, on four underwing hardpoints. Inner pylons stressed for 160kg (350lb), outer pylons 80kg (175lb).

Operators: France, Portugal, Togo.

History: The French Armée de l'Air's primary basic trainer, the Epsilon is based on the successful four seat TB 10 Tobago light aircraft.

Aerospatiale's General Aviation subsidiary Socata developed the Epsilon in response to meet an Armée d l'Air requirement for a basic trainer. Initially Socata looked at a jet powered aircraft, then a piston engined aircraft based on the Tobago with two seats side-by-side. When the Armée de l'Air decided it wanted a tandem seating arrangement, the basic design was redeveloped and all commonality with the Tobago was lost.

Socata proposed the Epsilon in two variants differing in powerplant fitted. It offered the 195kW (260hp) powered TB 30A and the 225kW (300hp) TB 30B, with only the latter, higher powered aircraft selected for development and production. The Armée de l'Air awarded the development contract in June 1979 and the resulting TB 30B prototype flew for the first time on December 22 that year.

Testing of the prototype revealed unacceptable pitch/yaw coupling characteristics, so Socata further refined the design to feature extended, rounded, upswept winglets and a redesigned rear fuselage and tail. The first and second prototypes were then modified and flew in this new, definitive configuration from late October 1980.

The first French production order was placed in March 1982 for 30 aircraft. Socata eventually delivered 150 Epsilons to the Armée de l'Air through to 1989, while Togo took delivery of a total of four machines and Portugal 18, assembled locally by OGMA.

The fully aerobatic Epsilon's fuel system allows it to fly inverted for up to two minutes. Togo's aircraft meanwhile are equipped with four external hardpoints, which can carry gun pods, rockets and light bombs in a counter insurgency role.

The TB 30 also formed the basis for the turboprop Turboméca Arrius powered TB 31 Omega, which first flew in 1985 but never entered production due to a lack of orders.

Photo: The Epsilon is France's standard basic trainer.

Aerospatiale Alouette II & Lama

Aerospatiale Alouette III

Country of origin: France

Type: Light utility helicopters

Powerplant: SA 313B Alouette II – One 270kW (360shp) Turboméca Artouste IIC6 turboshaft, driving a three blade main rotor and two blade tail rotor. SA 315B Lama – One 650kW (870shp) Turboméca Artouste IIIB turboshaft, derated to 410kW (550shp).

Performance: SA 313B – Max speed 185km/h (100kt), max cruising speed 165km/h (90kt). Max initial rate of climb 825ft/min. Hovering ceiling in ground effect 5400ft. Range with max fuel 300km (162nm), range with max payload 100km (54nm). SA 315B – Max cruising speed 192km/h (103kt). Max initial rate of climb 1080ft/min. Service ceiling 17,715ft. Hovering ceiling in ground effect 16,565ft, out of ground effect 15,090ft. Range with max fuel 515km (278nm).

Weights: SA 313B – Empty 895kg (1973lb), max takeoff 1600kg (3527lb). SA 315B – Empty 1020kg (2250lb), max takeoff 1950kg (4300lb), or 2300kg (5070lb) with external sling load.

Dimensions: SA 313B – Main rotor diameter 10.20m (33ft 5in), fuselage length 9.70m (31ft 10in), height 2.75m (9ft 0in). SA 315B – Main rotor diameter 11.02m (36ft 2in), length overall 12.92m (42ft 5in), fuselage length 10.26m (33ft 8in), height overall 3.09m (10ft 2in). Main rotor disc area 95.4m² (1026.7sq ft).

Accommodation: Typical seating for five. Can carry two stretchers in medevac role. Lama can lift a 1135kg (2500lb) external sling load.

Armament: None (officially).

Operators: Alouette II – operators include Belgium, Benin, Cameroon, Central African Republic, Congo, Dominican Republic, France, Guinea-Bissau, Ivory Coast, Lebanon, Senegambia, Tunisia. Lama – Argentina, Chile, Ecuador, India (Cheetah), Togo.

History: For a time the most successful western European helicopter in terms of numbers built, the Alouette II was based on the original Sud-Est Alouette SE 3120 which first flew on March 12 1955.

Two prototypes were built and these were powered by Salmson 9 piston engines. Production deliveries of the turbine powered SE 313B Alouette II occurred from 1957, the first machines bound for the French army. Most SA/SE 313B production was for military operators, many of whom had French links, while others went to civilian operators.

The Alouette II was soon followed by a more powerful Turboméca Astazou powered development. This aircraft was designated the SA 318C Alouette II Astazou, and flew for the first time on January 31 1961. Power was supplied by a 395kW (530shp) Astazou IIA derated to 270kW (360shp), which increased the type's maximum speed and max takeoff weight, but otherwise the Alouette II and Alouette II Astazou were similar.

The SA 315B Lama was developed initially as a utility helicopter with excellent hot and high performance for the Indian Army. Called Cheetah in Indian service, the Lama mated the Alouette II's airframe with the larger Alouette III's dynamic components including the Artouste IIIB engine. The Lama's first flight was on March 17 1969. Aerospatiale built 407 through to 1989, while HAL in India continues low rate licence production.

Photo: One of eight French navy Alouette IIs. (MAP)

Country of origin: France

Type: Light utility helicopter

Powerplant: SA 316B – One 425kW (570shp) Turboméca Artouste IIIB turboshaft, driving a three blade main rotor and three blade tail rotor. SA 319B – One 450kW (600shp) derated Turboméca Astazou XIV.

Performance: SA 316B – Max speed 210km/h (113kt), max cruising speed 185km/h (100kt). Max initial rate of climb 885ft/min. Hovering ceiling in ground effect 7380ft/min. Range with max fuel 480km (260nm). SA 319B – Max cruising speed 197km/h (106kt). Max initial rate of climb 885ft/min. Hovering ceiling in ground effect 10,700ft, out of ground effect 5575ft. Range with six passengers 605km (327nm).

Weights: SA 316B – Empty 1122kg (2474lb), max takeoff 2200kg (4850lb). SA 319B – Empty 1140kg (2513lb), max takeoff 2250kg (4960lb).

Dimensions: SA 316B & SA 319B – Main rotor diameter 11.02m (36ft 2in), length overall 12.84m (42ft 2in), fuselage length 10.03m (32ft 11in), height 3.00, (9ft 10in). Main rotor disc area 95.4m² (1026.7sq ft).

Accommodation: Typical seating for seven.

Armament: Can carry one 7.62mm machine gun mounted on a tripod firing through right hand doorway, a 20mm cannon fixed to the left hand side of the fuselage, or four or two AS.11 anti tank missiles, or two Mk.44 torpedoes.

Operators: Operators include Argentina, Austria, Cameroon, France, Ghana, Iraq, Ireland, Malaysia, Mexico, Netherlands, Pakistan, Portugal, Romania, South Africa, Switzerland, Tunisia and Venezuela. Chetak in service with India and Nepal.

History: The popular Alouette III is an enlarged development of the Alouette II series and remains in widespread service worldwide.

Like the Alouette II, the Alouette III traces its development back to the Sud-Est SE 3101 piston powered prototypes, the first of which flew for the first time on July 31 1951. The largest member of the Alouette series, the III flew as the SE 3160 on February 28 1959. Compared with the Alouette II, the Alouette III is larger and seats seven, but in its initial SA 316A form is also powered by a Turboméca Artouste turboshaft.

This SA 316A Alouette III remained in production for almost a decade until 1969, when it was replaced by the improved SA 316B, with strengthened transmission and a greater max takeoff weight, but the same Artouste III turboshaft.

Further development led to the SA 319 Alouette III Astazou, which as its name suggests, is powered by a 450kW (600shp) Turboméca Astazou XIV turboshaft. The more powerful Astazou engine conferred better hot and high performance and improved fuel economy. The SA 319 entered production in 1968.

The SA 319 and SA 316B remained in production side by side through the 1970s and into the 1980s. HAL of India continues to licence build Alouette IIIs as the Chetak, mainly for that country's military, while similarly 230 were built by ICA-Brasov in Romania through to 1989. The Romanians also developed a two seat anti tank attack helicopter based on the Alouette as the IAR-317 Skyfox, but this aircraft flew in prototype form only.

Photo: An Indian Navy HAL Chetak. (RAN)

Aerospatiale SA 321 Super Frelon

Country of origin: France

Type: Multirole utility helicopter

Powerplants: SA 321G – Three 1100kW to 1215kW (1475shp to 1630shp) Turboméca Turmo IIIC turboshafts, driving a six blade main rotor and five blade tail rotor.

Performance: SA 321G – Max cruising speed at sea level 248km/h (134kt). Max initial rate of climb (inclined) 1214ft/min, 480ft/min on two engines. Hovering ceiling in ground effect 7120ft. Service ceiling 10,170ft. Range 1020km (550nm). Endurance in ASW role 4hr.

Weights: SA 321G – Empty 6700kg (14,775lb), max takeoff 13,000kg (28,660lb).

Dimensions: Main rotor diameter 18.90m (62ft 0in), length overall 23.03m (75ft 7in), fuselage length 19.40m (63ft 8in), height 6.66m (21ft 10in). Main rotor disc area 280.6m² (3019sq ft).

Accommodation: Flightcrew of two. Original SA 321G ASW configuration seats three tactical/sonar operators. Transport configured Super Frelons can seat 30 troops or carry 15 stretcher patients in a medevac configuration.

Armament: As originally configured, SA 321Gs could carry four homing torpedoes or two AM 39 Exocet anti shipping missiles. Various export aircraft configured to launch Exocet.

Operators: Argentina, China, France, Iraq, Syria.

History: While only built in relatively small numbers (it is still built under licence in China), the Super Frelon has the distinction of being the largest helicopter to be built in quantity in western Europe.

The Super Frelon was developed from the smaller, mid size SA 3200 Frelon (Hornet), the first flight of which was on June 10 1959. The Frelon was intended to meet French military requirements for a mid size transport helicopter, and although four prototypes were built, it was not ordered into production. Instead the Frelon formed the basis for the much larger Super Frelon which Sud Aviation developed in conjunction with Sikorsky. Sikorsky helped primarily with the development of the main and tail rotor systems, while Fiat of Italy assisted with the gearbox and power transmission (and built those parts for production aircraft).

The SA 3210-01 prototype Super Frelon flew for the first time on December 7 1962, and 99 production aircraft were built in three basic models. The SA 321G was initially operated by the French navy as an anti submarine warfare and sanitization aircraft for French nuclear armed submarines, equipped with radar, dunking sonar and torpedoes. Similar SA 321GMs and SA 321Hs were delivered to Syria and Iraq respectively. The SA 321F and SA 321J were civil variants, while the SA 321J is a utility transport. Non amphibious transport versions were exported to South Africa (SA 321L) and Israel (SA 321K), while Libya's SA 321Ms were delivered for SAR and logistics support.

French production ceased in 1983, while Changhe Aircraft Industries Corporation in China continues to licence build the multirole Z-8 development, with 12 in service with the Chinese naval air force.

Photo: South Africa has retired its SA 321L Super Frelons. (MAP)

Agusta A 109

Country of origin: Italy

Type: Multirole light helicopter

Powerplants: A 109M – Two 423kW (567shp) Pratt & Whitney Canada PW206C turboshafts, driving a four blade main rotor and two blade tail rotor. A 109KM – Two 471kW (632shp) Turboméca Arriel 1K1s.

Performance: A 109M – Max cruising speed at sea level clean 263km/h (142kt). Max initial rate of climb 1860ft/min. Service ceiling 19,200ft. Hovering ceiling in ground effect 16,600ft, out of ground effect 11,800ft. Max range at long range cruising speed 910km (491nm). A 109KM – Max cruising speed at sea level clean 264km/h (143kt). Max initial rate of climb 1950ft/min. Service ceiling 20,000ft. Hovering ceiling in ground effect 18,300ft, out of ground effect 13,200ft. Max range at long range cruising speed 819km (442nm).

Weights: A 109M – Empty 1611kg (3548lb), max takeoff 2850kg (6280lb), max takeoff with an external load 3000kg (6608lb). A 109KM – Empty 1657kg (3650lb), max takeoff same.

Dimensions: Main rotor diameter 11.00m (36ft 1in), length rotors turning 13.03m (42ft 9in), fuselage length 11.44m (37ft 6in), height 3.50m (11ft 6in). Main rotor disc area 95.0m² (1023sq ft).

Accommodation: Seats up to eight in passenger configuration.

Armament: Various weapons on two external hardpoints each side of the fuselage on pylons. Options include eight TOW 2A anti armour missiles, Stinger or Mistral air-to-air missiles, machine gun pods, main doorway pintle mounted guns, and rocket launchers.

Operators: Argentina, Belgium, Italy, Peru, UK, Venezuela, Yugoslavia.

History: Although developed primarily for the civil market, the A 109 has been adopted for a range of military and para military roles.

The first of four prototype A 109s flew for the first time on August 4 1971. The first production machines were not delivered until 1976. Basic models since then include the initial A 109A, the A 109A Mk II with improvements to the dynamic systems, the A 109C with a further uprated transmission, composite rotor blades and greater max takeoff weight, and most recently the P&WC PW206 powered A 109E Power.

Argentina was an early operator. Two of its four aircraft were captured by the British during the Falklands War and then placed into service with the British Army in support of SAS operations.

The first major military A 109 customer was Italy, which initially ordered 24 A 109A based A 109EOA armed scout helicopters fitted with sliding main cabin doors, fixed landing gear, roof mounted day sight, laser range finder and the ability to carry a variety of weapons.

The A 109C based A 109CM is in Belgium army service which took delivery of 18 scout and 24 anti armour variants as A 109BAs (designated by Belgium as A 109HO and HA respectively). Similar to the A 109EOA, the scouts feature a roof mounted Saab sight, the attack aircraft Saab/ESCO HeliTOW 2 sights and the capability to carry eight Hughes TOW 2A anti tank missiles.

The A 109K is designed for hot and high operations and is fitted with Turboméca Arriel turboshafts. The land based A 109KM has sliding doors and a fixed undercarriage and is in service in South America. The A 109M is currently under development and is a military variant of the PW206 powered A 109 Power.

Photo: An Italian army A 109EOA with roof mounted sight. (Agusta)

Agusta A 129 Mangusta

Country of origin: Italy

Type: Two seat multirole attack and scout helicopter

Powerplants: A 129 – Two 615kW (825shp) max continuous rated Rolls-Royce Gem 2 Mk 1004D turboshafts (licence built by Piaggio), driving a four blade main rotor and two blade tail rotor. International – Two 946kW (1268shp) max continuous rated LHTEC CTS800-2 turboshafts driving a five blade main rotor and two blade tail rotor.

Performance: A 129 – Dash speed 294km/h (160kt), max speed at sea level 250km/h (135kt). Max initial rate of climb 2030ft/min. Hovering ceiling in ground effect 10,300ft, out of ground effect 6200ft. Combat radius with eight TOW missiles, reserves and a 90min loiter time on station 100km (55nm). Max endurance 3hr 5min. International – Max speed at sea level 298km/h (161kt). Hovering ceiling in ground effect 14,900ft, out of ground effect 9100ft. Max range on internal fuel 534km (288nm).

Weights: A 129 – Empty equipped 2530kg (5575lb), MTOW 4100kg (9040lb). Intl – Empty 2987kg (6585lb), MTOW 5000kg (11,023lb).

Dimensions: A 129 – Main rotor diameter 11.90m (39ft 1in), wing span 3.20m (10ft 6in), length overall rotors turning 14.29m (46ft 11in), fuselage length 12.28m (40ft 3in), height overall 3.35m (11ft 0in). Main rotor disc area 111.2m² (1197.0sq ft). International – Same except fuselage length 12.50m (40ft 11in).

Accommodation: Crew of two seated in tandem, pilot in rear seat.

Armament: A 129 – Up to 1200kg of stores including rocket and gun pods and TOW 2 and 2A anti tank missiles. International – One 20 mm gun in undernose turret. Options include rocket and gun pods and Stinger AAMs.

Operators: Italy

History: Developed against an Italian army requirement, go-ahead for what became the A 129 Mangusta (Mongoose) was given in 1978.

The prototype's first flight was on September 11 1983. Features of the aircraft include two Rolls-Royce Gem turboshafts, seating for a gunner/copilot and pilot in separate, stepped cockpits, four blade main rotor with some use of composite construction, a computerised and fully redundant integrated management system designed to reduce crew workload, stub wings with two weapons pylons each, and a Saab/ESCO HeliTOW weapons system with nose mounted sight.

Following funding delays with the HeliTOW system, the A 129 entered service with the Italian army in October 1990.

The only A 129 development to fly thus far has been the A 129 International, developed to attract export sales. Changes include the 20% more powerful LHTEC CTS800 turboshafts, uprated transmission, a higher max takeoff weight and optional three barrel 12.7mm gun turret. First A 129 International flight was in 1988, more latterly the prototype flew in 1995 with a five blade main rotor, while new armament and equipment options include Stinger AAMs, a Lockheed Martin/GIAT 20mm three barrelled cannon and FLIR.

Italy's last 15 of 60 Mangustas will feature the International's five blade main rotor, plus uprated transmission, 4600kg (10,141lb) MTOW, 20mm cannon and Stinger AAMs.

Photo: A 129 International prototype with five blade main rotor. (Agusta)

AIDC AT-3 Tzu-Chiang

Country of origin: Taiwan

Type: Two seat advanced trainer and light attack aircraft

Powerplants: AT-3 – Two 15.6kN (3500lb) Garrett TFE731-2-2L non-afterburning turbofans.

Performance: AT-3 – Max speed at 36,000ft 904km/h (488kt), or 900km/h (486kt) at sea level, max cruising speed at 36,000ft 880km/h (475kt). Max initial rate of climb 10,100ft/min. Service ceiling 48,000ft. Range with internal fuel 2280km (1230nm). Endurance with internal fuel 3hr 12min.

Weights: AT-3 – Empty equipped 3855kg (8500lb), normal takeoff (trainer, clean) 5215kg (11,500lb), max takeoff 7940kg (17,500lb).

Dimensions: AT-3 – Wing span 10.46m (34ft 4in), length including nose probe 12.90m (42ft 4in), height 4.83m (15ft 10in). Wing area 21.9m² (236.1sq ft).

Accommodation: Seating for two in tandem. AT-3A seats pilot only.

Armament: Can be fitted with gun pods in an internal weapons bay. Disposable armament can be carried on one centreline pylon, four underwing hardpoints and two wingtip launch rails. Can carry bombs, rockets, wingtip mounted AAMs and training bombs.

Operators: Taiwan

History: The AT-3 Tzu-Chiang was AIDC's second indigenous design to enter Taiwanese service behind the turboprop powered Chung Tsing, and serves with the Taiwanese air force as an advanced/weapons trainer and light attack and close support aircraft. Up until the development of the Ching-Kuo fighter, the AT-3 was the most advanced aircraft to be developed by Taiwan's emerging aircraft industry.

Serious design of the AT-3 began in 1975 with the placement of a development contract. The first of two prototypes flew for the first time on September 16 1980, while the first production aircraft flew on February 6 1984. In all, AIDC built 60 AT-3s for the Republic of China Air Force, the last of which was delivered in 1990.

All 60 production aircraft were designated AT-3. The AT-3A Lui Meng meanwhile was a single seat dedicated light ground and maritime attack development. Two prototypes were known to have been built (the first one being converted from a two seat AT-3) and flown in the late 1980s, but development is thought to have been suspended.

The AT-3A could have been cancelled in favour of the two seat AT-3B, which features the nav/attack system initially developed for the Lui-Meng. Twenty AT-3s were converted to AT-3B standard which features a Westinghouse AN/APG-66 radar and an internal weapons bay that can carry semi recessed machine gun packs. The aircraft can carry a variety of weaponry, including wingtip mounted infrared guided AAMs, in addition to bombs and rockets on four underwing and a centreline pylon. The AT-3B's maximum external stores load is 2720kg (6000lb).

Power for the AT-3 is supplied by two Garrett (now AlliedSignal) TFE731 turbofans, while the airframe is of conventional construction. Other features include zero/zero ejection seats and the ability to carry and deploy an aerial target towing system.

Photo: AT-3s are used by the RoCAF's display team based at Kangshan. In RoCAF service the AT-3 has largely replaced the piston powered T-CH-1 Chung Tsing.

AIDC Ching-Kuo

Country of origin: Taiwan

Type: Lightweight multirole fighter

Powerplants: Two 26.8kN (6025lb) dry and 41.8kN (9400lb) afterburning ITEC (AlliedSignal/AIDC) TFE1042-70 (F125) turbofans.

Performance: Max level speed at 36,000ft 1295km/h (700kt). Max initial rate of climb 50,000ft/min. Service ceiling 54,000ft. Range figures not published.

Weights: Operating empty 6485kg (14,300lb), max takeoff 12,245kg (27,000lb).

Dimensions: Wing span over wingtip missile rails 8.53m (28ft 0in), length overall including nose probe 14.21m (46ft 7in), length overall excluding nose probe 13.26m (43ft 6in), height overall 4.65m (15ft 3in). Wing area 24.3m² (261.1sq ft).

Accommodation: Pilot only, or two in tandem in trainers.

Armament: One 20mm M61A1 Vulcan cannon. Six hardpoints can carry a variety of missiles, bombs, guided bombs and cluster munitions including 500lb/225kg GBU-12, Rockeye, AGM-65B Maverick, Hsiung Feng II anti ship missile, Sky Sword I short range IR guided and Sky Sword II medium range radar homing AAMs.

Operators: Taiwan

History: The Ching-Kuo is by far Taiwan's most ambitious aircraft program, and is now providing Taiwan with a capable multirole fighter.

Development of the Ching-Kuo, initially known as the Indigenous Defensive Fighter (IDF), began in 1982 after a US arms embargo precluded Taiwan from ordering F-16s or Northrop F-20 Tigersharks to replace ageing F-5s and F-104s fighters for air superiority, anti shipping and ground attack roles. Despite the arms embargo, US companies were still able to provide technical support for the program. General Dynamics worked closely with AIDC to develop the airframe, and similarities to the F-16 are obvious, particular the blended fuselage/wing design. Other features such as the leading edge root extensions give the aircraft the appearance of a scaled down F/A-18.

The International Turbofan Engine Company (ITEC) TFE1042 afterburning turbofans were developed in partnership by AlliedSignal and AIDC. The Golden Dragon 53 radar (which has a search range of 150km/80nm) is based on the GE APG-67 originally developed for the F-20, with some elements based on the F-16A's APG-66 with air and sea search modes and lookdown, shootdown capability, while the specifically developed infrared guided Sky Sword I and radar guided Sky Sword II AAMs closely resemble the AIM-9 Sidewinder and AIM-7 Sparrow, respectively. Other features include a side stick controller, two multi function displays, a HUD and fly-by-wire.

The first prototype Ching-Kuo, a single seater, flew for the first time on May 28 1989, while three other prototypes – one single seater and two two-seaters – and 10 pre production aircraft followed. The first production Ching-Kuo was delivered to the Republic of China Air Force in January 1994, with production continuing through to late 1998

Taiwan's initial plan to buy 260 Ching-Kuos was halved when the lifting of arms embargoes during the early nineties allowed it to purchase F-16s and Mirage 2000-5s and cancel a developed version.

Photo: A production two seater Ching-Kuo.

Airbus A310 & MRTT

Country of origin: European consortium

Type: A310 – VIP/strategic transport. MRTT – tanker transport

Powerplants: A310 – Initially either two 213.5kN (48,000lb) Pratt & Whitney JT9D-7R4D1 or two 222.4kN (50,000lb) General Electric CF6-80A3 turbofans. Current choices of 238kN or 262kN (53,500lb or 59,000lb) GE CF6-80C2A2s or -80C2A8s, or 231kN or 249kN (52,000lb or 56,000lb) P&W PW4152 or PW4156 turbofans.

Performance: A310-200 – Max cruising speed 897kmh (484kt), long range cruising speed 850kmh (459kt). Range at typical airliner operating weight with reserves 6800km (3670nm). A310-300 (with CF6-80C2A2s) – Typical airliner range with reserves 7980km (4310nm), or up to 9580km (5170nm) for high gross weight version.

Weights: A310-200 with CF6-80C2A2s – Operating empty 80,142kg (176,683lb), max takeoff 142,000kg (313,055lb). A310-300 with CF6-80C2A8s – Operating empty 80,330kg (177,095lb), max takeoff up to 164,000kg (361,560lb).

Dimensions: A310 – Wing span 43.89m (144ft 0in), length 46.66m (153ft 1in), height 15.80m (51ft 10in). Wing area 219.0m² (2357.3sq ft).

Accommodation: Flightcrew of two. MRTT max palletised passenger seating 270. Max payload 35 tonnes (77,161lb).

Armament: None

Operators: Belgium*, Canada, France, Germany, Thailand.

History: The A310, a shortened development of Airbus' original A300 widebody airliner, is now in limited military service as a transport.

Based on the larger A300 airliner, the A310 introduced a shortened fuselage, a new higher aspect ratio wing, new and smaller horizontal tail surfaces and a two crew flightdeck.

The first flight of an A310 occurred on April 3 1982, after the program was launched in July 1978. The basic passenger aircraft is the A310-200, while the A310-300 is a longer range development and has been in production since 1985. The A310-200F freighter and A310-200C convertible are available as new build aircraft or as conversions of existing A310s.

Military A310s currently in service operate in a variety of transport functions. Thailand became the first military A310 operator when its sole A310 was delivered in 1991. Germany inherited its A310s from the former East German airline Interflug. France's replaced DC-8s.

Canada is the largest A310 operator with five in service with 437 Squadron. Designated the CC-150 Polaris, they are used for strategic transport. More recently Belgium has announced its intention to acquire two ex airline A310s to replace 727-100s.

Airbus offers new build and conversion Multi Role Tanker Transport (MRTT) configured A300s and A310s (MRTT 300 and MRTT 310 respectively). Features offered on the MRTT include both boom and probe and drogue refuelling with additional belly fuel tanks, and a quick change main deck layout for freight and/or palletised seating.

Germany launched the MRTT program in 1997 when it contracted DASA and Lufthansa to convert two of its aircraft. Initially they will not be equipped for air-to-air refuelling.

Additionally Raytheon E-Systems is offering Australia the A310 as an AEW&C platform fitted with Elta's phased array radar.

Photo: France flies two A310-300s. (Armée de l'Air)

Airbus Military Company FLA

Countries of origin: Belgium, France, Germany, Portugal, Spain, Turkey, UK

Type: Tactical transport

Powerplants: Four 6710kW (9000shp) class turboprops – possibly SNECMA, MTU and Fiat Avio M138s (a turboprop development of the M88), or BR700-TP turboprop developments of the BMW Rolls-Royce BR715, or the AlliedSignal AS812, driving eight blade propellers.

Performance: Cruising speed Mach 0.68. Soft field landing and takeoff run less than 1065m (3500ft). Tactical mission range with a 25,000kg (55,115lb) payload 3850km (2080nm), strategic mission range with a 32,000kg (70,547lb) payload 4445km (2400nm). Ferry range 7595km (4100nm).

Weights: Max zero fuel weight 84,250kg (185,740lb), max takeoff 110,850kg (244,380lb). Max payload 25,000kg (55,115lb), max overload payload 32,000kg (70,547lb).

Dimensions: Wing span 41.40m (135ft 10in), length 42.00m (137ft 10in), height 14.50m (47ft 7in).

Accommodation: Flightcrew of two, with provision for a third flightdeck crewmember, plus a loadmaster. Will carry up to 32 tonnes of payload, with options including a Super Puma helicopter, or two Tiger helicopters, a Patriot SAM system, six Land Rover 4WDs and trailers, nine 2.24 x 2.74m (88 x 108in) military pallets or two ISO 20ft (6.1m) containers.

Armament: None

Operators: Belgium, France, Germany, Italy, Portugal, Spain, Turkey and the UK have requirements for up to 300 FLAs.

History: The FLA has its origins in various European requirements to replace Transall C-160s and C-130 Hercules.

The FLA (or Future Large Aircraft) began life as the FIMA (Future International Military Aircraft) a high wing, propfan powered design which resulted from a four nation study group formed in December 1982. In 1989 FIMA evolved into the EUROFLAG (as in European Future Large Aircraft Group). At the time EUROFLAG envisaged that the aircraft would have a 90 to 99 tonne max takeoff weight and enter service in 2000 (with full scale development beginning in 1996). At the time up to 1000 new transports were required.

Initial studies of the aircraft carried on into the early 1990s, by which time it was envisaged that the aircraft would be powered by four turbofans, rather than turboprops. An Outline European Staff Target (OEST) was defined in 1991, a European Staff Target and intergovernmental MoU was signed in 1993, turbofans were dropped in preference to turboprops in 1994, and a full feasibility study was completed in 1995. EUROFLAG's (by then Euroflag srl) FLA work was taken over by the Airbus Military Company in 1995, with the aim that Airbus would develop and build the aircraft along commercial lines). Various funding problems and delays mean that a firm FLA launch is provisionally planned for mid 1998, which would mean a first flight sometime around 2003 with initial entry into service perhaps two years later.

Apart from transport, the basic FLA will be capable of being converted into a two point probe and drogue aerial tanker. The FLA could also be developed to fulfil AEW and maritime patrol missions and into a three point aerial tanker.

Photo: A computer generated image of the FLA. (Airbus)

Alenia G222

Country of origin: Italy

Type: Tactical transport

Powerplants: Two 2535kW (3400shp) General Electric T64-GE-P4D turboprops, licence built by Fiat, driving three blade Hamilton Standard propellers.

Performance: Max speed 540km/h (292kt), economical cruising speed 440km/h (240kt). Max initial rate of climb 1705ft/min. Service ceiling 25,000ft. Takeoff run at MTOW 662m (2172ft). Ferry range 4630km (2500nm), range with max payload 1370km (740nm), range with 36 litters and four medical attendants 2500km (1350nm).

Weights: Empty equipped 15,400kg (33,950lb), max takeoff 28,000kg (61,728lb).

Dimensions: Wing span 28.70m (94ft 2in), length 22.70m (74ft 6in), height 9.80m (32ft 2in). Wing area 82.0m² (882.7sq ft).

Accommodation: Flightcrew of two with provision for a loadmaster. Typical accommodation for 46 fully equipped troops, or 40 fully equipped paratroops. Can carry a 9600kg (21,165lb) payload comprising light vehicles and artillery. Two Libyan G222s equipped for VIPs.

Armament: None

Operators: Argentina, Congo, Italy, Libya, Nigeria, Somalia, Thailand, UAE (Dubai), USA, Venezuela.

History: The G222's origins date back to an early 1960's NATO requirement for a V/STOL tactical transport.

The NATO requirement spawned a number of exotic V/STOL concepts, none of which were practical. The Italian air force placed a contract with Fiat to develop its G222 V/STOL concept, but importantly that contract was later extended to cover a conventionally configured STOL development, which laid the ground work for the definitive G222 transport. The Italian air force placed a contract for two prototype G222s in 1968, and, after a number of delays caused by external forces, the first G222 made the type's first flight on July 18 1970.

The two prototypes were unpressurised and powered by two lower rated CT64-820 engines, but otherwise the prototype and production aircraft were similar. Design features of the G222 include its good short field performance, large double slotted flaps, barrel shaped fuselage, rear freight ramp and tandem main undercarriage wheels with levered suspension. Much of the Italian aerospace industry was involved in the construction of the G222, with Aermacchi building the outer wings, Piaggio the wing centre sections and SIAI-Marchetti responsible for the tail.

Almost all G222s built were the basic transport, although 20 G222Ts built for Syria are powered by 3635kW (4860shp) Rolls-Royce Tynes. Other variants are the Chrysler C-27A Spartan, procured via Chrysler in 1990 from Alenia to fulfil transport duties with the US Air Force in South America; the Elint configured G222VS; firefighting G222SAA; and the radio/radar calibration G222R/M.

The ultimate G222 development is the Allison AE 2100 powered C-27J Spartan, which is being developed by LMATTS (Lockheed Martin Alenia Tactical Transport Systems) and is described separately.

Photo: An Italian air force G222 in flight. (Alenia)

AMX International AMX

Countries of origin: Italy and Brazil

Type: Light attack aircraft

Powerplant: One 49.1kN (11,030lb) Rolls-Royce Spey Mk 807 non afterburning turbofan built under licence in Italy by Fiat, Piaggio and Alfa Romeo Avio, in co-operation with CELMA in Brazil.

Performance: Max speed 915km/h (493kt) at 36,000ft. Max initial rate of climb 10,250ft/min. Service ceiling 42,650ft. Combat radius at max takeoff weight with 2720kg (6000lb) of external payload lo-lo-lo 528km (285nm), hi-lo-hi 925km (500nm); combat radius at typical mission TO weight with 910kg (2000lb) of external stores lo-lo-lo 555km (300nm), hi-lo-hi 890km (480nm).

Weights: Operating empty 6700kg (14,770lb), max takeoff 13,000kg (28,660lb).

Dimensions: Wing span 8.87m (29ft 2in), length 13.23m (43ft 5in), height 4.55m (14ft 11in). Wing area 21.0m² (226.1sq ft).

Accommodation: Pilot only, seating for two in tandem in trainer.

Armament: One 20mm GE M61A1 Vulcan cannon in Italian aircraft, two 30mm DEFA cannons in Brazilian aircraft. External armament of up to 3800kg (8375lb) on four underwing, one centreline and two wingtip stations. Options include wingtip mounted AIM-9 or MAA-1 Piranha AAMs, unguided bombs, rockets and cluster munitions.

Operators: Brazil*, Italy*.

History: The AMX resulted from similar air force specifications for a replacement for the G91 and F-104 (in ground attack roles) in Italian service and the AT-26 Xavante (MB-326) in Brazilian use.

In the late 1970s Aermacchi was working with Embraer on the A-X, an Xavante replacement, while the Italian air force issued a formal requirement for a G91 replacement in 1977. Initial work on the AMX began in 1978 when Aeritalia (now Alenia) teamed with Aermacchi. Thus the involvement of Embraer, who joined the program in 1980 and who had been working with Aermacchi, was a logical development.

With an initial agreement for 266 production aircraft (79 for Brazil, 187 for Italy) reached in 1981, development of the AMX gathered pace and the first development prototype flew for the first time on May 15 1984. Construction of the first batch of 30 production aircraft and the design of a two seat AMX-T trainer began in mid 1986, while the first production aircraft, for Italy, first flew in May 1988.

Design of the AMX is fairly conservative, with power supplied by the proven Spey turbofan. Design features include HOTAS controls and HUD, multi function displays, INS navigation and ECM, with provision in the nose for FLIR or a radar. In addition, three different Aeroelectronica of Brazil developed reconnaissance pallets can be fitted in the forward fuselage, while recce pods can be fitted on the external hardpoints. The AMX-T could also be adopted for ECR and anti shipping.

Alenia is AMX program leader with a 46.7% share of production, Aermacchi has 23.6% and Embraer 29.7%. Component manufacture is not duplicated, however there are separate final assembly lines in Italy and Brazil. Deliveries are continuing of the 136 ordered by Italy and the 56 for Brazil (Brazil designates the AMX the A-1).

Photo: An AMX of the Italian air force's 14° Gruppo.

Antonov/PZL Mielec An-2

Countries of origin: Ukraine and Poland

Type: General purpose utility biplane

Powerplant: An-2P – One 745kW (1000hp) PZL Kalisz ASz-61IR nine cylinder radial piston engine driving an AW-2 four blade variable pitch propeller.

Performance: An-2P – Max speed 258km/h (139kt) at 5740ft, economical cruising speed 185km/h (100kt). Max initial rate of climb 690ft/min. Range at 3280ft with a 500kg (1100lb) cargo 900km (485nm).

Weights: An-2P – Empty 3450kg (7605lb), MTOW 5500kg (12,125lb).

Dimensions: Upper wing span 18.18m (59ft 8in), lower 14.24m (46ft 9in), length (tail down) 12.40m (40ft 8in). Upper wing area 43.5m² (468.7sq ft), lower 28.0m² (301.2 sq ft).

Accommodation: Flightcrew of one or two pilots. Passenger accommodation for 12 at three abreast.

Armament: None, although some aircraft have been modified to carry a small bomb load.

Operators: An-2 – Operators include Afghanistan, Angola, Azerbaijan, Byelorussia, Bulgaria, Croatia, Cuba, Czech Republic, Georgia, Laos, Latvia, Mali, Mongolia, Nicaragua, Poland, Romania, Russia, Slovak Republic, Tadjikistan, Turkmenistan, Ukraine, Uzbekistan, Vietnam. Y-5 – Albania, China, North Korea.

History: The An-2 was originally designed to a USSR Ministry of Agriculture and Forestry requirement, and as well as large scale civil use was adopted in significant numbers by air arms of numerous Soviet aligned countries for a multitude of utility roles.

First flown on August 31 1947, the An-2 entered production and service the following year. The unusual biplane configuration was chosen for its good takeoff performance, docile low speed handling and excellent climb rates, and the wings were fitted with leading edge slats and double slotted flaps, further improving performance, while power was supplied by a 745kW (1000hp) ASh-62 radial. Soviet production continued through until 1960, by which time a number of variants had been developed, including the base model An-2P, An-2S and -2M crop sprayers, An-2VA water bomber, An-2M floatplane and the An-2ZA high altitude meteorological research aircraft.

Production responsibility was transferred to Poland's PZL Mielec in 1960, with the first Polish An-2 flying on October 23 1960. Aside from the An-2P, Polish versions include the An-2PK VIP transport, An-2PR for TV relay work, An-2S ambulance, An-2TD paratroop transport, An-2P cargo/passenger version, An-2 Geofiz geophysical survey version, An-2T utility and An-2TP passenger aircraft.

Chinese production as the Y-5 commenced with Nanchang in 1957, before being transferred to Shijiazhuang Aircraft. The main Chinese version is the standard Y-5N, while the latest development is the Y-5C paratroop carrier for the PLA-AF with distinctive wingtip vanes.

An Antonov turboprop powered version, the An-3, was developed in the late 1980s, but did not enter production.

In military service the An-2 is used in a wide variety of missions including paratroop transport, special forces insertion, navigation trainer and general utility work.

Photo: A Croation An-2. (MAP)

Antonov An-12

Country of origin: Ukraine

Type: Tactical transport

Powerplants: An-12BP – Four 2985kW (4000ehp) Ivchenko (now Progress) AI-20K turboprops, driving four blade constant speed propellers.

Performance: An-12BP – Max speed 777km/h (420kt), max cruising speed 670km/h (360kt). Max initial rate of climb 1970ft/min. Service ceiling 33,465ft. Takeoff run at max takeoff weight 700m (2296ft). Range with max fuel 5700km (3075nm), range with max payload 3600km (1940nm).

Weights: An-12BP – Empty 28,000kg (61,728lb), max takeoff 61,000kg (134,480lb).

Dimensions: An-12BP – Wing span 38.00m (124ft 8in), length 33.10m (108ft 7in), height 10.53m (34ft 7in). Wing area 121.7m² (1310sq ft).

Accommodation: Flightcrew of two pilots, flight engineer, navigator (in glazed nose) and radio operator, plus loadmasters. Can carry up to 20 tonnes (44,060lb) of freight such as artillery, light armoured vehicles and missile carriers, or alternatively up to 90 equipped troops or paratroopers.

Armament: Two tail mounted 23mm cannon (not on all aircraft).

Operators: Czech Republic, Egypt, Ethiopia, Iraq, Russia, Ukraine, Yemen. Y-8 – China, Myanmar, Sudan.

History: For many years the An-12 (NATO codename 'Cub') provided the backbone of Soviet and Warsaw Pact air forces' medium lift transport capability, but the type, generally considered the Russian equivalent of the C-130, is now being replaced by more modern airlifters.

The origins of the An-12 lie in the An-8, a twin turboprop powered military transport which featured the classical military freighter configuration of a high wing and rear loading ramp. About 100 An-8s were built and the type formed the basis for the stretched, four engined An-10 airliner for Aeroflot. The An-10 in turn formed the basis for the An-12, the main differences between the two being the latter's more upswept rear fuselage and rear loading ramp.

The An-12 flew for the first time in 1958, powered by Kuznetsov NK-4 turboprops. The definitive production freighter meanwhile, the An-12BP, is powered by Ivchenko AI-20s. The An-12 remained in production until 1973, with a number also delivered to Aeroflot and Soviet aligned airlines. Its replacement in Russian service is the Il-76.

Various special missions variants of the An-12 have been developed, but details on these aircraft are sketchy. Many aircraft have been converted for Elint, festooned with various antennas, and these are covered by the NATO designations 'Cub-A', and 'Cub-B', while the 'Cub C' and more recent 'Cub-D' are ECM aircraft. Unconfirmed reports have suggested the development of a command post variant, while others have been used for research and development tasks.

Xian in China meanwhile developed the improved Y-8 from 1968. A number of variants have been developed (all built by Shaanxi Aircraft Company), including the Y-8A helicopter carrier, pressurised Y-8C (developed with assistance from Lockheed), Y-8D export aircraft with western avionics and Y-8E drone carrier. A single Y-8X maritime patrol and ASW aircraft has also flown. The Y-8 remains in production.

Photo: The Czech air force's sole An-12 transport. (Paul Merritt)

Antonov An-22 Antheus

Country of origin: Ukraine

Type: Strategic turboprop freighter

Powerplants: Four 11,185kW (15,000shp) Kuznetsov (now Kuibyshev) NK-12MA turboprops, driving eight blade counter rotating propellers.

Performance: Max speed 740km/h (400kt), cruising speed 520km/h (281kt). Range with max fuel and 45 tonne (99,200lb) payload 10,950km (5905nm), range with max payload 5000km (2692nm).

Weights: Typical empty equipped 114,000kg (251,325lb), max takeoff 250,000kg (551,160lb).

Dimensions: Wing span 64.49m (211ft 4in), length 57.92m (190ft 0in), height 12.53m (41ft 1in). Wing area 345m² (3713.0sq ft).

Accommodation: Flightcrew of up to six, comprising two pilots, navigator, flight engineer and a communications specialist. Up to 29 passengers can be accommodated on the upper deck behind the flightdeck. Total An-22 payload is 80,000kg (176,350lb).

Armament: None

Operators: Russia

History: The massive An-22 (NATO reporting name 'Cock') is by far the largest turboprop powered aircraft yet built and was a remarkable technological achievement for its time.

Antonov designed the An-22 in response to a Soviet military requirement for a strategic heavylift freighter, and when it made its first flight on February 27 1965 it was easily the largest aircraft in the world. Subsequent production of the An-22 lasted until 1974.

The An-22's NK-12 turboprops, which also power the Tu-95/Tu-142 'Bear' family of bombers and maritime patrol aircraft, are the most powerful turboprop engines in service. Other notable An-22 features include comprehensive navigation and precision drop avionics complete with three separate radars, 14 wheel undercarriage (tyre pressures can be adjusted from the flightdeck to optimise the aircraft for different runway surfaces), integral rear loading ramp, twin tails and double slotted flaps.

After entering service, the An-22 set 14 payload to height records in 1967, the pinnacle of which was the carriage of 100 tonnes (220,500lb) of metal blocks to an altitude of 25,748ft (7848m). It also established the record for a maximum payload lifted to a height of 2000m (6562ft), carrying a payload of 104,445kg (221,443lb). A number of speed records were also set in 1972, including a speed of 608.5km/h (328kt) around a 1000km (540nm) circuit with a 50,000kg (110,250lb) payload. Further speed with payload records were established in 1974 and 1975.

Almost all An-22s, while primarily built for the Soviet air force, wear Aeroflot colours. The An-22s' 'civilian' colours and status allowed them much freer access to landing and overflight rights than had they been operated in military markings. The aircraft have also widely been used for civil operations.

While the An-22 has been superseded by the larger, turbofan powered An-124 (described separately), the surviving aircraft are still heavily utilised as they offer rare payload carrying characteristics.

Photo: Note the 14 wheel undercarriage of the An-22 as it is about to touch down. (Dave Fraser)

Antonov An-26 & An-32

Country of origin: Ukraine

Type: Tactical transport

Powerplants: An-26B – Two 2075kW (2780ehp) ZMKB Progress (formerly Ivchenko) AI-24VT turboprops driving four blade propellers, and one auxiliary 7.85kN (1765lb) Soyuz (formerly Tumansky) RU-19A-300 turbojet. An-32 – Two 3760kW (5042ehp) ZMKB Progress AI-20D Series 5 turboprops.

Performance: An-26B – Cruising speed 435km/h (235kt). Max initial rate of climb 1575ft/min. Takeoff run on sealed runway 870m (2855ft). Range with max payload and no reserves 1240km (670nm), range with max fuel and no reserves 2660km (1435nm). An-32 – Max cruising speed 530km/h (285kt), economical cruising speed 470km/h (254kt). Service ceiling 30,840ft. Takeoff run on sealed runway 760m (2495ft/min). Range with max payload 1200km (645nm), range with max fuel 2520km (1360nm).

Weights: An-26B – Empty 15,850kg (34,943lb), max takeoff 24,000kg (52,910lb). An-32 – Empty 16,800kg (37,038lb), max takeoff 27,000kg (59,525lb).

Dimensions: An-24B – Wing span 29.20m (95ft 2in), length 23.80m (78ft 1in), height 8.58m (28ft 2in). Wing area 75.0m² (807.1sq ft). An-32 – Wing span 23.78m (78ft 0in), length 23.80m (78ft 1in), height 8.75m (28ft 9in). Wing area 75.0m² (807.1sq ft).

Accommodation: An-24B – Flightcrew of two pilots, flight engineer, navigator and radio operator, plus loadmaster. Seating for up to 40 troops or 24 stretcher patients. An-32 – Flightcrew of two pilots and navigator.

Armament: None, although some have been fitted with bomb racks.

Operators: An-26 – Afghanistan, Angola, Bangladesh, Benin, Bulgaria, Cape Verde, China, Cuba, Congo, Czech Republic, Ethiopia, Guinea Bissau, Hungary, Iraq, Laos, Libya, Madagascar, Mali, Mongolia, Mozambique, Nicaragua, Poland, Romania, Russia, Serbia, Slovakia, Ukraine, Vietnam, Yemen, Zambia. An-32 – Afghanistan, Cuba, Czech Republic, India; Mongolia, Peru, Tanzania.

History: The An-26 has been the standard light tactical transport aircraft of almost every former Soviet Bloc country since the 1970s.

The An-26 (NATO reporting name 'Curl') is a militarised development of the An-24 airliner, which first flew in April 1963. The pressurised An-26 (first flight in 1968) differs from the An-24 in featuring a rear loading freight ramp, more powerful Ivchenko turboprops and a turbojet APU which can serve as an auxiliary engine for takeoff. More than 1400 An-26s and An-26Bs (with improved freight handling system) were built until the type was replaced in production by the improved An-32 (NATO reporting name 'Cline').

The An-32 first flew in the 1976 and features much more powerful engines for improved hot and high performance (the type finding favour with air forces which operate in such environments). The An-32 features improved systems and is visually identifiable by its above wing mounted engines, which give greater ground clearance for the increased diameter propellers.

Meanwhile Xian in China has developed the Y7 and the Y7H from the An-24, and some are in Chinese military service.

Photo: A Czech An-26. (Paul Merritt)

Antonov An-70

Country of origin: Ukraine

Type: Heavy freighter

Powerplants: Four 10,290kW (13,800hp) Progress D-27 propfans driving counter rotating Stupino SV-27 14 blade propellers.

Performance: Cruising speed 750km/h (405kt). STOL takeoff required runway length 900m (2960ft). Range with 20,000kg (44,100lb) of cargo 7400km (3995nm) (3000km/1620nm with STOL takeoff and landing), or 3800km (2050nm) with a 35,000kg (77,161lb) payload.

Weights: Max takeoff 130,000kg (286,600lb).

Dimensions: Wing span 44.06m (144ft 7in), length 40.25m (132ft 1in), height 16.10m (52ft 10in).

Accommodation: Flightcrew of two pilots and a flight engineer, plus accommodation for two loadmasters. Designed to accept a large percentage of NATO and CIS military equipment. Standard payload 35 tonnes (77,161lb), or up to 300 troops.

Operators: None

Armament: None

History: The An-70 has been developed by Antonov as a replacement for its An-12, which is currently in widespread military and civilian use with operators throughout the CIS. Originally designed to be in production in 1988, delays mean it will enter service in 1998.

The An-70 is one of the most recent aircraft to be developed in the Commonwealth of Independent States and incorporates a range of modern technology design concepts. The most prominent feature of the An-70 is its four Russian designed propfans consisting of 14 blade Stupino counter rotating scimitar propellers and the Progress turboprops. Combined these are designed to offer very high speed combined with low fuel consumption. The Russian developed SV-27 all composite propellers are highly swept and are claimed to have a 90% efficiency in cruise, at near jet speeds.

Takeoff and landing speeds are also lower thanks to the propfans, while the An-70's ability to fly from relatively short fields means it can operate from 80% of all CIS airstrips, allowing shorter journeys and greater point to point flights.

Composite materials are used throughout the airframe, including the horizontal and vertical tails which are all composite. The An-70 also incorporates fly-by-wire and an advanced flightdeck with six full colour digital displays and a head up display used for landings on short strips. The digital avionics are also linked via a databus equivalent to US 1553B standard, believed to be another first for a CIS aircraft, and allowing far easier integration of western avionics in the future.

The An-70 program was thrown into doubt in February 1995 when the sole prototype collided with its An-72 chase plane while on a test flight. At that time completion of a second prototype was still some time of, but this aircraft was completed and flew for the first time on April 24 1997. Production aircraft will be built at Kiev with first deliveries planned for 1998.

An-70 models include the basic An-70 military freighter, two crew An-70-100, export An-77 and commercial An-70T. The proposed An-70TK would be a twin propfan convertible passenger/freight aircraft.

Photo: The second An-70 prototype.

Antonov An-72 & An-74

Country of origin: Ukraine

Type: STOL utility and (An-74) polar transport

Powerplants: Two 63.7kN (14,330lb) ZMKB Progress D-36 turbofans.

Performance: An-72 – Max speed 705km/h (380kt), cruising speed at 32,800ft 550 to 600km/h (295 to 325kt). Service ceiling 38,715ft. Range with max fuel and reserves 4800km (2590nm), with a 7500kg (16,535lb) payload 2000km (1080nm). An-74 – Range with a 1500kg (3310lb) payload 5300km (2860nm). An-72P – Patrol speed 300 to 350km/h (162 to 189kt). Ceiling 33,135ft. Max endurance 7hr 18min.

Weights: An-72 – Empty 19,050kg (41,997lb), max takeoff (from a 1800m/5900ft runway) 34,500kg (76,060lb), max TO from a 1000m (3280ft) runway 27,500kg (60,625lb). An-72P – Max takeoff 37,500kg (82,670lb).

Dimensions: An-72 – Wing span 31.89m (104ft 8in), length 28.07m (92ft 1in), height 8.65m (28ft 5in). Wing area 98.6m² (1062sq ft).

Accommodation: An-72 flightcrew of two pilots and a flight engineer, An-74 has provision for a radio operator. Can carry a payload of 10 tonnes (22,045lb). An-72 can also seat 68 on removable seats. An-72P – Crew of five.

Armament: An-72P – One 23mm gun pod, a UB-23M rocket launcher under each wing and four 100kg (220lb) bombs carried internally. Improved development offered by IAI can carry the Griffin laser guided bomb.

Operators: Iran, Kazakhstan, Peru, Russia, Ukraine.

History: The An-72 (NATO came 'Coaler') was designed as a replacement for the An-26 tactical transport in Soviet service.

The first of two An-72 prototypes flew for the first time on December 22 1977, although it was not until 1985 that the first of eight extensively revised pre production An-72s flew. Included in this pre production batch were two An-74s, differing from the An-72s in their ability to operate in harsh weather conditions in polar regions because of an improved avionics suite.

Transport versions of the An-72 family include the An-72A base model with extended wings and fuselage compared to the prototypes, the An-72AT which can carry international standard containers, and the An-72S VIP transport. Versions of the An-74 include the base An-74A with enlarged nose radome, the An-74T freighter, the An-74TK convertible passenger/freighter model, and the An-74P Salon VIP transport. A prototype AEW An-71 ('Madcap') has also flown.

The An-72P maritime patrol aircraft meanwhile is based on the basic An-72 fuselage with a 23mm gun, rocket pods, four light bombs carried internally, day and night downward looking and oblique optical cameras and an optical TV sight. In service with Ukraine, the An-72P is designed for close-in coastal surveillance. Antonov is now offering an improved development of the An-72P in conjunction with Israel Aircraft Industries. Changes include a glass cockpit, Elta EL/M 2022A radar, Electro Optical day and night long range observation system and Elisra electronic warfare suite.

The most significant design feature of the An-72 and An-74 is the use of engine exhaust gases blown over the wing's upper surface to improve STOL performance and lift.

Photo: An An-72P demonstrator, note rocket launcher. (Paul Merritt)

Antonov An-124 Ruslan

Country of origin: Ukraine

Type: Heavy lift strategic transport

Powerplants: Four 229.5kN (51,590lb) ZMKB Progress (Lotarev) D-18T turbofans.

Performance: Max cruising speed 865km/h (468kt), typical cruising speeds between 800 and 850km/h (430 to 460kt). Range with max payload 4500km (2430nm), range with full fuel load 16,500km (8900nm).

Weights: Operating empty 175,000kg (385,800lb), max takeoff 405,000kg (892,875lb).

Dimensions: Wing span 73.30m (240ft 6in), length 69.10m (226ft 9in), height 20.78m (68ft 2in). Wing area 628.0m² (6760sq ft).

Accommodation: Flightcrew of six consisting of two pilots, two flight engineers, navigator and communications operator. Upper deck behind the flightdeck area comprises a galley, rest room and two relief crew cabins. Upper deck area behind the wing can accommodate up to 88 passengers. Main deck cargo compartment is designed to carry an extremely large range of bulky and oversized cargos including 12 ISO standard containers, heavy artillery, main battle tanks, SAM systems, helicopters, SS-20 mobile IRBM, etc. The An-124's total payload in weight is 150 tonnes (330,695lb).

Armament: None

Operators: Russia, Ukraine.

History: The massive An-124 for a time held the mantle of the world's largest aircraft before the arrival of the An-225, a stretched six engine derivative, and is the largest aircraft in the world to achieve full production status.

The An-124 was developed primarily as a strategic military freighter to replace the turboprop powered An-22 (described separately) but also for use by the Soviet state airline Aeroflot for carriage of bulky and oversize cargos. The first prototype An-124 flew on December 26 1982, while a second prototype, named Ruslan after Pushkin's mythical giant, made the type's first western public appearance at the Paris Airshow in mid 1985, preceding the type's first commercial operations in January 1986. Since that time the An-124 has set a wide range of payload records.

Except for its low set tail, the An-124's configuration is similar to the United States Air Force's Lockheed C-5 Galaxy (described separately), which, with a maximum takeoff weight of 350 tonnes, is slightly smaller. Notable features include nose and tail cargo doors which allows simultaneous loading and unloading, 24 wheel undercarriage allowing operations from semi prepared strips, the ability to 'kneel' for easier front loading and a fly-by-wire control system.

An-124 models include the basic An-124, the commercial An-124-100 certificated in Russia in 1992, the An-124-100M with western avionics, and the EFIS equipped An-124-102.

Almost all An-124s built serve under Aeroflot markings, but these aircraft commonly perform military tasks, while a smaller number of Ruslans are assigned directly to the Russian air force (deliveries began in 1987). The An-124 has the NATO reporting name of 'Condor'.

Photo: While most An-124s operate in Aeroflot or other civil markings, this example wears the Russian air force's red star.

Avioane IAR-99 Soim & IAR-109 Swift

Country of origin: Romania

Type: Two seat basic and advanced trainer

Powerplant: IAR-99 – One 17.8kN (4000lb) Turbomecanica licence built Rolls-Royce Viper Mk 632-41M turbojet.

Performance: IAR-99 – Max speed at sea level 865km/h (467kt). Max initial rate of climb 6890ft/min. Service ceiling 42,325ft. Max range with internal fuel (trainer) 1100km (593nm), ground attack 967km (522nm). Combat radius with pilot only, ventral gun and four rocket pods lo-lo-lo 350km (190nm); with ventral gun, two rocket pods and 500kg (1100lb) of bombs hi-lo-hi 345km (185nm); with ventral gun and four 250kg (550lb) bombs hi-hi-hi 385km (208nm). Max endurance (trainer mission) 2hr 40min, (ground attack) 1hr 45min.

Weights: IAR-99 – Empty equipped 3200kg (7055lb), max takeoff (trainer) 4400kg (9700lb), (ground attack) 5560kg (12,258lb).

Dimensions: IAR-99 – Wing span 9.85m (32ft 4in), length 11.01m (36ft 2in), height 3.90m (12ft 10in). Wing area 18.7m² (201.4sq ft).

Accommodation: Two in tandem, though pilot only when flying ground attack missions.

Armament: Removable ventral gun pod contains a 23mm GSh-23 two barrel cannon. Four underwing hardpoints can carry a combined load of 1000kg (2205lb), including light bombs and rocket pods.

Operators: Romania

History: Romania's indigenously developed IAR-99 Soim (Falcon) is a two seat advanced trainer and light attack aircraft in a similar vein to the Aermacchi MB-339 and Aero Albatros.

Development of the Soim began at Romania's Institute de Aviate at Bucharest in the early 1980s, while the program's existence was first made public to the west at the 1983 Paris Airshow. Romania's state aviation enterprise IAv Croavia (renamed Avioane in 1991) was entrusted with Soim production, and IAv built the first prototype which flew for the first time on December 21 1985.

Production of the Soim began in 1987 against an initial order for 20 from the Romanian air force. A second order for 30 was placed, but only a small number are believed to have been delivered with production thought to have ceased.

The Soim replaced the Romanian air force's Aero L-29 Delfins, providing basic and advanced training, as well as having a secondary close air support/ground attack role, supplementing IAR-93s.

The IAR-109 Swift is an upgraded development of the Soim, aimed primarily at export orders. The Swift differs from the Soim in having advanced Israeli developed nav/attack avionics and modern cockpit (including HUD and multi function displays), expanded weapons carrying capability (including the capability to launch infrared guided AAMs and laser guided bombs), and Martin-Baker lightweight ejection seats. The airframe and engine remain unchanged. It is offered in IAR-109T basic trainer configuration and IAR-109TF armed combat trainer form.

Avioane announced development of the Swift in 1993, a converted IAR-99 served as the first prototype, while the first new build Swift flew for the first time in November 1993. None have been ordered.

Photo: The Avioane IAR-109. (Keith Anderson)

Beechcraft T-34 Mentor & Turbo Mentor

Country of origin: United States of America

Type: Two seat primary trainer

Powerplant: T-34A & B – One 170kW (225hp) Continental O-470 flat six piston engine, driving a two blade propeller. T-34C – One 535kW (715shp) Pratt & Whitney Canada PT6A-25 turboprop derated to 300kW (400shp) driving a three blade prop.

Performance: T-34A & B – Max speed 302km/h (163kt), max cruising speed 270km/h (145kt). Max initial rate of climb 1210ft/min. Service ceiling 21,200ft. Range 1240km (667nm). T-34C – Max speed 414km/h (224kt), max cruising speed 398km/h (215kt). Max initial rate of climb 1480ft/min. Service ceiling 30,000ft plus. Range 1310km (708nm) at 333km/h (180kt) cruising speed.

Weights: T-34A & B – Empty 932kg (2055lb), max takeoff 1315kg (2900lb). T-34C – Empty 1193kg (2630lb), max TOW 1938kg (4274lb).

Dimensions: T-34A & B – Wing span 10.01m (32ft 10in), length 7.87m (25ft 10in), height 2.92m (9ft 7in). Wing area 16.5m² (177.6sq ft). T-34C – Wing span 10.16m (33ft 4in), length 8.75m (28ft 9in), height 3.02m (9ft 11in). Wing area 16.71m² (179.9sq ft).

Accommodation: Seating for two in tandem.

Armament: T-34C-1 – Four underwing hardpoints can carry up to 545kg (1200lb) of practice and light bombs, rockets, miniguns, AGM-22A anti tank missiles or towed target equipment.

Operators: Mentor – Argentina, Colombia, Dominican Rep, Uruguay, Venezuela. Turbo Mentor – Argentina, Ecuador, Gabon, Indonesia, Morocco, Peru, Taiwan, Uruguay, USA.

History: Perhaps the most successful western, postwar, basic trainer built, the T-34 is based on one of civil aviation's most successful light aircraft types, the Beech 35 Bonanza.

The prototype four seat Beech Bonanza flew for the first time on December 22 1945, predating a production run that began in 1947 and continues to this day. In 1948 Beech took the Bonanza design as the basis for a military basic trainer. The private venture Model 45 Mentor differed from the Bonanza in having seating for two in tandem and a conventional tail unit (the Model 35 Bonanza is famous for its V-tail). The Model 45 Mentor flew for the first time on December 2 1948, arousing the interest of the newly formed US Air Force enough so that that service ordered three evaluation examples.

The three evaluation YT-34s were delivered in 1950, and successful testing led the USAF to order the first of an eventual 450 T-34As in 1953. That year the USN evaluated the T-34 and ordered 290 similar T-34Bs in mid 1954. Mentors were also built under licence in Canada and Japan and assembled in Argentina. In all over 1300 were built. USAF Mentors were retired in 1960.

The success of the Mentor led to a 1973 USN request for Beech to build a turboprop powered development to replace the T-34B and also the North American T-28 Trojan. The resulting Pratt & Whitney Canada PT6A powered T-34C Turbo Mentor (dubbed Tormentor) flew for the first time on September 21 1973. A total of 352 T-34Cs was built (the last of which, attrition replacements for the USN, were delivered in 1990), most of which were for the US Navy, but 129 armed T-34C-1s were exported.

Photo: A Morrocan air force T-34 Turbo Mentor.

Bell 47G/H-13 Sioux

Country of origin: United States of America

Type: Light utility, training and observation helicopter

Powerplant: 47G-3B-2A – One 210kW (280hp) Lycoming TVO-435-F1A flat six piston engine, driving a two blade main rotor and two blade tail rotor.

Performance: 47G-3B-2A – Max speed 170km/h (91kt), cruising speed 135km/h (73kt) at 5000ft. Max initial rate of climb 880ft/min. Service ceiling 19,000ft. Hovering ceiling in ground effect 17,700ft, out of ground effect 12,700ft. Range 395km (215nm) at 6000ft.

Weights: 47G-3B-2A – Empty 858kg (1893lb), max takeoff 1340kg (2950lb).

Dimensions: 47G-3B-2A – Main rotor diameter 11.32m (37ft 2in), length overall 13.30m (43ft 8in), fuselage length 9.63m (31ft 7in), height 2.83m (9ft 4in). Main rotor disc area 100.8m² (1085sq ft).

Accommodation: Seating for two or three occupants, side-by-side. Can carry two stretchers, one on each skid.

Armament: None

Operators: Greece, Malta, New Zealand, Pakistan, Peru, Taiwan, Turkey, Uruguay, Zambia.

History: Both in the military and civil spheres, the Bell 47 is recognised as being one of the first practical helicopters, and was the first to see widespread military use.

The lineage of the Bell dates back to 1943 and the Bell Model 30, an experimental helicopter ordered by the US Army for evaluation. The US Army ordered 10 Model 30s for evaluation, and the type formed the basis for the improved Model 47. The Model 47's first flight was on December 8 1945. The prototype 47 featured seating for two side by side, with a car style cabin and was powered by a Franklin piston engine, and in this initial form the 47 became the first helicopter to be certificated by the USA's Civil Aeronautics Administration.

The promise the Bell helicopter showed soon translated into military orders from the US services, the USAAF ordering 28 as YR-13s in 1947 for evaluation, some of which went to the US Navy as HTL-1 trainers. In 1948 the US Army ordered 65, designated H-13Bs. The name Sioux was adopted later.

By 1953 Bell was producing the definitive Model 47 variant, the 47G, which featured progressively more powerful engines, plus the previously introduced goldfish bowl canopy and uncovered tail, the two features which make the Bell 47 probably the most recognised helicopter in the world. The 47G remained in production through to the 1970s, and was also licence built by Agusta in Italy and Kawasaki in Japan.

The H-13 saw widespread US military service during the Korean War, where the type was used for a range of roles such as medevac (fitted with stretchers on either skid), observation and utility transport, and proved beyond doubt the utility of the helicopter.

Today the Bell 47 remains only in limited military service, having largely been replaced by more modern and more capable types, with most in use as trainers or for light utility work.

Photo: New Zealand's Sioux are used for pilot training. (RNZAF)

Bell UH-1B & UH-1C Iroquois

Country of origin: United States of America

Type: Troop transport & utility helicopter

Powerplant: UH-1B & UH-1C – One 820kW (1100shp) Lycoming T53-L-9 or L-11 turboshaft, driving two blade main rotor and tail rotors.

Performance: UH-1B – Max speed 222km/h (120kt), normal cruising speed 193km/h (104kt). Max initial rate of climb 1900ft/min. Service ceiling 16,700ft. Hovering ceiling out of ground effect 11,800ft. Range 463km (250nm). UH-1C – Max speed and max cruising speed 238km/h (130kt), normal cruising speed 230km/h (124kt). Max initial rate of climb 1400ft/min. Service ceiling 11,500ft. Hovering ceiling in ground effect 10,600ft, out of ground effect 10,000ft. Range with auxiliary fuel 615km (332nm).

Weights: UH-1B – Empty 2050kg (4520lb), max TOW 3855kg (8500lb). UH-1C – Empty 2300kg (5070lb), max TOW 4310kg (9500lb).

Dimensions: Main rotor diameter 13.41m (44ft 0in), length overall rotors turning 16.15m (53ft 0in), fuselage length 11.70m (38ft 5in), height 3.84m (12ft 7in). Main rotor disc area 141.3m² (1520sq ft).

Accommodation: Pilot and copilot or passenger side by side, with six troops in main cabin. Alternatively main cabin can accommodate three stretchers and a medical attendant.

Armament: UH-1B/C – Can be fitted with a variety of weaponry including a 7.62mm minigun. AB 204AS – Two Mark 44 torpedoes.

Operators: Austria, Colombia, Honduras, Indonesia, Singapore, South Korea, Sweden, Yemen.

History: The Iroquois has a very special place in modern military history. Produced in more numbers than any other western military aircraft since WW2, it is indelibly linked with the Vietnam War, where it proved beyond a doubt the importance and value of helicopter air mobility to land warfare.

The Iroquois, or Huey, began life in response to a 1954 US Army requirement for a turbine utility helicopter, primarily for medevac. Bell responded to the request with its Lycoming T53 powered Model 204, which was selected for development and the first of the XH-40 prototypes flew on October 22 1956. The XH-40s were followed by six larger, pre production YH-40s, representative of early production aircraft which up until 1962 were designated HU-1A, hence 'Huey'.

The HU-1B or UH-1B introduced a further enlarged cabin and a modified main rotor, and it was this model which was the first to see widespread service in Vietnam, both as a transport and fitted out as a gunship. War experience with gunship configured UH-1Bs led to the UH-1C with an improved rotor system and higher top speed. The UH-1E was similar but developed for the USMC as an assault support helicopter and also built in TH-1E (USMC) and TH-1L (USN) trainer versions. The UH-1F was developed for the USAF and used for missile range support duties and was powered by a General Electric T58 and featured the tailboom of the larger UH-1D (described separately).

Aside from Bell production, short fuselage UH-1s were built in Japan (Fuji) and Italy (by Agusta). Aside from the T53, Agusta built AB 204Bs were powered with the Bristol Siddeley Gnome or GE's T58. The T58 powered AB 204AS was developed specifically for ASW and was fitted with radar and sonar and could carry Mk 44 torpedoes.

Photo: An Austrian AB 204B. (Austrian Armed Forces)

Bell 205, UH-1D & UH-1H Iroquois

Country of origin: United States of America

Type: Utility and battlefield helicopters

Powerplant: UH-1H – One 1045kW (1400shp) Lycoming T53-L-13 turboshaft, driving a two blade main rotor and two blade tail rotor.

Performance: Max speed and max cruising speed 205km/h (110kt). Max initial rate of climb 1600ft/min. Service ceiling 12,600ft. Hovering ceiling out of ground effect 4000ft. Range with max fuel and typical payload 420km (225nm).

Weights: UH-1H – Empty equipped 2363kg (5210lb), normal takeoff 4100kg (9040lb), max takeoff 4310kg (9500lb).

Dimensions: UH-1H – Main rotor diameter 14.63m (48ft 0in), length overall rotors turning 17.62m (57ft 10in), fuselage length 12.77m (41ft 10in), height overall 4.41m (14ft 6in). Main rotor disc area 168.1m² (1809.6sq ft).

Accommodation: UH-1H – Flightcrew of one or two pilots, plus up to 14 equipped troops in the main cabin.

Armament: UH-1H – Pintle mounted machines guns, plus miniguns and rockets mounted on fuselage stub wings.

Operators: 205, UH-1D/H & AB 205 – Argentina, Australia, Bolivia, Brazil, Canada, Chile, Colombia, Dominican Rep, El Salvador, Germany, Greece, Guatemala, Honduras, Indonesia, Iran, Italy, Jamaica, Japan, Mexico, Morocco, Myanmar, New Zealand, Oman, Pakistan, Panama, Peru, Philippines, Saudi Arabia, Singapore, South Korea, Spain, Taiwan, Thailand, Tunisia, Turkey, UAE (Dubai), USA, Uruguay, Zambia.

History: With production of the UH-1B Huey in full swing in 1960, Bell approached the US Army about developing a larger and more powerful development.

The US Army ordered seven improved YUH-1D Iroquois (Bell model number 205), for trials and evaluation in July 1960. First flight of the improved Huey was on August 16 1961 and the type was subsequently ordered into production as the UH-1D.

Compared with the UH-1B and C, the D model featured an 820kW (1100shp) T53-L-11 turboshaft and an enlarged fuselage capable of seating 14 fully equipped troops, twice that of the earlier models. Deliveries of the first of 2008 UH-1Ds for the US Army began in August 1963. Further, Dornier licence built 352 for Germany.

The improved UH-1H introduced a more powerful T53-L-13 turboshaft, but otherwise remained basically unchanged from the UH-1D. Deliveries of the definitive UH-1H to the US Army began in September 1967, while the final Bell built UH-1H was delivered almost two decades later in 1986. Licence built UH-1Hs were built in Italy (by Agusta as the AB 205), Taiwan (by AIDC) and Japan where Fuji continues low rate production of the improved UH-1J with uprated engine and transmission from the AH-1S, Bell 212 main rotor and 212 style longer nose and wider fuselage.

The UH-1D and UH-1H both saw widespread service with the US military (and Australia) in Vietnam.

Bell offers an upgrade of the UH-1H, the AlliedSignal (nee Lycoming) T53-L-703 powered Huey II. Colombia is the launch customer. More significantly, the US Army plans to re-engine 131 ANG UH-1Hs with the LHTEC T800.

Photo: Greece operates over 100 UH-1Hs/AB 205s. (Greek MoD)

Bell 214 Huey Plus, Isfahan & BigLifter

Country of origin: United States of America

Type: Utility & battlefield helicopter

Powerplant: 214A – One 2185kW (2930shp) Lycoming LTC4B-8D turboshaft, driving a two blade main rotor and two blade tail rotor.

Performance: 214A – Max cruising speed clean 260km/h (140kt), max cruising speed with slung load 185km/h (100kt). Service ceiling clean 16,400ft, with sling load 12,400ft. Hovering ceiling out of ground effect clean 12,200ft, out of ground effect with sling load 5400ft. Range clean with reserves 475km (255nm), with sling load 167km (90nm). Endurance 2hr 35min.

Weights: 214A – Empty 3442kg (7588lb), normal takeoff 6260kg (13,800lb), max takeoff with slung load 6805kg (15,000lb).

Dimensions: 214A – Main rotor diameter 15.24m (50ft 0in), fuselage length 14.63m (48ft 0in), height overall 3.90m (12ft 10in). Main rotor disc area 182.4m² (1963.5sq ft).

Accommodation: 214A – Flightcrew of two pilots plus 14 equipped troops. In medevac role can carry six stretcher patients and two medical attendants.

Armament: Usually none.

Operators: Ecuador, Iran, Oman, Philippines, UAE (Dubai).

History: A further development of the ubiquitous Bell Iroquois, the 214 is the most powerful single engined helicopter in military service anywhere.

Bell announced it was developing the 214 Huey Plus on October 12 1970. The private development 214 was based on the basic airframe of the UH-1H Iroquois, but introduced a significantly more powerful 1415kW (1900shp) T53-L-702 turboshaft, a new, longer diameter main rotor and a strengthened fuselage to cope with the new rotor and increased torque. A prototype 214 flew for the first time in 1970 and it demonstrated a number of performance improvements such as a top speed at max weight of 306km/h (165kt), but the type failed to attract orders from the US Army.

The 214 did however arouse the interest of Iran, who saw the 214 as being able to meet its requirement for a troop and supply transport able to operate in its hot environment. Iran ordered 287 Bell 214As, which featured the vastly more powerful 2185kW (2930shp) Lycoming LTC4B-8 turboshaft, on December 22 1972. In addition to the 214As, which were named Isfahan after the town near the Iranian army's helicopter school, Iran also took delivery of 39 SAR configured 214Cs. Plans to establish a production line in Iran for the 214 and the larger 214ST (described separately) were terminated with the fall of the Shah in 1979 and the severing of diplomatic ties with the USA. The cutting of ties with the US also put an end to Bell's support for Iran's large fleet of 214s, and many may no longer be serviceable.

Bell commercially marketed the 214 as the 214B Biglifter and promoted the helicopter's ability to lift large sling loads. Several countries purchased 214Bs for military use.

Photo: One of 287 Bell 214As delivered to Iran during the reign of the Shah. The 214 has a different air intake and exhaust arrangement compared with the 205/UH-1H.

Bell 212, UH-1N & AB 212

Countries of origin: United States of America & Canada

Type: Battlefield & utility helicopter & ASW helo (AB 212ASW)

Powerplants: 212 – One 1340kW (1800shp) takeoff rated Pratt & Whitney Canada PT6T-3 or PT6T-3B Turbo Twin-Pac (two coupled PT6 turboshafts) driving two blade main and tail rotors.

Performance: 212 – Max cruising speed 206km/h (111kt), long range cruising speed 193km/h (104kt). Max initial rate of climb 1320ft/min. Range with standard fuel at long range cruising speed 450km (243nm).

Weights: 212 – Empty 2765kg (6097lb), max TOW 5080kg (11,200lb).

Dimensions: 212 – Main rotor diameter 14.69m (48ft 2in), length overall rotors turning 17.46m (57ft 3in), fuselage length 12.92m (42ft 5in), height overall 4.53m (14ft 10in). Main rotor disc area 168.1m² (1809.6sq ft).

Accommodation: 212 – Total seating for 15, including one or two pilots. In medevac role can house six stretchers and two medical attendants. AB 212ASW – Typical crew of three or four.

Armament: 212 – Can be fitted with pintle mounted machine guns in main cabin doors. AB 212ASW – Two Mk 44, Mk 46 or MQ 44 torpedoes, or AS 12 or Sea Killer ASMs.

Operators: Argentina, Austria, Bangladesh, Canada, Chile, Dominican Republic, Dubai, Ecuador, El Salvador, Ghana, Greece, Guatemala, Guyana, Iran, Israel, Italy, Japan, Lebanon, Libya, Malta, Mexico, Morocco, Panama, Philippines, Saudi Arabia, Singapore, South Korea, Spain, Sri Lanka, Sudan, Thailand, Tunisia, Turkey, Uganda, Venezuela, Yemen, Zambia.

History: Development of the Bell 212 was initiated after Bell, Pratt & Whitney Canada and the Canadian Government agreed to jointly fund development of a twin engine version of the Iroquois.

The early 1968 three way agreement paved the way to mate the basic UH-1H/205 fuselage with a Pratt & Whitney Canada PT6T Turbo Twin-Pac to significantly boost performance. The Twin-Pac mated two PT6 turboshafts through a single combining gearbox and single output shaft, and was fitted with torque sensors so that if one of the engines failed the other could be throttled up to compensate for the power loss. First flight was in 1968.

When the 1968 agreement was announced, Bell announced it held orders for the new helicopter from the Canadian Armed Forces for 50 CUH-1Ns (now CH-135 Twin Hueys) and the US military as UH-1Ns. The US Navy and Marines were the largest UH-1N operators, taking delivery of 221 between them. The USMC has recently contracted Bell to upgrade its UH-1Ns to feature a glass cockpit, four blade main rotor and twin GE T700 turboshafts under the H-1 upgrade. These will have a high degree of commonality with similarly upgraded USMC AH-1Ws.

The 212 is sold commercially as the Twin Two-Twelve and remains in production alongside other Bell civil helicopters in Canada.

In Italy, Agusta licence built the 212 as the AB 212, and developed the anti submarine warfare AB 212ASW. This unique 212 variant is the Italian navy's primary shipborne helicopter. It is equipped with MM/APS-705 search radar, sonar and ESM and can be armed with homing torpedoes or anti ship missiles.

Photo: A Canadian Forces CH-135 Twin Huey.

Bell 412, AB 412 Grifone & CH-146 Griffon

Countries of origin: United States of America & Canada

Type: Battlefield & utility helicopter

Powerplants: CH-146 – One 1425kW (1910shp) Pratt & Whitney Canada PT6T-3D Turbo Twin-Pac (two coupled PT6s), driving a four blade main rotor and two blade tail rotor.

Performance: CH-146 – Max cruising speed 240km/h (130kt), long range cruising speed 230km/h (124kt). Hovering ceiling in ground effect 10,200ft, out of ground effect 5200ft. Range at long range cruising speed with standard fuel and no reserves 745km (402nm).

Weights: CH-146 – Empty equipped 3065kg (6760lb), max takeoff 5397kg (11,900lb).

Dimensions: CH-146 – Main rotor diameter 14.02m (46ft 0in), length overall rotors turning 17.12m (56ft 2in), fuselage length 12.92m (42ft 5in), height overall 4.57m (15ft 0in). Main rotor disc area 154.4m² (1661.9sq ft).

Accommodation: Total seating for 15, including one or two pilots. In medevac role six stretcher patients and two medical attendants.

Armament: Military 412 – Offered with removable nose mounted turret gun, 7.62mm machine gun, 20mm cannon and rocket pods and pintle mounted machine guns in the main cabin doors.

Operators: 412 – Botswana, Canada, Honduras, Indonesia, Norway, Philippines, Poland, Slovenia, Sri Lanka, UK, Venezuela. AB 412 – Finland, Italy, UAE (Dubai), Venezuela, Zimbabwe.

History: The Bell 412 is the ultimate development of the world's most successful helicopter series which began in the late 1950s with the Bell 204 or UH-1A/B/C Iroquois.

The mating of the Pratt & Whitney Canada PT6T Turbo Twin-Pac with the Bell 205 to produce the Bell 212 was a significant commercial success for Bell. However, by the mid 1970s Bell was looking at further improving the breed, and in particular improving the 212's speed and range performance.

Not wanting to re-engine the 212 or make any major structural changes, Bell instead decided to increase performance by developing a four bladed main rotor for the 212. The shorter diameter four blade main rotor is of composite construction except between the leading edge and spar, and has a longer fatigue life and produces less vibration than Bell's earlier two bladed units. First flight of the 412 was in August 1979, while production was transferred to Canada in 1989.

Progressive development of the 412, spurred mainly by growing civil orders, led to the 412SP (Special Performance), 412HP (High Performance) and the current production 412EP (Enhanced Performance). The 412EP also forms the basis for the CH-146 Griffon (412CF), 100 of which have been ordered for the Canadian Forces. In the UK nine 412EPs now fly with the civilian operated Defence Helicopter Flying School, designated Griffin HT.1s.

Like the 204, 205 and 212, the 412 is licence built in Italy by Agusta-Bell as the AB 412. The military AB 412 Grifone features strengthened undercarriage skids to increase crash survivability, crew crash absorbing and armoured crew seats and can be fitted with impact absorbing seats for passengers. It is in service with the Italian army as a battlefield transport and the Italian navy for SAR.

Photo: Italian army AB 412 Grifones.

Bell 206, OH-58, TH-67 & TH-57

Country of origin: United States of America

Type: Light observation (OH-58), utility transport and training helicopter (TH-67 & TH-57)

Powerplant: OH-58A – One 237kW (317shp) Allison T63-A-700 (Allison 250) turboshaft, driving two blade main and tail rotors.

Performance: OH-58A – Max cruising speed at sea level 196km/h (106kt), economical cruising speed 188km/h (102kt), loiter speed for max endurance 91km/h (49kt). Max initial rate of climb 1780ft/min. Service ceiling 19,000ft. Hovering ceiling in ground effect 13,750ft, out of ground effect 9000ft. Max range at sea level with reserves 480km (260nm). Endurance at sea level with no reserves 3hrs 30mins.

Weights: OH-58A – Empty equipped 718kg (1582lb), max takeoff 1360kg (3000lb).

Dimensions: OH-58A – Main rotor disc diameter 10.77m (35ft 4in), length overall with rotors turning 12.49m (41ft 0in), fuselage length 9.84m (32ft 4in), height overall rotors turning 2.91m (9ft 7in). Main rotor disc area 91.1m² (980.5sq ft).

Accommodation: Total seating for five including pilot.

Armament: Usually none, but can be fitted with pintle mounted MGs.

Operators: 206 – Includes Brazil, Brunei, Chile, Columbia, Cyprus, Ecuador, Guatemala, Guyana, Indonesia, Israel, Ivory Coast, Mexico, Myanmar, Pakistan, Peru, South Korea, Sri Lanka, Thailand, UAE (Abu Dhabi & Dubai), Venezuela. OH-58 – Australia, Austria, Canada, USA. TH-67 – USA. TH-57 – USA. 206L – Includes Bangladesh, Cameroon, Guatemala, Mexico, UAE (Dubai), Venezuela.

History: The world's most successful light turbine helicopter grew out of Bell's failed submission to meet a 1960 US Army requirement for a four seat light observation helicopter.

While Bell lost that contract to Hughes with what became the OH-6 Cayuse (described separately), the company set about developing a five seat commercial light helicopter based on the general design of the four OH-4 prototypes which had flown for the first time in December 1962. The civil Bell 206 JetRanger flew for the first time on January 10 1966, and production aircraft were delivered from later that year. Since that time the JetRanger has been in continuous production in progressively modernised forms and has seen widespread military use, as has, to a lesser extent, the stretched 206L LongRanger.

The wheel turned full circle for Bell when in 1967 the US Army reopened the Light Observation Helicopter competition because of the rising costs and late deliveries of the OH-6, and ordered the 206A into production as the OH-58A Kiowa. In all, 2200 Kiowas were delivered to the US Army from May 1968. Many were upgraded to OH-58C standard with an uprated engine. Canada ordered 72 COH-58A Kiowas (subsequently redesignated CH-139), while Austria acquired 12 similar OH-58Bs. Finally Australia's Commonwealth Aircraft Corporation assembled 57 206B-1 Kiowas locally.

The US Navy and Army also use the 206 for training, the former's (delivered from 1968) aircraft designated TH-57 SeaRangers, the latter's, TH-67 Creeks (delivered from 1993).

Photo: The first TH-67 Creek for the US Army. (Bell)

Bell Kiowa Warrior & Combat Scout

Country of origin: United States of America

Type: Armed observation & light attack helicopters

Powerplant: OH-58D – One 485kW (650shp) intermediate rating Allison T703-AD-700 (Allison 250-C30R) turboshaft, driving a four blade main rotor and two blade tail rotor.

Performance: OH-58D Kiowa Warrior – Max level speed at 4000ft 237km/h (128kt), max cruising speed at mission weight 211km/h (114kt), economical cruising speed 204km/h (110kt). Max initial rate of climb 1540ft/min. Service ceiling 15,000ft. Hovering ceiling out of ground effect 4000ft. Range 413km (223nm). Endurance 2hr 24min.

Weights: OH-58D Kiowa Warrior – Empty 1492kg (3289lb), max takeoff 2495kg (5500lb).

Dimensions: OH-58D – Main rotor diameter 10.67m (35ft 0in), length overall rotors turning 12.85m (42ft 2in), fuselage length 10.48m (34ft 5in), height overall 3.93m (7ft 10in). Main rotor disc area 89.4m² (962.0sq ft).

Accommodation: Seating for pilot and observer side by side in OH-58D Kiowa and Kiowa Warrior. Seating for five in Combat Scout.

Armament: OH-58D Kiowa Warrior – Four Stinger AAMs, or four AGM-114C Hellfire anti armour missiles, two seven round rocket pods, or podded 7.62mm or 0.50in machine guns.

Operators: OH-58D – Taiwan, USA. Combat Scout – Saudi Arabia.

History: The OH-58D development of the Kiowa resulted from the US Army's Army Helicopter Improvement Program of 1979.

The Army Helicopter Improvement Program (AHIP) was designed to result in a relatively low cost scout and observation helicopter to support attack AH-64 Apaches. The contract for the AHIP was awarded to Bell for a development of the OH-58 Kiowa.

The resulting OH-58D Kiowa flew for the first time on October 6 1983. Unlike the fairly basic Kiowa, the OH-58D introduced the McDonnell Douglas Astronautics developed mast mounted sight which features TV and infrared sensors, plus a new, four blade main rotor to enhance performance. OH-58D deliveries began in December 1985. Initially the US Army planned to convert 592 OH-58A/Cs to OH-58D standard, this total now stands at 507 (with 398 ordered).

Originally the OH-58D was to be unarmed, but all aircraft are being progressively upgraded to OH-58D Kiowa Warrior status, capable of carrying Stinger AAMs, Hellfire ASMs, rockets and gun pods. The Kiowa Warrior also features uprated transmission, higher max takeoff weight, RWR, IR jammer, laser warning receiver and lightened structure.

The Multi Purpose Light Helicopter (MPLH) development has squatting landing gear and quick folding rotors and is designed to fit into the cargo holds of C-130s and C-141s and be ready to fly 10 minutes after unloading. 81 conversions are on order.

Prototype OH-58Xs with night flying chin turret, colour digital maps, GPS and other improvements have flown. One had some stealth features (including chisel nose, blade root cuffs, composite main doors and RAM coating)

The 406CS Combat Scout is a downgraded export version of the OH-58D without the mast mounted sight (instead, Saudi aircraft are fitted with a Saab-Emerson HeliTOW sight) and lacking some sensitive avionics.

Photo: An armed US Army OH-58D Kiowa Warrior. (Bell)

Bell AH-1F & AH-1S HueyCobra

Country of origin: United States of America

Type: Attack helicopter

Powerplant: AH-1F – One 1340kW (1800shp) Textron Lycoming T53-L-703 turboshaft driving two blade main and tail rotors.

Performance: AH-1F – Max level speed 227km/h (123kt). Max initial rate of climb 1620ft/min. Service ceiling 12,200ft. Hovering ceiling in ground effect 12,200ft. Range 507km (275nm).

Weights: AH-1F – Operating empty 2993kg (6598lb), normal takeoff 4525kg (9975lb), max takeoff 4535kg (10,000lb).

Dimensions: AH-1F – Main rotor diameter 13.41m (44ft 0in), length overall rotors turning 16.18m (53ft 1in), fuselage length 13.59m (44ft 7in), height to top of rotor head 4.09m (13ft 5in). Main rotor disc area 141.3m² (1520.2sq ft).

Accommodation: Copilot/gunner (in front cockpit) and pilot in tandem.

Armament: Eight Hughes TOW anti armour missiles on the outboard stations of two stub wings. Can carry rockets and machine gun pods. General Electric nose mounted three barrel 20mm gun turret can be slaved to helmet mounted sights.

Operators: Bahrain, Israel, Japan, Jordan, Pakistan, South Korea, Thailand, Turkey, USA.

History: The world's first operational dedicated two seat helicopter gunship, the HueyCobra was initially intended to be an interim design pending the introduction into service of the subsequently cancelled Lockheed AH-56 Cheyenne.

The HueyCobra began life as a private venture when in 1965 Bell took the powerplant, transmission and rotor system of the UH-1B/C Iroquois and matched them to a new fuselage featuring seating for two in tandem, stub wings to carry weapons and a nose gun, to result in the Bell 209. The prototype flew for the first time on September 7 1965, just six months after design work had begun. The US Army subsequently ordered the 209 into production as the AH-1G HueyCobra to fulfil an urgent need for an attack helicopter primarily to escort troop carrying UH-1 Iroquois in Vietnam, pending delivery of the troubled AH-56. In all 1078 AH-1Gs were built, many of which saw service in Vietnam, while the AH-56 program was cancelled.

The AH-1G was followed up by the AH-1Q, an interim anti armour version capable of firing Hughes TOW anti tank missiles. First flown in 1973, 92 AH-1Gs were converted to AH-1Qs. Combat experience found the AH-1Q's hot and high performance lacking, and resulted in the AH-1S. The AH-1S designation covers staged improvements to the AH-1's powerplant and transmission, armament, avionics and cockpit. New build production AH-1Ss and conversions of the AH-1Qs and AH-1Gs resulted in four separate AH-1S subvariants, the AH-1S(MC) being the definitive standard incorporating all the planned improvements.

In 1989 the US Army redesignated the AH-1S to reflect the different variants. Thus AH-1F covers the AH-1S(MC), while the AH-1S designation now covers AH-1S(MOD) aircraft (converted AH-1Qs), AH-1P covers early build AH-1Ss, and AH-1E covers AH-1Ss with improved weapon systems. In 1995 Bell and IAR Brasov signed an agreement covering the licence construction of 96 AH-1Fs in Romania, but in 1996 this agreement was altered to cover the AH-1W instead.

Photo: The Israeli air force flies 40 Cobras.

Bell AH-1W SuperCobra

Country of origin: United States of America

Type: Attack helicopter

Powerplants: AH-1W – Two 1285kW (1723shp) General Electric T700-GE-401 turboshafts driving two blade main and tail rotors.

Performance: AH-1W – Max level speed 282km/h (152kt), max cruising speed 278km/h (150kt). Max initial rate of climb on one engine 800ft/min. Service ceiling 14,000ft plus. Hovering ceiling in ground effect 14,750ft, out of ground effect 3000ft. Range with standard fuel and no reserves 587km (317nm). Max endurance 3hr.

Weights: AH-1W – Empty 4635kg (10,215kg), MTOW 6690kg (14,750lb).

Dimensions: AH-1W – Main rotor diameter 14.63m (48ft 0in), length overall rotors turning 17.68m (58ft 0in), fuselage length 13.87m (45ft 6in), height to top of rotor head 4.11m (13ft 6in), height overall 4.44m (14ft 7in). Main rotor disc area 168.1m² (1809.6sq ft).

Accommodation: Copilot/gunner (front cockpit) and pilot in tandem.

Armament: AH-1W – General Electric nose mounted turret houses three barrel 20mm M197 gun. Can carry up to eight Hughes TOW or AGM-114 Hellfire anti armour missiles on outboard stations of stub wings, plus rocket or gun pods on inboard stations. Other armament options include fuel air explosives, iron bombs, two AIM-9L Sidewinder air-to-air missiles or AGM-122A Sidearm ASMs.

Operators: AH-1J – Iran. AH-1W – Romania*, Taiwan*, Turkey, USA.

History: The twin engine variants of the Cobra were developed specifically for the US Marine Corps, and have resulted in the ultimate Cobra development so far, the AH-1W SuperCobra.

The AH-1 HueyCobra aroused USMC interest early on in its career, and that service's evaluation of the US Army's AH-1G led to a 1968 order for 49 similar AH-1J SeaCobras. The AH-1J was similar to the AH-1G except for the powerplant, the Marines specifying the 1340kW (1800shp) (flat rated to 820kW/1100shp) Pratt & Whitney Canada T400-CP-400, the military version of the PT6T Turbo Twin-Pac, an installation that coupled two PT6 turboshafts through a combining transmission. The AH-1J also introduced the three barrel M197 20mm cannon in the nose turret. Iran also ordered 202 AH-1Js.

The improved AH-1T (initially known as the Improved Sea Cobra) was first ordered in 1974 and differed from the J in having a 1470kW (1970shp) T400-WV-402, a new rotor system based on that for the Bell 214, uprated transmission and lengthened fuselage and tail.

The AH-1W started life as a proposal to Iran for an AH-1T powered by two General Electric T700s. A so powered demonstrator was flown in 1983 and designated AH-1T+ and the type, with further improvements, was ordered into production for the USMC as the AH-1W SuperCobra, or Whiskey Cobra. Aside from new build AH-1Ws, AH-1Ts have been converted to the new configuration.

In 1996 Bell and IAR Brasov signed an agreement which will see 96 AH-1Ws built in Romania from 1999, called the AH-1RO Dracula, but at late 1997 this program looked unlikely to go ahead.

The US Marine Corps is upgrading its AH-1Ws to four blade AH-1W (4BW) configuration under the H-1 upgrade program. Other new features include new stub wings able to carry more weapons, glass cockpits with HOTCC and a new EW suite.

Photo: A Turkish AH-1W. (Bell)

Bell 214ST

Country of origin: United States of America

Type: Medium transport helicopter

Powerplants: 214ST – Two 1215kW (1625shp) General Electric CT7-2A turboshafts linked through a combining gearbox driving a two blade main rotor and two blade tail rotor.

Performance: 214ST – Max cruising speed 260km/h (140kt) at 4000ft, or 264km/h (143kt) at sea level. Max initial rate of climb 1780ft/min. Service ceiling with one engine out 4800ft. Hovering ceiling in ground effect 6400ft. Ferry range with auxiliary fuel 1020km (550nm), range with standard fuel and no reserves 805km (435nm).

Weights: 214ST – Empty 4300kg (9481lb), max takeoff 7938kg (17,500lb).

Dimensions: 214ST – Main rotor diameter 15.85m (52ft 0in), length overall rotors turning 18.95m (62ft 2in), fuselage length 15.03m (49ft 4in), height overall 4.84m (15ft 11in). Main rotor disc area 197.3m² (2124sq ft).

Accommodation: 214ST – Pilot and copilot and up to 16 or 17 passengers. Freight volume of 8.95m³ (316cu ft). Can carry an external sling load of 3630kg (8000lb).

Armament: Typically none, but can be fitted with pintle mounted machine guns in main cabin door.

Operators: Brunei, Iraq, Oman, Peru, Thailand, Venezuela.

History: Despite sharing a common model number with the 214 Huey Plus and Big Lifter (described separately), the Bell 214ST is a much larger helicopter.

Bell's biggest helicopter yet (excluding the V-22) was developed in response to an Iranian requirement for a larger transport helicopter with better performance in its hot and high environment than its 214 Isfahans. Bell based its proposal on the 214 but made substantial design changes, resulting in what is essentially an all new helicopter with little commonality with the smaller 214 series.

The 214ST featured two General Electric CT7 turboshafts (the commercial equivalent of the military T700 which powers the AH-1W and UH-60), a stretched fuselage seating up to 17 in the main cabin and stretched main rotor blades from the 214 with composite construction. The 214ST designation originally stood for Stretched Twin, reflecting the changes over the 214, but this was later changed to stand for Super Transporter.

The 214ST was to have been built under licence in Iran as part of that country's plans to establish a large army air wing (other aircraft ordered in large numbers under this plan were the 214A Isfahan and AH-1J SeaCobra, both described separately), but the Islamic revolution and fall of the Shah in 1979 put paid to these plans.

Undeterred, Bell continued development of the 214ST for civil and military customers. The 214ST flew for the first time on July 21 1979 and 100 production aircraft were built through to 1990.

Most 214ST sales were to military customers. Ironically, Iraq was the 214ST's largest customer, taking delivery of 45 during 1987 and 1988, some most likely seeing service in the Gulf War. Other customers include Peru, Thailand and Venezuela.

Photo: The 214ST differs considerably from the 214A and 214B.

Bell/Boeing V-22 Osprey

Country of origin: United States of America

Type: Tiltrotor tactical transport

Powerplants: Two 4590kW (6150shp) Allison T406-AD-400 turboshafts driving three blade proprotors.

Performance: Max cruising speed in aeroplane mode 638km/h (345kt), at sea level in helicopter mode 185km/h (100kt). Service ceiling 26,000ft. Takeoff run in short takeoff mode less than 150m (500ft). Ferry range 3890km (2100nm). Range with a 5445kg (12,000lb) payload and vertical takeoff 2225km (1200nm). Range with a 9075kg (20,000lb) payload and short takeoff 3335km (1800nm).

Weights: Empty 14,800kg (32,628lb), normal mission takeoff weight for a vertical takeoff 21,545kg (47,500lb), normal mission takeoff weight with short takeoff 24,947kg (55,000lb), max takeoff with short takeoff for self ferry 27,442kg (60,500lb).

Dimensions: Prop rotor diameter 11.58m (38ft 0in), wing span including nacelles 15.52m (50ft 11in), fuselage length excluding probe 17.47m (57ft 4in), height overall nacelles vertical 6.63m (21ft 8in), height at top of tail fins 5.38m (17ft 8in). Proprotor disc area each 105.4m² (1134sq ft), wing area 35.5m² (392.0sq ft).

Accommodation: Flightcrew of two plus loadmaster/crew chief. Seating for up to 24 fully combat equipped troops in main cabin.

Armament: None, although special mission aircraft would be armed.

Operators: None

History: Despite weight and cost problems, the revolutionary V-22 nevertheless is set to become the first operational tilt rotor aircraft in the world.

Development of the Osprey dates back to the early 1980s' joint services program to develop a tiltrotor transport based on the successful Bell/NASA XV-15 demonstrator. The US Navy awarded a teaming of Bell and Boeing an initial development contract in April 1983, while an order for six flying prototypes (later reduced to five) was signed in May 1986. First flight was on March 19 1989.

Since that time the Osprey program has suffered its share of problems, with two of the prototypes crashing, planned production orders reduced and the whole program coming close to cancellation in 1992 as an economy measure. The second of four production standard V-22s was delivered to the Naval Air Warfare Centre in September 1997. The first of 360 MV-22s for the USMC (to replace CH-46s and CH-53s) is due to be delivered in mid 1999. The MV-22 will be able to perform all the missions a comparable helicopter will, yet it can cruise at twice the speed and carry twice the payload.

The V-22 features two Allison T400 turboshafts (with FADEC) mounted in tilting nacelles. The engines are also linked via a cross-shaft that allows both proprotors to be powered in the event of an engine failure. Other features include 59% composite construction by weight, digital fly-by-wire, four screen EFIS and AAQ-16 FLIR, while the wings swivel to be parallel to the fuselage for stowage on ships.

Upcoming Osprey variants will include the USAF's 55 planned CV-22 special operations aircraft to be fitted with long range fuel tanks and APQ-174 terrain following/avoidance radar, and the USN's HV-22 Combat SAR HH-3 replacement (48 planned).

Photo: The US Marines remain committed to the V-22.

Beriev Be-12 Tchaika

Country of origin: Russia

Type: Maritime patrol and ASW amphibian

Powerplants: Two 3125kW (4190ehp) Ivchenko (now Progress) AI-20D turboprops, driving four blade propellers.

Performance: Max level speed 608km/h (328kt), typical patrol speed 320km/h (173kt). Max initial rate of climb 2990ft/min. Service ceiling 37,000ft. Ferry range 7500km (4050nm), range with combat load 4000km (2160nm).

Weights: Empty 21,700kg (47,840lb), max takeoff 31,000kg (68,342lb).

Dimensions: Wing span 29.71m (97ft 6in), length 30.17m (99ft 0in), height 7.00m (23ft 0in). Wing area 105.0m² (1130.3sq ft).

Accommodation: Five crew complement consists of pilot, copilot, navigator, radar operator and MAD operator.

Armament: Internal weapons bay and two underwing hardpoints can carry a variety of weaponry including torpedoes, depth charges and mines.

Operators: Russia, Vietnam, Ukraine.

History: One of the few amphibians in military service, the Tchailka (or gull) still remains in Russian naval aviation service performing close in maritime patrol, ASW and SAR work.

The Be-12 (NATO name 'Mail') was developed as a replacement for the earlier piston powered Be-6, which first flew in 1949. The turbo-prop Be-12 meanwhile first flew during 1960, and made its public debut at the 1961 Soviet Aviation Day Display at Tushino, Moscow. The Be-12 was of the same basic configuration as the smaller Be-6, with twin tails and a high cranked wing to give the propellers and engine maximum clearance from the water. Other Be-12 features include the powerful Ivchenko AI-20D turboprops (AI-20s also power the land based Il-38 'May' maritime patrol and ASW aircraft), a stepped hull with spray dams along the nose to minimise engine water ingestion, retractable undercarriage, a nose mounted search radar and tail mounted Magnetic Anomaly Detector (MAD) boom.

The Be-12 was selected for Soviet naval service in 1964 ahead of another Beriev design, the jet powered Be-10. The Be-10 aircraft established a number of seaplane world records, but only three or four are thought to have been built, mainly for trials purposes. The Be-12 itself set or broke all 44 FAI (Federation Aeronautique Internationale) records covering turboprop powered amphibians and seaplanes between 1964 and 1983.

Exact production of the Be-12 is unknown, though it is thought to have run to around 100 aircraft. The main role of the Be-12 is ASW and maritime patrol within 370km (200nm) of shore bases, however Be-12s have performed a variety of different tasks including Arctic and Siberian exploration and resource exploration, geophysical mapping and search and rescue.

While the brunt of Russian ASW and maritime patrol tasks are now borne by the Il-38 and Tu-142, the majority of Be-12s are still in service with the Russian northern fleet and probably with Ukraine. The Be-12 is also in service in Vietnam.

Photo: This ex Russian navy Be-12 was returned to Beriev in 1993 to serve as a demonstrator firebomber for civil/government use. (Beriev)

Beriev A-40 & Be-42 Albatross

Country of origin: Russia

Type: Maritime patrol & ASW (A-40) and SAR (Be-42) amphibian

Powerplants: A-40 – Two 117.7kN (26,455lb) Aviadvigatel D-30KPV turbofans and two 24.5kN (5510lb) RKBM (formerly Klimov) RD-60K booster turbojets.

Performance: A-40 – Max level speed 760km/h (410kt), max cruising speed 720km/h (388kt). Max initial rate of climb on one engine 5900ft/min. Service ceiling 31,825ft. Range with max payload 4100km (2210nm), range with max fuel 5500km (2965nm).

Weights: A-40 – Max payload 6500kg (14,330lb), max takeoff 86,000kg (189,595lb).

Dimensions: A-40 – Wing span 41.62m (136ft 7in), length overall including nose probe 43.84m (143ft 10in), fuselage length 38.92m (127ft 8in), height 11.07m (36ft 4in). Wing area 200.0m² (2153sq ft).

Accommodation: A-40 – Crew complement of eight consisting of pilot, copilot, flight engineer, radio operator, navigator/observer and three observers. Be-42 – Flightcrew of five, plus three medical attendants, and accommodation for 54 rescued survivors.

Armament: A-40 – Internal weapons bay could carry a range of weapons maritime such as torpedoes, mines and depth charges. Be-42 – None.

Operators: Russia*

History: The Beriev Albatross is the world's largest amphibious aircraft and was designed, initially at least, to replace the Be-12 and Il-38 in maritime patrol and ASW roles.

Design work on the Albatross (NATO identification name 'Mermaid') began in 1983, but it was not until 1988 that the type was made publicly known in the west when the US announced it had taken satellite photographs of a jet powered amphibian under development in Russia. The Albatross made its first flight in December 1986, while its first public appearance was a fly-by at the 1989 Soviet Aviation Day Display at Tushino, Moscow.

The exact future of the Albatross is in some doubt. As many as 20 A-40 Albatrosses have been ordered for CIS naval service, but the status of this order is unclear, with construction believed to be delayed due to funding difficulties. Other versions of the aircraft include the Be-42, which is optimised for search and rescue and the proposed twin propfan powered A-45, Be-40P 105 seat airliner and Be-40PT combi airliner/freighter. The aircraft also forms the basis of the slightly smaller civil Be-200, which is being promoted for various missions including firefighting.

Design features of the Albatross include its unique 'variable rise' single step hull, which is designed to improve stability and controllability in the water, and a unique powerplant combination of two D-30KPV turbofans with a booster turbojet in each of the engine pylons.

The Be-42 SAR aircraft would be able to take 54 survivors of a marine accident and would be equipped with liferafts, powerboats and a range of specialised medical equipment including a transfusion machine, defibrillator and ECG. It would also be equipped with various infrared sensors and a searchlight.

History: The Albatross has the distinction of being the only jet powered amphibian currently flying. (Peter Clark)

Beriev/Ilyushin A-50

Country of origin: Russia

Type: Airborne Early Warning & Control aircraft

Powerplants: Four 117.7kN (26,455lb) Aviadvigatel (Soloviev) D-30KP turbofans.

Performance: Generally similar to the Il-76, described separately under Ilyushin, with cruising speed between 750 and 800km/h (405 and 432kt). Generally operates at 33,000ft flying figure of eight search tracks, with 100km (54nm) between the centre of each circle.

Weights: Unpublished, but similar to Il-76.

Dimensions: Wing span 50.50m (165ft 8in), length 46.59m (152ft 10in), height 14.76m (48ft 5in). Wing area 300.0m² (3229.2sq ft).

Accommodation: Normal crew complement of 15, including two pilots, flight engineer and navigator.

Armament: None

Operators: Russia

History: The A-50 (NATO name 'Mainstay') was developed to replace Russia's first operational AEW&C aircraft, the Tupolev Tu-126 'Moss'.

The Tu-126 was a conversion of the Tu-114 airliner (the Tu-114 was an airliner development of the Tu-95) and about a dozen Tu-126 conversions are thought to have seen service since the mid 1960s.

Development of an improved AEW&C aircraft to replace the Tu-126 began during the 1970s, resulting in the A-50. The A-50 is based on the Ilyushin Il-76 freighter, the most obvious difference being the large Sentry style rotating rotodome mounted above the fuselage housing the Liana radar.

Other external features include a nose mounted refuelling probe (although refuelling is difficult because of the buffet caused by the rotodome), horizontal blade antennas mounted on each main undercarriage fairing, the glazed nose navigator station of the Il-76 has been deleted, a dorsal fin forward of the wing, an intake in the root of the tail to supply air to cool avionics, and a number of smaller antennas.

Inside the A-50, crew facilities are spartan, with no rest bunks and high noise levels. A single large colour CRT screen and station is used for controlling fighters, while other screens (also colour CRTs) display data about the air and ground tactical situations.

The A-50 first entered service in 1984 and around 20 have been built. It represents the state of the art in Russian electronics, as its capabilities are reportedly comparable to that of the Sentry in some areas. The A-50 can detect low flying cruise missiles, control fighters, and download tactical information to ground stations and fighters automatically. The improved A-50U, which first appeared in 1995, features the Vega Shmel-M radar.

Beriev is also building an A-50I, a bare A-50 airframe in which IAI will install the Elta phased array AEW radar for a potential candidate to meet a Chinese requirement for four AEW aircraft.

Iraq has independently developed two AEW versions of the Il-76. The failed Baghdad 1 featured a Thomson-CSF radar mounted in the lower tail, while the Adnan conversion features a rotodome above the fuselage. Of the three Adnans converted, one was destroyed on the ground during the Gulf War.

Photo: A Russian air force A-50U. (MAP)

Boeing B-52 Stratofortress

Country of origin: United States of America

Type: Strategic bomber

Powerplants: B-52H – Eight 75.6kN (17,000lb) Pratt & Whitney TF33-P-3 turbofans.

Performance: B-52H – Max level speed Mach 0.90 or 957km/h (516kt), cruising speed 820km/h (442kt), low level penetration speed 650 to 675km/h (352 to 365kt). Service ceiling 55,000ft. Range with max fuel without inflight refuelling over 16,095km (8685nm).

Weights: B-52H – Empty 78,355kg (172,740lb), max takeoff 229,088kg (505,000lb).

Dimensions: B-52H – Wing span 56.39m (185ft 0in), length 49.05m (160ft 11in), height 12.40m (40ft 8in). Wing area 371.6m² (4000sq ft).

Accommodation: B-52H – Crew complement of five, comprising pilot, copilot, navigator, bombardier/radar navigator and ECM operator.

Armament: B-52H – Tail mounted 20mm M61A1 cannon no longer in use. In nuclear strike role can be fitted with 20 AGM-86B or AGM-129 cruise missiles in the internal bomb bay and two underwing stations. Can be fitted with free fall nuclear bombs. Conventional munitions include up to 12 AGM-84 Harpoon or AGM-142A ASMs, AGM-86C cruise missiles or up to 51 750lb (340kg) class bombs or mines.

Operators: USA

History: The mighty B-52 began life in the 1940s as a proposed replacement for Strategic Air Command's B-36s and B-50s (the B-50 was a development of the B-29 Superfortress).

Originally the B-52 was to be powered by turboprops as they offered the best compromise between high performance and long range, but the availability of the Pratt & Whitney J57 turbojet (which offered a quantum leap forward in performance and economy over earlier jets) resulted in the definitive eight jet arrangement. A prototype XB-52 flew for the first time on April 15 1952. Successful evaluation of the B-52 led to the first production contracts and an entry into service in March 1955.

In all, 744 B-52s were built through to 1962 in eight major sub-types, the most important numerically being the B-52D (which saw extensive use as a conventional bomber in Vietnam), the B-52G which introduced a shorter vertical tail, remote control tail guns and a wet wing, and the B-52H with turbofan engines.

While all versions of the B-52 were progressively upgraded throughout their service lives to keep pace with new roles, mission profiles and technologies, the only model now in service is the TF33 turbofan powered B-52H (the switch to more economical turbofan engines increased the B-52's range by a third). The B-52H also introduced a tail mounted 20mm cannon, although this is no longer used. B-52H features include a terrain following radar, comprehensive ECM protection and Electro-Optical Viewing System.

About 90 B-52Hs were on Air Combat Command strength in 1997 when Boeing was proposing to re-engine 71 with four Allison assembled 192kN (43,000lb) Rolls-Royce RB211-535 turbofans. Boeing claimed the re-engine would save the USAF billions of dollars in maintenance costs over a service life extending to 2030, in addition to giving improved performance and range.

Photo: A USAF B-52H – a symbol of US military might. (John Sise)

Boeing KC-135 Stratotanker

Country of origin: United States of America

Type: Air-to-air refuelling tanker

Powerplants: KC-135R – Four 97.9kN (22,000lb) CFM F108 turbofans.

Performance: KC-135R – Max speed 982km/h (530kt), cruising speed at 35,000ft 855km/h (462kt). Max initial rate of climb 1290ft/min. Service ceiling 45,000ft. Operational radius 4635km (2500nm).

Weights: KC-135R – Operating empty 48,220kg (106,305lb), max takeoff 146,285kg (322,500lb).

Dimensions: Wing span 39.88m (130ft 10in), length 41.53m (136ft 3in), height 12.70m (41ft 8in). Wing area 226.0m^2 (2433.0sq ft).

Accommodation: Standard crew complement for tanking of four, comprising pilot, copilot, navigator and boom operator. Fuel capacity 92,210kg (203,288lb).

Armament: None

Operators: France, Singapore*, Turkey*, USA.

History: The KC-135 Stratotanker is a very significant aircraft, having paved the way for Boeing's unparalleled success as the world's premier jet airliner manufacturer, while also considerably boosting the USAF's ability to conduct war by substantially increasing aircraft range.

In the early 1950s Boeing made the daring decision to develop as a private venture a four jet engined transport that could be developed into an airliner, but also meet a USAF requirement for an inflight refuelling tanker with jet aircraft speeds. The resulting 367-80 demonstrator first flew on July 15 1954. Just one month later in August 1954 the USAF ordered it into production as the KC-135 Stratotanker inflight refueller with a Boeing developed flying boom. Features of the KC-135A included four J57 turbojets, fuel in belly and wing tanks and a side loading cargo door for freight on the main deck.

Some 820 KC-135s and variants were built, giving Boeing considerable experience in building jet transports, while the KC-135 (which has the Boeing model number of 717) forms the basis of the 707.

Aside from the KC-135A, 45 C-135 Stratolifter freighters were built without tanking equipment, pending the delivery of the Lockheed C-141 Starlifter. A handful survive as transports in support roles with special USAF units. The KC-135Q designation applies to 56 KC-135As modified to refuel SR-71s (now re-engined with F108s as KC-135Ts), while France took delivery of 12 C-135F tankers (also later re-engined with F108s as C-135FRs).

The KC-135 has been the subject of two major re-engining programs. Over 160 Air Force Reserve and Air National Guard KC-135s were re-engined with TF33 turbofans sourced from retired 707 airliners as KC-135Es. The KC-135R designation applies to KC-135s re-engined with CFM International F108 (CFM56) turbofans. More than 400 KC-135Rs have been delivered, mainly to active duty USAF AMC units, while 33 will be modified with hose and drogue pods.

Both turbofan re-engining programs significantly increase the KC-135's takeoff performance, range and fuel offload capabilities, and, particularly in the case of the KC-135R, make the aircraft significantly quieter than the turbojet powered KC-135A. All surviving USAF KC-135As that were not re-engined have been retired.

Photo: A TF33 powered KC-135E. (Doug Mackay)

Boeing EC-135 & RC-135

Country of origin: United States of America

Type: Series of special missions adaptations of basic C-135 airframe

Powerplants: EC-135C – Four 80.1kN (18,000lb) Pratt & Whitney TF33-P-9 turbofans.

Performance: EC-135C – Max speed 990km/h (535kt), cruising speed (at 35,000ft) 900km/h (485kt). Max initial rate of climb 2000ft/min. Service ceiling 40,600ft. Ferry range 9100km (4910nm), operational radius 4310km (2325nm).

Weights: EC-135 – Basic empty 46,403kg (102,300lb), max takeoff 135,625kg (299,000lb).

Dimensions: EC-135 – Wing span 39.88m (130ft 10in), length 41.53m (136ft 3in), height 12.70m (41ft 8in). Wing area 226.0m^2 (2433sq ft).

Accommodation: Various, depending on aircraft fit out and mission.

Armament: None

Operators: USA

History: The basic C-135 airframe forms the basis for one of the most prolific families of variants and subtypes in military aviation, with aircraft performing a diverse range of missions.

The EC-135 was originally developed to serve as an airborne command post for the then Strategic Air Command's B-52 nuclear bomber fleet, and some 40 C-135s were converted as EC-135s at various stages. The aircraft are fitted with a comprehensive communication suite which allows the battle commander to communicate with the national command structure, other command post and intelligence aircraft and ground forces. The EC-135s feature a trailing wire antenna which is reeled out behind it, various antennas along the fuselage, and in the case of four EC-135Cs, a Milstar satcom antenna mounted in a bulge on top of the fuselage. Most surviving EC-135s are EC-135Cs, most other subvariants have been retired because of a reduced requirement for these aircraft. The EC-135Cs themselves are scheduled to be retired, with most of their missions taken over by the US Navy's E-6 Mercury TACAMO platform. Another EC-135 variant is the EC-135E range instrumentation aircraft.

RC-135U, RC-135V Rivet Joint and RC-135W signals intelligence variants still form an important part of the USA's intelligence gathering assets. All three RC-135 variants feature slab sided cheek fairings covering the antennas for the Automatic Elint Emitter Locator System (AEELS) which intercepts transmissions on a broad range of frequencies and sorts out those which may be of interest to the aircraft's operators. The RC-135V and RC-135W also feature a thimble nose featuring further sensors. The TC-135W is a similar variant used for RC-135 crew training. The RC-135S Cobra Ball records foreign missile launches and testing and may be used tactically for ballistic missile launch detection.

The NC-135 and NKC-135 designations apply to aircraft used for various test and trials purposes, including inflight refuelling tests. The USN operates two NKC-135As electronic warfare aircraft, used to create simulated electronic warfare environments for fleet training.

Other variants on the C-135 theme include the WC-135M weather research platform and the OC-135 which is used for Open Skies treaty verification reconnaissance and is fitted with panoramic, oblique and vertical cameras.

Photo: A RC-135S Cobra Ball. (Les Bushell)

Boeing 707

Country of origin: United States of America

Type: Strategic & VIP transport, tanker and special mission aircraft

Powerplants: 707-320B – Four 80kN (18,000lb) Pratt & Whitney JT3D-3 turbofans or four 84.4kN (19,000lb) P&W JT3D-7s.

Performance: 707-320B – Max speed 1010km/h (545kt), max cruising speed 974km/h (525kt), long range cruising speed 885km/h (478kt). Max initial rate of climb 4000ft/min. Range with max passenger load 6920km (3735nm), range with max fuel and 147 passengers and reserves 9265km (5000nm).

Weights: 707-320B – Empty 66,408kg (146,400lb), max takeoff 151,315kg (333,600lb).

Dimensions: 707-320B – Wing span 44.42m (145ft 9in), length 46.61m (152ft 11in), height 12.94m (42ft 5in). Wing area 283m² (3050sq ft).

Accommodation: Flightcrew of two pilots and flight engineer. In passenger service could seat up to 190 passengers. Alternatively can carry freight on main deck in freighter and combi versions.

Armament: None

Operators: Angola, Argentina, Australia, Brazil, Chile, Columbia, Germany, India, Indonesia, Israel, Italy, Morocco, NATO, Pakistan, Peru, South Africa, Spain, Togo, Venezuela, Yugoslavia.

History: The 707 is widely recognised as one of the two most significant postwar commercial airliners, and with over 1000 built including military versions was highly successful.

Boeing's model 707 was based on the Model 367-80 jet transport development aircraft, which flew for the first time on July 15 1954. The 367-80 or Dash 80 demonstrator led to the KC-135 tanker and then the larger 707 airliner. The 707 flew for the first time on December 20 1957 and entered service the next year. Compared with the KC-135, the initial 707-120 featured a wider, longer fuselage. Power was supplied by JT3 turbojets, the commercial equivalent of the J57.

Military 707s are all converted 707-320Bs or 320Cs. The -320B differs from the original 120 in having four JT3D turbofan engines (equivalent to the TF33) and a stretched fuselage. The 707-320B and the 707-320C convertible passenger/freighter aircraft are the definitive 707 models and were delivered to airlines around the world between 1962 and 1977. Most military 707s are ex civilian aircraft, although Canada, Germany and Iran purchased new build 707s direct from Boeing (the Iranian aircraft delivered with KC-135 style flying boom refuelling equipment and Beech probe and drogue wingtip pods).

Aside from Iran, many other 707 operators have fitted their 707s with air-to-air refuelling equipment. Australia, Brazil, Israel, Italy, Morocco, Peru, Spain and Venezuela all operate 707 tankers.

Israel has adopted the 707 for Elint and AEW missions. Some serve as command posts, others combined tanker/Elint aircraft. The AEW Phalcon is the most extensive non US military development of the 707 with Elbit phased array radar mounted in a nose radome and conformal cheeks along the sides of the fuselage. Aside from Israel, Chile and possibly South Africa operate Phalcons.

Ireland based Omega is one of a number of companies to offer 707 tanker conversions, but is also offering the 7Q7 97kN (21,650lb) P&W JT8D-200 re-engine program.

Photo: One of five Australian 707s. (Rob Finlayson)

Boeing E-6 Mercury, VC-137 & EC-18

Country of origin: United States of America

Type: E-6 – Sub communications and command post. VC-137 – VIP transport. EC-18 – Range instrumentation & cruise missile control aircraft

Powerplants: E-6A – Four 97.9kN (22,000lb) CFM International F108-CF-100 turbofans.

Performance: E-6A – Dash speed 980km/h (530kt), max cruising speed at 40,000ft 842km/h (455kt). Patrol altitude between 25,000 and 30,000ft. Service ceiling 42,000ft. Mission range without inflight refuelling 11,760km (6350nm). Operational radius 1855km (1000nm) on a 10hr 30min without refuelling, or 28hr 55min with one refuelling, or 72hr with multiple refuellings. Unrefuelled endurance 15hr 25min.

Weights: E-6A – Operating empty 78,378kg (172,795lb), max takeoff 155,130kg (342,000lb).

Dimensions: E-6A – Span 45.16m (148ft 2in), length 46.61m (152ft 11in), height 12.93m (42ft 5in). Wing area 283.4m² (3050.0sq ft).

Accommodation: E-6A – Flightcrew of four. Has eight bunks in rest area for relief crew and four communications work stations.

Armament: None

Operators: USA

History: The E-6, EC-18 and VC-137 are military variants of the 707.

The first US military development of the 707 airliner to see service was the VC-137. Three VC-137As were first delivered for VIP transport use in 1959. These aircraft were based on the 707-120 airframe and were powered by J57 (JT3) turbojets, but later became VC-137Bs when re-engined with TF33 turbofans. The VC-137Bs were redesignated C-137Bs in the late 1970s. The VC-137C designation applies to two larger TF33 powered 707-320 based VIP transports, used as the presidential Air Force One aircraft until replaced by the VC-25. The VC-137s are to be replaced by the 757 based C-32A from 1998.

The EC-18 designation applies to ex American Airlines 707-320Bs purchased in 1981. Eight were originally delivered as C-18s – of those one was scrapped for parts and one was retained for general transport duties. Four were converted as EC-18B Advanced Range Instrumentation Aircraft (ARIA) with a steerable telemetry-receiving antenna in a bulbous nose radome (similar to the EC-135E). The remaining two are EC-18D Cruise Missile Mission Control Aircraft, fitted with an APG-63 radar (as on the F-15) and telemetry receiver.

The E-6 Mercury was developed for the US Navy as a replacement for EC-130Q TACAMO (TAke Charge And Move Out) Hercules. These 16 new build aircraft are tasked with providing a communications link between the US national command structure, other command post aircraft such as the E-4 and the US Navy's submarine fleet – primarily ballistic nuclear missile armed submarines. The E-6 (initially named Hermes) is powered by CFM F108 turbofans and is equipped with a comprehensive secure communications suite, including HF, VHF and UHF radio comms and UHF satellite comms (two underwing pods house ESM receivers and the UHF satellite antennas). The aircraft is also equipped with two trailing wire antennas. First flight was on February 19 1987. The E-6s are now being upgraded to E-6B standard, gaining some EC-135 equipment and gradually taking over the EC-135's airborne command post role. The first was delivered in May 1997.

Photo: The E-6 Mercury. (Boeing)

Boeing E-3 Sentry

Country of origin: United States of America

Type: Airborne Warning & Control System (AWACS) aircraft

Powerplants: E-3A/C – Four 93.4kN (21,000lb) Pratt & Whitney TF33-P-100 turbofans. E-3D/F – Four 106.8kN (24,000lb) CFM56-2A-3s.

Performance: E-3C – Max speed 853km/h (460kt). Service ceiling over 29,000ft. Operational radius 1610km (870nm) for a 6 hour patrol without inflight refuelling. Endurance without inflight refuelling over 11 hours. E-3D/F – Service ceiling over 30,000ft. Endurance without inflight refuelling over 10 hours.

Weights: E-3C – Operating empty 77,995kg (171,950lb), max takeoff 147,420kg (325,000lb). E-3D – Max takeoff 150,820kg (332,500lb).

Dimensions: E-3A/C/F – Wing span 44.42m (145ft 9in), length 46.61m (152ft 11in), height 12.73m (41ft 9in). Wing area 283.4m² (3050.0sq ft). E-3D – Same except wingspan 44.98m (147ft 7in).

Accommodation: E-3C/D/F – Total crew complement of 17.

Armament: None, although could carry self defence AAMs.

Operators: France, NATO, Saudi Arabia, UK, USA.

History: The E-3 Sentry is a flying command post detecting enemy aircraft and missiles, and directing and warning friendly aircraft of their positions.

The Sentry was developed as a replacement for the ageing Lockheed Super Constellation based EC-121 Warning Star. Development of a replacement based upon Boeing's 707-320 airframe resulted in the first flight of a prototype EC-137 on February 5 1972. The first operational E-3A Sentry was delivered in March 1977.

The basis of the Sentry's detection abilities is the massive Westinghouse APY-1 (first 25 aircraft) or APY-2 radar mounted in the rotodome affixed above the rear fuselage. The rotodome rotates six times per minute and can be operated in various modes such as over the horizon, pulse doppler scan, passive and maritime. The APY-2 is capable of tracking up to 600 low flying aircraft at one time.

Internally the E-3 is equipped with operator stations for the radar and comms suite, galley, rest area and bunks for rest/relief crew.

The USAF's original EC-137s and 22 E-3A Core aircraft were upgraded to E-3B Block 20 standard with a limited maritime surveillance capability, provision for self defence measures, ECM resistant communications equipment, more UHF radios, five more operator stations and a more powerful central computer. A later upgrade was for 10 E-3A Standards to E-3C Block 25 level with more operator consoles, more UHF radios and provision for Have Quick anti jamming radio.

NATO operates 18 E-3A Standard Sentries, while Saudi Arabia took delivery of five E-3A Standards powered by CFM56 engines plus eight KE-3A tankers without AWACS equipment. British E-3D Sentry AEW.1s and French E-3Fs are powered by CFM56s and have a refuelling probe, while E-3Ds have wingtip mounted Loral ESM pods.

Boeing has developed a Multi Stage Improvement Program which involves upgrading the communications suite, fitting GPS, upgrading the radar and the central computer. Additionally, US and NATO E-3s are being fitted with ESM with sensors in side mounted canoe type fairings. Boeing is also studying fitting the E-3 with the 737-700's modern EFIS two crew cockpit.

Photo: France operates four E-4Fs. (Armée de l'Air)

Boeing 727 & C-22

Country of origin: United States of America

Type: Passenger & VIP transport

Powerplants: C-22B/727-100 – Three 62.3kN (14,000lb) Pratt & Whitney JT8D-7 turbofans.

Performance: C-22B/727-100 – Max speed 1017km/h (550kt), max cruising speed 960km/h (518kt). Range with max payload 5000km (2700nm).

Weights: C-22B/727-100 – Empty equipped 36,560kg (80,600lb), max takeoff 72,570kg (160,000lb).

Dimensions: C-22B/727-100 – Wing span 39.92m (108ft 0in), length 40.59m (133ft 2in), height 10.36m (34ft 0in). Wing area 157.9m² (1700sq ft).

Accommodation: C-22B/727-100 – Flightcrew of three (two pilots and flight engineer). Typical two class 727-100 airline seating for 94, max seating for 131. Most are configured with customised VIP/presidential transport interiors. C-22Bs configured to seat 90, including 24 in first class leather seats. All seats face rearwards.

Armament: None

Operators: 727-100 – Belgium, Congo, Mexico, New Zealand, Taiwan. 727-200 – Senegambia. C-22 – USA.

History: The 727 was built in greater numbers than any other jet engined airliner except the 737. When production was completed in 1984 more 727s had been built than any other commercial jetliner, but only a handful have ever seen military service.

The 727 began life as a short to medium range medium capacity airliner to slot beneath Boeing's four engined 707 (described separately) and 720. Initial design studies began as early as 1956, and the resulting Boeing Model 727, which first flew on February 9 1963, featured three engines (for good field performance), the 707's fuselage cross section but with a redesigned lower fuselage, and limited commonality with the 707 and 720. The first 727 was delivered in February 1964. Relatively slow initial sales led to various sub variants with higher gross weight options, plus the 727-100C Convertible and 727-200QC Quick Change.

The stretched 727-200 was announced in August 1965 in response to demand for a higher capacity model. The 6.10m (20ft) stretch involved equal length plugs fore and aft of the main undercarriage, but no increased fuel capacity, adversely affecting range. This issue was addressed with the higher gross weight and longer range Advanced 727-200, which entered service in June 1971. The 727-200F freighter flew in 1983 and was the last variant of this highly successful airliner.

While its success as an airliner is almost without parallel, only a small number have filtered down into military service. Nevertheless a number of nations use 727-100s for passenger transport, some equipped with customised VIP or presidential/head of state interiors.

The US Air Force's 201st Airlift Squadron operates four ex PanAm and National Airlines 727-100s as C-22B staff transports (a single ex Lufthansa 727-100 C-22A was retired). A single ex Singapore Airlines 727-200 is also operated, designated C-22C.

Photo: The Fuerza Aerea Mexicana (Mexican air force) flies three VIP configured 727-100s. (David Daw)

Boeing 737, CT-43 & Surveiller

Country of origin: United States of America

Type: 737 – VIP and general transport. CT-43 – Navigation trainer. Surveiller – Maritime reconnaissance/transport

Powerplants: 737-200 – Two 64.5kN (14,500lb) Pratt & Whitney JT8D-9A turbofans, or two 69.0kN (15,500lb) JT8D-15s, or two 71.2kN (16,000lb) JT8D-17s, or two 77.4kN (17,400lb) JT8D-17Rs.

Performance: 737-200 – Max speed 943km/h (509kt), max cruising speed 927km/h (500kt), economical cruising speed 795km/h (430kt). Max initial rate of climb 3760ft/min. Range with 155 passengers and reserves between 3520km (1900nm) and 4260km (2300nm) depending on weight options and engines.

Weights: 737-200 – Operating empty 27,690kg (61,050lb), max takeoff 58,105kg (128,100lb).

Dimensions: 737-200 – Wing span 28.35m (93ft 0in), length 30.48m (100ft 0in), height 11.28m (37ft 0in). Wing area 91.1m² (980sq ft).

Accommodation: Flight crew of two pilots. CT-43 – Configured for 12 students, four advanced students and three instructors. Surveiller – Indonesia's 737s fitted with 14 first class and 88 economy seats.

Armament: None

Operators: 737 – Brazil, India, Kuwait, Mexico, Niger, South Korea, Venezuela. CT-43 – USA. Surveiller – Indonesia.

History: With over 3800 737s of all variants sold, Boeing's smallest airliner is the world's most successful jet airliner in terms of sales. A small number of these are in military service as transports, while the 737 also forms the basis of the USAF's CT-43 navigation trainer, and is in use for maritime patrol duties with Indonesia.

The 737 was conceived as a short range small capacity airliner to round out the Boeing jet airliner family, slotting beneath the 727 (described separately), 720 and 707. Announced in February 1965, the 737 was originally envisioned as seating between 60 to 85, although a 100 seater was finally settled upon.

The first 737-100 made its first flight on April 9 1967. Further development led to the stretched 737-200, which became the main production model through to the mid 1980s. The -200 was replaced by the CFM International CFM56 powered 110 seat 737-500, 130 seat 737-300 and 145 seat 737-400. Further development has led to the similarly sized Next Generation 737s, the 737-600, -700 and -800, with new glass cockpits and other improvements. Boeing is offering the 737-700 as an AEW platform with Northrop Grumman phased array radar to meet an Australian requirement.

The US Air Force took delivery of 19 T-43 navigation trainers from mid 1973. These aircraft are based on the 737-200 with the specialised trainer featuring accommodation for 12 student navigators, four advanced student navigators and three instructors. Navigation stations are fitted along the starboard side of the fuselage. The T-43 was later redesignated CT-43, reflecting the fact that many of these aircraft also have a passenger transport role.

Indonesia operates three 737-200 Surveillers for maritime reconnaissance, fitted with a Motorola Side Looking Airborne Modular Multi Mission Radar, with antennas fitted in blade fairings on the rear fuselage. Other nations operate 737s in VIP and staff transport roles.

Photo: A USAF CT-43. (MSgt Serna, USAF)

Boeing 747, E-4, VC-25 & AL-1A

Country of origin: United States of America

Type: 747 – VIP transport, command post and strategic transport. E-4 – Command post aircraft. VC-25 – Presidential transport. AL-1A – Anti missile aircraft

Powerplants: E-4B – Four 233.5kN (52,500lb) GE F103-GE-100 turbofans. VC-25 – Four 252.4kB (56,750lb) F103-GE-102s.

Performance: E-4B – Max speed 970km/h (523kt), economical cruising speed 907km/h (490kt). Cruise ceiling 45,000ft. Ferry range 12,600km (6800nm). Mission endurance 12 hours, with refuelling 72 hours. VC-25 – Range 11,490km (6200nm).

Weights: E-4B – Max takeoff 362,875kg (800,000lb).

Dimensions: E-4B, VC-25 & 747-200 – Span 59.64m (195ft 8in), length 70.51m (231ft 4in), height 19.33m (63ft 5in). Wing area 511m² (5500sq ft).

Accommodation: E-4B – Flightcrew of four. Crew rest area in upper deck. Main deck fitted with command area, a conference room, battle staff area and command, control and communications area. VC-25 – Accommodation for the president with 70 passenger seats and accommodation for 23 crew. 747-200/400 – Seating for up to 400 troops.

Armament: None

Operators: 747 – Japan, Iran, Israel, Saudi Arabia. E-4 – USA. VC-25 – USA. AL-1A – USA*.

History: Developed as a private venture at enormous financial risk, the 747 was over twice the size of any airliner preceding it.

The 747 first flew on February 9 1969. Since that time it has been produced in five basic versions, the initial 747-100, the heavier 747-200, long range, shorter fuselage 747SP (one is operated by the Saudi Royal Flight), the 747-300 which introduced the stretched upper deck, and the current ultra long range, two crew 747-400.

The USAF selected the 747-200 as the basis for its E-4 Advanced Airborne National Command Post aircraft (alternatively the National Emergency Airborne Command Post – NEACP or Kneecap). Nicknamed the Doomsday Plane, the E-4 is tasked with providing an airborne base from which the US president and senior government officials can operate during war – in particular nuclear war. Three E-4As were delivered from late 1974, while a single E-4B with greatly improved communications and a revised interior was delivered in 1979. The E-4As were later modded to E-4B standard.

The VC-25 designation applies to two 747-200s delivered to the USAF in 1990 to serve as presidential transports – Air Force One when the US president is onboard. The VC-25 features a comprehensive communications fit, presidential stateroom, conference room and accommodation for senior staffers, press and flight and cabin crews.

The C-19 designation applies to US 747 airliners which are part of the Civil Reserve Air Fleet, which the military can call upon in war.

Japan operates two 747-400s as VIP and troop transports. Iran operates 747-100 tanker/transports and 747-100F Freighters.

The AL-1A is an anti ballistic and cruise missile aircraft based on the 747-400F and equipped with a TRW laser to be mounted in the nose. The prototype YAL-1A is due to fly in 1999 and seven will be in operational USAF service by 2007 (comprising five production aircraft, and the reworked prototype and EMD aircraft).

Photo: One of two Japanese VIP 747-400s. (Boeing)

Boeing 757 & C-32

Country of origin: United States of America

Type: Medium range VIP and government transport

Powerplants: 757-200 – Two 166.4kN (37,400lb) Rolls-Royce RB211-535C turbofans, or two 178.4kN (40,100lb) RB211-535E4s, or two 170kN (38,200lb) Pratt & Whitney PW2037s, or two 185.5kN (41,700lb) PW2040s.

Performance: 757-200 – Max cruising speed 914km/h (493kt), economical cruising speed 850km/h (460kt). Range with P&W engines and 186 passengers 5522km (2980nm), with RR engines 5226km (2820nm). Range at optional max takeoff weight with P&W engines 7410km (4000nm), with RR engines 6857km (3700nm).

Weights: 757-200 – Operating empty with P&W engines 57,040kg (125,750lb), with RR engines 57,180kg (126,050lb). Medium range max takeoff weight 104,325kg (230,000lb), long range max takeoff weight 113,395kg (250,000lb).

Dimensions: Wing span 38.05m (124ft 10in), length 47.32m (155ft 3in), height 13.56m (44ft 6in). Wing area 185.25m^2 (1994sq ft).

Accommodation: 757-200 – Flightcrew of two. Typical passenger arrangements vary from 16 first & 162 economy passengers to 214 to 239 in an all economy class configuration. Argentinean and Mexican aircraft have customised interiors.

Armament: None

Operators: 757 – Argentina, Mexico. C-32 – USA*.

History: While only two 757s were in military service in 1997, the USAF has ordered four as C-32A VIP transports.

Boeing considered a number of proposals for a successor to the 727 trijet airliner during the 1970s, many of these designs featuring the nose and T-tail of the earlier jet. It was not until later in that decade however that Boeing settled on a more conventional design featuring the same cross section as the 727, but considerably longer in length, with an all new wing, fuel efficient high bypass turbofan engines and a new nose section housing an advanced cockpit. Development of the 757 was launched in 1978 in tandem with the widebody 767 (described separately). The 767 first flew a few months earlier, but the two types share a number of systems and technology, including a common flightdeck.

First flight was on February 19 1982, with the 757-200 entering airline service in January the following year. Subsequent versions to appear include the 757-200PF freighter, and the 757-200M Combi. The stretched 240 seat 757-300 is due to fly in mid 1998.

In terms of commercial orders, the 757 has been a great success story for Boeing, with over 890 ordered by late 1997. As yet though it has only found limited applications in the military role. Just two wore military colours in 1997, an example each serving with the air forces of Argentina and Mexico. Both these aircraft are used for VIP and government transport tasks, and are fitted with customised interiors.

In August 1996 the USAF ordered four 757-200s for VIP use to replace ageing VC-137s. Allocated the USAF designation C-32A, the PW2040 powered Boeings will be delivered to the 89th Airlift Wing at Andrews AFB from early 1998. In service, the C-32s will be used to transport US cabinet and congress members and the vice president.

Photo: Mexico's 757 presidential transport. (Julian Green)

Boeing E-767 & 767T/T

Country of origin: United States of America

Type: Airborne Early Warning & Control System (AWACS) aircraft

Powerplants: Two 273.6kN (61,500lb) General Electric CF6-80C2 turbofans.

Performance: Estimated – 767 airliner max cruising speed 914km/h (493kt), 767 airliner cruising speed 854km/h (461kt). Service ceiling 34,000 to 43,000ft. Unrefuelled range 8335 to 9260km (4500 to 5000nm). Endurance at 1850km (1000nm) patrol radius eight hours, endurance at 555km (300nm) 12 hours. Endurance with inflight refuelling 22 hours. (AAR receptacle not fitted to JASDF aircraft.)

Weights: Max takeoff 174,635kg (385,000lb).

Dimensions: Wing span 47.47m (156ft 1in), length 48.51m (159ft 2in), height 15.85m (52ft 0in). Wing area 283.3m^2 (3050sq ft).

Accommodation: Full 20 crew complement consists of two pilots, mission director, tactical director, fighter allocator, two weapon controllers, surveillance controller, link manager, seven surveillance operators, communications operator, radar technician, communications technician and computer display technician. Crew rest area and galley in rear of cabin. Reserve crew also carried.

Armament: None

Operators: Japan*

History: The Boeing E-767 is an adaptation of the 767-200 airliner fitted with the radar and systems of the E-3 Sentry for Japan.

Development of the E-767 was spurred by a Japanese requirement for four AWACS aircraft, with the natural choice being the E-3 Sentry (described separately). However, the closure of the 707/E-3 production line in 1991 led Boeing and Japan to look at developing an AWACS platform using the Sentry's core systems and the airframe of the 767-200ER airliner. Boeing announced it was performing definition studies of such a combination to meet the Japanese requirement in December 1991.

Japan ordered two E-767s in November 1993, and now its required four are on order. The first 'green' E-767 airframe flew in October 1994. It was then fitted with a dummy radome for aerodynamic testing and first flew in this configuration on August 9 1996, before being fitted with the AWACS radar and avionics suite. The first two aircraft are scheduled to be delivered in March 1998, with the third and fourth aircraft following in 1999.

Central to the E-767 is the Westinghouse APY-2 surveillance radar, as on the E-3. Internally the E-767 will be configured with stations for communications, data processing, eight multifunction operator consoles in two rows, equipment bays, galley and crew rest area.

Aside from Japan, Boeing sees a small but significant market for further E-767 sales to countries such as Italy and Saudi Arabia.

In addition, Boeing has also selected the 767-200 and stretched -300 for development for a family of military transports to replace the large numbers of converted 707s currently in service. The most obvious roles for the 767T/T are aerial tankers and strategic transports. Boeing studies found that the 767 was the best Boeing airliner platform suitable for adaptation for the majority of anticipated military missions.

Photo: The E-767. (Boeing)

Boeing C-17 Globemaster III

Country of origin: United States of America

Type: Strategic and intra theatre transport

Powerplants: Four 181.0kN (40,700lb) Pratt & Whitney F117-PW-100 turbofans.

Performance: Normal cruising speed at 28,000ft Mach 0.77, max cruising speed at low altitude 648km/h (350kt) CAS. Airdrop speed at sea level 215 to 465km/h (115 to 250kt) CAS. Max ferry range 9432km (5095nm). Operational radius with a 36,785kg (81,000lb) payload and a 975m (3200ft) TO, land in 823m (2700ft), takeoff again with a similar payload in 853m (2800ft) and land in 792m (2600ft) – 925km (500nm). Range with a 68,040kg (150,000lb) payload, a 2320m (7600ft) TO run and a 885m (2900ft) landing – 5185km (2800nm).

Weights: Operating empty 125,645kg (277,000lb), max takeoff 265,350kg (585,000lb).

Dimensions: Span over winglets 51.76m (169ft 10in), length 53.04m (174ft 0in), height 16.79m (55ft 1in). Wing area 353m² (3800.0sq ft).

Accommodation: Flightcrew of two, plus loadmaster. Max payload 77,290kg (170,400lb). Can carry standard freight pallets, air droppable pallets, 100 passengers on seating pallets and 54 along fuselage sides, 48 stretcher patients, or 75 troops on temporary fuselage side and centreline seats, or 102 paratroops, 4WD vehicles, an M1A1 Abrams MBT plus other vehicles, or up to three AH-64s.

Armament: None

Operators: USA*

History: The C-17 airlifter suffered a controversial, prolonged and often troublesome development, but in service is proving to be highly reliable and very versatile.

The USAF selected the McDonnell Douglas C-17 to meet its C-X requirement for a heavy airlifter in August 1981. The C-X requirement called for a transport capable of strategic and intra theatre missions, with good STOL performance from semi prepared strips, good ground manoeuvrability and a voluminous cargo hold capable of accommodating attack helicopters and the M1 Abrams main battle tank.

The original C-17 full scale development contract was cancelled in 1982 and replaced with low priority development. The first flying prototype was ordered in late 1985 while the first production contract was signed in January 1988. First flight was on September 15 1991.

The C-17 is of conventional military freighter configuration with a high wing, T-tail and rear loading freight ramp. Power is supplied by four Pratt & Whitney F117 turbofans, developments of the commercial PW2000 series used for the Boeing 757 airliner. Notable design features include fly-by-wire flight controls (the first on a US transport aircraft), a two crew glass cockpit with HUDs, externally blown flaps and STOL performance equivalent to the C-130's.

The USAF originally required 210 C-17s, but will take delivery of 120 from Boeing through to 2006. The 35th was delivered in November '97.

Apart from the basic C-17A, Boeing has proposed the KC-17, a tanker transport fitted with a palletised fuel tank carried on the main deck and KC-10 style boom and/or hose and drum units. A stretched C-17 has also been proposed as a C-5 replacement, but seems unlikely. The MD-17 is a commercial variant on offer.

Photo: The C-17 Globemaster III. (Doug Mackay)

Boeing/BAe AV-8B/GR.7 Harrier II

Countries of origin: United States of America and United Kingdom

Type: STOVL ground attack fighter

Powerplant: AV-8B – One 95.4kN (21,450lb) Rolls-Royce F402-RR-406A turbofan, or a 105.9kN (23,800lb) F402-RR-408 from 1990.

Performance: AV-8B – Max speed 1065km/h (575kt). Max initial rate of climb 14,715ft/min. Service ceiling over 50,000ft. Short takeoff run at MTOW 435m (1437ft). Ferry range with external fuel 3640km (1965nm). Combat radius from a STO with 12 500lb Mk 82 Snakeye bombs with a 1hr loiter 167km (90nm). Combat radius from a STO with seven Mk 82 Snakeye bombs and external fuel, hi-lo-hi 1100km (595nm). Endurance with two AIM-9 Sidewinders on a CAP 185km (100nm) from the carrier 3hr.

Weights: AV-8B – Operating empty 6336kg (13,968lb), max takeoff (with a STO) 14,060kg (31,000lb).

Dimensions: AV-8B – Wing span 9.25m (30ft 4in), length 14.12m (46ft 4in), height 3.55m (11ft 8in). Wing area with LEXes from 1990 22.6m² (243.4sq ft).

Accommodation: Pilot only, or two in tandem in TAV-8B and T.10.

Armament: AV-8B – One 25mm GAU-12/A Equaliser five barrel cannon in ventral pod. Max external stores load of 6003kg (13,235lb) can include AIM-9s, AGM-65s and various bombs.

Operators: Italy, Spain, UK, USA.

History: Hawker Siddeley (now BAe) pulled out of initial Anglo/America development of the 'big wing' Harrier in 1975.

Instead later that decade McDonnell Douglas (under a new collaborative agreement with Hawker Siddeley) began development of the Super Harrier for the US Marines, with a much larger supercritical wing with two additional underwing hardpoints. The new wing was flown for the first time on an AV-8A (designated YAV-8B) on November 9 1978. The raised cockpit was introduced on the first of four full scale development aircraft, the first of which flew on November 5 1981.

After a batch of 12 pilot production AV-8Bs were built, production AV-8Bs were delivered to the US Marines from early 1984. That same year the first full scale development GR.5 Harrier for the RAF had its first flight. AV-8Bs and GR.5s differed in that the British Harriers have two 25mm cannons, rather than one in the AV-8B, while the RAF's machines are powered by 95.6kN (21,500lb) RR Pegasus Mk 105s.

Also in 1984 development work began on the AV-8B Night Attack for the USMC, which differs in having a GEC Marconi FLIR mounted on the nose, a head down display and a colour moving map. Deliveries were from 1989. Similarly the RAF has upgraded all its aircraft to GR.7 standard, with a nose mounted FLIR for night attack. Fitted with a TIALD pod the GR.7 can also autonomously launch guided PGMs.

The USMC has ordered a total of 280 AV-8Bs (including 24 TAV-8Bs two seaters), while the RAF has ordered 109 GR.5/GR.7s, including 13 T.10s. The T.10 two seater differs from the TAV-8B in having eight underwing pylons (not two) and FLIR.

The most advanced Harrier development thus far is the APG-65 radar equipped Harrier II Plus. Spain, Italy and the US Marines are all taking delivery of rebuilt or new build Harrier II Pluses.

Photo: A USMC AV-8B. (Paul Merritt)

Boeing F/A-18 Hornet

Country of origin: United States of America

Type: Multirole fighter

Powerplants: F/A-18C – Two 71.2kN (16,000lb) with afterburning General Electric F404-GE-400 turbofans, or since 1992 two 78.7kN (17,700lb) F404-GE-402 EPEs.

Performance: F/A-18C – Max speed over Mach 1.8 or approx 1915km/h (1033kt). Max initial rate of climb 45,000ft/min. Combat ceiling approx 50,000ft. Unrefuelled ferry range over 3335km (1800nm). Interdiction combat radius hi-lo-hi 537km (290nm), attack mission combat rad 1065km (575nm), combat rad on an air-to-air mission 740km (400nm). CAP endurance from a carrier 1hr 45min.

Weights: F/A-18C – Empty 10,810kg (23,832lb), max takeoff approx 25,400kg (56,000lb).

Dimensions: Wing span 11.43m (37ft 6in), length 17.07m (56ft 0in), height 4.66m (15ft 4in). Wing area 37.2m^2 (400.0sq ft).

Accommodation: Pilot only, or two in tandem in F/A-18B/D.

Armament: One M61A1 Vulcan 20mm cannon. F/A-18C can carry 7030kg (15,500lb) of ordnance, including AIM-9 Sidewinder, AIM-7 Sparrow and AIM-120 Amraam AAMs, AGM-65 Maverick ASMs, AGM-88 HARM anti radiation missiles, AGM-84 Harpoon anti ship missiles, bombs, cluster bombs, rockets and laser guided bombs.

Operators: Australia, Canada, Finland*, Kuwait, Malaysia, Spain, Switzerland*, USA.

History: Designed for both air-to-air and air-to-ground missions, the multirole Hornet is a potent fighter and accurate attack aircraft.

In August 1974 the US Congress cancelled the US Navy's VFAX program for a new low cost lightweight multirole fighter, and instead recommended that the service should study developments of the General Dynamics YF-16 and Northrop YF-17 developed for the US Air Force. Neither of these companies had experience building carrier aircraft, so McDonnell Douglas (now Boeing) teamed with Northrop to offer a developed F-17 while Vought teamed with GD.

McDonnell Douglas, with Northrop as a major associate (major contractor from 1985), was selected to develop its enlarged YF-17 proposal on May 2 1975. Initially the aircraft was to be built in F-18 fighter and ground attack A-18 versions, but the two roles were combined into the one airframe, resulting in the F/A-18 Hornet. The first of 11 development Hornets first flew on November 18 1978.

The F/A-18 is bigger and heavier than the YF-17. Features include fly-by-wire, an advanced cockpit with a HUD and HOTAS, a multi mode Hughes APG-65 radar, folding wingtips and two GE F404 turbofans.

The improved F/A-18C first flew in 1986. Changes include improved avionics, a new central computer and AIM-120 and AGM-65 compatibility. The US Marines operate Night Attack F/A-18C/Ds with NVG compatibility and carrying FLIR and laser designator pods. Marine and Malaysian F/A-18D two seaters have a dedicated mission capable rear cockpit with two large colour multi function displays and a colour moving map with no flight controls (although these can be added), while USMC F/A-18D(RC)s are wired to carry a reconnaissance pod. Uprated GE F404-GE-402 engines were introduced from 1992, the improved APG-73 radar from 1994.

Photo: A Malaysian F/A-18D. (Boeing)

Boeing F/A-18E Super Hornet

Country of origin: United States of America

Type: Multirole fighter

Powerplants: Two 98.0kN (22,000lb) approx with afterburning General Electric F414-GE-400 turbofans.

Performance: F/A-18E – Max level speed more than Mach 1.8 or approx 1915km/h (1033kt). Service ceiling 50,000ft. Required combat radius specification on a hi-lo-lo-hi interdiction mission with four 455kg/1000lb bombs, two AIM-9 Sidewinders and external fuel 720km (390nm). Fighter escort combat radius with two AIM-9s and two AIM-120s 760km (410nm). Maritime air superiority endurance with six AAMs and external fuel 280km (150nm) from the ship 2hr 15min.

Weights: F/A-18E – Design target empty weight 13,387kg (29,574lb), TO weight on an attack mission 29,937kg (66,000lb).

Dimensions: Span over missiles 13.62m (44ft 9in), length 18.31m (60ft 1in), height 4.88m (16ft 0in). Wing area 46.5m^2 (500.0sq ft).

Accommodation: Pilot only or two in tandem in F/A-18F.

Armament: One M61A1 Vulcan 20mm cannon. 11 external hardpoints (three underwing, one centreline and two fuselage side) can carry 8050kg (17,750lb) of stores. Armaments would be similar to those carried on the F/A-18A/C.

Operators: USA*

History: The success of the multirole Hornet on US carrier decks meant development of an improved and heavier version was logical.

McDonnell Douglas (now Boeing) proposed an enlarged Hornet as a successor for the cancelled General Dynamics/McDonnell Douglas A-12 Avenger II (which was to have been a stealthy successor to the A-6) in 1991. Official interest was such that a $US3.8bn contract covering the development of the F/A-18E and two seat F/A-18F and the construction of seven development aircraft was signed on December 7 1992. The first of these aircraft was rolled out on September 18 1995 (when the Super Hornet name was adopted), with first flight on November 18 that year.

Compared with the F/A-18C the F/A-18E is significantly larger. The fuselage is stretched 86cm (2ft 10in) while the wings are of the same layout but are 1.31m (4ft 4in) longer and 9.3m^2 (100.0sq ft) greater in area. The LEXes have been enlarged to retain the Hornet's excellent high alpha performance and the horizontal tails are bigger. The larger airframe substantially increases fuel capacity, so much so that range is increased by 40% over the F/A-18C. The engine intakes have also been redesigned to increase the airflow to the more powerful GE F414 engines (a development of the F404).

Internally the E's avionics suite is based on the F/A-18C's, including the APG-73 radar, although the cockpit has been improved to feature a large touch panel LCD display, a second LCD colour display and three monochrome displays.

The USN planned to acquire as many as 1000 F/A-18E/Fs to replace F/A-18A/Cs and F-14s, delivered from late 1998, but following the 1997 QDR the buy is likely to be reduced to between 550 to 785. This number may be further boosted if the USN orders the Boeing/Northrop Grumman proposed F/A-18C^{2}W (or F/A-18G) electronic warfare variant of the F/A-18F to replace the EA-6B Prowler.

Photo: A F/A-18F, one of seven development Super Hornets. (Boeing)

Boeing F-15E Eagle

Country of origin: United States of America

Type: Long range strike fighter

Powerplants: F-15E (later aircraft) – Two 79.2kN (17,800lb) dry and 129.4kN (29,100lb) with afterburning Pratt & Whitney F100-PW-229 turbofans.

Performance: F-15E – Max speed Mach 2.5 or approx 2655km/h (1433kt), cruising speed 917km/h (495kt). Service ceiling 60,000ft. Max range 4445km (2400nm). Combat radius 1270km (685nm).

Weights: F-15E – Operating empty 14,515kg (32,000lb), max takeoff 36,740kg (81,000lb).

Dimensions: Wing span 13.05m (42ft 10in), length 19.43m (63ft 9in), height 5.63m (18ft 6in). Wing area 56.5m^2 (608.0sq ft).

Accommodation: Pilot and Weapon Systems Operator in tandem.

Armament: One M61A1 20mm Vulcan cannon. Max weapon load of 11,115kg (24,500lb). Options include AIM-9 Sidewinder, AIM-7 Sparrow and AIM-120 Amraam AAMs, GBU-10, GBU-12 and GBU-24 laser guided bombs, electro optically guided GBU-15 and powered AGM-130 bombs, conventional bombs, cluster munitions, B51 and B61 nuclear bombs and AGM-88 HARM (from 1996) and AGM-65 ASMs.

Operators: Israel (F-15I), Saudi Arabia (F-15S), USA.

History: While 'not a pound for air to ground' epitomised the role of the McDonnell Douglas F-15A/C, the multirole F-15E was developed specifically to supplant the long ranging F-111 strike bomber.

McDonnell Douglas (now Boeing) had long promoted the bomb carrying ability of the F-15, even though an official requirement for an air-to-ground capability was dropped in 1975. In the early 1980s the USAF had a requirement for a new multirole fighter the ETF (Enhanced Tactical Fighter) to supplement the F-111. The USAF selected a two seat development of the F-15, the F-15E, in preference to the F-16XL (an enlarged F-16 featuring a cranked delta wing) in February 1984. First flight was on December 11 1986.

Changes to the F-15E over the F-15D reflect not only the change in role but also advances in technology. Features include the APG-70 radar with synthetic aperture ground mapping, a wide angle HUD, three colour multi function CRTs in the front cockpit and four in the rear, permanent CFTs (conformal fuel tanks) fitted with tangential stores stations, more powerful F100-PW-229 engines (-220s in initial aircraft) and removable Martin Marietta (now Lockheed Martin) LANTIRN navigation and target designation pods. The AAQ-13 LANTIRN pod beneath the port intake comprises a wide angle FLIR and Texas Instruments terrain following radar. The AAQ-14 (underneath the starboard intake) features FLIR and a laser rangefinder/designator.

Small numbers of F-15Es (up to 16) are being built for the USAF on top of the 209 delivered by mid 1994. Many saw extensive service during the Gulf War in 1991.

F-15E derivative production continues for Saudi Arabia and Israel. The Saudi F-15S features downgraded avionics, a simplified APG-70 without ground mapping and a Lockheed Martin Sharpshooter targeting pod in place of the AAQ-14. First flight was in June 1995 and 72 are on order. Twenty five F-15I Thunders are being delivered to Israel (ff Sept '97), differing from the F-15E only in their Israeli EW suites.

Photo: The F-15E is nicknamed Beagle (Bomber Eagle). (Paul Merritt)

Boeing X-32 JSF

Country of origin: United States of America

Type: Advanced multirole fighter prototype

Powerplants: One 155kN (35,000lb) class Pratt & Whitney SE614 (F119 derivative) turbofan.

Performance: Boeing claims its JSF contender will, compared with current "US strike fighters", have a 33% improved combat radius on internal fuel, 27% faster acceleration, 33% better agility, 13% greater sustained g turns, up to 51% higher specific excess power.

Weights: CTOL empty approx 9990kg (22,000lb). CV & STOVL empty approx 10,900kg (24,000lb). Max takeoff for all variants approximately 22,700kg (50,000lb).

Dimensions: CTOL & CV – Wing span 11m (36ft), length 13.7m (45ft). STOVL – Same except wing span 9.2m (30ft).

Accommodation: Pilot only, two seater conversion trainer planned.

Armament: Internal gun for USAF aircraft. Production aircraft armament would include AIM-9Xs, AIM-120s and JDAMs.

Operators: Planned for service with the USAF, USN, USMC & RN.

History: The X-32 is Boeing's contender for the US Joint Strike Fighter program, potentially the world's largest arms project, with a total development and production pricetag of over $US165bn.

The JSF resulted from the merger of the JAST program to replace USAF F-16s and USN F/A-18s and the CALF ASTOVL program to replace USMC AV-8s. The stealthy, multirole JSF is intended to be built in conventional, carrier capable and STOVL versions, using a common basic aircraft for maximum commonality to keep costs low. In December 1995 the UK became a 10% development partner in JSF, with the aim of replacing RN Sea Harriers.

By June 1996 Boeing, Lockheed Martin and McDonnell Douglas had submitted their design proposals to the JSF project office, with Boeing and Lockheed Martin then selected to build two JSF demonstrators each (one a conventional air force variant later to be converted to carrier capable configuration, the second in STOVL form).

Boeing's X-32s and Lockheed Martin's X-35 demonstrators are scheduled to fly in 2000 for comparative evaluation, with the winning design selected in 2001. To the winner the spoils will be enormous, current planning envisages the USAF taking 2036 JSFs, the USMC 642, the USN 300 and RN 60, in addition to exports. IOC with the USAF is planned for 2007.

Boeing's X-32 blended delta contender will be powered by a P&W SE614 (F119 derivative), while the STOVL variant will use a Harrier style thrust vectored direct lift system designed by Rolls-Royce. Boeing is projecting 93% overall commonality between its three JSF variants. The basic wing, forebody (nose) and tail of the aircraft would be common, with the fuselage adapted to the three models (although the STOVL variant's wing would be shortened).

Other common features of Boeing's JSF design include the variable geometry chin inlet, side fuselage internal weapons bays, leading edge flaps and flapperons, twin outward canted fins and 2-D thrust vectoring.

Boeing plans to take advantage of its extensive commercial airliner production experience to keep down JSF manufacturing costs.

Photo: Boeing's USN JSF version. (Boeing)

Boeing/BAe T-45 Goshawk

Countries of origin: United Kingdom and United States of America

Type: Advanced carrier-capable trainer.

Powerplant: T-45A – One 26.0kN (5845lb) Rolls-Royce Turboméca F405-RR-401 (navalised Adour).

Performance: T-45A – Max speed at 8000ft 1005km/h (543kt). Max initial rate of climb 8000ft/min. Time to 30,000ft clean 7min 40sec. Service ceiling 40,000ft. Ferry range with int fuel 1532km (826nm).

Weights: T-45A – Empty 4460kg (9834lb), max TOW 6387kg (14,081lb).

Dimensions: T-45A – Wing span 9.39m (30ft 10in), length incl nose probe 11.99m (39ft 4in), fuselage length 10.89m (35ft 9in), height 4.08m (13ft 5in). Wing area 17.7m² (190.1sq ft).

Accommodation: Two in tandem.

Armament: Usually none. One hardpoint under each wing can be used to carry practice bomb racks, rocket pods or fuel tanks.

Operators: USA*

History: One of the rare instances where the US military has ordered a foreign aircraft, albeit heavily modified and built under licence in the USA, the Goshawk is a navalised carrier-capable variant of the British Aerospace Hawk (described separately).

The lengthy evolution of the basic Hawk into the Goshawk began in the late 1970s. The US Navy's VTXTS (later T45TS) program to find a replacement for both the TA-4J Skyhawk and T-2 Buckeye evaluated a number of aircraft including the BAe Hawk and the Dassault/Dornier Alpha Jet in 1978. This evaluation proved the Hawk's relatively economic operation and it was selected for development to tailor it to US Navy requirements in November 1981, with McDonnell Douglas (now Boeing) as prime contractor and British Aerospace as principal subcontractor.

The redesign of the Hawk 60 to make it capable of carrier operations was fairly extensive, and involved strengthening of the airframe and undercarriage with a twin wheel nose gear that retracts into a slightly enlarged forward fuselage, adding a tail arrester hook, two side mounted airbrakes, a ventral fin and US Navy standard cockpit displays and radios. The crew sit on two Martin-Baker Mk 14 NACES ejection seats. The Hawk's Adour turbofan has been modified for operations from carriers and under the US system is designated F405.

The first full scale development T-45 first flew on April 16 1988. Deliveries were originally planned for 1989, but this was delayed when the USN requested further changes to the airframe and engine. Production T-45A aircraft were delivered from January 1992. These aircraft are completed at St Louis, while BAe builds the wings, centre and rear fuselage, tail, canopy and flying controls.

From the 84th production aircraft in late 1997 the Goshawk is being fitted with the 'Cockpit 21' glass cockpit, with two Elbit multi function displays in each cockpit, as the T-45C (with As to be upgraded to C standard). Another possible future change is the substitution of the Adour with the AlliedSignal F124 turbofan. An F124 powered T-45 flew on October 6 1996 (the F124 T-45 was unsuccessfully offered to Australia) but the USN has decided against fitting undelivered T-45s with the new engine.

The US Navy plans to acquire 170 production with deliveries continuing through to 2006.

Photo: The first T-45C gets airborne. (Boeing)

Boeing/Hughes OH-6 Cayuse & MD 500

Country of origin: United States of America

Type: Observation, light attack, training and utility helicopter

Powerplant: OH-6A – One 189kW (253shp) takeoff rated Allison T63-A-5A turboshaft driving a five blade main rotor and two blade tail rotor.

Performance: OH-6A – Econ cruising speed 215km/h (116kt). Max initial rate of climb with mil power 1840ft/min. Service ceiling 15,800ft. Hovering ceiling in ground effect 11,800ft, out of ground effect 7300ft. Range at 5000ft 610km (330nm). Ferry range 2510km (1355nm).

Weights: OH-6A – Empty equipped 557kg (1229lb), max takeoff 1090kg (2400lb), max overload takeoff 1225kg (2700lb).

Dimensions: OH-6A – Main rotor diameter 8.03m (26ft 4in), length overall rotors turning 9.24m (30ft 4in), fuselage length 7.01m (23ft 0in), height to top of rotor head 2.48m (8ft 2in). Main rotor disc area 50.6m² (544.6sq ft).

Accommodation: OH-6A – Typical seating for four, but rear two seats can be removed to make room for four troops to sit on the floor.

Armament: OH-6A – Provision for various machine guns and rocket pods.

Operators: OH-6 – Brazil, Colombia, Taiwan, USA. 500 – Argentina, Bahrain, Bolivia, Colombia, Costa Rica, Cyprus, Dominican Republic, El Salvador, Finland, Greece, Indonesia, Israel, Italy, Japan, Jordan, Kenya, Mauritania, Mexico, North Korea, Philippines, South Korea, Spain.

History: One of the most successful light turbine helicopters built, the Hughes, McDonnell Douglas and now Boeing 500 series began life in response to a US Army requirement for an observation helicopter.

Hughes won the US Army observation helicopter contest against competition from Bell and Hiller, resulting in the Allison 250 powered OH-6 Cayuse, which first flew in February 1963. Several thousand OH-6s (or Loaches) have served widely with the US Army in observation and special mission roles since the mid 1960s (including in Vietnam). The OH-6 was marketed in civil guise as the Hughes 500, which formed the basis for a number of export orientated military variants.

The first Hughes 500 export military variant was the 500M Defender, which was delivered to Colombia and built under licence by Kawasaki in Japan as the OH-6J. The 500M was followed by the 500MD Defender in 1976, an improved variant with a more powerful engine, small T-tail and new five blade main rotor. Apart from the basic Defender, it was offered in 500D Scout Defender, anti tank 500MD/TOW Defender and torpedo carrying 500MD/ASW Defender (with search radar and towed MAD) variants.

The 500MG Defender is the military variant of the 500E (with a recontoured nose and an Allison 250-C20B). The 530F is a more powerful version optimised for hot and high work and the equivalent military model is the 530MG Defender. Current production 500MG and 530MGs are offered with a FLIR, mast mounted TOW sight and a laser rangefinder. Built alongside these models is the revolutionary NOTAR equipped MD 520N, and while none are in military service, small numbers of US Army special ops MH-6Js and machine gun and rocket armed AH-6Js have been fitted with NOTAR tails (these may have been refitted with conventional tail rotors).

Photo: A Mexican air force 530MG Defender. (Boeing)

Boeing AH-64 Apache

Country of origin: United States of America

Type: Attack helicopter

Powerplants: AH-64A – Two 1265kW (1696shp) General Electric T700-GE-701 turboshafts, or from 1990 two 1410kW (1890shp) T700-GE-701Cs, driving four blade main and tail rotors.

Performance: AH-64A (with T700-GE-701s) – Max speed and max cruising speed 293km/h (158kt), cruising speed approx 278km/h (150kt). Max vertical rate of climb 2500ft/min. Service ceiling 21,000ft. Hovering ceiling in ground effect 15,000ft, out of ground effect 11,500ft. Ferry range with external fuel 1900km (1025nm). Max range with internal fuel 480km (260nm). Max endurance 3hr 9min.

Weights: AH-64A – Empty 5165kg (11,387lb), max takeoff 9525kg (21,000lb).

Dimensions: Main rotor diameter 14.63m (48ft 0in), wing span 5.23m (17ft 2in), length overall rotors turning 17.76m (58ft 3in), fuselage length 14.97m (49ft 2in), height overall 4.66m (15ft 4in). Main rotor disc area 168.1m² (1809.1m²).

Accommodation: Copilot/gunner in front cockpit, with pilot behind.

Armament: One M230 Chain Gun 30mm automatic cannon under forward fuselage with 1200 rounds. Four underwing hardpoints can carry up to 16 AGM-114 Hellfire anti armour missiles, or rocket pods, Stinger or Sidewinder AAMs, or Sidearm anti radiation missiles.

Operators: Egypt, Greece, Israel, Netherlands*, Saudi Arabia, UAE (Abu Dhabi), UK*, USA.

History: The Boeing (nee McDonnell Douglas) Apache was developed to meet the US Army's Advanced Attack Helicopter requirement.

To meet the AAH requirement the US Army sponsored the development of the Bell YAH-63 and the Hughes YAH-64 for a competitive fly-off. Hughes' YAH-64 flew for the first time on September 30 1975, and it was selected for further development ahead of the Bell design in December 1976. Full scale development followed, although it was not until March 1982 that final production approval was given, with a US Army order for an initial 11 AH-64 Apaches. Apaches were delivered from 1984 and the first unit became operational in 1986.

Apache design features include two shoulder mounted GE T700 turboshafts, crew armour, aerobatic capability, a high degree of survivability and the nose mounted Lockheed Martin (Martin Marietta) AAQ-11 TADS/PNVS (Target Acquisition and Designation Sight/Pilot Night Vision Sensor). TADS comprises a FLIR, TV camera, laser spot tracker and laser rangefinder/designator and is used for target location and designation. The PNVS FLIR allows nap of the earth flying.

Over 800 AH-64As have been built for the US Army and export and the type proved very successful in combat in the Gulf War. The interim AH-64B with improvements from combat experience was cancelled.

More than 500 US Army AH-64A Apaches are being upgraded to AH-64D standard, of which 227 will be to AH-64D Longbow Apache standard. The AH-64D features improved avionics housed in enlarged cheek fairings, while full standard AH-64D Longbow Apaches will feature the Northrop Grumman mast mounted millimetre wave radar, able to guide a radio frequency seeker Hellfire missile. Deliveries began in March '97. UK built WAH-64Ds will feature RTM332s.

Photo: The UK's WAH-64Ds will be delivered from 1998. (Westland)

Boeing/Sikorsky RAH-66 Comanche

Country of origin: United States of America

Type: Two seat scout and reconnaissance attack helicopter

Powerplants: Two 1068kW (1432shp) LHTEC T800-LHT-801 turboshafts, driving a five blade main rotor and eight blade fan-in-fin shrouded tail rotor.

Performance: Max level speed (dash) 324km/h (175kt). Max vertical rate of climb 1418ft/min. Time to turn 180° to target 4.7 seconds. Time to snap turn at target at 148km/h (80kt) 4.5 seconds. Ferry range with external fuel 2335km (1260nm). Endurance with standard fuel 2 hours 30 minutes.

Weights: Empty 3522kg (7765lb), mission takeoff 4807kg (10,597lb), max takeoff 7896kg (17,408lb).

Dimensions: Main rotor diameter 11.90m (39ft 1in), length overall rotor turning 14.28m (46ft 10in), fuselage length excluding gun 13.20m (43ft 4in), height over tailplane 3.37m (11ft 1in). Main rotor disc area 111.2m² (1197.0sq ft).

Accommodation: Pilot (front) and Weapon Systems Operator (rear) in stepped, tandem cockpits.

Armament: One 20mm, three barrel General Electric cannon in undernose Giat turret. Two weapons bay doors can hold three Hellfire or Stinger missiles each, with four Hellfires or eight Stingers on each optional stub wing.

Operators: USA*

History: The Comanche is without doubt the most advanced (and most expensive) combat helicopter currently under development.

As early as 1982 the US Army devised the LHX (Light Helicopter Experimental) program to replace 5000 UH-1s, AH-1s, OH-6s and OH-58s. By 1988 though when a request for proposals was issued to the Boeing/Sikorsky First Team and Bell/McDonnell Douglas Super Team, the requirement had been refined to just a scout/reconnaissance helicopter, with the requirement brought back to 1292 aircraft.

The Boeing Sikorsky teaming's proposal was selected for development as the RAH-66 Comanche in April 1991. Advanced features of the RAH-66 include stealth with airframe faceting to reduce radar cross section; a five blade, composite main rotor with swept tips and bearingless hub; Sikorsky developed eight blade fan-in-fin shrouded tail rotor; internal weapons bays; retractable undercarriage; two specially developed LHTEC (AlliedSignal and Allison) T800 turboshafts; detachable stub wings; NVG compatible EFIS cockpits with 3D digital moving map displays; triple redundant fly-by-wire flight controls; sidestick cyclics; helmet mounted sights; Longbow millimetre wave radar; FLIR and laser designator. First flight was on January 4 1996 from West Palm Beach in Florida.

Unfortunately for Boeing, Sikorsky and the US Army, the RAH-66 program has suffered a number of delays and setbacks, mainly because of budget cutbacks. Current plans envisage two YRAH-66 prototypes (the second to fly in '98) and six (initially unarmed) early operational capability aircraft to enter US Army service with a trials unit from 2001. These aircraft and the refurbished prototypes would then enter operational service in 2007. A decision on funding production aircraft is now planned for 2004.

Photo: The first prototype RAH-66.

Boeing Helicopters CH-46 Sea Knight

Country of origin: United States of America

Type: Medium lift multirole helicopter

Powerplants: CH-46E – Two 1395kW (1870shp) General Electric T58-GE-16 turboshafts, driving two three-blade rotors.

Performance: CH-46E – Max speed at sea level 267km/h (144kt), max cruising speed at sea level 266km/h (143kt). Max initial rate of climb 1715ft/min. Hovering ceiling in ground effect 9500ft, out of ground effect 5750ft. Ferry range 1110km (600nm), range with a 1090kg (2400lb) payload 1020km (550nm).

Weights: CH-46E – Empty 5255kg (11,585lb), max takeoff 11,022kg (24,300lb).

Dimensions: CH-46E – Rotor diameter each 15.24m (50ft 0in), length overall with rotors turning 25.40m (83ft 4in), fuselage length 13.66m (44ft 10in), height to top of rear rotor head 5.09m (16ft 9in). Total rotor disc area 364.8m² (3927.0sq ft).

Accommodation: Crew of three, with 25 troops and troop commander. Standard USMC CH-46E load of 17 troops or 15 casualty litters. CH-46E max payload 3175kg (7000lb). Can carry external sling loads.

Armament: None

Operators: Canada, Japan, Saudi Arabia, Sweden, USA.

History: The United States Marine Corps' primary assault troop transport, the CH-46 Sea Knight began life as a private venture.

In the mid 1950s the Vertol company (later acquired by Boeing) began design studies of a medium lift twin engine transport helicopter, taking advantage of the lifting capabilities offered by turboshaft engines. The resulting Model 107 helicopter flew in prototype form for the first time on April 22 1958. This initial prototype was powered by two 640kW (860shp) Lycoming T53 turboshafts, and featured tandem main rotors (negating the need for an anti torque tail rotor), an unobstructed main cabin and rear loading freight ramp.

The Model 107 originally aroused the interest of the US Army, who ordered three as YCH-1As for evaluation, but this service went on to order the larger CH-47 Chinook. Instead it was the US Marines who ordered the 107 into production in June 1961, as the HRB-1 (CH-46 after 1962), to replace its UH-34s.

The first of 160 USMC CH-46As entered service in June 1964, these aircraft powered by 935kW (1250shp) General Electric T58-GE-8 turboshafts. The US Navy took delivery of 14 similar UH-46As for vertical replenishment of ships at sea. The USMC's CH-46D and USN's UH-46D introduced 1045kW (1400shp) T58-GE-10s, while the similar CH-46F introduced more avionics.

The Marines' current CH-46 model is the E, an upgrade of CH-46D and F models with 1395kW (1870shp) T58-GE-16s and improved crash survivability. Deliveries of upgraded Es began in 1977.

Canada took delivery of six CH-46A based CH-113 Labradors for SAR and 12 CH-113A Voyageurs for transport. Sweden's HKP-4s feature Rolls-Royce Gnome engines. In Japan Kawasaki has licence built (through to 1990) the 107 and further developed the 107 as the KV 107 for military and commercial operators. Uses include SAR, mine countermeasures and transport, while some were exported to Saudi Arabia and Sweden.

Photo: A Canadian Forces CH-113 Labrador. (Canadian Forces)

Boeing Helicopters CH-47 Chinook

Country of origin: United States of America

Type: Medium lift transport helicopter

Powerplants: CH-47D – Two 2795kW (3750shp) takeoff rated AlliedSignal T55-L-712 turboshafts driving two three-blade rotors. MH-47E – Two 3108kW (4168shp) continuous rated T55-L-714s.

Performance: CH-47D – Max cruising speed at sea level 290km/h (156kt), average cruising speed 256km/h (138kt). Max initial rate of climb 1522ft/min. Service ceiling 8450ft. Hovering ceiling out of ground effect 10,550ft. Range 425km (230nm). MH-47E – Ferry range 2333km (1260nm), operational radius 935km (505nm).

Weights: US Army CH-47D – Empty 10,615kg (23,400lb), max takeoff 22,680kg (50,000lb). International CH-47D – Empty 10,578kg (23,231lb), max takeoff 24,495kg (54,000lb). MH-47E – Empty 12,210kg (26,918lb), max takeoff 24,495kg (54,000lb).

Dimensions: CH-47D – Rotor diameter each 18.29m (60ft 0in), length overall rotors turning 30.18m (99ft 0in), fuselage length 15.55m (51ft 0in), height to top of rear rotor head 5.77m (18ft 11in). Total rotor disc area 525.3m² (5654.9sq ft). International CH-47D & MH-47E – Same except fuselage length 15.87m (52ft 1in).

Accommodation: Two flightcrew with main cabin seating for up to 44 troops or 24 casualty litters.

Armament: MH-47E – Two window mounted 0.50in M2 machine guns, with provision for Stinger AAMs. Some mount miniguns.

Operators: Argentina, Australia, Egypt, Greece, Iran, Italy Japan, Libya, Morocco, Netherlands, Singapore, South Korea, Spain, Taiwan, Thailand, UK, USA.

History: Although the US Army was originally interested in the smaller Vertol 107 (which became the CH-46 Sea Knight), in June 1959 the service selected the much larger Vertol Model 114 for development as its battlefield mobility helicopter.

First flight was on September 21 1961, with service entry of the CH-47A Chinook in August 1962. Large numbers of CH-47As and CH-47Bs (with uprated engines and larger diameter rotors) saw service in Vietnam, as did to a lesser extent CH-47Cs (with further uprated engines and additional fuel capacity), which first flew in 1968. Large numbers of US Army CH-47As and Bs were upgraded to C standard, while new build Cs were widely exported and built in Italy under licence by Agusta.

The current CH-47D Chinook first flew in February 1982. Improvements include yet more powerful T55-L-712 turboshafts, NVG compatible flightdeck and triple external cargo hooks. All US Army CH-47s have now been rebuilt to CH-47D standard (plus 11 modified to special ops MH-47D configuration) while new build and upgraded CH-47D Internationals have been delivered to a number of countries.

The US Army's special operations MH-47Es are used for covert troop insertion and extraction. Features include NVG compatible EFIS flightdeck, GPS, FLIR, terrain following radar, refuelling probe, greater fuel capacity and a missile warning/countermeasures suite. Twenty five were built for the US Army and eight are on order for the RAF as HC.3s.

At least 300 US Army CH-47s will be upgraded under the CH-47 Improved Cargo Helicopter (ICH) program to extend their service lives beyond 2030, with T55-GA-714A turboshafts.

Photo: The Australian Army operates four CH-47Ds with two on order.

Breguet Alizé

Country of origin: France

Type: Carrier borne anti submarine warfare aircraft

Powerplant: One 1475kW (1975shp) Rolls-Royce Dart RDa.7 Mk 21 turboprop, driving a four blade propeller.

Performance: Max speed 520km/h (281kt) at 9900ft, 460km/h (248kt) at sea level, cruising speed 370km/h (200kt), patrol speed 232km/h (125kt). Max initial rate of climb 1380ft/min. Service ceiling above 20,500ft. Ferry range with auxiliary fuel 2870km (1550nm), or 2500km (1350nm) with standard fuel. Endurance with auxiliary fuel 7hr 40min, or 5hr 5min with standard fuel.

Weights: Empty 5700kg (12,565lb), max takeoff 8250kg (18,190lb).

Dimensions: Wing span 15.60m (51ft 2in), length 13.86m (45ft 6in), height 5.00m (16ft 5in). Wing area 36.0m^2 (387.5sq ft).

Accommodation: Crew of three, comprising pilot, radar operator and a sensor operator.

Armament: Internal weapons bay can carry a homing torpedo or three 160kg (353lb) depth charges. Two underwing hardpoints can carry an air-to-surface missile each, or rockets, bombs or depth charges.

Operators: France

History: The Alizé looks set to see service in the harsh carrier environment past the turn of the century, a tribute to the longevity of a design that was conceived in 1948 and flew for the first time in 1956.

Design work on what evolved into the Alizé began in 1948 against a French navy requirement for a carrier based strike aircraft. Breguet's resulting Br.990 Vultur (vulture) featured a nose mounted Armstrong Siddeley Mamba turboprop plus an auxiliary Rolls-Royce Nene turbojet in the rear fuselage which would be shut down in cruise flight to boost endurance. Although the Vultur was successfully test flown, the French navy never ordered it into production, and instead Breguet used the basic design as the basis for a carrier borne ASW platform.

The evolution to an ASW platform began in 1954 and involved dropping the Nene, substituting a Rolls-Royce Dart for the Mamba turboprop and the addition of a search radar mounted in a retractable radome. The changes to the Vultur justified the adoption of a new name – Alizé (tradewind).

The Alizé's main undercarriage retracts forwards into underwing pods which also contain sonobuoys, while the pilot and radar operator sit side-by-side, with a sensor operator seated behind them.

The Alizé flew for the first time in prototype form on October 6 1956. Deliveries of production aircraft began in May 1959, with 75 built for the French navy and 12 for India. (Breguet merged with Dassault in December 1961.)

Since then France's surviving Alizé fleet has been upgraded twice. In 1980 they were fitted with a Thomson-CSF Iguane radar, plus new navigation and communications systems and an ESM capability. In 1990 the 24 surviving French Alizés were fitted with a datalink and other minor modifications, extending their service lives beyond 2000.

India's Alizés were retired in 1992, after having been shore based since 1987 (when the carrier *Vikrant* was fitted with a ski jump thus preventing Alizé carrier ops).

Photo: A French navy Alizé. Note the folded wings.

British Aerospace 146

Country of origin: United Kingdom

Type: VIP transport

Powerplants: BAe 146-100 – Four 30.0kN (6700lb) Textron Lycoming ALF 502R-3s or four 31.0kN (6970lb) ALF 502R-5 turbofans.

Performance: BAe 146-100 – Cruising speed 767km/h (414kt), long range cruising speed 670km/h (361kt). Range with standard fuel 3000km (1620nm), range with max payload 1630km (880nm).

Weights: 146-100 – Operating empty 23,288kg (51,342lb), max takeoff 38,100kg (84,000lb).

Dimensions: 146-100 – Wing span 26.21m (86ft 0in), length 26.20m (86ft 0in), height 8.61m (28ft 3in). Wing area 77.3m^2 (832.0sq ft).

Accommodation: 146-100 – Flightcrew of two, plus seating for up to 94 passengers six abreast in an airliner configuration. RAF CC.Mk 2s and Saudi Statesman aircraft fitted with VIP interiors.

Armament: None

Operators: Saudi Arabia, UK.

History: The BAe 146 regional jet is only in limited military service.

The origins of the 146 date to August 1973 when the then Hawker Siddeley Aviation announced it was designing a short range quiet airliner powered by four small turbofans. Under the designation HS.146, large scale development was to last just a few months before a worsening economic recession made the risk of the project seem unjustifiable. Development then continued on a limited scale, but it was not until July 1978 when the project was relaunched, by which time Hawker Siddeley had been absorbed into the newly created British Aerospace.

The resulting BAe 146 made its first flight on September 3 1981. Certification was granted in early 1983, with first deliveries following shortly afterwards in May 1983. Initial deliveries were of the 146-100, later versions included the stretched, 85 to 100 seat 146-200 and further stretched, 100 to 112 seat 146-300. Because of the type's low noise characteristics the 146 series has been quite successful as a freighter, designated QT – Quiet Trader.

The 146QT also formed the basis of the 146STA Small Tactical Airlifter, which features a cargo door in the rear fuselage. Proposed payloads included up to 60 fully equipped paratroops, or 24 stretchers. Although a demonstrator 146STA was flown in the late 1980s, none were ordered.

The 146 series is now marketed by the AI(R) consortium as the Avro RJ series, with improved engines and other systems. The 146-100 is now the RJ70, the 146-200 the RJ85 and the 146-300 the RJ100.

Military use of the 146 is limited to the UK and Saudi Arabia. The RAF leased three BAe 146-100s as CC.1s for evaluation as replacement for Andovers for the Queen's Flight. Two 146-100s were then ordered as CC.2s for service with the Queen's Flight. These were delivered from 1986 and have been fitted with Loral Matador infrared jamming equipment. A third was delivered in 1990.

Saudi Arabia operates four 146s, named Statesman, as VIP transports with its Royal Flight.

Photo: The Royal Air Force's BAe 146 CC.2s are fitted with infrared jammers. (Dave Fraser)

Country of origin: United Kingdom

Type: Utility and VIP transport

Powerplants: Srs 2A – Two 1700kW (2280ehp) Rolls-Royce Dart RDa.7 Mk 534-2 or 535-2 turboprops, driving four blade propellers.

Performance: Srs 2A – Cruising speed 452km/h (244kt). Max initial rate of climb 1320ft/min. Service ceiling 25,000ft. Range with max payload and reserves 1360km (735nm), range with max fuel and reserves 3130km (1690nm).

Weights: Srs 2A – Operating empty 12,160kg (26,805lb), max takeoff 21,092kg (46,500lb).

Dimensions: Srs 2A – Wing span 30.02m (98ft 6in), length 20.42m (67ft 0in), height 7.57m (24ft 10in). Wing area 75.4m² (810.8sq ft).

Accommodation: Flightcrew of two. Seating for up to 58 troops in airliner style seating. Can carry 48 paratroopers or 24 stretcher patients and nine medical attendants. Can be fitted with VIP interior. Australian nav trainers fitted with side facing workstation for two students and an instructor, plus passenger seating.

Armament: None

Operators: Australia, Belgium, Brazil, Ecuador, India, Nepal, South Korea, Tanzania, Thailand.

History: The HS.748 began life as an Avro design effort to re-enter the civil market in anticipation of a decline in military business.

The HS.748 has proven to be reasonably successful sales wise, and popular in third world nations with poor infrastructure, mainly as an airliner, but also as a military transport. Of the 382 built, 52 were delivered new to military customers.

First surfacing as the Avro 748 in 1958, Hawker Siddeley took over the 748 design in 1959 (Avro being a part of the Hawker Siddeley Group). The new aircraft first flew on June 24 1960.

The Series 2, in its 2, 2A and 2C variants, was the most successful of the line, the first flying on November 6 1961. The Series 2 differed from the 1 in having progressively higher weights and more powerful engines. The Series 2B appeared in 1977, offering a range of aerodynamic and other improvements, including an increased wing span.

The most advanced variant of the 748 to appear, the Super 748, made its first flight in July 1984. It introduced an advanced flightdeck, more efficient and hushkitted engines, and new interior fitout.

Two specific military versions offered were the BAe 748 Military Transport and the Coast Guarder. The Military Transport features a large cargo door in the rear fuselage, strengthened floor for freight and optional higher max takeoff weights. Customers included Belgium, Brazil and Ecuador. India licence built 20 similar aircraft.

The Coastguarder was optimised for maritime patrol and SAR and was fitted with a search radar, but was never sold. Meanwhile India has flown a 748 modified with an AEW style rotodome above the fuselage for aerodynamic testing.

Australia is one of the largest 748 operators. The RAAF operates two as light transports (due to be retired) and eight as navigation trainers. The Royal Australian Navy operates a further two configured as EW trainers to simulate an electronic warfare environment as a training aid for ships and aircraft.

Photo: A Belgium BAe 748 Military Transport. (Belgium SID)

Country of origin: United Kingdom

Type: Tactical transport

Powerplants: Two 2420kW (3245ehp) Rolls-Royce RDa.12 Dart turboprops, driving four blade propellers.

Performance: Max speed 490km/h (265kt), normal cruising speed 450km/h (243kt). Max initial rate of climb 1200ft/min. Service ceiling 24,000ft. STOL takeoff run 315m (1030ft). Range with max fuel and reserves 3620km (1955nm), range with max payload 795km (430nm).

Weights: Basic operating 12,550kg (27,665lb), max takeoff 22,680kg (50,000lb).

Dimensions: Wing span 29.87m (98ft 0in), length 23.75m (77ft 11in), height 8.97m (29ft 5in). Wing area 77.2m² (831.4sq ft).

Accommodation: Flightcrew of two pilots, can also carry a navigator/radio operator. Main cabin can seat up to 52 troops, or 40 paratroops or 25 stretcher patients plus medical attendants or up to three Land Rover 4WDs. Some New Zealand aircraft fitted with a customised VIP interior.

Armament: None

Operators: New Zealand

History: The Andover is a dedicated STOL capable military tactical transport, complete with rear loading ramp, developed from the basic HS.748 transport.

Avro began design work on its Model 780 to meet a Royal Air Force requirement for a STOL tactical transport capable of operating from dirt or roughly prepared 275m length airstrips from 1963. The resulting aircraft was based closely on the HS.748 Series 2 airliner, but differed in a number of key areas to tailor it to its military role. The most obvious change was to the rear fuselage, which was redesigned to feature a rear loading ramp. The fuselage was also stretched slightly, and the tailplane repositioned (with dihedral added to the horizontal tail) to allow for the rear ramp. One innovative feature was the Dowty Rotol kneeling main undercarriage, designed to allow the cabin floor sill to be adjusted in height and horizontally to align with the trays of loading/unloading trucks.

The Andover also features more powerful Dart turboprops compared with the HS.748, and larger diameter propellers.

The first Andover was in fact the HS.748 prototype converted to the new configuration, and it flew for the first time on December 21 1963. In all, 31 were built and all were delivered to the RAF's Air Support Command. Apart from UK based squadrons, RAF Andovers were based in Singapore and Aden (Yemen). All have now been retired.

The UK's 1975 budget cuts resulted in a number of Andovers becoming surplus and 10 were sold to New Zealand. Five of NZ's nine survivors were retired at the end of 1996 when the aircraft's operating unit 40 Squadron relinquished its tactical transport role. The four survivors will remain in service for twin transport training until they are replaced in mid 1998 by commercially operated twin turboprops.

Photo: A New Zealand Andover over Auckland. This aircraft's white paint scheme is a legacy of UN service at some stage. Other RNZAF aircraft feature a tactical camouflage scheme (RNZAF)

British Aerospace Bulldog

Country of origin: United Kingdom

Type: Two seat basic trainer

Powerplant: T.1 – One 150kW (200hp) Lycoming IO-360-A1B6 fuel injected flat four piston engine, driving a two blade constant speed propeller.

Performance: T.1 – Max speed 240km/h (130kt), max cruising speed 222km/h (120kt), economical cruising speed 195km/h (105kt). Max initial rate of climb 1035ft/min. Service ceiling 16,000ft. Range with max fuel at 55% power 1000km (540nm). Endurance with max fuel 5 hours.

Weights: T.1 – Empty equipped 650kg (1430lb), normal and semi aerobatic max takeoff 1065kg (2350lb), fully aerobatic max takeoff 1015kg (2238lb).

Dimensions: T.1 – Wing span 10.06m (33ft 0in), length 7.09m (23ft 3in), height 2.28m (7ft 6in). Wing area 12.0m² (129.4sq ft).

Accommodation: Seating for two side by side, with room for an observer behind them.

Armament: Provision for weapons on four optional underwing hardpoints, including rocket and gun pods, practice and live bombs.

Operators: Ghana, Jordan, Kenya, Lebanon, Sweden, UK.

History: The Bulldog two seat primary trainer has its origins in the civil Beagle B.121 Pup, a two place light aircraft.

The Beagle Pup flew for the first time on April 8 1967 and established the basic design and configuration that was to characterise the Bulldog. While the Pup was popular with pilots for its good flying characteristics the Beagle company was experiencing continuing financial difficulties that forced it to close its doors in January 1970, with production of the Pup ceasing after just 150 had been built.

Before then though, Beagle had flown a military trainer variant called the Bulldog on May 19 1969. Based closely on the Pup, features of the Bulldog included a rearward sliding cockpit canopy, seating for two side by side (with room for an observer behind them), a Lycoming IO-360 four cylinder piston engine driving a two blade constant speed prop and fixed undercarriage.

Following Beagle's collapse, Scottish Aviation (itself since merged into British Aerospace) purchased the Bulldog's design rights, and flew its own Bulldog prototype on February 14 1971. The first Series 100 production aircraft flew on June 22 1971 and a total of 98 was built for Kenya, Malaysia and Sweden (both air force and army).

The Series 120 was built in larger numbers, and introduced increased aerobatic capability at maximum weight and full aerobatic capability up to a higher weight. The largest Bulldog customer was the RAF, who took delivery of 130 Model 121s designated the T.1. The survivors equip University Air Squadrons to train sponsored undergraduate students, plus other miscellaneous units. The 120 was also widely exported, and production ceased in 1981.

A developed version of the Bulldog was the Bullfinch, which featured a retractable undercarriage. It was flown in 1976 but was not put into production.

Photo: An RAF Bulldog T.1. Note the good visibility offered by the rearward sliding canopy. (Bruce Malcolm)

British Aerospace Strikemaster

Country of origin: United Kingdom

Type: Advanced jet trainer and light attack aircraft

Powerplant: Mk 80 – One 15.2kN (3140lb) Rolls-Royce Viper Mk 535 turbojet.

Performance: Mk 80 – Max speed at 18,000ft 775km/h (418kt), at sea level 725km/h (320kt). Max initial rate of climb 5250ft/min. Time to 30,000ft 8min 45sec. Service ceiling 40,000ft. Combat radius on a hi-lo-hi attack mission with 1360kg (3000lb) payload 397km (215nm), with a 455kg (1000lb) payload 925km (500nm). Combat radius on a lo-lo-lo attack mission with 455kg (1000lb) payload 445km (240nm).

Weights: Mk 80 – Operating empty 2810kg (6195lb), max takeoff 5215kg (11,500lb).

Dimensions: Mk 80 – Wing span 11.23m (36ft 10in), length 10.27m (33ft 9in), height 3.10m (10ft 2in). Wing area 19.9m² (213.7sq ft).

Accommodation: Seating for two, side by side.

Armament: Mk 80 – Two internal 7.62mm FN machine guns. Max permissible external stores load 1360kg (3000lb) on four underwing hardpoints, including rockets, bombs, practice bombs, gun and cannon pods, plus reconnaissance pods.

Operators: Botswana, Kenya, Oman, Saudi Arabia, Sudan.

History: The Strikemaster is the final and most potent development of a family of two seat trainers that began with the radial piston engine powered Percival Provost.

The Strikemaster is a direct development of the Hunting Percival (later BAC) Jet Provost. The Jet Provost began life as a low cost, minimum change development of the piston engined Provost, although the metamorphosis to jet power involved a much greater redesign than first planned. The Jet Provost (or JP) established the basic configuration of the Strikemaster, and flew for the first time on June 26 1954. The first major production JP was the T.3, the T.4 introduced two Martin Baker ejection seats and wingtip tanks. The definitive Jet Provost, the T.5, featured a redesigned, longer nose with a larger canopy, and formed the basis for the Strikemaster.

The development of an armed Jet Provost T.5 was logical, considering the JP's reasonable success with export customers. The resulting private venture Strikemaster was based closely on the Jet Provost T.5, but introduced a more powerful Viper turbojet, structural strengthening and four underwing hardpoints. BAC gave the Strikemaster its model number 167. The first Strikemaster made its first flight in October 1967 and production of the Mk 80 began a year later. All but 10 of the 146 built were Mk 80s, Sudan took delivery of 10 similar Mk 90s (the last Strikemaster built) in 1984.

The Strikemaster appealed to a number of air arms because of its ability to conduct advanced pilot training and light attack missions. The largest current Strikemaster operator is Saudi Arabia, where the aircraft is used for refresher training and liaison tasks now that Hawks have been delivered, but they are being phased out. Other important Strikemaster customers who have since retired their aircraft include New Zealand (its Strikemasters were nicknamed Bluntys), Kuwait and Singapore.

Photo: Kuwait replaced its Strikemasters with Hawk 64s.

British Aerospace/MDC AV-8S Harrier

Country of origin: United Kingdom

Type: V/STOL light attack aircraft

Powerplant: AV-8S – One 95.6kN (21,500lb) Rolls-Royce F402 (Pegasus) turbofan.

Performance: AV-8S – Max speed 1175km/h (635kt). Max initial rate of climb 29,000ft/min. Time to 40,000ft after vertical takeoff 2min 23sec. Service ceiling 51,000ft. Takeoff run with 2270kg (5000lb) warload 305m (1000ft). Ferry range with external fuel 3430km (1850nm). Combat radius with 1995kg (4400lb) warload, hi-lo-hi, 665km (360nm).

Weights: AV-8S – Empty equipped 5530kg (12,190lb), normal VTO 7735kg (17,050lb), max takeoff STO 10,115kg (22,300lb).

Dimensions: AV-8S – Wing span 7.70m (25ft 3in), length 13.87m (45ft 6in), height 3.63m (11ft 11in). Wing area 18.7m² (201.1sq ft).

Accommodation: Pilot only in AV-8S, two in tandem in T.4 and TAV-8S.

Armament: Two 30mm Aden cannons mounted in underfuselage fairings. Four underwing stations can carry up to 2405kg (5300lb) of ordnance, including AIM-9 Sidewinder AAMs, rockets and bombs.

Operators: Thailand

History: The revolutionary Harrier was the world's first practical V/STOL (vertical/short takeoff and landing) fixed wing aircraft.

The origins of the Harrier lie in the Hawker P.1127, design of which began in 1957 to take advantage of the Bristol BS.53 turbofan engine. The BS.53 was able to vector or direct thrust from its four exhaust nozzles which could pivot more than 90° from the horizontal, and evolved into the Rolls-Royce Pegasus.

The first of six P.1127 prototypes successfully made its first hovering flight on October 21 1960, while the first transition from vertical to horizontal flight occurred on September 12 1961. The P.1127s were followed by nine pre production development aircraft named Kestrel, which were operated for a time by a special tri nation squadron with pilots from the RAF, Germany and the USA. Britain ordered a further six development aircraft in February 1965, which it named Harrier. The first of these original Harriers first flew in August 1966.

While the planned P.1154 multirole supersonic fighter development for the RAF and RN was scrapped, the Harrier entered production for the RAF as a light strike aircraft, the first of these, designated GR.1, flying on December 28 1967. 132 were ordered, including T.2 trainers. RAF Harriers were delivered as GR.3s and T.4s from 1976 when the aircraft were fitted with a Marconi laser ranger and marked target seeker in a lengthened nose. All have been retired.

The US Marine Corps took delivery of 110 McDonnell Douglas built AV-8As and two seat TAV-8As, similar in specification to the GR.1. Later upgraded to AV-8C standard, the last of these earlier Harriers was retired in 1987.

The only other customer for early Harriers was the Spanish navy, who ordered 11 AV-8S single seaters and two TAV-8S two seaters from MDC. Designated VA.1 and VAE.1 respectively and named Matador, these aircraft have since been replaced by Harrier IIs and Harrier II Pluses and sold to the Thai navy for service aboard its newly delivered Spanish built aircraft carrier. Thailand took delivery of the aircraft during 1996.

Photo: A Royal Thai Navy AV-8S. (RTN)

British Aerospace Sea Harrier

Country of origin: UK

Type: V/STOL naval multirole fighter

Powerplant: One 95.6kN (21,500lb) Rolls-Royce Pegasus Mk 104 turbofan.

Performance: FRS.1 – Max speed 1185km/h (640kt) plus at low level, cruising speed at 36,000ft 850km/h (460kt), cruising speed at low level 640 to 835km/h (350 to 450kt). Combat radius on a high altitude interception mission 750km (405nm), combat radius on a low level attack mission 565km (305nm).

Weights: FRS.1 – Operating empty 6375kg (14,052lb), max takeoff 11,880kg (26,200lb).

Dimensions: FRS.1 – Wing span 7.70m (25ft 3in), length overall 14.50m (47ft 7in), height 3.71m (12ft 2in). Wing area 18.7m² (201.1sq ft).

Accommodation: Pilot only.

Armament: FRS.1 – Two underfuselage pod mounted 30mm Aden cannons. Four underwing pylons can carry up to 3630kg (8000lb) but cleared for 2270kg (5000lb) of armament including AIM-9 Sidewinders, bombs, rockets and BAe Sea Eagle anti shipping missiles. Indian FRS.51s wired for Matra AAMs.

Operators: India

History: The Sea Harrier has one of the best air-to-air combat records in recent military history, shooting down 28 Argentinean warplanes in the Falklands War for no loss.

The suitability of the basic Harrier design for use from small aircraft carriers was obvious from the program's inception. A P.1127 (Harrier predecessor) first demonstrated the type's suitability for carrier operations by flying off HMS *Ark Royal*, although official Royal Navy interest was not forthcoming until the mid 1970s when the Phantom and Buccaneer equipped *Ark Royal* was nearing retirement without a planned replacement. Thus the RN sanctioned development of a navalised Harrier for operation off the forthcoming ASW helicopter carriers (fitted with ski jump ramps), with 24 Sea Harrier FRS.1s ordered in May 1975. This far sighted decision was to pay huge dividends as the Sea Harrier came into its own during the 1982 Falklands War, providing vital air cover for British ground forces and ships, and consistently outclassing Argentine Daggers in air-to-air engagements.

The FRS.1 Harrier is similar to the RAF GR.3 except for the forward fuselage. The cockpit was raised, increasing room for additional avionics in the forward fuselage and giving the pilot much greater all round vision, while the FRS.1's nose contains an oblique reconnaissance camera and a Ferranti Blue Fox multimode radar (a development of the Lynx helicopter's Sea Spray radar). The FRS.1's Pegasus Mk 104 engine is a navalised version of the GR.3's Mk 103 with minor changes for operations in a marine environment, including anti corrosive coatings on some ferrous components.

The RN took delivery of a total of 57 FRS.1s plus four T.4N two seat conversion trainers (without Blue Fox radar). Surviving FRS.1s were retired from RN service in 1995 to be upgraded to F/A.2 standard.

India is the only Sea Harrier export customer, ordering the first of 21 Sea Harrier FRS.51s and four T.60 trainers in 1978 (22 survive).

Photo: A RN FRS.1 hovers above HMS *Invincible*. (BAe)

British Aerospace Sea Harrier F/A.2

Country of origin: United Kingdom

Type: V/STOL naval multirole fighter

Powerplant: One 95.6kN (21,500lb) Rolls-Royce Pegasus Mk 106 turbofan.

Performance: F/A.2 – Max speed 1185km/h (640kt) plus, cruising speed at 36,000ft 850km/h (460kt). Max initial rate of climb 50,000ft/min. Service ceiling 51,000ft. Takeoff run without ski ramp approx 305m (1000ft). Combat radius on a 90min time on station CAP with four AIM-120s and two drop tanks 185km (100nm). Hi-lo-hi combat radius with two Sea Eagle missiles and two 30mm cannons 370km (200nm). Hi-lo-hi reconnaissance mission radius with two drop tanks 970km (525nm).

Weights: Max takeoff 9843kg (21,700lb).

Dimensions: F/A.2 – Wing span 7.70m (25ft 3in), length overall 14.17m (46ft 6in), height 3.71m (12ft 2in). Wing area 18.7m² (201.1sq ft).

Accommodation: Pilot only.

Armament: Stressed to carry up to 3630kg (8000lb) of external ordnance, although only cleared for 2270kg (5000lb) on four underwing and two underfuselage hardpoints. Can carry up to four AIM-120 Amraams on outboard and underfuselage stations, or two AIM-120s and four AIM-9s. Underfuselage stations can also carry two 30mm Aden cannons. Other weapons include bombs, rockets and Sea Eagle anti ship missiles.

Operators: UK

History: The F/A.2 is a midlife upgrade of the Sea Harrier FRS.1, with changes to the airframe, cockpit, avionics, radar and armament.

Work on a midlife upgrade of the Sea Harrier first began in January 1985 when BAe was contracted to do a project definition study. British Aerospace initially proposed a number of aerodynamic refinements plus wingtip Sidewinder missile rails that were not adopted, with changes instead focusing around a new radar and modernised cockpit.

The first modified Sea Harrier, designated FRS.2, was an aerodynamic prototype without radar installed and it flew for the first time in its new configuration on September 19 1988. In all, British Aerospace has been converting 34 FRS.1s to the new standard (the FRS.2 designation was dropped in favour of F/A.2), while 18 new build F/A.2s have been ordered to cover attrition losses. The first production conversions were delivered from April 1993, the last in 1997.

The most obvious change with the F/A.2 is the Blue Vixen radar mounted in a new, rounded radome. The GEC-Marconi Blue Vixen is a pulse doppler multimode radar featuring all weather lookdown/shootdown capability, track-while-scan, multiple target tracking and improved surface target detection abilities. The F/A.2's nose contains an additional avionics bay, while the upgrade to the cockpit involves fitting HOTAS controls and multi function CRT displays. The fuselage is also stretched slightly, with a 35cm (1ft 2in) plug behind the wing.

The F/A.2 program suffered a number of delays and an increase in cost of 20%, largely due to problems with integrating the Blue Vixen radar with the AIM-120 Amraam. However these problems have been overcome, and the Royal Navy now has a very capable medium range fire and forget missile armed fighter.

Photo: A 801 Sqn F/A.2. (Pete Battye, RAAF)

British Aerospace Hawk

Country of origin: United Kingdom

Type: Two seat advanced trainer and light attack aircraft

Powerplant: 60 – One 25.4kN (5700lb) Rolls-Royce Turboméca Adour 861 turbofan. 100 – One 26.0kN (5845lb) Adour 871.

Performance: 60 – Max level speed at sea level 1010km/h (545kt). Max initial rate of climb 11,800ft/min. Service ceiling 46,000ft. Combat radius with 907kg (2000lb) external load 1448km (781nm), with a 2270kg (5000lb) external load 1000km (538nm). 100 – Max speed 1038km/h (560kt) at 36,000ft, at sea level 1001km/h (540kt). Max initial rate of climb 11,800ft/min. Service ceiling 44,500ft. Combat radius on a hi-lo-hi mission with seven BL755 cluster bombs 510km (275nm).

Weights: 60 – Empty 4012kg (8845lb), max TOW 9100kg (20,060lb). 100 – Empty 4400kg (9700lb), max takeoff 9100kg (20,060lb).

Dimensions: 60 – Wing span 9.39m (30ft 10in), fuselage length 10.78m (35ft 4in), height 3.98m (13ft 1in). Wing area 16.7m² (179.6sq ft). 100 – Wing span 9.94m (32ft 8in) with wingtip AIM-9 missiles, fuselage length including nose probe 12.10m (39ft 8in), height 3.99m (12ft 1in). Wing area 16.7m² (179.6sq ft).

Accommodation: Seating for two in tandem.

Armament: 60 & 100 – Up to 3000kg (6615lb) of external ordnance, including rocket pods, bombs and cluster bombs, AIM-9 Sidewinder AAMs and a centreline 30mm Aden cannon.

Operators: Australia*, Finland, Indonesia, Kenya, Kuwait, Malaysia, Oman, Saudi Arabia, Switzerland, South Korea, UAE (Abu Dhabi & Dubai), UK, Zimbabwe.

History: The Hawk is one of the most successful trainer families of the past 25 years.

Hawker Siddeley began initial design studies of a two seat jet trainer in 1968 under the designation P.1182, at a time when the RAF had a marked shortfall in trainer aircraft. Hawker's design was subsequently formally adopted by the RAF in 1970, and the first aircraft first flew on August 21 1971.

In all the RAF took delivery of 176 Hawk T.1s from 1976. In the mid 1980s 89 RAF Hawks were modified as T.1As, wired to accept Sidewinders on the inboard pylons for emergency wartime use as air defence fighters. A small number of rewinged RAF T.1Ws can carry stores on two underwing pylons.

The first export Hawk was the Mk 50 which introduced a more powerful engine, a higher max takeoff weight and greater stores carriage on four underwing pylons. The Mk 60 features a further increase in engine power, an improved wing with leading edge fences and a revised flap layout, giving improved airfield performance, and Sidewinder and Matra AAM capability.

The ultimate Hawk two seat development is the 100. Changes are many and include a more powerful Adour 871 turbofan; a revised wing with fixed leading edge droop to improve manoeuvrability, full width flaps and optional wingtip missile rails; an extended nose, optionally housing FLIR and/or a laser ranger; and revised avionics, including multi function displays, plus HUD and HOTAS controls. Australia's 33 Hawk 127 LIFs will be delivered from 1999 and will feature three colour CRT displays in each cockpit.

Photo: A Royal Air Force of Oman Hawk 103. (BAe)

British Aerospace Hawk 200

Country of origin: United Kingdom

Type: Light multirole single seat fighter

Powerplant: One 26.0kN (5845lb) Rolls-Royce/Turboméca Adour Mk 871 turbofan.

Performance: Max speed at sea level 1000km/h (540kt), economical cruising speed 795km/h (430kt). Max initial rate of climb 11,510ft/min. Service ceiling 45,000ft. Ferry range with two drop tanks 2390km (1365nm). Combat radius with a recce pod and two drop tanks, hi-hi-hi 1600km (862nm); combat radius with 1360kg (3000lb) ordnance hi-lo-hi 945km (510nm); combat radius on a hi-hi-hi interception with two AIM-9s and two drop tanks 1335km (720nm).

Weights: Basic empty 4450kg (9810lb), max takeoff 9100kg (20,060lb).

Dimensions: Wing span 9.94m (32ft 8in) with wingtip missiles, normal wingspan 9.39m (30ft 10in), fuselage length 10.95m (35ft 11in), height 4.13m (13ft 7in). Wing area 16.7m² (179.6sq ft).

Accommodation: Pilot only.

Armament: Up to 3495kg (7700lb) of ordnance externally on one centreline, four underwing and two wingtip stations. Weapon options include up to four AIM-9 Sidewinder AAMs, a centreline Aden 30mm cannon, bombs and rockets.

Operators: Indonesia*, Malaysia, Oman.

History: The ultimate development of the Hawk family so far, the single seat Hawk 200 fighter has found a small but ready market from existing two seat Hawk customers.

The original two seat Hawk flew for the first time on August 21 1971, since which time over 450 have been ordered. This commercial success in part contributed to British Aerospace's announcement in 1984 that it was to build a single seat light fighter development known as the Hawk 200. This demonstrator first flew on May 19 1986.

While the first Hawk 200 demonstrator crashed two months after its first flight (through g-induced loss of consciousness), a preproduction 200 flew in April 1987, and a production representative, radar equipped Hawk 200RDA demonstrator flew in February 1992.

Compared with the two seater Hawks, the Hawk 200 differs mainly in the redesigned forward fuselage and nose to accommodate the single seat cockpit. Otherwise the Hawk 200 and equivalent Hawk 100 two seater retain 80% commonality. Like the 100, the single seater features the advanced combat wing with leading edge droop for improved manoeuvrability, full span flaps and wingtip rails for air-to-air missiles (typically the Sidewinder). The wingtip rails, four underwing and one centreline station can carry between them over three tonnes of ordnance.

The redesigned nose houses a Westinghouse APG-66H multimode radar (similar to that fitted to the F-16). The FLIR/laser range finder nose of the Hawk 100 was also offered as an option for the single seater for a time, but was dropped. In the cockpit the 200 features modern avionics, a single colour multi function display, a HUD and optional HOTAS controls.

So far all Hawk 200 orders have been placed in conjunction with two seat orders. Oman was the first customer, and its initial 200 flew for the first time in September 1993.

Photo: A Royal Malaysian Air Force Hawk 200. (BAe)

British Aerospace Nimrod

Country of origin: United Kingdom

Type: Maritime patrol and Elint aircraft

Powerplants: Four 54.0kN (12,140lb) Rolls-Royce RB.168-20 Spey Mk 250 turbofans.

Performance: MR.2 – Max cruising speed 880km/h (475kt), economical cruising speed 787km/h (425kt), typical patrol speed at low level on two engines 370km/h (200kt). Service ceiling 42,000ft. Typical endurance 12 hours. Max endurance without refuelling 15 hours, with one refuelling 19 hours. Ferry range 9265km (5000nm).

Weights: MR.2 – Typical empty 39,010kg (86,000lb), max normal takeoff 80,515kg (177,500lb), max overload takeoff 87,090kg (192,000lb).

Dimensions: Wing span 35.00m (114ft 10in), length 38.63m (126ft 9in), height 9.08m (29ft 9in). Wing area 197.0m² (2121.0sq ft).

Accommodation: Normal crew of 12 comprising two pilots and flight engineer on flightdeck with navigator, tactical navigator, radio operator, two sonic system operators, ESM/MAD operator and two observers/stores loaders in main cabin.

Armament: Total of 6125kg (13,500lb) of ordnance can be carried in the internal weapons bay and on two underwing hardpoints. Options include AGM-84 Harpoon ASMs, Stingray torpedoes, bombs and depth charges, plus up to four AIM-9 Sidewinders for self defence.

Operators: UK

History: The Nimrod was developed to meet an RAF requirement for a replacement for the ageing Avro Shackleton.

In 1964 two unsold Comet 4 airliners were selected as prototype airframes for the new maritime patrol aircraft. These two prototypes were given the Hawker Siddeley model number 801, and the first flew in converted form on May 23 1967. Changes to the Comet included the replacement of the airliner's RR Avon turbojets with Spey turbofans (increasing fuel efficiency, and thus range – the Nimrod can cruise while on patrol on two of its four Speys) and a new lower fuselage with an internal weapons bay and extended nose to contain a search radar. Other changes included a Magnetic Anomaly Detector (MAD) mounted in a boom extending from the rear fuselage, and ESM sensors mounted in a fairing on top of the tail. The first of 46 Nimrod MR.1s ordered entered RAF service in October 1969.

The MR.2 designations applies to an upgrade applied to 32 Nimrods from 1975. The upgrade involved a new central tactical system with a new computer and processors, new communications suite and EMI's Searchwater radar. Subsequently the fleet was modified to MR.2P standard with the addition of an inflight refuelling probe, and more recently Nimrods have been fitted with Loral wingtip ESM pods.

A mid 1980s program to adapt the Nimrod as an AEW aircraft, (designated AEW.3) was cancelled due to technical problems.

Two further Nimrods (a third made a successful ditching off the coast of Scotland in May 1995) serve as R.1P Elint platforms. Identifiable by the lack of MAD boom, the R.2s are still officially identified as radar calibration aircraft, but are fitted with sensors to detect and record electronic emissions. A third, previously stored Nimrod airframe is being converted to R.1P configuration.

Photo: A Nimrod MR.2P in flight.

British Aerospace Nimrod 2000

Country of origin: United Kingdom

Type: Maritime patrol aircraft

Powerplant: Four 66.3kN (14,900lb) BMW Rolls-Royce BR710 turbofans.

Performance: Max operating Mach number Mach 0.77. Service ceiling 42,000ft. Range with max internal fuel over 11,110km (6000nm). Endurance over 15hr.

Weights: Empty 46,500kg (102,515lb), max takeoff 104,855kg (231,165lb).

Dimensions: Wing span over tip pods 38.71m (127ft 0in), length excluding refuelling probe 38.63m (126ft 9in), height 9.14m (30ft 0in). Wing area 235.8m² (2538.0sq ft).

Accommodation: Flightcrew of two, with an Air Electronics Officer and seven tactical mission crew, and optionally two observers and a sonobuoy loader, with accommodation for up to 13 relief crew or support personnel.

Armament: Will be able to carry a wide variety of current and planned anti ship and anti submarine weapons (such as ASMs, torpedoes and mines) in the internal weapons bay and four underwing hardpoints. External hardpoints will also carry Sidewinder or ASRAAM AAMs for self defence.

Operators: United Kingdom*

History: The BAe Nimrod 2000 is a substantial rebuild of the current MR.2P Nimrod, with changes to the airframe, engines, cockpit, mission systems and radar.

The Nimrod 2000 was British Aerospace's response to the Royal Air Force's Nimrod replacement program. The RAF selected BAe's offering of a re-engined and rebuilt Nimrod ahead of offerings from Lockheed Martin (with its Orion 2000), Dassault (Atlantique 3) and Loral (P-3 Valkyrie – rebuilt and re-engined ex USN P-3A/Bs). The selection of the Nimrod 2000 was announced on July 25 1996.

The transformation to Nimrod 2000 involves refurbishing the existing fuselage and fitting new build larger area wings and wing box, new Messier-Dowty undercarriage, new hydraulic, fuel and electrical systems, four new, 23% more powerful and 20% more fuel efficient BMW Rolls-Royce BR710 turbofans (which, together with additional fuel capacity significantly increases the Nimrod's range), a two crew flightdeck and a new fully integrated mission system.

The British Aerospace integrated mission system will comprise a Boeing supplied tactical command sensor sub-system, Telephonics communication sub-system, Loral Defensive Aids Sub-System and a Smiths Industries Armaments Control System. Sensors will include a Racal Searchwater 2000MR radar, Elta ESM, FLIR and the current Nimrod's MAD. The current UYS-503 processor is also retained.

The flightdeck will feature seven Sextant Avionique colour LCD displays, compatible with NVGs, EICAS, a ring laser gyro INS with GPS nav system and a microwave landing system.

Work began on the first three of 21 Nimrods to be rebuilt in early 1997. First deliveries to the RAF will begin in 2002. BAe is also marketing new build Nimrod 2000s on the world market.

Photo: An artist's impression of the Nimrod 2000. The Nimrod's buried engine configuration significantly reduces radar cross compared with turboprop powered maritime patrol aircraft. (BAe)

Canadair CT-114 Tutor

Country of origin: Canada

Type: Two seat advanced jet trainer

Powerplant: CL-41A – One 13.1kN (2950lb) Orenda licence built General Electric J85-CAN-J4 turbojet. CL-41G – One 11.8kN (2633lb) J85-CAN-40.

Performance: CL-41A – Max speed at 28,500ft 801km/h (432kt). Service ceiling 43,000ft. Range 1000km (540nm).

Weights: Empty equipped 2220kg (4895lb), max takeoff 3532kg (7788lb).

Dimensions: Wing span 11.13m (36ft 6in), length 9.75m (32ft 0in), height 2.84m (9ft 4in). Wing area 20.4m² (220.0sq ft).

Accommodation: Seating for two, side by side.

Armament: Usually none in Canadian service. Malaysian (CL-41G) aircraft were fitted with six hardpoints which could carry a total 1815kg (4000lb) of ordnance, including bombs, rockets, gun pods and air-to-air missiles.

Operators: Canada

History: Despite flying for the first time in 1960, and with the average age of those remaining in service being over three decades, the Canadair Tutor looks set to remain Canada's primary advanced trainer into the next century.

The Tutor was initially developed as a private venture due to a lack of official Canadian Government interest in the project. Regardless of the lack of support, development continued, resulting in a first flight on January 13 1960. This first prototype CL-41 was powered by a 10.8kN (2400lb) Pratt & Whitney JT12A-5 turbojet, while the design as a whole differed from most of its contemporaries in having side by side seating and a T-tail. Another design feature is the two airbrakes on either side of the rear fuselage.

The Canadian Government ordered 190 production CL-41s for the then Royal Canadian Air Force in September 1961 after an evaluation of contemporary trainers. Unlike the prototype these production aircraft are powered by a General Electric J85 turbojet, built under licence in Canada by Orenda. In Canadian service the CL-41 is designated the CT-114 Tutor.

The 190 production Tutors were delivered between December 1963 and September 1966. More than 130 remain in Canadian Forces service, although a number are in storage. The principle operator of the Tutor is 2 Flying Training School at Moose Jaw in Saskatchewan, with whom pilots are trained up to wings standard. Those pilots bound for fast jets then have further Tutor training. Other CT-114s are in service with the Central Flying School for instructor training. The most famous operator of the Tutor is the Snowbirds aerobatic display team whose aircraft are fitted with smoke generators.

The only country outside Canada to operate the Tutor was Malaysia. The Royal Malaysian Air Force took delivery of 20 CL-41Gs, which compared with the basic CL-41 were equipped with six hardpoints capable of carrying a range of armaments including rockets and bombs. Named the Tebuan, or Wasp, the CL-41Gs were delivered in 1967-68, but were retired from service in the mid 1980s, due to fatigue and corrosion problems.

Photo: A Tutor of Canada's Snowbirds display team. (Alan MacDonald)

Canadair CL-215, CL-215T & CL-415

Country of origin: Canada

Type: Firefighting, SAR and multirole transport amphibian

Powerplants: CL-215 – Two 1565kW (2100hp) Pratt & Whitney R-2800-CA3 18 cylinder radial piston engines, driving three blade constant speed propellers.

Performance: CL-215 – Max cruising speed 290km/h (157kt). Max initial rate of climb 1000ft/min. Takeoff run from water at 17,100kg (37,700lb) all up weight 800m (2625ft). Range with a 1590kg (3500lb) payload at max cruising speed 1715km (925nm), or 2095km (1130nm) at long range cruise power.

Weights: CL-215 – Empty 12,220kg (26,940lb), typical operating empty 12,740kg (28,080lb), max takeoff from water 17,100kg (37,700lb), max takeoff from land 19,730kg (43,500lb).

Dimensions: CL-215 – Wing span 28.60m (93ft 10in), length 19.82m (65ft 1in), height 8.98m (29ft 6in) on land or 6.88m (22ft 7in) on water. Wing area 100.3m² (1080sq ft).

Accommodation: Flightcrew of two, plus accommodation in special missions variants for a third flightdeck member, a mission specialist and two observers. Passenger configuration for 30, or in a combi configuration for 11, with firebombing tanks retained and freight in forward fuselage. Fire retardant capacity of 6125kg (13,500lb).

Armament: None

Operators: CL-215 – Greece, Spain, Thailand, Venezuela.

History: While most production CL-215/415s have been for civilian/ government agency work where they serve as firebombers, a number have also been acquired for a range of military roles including maritime patrol, search and rescue and transport.

The CL-215 first flew on October 23 1967, and 125 were built in different batches through to 1990. Primary customers were government agencies, including various Canadian province governments and France, plus the air forces of Greece, Spain, Italy and Yugoslavia. The status of the aircraft delivered to what was then Yugoslavia is unclear, while the Italian AF CL-215s have been transferred to a government agency. In the firefighting role the CL-215's capabilities are impressive, it can scoop up 5455 litres (1200 Imp gal/1440US gal) of water from a flat water source such as a lake in 12 seconds.

Spain took delivery of a total of 20 CL-215s, of which eight were configured for maritime patrol and search and rescue work, while the Royal Thai Navy operates two CL-215s, also configured for SAR. Another military CL-215 operator is Venezuela, its two aircraft are configured as passenger transports.

Canadair offers retrofit kits for CL-215s to the new Pratt & Whitney Canada PW123 turboprop powered CL-215T standard. Spain has ordered 15 retrofit kits for its aircraft.

The improved, new build CL-415 features the PW123s, but also an EFIS cockpit, higher weights and an increased capacity firebombing system. Its principle mission is that of a firebomber, but various special mission (including SAR and maritime patrol) and transport configurations are offered. The first CL-415 flew on December 6 1993.

Photo: Greece is the largest military CL-215 operator, with 15 on air force strength for firefighting. (Greek MoD)

Canadair Challenger

Country of origin: Canada

Type: Special missions and VIP transport

Powerplants: 600 – Two 33.6kN (7500lb) Avco Lycoming ALF 502L turbofans. 601 – Two 40.66kN (9140lb) General Electric CF34-3As.

Performance: 600 – Max speed 904km/h (488kt), max cruising speed 890km/h (480kt), long range cruising speed 800km/h (432kt). Range with reserves (latter build aircraft) 6300km (3402nm). 601-1A – Max cruising speed 851km/h (460kt), typical cruising speed 820km/h (442kt), long range cruising speed 786km/h (424kt). Range with max fuel and reserves 6208km (3352nm).

Weights: 600 latter build aircraft – Empty 8370kg (18,450lb), operating empty 10,285kg (22,675lb), max takeoff 18,200kg (40,125lb). 601-1A – Empty 9050kg (19,950lb), operating empty 11,605kg (25,585lb). Max takeoff 19,550kg (43,100lb).

Dimensions: 600 – Wing span 18.85m (61ft 10in), length 20.85m (68ft 5in), height 6.30m (20ft 8in). Wing area 41.8m² (450sq ft). 601 – Same except wing span 19.61m (64ft 4in). Wing area 48.3m² (520.0sq ft).

Accommodation: Flightcrew of two. Various seating options available depending on customer preference, max seating for 19.

Armament: None

Operators: Canada, China, Croatia, Germany, Malaysia.

History: The Challenger family of business jets has seen limited military service, mainly as a VIP transport.

Canadair purchased the rights to an all new business jet developed by Bill Lear, original designer of the Lear Jet, in 1976. Known as the LearStar 600 this design was notable for its large cabin, long range and good operating economics. As the CL-600, Canadair launched development of the LearStar design in October 1976.

The first CL-600 flew on November 8 1978. Unfortunately for Canadair the aircraft suffered a number of early problems. Overweight, a major weight and drag reduction program paired back the CL-600's weight, improving range, but the troubled ALF 502 turbofans failed to meet predicted performance levels.

Troubles with the ALF 502 powered CL-600 led Canadair to develop a vastly improved variant in the form of the General Electric CF34 powered Challenger 601 (the CF34 also powers the USAF's A-10 Thunderbolt II and USN's S-2 Viking). Other detail changes included winglets, which are also offered as a retrofit to earlier aircraft. The 601 first flew on April 10 1982 and for a time was offered alongside the CL-600. The CL-600 was dropped from the model line in 1983. The 601 has been offered in progressively improved variants, the latest is the 604.

Canada is the largest Challenger military operator. The Canadian Forces uses CE-144s as high speed, high altitude threat simulators for developing fighter pilot interception skills. One is a CX-144 electronics and avionics testbed while others serve as CC-144 VIP transports. All Canadian CL-600s have been fitted with the winglets of the 601.

Other military operators are Malaysia (CL-600), Croatia (601), Germany (601) and China (601), all used as VIP transports.

Photo: A Canadian Forces CC-144 (Challenger 601). (Bill Lines)

CASA C-101 Aviojet

Country of origin: Spain

Type: Two seat basic and advanced trainer and light attack aircraft

Powerplant: C-101CC/DD – One 20.9kN (4700lb) with max reserve power or 19.1kN (4300lb) without reserve Garrett TFE731-5-IJ turbofan.

Performance: C-101CC/DD – Max speed with max reserve power 835km/h (450kt) at 15,000ft, max speed at sea level 785km/h (423kt), economical cruising speed 612km/h (330kt). Max initial rate of climb 6360ft/min (with max reserve power), normal max initial rate of climb 4975ft/min. Time to 25,000ft 6min 30sec. Service ceiling 44,000ft. Lo-lo-lo attack radius with four 250kg bombs and 30mm cannon with 5min over target and reserves 482km (260nm). Ferry range with reserves 3705km (2000nm). Max endurance 7 hours.

Weights: C-101CC – Empty equipped 3470kg (7650lb), max takeoff 6300kg (13,890lb).

Dimensions: Wing span 10.60m (34ft 10in), length 12.50m (41ft 0in), height 4.25m (14ft 0in). Wing area 20.0m² (215.3sq ft).

Accommodation: Two in tandem.

Armament: C-101CC – Can carry a 30mm DEFA 533 cannon or twin 12.7mm Browning M3 machine gun pod in lower fuselage. Six underwing hardpoints can carry a total of 2250kg (4960lb) of ordnance, including bombs, rocket pods, plus up to two AGM-65 Maverick ASMs, or two AIM-9 Sidewinder of Matra Magic AAMs on C-101DD.

Operators: Chile, Honduras, Jordan, Spain.

History: At the lower end of the jet trainer/light attack platform spectrum, the CASA C-101 Aviojet is nevertheless a relatively inexpensive and capable aircraft.

Design of the Aviojet began in 1975 to replace the Hispano Saeta after CASA signed a development contract with the Spanish Air Ministry. As CASA's first foray into the jet engined trainer field, the company enrolled the help of Northrop of the USA and Germany's MBB (now Northrop Grumman and Daimler Benz Aerospace respectively). Northrop designed the unswept wing and inlet area, but CASA assumed all design responsibility after the first flight of the first of four prototypes on June 27 1977.

Notable features of the Aviojet include modular construction, the Garrett TFE731 high bypass turbofan, an engine widely used on business jets and known for its reliability and fuel efficiency (conversely the high bypass contributes to ordinary high altitude performance), and a weapons bay in the forward fuselage which can house cannon or gun packs, a reconnaissance pod, an ECM package or a laser designator.

Initial production of the C-101 was for Spain, whose C-101EB trainers are designated E.25 Mirlo, or Blackbird. The C-101BB features a more powerful engine and was sold to Chile as the T-36 (subsequently fitted with a ranging radar) and Honduras. The C-101CC introduced a more powerful engine than the C.101BB with a five minute military reserve power thrust rating of 20.9kN (4700lb). It was sold to Chile as the A-36 Halcón (Hawk) and Jordan. The C-101DD features nav/attack avionics improvements, including a HUD, HOTAS controls, weapon aiming controls and AGM-65 compatibility. First flown in May 1985, none were ordered. In all 149 C-101s were built before production wound up.

Photo: A Chilean A-36 Halcón. (Fuerza Aerea de Chile).

CASA C-212 Aviocar & Patrullero

Country of origin: Spain

Type: Aviocar – STOL utility transport. Patrullero – Maritime patrol and Elint/ECM platform

Powerplants: 200 – Two 670kW (900shp) Garrett TPE311-10-501Cs turboprops driving four blade constant speed propellers. 300 – Two 670kW (900shp) AlliedSignal TPE331-10R-513Cs.

Performance: 200 – Max cruising speed 365km/h (197kt), cruising speed 346km/h (187kt). Range with max payload 410km (220nm), range with max fuel 1760km (950nm). 300 – Max cruising speed 354km/h (190kt), economical cruising speed 300km/h (162kt). Max initial rate of climb 1630ft/min. STOL takeoff run 385m (1260ft). Range with 25 passengers at max cruising speed 440km (237nm), range with a 1700kg (3770lb) payload 1435km (775nm).

Weights: 200 – Empty 3780kg (8333lb), MTOW 7450kg (16,424lb). 300 – Empty 3780kg (8333lb), max takeoff 7700kg (16,975lb).

Dimensions: 200 – Wing span 19.00m (62ft 4in), length 15.16m (49ft 9in), height 6.30m (20ft 8in). Wing area 40.0m² (430.6sq ft). 300 – Wing span 20.28m (66ft 7in), length 16.15m (53ft 0in), height 6.60m (21ft 8in). Wing area 41.0m² (441.3sq ft).

Accommodation: Aviocar – Flightcrew of two. Max passenger seating for 26 troops or 12 stretchers and four medical attendants. Patrullero – Four systems operators in maritime patrol configuration, or radar operator and two observers in ASW configuration.

Armament: Aviocar – Two underwing hardpoints of 250kg (550lb) capacity each can carry light gun or rocket pods. Patrullero – Can carry torpedoes (such as Mk 46s or Stingray), rockets and anti shipping missiles (including Aerospatiale AS 15TT and Sea Skua).

Operators: Angola, Bolivia, Chile, Columbia, Djibouti, Equatorial Guinea, Ghana, Indonesia, Jordan, Mexico, Myanmar, Nicaragua, Panama, Paraguay, Portugal, South Africa, Sweden, Sudan, UAE (Abu Dhabi), Uruguay, Venezuela, Zimbabwe.

History: Conceived as a light STOL transport for Spain, the C-212 has found a large military market worldwide.

The C-212 was designed to replace the Spanish air force's mixed fleet of Douglas C-47 Dakotas and Junkers Ju 52s still in service in the 1960s. Design work began in the late 1960s (features including good STOL performance and a rear cargo ramp), the first prototype flying on March 26 1971. The type entered air force service in 1974.

The initial civil version was designated the C-212C, the military version the C-212-5. Production of these models ceased in 1978, CASA switching to the Series 200 with more powerful engines and higher operating weights. The Series 200 first flew in converted C-212C prototype form on April 30 1978. IPTN in Indonesia continues to build small numbers of -200s under licence.

A third development of the Aviocar is the Series 300 which first flew in 1984. Improvements include improved engines and winglets.

The Series 300 is also offered in special mission Patrullero form, as the radar and sonobuoy equipped maritime 300MP patrol form, anti submarine 300ASU and signal interception, classification, identification and jamming equipped ECM/Elint 300DE.

Photo: The IPTN NC-212-200 maritime patrol demonstrator. Indonesia's navy has 10 on order. (Robert Wiseman)

CASA CN-235

Countries of origin: Indonesia & Spain

Type: Tactical transport and maritime patrol aircraft

Powerplants: Two 1305kW (1750shp) General Electric CT7-9C turboprops, driving four blade Hamilton Standard propellers.

Performance: CN-235 M – Max cruising speed at 15,000ft 460km/h (248kt). Max initial rate of climb 1900ft/min. Service ceiling 26,600ft. Takeoff distance to 50ft at MTOW 1290m (4235ft). Range (srs 200) with max payload 1500km (810nm), with a 3550kg (7825lb) payload 4445km (2400nm).

Weights: CN-235 M – Operating empty 8800kg (19,400lb), max takeoff 16,500kg (36,375lb).

Dimensions: CN-235 M – Wing span 25.81m (84ft 8in), length 21.40m (70ft 3in), height 8.18m (26ft 10in). Wing area 59.1m² (636.1sq ft).

Accommodation: CN-235 M – Flightcrew of two, plus typically a loadmaster. Can accommodate 48 equipped troops or 46 paratroopers.

Armament: CN-235 MP – Six underwing hardpoints allow the carriage of anti shipping missiles such as Exocet and Harpoon.

Operators: Botswana, Chile, Ecuador, France, Gabon, Ireland, South Africa, South Korea, Morocco, Panama, Papua New Guinea, Saudi Arabia, Spain, Turkey*.

History: CASA of Spain and Indonesia's IPTN jointly developed the CN-235 under the Airtech banner, but since 1992 both companies have developed the aircraft separately.

With development shared equally between the two companies, one prototype in each country was rolled out simultaneously on September 10 1983. The Spanish built prototype was the first to fly, taking to the skies for the first time on November 11 1983, while the Indonesian prototype flew for the first time on December 30 that year.

CN-235 final assembly lines are located in both Indonesia and Spain, but all other construction is not duplicated. CASA builds the centre and forward fuselage, wing centre section, inboard flaps and engine nacelles, while IPTN is responsible for the outer wings and flaps, ailerons, rear fuselage and tail.

Initial production was of the CN-235-10, subsequent and improved developments including the CN-235-100 and the current production -200, with more powerful engines and structural improvements respectively.

While commercial developments of the CN-235 (including the QC – quick change) have sold in modest numbers, the military CN-235 M transport has been quite successful with over 160 in service with 17 countries, most built by CASA. Features of the M include good field performance, a rear loading ramp and spacious interior.

CASA's CN-235 MP Persuader maritime patrol aircraft has been sold to Ireland and features a Litton APS-504 search radar, FLIR and ESM.

CASA's ultimate development of the CN-235 thus far is the stretched and Pratt & Whitney Canada PW127 powered C-295, described separately.

Photo: Spain is one of the largest CN-235 operators.

CASA C-295

Country of origin: Spain

Type: Tactical transport

Powerplants: Two 2172kW (2920shp) Pratt & Whitney Canada PW127G turboprops, driving six blade Hamilton Standard propellers.

Performance: Max cruising speed at altitude 480km/h (260kt). Service ceiling 25,000ft. Takeoff run (ISA, at sea level) 800m (2625ft). Landing run 490m (1610ft). Range with max payload 1348km (728nm), range with max fuel and a 4000kg (8818lb) payload 4535km (2450nm), range with a 6000kg (13,228lb) payload 4165km (2250nm).

Weights: Max takeoff 21,000kg (46,297lb), max overload takeoff 23,200kg (51,147lb).

Dimensions: Wing span 25.81m (84ft 8in), length 24.45m (80ft 3in), height 8.15m (26ft 9in). Wing area 59.1m² (636.1sq ft).

Accommodation: Flightcrew of two. Typical accommodation for 69 fully equipped troops, or 78 troops in a high density configuration, or 48 paratroops, or 27 stretcher patients and four attendants. Max payload 7500kg (16,535lb), max overload payload 9700kg (21,385lb). Can carry up to five 2.24 x 2.74m (88 x 108in) pallets including one on the rear ramp, or one 2.24 x 2.74m (88 x 108in) pallet and three 2.24 x 3.18m (88 x 125in) pallets, or three 4WDs.

Armament: None, but provision for three hardpoints under each wing to carry up to 3200kg of ordnance.

Operators: None ordered at the time of writing.

History: The CASA C-295 is a stretched and re-engined development of the successful CN-235 tactical transport.

The CN-235 transport was developed jointly by CASA of Spain and IPTN of Indonesia, but since 1992 each company has pursued development of the basic aircraft independently. CASA began studies of a stretched and re-engined CN-235 in 1995. Other than performance improvements the C-295 will further distinguish CASA's tactical transport offerings from IPTN's versions of the CN-235.

Development of the C-295 began in November 1996 following CASA market surveys confirming sufficient demand for the aircraft. At the time of writing a prototype aircraft was under construction and was expected to achieve its first flight in March 1998. It will be followed by the first production aircraft, which is due to fly in 1999. Civil and military certification is expected in late 1999, permitting first customer deliveries in early 2000.

Compared with the basic CN-235, the C-295's fuselage will be stretched by six fuselage frames (three forward and three aft of the wing) taking length from 21.40m (70ft 3in) to 24.45m (80ft 3in), increasing the aircraft's payload. The C-295 will be powered by two P&WC PW127 turboprops driving six blade composite propellers, improving cruising speed and the takeoff run required. The basic CN-235 wing is strengthened with increased fuel capacity, while the undercarriage is also strengthened for the increased weights with a dual wheel nosewheel. Other changes include a higher pressurisation differential and a five screen NVG compatible EFIS flightdeck.

Photo: A model of the C-295 development of the CN-235. (CASA)

Cessna O-1 Bird Dog

Country of origin: United States of America

Type: Observation, liaison and forward air control aircraft

Powerplant: O-1E – One 159kW (213hp) Continental O-470-11 flat six piston engine, driving a two blade constant speed propeller.

Performance: O-1E – Max speed at sea level 243km/h (131kt), economical cruising speed 167km/h (90kt). Max initial rate of climb 1150ft/min. Service ceiling 18,500ft. Range 853km (460nm).

Weights: O-1E – Empty 732kg (1614lb), max takeoff 1102kg (2430lb).

Dimensions: O-1E – Wing span 10.97m (36ft 0in), length 7.85m (25ft 9in), height 2.22m (7ft 4in). Wing area 16.2m² (174.0sq ft).

Accommodation: Pilot and observer in tandem. Alternatively stretcher patient (with no observer) can be carried.

Armament: O-1E – None. O-1C – Two underwing hardpoints for a 113kg (250lb) bomb each, or unguided rockets.

Operators: Italy, Malta, Pakistan, South Korea, Thailand.

History: Of the more than 3500 Bird Dogs built from 1950, over 200 remain in military service today, testament to the utility of this Korean and Vietnam wars veteran.

During WW2 the US Army successfully employed many thousands of light aircraft, mainly Piper L-4s and Taylorcraft L-2 'Grasshoppers', for observation, artillery direction, tactical reconnaissance and liaison duties. Both the L-2 and L-4 were simple conversions of existing civil aircraft, and their success in their many roles led the US Army post-war to seek a standard observation aircraft, tailored closely to its specific needs.

Anticipating such a requirement, Cessna developed its Model 305 as a private venture, and this flew for the first time in December 1949. In April 1950 the official US Army competition for an observation aircraft saw Cessna's 305 selected over designs from a number of other manufacturers. The US Army ordered an initial 418 Model 305s as L-19As (O-1A from 1962).

The 305 was based loosely on the Cessna 170, a taildragger that formed the basis for the Cessna 172 (from which was developed the T-41 Mescalero – described separately). Compared with the 170 though, Cessna cut down the rear fuselage, giving 360° vision, while a transparency was fitted in the wing centre section above the main fuselage. Seating was for two in tandem. At the US Army's request the 305 was also fitted with electrically operated, slotted trailing edge flaps (later fitted to civil Cessnas) to improve STOL performance.

Bird Dog variants included the instrument trainer L-19A-ITs and TL-19Ds (TO-1D – many of these were later converted to O-2D and O-2F standards), the US Marines' OE-1 (O-1B) and improved OE-2 (O-1C), the TL-19A (TO-1A) dual control trainer (many of which were converted to O-1G FAC standard), and the definitive L-19E/O-1E, and improved L-19A/O-1A with more modern equipment. L-19E production initially ceased in 1959, but a further batch was built from 1961.

The O-1A saw service in the Korean War, while the O-1E was used extensively in Vietnam, primarily directing air strikes.

Photo: An O-1A Bird Dog in Thai markings. Note the cut down rear fuselage. (Bill Lines)

Cessna T-41 Mescalero & 172

Country of origin: United States of America

Type: Basic trainer, liaison and observation aircraft

Powerplant: T-41A – One 108kW (145hp) Continental O-300-C flat six piston engine, driving a two blade fixed pitch propeller.

Performance: T-41A – Max speed 224km/h (121kt), max cruising speed at 9000ft 211km/h (114kt). Max initial rate of climb 645ft/min. Service ceiling 13,100ft. Ferry range 1030km (555nm), standard range 990km (535nm).

Weights: T-41A – Operating empty 565kg (1245lb), max takeoff 1043kg (2300lb).

Dimensions: T-41A – Wing span 10.92m (35ft 10in), length 8.20m (26ft 11in), height 2.68m (8ft 10in). Wing area 16.2m² (174.0sq ft).

Accommodation: Seating for pilot and instructor side-by-side, with seats for two passengers behind them.

Armament: None

Operators: Includes Angola, Bolivia, Chile, Columbia, Dominican Republic, Ecuador, El Salvador, Greece, Guatemala, Honduras, Indonesia, Ireland, Liberia, Pakistan, Peru, Philippines, Saudi Arabia, South Korea, Trinidad and Tobago, Turkey.

History: The Cessna 172 is by far and away the world's most successful light aircraft, and so it is not surprising that a significant portion of the nearly 42,000 built found their way into military service.

The 172 began life as a tricycle undercarriage development of the four place Cessna 170, the aircraft that also formed the basis of the O-1 Bird Dog (described separately). The prototype 170 flew in September 1947, the prototype 172 in November 1955. The type was a success almost instantly, and through to 1986 the 172 was built in successively improved variants. An improved 172, aimed principally at civil customers, entered production in 1996.

US military interest resulted in the July 1964 US Air Force order for Cessna 172Fs for pilot flight screening performed by civil firms under contract, designated the T-41A Mescalero. These aircraft differ little from the civil 172F, and production took place between 1964 and 1967. The US Army also ordered 172s for pilot training, its T-41Bs based on the R172E with a 155kW (210hp) Continental IO-360 driving a constant speed prop. The USAF's T-41C was similar to the T-41B except for its fixed pitch propeller, and 52 were built for the USAF Academy. The T-41D, based on the T-41C but with a 28 volt electrical system, was procured for a number of countries under the US's Military Assistance Program (MAP). Some 311 T-41Ds were built between 1968 and 1978.

Replacement of the USAF's Mescaleros with Slingsby T-3 Fireflies (described separately) was completed in 1995.

Apart from 172s built as T-41s, several other countries procured civil 172s direct from Cessna or from Reims-Cessna in France (which built several thousand FR172s under licence). In all, over 30 countries have operated military 172s or T-41s.

Apart from basic pilot training, the 172 is also widely used for a number of secondary duties such as observation, liaison and border patrol.

Photo: The Greek air force operates 19 T-41Ds in the initial pilot training role. (MAP)

Cessna T-37 Tweet

Country of origin: United States of America

Type: Two seat basic and advanced trainer

Powerplants: T-37B/C – Two 4.56kN (1025lb) Continental J69-T-25 turbojets.

Performance: T-37B – Max speed 684km/h (370kt) at 25,000ft, cruising speed 612km/h (330kt). Max initial rate of climb 3370ft/min. Service ceiling 39,200ft. Range 1500km (810nm). T-37C – Max speed 650km/h (350kt), cruising speed 575km/h (310kt). Max initial rate of climb 2390ft/min. Service ceiling 29,900ft. Ferry range 1517km (820nm) with tip tanks, range with standard fuel 1367km (738nm).

Weights: T-37B – Empty 1755kg (3870lb), max takeoff 2993kg (6600lb). T-37C – Max takeoff 3402kg (7500lb).

Dimensions: Wing span 10.30m (33ft 9in), length 8.92m (29ft 3in), height 2.80m (9ft 2in). Wing area 17.1m² (183.9sq ft).

Accommodation: Seating for two, side by side.

Armament: T-37C – Up to 227kg (500lb) of armament on two underwing hardpoints, comprising two 113kg (250lb) bombs or rockets.

Operators: Chile, Columbia, Germany, Greece, Pakistan, Thailand, Turkey, USA.

History: Cessna's viceless T-37 Tweet has four decades of service behind it, and seems likely to see out the 1990s in use with a number of operators.

In 1952 the US Air Force formulated a requirement for an 'all through' jet trainer that would train pilots from basic through to wings standard. The winner of this contest was Cessna, whose Model 318 featured seating for two side by side, two small turbojets and a straight wing. The first of two prototype Model 318s, designated XT-37, flew for the first time on October 12 1954.

The initial production model was the 4.1kN (920lb) Continental J69-T-9 turbojet (licence built Turboméca Mabore) powered T-37A, which first flew in September 1955, although some problems with the aircraft delayed service entry until 1957. In all 534 T-37As were built, all of which were delivered to the USAF. In 1959 production switched to the T-37B, which introduced more powerful J69-T-25s, improved avionics and optional wingtip tanks. Some 449 T-37Bs were built. Surviving T-37As were subsequently upgraded to T-37B standard.

The final production Tweet or 'Tweetie Bird' (named after the cartoon character) model was the T-37C, 269 of which were built specifically for export. It differs from the T-37B in having a higher max takeoff weight and two underwing hardpoints for bombs or rockets.

The US Air Force began all through jet training with the T-37 in 1961, however the cost of operations led that service to reintroduce piston engined T-41 Mescaleros for initial training in 1965.

Plans to replace the USAF's T-37s with an all new jet trainer faltered when the Fairchild T-46 Eaglet was cancelled in 1986 due to program management problems. Cessna then proposed substantially upgrading the T-37 to Garrett turbofan powered T-48 standard, but instead the aircraft's replacement will be the long awaited JPATS winner, the Pilatus PC-9 based Raytheon Beech T-6 Texan II.

In the meantime, USAF T-37s have been undergoing a service life extension program (SLEP) engineered by Sabreliner.

Photo: A Vance AFB based USAF T-37. (USAF)

Cessna A-37 Dragonfly

Country of origin: United States of America

Type: Two seat light attack aircraft

Powerplants: A-37B/OA-37B – Two 12.7kN (2850lb) General Electric J85-GE-17A turbojets.

Performance: A-37/OA-37B – Max speed 816km/h (440kt) at 16,000ft, max cruising speed 787km/h (425kt). Max initial rate of climb 6990ft/min. Service ceiling 41,765ft. Range with max fuel and reserves 1630km (880nm), range with max payload including 1860kg (4100lb) of external ordnance 740km (400nm).

Weights: A-37B – Empty equipped 2817kg (6211lb), max takeoff 6350kg (14,000lb).

Dimensions: Wing span 10.93m (35ft 11in), length excluding refuelling probe 8.93m (29ft 4in), height 2.71m (8ft 11in). Wing area 17.1m² (183.9sq ft).

Accommodation: Seating for two, side-by-side.

Armament: One 7.62mm GAU-2 minigun in forward fuselage. Eight underwing hardpoints can carry a total ordnance load of 1860kg (4100lb), including bombs, rockets and gun pods.

Operators: Chile, Columbia, Ecuador, El Salvador, Guatemala, Honduras, Peru, South Korea, Uruguay.

History: The US Air Force's decision to evaluate the suitability of an armed version of the T-37 Tweet jet trainer for light attack/counter insurgency work was a fruitful one, as the resulting A-37 saw widespread active service in Vietnam where it was well suited to the type of conflict fought there.

In 1962 the USAF's Special Air Warfare centre began evaluating two T-37Bs to test the type's suitability for the counter insurgency (COIN) role. After initial testing the two T-37Bs were modified to YAT-37D standard (first flight October 22 1963) and fitted with two 10.7kN (2400lb) General Electric J85-GE-5 turbojets. Testing proved positive but initially nothing came of the concept until the Vietnam War intensified. In 1966 the USAF contracted Cessna to convert 39 T-37Bs to light attack A-37A Dragonfly standard. Apart from the GE J85 turbojets, the A-37As introduced eight underwing hardpoints, extra fuel capacity in wingtip tanks, armour protection, attack avionics, larger wheels and tyres and an internal 7.62mm minigun.

Twenty five A-37As were successfully evaluated in operational conditions in Vietnam from mid 1967, these aircraft were later transferred to full operational service, and were passed to the South Vietnamese air force in 1970.

The success of the A-37A led to the definitive A-37B, with uprated engines, an inflight refuelling probe and increased internal fuel capacity, while the airframe was stressed for 6g rather than 5g. In all 577 A-37Bs were delivered to the USAF and export customers between May 1968 and 1975. A-37Bs saw widespread service with the US and South Vietnamese air forces during the Vietnam War, and captured examples even saw brief service with the North Vietnamese air force during the closing stages of that conflict.

The USAF fitted 130 A-37Bs as OA-37Bs with avionics for forward air control work, although the last of these was retired in 1992. Ex USAF A-37 and OA-37s serve widely in South America.

Photo: A Chilean A-37B Dragonfly. (Fuerza Aerea de Chile)

Chengdu J-7 & F-7

Country of origin: China (based on Russian designed MiG-21)

Type: Single seat fighter

Powerplant: F-7M – One 43.2kN (9700lb) dry and 64.7kN (14,550lb) with afterburner Liyang WP7BM turbojet.

Performance: F-7M – Max speed 2175km/h (1175kt). Max initial rate of climb 35,433ft/min. Service ceiling 59,700ft. Max ferry range with external fuel 2230km (1203nm). Combat radius with two 150kg (330lb) bombs and drop tanks on a hi-lo-hi interdiction mission 600km (325nm), combat radius on a long range intercept mission with two AAMs and three drop tanks 650km (350nm).

Weights: F-7M – Empty 5275kg (11,630lb), max takeoff 8888kg (19,577lb).

Dimensions: F-7M – Wing span 7.15m (23ft 6in), length (excl probe) 13.95m (45ft 9in), height 4.10m (13ft 6in). Wing area 23.0m² (247.6sq ft).

Accommodation: Pilot only, except for two in tandem in JJ-7/FT-7.

Armament: F-7M – Two Type 30-1 30mm cannons. Max external ordnance of 1000kg (2205lb) on four underwing hardpoints and on centreline fuel tank station. Two inner hardpoints can carry PL-2, -2A or -7 infrared guided AAMs, or Matra R550 Magic AAMs. Inner and outer pylons can carry rockets and bombs.

Operators: Albania, Bangladesh, China, Egypt, Iran, Iraq, Myanmar, Pakistan, Sri Lanka, Tanzania, Zimbabwe.

History: China's copy of the MiG-21 forms an important part of the People's Liberation Army Air Force inventory and has been widely exported to a number of non aligned countries.

In 1961 China acquired a licence to build the MiG-21F-13 ('Fishbed C') and its Tumansky R-11F-300 turbojet. However, the severing of ties with Russia left the Chinese with incomplete technical drawings, and they instead were forced to reverse engineer pattern aircraft. This meant the first Chinese built aircraft, designated J-7, didn't fly until January 17 1966. The J-7 entered production the following year with Shenyang despite the turmoil of the cultural revolution, and some were exported as the F-7A to Albania and Tanzania.

Production was subsequently transferred to Chengdu as the J-7I. In 1975 development work began on the improved J-7II, which introduced a more powerful engine with double the time between overhaul. It was exported to Egypt and Iraq in the early 1980s as the F-7B.

The export F-7M Airguard features a GEC-Marconi HUD and weapons aiming computer, an improved ranging radar, radar altimeter, IFF and an improved engine. It has been exported to Bangladesh, Iran and Zimbabwe. The F-7P and F-7MP are similar, but with a number of minor modifications (including Martin-Baker ejection seat and Sidewinder compatibility) specifically for the Pakistan Air Force.

Other variants include the J-7E, thought to have first flown in 1990 and featuring a cranked delta wing, more powerful engine and extra hardpoints, and the J-7III, loosely equivalent to the MiG-21MF and featuring an all weather radar in an enlarged radome. Two seater JJ-7s and FT-7s meanwhile are built by Guizhou.

The latest development on offer is the F-7MG which features the J-7E's cranked delta wing fitted with leading and trailing edge flaps, Super Skyranger look down/shoot down radar, HUD and optional GPS.

Photo: Pakistan's F-7Ms were initially dubbed Skybolt. (Chengdu)

Chengdu FC-1

Country of origin: China

Type: Multirole fighter

Powerplants: One 81.4kN (18,300lb) with afterburning Klimov RD-93 turbofan.

Performance: Max speed at altitude Mach 1.6 to 1.8. Service ceiling 52,000ft. Fighter mission combat radius 1200km (650nm), ground attack combat radius 700km (378nm), max range on internal fuel 2200km (1200nm).

Weights: Operating empty 9300kg (20,530lb), max takeoff 12,500kg (27,557lb).

Dimensions: Wing span over wingtip missiles 9.50m (31ft 2in), length 13.95m (45ft 9in), height 5.02m (16ft 6in).

Accommodation: Pilot only, two seat conversion trainer planned.

Armament: Four underwing, two wingtip and one centreline hardpoints for a variety of air-to-air and air-to-ground weapons, including a GSh-23-2 23mm twin barrel cannon pod on the centreline station, PL-7 and PL-10 AAMs, rockets, bombs and missiles.

Operators: Not in service at the time of writing.

History: Chengdu Aircraft Corporation's FC-1 is being developed as a modern replacement for China's big fleet of ageing J-7s and for Pakistan in lieu of its suspended F-16 order.

The FC-1 (Fighter China) program began in 1991, following the USA's withdrawal from Super-7 development. The aircraft was designed with the assistance of Mikoyan, possibly using the MiG designer's experience on the original 1980s MiG-33, a single engine version of the MiG-29.

China publicly revealed the existence of the FC-1 at 1995's Paris Airshow. At the time the FC-1's first flight was planned for early 1997 with first deliveries of production aircraft in 1999. However first flight has been delayed and in late 1997 the program appeared to be on hold for a year or two due to funding problems.

The FC-1 is a tailed delta design and will be of conventional construction. It will have conventional flight controls with a backup analog fly-by-wire system. Power will be from a single Klimov RD-93 turbofan, a development of the RD-33 which powers the MiG-29. The delta wing will carry AAMs on wingtip stations in addition to the four underwing hardpoints and one centreline station. Chinese aircraft are expected to have locally developed or Russian avionics and radar.

Pakistan is participating in the FC-1 program as it requires a modern fighter in lieu of the USA's suspension of its F-16 order and to replace F-6s and early model F-7s. Subassemblies may be made at Pakistan's Aeronautical Complex at Kamra. If Pakistan orders the FC-1 a final assembly line may also be set up in that country.

Pakistani and other export FC-1s would most likely be fitted with western origin avionics built on a MIL STD 1553B databus. GEC-Marconi is pitching its Blue Hawk radar for the FC-1, Alenia the Grifo S7 and Thomson-CSF/Sagem the RC-400, with other western features likely to include a HUD and multifunction displays, a mission computer and inertial navigation system.

Photo: An airshow model of the FC-1. Apart from China and Pakistan, potential FC-1 customers could include current F-7 operators such as Myanmar, Bangladesh and Iran.

Countries of origin: Israel and China

Type: Multirole fighters

Powerplant: Lavi – One 55.5kN (12,500lb) dry and 82.7kN (18,600lb) with afterburning (approx ratings) Pratt & Whitney PW1120 afterburning turbojet (a turbojet development of the F100).

Performance: Lavi estimated – Max speed above 36,000ft 1969km/h (1063kt) or Mach 1.85. Low level penetration speed with two AAMs and eight 340kg/750lb bombs 997km/h (538kt). Combat radius on an air-to-ground mission, lo-lo-lo 1110km (600nm), or hi-lo-hi with six 113kg/250lb bombs 2130km (1150nm). Combat air patrol radius 1850km (1000nm).

Weights: Lavi – Empty approx 7030kg (15,500lb), max takeoff 18,370kg (40,500lb).

Dimensions: Lavi – Wing span 8.78m (28ft 10in), length 14.57m (47ft 10in), height 4.78m (15ft 8in). Wing area 33.1m^2 (355.8sq ft).

Armament: Lavi – One internal 30mm cannon. Two wingtip pylons for AAMs. Four underwing and seven underfuselage hardpoints can carry air-to-surface missiles, bombs, laser guided bombs and rockets.

Accommodation: Pilot only or two in tandem Lavi TD.

Operators: None

History: The Lavi (Young Lion) was originally developed as a multirole fighter for the Israeli air force before program cancellation saw the prototypes used as technology demonstrator airframes. However the Lavi may also form the basis for China's Chengdu J-10 multirole fighter due to enter service early next decade.

The Lavi story begins in the early 1980s when IAI began development work on a multirole fighter to meet an IDF requirement for 300 or so such aircraft. Program go-ahead was given in 1980, while full scale development began in October 1982. The first prototype (B-1) flew for the first time on December 31 1986, the second (B-2) flew on March 30 1987. Both prototypes were two seaters, with test avionics occupying the second seat.

Despite promising results, the Lavi program was cancelled in August 1987, mainly due to budget restrictions, coupled with some US opposition and the availability of extra, cheaper F-16s.

Design features of the Lavi include F-16 style ventral air intake, canard delta configuration, a single PW1120 turbojet, an Elta multimode radar, HUD, HOTAS and three multi function displays.

Following cancellation IAI elected to use the Lavi as a technology demonstrator and testbed for Israeli developed avionics and systems. To this end the third prototype (B-3) was completed as the Lavi TD. Another two seater (but this time with no test avionics in the second seat), it first flew on September 25 1989.

In the mid 1990s a number of reports surfaced suggesting that IAI was co-operating with China to develop the J-10, a new multirole fighter that strongly resembles the Lavi in configuration and allegedly based on Lavi developed technologies (possibly including the EL\M-2032 radar). The J-10 is believed to be powered by a 122.6kN (27,650lb) with afterburning Saturn AL-31F turbofan and is understood to be in an advanced stage of development. The PLA-AF reportedly requires around 300 J-10s.

Photo: IAI's Lavi TD technology demonstrator. (IAI)

Country of origin: France

Type: Maritime patrol aircraft

Powerplants: ATL2 – Two 4550kW (6100ehp) Rolls-Royce Tyne RTy.20 Mk 21 turboprops, driving four blade propellers.

Performance: ATL2 – Max level speed 648km/h (350kt) at altitude or 592km/h (320kt) at sea level, max cruising speed 555km/h (300kt), normal patrol speed 315km/h (170kt). Max initial rate of climb at 30,000kg (66,140lb) AUW 1200ft/min, or at 40,000kg (88,185lb) AUW 700ft/min. Service ceiling 30,000ft. Ferry range with max fuel 9075km (4900nm). Combat radius with two hours on station on anti shipping mission with one AM 39 Exocet missile 3333km (1800nm). Radius with 8hr patrol and four torpedoes 1110km (600nm), or with 5hr patrol 1850km (1000nm). Max endurance 18hr.

Weights: ATL2 – Empty equipped standard mission 25,700kg (56,660lb), max takeoff 46,200kg (101,850lb).

Dimensions: Span incl wingtip pods 37.42m (122ft 9in), length 33.63m (110ft 4in), height 10.89m (35ft 9in). Wing area 120.3m^2 (1295.3sq ft).

Accommodation: Normal crew complement of 10 to 12, comprising pilot, copilot, flight engineer, nose observer, radio navigator, ESM/ECM/MAD operator, radar & IFF operator, tactical co-ordinator, two acoustic operators and optionally two observers in rear fuselage.

Armament: ATL2 – Up to eight Mk 46 torpedoes, or seven Murène torpedoes or two AM 39 Exocet or AS 37 Martel ASMs (typical load three torpedoes and one missile), or NATO standard bombs in weapons bay. Four underwing hardpoints for ASMs and AAMs.

Operators: France, Germany, Italy, Pakistan.

History: The Atlantic resulted from a NATO requirement to find a replacement for the Lockheed P-2 Neptune.

The NATO requirement for a long range maritime patrol aircraft was issued in 1958. Breguet (who merged with Dassault in 1971) was the successful bidder, with its Br 1150 design selected over 24 other designs submitted from nine countries.

The Atlantic first flew in prototype form on October 21 1961 and entered service with the navies of France and Germany in 1965. In all, 87 production Altantics were built through to 1974 by a European consortium led by Breguet. Other customers were Italy and the Netherlands while Pakistan's three ex French navy Atlantics were delivered in the mid 1970s.

Design features of the basic Atlantic include a double bubble fuselage, the lower portion of which is unpressurised and includes the weapons bay, US sourced ASW equipment and a Thomson-CSF search radar in a retractable radome. Germany also operates five Atlantics modified for Elint, while Thomson-CSF is upgrading Pakistan's aircraft.

Twenty eight new build Atlantique 2s have been ordered for the French navy. These aircraft feature modern avionics and systems including a Thomson-CSF Iguane radar, a pod mounted FLIR in the nose, a new MAD, new ESM equipment, processors and navigation equipment. First flight was in 1981, with deliveries beginning in 1988 and concluding in 1997.

The proposed Allison AE 2100 powered Atlantique 3 would feature a two flightcrew cockpit and new avionics and systems.

Photo: A German navy Atlantic. (Paul Merritt)

Dassault Mystère/Falcon 200 & Gardian

Country of origin: France

Type: VIP transport, ECM trainer, maritime patrol and utility transport.

Powerplants: 200 – Two 23.1kN (5200lb) Garrett ATF 3-6A-4C turbofans.

Performance: 200 – Max cruising speed 870km/h (470kt) at 30,000ft, economical cruising speed 780km/h (420kt). Service ceiling 45,000ft. Range with max fuel, eight passengers and reserves 4650km (2510nm).

Weights: 200 – Empty 8250kg (18,290lb), max takeoff 14,515kg (32,000lb).

Dimensions: Wing span 16.32m (53ft 7in), length 17.15m (56ft 3in), height 5.32m (17ft 6in). Wing area 41.0m² (441.3sq ft).

Accommodation: Flightcrew of two. Typical main cabin seating for between eight and 10 passengers, or up to 14 in a high density configuration. Aerial ambulance can be fitted with three stretchers.

Armament: The Gardian was offered with the capability of carrying two AM 39 Exocet anti shipping missiles.

Operators: Belgium, Chile, Egypt, France, Iran, Morocco, Norway, Pakistan, Peru, Portugal, Sudan, Syria.

History: The Mystère or Falcon 20 and 200 is Dassault's most successful business jet thus far, with more than 500 built. Many serve as VIP transports with others used in a variety of special missions roles.

Development of the original Mystère 20 traces back to joint collaboration between Sud Aviation (which later merged into Aerospatiale) and Dassault in the late 1950s. Development progressed to the stage where prototype construction began in January 1962, with a first flight on May 4 1963. This prototype shared the type's overall configuration with production aircraft, but differed in that it was powered by 14.8kN (3300lb) Pratt & Whitney JT12A-8 turbojets, whereas production Mystère 20s (or Falcon 20s outside France) were powered with General Electric CF-700 turbofans.

The 200, or initially the 20H, features Garrett turbofans, greater fuel tankage and much longer range. This version remained in production until 1988, while production of the 20 ceased in 1983.

The majority of military Falcon 20 and 200 operators use them as VIP transports. However, France's sizeable fleet is an exception. The French navy operates five maritime patrol Gardians from its New Caledonia and Tahiti territories in the Pacific. These aircraft are fitted with a Thomson-CSF Varan radar and large observation windows. Chile has also upgraded two ex civil Falcon 200s to a similar standard. The French Armée de l'Air meanwhile operates a variety of combat radar and navigation system equipped Mystère 20NAs to train crews bound for Mirage IVs and 2000s, while a single Mystère 20NR trains pilots bound for the Mirage F1CR.

Other military applications include target towing, aerial ambulance and electronic warfare training aircraft. In the USA the Coast Guard operates a number of HU-25s Guardians for search and rescue. A number are equipped with Motorola SLAR and Texas Instruments linescan for maritime pollution detection, while others are fitted with a Westinghouse APG-66 radar (as on the F-16) and FLIR and used for tracking suspicious sea and air traffic.

Photo: One of Belgium's two VIP Falcon 20s. (Belgium SID)

Dassault Falcon 50

Country of origin: France

Type: VIP & government transport

Powerplants: Three 16.5kN (3700lb) AlliedSignal TFE731-3 turbofans.

Performance: Max cruising speed 880km/h (475kt), long range cruising speed 797km/h (430kt). Max operating altitude 45,000ft. Range at Mach 0.75 with eight passengers and reserves 6480km (3500nm).

Weights: Empty equipped 9150kg (20,170lb), standard max takeoff 17,600kg (38,800lb), or optionally 18,500kg (40,780lb).

Dimensions: Wing span 18.86m (61ft 11in), length 18.52m (61ft 9in), height 6.97m (22ft 11in). Wing area 46.8m² (504.1sq ft).

Accommodation: Flightcrew of two pilots. A number of cabin seating arrangements are available, depending on the toilet location. Seating for eight or nine with aft toilet, or for up to 12 with forward toilet. Can accommodate three stretchers, two doctors or attendants and medical equipment in a medevac role.

Armament: None

Operators: France*, Italy, Morocco, Portugal, Spain, South Africa, Sudan.

History: The long range trijet Falcon 50 is based loosely on the earlier twinjet Mystère/Falcon 20 and 200 family, and like the 20 and 200, has found a military market as a VIP transport.

The Dassault Falcon 50 was developed for long range trans Atlantic and transcontinental flight sectors, using the Falcon 20 as the design basis. To meet the required 6440km (3475nm) range requirement though significant changes mean that the Falcon 50 is for all intents and purposes an all new aircraft.

Key new features to achieve the range were the selection of three 16.5kN (3700lb) Garrett (now AlliedSignal) TFE731 turbofans, mounted on a new rear tail section, plus a new supercritical wing of greater area than that on the 20 and 200. Many Falcon 20 features and components were retained, the most obvious of these being the nose and fuselage cross section.

The prototype Falcon 50 flew in November 1976 but it wasn't until 1979 that production deliveries began. In the meantime the wing design was changed to incorporate the supercritical wing that still retained the original wing's planform. A second prototype flew on February 18 1978 and the first preproduction aircraft flew on June 13 1978. Like others in the Falcon family, Aerospatiale participates in the Falcon 50 manufacturing program, building the fuselage and tail surfaces. The first major Falcon 50 development is the extended range 50EX. It first flew in 1996 and features a new EFIS flightdeck.

Most military operated Falcon 50s serve as VIP and government transports, fitted with four or five seats in the main cabin. Italy's Falcon 50s are also convertible to an air ambulance configuration.

The French navy has ordered four maritime surveillance Falcon 50 Surmars, with Thomson CSF Ocean Master radar, observation windows and the ability to drop SAR equipment. They will be delivered from 2000.

Photo: A Portuguese air force Falcon 50. (MAP)

Dassault Falcon 900

Country of origin: France

Type: VIP & head of state transport & maritime patrol aircraft

Powerplants: 900 – Three 20.0kN (4500lb) Garrett (now AlliedSignal) TFE731-5AR-1C turbofans. 900B – Three 21.1kN (4750lb) TFE731-5BRs.

Performance: 900 – Max cruising speed 927km/h (500kt), economical cruising speed Mach 0.75. Max cruising altitude 51,000ft. Range with max payload and reserves 6412km (3460nm), range with 15 passengers and reserves 6968km (3760nm), with eight pax and reserves 7227km (3900nm). 900B – Same except for range with 15 pax and reserves 7115km (3840nm).

Weights: 900 – Empty equipped 10,545kg (23,248lb), max takeoff 20,640kg (45,500lb). 900B – Empty equipped 10,240kg (22,575kg), max takeoff 20,640kg (45,500lb).

Dimensions: Wing span 19.33m (63ft 5in), length 20.21m (66ft 4in), height 7.55m (24ft 9in). Wing area 49.0m2 (527.4sq ft).

Accommodation: Flightcrew of two. Main passenger cabin accommodation for between eight or 15 passengers, or as many as 18 in a high density configuration.

Armament: None

Operators: Algeria, Australia, France, Gabon, Japan, Malaysia, Nigeria, South Africa, Spain, Syria.

History: Of the more than 190 transcontinental Falcon 900s sold so far, a significant number are operated as military VIP transports.

Dassault announced it was developing a new intercontinental range large size business jet based on its Falcon 50 trijet at the 1983 Paris Airshow. Development culminated in the prototype, *Spirit of Lafayette*, flying for the first time on September 21 1984. A second prototype flew on August 30 1985.

While of similar overall configuration to the Falcon 50, the Falcon 900 features an all new widebody fuselage, which can seat three passengers abreast and is also considerably longer and wider. The main commonality with the Falcon 50 is the wing, which despite being originally designed for a considerably lighter aircraft, was adapted almost directly unchanged (and incidentally also appears on the new Falcon 2000 twin). In developing the Falcon 900 Dassault made extensive use of computer aided design, while the aircraft's structure incorporates a high degree of composite material.

From 1991 the standard production model was the Falcon 900B, which differs from the earlier 900 in having more powerful engines, increased range, the ability to operate from unprepared strips and Category II visibility approach clearance. A further improved development is the 8335km (4500nm) range 900EX with EFIS and other improvements and delivered from late 1996.

Like the smaller Falcons (Mystères in France), the 900 has proven popular with a number of countries as military VIP transports, particularly so for its large cabin and transcontinental range. Japan operates a unique maritime surveillance version of the Falcon 900 with a US sourced search radar, HU-25 Guardian/Gardian-like large observation windows, a dedicated operator station and a hatch to drop sonobuoys, markers and flares.

Photo: A French Falcon 900. (Armée de l'Air)

Dassault Mirage III

Country of origin: France

Type: Multirole fighter

Powerplant: IIIE – One 41.2kN (9435lb) dry and 60.8kN (13,670lb) afterburning SNECMA Atar 9C-3 turbojet, plus optional (although rarely used) 14.7kN (3305lb) SEPR jettisonable booster rocket.

Performance: IIIE – Max speed 2350km/h (1268kt), cruising speed at 36,100ft 955km/h (516kt). Time to 26,090ft 3min 0sec. Service ceiling 55,775ft, or 75,460ft with booster rocket. Ferry range with three drop tanks 4000km (2150nm). Combat radius on a hi-lo-hi attack mission 1200km (647nm).

Weights: IIIE – Empty 7050kg (15,542lb), max takeoff 13,700kg (30,205lb).

Dimensions: Wing span 8.22m (27ft 0in), length 15.03m (49ft 4in), height 4.50m (14ft 9in). Wing area 35.0m2 (376.8sq ft).

Accommodation: Pilot only, or two in tandem in IIIB and IIID.

Armament: Two 30mm DEFA 552A cannons in lower fuselage. IIIE has four underwing and one centreline hardpoints capable of carrying up to 4000kg (8818lb) of armaments, including one radar guided Matra R.350 AAM, Matra R.550 Magic or AIM-9 Sidewinder infrared guided AAMs, AS 30 and AS 37 ASMs, bombs and rockets.

Operators: Argentina, Brazil, Pakistan, Switzerland.

History: The first of Dassault's famous Mirage series of fighters to enter production, the Mirage III enjoyed considerable export success and propelled France to the forefront of combat aircraft design.

The Mirage name was first applied to a design to meet a 1952 French Armée de l'Air requirement for a light, high speed interceptor. The Mirage I was a small delta wing design powered by two Armstrong Siddeley Viper turbojets and first flew in June 1955. While the Mirage I was too small to be practical, test experience gained was invaluable for the much larger SNECMA Atar powered Mirage III. The prototype Mirage III-001 flew for the first time on November 17 1956 and later became the first western European aircraft to reach Mach 2 in level flight. Ten pre production Mirage IIIAs were built before the first Mirage IIICs were delivered to the Armée de l'Air in July 1961. IIICs were also built for South Africa (IIICZ) and Israel (IIICJ – veterans of Israel's Middle East wars, survivors were sold to Argentina in 1982). The equivalent two seater is the IIIB.

The multirole Mirage IIIE retains the Thomson-CSF Cyrano II radar but has nav/attack avionics and Doppler navigation radar (in a bulge beneath the cockpit), while French aircraft had the ability to carry an AN 52 nuclear bomb. The two seat IIID does not have the Cyrano radar.

The IIIE was a significant export success, and was built under licence in Australia (IIIO) and Switzerland (as the IIIS with a Hughes TARAN 18 radar). The reconnaissance Mirage IIIR is based on the IIIE, but features cameras (and no radar) in a modified nose (four South African IIIR2Zs were delivered with Atar 9K-50s).

France has retired its Mirage IIIs, while most remaining Mirage III operators have upgraded their aircraft (Swiss and Brazilian aircraft have canards). The radar-less, ground attack optimised Mirage 5 is described separately.

Photo: One of four Brazilian Mirage IIIDBRs. Note retrofitted canards. (Francois Robineau, Dassault/Aviaplans)

Dassault Mirage 5 & 50

Country of origin: France

Type: Ground attack and day fighter

Powerplant: 50M – One 49.0kN (11,025lb) dry and 70.8kN (15,875lb) afterburning SNECMA Atar 9K-50 turbojet.

Performance: 50M – Max speed 2338km/h (1262kt) at 39,370ft, cruising speed at 36,100ft 955km/h (516kt). Max initial rate of climb 36,615ft/min. Time to 45,000ft 4min 42sec. Service ceiling 59,055ft. Interception combat radius with two AAMs and three drop tanks, hi-hi-hi 1315km (710nm). Combat radius with two 400kg (880lb) bombs and three drop tanks, hi-lo-hi 1260km (680nm), or with same load and lo-lo-lo 630km (340nm).

Weights: 50M – Empty equipped 7150kg (15,763lb), max takeoff 14,700kg (32,407lb).

Dimensions: 50M – Wing span 8.22m (27ft 0in), length 15.56m (51ft 1in), height 4.50m (14ft 9in). Wing area 35.0m² (376.8sq ft).

Accommodation: Pilot only, except two in tandem in two seaters.

Armament: 5 – Two 30mm DEFA 552A cannon in lower fuselage. Can carry up to 4000kg (8818lb) of armament on four underwing and three underfuselage hardpoints, comprising rockets, bombs and infra-red guided missiles. Cyrano radar equipped 5s can fire the radar guided Matra R.350. Venezuelan and some Pakistani aircraft can fire AM 39 Exocet anti shipping missiles.

Operators: Argentina, Chile, Columbia, Egypt, Gabon, Libya, Pakistan, Peru, UAE (Abu Dhabi), Venezuela.

History: Dassault developed the Mirage 5 at the request of Israel, who was seeking a low cost, day ground attack fighter version of the Mirage III.

First flown in May 1969, the Mirage 5 originally differed from the IIIE in the deletion of the Cyrano radar, which allowed simplified avionics to be carried in a slimmer and longer nose and creating space for extra internal fuel, and the addition of two extra hardpoints under the fuselage. Otherwise the Mirage 5 was identical to the III. Variants other than the basic single seater were the two seat 5D and reconnaissance 5R.

France's then president Charles de Gaulle embargoed the delivery of the 50 Mirage 5Js on order for Israel, and instead these aircraft were delivered to the Armée de l'Air as Mirage 5Fs. Other customers were soon attracted to the Mirage 5 and in all 525 were built.

The Mirage 5 was offered with increasingly more sophisticated avionics and systems (including ranging radar and laser rangefinders) as production progressed, and a number were fitted with lightweight Cyrano IV, Agave or Aida 2 radars.

The last major production version of the line that began with the Mirage III was the Mirage 50, which features a 20% more powerful Atar 9K-50 turbojet, as fitted on the Mirage F1. First flown on April 15 1979, customers were Chile and Venezuela. Dassault also offers the 50M as an upgrade of existing Mirage IIIs and 5s.

Like the Mirage III, several nations have Mirage 5 upgrade programs, typically including modern avionics and canards.

Photo: An upgraded Venezuelan Mirage 50EV, with canards, refuelling probe and Cyrano IV radar. (Francois Robineau, Dassault/Aviaplans)

Dassault Super Etendard

Country of origin: France

Type: Carrier borne strike fighter

Powerplant: One 49.0kN (11,025lb) SNECMA Atar 8K-50 non afterburning turbojet.

Performance: Max speed 1118km/h (603.5kt), max speed at sea level 1180km/h (637kt). Max initial rate of climb 19,685ft/min. Service ceiling over 45,000ft. Combat radius on an anti shipping mission with one AM 39 Exocet and two drop tanks, hi-lo-hi 850km (460nm).

Weights: Empty equipped 6500kg (14,330lb), MTOW 12,000kg (26,455lb).

Dimensions: Wing span 9.60m (31ft 6in), length 14.31m (47ft 0in), height 3.86m (12ft 8in). Wing area 28.4m² (305.7sq ft).

Accommodation: Pilot only

Armament: Two internal 30mm DEFA cannons. Up to 2100kg (4630lb) of ordnance on two under fuselage and four underwing hardpoints, including rocket pods, bombs, laser guided bombs, Magic AAMs, two Exocets, or one ASMP guided stand-off nuclear missile (under one wing, offset by a fuel tank under the other wing).

Operators: Argentina, France.

History: As its name suggests, the Super Etendard is a developed version of the smaller Etendard IV.

The original Etendard (meaning standard, as in flag) was designed in response to the same NATO requirement for a light attack fighter as the Fiat G91. While the original Bristol Orpheus powered Etendard was looked over in favour of the G91, Dassault, convinced of the design's potential, launched the Etendard IV powered by a SNECMA Atar turbojet (first flight July 24 1956). The IV attracted the attention of the French navy, who, after some delays, took delivery of the attack IVM and reconnaissance IVR.

The early 1970s Etendard replacement requirement was originally to be met by about 100 navalised SEPECAT Jaguar Ms. However politics and cost interfered, and instead, after evaluation of the Skyhawk and Corsair, the French navy ordered Dassault's proposed Super Etendard.

The Super Etendard introduced a more powerful Atar 8K-50 turbojet, a non afterburning version of the Mirage F1's 9K-50, a strengthened and revised structure for operations at higher speeds and weights, a Thomson-CSF/Dassault Agave radar, inertial navigation, improved avionics and a retractable inflight refuelling probe.

The first of three converted Etendard IVM Super Etendard prototypes flew for the first time on October 29 1974, while the first of 71 production Super Etendards were delivered from June 1978. In the mid 1980s France's Super Etendards were subjected to an upgrade that featured a life extension out to 2008, the ability to launch the ASMP standoff nuclear missile, a new Dassault Electronique Anemone radar, new cockpit instrumentation, HUD, HOTAS and other systems.

While Iraq leased five Super Etendards pending the delivery of Mirage F1EQs from 1983, the only export customer was Argentina. Argentine navy Super Etendards gained some notoriety when they sunk HMS *Sheffield* and the *Atlantic Conveyer* with Exocets during the Falklands War in 1982.

Photo: A Super Etendard launches from aircraft carrier *Foch*. (Francois Robineau, Dassault/Aviaplans)

Dassault Mirage F1

Country of origin: France

Type: Multirole fighter

Powerplant: F1C – One 49.0kN (11,025lb) dry and 70.2kN (15,785lb) afterburning SNECMA Atar 9K-50 turbojet.

Performance: F1C – Max speed 2338km/h (1262kt). Max initial rate of climb 41,930ft/min. Service ceiling 65,600ft. Combat radius with 14 250kg (550lb) bombs hi-lo-hi 425km (230nm), or lo-lo-lo with one AM 39 Exocet anti shipping missile and two drop tanks 700km (378nm). Combat air patrol with two Super 350 AAMs, one underfuselage tank and one combat engagement 2hr 15min.

Weights: F1C – Empty 7400kg (16,315lb), max takeoff 16,200kg (35,715lb).

Dimensions: F1C – Wing span without wingtip missiles 8.40m (27ft 7in), length 15.30m (50ft 3in), height 4.50m (14ft 9in). Wing area 25.0m² (269.1sq ft). F1C-200 – Same except length 15.30m (50ft 3in).

Accommodation: Pilot only, or two in tandem in F1B.

Armament: F1C – Two 30mm DEFA 553 cannons in lower fuselage. Theoretically can carry 6300kg (13,890lb), or in practice 4000kg (8818lb) of ordnance on four underwing, one centreline and two wingtip hardpoints including wingtip AIM-9 or Magic infrared guided AAMs, R.530 or Super 530F radar guided AAMs, rockets, bombs and ASMs, including the AM 39 Exocet, or Armat anti radiation missile.

Operators: Ecuador, France, Greece, Iraq, Jordan, Libya, Morocco, South Africa, Spain.

History: When developing a successor for the popular Mirage III, Dassault dropped the tailless delta configuration and instead adopted a conventional swept wing for its Mirage F1.

In 1964 the French Government awarded Dassault a development contract to begin work on an all weather interceptor. Work was initially on the Mirage F2, a 20 tonne class fighter powered by a TF306 turbofan. At the same time though Dassault worked on a private venture fighter that was similar to the F2, but smaller overall and to be powered by an Atar turbojet. This design was the Mirage F1, which flew as a privately funded prototype on December 23 1966.

The Mirage F1 was not a great technological advance, yet it was quite a big improvement over the Mirage III, in that the Atar 9K-50 was considerably more powerful, it had 43% more internal fuel (doubling the ground attack radius), improved manoeuvrability, 30% better field performance, slower approach speed and an improved Cyrano IV radar.

Production of the F1 began with 100 F1C interceptors for the Armée de l'Air which were delivered from May 1973. From 1977 deliveries to the Armée de l'Air were of the F1C-200 which introduced a fixed refuelling probe and a minor fuselage stretch. Fifty five F1Cs were later modified for ground attack as F1CTs.

France also took delivery of 64 reconnaissance F1CRs fitted with infrared linescan installed in place of the cannons, optical cameras in a small nose fairing and various centreline recce pods. Also in French service are two seat F1Bs – with less external fuel and a slight stretch.

The Mirage F1 has been exported widely, mostly F1Cs. The F1A is simplified for day ground attack without the Cyrano radar, while the multirole F1E and equivalent F1D two seater achieved some success.

Photo: A Spanish F1 of Ala 14. (Paul Merritt)

Dassault Mirage 2000

Country of origin: France

Type: Multirole fighter

Powerplant: 2000C – One 64.3kN (14,460lb) dry and 95.1kN (21,835lb) afterburning SNECMA M53-P2 turbofan.

Performance: 2000C – Max speed over 2338km/h (1262kt). Max initial rate of climb 56,000ft/min. Service ceiling 54,000ft. Time to 49,215ft 4min. Ferry range with drop tanks 3335km (1800nm). Combat range with four 250kg (550lb) bombs 1480km (800nm) without drop tanks, or over 1850km (1000nm) with drop tanks.

Weights: 2000C – Empty 7500kg (16,535lb), MTOW 17,000kg (37,478lb).

Dimensions: 2000C – Wing span 9.13m (30ft 0in), length 14.36m (47ft 1in), height 5.20m (17ft 1in). Wing area 41.0m² (441.3sq ft).

Accommodation: Pilot only, or two in tandem in 2000B.

Armament: 2000C – Two 30mm DEFA 554 cannons in lower fuselage. Up to 6300kg (13,890lb) of external ordnance can be carried on four underwing and five underfuselage hardpoints, including Matra Magic 2 and Super 530D AAMs, laser guided bombs, dumb bombs, anti runway bombs, cluster bombs, two AS 30L ASMs, two Armat anti radiation missiles or two AM 39 Exocet anti ship missiles. Typical interceptor load two Magic 2s and two Super 530Ds.

Operators: Egypt, France, Greece, India, Peru, Qatar*, Taiwan*, UAE (Abu Dhabi).

History: The Mirage 2000 combines the proven benefits of the delta wing layout with technological improvements such as fly-by-wire.

A delta wing configuration boasts a number of advantages such as a large wing area and large internal fuel volume, but has also a number of shortcomings including poor field performance and manoeuvrability due to wing sweep angle. However the Mirage 2000's use of fly-by-wire with inherent instability and leading edge slats dramatically improves manoeuvrability compared with the Mirage III.

Development work on the Mirage 2000 began when a lack of funding forced the cancellation of the larger, twin engined Super Mirage in 1975. Even though the Mirage 2000 was intended as a smaller and simpler fighter than the Super Mirage, the program was still ambitious, as the aircraft was to incorporate advances in radar, cockpit, armament, airframe and powerplant technologies. The official specification written for the Mirage 2000 was issued in 1976, with the first prototype flying for the first time on March 10 1978 and with deliveries of production 2000Cs (and later two seat 2000B) occurring from April 1983, only a year behind the original schedule.

Apart from fly-by-wire (a technology in which France had little prior experience), the Mirage 2000 introduced the new SNECMA M53 turbofan, a Thomson-CSF RDM multimode radar, a CRT, HUD and HOTAS.

Other than Taiwan and Qatar, all export customers have ordered the 2000E (and recce pod carrying 2000R), a multirole development powered by the M53-P2. Taiwan and Qatar have ordered the 2000-5, a modernised multirole development and France is upgrading 37 Mirage 2000s to 2000-5 standard, delivered from late 1997.

The 2000-5 features five LCD cockpit displays (as developed for Rafale), a multimode Thomson-CSF RDY radar, Matra Mica AAM compatibility and an uprated M53-P20 powerplant.

Photo: France is upgrading 37 Mirage 2000Cs to 2000-5Fs.

Dassault Mirage 2000N & 2000D

Country of origin: France

Type: Nuclear & conventional strike fighters

Powerplant: 2000D – One 64.3kN (14,460lb) dry and 95.1kN (21,385lb) afterburning SNECMA M53-P2 turbofan.

Performance: 2000D – Max speed 2390km/h (1290kt). Penetration speed at 195ft 1112km/h (600kt). Max initial rate of climb 59,055ft/min. Service ceiling 59,055ft. Range with max external fuel 3335km (1800nm), combat radius with two Magic 2 AAMs, 1000kg (2205lb) of ordnance and two drop tanks 1500km (810nm).

Weights: 2000D – Empty equipped 7750kg (17,085lb), max takeoff 17,300kg (38,140lb).

Dimensions: 2000D – Wing span 9.13m (30ft 0in), length 14.55m (47ft 9in), height 5.15m (16ft 11in). Wing area 41.0m² (441.3sq ft).

Accommodation: Crew of two in tandem.

Armament: Nine hardpoints (one centreline, four underfuselage and four underwing) can carry a total payload of 6300kg (13,890lb). Weapon options include Matra BGL laser guided bombs, Aerospatiale AS 30L laser guided ASMs, Matra Armat anti radiation missiles, two AM 39 Exocet anti ship missiles, bombs, cluster bombs, gun pods with two 30mm cannon each and dispensers with anti runway and anti armour munitions. Two Matra Magic 2 AAMs typically carried on outboard wing stations. 2000N can carry a single Aerospatiale 150kT or 300kT yield ASMP 850kg (1875lb) stand-off guided nuclear missile.

Operators: France

History: The two seat strike variants of Dassault's Mirage 2000 originate from efforts to find a replacement for the Mirage IV.

As early as 1979 Dassault received a contract to build a nuclear attack development of the 2000, designated the 2000P (Pénétration). This designation was subsequently changed to 2000N (Nucléaire), to better reflect its role, and the first of the two prototypes flew for the first time on February 3 1983.

The 2000N is closely based on the airframe of the 2000B conversion trainer. Changes to the airframe were restricted mainly to structural strengthening for low level operations. However the 2000N does have a considerably different avionics suite to reflect its offensive roles. The key difference is the Dassault Electronique/Thomson-CSF Antilope 5 radar, with terrain following (down to 300ft and speeds of 1110km/h/600kt), ground mapping, navigation, air-to-sea and air-to-air modes. The primary weapon of the 2000N is the Aerospatiale ASMP stand-off guided nuclear missile which is carried on the centreline station. A typical nuclear attack configuration would be the ASMP, two 2000 litre tanks and two Magic 2 AAMs.

To augment the Mirage IVP, France ordered 75 2000Ns in two variants, the nuclear only 2000N-K1 and nuclear and conventional capable 2000N-K2. These were delivered between the late 1980s and 1993.

The 2000D is basically similar to the 2000N-K2 except that it can only carry conventional munitions (it can be identified by its lack of nose probe). It first flew on February 19 1991, and France has 90 on order. Finally the 2000S (Strike) was an offered export version of the 2000D, with Antilope 5 radar that is no longer marketed.

Photo: A Mirage 2000D with laser designator, AS 30L and Magic missiles. (Francois Robineau, Dassault/Aviaplans)

Dassault Rafale

Country of origin: France

Type: Advanced multirole fighter

Powerplants: Two 48.7kN (10,950lb) dry and 87.0kN (19,555lb) with afterburning SNECMA M88-3 turbofans.

Performance: Rafale C – Max speed 2125km/h (1147kt), max speed at low level 1390km/h (750kt). Combat radius on a low level penetration mission with 12 250kg (550lb) bombs, four Mica AAMs and three drop tanks 1055km (570nm). Air-to-air combat radius with eight Mica AAMs and four tanks 1760km (950nm).

Weights: Rafale C – Empty equipped approx 9060kg (19,975lb), max TOW initially 19,500kg (47,399lb), developed version 21,500kg (47,400lb).

Dimensions: Rafale C – Wing span incl wingtip missiles 10.90m (35ft 9in), length 15.30m (50ft 3in), height 5.34m (17ft 6in). Wing area 46.0m² (495.1sq ft).

Accommodation: Pilot only in Rafale C & M, two crew in Rafale B.

Armament: One internal 30mm Giat DEFA 791B cannon. Normal external laod up to 6000kg (13,230lb) on six underwing, two wingtip, two centreline and four underfuselage stations. Options include an ASMP nuclear standoff missile, up to eight Matra Mica AAMs, AM 39 Exocets, laser guided bombs, AS 30L laser guided ASMs, or Apache dispensers with anti armour or anti runway munitions.

Operators: France*

History: When the Mirage 2000 was just entering service in the early 1980s France was already casting its eye on a successor.

When France withdrew as a participant of the EFA (now Eurofighter) consortium, development instead focused on Dassault's Avions de Combat Experimentale (ACX) design.

As the Rafale A, the ACX was built in demonstrator form which first flew on July 4 1986. The Rafale A was used to validate much of the design of the definitive Rafale, including the airframe, fly-by-wire system and SNECMA M88 turbofan.

The definitive Rafale is slightly smaller than the Rafale A, has some stealth measures and greater use of composite materials by weight. It will be built in three versions, the single seat Rafale C (first flight May 19 1991) and two seat Rafale B for the Armée de l'Air (the two types have the generic Rafale D designation), and the navalised Rafale M single seater for the French navy. Current plans envisage 212 C and Ds for the air force to replace Jaguars and Mirage F1s and 60 Ms for the navy to replace Super Etendards and Crusaders. On top of the 13 production aircraft previously funded, Dassault was awarded a multi year contract for the first 48 of these aircraft in early 1997.

Features of the Rafale include its blended fuselage/wing airframe, comprehensive Spectra integrated defensive aids subsystems, Dassault Electronique/Thomson-CSF RBE2 radar (with electronic scanning, air-to-air, air-to-ground, navigation and terrain following functions), LCD cockpit displays, a helmet mounted sight, voice commands, FLIR, IRST and laser rangefinder. Rafale Ms will be the first to enter service, currently planned for 2000, with air force aircraft following two years later.

Photo: Most Armée de l'Air Rafales will be ground attack orientated B two seaters. (Francois Robineau, Dassault/Aviaplans)

Dassault Mirage IV

Country of origin: France

Type: Strategic nuclear bomber and reconnaissance aircraft

Powerplants: Two 49.0kN (11,025lb) dry and 70.6kN (15,875lb) afterburning SNECMA Atar 9K-50 turbojets.

Performance: Max speed 2338km/h (1262kt) at 36,100ft, max speed at sea level approx 1350km (728kt), normal penetration speed 1913km/h (1172kt). Time to 36,100ft 4min 14sec. Service ceiling 65,615ft. Ferry range with drop tanks 4000km (2158nm). Typical combat radius 1240km (668nm).

Weights: Empty equipped 14,500kg (31,965lb), max takeoff 31,600kg (69,665lb).

Dimensions: Wing span 11.85m (38ft 11in), length 23.50m (77ft 1in), height 5.65m (18ft 6in). Wing area 78.0m^2 (839.6sq ft).

Accommodation: Crew of two in tandem.

Armament: One 30kT or 150kT yield 900kg (1985lb) Aerospatiale ASMP stand-off supersonic nuclear ASM. Alternatively can carry up to 7200kg (15,873lb) of conventional ordnance, including bombs or AS 37 Martel anti radar missiles on underwing and underfuselage hardpoints.

Operators: France

History: The Mirage IV was the end result of France's 1954 decision to field a nuclear deterrent force.

Dassault looked at a number of proposals for a strategic nuclear bomber before settling on the Mirage IVA, including developments of the Vautour through to a design approaching the B-58 Hustler in size and powered by two Pratt & Whitney J75 turbojets. In the end the much smaller Mirage IVA design was settled upon, to be powered by two SNECMA Atar turbojets and incapable of launching a strike to the Soviet Union and returning without the aid of inflight refuelling. First flight was on June 17 1959.

Resembling a scaled up Mirage III, the Mirage IV features a delta wing, a crew of two in tandem, an inflight refuelling probe extending from the nose (for refuelling either from KC-135FRs or Mirage IV buddy tankers), surveillance and doppler radars for navigation more latterly augmented by dual INS, while the original 60kT nuclear bomb would be carried semi recessed under fuselage. Twelve booster rockets (six under each wing) are often used to improve field performance.

The successful flight trials of one prototype and three revised pre production Mirage IVs led to an Armée de l'Air order for 50 production aircraft. In all France took delivery of 62 production Mirage IVAs, and these were subjected to numerous upgrades and modifications throughout their service lives. Twelve IVs were modified for reconnaissance with the fitment of semi recessed cameras and SLAR. In the late 1980s 19 Mirage IVs were modified to IVP standard, which involved fitting modern avionics including dual INS, plus new RWR and the ability to launch the Aerospatiale ASMP stand-off nuclear missile (which has a range of 80km/43nm at low level, or 250km/135nm from high altitude).

In 1996 all but five of the surviving IVPs were retired, with the survivors providing a limited strategic reconnaissance capability.

Photo: A Mirage IVP in flight. (SIRPA - AIR)

Dassault/Dornier Alpha Jet

Countries of origin: France and Germany

Type: Two seat advanced trainer and close support aircraft

Powerplants: Alpha Jet A – Two 14.1kN (3175lb) SNECMA/Turboméca Larzac 04-C20 turbofans. E – Two 13.2kN (2975lb) Larzac 04-C6s.

Performance: A – Max speed Mach 0.86. Max initial rate of climb 12,000ft/min. Time to 30,000ft less than 7min. Service ceiling 48,000ft. Ferry range with four external tanks over 4000km (2160nm). Combat radius with gun pod and underwing weapons hi-lo-hi 585km (315nm), or lo-lo-lo 390km (210nm). Combat radius with gun pod, weapons and two tanks hi-lo-hi 1075km (580nm), or lo-lo-lo 630km (340nm). E – Same except max speed 1000km/h (540kt). Radius on a lo-lo-lo training mission with two drop tanks 670km (360nm). Endurance with internal fuel over 3hr 30min.

Weights: A – Empty equipped 3515kg (7750lb), max takeoff 8000kg (17,637lb). E – Empty equipped 3345kg (7375lb), max takeoff same.

Dimensions: A – Wing span 9.11m (29ft 11in), length 13.23m (43ft 5in), height 4.19m (13ft 9in). Wing area 17.5m^2 (188.4sq ft). E – Same except length 11.75m (38ft 7in).

Accommodation: Two in tandem.

Armament: More than 2500kg (5510lb) of external ordnance, including centreline 30mm DEFA or 27mm Mauser cannon pod, bombs and rockets, AAMs (such as AIM-9 or Magic) and ASMs (such as AGM-65).

Operators: Belgium, Cameroon, Egypt, France, Ivory Coast, Morocco, Nigeria, Portugal, Qatar, Togo.

History: France and Germany agreed to jointly develop a new subsonic advanced trainer in the late 1960s.

The TA501 design, which was submitted by Dassault, Breguet (the two French companies merged in 1971) and Dornier, was chosen in 1970 over two other competing designs, all of which were to be powered by two small Larzac turbofans, (the twin configuration a legacy of Germany's bad experiences with single engine F-104s). The TA501 was named Alpha Jet, and a change in Germany's requirement for the aircraft saw it being developed in advanced trainer and close support/battlefield reconnaissance forms.

Official development go-ahead for the program was given in February 1972, resulting in the first flight of a prototype on October 26 1973. French Alpha Jet E (Ecole – school) deliveries to replace Magisters began in 1978, while Germany's first Alpha Jet A (Appui-tactique) first flew in April 1978. Most new build Alpha Jet export customers took delivery of aircraft similar to the French standard.

Germany's were fitted with a comprehensive nav/attack suite including twin gyro INS and a doppler navigation radar. Germany took delivery of 175 Alpha Jets which primarily replaced G91s for close air support. These aircraft were later re-engined with uprated engines. Germany has now retired all its Alpha Jets (50 went to Portugal).

The Alpha Jet NGEA (new generation attack/trainer) was launched in 1980 and features a HUD, cockpit CRTs, laser rangefinder and compatibility with the Matra Magic AAM. It was sold to Cameroon and Egypt. The current offering Alpha Jet ATS would feature LCD displays, HOTAS controls, a small radar and FLIR.

Photo: Belgium flies 31 Alpha Jet Es. (Belgium SID)

De Havilland Canada DHC-4 Caribou

Country of origin: Canada

Type: STOL tactical transport

Powerplants: DHC-4A – Two 1080kW (1450shp) Pratt & Whitney R-2000-7M2 14 cylinder twin row radial piston engines driving three blade propellers.

Performance: DHC-4A – Max speed 347km/h (187kt), normal cruising speed 293km/h (158kt). Max initial rate of climb 1355ft/min. Service ceiling 24,800ft. Takeoff run to 50ft at MTOW 360m (1185ft). Range with max payload 390km (210nm), range with max fuel 2105km (1135nm).

Weights: DHC-4A – Basic operating 8293kg (18,260lb), standard max takeoff 12,930kg (28,500lb), military overload max takeoff 14,195kg (31,300lb).

Dimensions: DHC-4A – Wing span 29.15m (95ft 8in), length 22.13m (72ft 7in), height 9.68m (31ft 9in). Wing area 84.7m² (912.0sq ft).

Accommodation: Crew of two and a loadmaster. Can carry almost 4 tonnes (8000lb) of cargo (including two jeeps or Land Rovers, or light artillery pieces). Can seat 32 equipped troops, or 22 stretcher patients plus medical attendants in air ambulance configuration.

Armament: None

Operators: Australia, Cameroon, Liberia, Malaysia, Uganda, Zambia.

History: De Havilland Canada's fourth design was a successful attempt at combining the payload of the DC-3 with the STOL performance of the earlier single engine DHC-2 Beaver and DHC-3 Otter.

De Havilland Canada (DHC) originally designed the DHC-4 as a private venture with an eye on Canadian and US military requirements. DHC built a prototype demonstrator (with assistance from Canada's Department of Defence Production) that first flew on July 30 1958. Impressed with the DHC-4's STOL capabilities and potential, the US Army ordered five for evaluation as the YAC-1 to meet its requirement for a tactical airlifter to supply the battlefront with troops and supplies and evacuate casualties on the return journey.

The US Army went on to become the largest Caribou operator, taking delivery of 159. The initial AC-1 designation was later changed to CV-2, and then C-7 when the US Army's CV-2s were transferred to the US Air Force in 1966 (the Caribou was the largest aircraft ever operated by the US Army up to that time). Caribou production ended in 1973 after 307 had been built, mostly for military customers.

US Army CV-2s, Air Force C-7s and Australian DHC-4A Caribou saw extensive service during the Vietnam conflict, where the type came into its own. The Caribou was well suited to Vietnam's demanding conditions and its STOL performance (unmatched by few types before or since) saw it operate into areas otherwise the domain of helicopters. Interestingly many US Caribou were captured by North Vietnamese forces in 1975 and remained in service with that country through the late 1970s. Other former military operators include Canada, Colombia, India, Spain and Tanzania.

Today a dwindling number of Caribou survive in military service, notably with Australia and Malaysia. Malaysia already has IPTN built CN-235s on order as a replacement, while Australia is evaluating the LMATTS C-27J, C-295 and CN-235 to replace its long serving fleet.

Photo: An Australian Caribou. (RAAF Richmond)

De Havilland Canada DHC-5 Buffalo

Country of origin: Canada

Type: STOL tactical transport

Powerplants: DHC-5D – Two 2335kW (3133shp) General Electric CT64-820-4 turboprops driving three blade propellers.

Performance: DHC-5D – Max cruising speed 467km/h (252kt). Max initial rate of climb 2330ft/min. Service ceiling 31,000ft. Takeoff run with a 5445kg (12,000lb) payload 290m (950ft). Max range with ferry tanks 6115km (3300nm).

Weights: DHC-5D – Operating empty 11,410kg (25,160lb), max takeoff weight from an unprepared strip 18,597kg (41,000lb), max takeoff from prepared strip 22,315kg (49,200lb).

Dimensions: DHC-5D – Wing span 29.26m (96ft 0in), length 24.08m (79ft 0in), height 8.73m (28ft 8in). Wing area 87.8m² (945sq ft).

Accommodation: Crew of two pilots plus loadmaster. Cabin can seat 41 equipped troops, or 35 paratroops, or 24 stretcher patients and six medical attendants. Max payload 8165kg (18,000lb). Max air droppable unit 2720kg (6000lb).

Armament: None

Operators: Cameroon, Canada, Ecuador, Indonesia, Kenya, Mauritania, Mexico, Peru, Sudan, Tanzania, Togo, UAE (Abu Dhabi), Zaire, Zambia.

History: The Buffalo is a turboprop powered development of the earlier Caribou, and was developed specifically to meet a 1962 US Army requirement.

The US Army selected the Buffalo for development ahead of 24 other contenders for a STOL transport requirement. Funding for the development of the DHC-5 (initially called Caribou II) was split equally between de Havilland Canada, the Canadian Government and the US Army. The resulting aircraft was closely based on the Caribou, but introduced two General Electric CT64 turboprops, an increased maximum lift coefficient, a T-tail and a significantly higher max takeoff weight.

The US Army funded the development of four CV-7A evaluation Buffalos, the first of which flew for the first time on April 9 1964. Unfortunately for de Havilland Canada, the same change of US policy that saw the US Army transfer its CV-2s to the US Air Force saw the cancellation of plans to procure production CV-7s. The four CV-7As were thus transferred to the USAF as C-8s.

A Canadian Armed Forces order for 15 CC-113 Buffalos for search and rescue saved the program from an uncertain future, and export orders were soon placed in (the first coming from Brazil). In all 59 Buffalos were built through to 1972 when production ceased for the first time.

Proposed but unbuilt Buffalo variants were the DHC-5B with CT64-P4Cs and the DHC-5C with either CT64-P4Cs or Rolls-Royce Darts.

DHC reopened the Buffalo line in 1974 when it introduced the improved DHC-5D. The DHC-5D features more powerful CT64-820-4s (in place of the DHC-5A's 2280kW [3055ehp] CT64-820-1s), increasing payload range. DHC-5D production continued for a number of overseas customers through to 1986, by which time total Buffalo production reached 126.

Photo: Canada's 14 surviving CC-115 Buffalos are used for SAR. Note the nose mounted weather radar. (Paul Merritt)

De Havilland Canada DHC-6 Twin Otter

Country of origin: Canada

Type: STOL utility transport

Powerplants: 100 – Two 430kW (579shp) Pratt & Whitney Canada PT6A-20 turboprops. 300 – Two 460kW (620shp) PT6A-27s.

Performance: 100 – Max cruising speed 297km/h (160kt). Range with max fuel 1427km (770nm), range with a 975kg (2150lb) payload 1344km (727nm). 300 – Max cruising speed at 10,000ft 338km/h (182kt). Max initial rate of climb 1600ft/min. STOL takeoff run 104m (304ft). Range with 1135kg (2500lb) payload 1297km (700nm), range with a 860kg (1900lb) payload and wing tanks 1705km (920nm).

Weights: 100 – Basic operating empty 2653kg (5850lb), max takeoff 4765kg (10,500lb). 300 – Operating empty 3363kg (7415lb), max takeoff 5670kg (12,500lb).

Dimensions: 100 – Wing span 19.81m (65ft 0in), length 15.09m (49ft 6in), height 5.94m (19ft 6in). Wing area 39.0m² (420sq ft). 300 – Same except for length 15.77m (51ft 9in), or 15.09m (49ft 6in) for floatplane variants.

Accommodation: Flightcrew of two. Standard airliner interior seats 20 at three abreast.

Armament: None, though DHC-6-300M(COIN) was offered with a cabin mounted machine gun and capability to carry underwing ordnance.

Operators: Argentina, Australia, Canada, Chile, Ecuador, Ethiopia, France, Haiti, Nepal, Norway, Paraguay, Peru, Uganda, USA.

History: De Havilland Canada's most successful design in terms of sales, the Twin Otter has sold widely to the world's military air arms due to its rugged construction and STOL performance.

Development of the Twin Otter dates back to January 1964 when de Havilland Canada started design work on a new STOL twin turboprop commuter airliner (seating between 13 and 18) and utility transport. Designated the DHC-6, construction of the prototype began in November that year, resulting in the type's first flight on May 20 1965.

The first production aircraft were Series 100s, design features including double slotted trailing edge flaps and ailerons on the wings that can act in unison to boost STOL performance. In comparison with the later Series 200 and 300s, the 100s are distinguishable by their blunt noses, while in common with the later aircraft skis and floats can be fitted. Canada was the only military customer for the Series 100, taking delivery of eight CC-138s for search and rescue.

The Series 200, which was debuted in April 1968, introduced the extended nose, which together with a reconfigured storage compartment in the rear cabin greatly increased baggage stowage area. The Series 300 was introduced from the 231st production aircraft in 1966. It too features the lengthened nose, but also introduced more powerful engines, thus allowing a 450kg (1000lb) increase in takeoff weight. Production ceased in 1988 and comprised 115 Series 100 aircraft, 115 Series 200s and 614 Series 300s.

Dedicated military variants of the 300 were offered in 1982. The DHC-6-200M was a 15 seat troop transport with optional air ambulance and paratroop configurations; armed and armoured DHC-6-300M(COIN) for counter insurgency missions; and the DHC-6-300MR maritime patrol variant fitted with searchlight and radar.

Photo: Norway flies its Twin Otters for transport and SAR. (Les Bushell)

De Havilland Dash 8 & E-9

Country of origin: Canada

Type: Utility transport, navigation trainer and range support aircraft

Powerplants: 100 – Two 1490kW (2000shp) Pratt & Whitney Canada PW120A turboprops driving four blade propellers.

Performance: 100A – Max cruising speed 491km/h (265kt), long range cruising speed 440km/h (237kt). Max initial rate of climb 1560ft/min. Certificated service ceiling 25,000ft. Range with full passenger load, max fuel and reserves 1520km (820nm), range with a 2720kg (6000lb) payload 2040km (1100nm).

Weights: 100A – Operating empty 10,251kg (22,600lb), max takeoff 15,650kg (34,500lb).

Dimensions: Wing span 25.91m (85ft 0in), length 22.25m (73ft 0in), height 7.49m (24ft 7in). Wing area 54.4m² (585.0sq ft).

Accommodation: Flightcrew of two. Typical passenger seating for 37 at four abreast, or max seating for 40.

Armament: None

Operators: Canada, Kenya, USA.

History: De Havilland's Dash 8 has carved itself a significant slice of the fiercely competitive regional airliner market, but has also found its way in small numbers into military colours.

De Havilland began development of the Dash 8 in the late 1970s in response to what it saw as a considerable market for a new generation 30 to 40 seat commuter airliner. The first flight of the new airliner was on June 20 1983, while the first airline Dash 8 customer delivery took place on October 23 1984.

Like the four engined 50 seat Dash 7 before it, the Dash 8 features a high mounted wing and T-tail and has an advanced flight control system and large full length trailing edge flaps. Power is supplied by two Pratt & Whitney Canada PW120 (originally PT7A) turboprops.

The initial Dash 8 production model was the Series 100, which was followed by the PW120A powered Series 100A in 1990. The Series 100B has been on offer since 1992 and has more powerful PW121s for better climb and airfield performance. Significant performance benefits are offered by the Series 200 which was announced in 1992 and has been available for delivery since 1994. It features more powerful PW123C engines, and thus has a higher cruising speed, plus greater commonality with the stretched Dash 8-300. The 200B has PW123Bs for better hot and high performance. Four Dash 8-200s are being fitted with search radar and FLIR for Australian Customs use.

The stretched, 50 seat Dash 8-300 is powered by PW123s and is greater in length by 3.43m (11ft 3in). A further development is the Dash 8-400, a 70 seat regional airliner available from 1999.

Dash 8 military service is currently limited to variants of the Dash 8-100. Canada is the largest operator with two CC-142 transports (Dash 8M) and three modified CT-142 navigation trainers, which feature a mapping radar housed in a bulged nose radome. Kenya meanwhile operates three standard Dash 8s as transports.

The US Air Force uses two modified Dash 8s for missile range control, designated E-9As. These two aircraft feature a large phased array radar mounted along the right hand side of the fuselage, telemetry equipment and an APS-128D surveillance radar in a ventral dome.

Photo: A Canadian Forces CT-142 navigation trainer.

Denel CSH-2 Rooivalk

Country of origin: South Africa

Type: Attack helicopter

Powerplants: Two 1376kW (1845shp) takeoff rated Turboméca Makila 1K2 turboshafts, driving a four blade main rotor and five blade tail rotor.

Performance: (ISA at S/L) – Max cruising speed 252km/h (136kt). Max initial rate of climb 3620ft/min. Service ceiling 20,000ft. Hovering ceiling out of ground effect 7900ft. Range with max internal fuel and no reserves 705km (380nm), range at max takeoff weight with external fuel 1260km (680nm). Endurance with max internal fuel 3hr 35min, endurance with external fuel 6hr 50min.

Weights: Empty 5910kg (13,030lb), max takeoff 8750kg (19,290lb).

Dimensions: Main rotor diameter 15.58m (51ft 2in), length overall 18.73m (61ft 5in), fuselage length (incl tail rotor, excl gun) 16.39m (53ft 9in), height 5.19m (17ft 0in). Main rotor disc area 190.6m² (2051sq ft).

Accommodation: Copilot/weapons operator and pilot in tandem.

Armament: Steerable chin mounted 20mm Armscor MG 151. Six underwing stores pylons (three a side) can carry 70mm rocket launchers, and Mokopa anti tank missiles on inner four pylons. Wingtip stations can carry V3P Darter or Mistral infrared air-to-air missiles.

Operators: South Africa*

History: Born out of necessity because of the now lifted UN arms embargo, the Rooivalk (or Red Kestrel) was designed in response to a South African Air Force requirement for a combat support helicopter.

The Rooivalk design is based on experience Atlas (now Denel) gained from building and flying the XH-1 Alpha concept demonstrator, a one-off attack helicopter configured testbed based on the Alouette III. Development of the XH-1 began in 1981, resulting in a first flight on February 27 1986. The XH-1 retained the Alouette's engine, rotor and transmission systems combined with a new tandem two seat fuselage.

Design of the Rooivalk began in 1984, and subsequent experience with the XH-1, plus two Puma testbeds modified as gunships and designated XTP-1 Beta, allowed a first flight of the XH-2 Rooivalk prototype on February 11 1990. The XH-2 was later redesignated XDM (Experimental Development Model). It was joined by a second flying prototype, the ADM (Advanced Development Model), which is tasked with avionics and weapons development, in 1992, and the production representative EDM (Engineering Development Model) which first flew in November 1996.

The Rooivalk uses the same, although uprated, Turboméca Makila 1A1 turboshafts, transmission and rotor system of the SA 330 Puma. Otherwise the Rooivalk is an all new aircraft, featuring stepped cockpits, extensive armouring, and a gyro stabilised nose mounted turret with FLIR and TV sensors and laser rangefinder which make up an automatic target detection and tracking system. Production aircraft will feature cheeks on the side of the fuselage (fitted to the EDM aircraft) housing ammunition and avionics, two colour LCDs in each cockpit, helmet mounted sights and a laser ring gyro nav system.

South Africa has ordered 16 Rooivalks for one squadron.

Photo: The EDM Rooivalk flew in November 1996. (Denel)

Denel Cheetah

Countries of origin: South Africa and France

Type: Multirole fighter

Powerplant: EZ – One 42.0kN (9435lb) dry and 60.8kN (13,670lb) with afterburning SNECMA Atar 9C turbojet. Some two seaters and R2Z recce aircraft are powered by a 49.0kN (11,025lb) dry and 70.6kN (15,875lb) with afterburning Atar 9K-50.

Performance: EZ – Max speed 2338km/h (1262kt), max cruising speed 956km/h (516kt). Range and payload radius figures unpublished.

Weights: Unpublished.

Dimensions: EZ – Wing span 8.22m (27ft 0in), length including nose probe 15.65m (51ft 4in), height 4.55m (14ft 11in). Wing area 34.8m² (374.6sq ft).

Accommodation: Pilot only in EZs and RZs, two in DZ trainers.

Armament: Fixed armament comprises two 30mm DEFA cannons. Disposable stores carried on four underwing and three underfuselage stations including indigenously developed Armscor V3B Kukri and V3C Darter air-to-air missiles, AS20 air-to-ground missiles, bombs, cluster bombs and rockets, plus AIM-9 Sidewinder and Matra R550 AAMs.

Operators: South Africa

History: The Denel Cheetah is one of the most comprehensive upgrades of the venerable Mirage III yet, with significant changes and improvements to the airframe, avionics and, in the case of two seaters, powerplant.

Like a number of South African developed weapon systems, the Cheetah was born out of necessity. A 1977 United Nations arms embargo prevented South Africa from buying military equipment from the rest of the world, thus thwarting any South African Air Force plans for a replacement of its ageing fleet of 1960s vintage Mirage IIIs coming to fruition. Instead, South Africa instigated its own mid life update program, reportedly with assistance from IAI in Israel.

The Cheetah upgrade was first publicly announced in 1986 when Atlas (now Denel) unveiled an upgraded Mirage two seater, the Cheetah D (or DZ). Main aerodynamic features of the Cheetah upgrade include structural modifications to extend fatigue life, canards, a stretched nose to house new avionics, dog tooth leading edge extensions, small strakes on the nose and small fences on the wing replacing leading edge slats. The two seaters also feature strakes along the lower fuselage below the cockpit. Internally the Cheetah features new avionics, believed to be of Israeli origin and including a MIL STD 1553B databus, a head-up display, HOTAS (Hands On Throttle And Stick) controls and a new nav/attack system with inertial navigation. The extended nose houses avionics plus an Elta EL/M-2001B radar.

Single seat Cheetahs are known as Cheetah Es or EZs, and retain the original SNECMA Atar 9C turbojet. Some of the two seaters have been fitted with the more powerful Atar 9K-50 turbojet as on the Mirage F1, for which Denel has a manufacturing licence. Reconnaissance Cheetah R2s are already powered by the 9K-50.

A prototype Cheetah ACW with an advanced combat wing flew for the first time in 1992, while 12 EZs were due to be fitted with the Israeli Elta EL/M-2035 fire control radar and the Atar 9K-50.

Photo: The two seat Atar 9K-50 powered Cheetah. (Paul Merritt)

Dornier Do 27

Country of origin: Germany

Type: Light STOL utility transport, trainer and liaison aircraft

Powerplant: Do 27H-2 – One 255kW (340hp) Lycoming GSO-480-B1B6 flat six piston engine, driving a three blade propeller. Do 27Q-5 – One 200kW (270hp) GSO-480-B1A6 driving a two blade prop.

Performance: Do 27H-2 – Max speed 245km/h (132kt), high speed cruise 212km/h (115kt), economical cruising speed 180km/h (97kt). Max initial rate of climb 965ft/min. Service ceiling 22,000ft. Range with max fuel 1360km (735nm). Do 27Q-5 – Max speed 232km/h (125kt), 75% power cruising speed 211km/h (114kt), 60% power cruising speed 190km/h (103kt), economical cruising speed 175km/h (95kt). Max initial rate of climb 650ft/min. Service ceiling 10,800ft. Range with max fuel and no reserves 1102km (595nm).

Weights: Do 27H-2 – Empty equipped 1170kg (2580lb), max takeoff 1848kg (4070lb). Do 27Q-5 – Empty equipped 1130kg (2490lb), max takeoff 1848kg (4070lb).

Dimensions: Do 27H-2 & Q-5 – Wing span 12.00m (39ft 5in), length 9.60m (31ft 6in), height 2.80m (9ft 2in). Wing area 19.4m² (208.8sq ft).

Accommodation: Pilot and passenger with between four and six passengers behind them. Can be configured for freight or stretchers.

Armament: Usually none.

Operators: Angola, Burundi, Switzerland, Togo.

History: The Dornier Do 27 was the first military aircraft to be built in any numbers in West Germany since World War 2 (577 in all), and marked the re-emergence of Dornier as an aircraft designer and manufacturer.

The Do 27 traces back to the Do 25, which Professor Claude Dornier (Dornier was responsible for the Do 17 medium bomber in WW2) designed in Spain for a Spanish military requirement for a light general purpose utility aircraft. Two prototype Do 25s were built, the first was powered by a 110kW (150hp) ENMA Tigre G-IVB engine and flew for the first time on June 25 1954. Subsequently CASA built 50 production aircraft, as Do 27As for the Spanish air force (Spain designated the type the C-127).

Following this success the German army and air force ordered the Do 27 in large numbers. A total of 428 were delivered to German forces from the mid 1950s to 1960, although these aircraft have now been retired. Small numbers were built for other military customers, while many ex German aircraft went to other military customers, including the air arms of Portugal, Nigeria, Israel, Sudan and Turkey. In turn some of the Portuguese aircraft ended up in Angolan military service, while other second hand Do 27s were purchased by a number of African nations.

Features of the Do 27 design include a flat six Lycoming piston engine, a wide and relatively roomy cabin, wide track tricycle undercarriage and excellent STOL performance, the latter especially ensuring its popularity in developing nations.

Do 27 models include the initial Do 27A and dual control Do 27B for Germany; the Do 27-H series that was based on the A-4 but with a more powerful engine and three blade prop; and the Do 27Q series, equivalent to the Do 27A.

Photo: Germany's Do 27 have long been retired. (Dornier)

Dornier Do 28 & 128

Country of origin: Germany

Type: STOL utility and transport and liaison aircraft

Powerplants: Do 28 D-2 – Two 285kW (380hp) Lycoming IGSO-540-A1E flat six piston engines driving three blade constant speed propellers. 128-6 – Two 300kW (400shp) Pratt & Whitney Canada PT6A-110 turboprops.

Performance: Do 28 D-2 – Max speed 325km/h (175kt), max cruising speed 306km/h (165kt), economical cruising speed 241km/h (130kt). Max initial rate of climb 1160ft/min. Service ceiling 25,200ft. Takeoff run 280m (920ft). Range with max payload 1050km (566nm). 128-6 – Max speed 340km/h (183kt), max cruising speed 330km/h (178kt), economical cruising speed 256km/h (138kt). Max initial rate of climb 1260ft/min. Service ceiling 32,600ft. Takeoff run to 50ft altitude 554m (1820ft). Range with max fuel 1825nm (985nm), with a 805kg (1774lb) payload 1460km (788nm).

Weights: Do 28 D-2 – Empty 2328kg (5132lb), max takeoff 3842kg (8470lb). 128-6 – Empty 2540kg (5600lb), max takeoff 4350kg (9590lb).

Dimensions: Do 28 D-2 – Wing span 15.55m (51ft 0in), length 11.41m (37ft 5in), height 3.90m (12ft 10in). Wing area 29.0m² (312sq ft). 128-6 – Same except for wing span 15.85m (52ft 0in).

Accommodation: One or two pilots on flightdeck and up to 13 troops on inward facing folding seats. In air ambulance configuration can accommodate five stretchers. Also used to carry freight.

Armament: Usually none.

Operators: Do 28 – Croatia, Greece, Israel, Kenya, Malawi, Morocco, Niger, Zambia. Do 128 – Cameroon, Nigeria.

History: The Skyservant followed from the success of the Do 27 single in the liaison and light transport roles, and over 200 were built almost exclusively for military customers.

The Do 28 Skyservant was the second aircraft to bear the Do 28 designation, but is similar only in configuration to the original Do 28 (the first Do 28 flew in 1959 and was a twin engine development of the Do 27). The Do 28 Skyservant first flew on February 23 1966, and while it retained the earlier Do 28's high wing and side mounted engine configuration, was an all new and much larger aircraft. Other design features were the fixed tailwheel undercarriage and the faired mainwheels mounted beneath the engines.

The Do 28 was developed into a number of progressively improved variants, from the original D, through the D-1 and D-2, to the 128-2, introduced in 1980. Each variant introduced a number of detail changes. Most Do 28 production was for military customers, notably Germany, although small numbers were sold to commercial operators.

A turboprop version of the Do 28, designated the Do 28 D-5X, first flew in April 1978, fitted with two Avco Lycoming LTP 101-600-1As derated to 300kW (400shp). Production turboprop Dornier 128-6s however feature Pratt & Whitney Canada PT6As, the first such configured aircraft flying in March 1980. Only a small number were built between then and 1986, notably for Peru, which ordered 16, and Cameroon, whose three (two survive) Do 128s were fitted with a MEL Marec search radar for maritime patrol.

Photo: Germany was the largest Do 28 operator. (Dornier)

Douglas C-47 Skytrain/Dakota

Country of origin: United States of America

Type: Tactical transport, gunship and utility transport

Powerplants: C-47A – Two 895kW (1200hp) Pratt & Whitney R-1830-92 14 cylinder two row radial piston engines, driving three blade propellers. Jet Prop DC-3 – Two 1060kW (1425shp) Pratt & Whitney Canada PT6A-65AR turboprops, driving five blade propellers.

Performance: C-47A – Max speed 346km/h (187kt), max cruising speed 298km/h (161kt), economical cruising speed 280km/h (151kt). Max initial rate of climb 1160ft/min. Service ceiling 24,000ft. Range 2415km (1305nm). Jet Prop DC-3 – Max cruising speed 343km/h (185kt). Max initial rate of climb 1000ft/min. Range with max payload 648km (350nm), max range 3705km (2000nm). Max endurance 14hr.

Weights: C-47A – Empty equipped 8250kg (18,190lb), max takeoff 13,290kg (29,300lb). Jet Prop DC-3 – Empty 7257kg (16,000lb), max takeoff 12,202kg (26,900lb).

Dimensions: C-47A – Wing span 28.95m (95ft 0in), length 19.62m (64ft 6in), height 5.15m (16ft 11in). Wing area 91.7m² (987sq ft). Jet Prop DC-3 – Same except length 20.68m (67ft 10in).

Accommodation: C-47 – Flightcrew of two. Up to 28 troops on inward facing seats, or 18 stretchers and three medical attendants. Jet Prop DC-3 – Up to 40 troops.

Armament: AC-47 – Three 7.62mm MGs through left side windows.

Operators: In service with over 20 countries including Australia, Bolivia, Chile, Colombia, El Salvador, Greece, Honduras, Mexico, Paraguay, South Africa, Taiwan, Thailand, Turkey, Zaire, Zambia

History: The C-47 was the most important military transport of WW2, and yet today, five decades later, it remains in service with the air arms of more than 20 countries around the world.

The C-47 traces back to the DC-3 airliner, an improved development of the earlier DC-2 which made its first flight in 1934. The DC-3 flew for the first time on December 17 1935 and went on to become the mainstay of US domestic airlines in the years prior to World War 2.

The entry of the US into WW2 in December 1941 would have a profound effect on the fortunes of the already successful DC-3 (more than 400 had been built by then). The US Army Air Force's requirements for transport aircraft were well met by the in-production DC-3, with the result that as the C-47 Skytrain it became the standard USAAF transport during the war. More than 10,000 were built for service with US and foreign air arms; in British and Commonwealth service it was named Dakota.

Postwar surplus C-47s became the standard equipment of almost all the world's airlines, while many US surplus C-47s were also sold or donated to the world's air forces. In the USSR it was built in quantity as the Lisunov Li-2.

The C-47's longevity has resulted in a number of turboprop conversion programs to improve its performance. Two notable conversions are the Basler Turbo-67 and Professional Aviation Jet Prop DC-3, both of which feature a small fuselage stretch and two Pratt & Whitney Canada PT6A turboprops. A small number of operators have converted their C-47s to Turbo-67 standard, while South Africa is converting 30 or so to Jet Prop standard.

Photo: A Royal Thai Air Force C-47. (Matthew Accred)

Douglas DC-6 & C-118

Country of origin: United States of America

Type: Medium haul transport

Powerplants: DC-6 – Four 1340kW (1800hp) Pratt & Whitney Double Wasp R-2800-CA15 18 cylinder twin row radial piston engines with a maximum output rating of 1790kW (2400hp) with water injection, driving three blade constant speed Hamilton Standard propellers. DC-6B – Four 1685kW (2500hp) R-2800-CB17s.

Performance: DC-6 – Max speed 570km/h (425kt), cruising speed 501km/h (270kt). Initial rate of climb 1070ft/min. Max range 7376km (3983nm). DC-6B – Cruising speed 507km/h (274kt). Service ceiling 25,000ft. Range with max payload 4835km (2610nm), range with max fuel 7595km (4100nm).

Weights: DC-6 – Empty 23,840kg (52,567lb), max takeoff 44,130kg (97,200lb). DC-6B – Empty 25,110kg (55,357lb), max takeoff 48,535kg (107,000lb).

Dimensions: DC-6 – Wing span 35.81m (117ft 6in), length 30.66m (100ft 7in), height 8.66m (28ft 5in). Wing area 135.9m² (1463sq ft). DC-6B – Same except length 32.18m (105ft 7in), height 8.74m (28ft 8in).

Accommodation: DC-6 – Flightcrew of three or four. Passenger accommodation typically for between 48 to 56, but aircraft now usually equipped to carry freight. DC-6B – Typical passenger seating for 54, with max seating for 102, but usually configured for freight.

Armament: None

Operators: Colombia, El Salvador, Mexico, South Korea.

History: The DC-6 was conceived in response to a WW2 military airlift requirement and went on to become Douglas's most successful four engined piston airliner in terms of civil sales.

During WW2 the USAAF's C-54 fleet's long range and payload capabilities so impressed the service that it ordered development of a larger and improved variant. Designated YC-112, this long range transport featured more powerful 1565kW (2100hp) R-2800-22W engines and a lengthened fuselage. The development timetable of the YC-112 though was such that it did not fly for the first time until February 15 1946, by which time the war ended and the USAAF requirement no longer stood.

Instead Douglas continued development of the type as a long range airliner, resulting in the DC-6. The YC-112 served as the prototype for the DC-6 program, and the first civil production aircraft were delivered to US airlines in March 1947. Entry into service however was not smooth with the fleet grounded for four months from later that year after a spate of inflight engine fires.

Development work on the stretched DC-6A with more powerful engines began in 1947. The DC-6A was optimised for freight work, the equivalent passenger version was the DC-6B. The DC-6C was a convertible passenger/freight model.

Renewed military interest in the DC-6 was sparked by the Korean War, with the result that large numbers of USAF C-118s and USN R6D-1s were built. Many of these aircraft later found their way into civil hands. A handful of both former airliner DC-6s and ex US military C-118s still remain in service with a number of air arms, principally in Latin America.

Photo: An El Salvadorean air force DC-6. (MAP)

Douglas DC-8 & EC-24

Country of origin: United States of America

Type: Strategic & VIP transport, ECM and Elint aircraft

Powerplants: Series 50 – Four 80.6kN (18,000lb) Pratt & Whitney JT3D-3 turbofans. Super 70 Series – Four 97.9kN (22,000lb) CFM International CFM56-2-C5 turbofans.

Performance: Series 50 – Max recommended cruising speed 933km/h (504kt). Range with max payload 9205km (4970nm), max range 11,260km (6078nm). Super 70 – Max cruising speed 887km/h (479kt), economical cruising speed 850km/h (460kt). Range with max payload (Super 73) 8950km (4830nm).

Weights: Series 50 – Operating empty 60,020kg (132,325lb), max takeoff 147,415kg (325,000lb). Super 73 – Operating empty 75,500kg (166,500lb), max takeoff 162,025kg (355,000lb).

Dimensions: Wing span 43.41m (142ft 5in), length 45.87m (150ft 6in), height 12.91m (42ft 4in). Wing area 257.6m^2 (2773sq ft) on early aircraft, or 266.5m^2 (2868sq ft) on later aircraft. Super 63 & 73 – Wing span 45.23m (148ft 5in), length 57.12m (187ft 5in), height 12.92m (45ft 5in). Wing area 271.9m^2 (2927sq ft).

Accommodation: Flightcrew of three. Series 50 can seat up to 179, and Series 71 and 73 can seat up to 220 in high density passenger configurations. Some of the French and Peruvian aircraft configured as VIP transports.

Armament: None

Operators: France, Peru, USA.

History: The DC-8 was Douglas' first jet powered airliner, and arch rival of the more successful Boeing 707. Compared with the 707, only a small number have ever seen military service.

Douglas was slower and more cautious to move into the then radical field of jet powered transports than Boeing, announcing the DC-8 project in 1955, the year after Boeing had flown its Dash 80 707/KC-135 predecessor. The first DC-8 flew on May 30 1958, and after a concentrated certification program the first production aircraft entered airliner service in September 1959, a year later than the 707.

Over 550 DC-8s were in built in a number of different variants, and two distinct fuselage lengths. Original short fuselage models included the turbojet powered Series 10, 20, 30 and 40, and the turbofan powered 50 series.

The stretched Super 60 series was built from the late 1960s, and comprised the long range 47.98m (157ft 5in) length 62, and the 57.12m (187ft 5in) length 61 and 63. When re-engined with CFM56s, the Super 60 series are known as Super 70s.

France continues to be the largest military operator, currently with a Series 55 and three Series 72s used for strategic and VIP transport duties, while a modified Series 53, the DC-8 SARIGUE, is used for ECM/Elint reconnaissance. It features wingtip pods and a dorsal fairing. All current French Armée de l'Air DC-8s are ex civil airliners, as are Peru's two DC-8-62CFs which are used as VIP transports.

In the USA Chrysler Technologies operates a single converted DC-8-54F freighter for the US Navy for ECM training. Designated EC-24, the DC-8 is used to simulate a realistic Electronic Warfare (EW) environment for fleet training exercises.

Photo: A French DC-8-72CF transport. (Armée de l'Air)

EH Industries EH 101 Merlin & Cormorant

Countries of origin: Italy and United Kingdom

Type: Medium lift utility transport and shipborne ASW helicopter

Powerplants: HM.1 – Three 1725kW (2312shp) Rolls-Royce Turbo-méca RTM322-01 turboshafts, driving a five blade main rotor and four blade tail rotor.

Performance: HM.1 – Cruising speed 278km/h (150kt), long range cruising speed 260km/h (140kt), best endurance speed 167km/h (90kt). Ferry range with auxiliary tanks 1853km (1000nm). Endurance with max weapon load, 5hr on station.

Weights: HM.1 – Operating empty 10,500kg (23,149lb), max takeoff 14,600kg (32,188lb).

Dimensions: Main rotor diameter 18.59m (61ft 0in), length overall rotors turning 22.81m (74ft 10in), length main rotor and tail folded (HM.1) 15.75m (51ft 8in), height overall rotors turning 6.65m (21ft 10in), height main rotor and tail folded (HM.1) 5.21m (17ft 1in). Main rotor disc area 271.5m^2 (2922.5sq ft).

Accommodation: Flightcrew of one or two. HM.1 will have a crew comprising one or two pilots, an acoustic sensor operator and observer. Utility version will accommodate 30 equipped troops, or 16 stretchers and medical attendants. Max external sling load 5445kg (12,000lb).

Armament: Merlin can be fitted with four homing torpedoes in addition to anti ship missiles. Utility version can be fitted with stub wings for rocket pods and a 12.7mm machine gun in a nose turret. HC.3 will have provision for pintle mounted machine guns in main doors.

Operators: Italy*, UK*.

History: The three engined EH 101 was initially conceived as a replacement for the Sikorsky/Westland Sea King, but is also on offer in a number of civil and military versions.

EH (or European Helicopter) Industries is a collaborative venture between Westland of the UK and Agusta of Italy, and was formed primarily to develop an anti submarine warfare helicopter for the Royal Navy and Italian navy, plus utility and civil variants. The partnership was formed in 1980, and both companies have a 50% holding. The development history of this aircraft is protracted and dates back to the late 1970s when Westland was working on its WG 34 Sea King replacement. The WG 34 was cancelled, paving the way for the joint Anglo Italian EH 101 program. Full scale program go ahead of the EH 101 was announced in March 1984. First flight of an EH 101 (the Westland built PP1) was on October 9 1987.

The lead customer for the EH 101 is the Royal Navy, which is taking delivery of 44 ASW configured Merlin HM.1s (previously HAS.1) equipped with Blue Kestrel search radar, dipping sonar and ESM (the first was rolled out in 1996). The RAF has ordered 22 utility Merlin HC.3s (with provision for FLIR and AAR probe) EH 101s for delivery from 1998, while the Italian navy has ordered eight ASW EH 101s similar in configuration to the Merlin and four EH 101 utility transports, and has a requirement for an AEW variant.

The EH 101 is offered with a choice of engines, either the Rolls-Royce Turboméca RTM322 or General Electric T700. British Merlins will have RTM322s, civil and Italian EH 101s will have General Electric CT7 engines.

Photo: A production Royal Navy Merlin HM.1. (Westland)

Embraer EMB-110 & EMB-111

Country of origin: Brazil

Type: Light utility transport & maritime patrol aircraft (EMB-111)

Powerplants: Two 560kW (750shp) Pratt & Whitney Canada PT6A-34 turboprops, driving three blade Hartzell propellers.

Performance: EMB-111 – Max cruising speed 360km/h (194kt), economical cruising speed 347km/h (187kt). Max initial rate of climb 1190ft/min. Service ceiling 25,500ft. Range 2945km (1590nm).

Weights: EMB-111 – Empty equipped 3760kg (8289lb), max takeoff 7000kg (15,432lb).

Dimensions: EMB-111 – Wing span over tip tanks 15.95m (52ft 4in), length 14.91m (48ft 11in), height 4.91m (16ft 2in). Wing area 29.1m² (313sq ft).

Accommodation: Flightcrew of two. Can carry up to 18 troops or six stretchers.

Armament: EMB-111 – Four underwing pylons can carry rockets, smoke bombs, flares, chaff dispenser and a searchlight.

Operators: EMB-110 – Brazil, Cape Verde, Chile, Colombia, Gabon, Peru, Uruguay. EMB-111 – Angola, Brazil, Chile, Gabon, Senegambia.

History: The EMB-110 Bandeirante, or 'Bandit', was Embraer's first and thus far most successful indigenous aircraft program and is in widespread civil and military service.

Design of the EMB-110 was undertaken in response to a Brazilian Ministry of Aeronautics specification for a general purpose light transport suitable for both military and civilian duties. The new design was developed with the assistance of well known French designer Max Holste, and the first of three prototypes, designated YC-95s, flew for the first time on October 26 1968.

Embraer (or Empresa Brasilera de Aeronáutica SA) was established the following year, and development and production of the YC-95 became one of the company's first responsibilities.

The first of the larger production standard EMB-110 Bandeirantes (Bandeirante is Portugese for Pioneer) flew on August 9 1972 and the type entered Brazilian air force service in February 1973.

Brazilian military transport versions of the basic EMB-110 are designated C-95, including 60 early build, 12 seat C-95s and 31 stretched C-95Bs, equivalent to the EMB-110P, the definitive civil version. Brazil also operates a small number of navigation aid calibration EC-95s and photographic survey RC-95s.

The most heavily modified Bandeirante is the EMB-111 maritime patrol variant, which features an Eaton-AIL APS-128 Sea Patrol radar mounted in a nose radome, ESM, wingtip tanks and four underwing hardpoints. The last 10 EMB-111s built for Brazil feature improved avionics including a MEL Super Searchmaster radar and EFIS. Brazil's EMB-111s are designated P-95s.

Production of the Bandeirante ceased in May 1990 (the last aircraft was delivered to the Brazilian air force). In all over 500 Bandeirantes were built, including 29 EMB-111s.

Photo: A Brazilian navy EMB-111. In Brazilian service these aircraft are nicknamed Bandeirulha, a contraction of Bandeirante Patrulha.

Embraer EMB-120 Brasilia

Country of origin: Brazil

Type: Twin turboprop VIP transport

Powerplants: Two 1340kW (1800shp) Pratt & Whitney Canada PW118 or PW118A turboprops, driving four blade Hamilton Standard propellers.

Performance: EMB-120 with PW118As – Max cruising speed 574km/h (310kt), long range cruising speed 482km/h (260kt). Max initial rate of climb 2120ft/min. Service ceiling 32,000ft. Range with max passengers and reserves 926km (500nm). EMB-120ER with PW118As – Max cruising speed 580km/h (313kt), long range cruising speed 500km/h (270kt). Max initial rate of climb 2500ft/min. Service ceiling 32,000ft. Range with max pax and reserves 1500km (810nm).

Weights: EMB-120 – Empty equipped 7100kg (15,655lb), max takeoff 11,500kg (25,353lb). EMB-120ER – Empty equipped 7140kg (15,741lb), max takeoff 11,990kg (26,433lb).

Dimensions: EMB-120 – Wing span 19.78m (64ft 11in), length 20.00m (65ft 8in), height 6.35m (20ft 10in). Wing area 39.4m² (424.42sq ft). EMB-120ER – Same except for length 20.07m (65ft 10in).

Accommodation: Flightcrew of two. Standard main cabin seating for 30 at three abreast. Brazilian VC-97s configured as VIP transports.

Armament: None

Operators: Brazil, Peru.

History: Although in only limited military service, the Brasilia, a high speed yet relatively inexpensive to operate and purchase commuter, is proving to be a considerable commercial sales success, following in the highly successful footsteps of the earlier and smaller Bandeirante.

Design work of the Brasilia dates back to the late 1970s when Embraer investigated stretching its EMB-121 Xingu corporate turboprop to a 25 seat regional airliner. While this was the first aircraft to bear the EMB-120 designation (it was named the Araguia), the resulting EMB-120 is an all new aircraft. Design studies began in September 1979, first flight of a PW115 powered prototype took place on July 27 1983, and entry into service was in October 1985.

Models include the basic EMB-120, the extended range EMB-120ER, EMB-120 Combi, EMB-120 Convertible, and current production EMB-120ER Advanced. Hot and high models are powered by two PW118As.

Brazil operates 10 VIP transport configured Brasilias, designated VC-97. These were delivered to the Brazilian air force from 1987.

Brazil also ordered five Airborne Early Warning and three Synthetic Aperture Radar configured Brasilias for its Amazon Surveillance System program. The EMB-120AEWs would have been fitted with an Ericsson Erieye phased array surveillance radar and three multi function operator work stations and an onboard command and control system. The EMB-120SRs would have been fitted with a Synthetic Aperture Radar, an ultraviolet/visible/infrared line scanner and a high sensitivity TV/FLIR.

First deliveries were planned for 1997 but in 1996 the EMB-145 regional jet airliner (described separately) was chosen as the platform for the two systems in place of the Brasilia.

Photo: A Brazilian air force VC-97 (EMB-120RT) VIP transport.

Embraer EMB-121 Xingu

Country of origin: Brazil

Type: Liaison, VIP transport and multi engine trainer aircraft

Powerplants: Xingu I – Two 505kW (600shp) Pratt & Whitney Canada PT6A-28 turboprops, driving three blade props. Xingu II – Two 635kW (850shp) PT6A-42s driving four blade props.

Performance: Xingu I – Max cruising speed 450km/h (243kt), economical cruising speed 365km/h (197kt). Max initial rate of climb 1400ft/min. Service ceiling 26,000ft. Range with max fuel 2352km (1270nm). Xingu II – Max cruising speed 465km/h (251kt), economical cruising speed 380km/h (205kt). Max initial rate of climb 1800ft/min. Range with max fuel 2278km (1230nm), with max payload 1630km (880nm).

Weights: Xingu I – Empty equipped 3620kg (7984lb), max takeoff 5670kg (12,500lb). Xingu II – Empty equipped 3500kg (7716lb), max takeoff 6140kg (13,536lb).

Dimensions: Xingu I – Wing span 14.45m (47ft 5in), length 12.25m (40ft 2in), height 4.74m (15ft 7in). Wing area 27.5m² (296.0sq ft). Xingu II – Wing span 14.83m (48ft 8in), length 13.44m (44ft 1in). Wing area 27.9m² (300.3sq ft).

Accommodation: Xingu I – Flightcrew of one or two, plus typical main cabin seating for five or six passengers. Xingu II – Flightcrew of two. Main cabin seating for seven, eight or nine passengers.

Armament: None

Operators: Brazil, France.

History: The sleek looking Xingu combined the Bandeirante's wing and engines with an all new fuselage and was intended as a fast corporate transport for the civil market, but in the end almost half of all EMB-121 production was for the Brazilian and French militaries.

The Xingu flew for the first time on October 10 1976, with a production aircraft following on May 20 1977 and customer deliveries starting later that year.

Several derivatives of the Xingu design were proposed that did not see the light of day, including the original EMB-120, the Araguia, a commuter airliner which would have seated 25, and the EMB-123 Tapajós. The Tapajós would have had more powerful 835kW (1120shp) PT6A-45 engines (which also would have powered the Araguia), increased wing span and lengthened fuselage.

A more modest development did enter production, the EMB-121B Xingu II. This features more powerful engines, four blade props, increased fuel tankage and greater seating capacity courtesy of a slightly stretched fuselage. The Xingu II made its first flight on September 4 1981. Xingu production ceased in August 1987 after 105 had been built.

The first six production Xingus were all delivered to the Brazilian air force in late 1977, designated VU-9 and used for VIP transport. Brazil later acquired a further six second hand EMB-121s, and these are designated EC-9.

Some 41 EMB-121s, almost half of all Xingu production, were delivered to the French Armée de l'Air and navy where they are used for aircrew training and liaison duties. They were ordered in September 1980 and the last was delivered in 1983.

Photo: A French navy Xingu. (Embraer)

Embraer RJ-145SA & RJ-145RS

Country of origin: Brazil

Type: Surveillance aircraft

Powerplants: Two 31.3kN (7040lb) Allison AE 3007A turbofans.

Performance: RJ-145 airliner – Max cruising speed 797km/h (430kt), economical cruising speed 667km/h (360kt). Service ceiling 37,000ft. Range with 50 passengers and reserves 1480km (800nm), range with max fuel and 20 passengers 2575km (1390nm).

Weights: RJ-145 airliner – Basic operating empty 11,585kg (25,545lb), max takeoff 19,200kg (42,336lb).

Dimensions: RJ-145 airliner – Wing span 20.04m (65ft 9in), length 29.87m (98ft 0in), height 6.71m (22ft 0in). Wing area 51.2m² (550.9sq ft).

Accommodation: Flightcrew of two. Standard airliner passenger accommodation for 50 at three abreast and 79cm (31in) pitch. RJ-145SA will have multifunction operator displays, with accommodation for a relief flightcrew.

Armament: None

Operators: Brazil*

History: Embraer's RJ-145 (formerly EMB-145) is a 50 seat regional airliner that is growing in popularity with airline customers but has also been selected as the platform for Brazil's SIVAM Amazon surveillance program.

Embraer first began looking at a stretched and jet engined development of its successful Brasilia turboprop in the mid 1980s. In late 1991 Embraer froze the 145's basic configuration (after having previously studied a straight wing design with above wing mounted engines design) with rear fuselage mounted engines. Other features include Allison AE 3007A turbofans (a turbofan development of the AE 2100 turboprop which powers the C-130J) and a Honeywell Primus 1000 EFIS avionics suite.

The RJ-145's first flight took place on August 11 1995 with first customer deliveries from December 1996.

Brazil's SIVAM (SIstema de Vigilancia da AMazonia) program was originally going to be met by modified EMB-120 Brasilias, however in late 1996 the Brazilian government decided to use the 145 as the SIVAM platform.

Raytheon is the SIVAM program prime contractor. Two versions of the RJ-145 are being developed under SIVAM, the AEW RJ-145SA and the synthetic aperture radar equipped RJ-145RS. The RJ-145SA will be fitted with a civilian spec Ericsson Erieye phased array radar mounted above the fuselage which will provide surveillance from low altitude up to 82,000ft, and out to distances of over 300km (160nm).

The RJ-145RS meanwhile will be fitted with a Canadian MacDonald Dettwiler IRIS (Integrated Radar Imaging System) synthetic aperture radar mounted in a canoe fairing beneath the fuselage, Skyball TV/FLIR and an ultraviolet/visible/infrared light linescanner.

The Brazilian air force will use the RJ-145SAs to detect and track illegal aircraft movements over the Amazon basin, while the RJ-145SRs will be used for resource exploitation and pollution detection and control and illegal activities surveillance.

The AEW RJ-145SA also shows promise for international sales.

Photo: A retouched photo showing the RJ-145SA. (Embraer)

Embraer EMB-312 Tucano

Country of origin: Brazil

Type: Two seat basic/advanced trainer

Powerplant: EMB-312 – One 560kW (750shp) Pratt & Whitney Canada PT6A-25C turboprop, driving a three blade propeller.

Performance: EMB-312 – Max speed 448km/h (242kt), max cruising speed 411km/h (222kt), economical cruising speed 319km/h (172kt). Max initial rate of climb 2330ft/min. Service ceiling 30,000ft. Ferry range with two underwing tanks 3330km (1797nm), typical range on internal fuel 1845km (995nm). Endurance on internal fuel approx 5hr.

Weights: EMB-312 – Basic empty 1810kg (3990lb), max takeoff 3175kg (7000lb).

Dimensions: EMB-312 – Wing span 11.14 (36ft 7in), length 9.86m (32ft 4in), height 3.40m (11ft 2in). Wing area 19.4m² (208.8sq ft).

Accommodation: Two in tandem, except in ALX single seater.

Armament: EMB-312 – Up to 1000kg (2205lb) on four underwing pylons, including bombs, rockets, gun pods and practice bombs.

Operators: Argentina, Brazil, Columbia, Egypt, France, Honduras, Iran, Kenya, Kuwait, Paraguay, Peru, Venezuela, UK.

History: What started as a replacement program for Brazil's fleet of T-37 trainers has resulted in South America's most successful military aircraft program, with over 600 sold to 14 different nations.

Development of the Tucano (Toucan) began in late 1978 when the Brazilian Ministry of Aeronautics awarded Embraer a development contract to design and fly a turboprop powered trainer to replace the Brazilian air force's Cessna T-37s. What resulted was the Tucano, a tandem two seater (with ejection seats) powered by a Pratt & Whitney Canada PT6A turboprop, featuring four underwing hardpoints for light armament or practice bombs. First flight was on August 16 1980.

Brazil originally ordered 133 Tucanos (service designation T-27) which were delivered between 1983 and 1986. Egypt became the first export customer, when in 1983 it ordered a total of 134, all but 10 of which were to be assembled by Helwan in Egypt. Of those 134, 80 were built for Iraq.

In 1985 the British RAF selected a Garrett TPE331 powered variant of the Tucano to replace its Jet Provosts. These aircraft were licence built by Shorts in Northern Ireland as the S312 (Tucano T.1 in RAF service), and feature a significantly more powerful 820kW (1100shp) TPE331-12B engine, improved systems and structural strengthening for improved fatigue life. Kuwait and Kenya have also ordered Shorts built, Garrett powered Tucanos.

France ordered 80 Embraer built EMB-312F Tucanos in 1991 to replace Magisters. Delivered from 1993, EMB-312Fs feature structural strengthening and French avionics.

The EMB-312H Super Tucano is a stretched (11.41m/37ft 6in long), more powerful development (featuring a 930kW/1250shp PT6A-68 driving a five blade prop). This aircraft was an unsuccessful contender in the USA's JPATS competition, but the armed single (A-29) and two seat (AT-29) Tucano ALX versions are being developed for the Brazilian air force. They will be used for anti narcotics and anti smuggling operations.

Photo: A Tucano of Brazil's Smoke Squadron aerobatic display team, (Doug Mackay)

ENAER T-35 Pillán

Countries of origin: Chile and United States of America

Type: Two seat basic trainer

Powerplant: T-35A – One 225kW (300hp) Textron Lycoming IO-540-K1K5 fuel injected flat six piston engine driving a three blade constant speed propeller. T-35TD – One 315kW (420shp) Allison 250-B17D turboprop driving a three blade constant speed propeller.

Performance: T-35A – Max speed 311km/h (268kt), max cruising speed 266km/h (144kt). Max initial rate of climb 1525ft/min. Time to 10,000ft 8min 48sec. Service ceiling 19,160ft. Range at 55% power 1205km (650nm), range at 75% power 1095km (590nm). Endurance at 55% power 5hr 35min, endurance at 75% power 4hr 25min. T-35DT – Max speed 425km/h (230kt), 75% power cruising speed 337km/h (182kt), 55% power cruising speed 313km/h (170kt). Max initial rate of climb 2850ft/min. Time to 9850ft 5min 36sec. Service ceiling 25,000ft. Range at 55% power 760km (410nm), range at 75% power 648km (350nm).

Weights: T-35A – Empty equipped 930kg (2050lb), max takeoff 1338kg (2950lb). T-35DT – Empty 943kg (2080lb), max takeoff 1338kg (2950lb).

Dimensions: T-35A – Wing span 8.84m (29ft 0in), length 8.00m (26ft 3in), height 2.64m (8ft 8in). Wing area 13.7m² (147.3sq ft). T-35DT – Same except length 8.60m (28ft 3in).

Accommodation: Seating for two in tandem.

Armament: Usually none.

Operators: Chile, Panama, Paraguay, Spain.

History: The Pillán (devil) basic trainer resulted from a Chilean air force requirement for a two seat, aerobatic basic trainer.

Responding to the requirement Piper designed a new trainer based on its PA-28R Saratoga, a six seater with retractable undercarriage (itself based on the PA-28 four seater family). Piper designated its new two seater the PA-28R-300, and while based on the Saratoga it featured a new fuselage centre section and structural strengthening for aerobatics. Like the Saratoga it featured a 225kW (300hp) six cylinder Lycoming IO-540 engine.

Piper built two prototypes, the first flying on March 6 1981, while the first of three ENAER assembled prototypes flew in January 1982. From 1979 ENAER (Empresa Nacional de Aeronáutic de Chile) had assembled under licence 27 Piper PA-28 Dakota four seat light aircraft for the Chilean air force and various local flying clubs and so was already experienced in building Piper aircraft.

ENAER production of the T-35 began in 1985. In all 80 were built for Chile, 60 T-35As and 20 IFR equipped T-35Bs. The most significant export customer for the T-35 was Spain, who ordered 41 T-35Cs. Designated the E.26 Tamiz in Spanish service, these aircraft were assembled in Spain by CASA from ENAER built kits. Other customers were Panama (10 IFR equipped T-35Ds) and Paraguay (15 T-35Ds). Final T-35 deliveries were completed in 1991.

The turboprop T-35DT Turbo Pillán was a development of the original T-35TX Aucán which first flew in February 1986. The T-35DT featured a new one piece canopy, oxygen system and improved instrumentation. None were sold.

Photo: A Pillan in Chilean markings. (Fuerza Aerea de Chile)

English Electric Canberra

Country of origin: United Kingdom

Type: Bomber, target tug and reconnaissance aircraft

Powerplants: B(I).8 – Two 33.2kN (7400lb) Rolls-Royce Avon 109 turbojets.

Performance: B(I).8 – Max speed 871km/h (470kt) at 40,000ft, max speed at sea level 827km/h (447kt). Max initial rate of climb 3400ft/min. Service ceiling 48,000ft. Range with max fuel 5840km (3155nm), range with max load and 10 minutes over target 1295km (700nm).

Weights: B(I).8 – Basic operating 12,678kg (27,950lb), max takeoff 24,925kg (54,950lb).

Dimensions: B(I).8 – Wing span over tip tanks 19.96m (65ft 6in), wing span 19.51m (64ft 0in), length 19.96m (65ft 6in), height 4.77m (15ft 8in). Wing area 89.2m² (960sq ft).

Accommodation: B(I).8 – Flightcrew of two. Pilot seated under fighter style canopy, navigator in nose.

Armament: Up to six 1000lb (455kg) bombs in weapons bay, or alternatively one 4000lb (1815kg) and four 1000lb (455kg) bombs, or eight 500lb (227kg) bombs, or three 1000lb (455kg) bombs and four Hispano cannons. Two underwing wingtip stations can carry 455kg (1000lb) each.

Operators: Argentina, Chile, India, Peru, UK.

History: The Canberra was Britain's primary medium bomber during the 1950s and into the 1960s, in addition to being widely exported, and today continues to serve, albeit in dwindling numbers.

As far back as 1944 English Electric (a large British industrial company that had built Halifax bombers under licence in WW2) was shortlisted along with a number of higher profile British aircraft manufacturers to design the RAF's first jet bomber. English Electric's design was selected and it flew for the first time on Friday May 13 1949.

Features of the Canberra included its very large, broad wing which was designed for high altitude operations but gave the aircraft fighter like agility, plus its two Rolls-Royce Avon turbojets (one in each wing) and an internal bomb bay. In all, 27 variants were built, including those built under licence in the USA by Martin as the B-57 Canberra, and 48 in Australia by GAF (some saw combat in Vietnam). Significant models include the B.2 bomber, PR.3 and PR.7 reconnaissance aircraft, and the B.6 bomber.

In October 1994 the RAF retired its last T.17s, originally built as trainers but later used for Electronic Warfare training. Others remain in RAF service for test and trials duties and reconnaissance.

The Shorts developed PR.9 remains in RAF service as a reconnaissance platform. Features of this aircraft include more powerful engines, an offset fighter style tear drop canopy under which sits the pilot (with the navigator in the nose) and increased span wings. The B(I).8 Interdictor also featured the offset fighter style canopy.

India is the largest current Canberra operator with a mixed fleet including B(I).58s (B(I).8s) and PR.57s (PR.7s). Argentina and Peru also operate Canberras as bombers, while until recently Germany operated two PR.9s. Chile flies two PR.9s.

Photo: The RAF's five PR.9s are used for photo survey work and should remain in service through to 2000.

Eurocopter Gazelle

Country of origin: France

Type: Reconnaissance, training, anti tank and multirole helicopter

Powerplant: SA 342L – One 640kW (858shp) Turboméca XIVM turboshaft, driving a three blade main rotor and Fenestron shrouded tail rotor.

Performance: SA 342L – Max cruising speed at sea level 260km/h (140kt). Max initial rate of climb 1535ft/min. Service ceiling 13,450ft. Hovering ceiling in ground effect 9975ft, out of ground effect 7775ft. Range at sea level with standard fuel 710km (383nm).

Weights: SA 342L – Empty 999kg (2202lb), max takeoff 2000kg (4410lb).

Dimensions: SA 342L – Main rotor diameter 10.50m (34ft 6in), length overall 11.97m (39ft 3in), fuselage length 9.53m (31ft 3in), height overall 3.19m (10ft 6in). Main rotor disc area 86.6m² (932.1sq ft).

Accommodation: Seating for five including pilot.

Armament: Armament options include rocket pods, four or six HOT wire guided anti armour missiles, two forward firing 7.62mm machine guns, and a single 20mm Giat cannon on starboard side. Yugoslav SA 342Ls equipped four AT-3 'Sagger' ASMs and two SA-7 AAMs.

Operators: Military operators include Angola, Burundi, Cameroon, Cyprus, Ecuador, Egypt, France, Gabon, Guinea Republic, Iraq, Ireland, Kenya, Kuwait, Lebanon, Libya, Morocco, Qatar, Senegambia, Syria, Tunisia, UAE (Abu Dhabi), UK, Yugoslavia.

History: Widely sold around the world to various military air arms, the Gazelle was developed as a replacement to the Alouette II.

The Gazelle pioneered a number of significant technological features, namely a rigid main rotor head, composite construction rotor blades and the Fenestron shrouded tail rotor, a feature of a number of Aerospatiale/Eurocopter helicopters since.

The prototype was designated SA 340-01, had conventional rotor blades and first flew on April 7 1967. A second prototype introduced composite blades, while improved pre production aircraft with a larger cabin were designated the SA 341 and named Gazelle.

The 1967 Anglo French agreement between Sud Aviation (Aerospatiale from 1970) and Westland covering the Gazelle, Lynx and Puma helicopters resulted in the Gazelle becoming a joint production effort between both nations. Initial production Gazelles were the SA 341B Gazelle AH.1 for the British Army, SA 341C Gazelle HT.2 for the Royal Navy, SA 341D Gazelle HT.3 trainer and SA 341E Gazelle HCC.4 transport for the RAF, the French army's SA 341F, civil SA 341G and military export SA 341H.

Over 600 SA 341s of different versions were built before production switched to the more powerful Astazou XIVH powered SA 342. Versions are the civil SA 342J and export optimised SA 342K. Final versions are the export military SA 341L and French army SA 342M, which remained in production through to the mid 1990s (total civil and military Gazelle production reached 1255). French SA 342Ms are equipped with HOT anti armour missiles, while earlier SA 341Fs have been converted to fire HOTs. France has also equipped 30 Gazelles (the SA 342M ATAM) to fire Matra Mistral AAMs.

Photo: A British Army Gazelle AH.1. (Paul Merritt)

Eurocopter/Aerospatiale SA 330 Puma

Country of origin: France

Type: Multirole medium lift helicopter transport

Powerplants: SA 330L – Two 1175kW (1575shp) Turboméca Turmo IVC turboshafts, driving a four blade main rotor and five blade tail rotor.

Performance: SA 330L – Max cruising speed 271km/h (146kt). Max initial rate of climb 1810ft/min. Service ceiling 19,685ft. Hovering ceiling in ground effect 13,940ft, out of ground effect 13,940ft. Range 572km (309nm).

Weights: SA 330L – Empty 3615kg (7970lb), normal MTOW 7405kg (16,315lb), max takeoff with sling load 7500kg (16,534lb).

Dimensions: SA 330L – Main rotor diameter 15.00m (49ft 3in), length overall rotors turning 18.15m (59ft 7in), fuselage length 14.06m (46ft 2in), height overall 5.14m (16ft 11in). Main rotor disc area 176.7m² (1902.2sq ft).

Accommodation: Flightcrew of two. Up to 20 troops or six stretchers and six seated patients or medical attendants in main cabin.

Armament: Options include 7.62mm gun pods, rockets and ASMs mounted on the fuselage sides, and pintle mounted machine guns in cabin doors.

Operators: Operators include Argentina, Chile, Ecuador, France, Gabon, Indonesia, Kuwait, Lebanon, Malawi, Morocco, Nepal, Nigeria, Portugal, Romania, Senegambia, Spain, UAE (Abu Dhabi), UK, Zaire.

History: The Puma was designed to meet a French army requirement for an all weather medium lift helicopter.

The first of two SA 330 prototypes flew for the first time on April 15 1965, with the first production aircraft flying in September 1968. A 1967 Royal Air Force decision to order the Puma as its new tactical helicopter transport resulted in substantial Westland participation in design and construction. This was a result of the Westland/Sud Aviation helicopter co-operation agreement covering the Puma, Gazelle and Lynx signed in 1967.

Early military versions of the Puma were the French army SA 330B, export SA 330C, SA 330E Puma HC.1 transport for the RAF, and the hot and high Turmo IVC powered SA 330H (designated SA 330Ba in French service). The initial civil variants were the SA 330F passenger and SA 330G freight versions The SA 330L is the definitive military version, and compared to the earlier models has composite main rotors and an increased maximum takeoff weight. The SA 330J is the civil equivalent.

IPTN of Indonesia assembled a small number of SA 330Js as the NSA-330 before switching to the Super Puma. When Aerospatiale ceased production in 1987, the sole source for the Puma became IAR of Romania.

Since it was isolated by a UN arms embargo, South Africa has developed its own Puma derivatives. Two Makila powered, armed XTP-1 Beta prototypes were used as testbeds during the 1980s for the Rooivalk attack helicopter program, while the Oryx is a Makila powered upgrade of South Africa's Puma fleet. The Oryx was originally named Gemsbok, and entered service in 1988. Other changes include single pilot operation, weather radar and Super Puma style tail.

Photo: Combined, France's army and air force fly over 160 Pumas. (Armée de l'Air)

Eurocopter Super Puma & Cougar

Country of origin: France

Type: Multirole medium lift helicopter transport

Powerplants: AS 532U2 – Two 1375kW (1845shp) takeoff rated Turboméca Makila 1A2 turboshafts driving a four blade main rotor and four blade tail rotor.

Performance: AS 532U2 – Fast cruising speed 273km/h (147kt), economical cruising speed 242km/h (131kt). Rate of climb 1260ft/min. Service ceiling 13,450ft. Hovering ceiling in ground effect 8333ft, out of ground effect 6235ft. Range with standard fuel 795km (430nm), range with max fuel 1175km (635nm). Endurance 4hr 12min.

Weights: AS 535U2 – Empty 4760kg (10,493lb), max takeoff 9750kg (21,495lb).

Dimensions: AS 532U2 – Main rotor diameter 16.20m (53ft 2in), length overall 19.50m (63ft 11in), length overall main rotor folded 16.79m (55ft 1in), height overall 4.97m (16ft 4in). Main rotor disc area 206.0m² (2217.4sq ft).

Accommodation: AS 532U2 – One pilot VFR or two pilots IFR operations. Main cabin seats up to 29 troops, or 14 stretchers, four seated patients and a medical attendant. Max slung load 4500kg (9920lb).

Armament: Options include 7.62mm gun pods, rockets and ASMs (including AM 39 Exocet anti ship missiles) mounted on the fuselage sides, and pintle mounted machine guns in cabin doors.

Operators: Military operators include Argentina, Brazil, Cameroon, Chile, China, Ecuador, France, Germany*, Indonesia, Japan, Jordan, Kuwait, Mexico, Nepal, Netherlands*, Nigeria, Qatar, Saudi Arabia, Singapore, South Korea, Spain, Sweden, Switzerland, Thailand, Togo, Turkey, UAE (Abu Dhabi), Venezuela, Zaire.

History: The Super Puma and Cougar are stretched and re-engined developments of the Puma.

The original Super Puma first flew in September 1978 and was simply a more powerful version of the original Puma, featuring 1270kW (1700shp) Turboméca Makila turboshafts, new avionics and composite rotor blades. Military versions were designated AS 332Bs, commercial versions AS 332Cs.

The AS 332M Super Puma (and civil AS 332L) introduced the stretched fuselage and was first flown on October 10 1980. Uprated Makila 1A1 engines were introduced in 1986. Indonesia's IPTN has licence built a small number of AS 332Ls for that country's military.

In 1990 Aerospatiale (Eurocopter from 1992) renamed military Super Pumas the AS 532 Cougar Mk I series. Various suffixes denote the different military versions – U for unarmed, A for armed, C for the shorter version, L for the slightly stretched fuselage variant. Further variants are the SAR/surveillance AS 532MC and ASW AS 532SC – both feature the shorter fuselage.

The standard current production model is the AS 532U2 Cougar Mk II (although the Cougar Mk I remains available). The unarmed U2, armed A2 and civil L2 feature a further fuselage stretch allowing an extra row of seats (and making them the longest members of the Super Puma/Cougar family), EFIS cockpit and longer main rotor blades with parabolic tips. It has been available since 1993. The latest version to fly is the simplified, fixed gear AS 532UB Cougar 100.

Photo: The shipborne AS 532SC Cougar. (Eurocopter)

Eurocopter Ecureuil & Fennec

Country of origin: France

Type: Multirole light helicopter

Powerplants: AS 555N – Two 340kW (455shp) takeoff rated Turboméca TM 319 Arrius turboshafts, driving a three blade main rotor and two blade tail rotor.

Performance: AS 555N – Max cruising speed 225km/h (121kt). Max initial rate of climb 1340ft/min. Service ceiling 13,125ft. Hovering ceiling in ground effect 8530ft, out of ground effect 5085ft. Range 722km (390nm). Endurance with one torpedo 2hr 20min.

Weights: AS 555N – Empty 1382kg (3046lb), max takeoff 2600kg (5732lb).

Dimensions: AS 555N – Main rotor diameter 10.69m (35ft 1in), length overall 12.94m (42ft 6in), fuselage length 10.93m (35ft 11in), height overall 3.34m (11ft 0in). Main rotor disc area 89.8m² (966.1sq ft).

Accommodation: Seating for up to six.

Armament: Options include a pintle mounted 7.62mm machine gun, a 20mm Giat gun pod, twin 7.62mm gun pods, rockets, HeliTOW anti tank missiles and up to two torpedoes on naval variants.

Operators: Australia, Benin, Botswana, Brazil, Central African Republic, China, Denmark, Djibouti, Ecuador, France, Malawi, Paraguay, Peru, Sierra Leone, Singapore, UAE (Abu Dhabi).

History: The Ecureuil was conceived as a replacement for the Alouette II.

Development in the early 1970s culminated in the first flights of the Lycoming LTS 101 powered prototype on June 27 1974 and the Turboméca Arriel powered prototype on February 14 1975. Customer deliveries began in April 1978.

Initial models offered were the Arriel powered AS 350B, which was marketed outside North America, and the LTS 101 powered AS 350C and A350D Astar sold in the USA. Developments include the AS 350BA fitted with the larger main rotors of the AS 350B2 and the AS 350B2 with a more powerful Arriel 1D1 turboshaft and the main and tail rotors developed for the AS 355F Ecureuil 2, and most recently the Arriel 2 powered AS 350B3.

The twin engined Ecureuil 2 first flew on September 28 1979. Powered by two Allison 250-C20F turboshafts, the Ecureuil 2 entered production as the AS 355E. In common with the AS 350, the AS 355 features the maintenance free Starflex main rotor hub and main rotor blades of composite construction. The AS 355F replaced the AS 355E from early 1982, while the current production model is the AS 350N (TwinStar in the US) with Turboméca Arrius turboshafts.

Aerospatiale adopted the name Fennec for dedicated military Ecureuils in 1990. Single engine military versions are based on the AS 350B2 and include the utility AS 550U2, gun and rocket armed AS 550A2, HeliTOW missile armed AS 550C2, unarmed maritime AS 350M2 and armed anti shipping AS 550S2. Corresponding models of the AS 350B3 will become available soon. Twin engine Fennec variants include the AS 555UN utility, armed AS 555AN, missile armed AS 555CN, unarmed maritime AS 555MN (with optional chin mounted radar) and armed maritime AS 555SN.

Photo: An Argentine navy AS 555SN Fennec. (Eurocopter)

Eurocopter Dauphin 2 & Panther

Country of origin: France

Type: Multirole helicopter

Powerplants: AS 565UB – Two 558kW (749shp) Turboméca Arriel 2C turboshafts driving a four blade main rotor and Fenestron shrouded tail rotor.

Performance: AS 565UB – Max cruising speed at sea level 278km/h (150kt). Max initial rate of climb 1535ft/min. Hovering ceiling in ground effect 8540ft, out of ground effect 8200ft. Range with max standard fuel 820km (443nm).

Weights: AS 565UB – Empty 2305kg (5082lb), max takeoff 4250kg (9040lb).

Dimensions: AS 565UB – Main rotor diameter 11.94m (39ft 2in), length overall 13.68m (44ft 11in), fuselage length 12.11m (39ft 9in), height 3.98m (13ft 1in). Main rotor disc area 111.9m² (1204.5sq ft).

Accommodation: AS 565 – Two pilots and eight to 10 troops in assault transport role or four stretchers plus medical attendants.

Armament: AS 565AA – Two rocket packs, or 20mm Giat M621 gun pods, or up to eight Matra Mistral AAMs in four two-round packs, on two fuselage outriggers. AS 565SA – Can carry four side mounted AS 15TT radar guided ASMs.

Operators: Angola, Brazil, Cameroon, China, Dominican Republic, France, Ireland, Ivory Coast, Saudi Arabia, South Africa, UAE (Abu Dhabi).

History: The Dauphin 2 is a twin engined development of the original single Turboméca Astazou powered SA 360 and SA 361 Dauphin, which first flew on June 2 1972.

A dedicated military anti tank variant of the SA 361 was offered, the HOT anti tank missile equipped SA 361F, but none were sold.

Compared with the SA 360, the SA 365 Dauphin 2 introduced twin Turboméca Arriel turboshafts and a new engine fairing, Starflex main rotor hub and higher max takeoff weight, but retained the same basic fuselage. The Dauphin 2's first flight was on January 24 1975, while production deliveries of SA 365Cs began in early 1978. Few SA 365Cs are in military service.

The SA 365 was soon replaced by the AS 365N, with more powerful Arriel 1C turboshafts, enlarged tail surfaces, revised transmission and main rotor, new rotor mast fairing and engine cowling, and retractable tricycle undercarriage. The US Coast Guard took delivery of 99 AS 365N based HH-65 Dolphins, optimised for search and rescue. These aircraft are powered by two Lycoming LTS 101s.

The civil AS 365N2 forms the basis for the military AS 565 Panther family. Released in 1990, features of the AS 365N2 and Panther include upgraded Arriel engines, increased max takeoff weights, redesigned cabin doors and optional EFIS displays. The improved N3 and equivalent Panthers feature Arriel 2Cs, while the latest civil version is the 'widebody' AS 365N4.

Current Panther models are based on the AS 365N3 and include the AS 565UB unarmed assault transport and AS 565AB armed transport. Naval variants comprise the unarmed AS 565MB and armed AS 565SB. Equipment options include sonar, MAD, searchlight, and search radar.

Photo: Saudi Arabia's navy operates AS 15TT firing AS 565SAs Panthers. (Eurocopter)

Eurocopter BO 105

Country of origin: Germany

Type: Observation, utility and anti tank helicopter

Powerplants: BO 105 CB – Two 320kW (429shp) Allison 250-C20B turboshafts, driving a four blade main rotor and two blade tail rotor.

Performance: BO 105 CB – Max cruising speed 245km/h (137kt), cruising speed 232km/h (125kt). Max initial rate of climb 1773ft/min. Service ceiling 17,000ft. Hovering ceiling out of ground effect 6500ft, in ground effect 9515ft. Range with max payload 655km (354nm), ferry range 1110km (600nm).

Weights: BO 105 CB – Empty equipped 1280kg (2820lb), max takeoff 2400kg (5290lb).

Dimensions: BO 105 CB – Main rotor diameter 9.84m (32ft 4in), length overall 11.86m (38ft 11in), fuselage length 8.56m (28ft 1in), height 3.00m (9ft 10in). Main rotor disc area 76.1m² (818.6sq ft).

Accommodation: Pilot and observer/copilot side by side, with three passengers or two stretchers behind them. Behind rear seats and below the engine is a cargo compartment, accessible by two clamshell doors in the rear fuselage.

Armament: PAH-1 – Six Euromissile HOT anti tank missiles in two three-tube launchers mounted on fuselage outriggers. Majority have been modified to fire HOT 2. Swedish BO 105 CBS can fire ESCO HeliTow anti tank missiles.

Operators: Bahrain, Brunei, Chile, Colombia, Germany, Indonesia, Iraq, Kenya, Mexico, Netherlands, Peru, Philippines, Sierra Leone, Spain, Sweden, Trinidad and Tobago, UAE (Dubai).

History: Well regarded for its agility, twin engine safety and performance, the BO 105 serves widely as a multirole observation and anti tank attack helicopter.

The first of three BO 105 prototypes made the type's maiden flight on February 16 1967. This aircraft was powered by two 236kW (317shp) Allison 250-C18 turboshafts and featured a conventional main rotor hub, but the subsequent prototypes incorporated a new rigid hub with feathering hinges, composite blades and MAN-Turbo 6022 engines. The BO 105 reverted to Allison 250 power with the second of two preproduction aircraft, flying in this form in January 1971. Initial production was of the BO 105 C, available from 1970, while Allison 250-C20 turboshafts became standard from 1973.

The BO 105 CB was introduced in 1975 with uprated engines and a strengthened transmission. The current BO 105 CBS has a slight 25cm (10in) fuselage stretch and an additional window, allowing an extra passenger to be carried. The BO 105 L has more powerful engines and a higher takeoff weight. The BO 105 LS is a hot and high version with Allison 250-C28C engines and built exclusively in Canada by Eurocopter Canada, the BO 105 LSA Super Lifter is design to carry external loads.

Easily the largest BO 105 operator is the German army, which took delivery of 212 HOT armed BO 105 Ps as PAH-1s and 100 BO 105 M scouts as the VBH. Both these models are similar to the BO 105 CB, and were upgraded with new rotor blades and other improvements. These modifications also formed the basis of the civil EC Super Five, the primary current production model.

Photo: Sweden's army flies 20 anti tank BO 105 CBs. (Les Bushell)

Eurocopter/Kawasaki BK 117

Countries of origin: Germany and Japan

Type: Multirole helicopter

Powerplants: BK 117 B-2 – Two 410kW (550shp) Textron Lycoming LTS 101-750B-1 turboshafts driving a four blade main rotor and two blade tail rotor.

Performance: BK 117 B-2 – Max cruising speed 248km/h (134kt). Max initial rate of climb 1900ft/min. Hovering ceiling in ground effect 7000ft, out of ground effect 7500ft. Range with internal long range tank 706km (381nm).

Weights: BK 117 B-2 – Empty 1745kg (3846lb), max takeoff 3350kg (7385lb).

Dimensions: Main rotor diameter 11.00m (36ft 1in), length overall 13.00m (42ft 8in), fuselage length 9.98m (32ft 9in), height rotors turning 3.85m (12ft 8in). Main rotor disc area 95.0m² (1023sq ft).

Accommodation: One pilot and maximum seating for 10 passengers.

Armament: Usually none, although the BK 117 A-3M was offered with eight HOT 2 or four TOW anti tank missiles.

Operators: Japan, Iraq, South Africa.

History: The BK 117 was developed under a joint collaborative effort between MBB of Germany (now part of Eurocopter) and Kawasaki of Japan.

The BK 117 program replaced the separate MBB BO 107 and Kawasaki KH-7 design studies. Retaining the former's overall configuration, Eurocopter is responsible for the helicopter's rotor system (which uses a scaled up version of the BO 105's four blade rigid main rotor), tail unit, hydraulic system and power controls, while Kawasaki is in charge of the fuselage, transmission and undercarriage.

Development led to the BK 117's first flight on June 13 1979, the first production aircraft (built in Japan) flew December 1981, civil certification was awarded in December 1982, and first deliveries took place early in 1983. Initial production was of the BK 117 A-1, while the BK 117 A-3 with higher max takeoff weight and enlarged tail rotor with twisted blades was certificated in March 1985.

The BK 117 A-3 also formed the basis of the only specific military development offered, the BK 117 A-3M. It was offered with a roof mounted sight, either TOW or HOT 2 anti tank missiles, a trainable nose mounted machine gun, rocket pods, RWR and ECM. However, the BK 117 A-3M was dropped in 1988 due to a lack of interest.

The BK 117 A-4 introduced from 1987 features enhanced performance through an increased transmission limit at takeoff power, improved tail rotor head and on German built aircraft increased fuel. The BK 117 B-1 (certificated in 1987) has more powerful engines and better performance, the BK 117 B-2 is currently in production and has an increased max takeoff weight, while the BK 117 C-1 is a German development with a new cockpit and Turboméca Arriel engines. Indonesia's three licence built aircraft are known as NBK-117s.

The BK 117 has not emulated the military sales success of its smaller BO 105 brother, and is only in small scale military use. The largest operator is Iraq, which took delivery of 16 SAR configured BK 117 B-1s. Others are in government and quasi military service.

Photo: MBB's BK 117 A-3M armed with four TOW anti tank missiles.

Eurocopter EC 635

Countries of origin: Germany and France

Type: Seven place light twin turbine utility helicopter

Powerplants: EC 135 – Either two 435kW (583shp) takeoff rated Turboméca Arrius 2Bs or two 463kW (621shp) takeoff rated Pratt & Whitney Canada PW206B turboshafts, driving a four blade main rotor and 10 blade shrouded Fenestron tail rotor.

Performance: EC 135 – Max cruising speed 261km/h (141kt). Max initial rate of climb 1595ft/min. Service ceiling 20,000ft. Hovering ceiling in ground effect 15,585ft, out of ground effect 13,450ft. Range with standard fuel 715km (385nm), ferry range with long range tank 925km (500nm). Endurance with standard fuel 4hr.

Weights: EC 135 – Empty with Arrius 2Bs 1370kg (3020lb), empty with PW206s 1390kg (3064lb), max takeoff 2500kg (5511lb) or 2700kg (5952lb) with an external sling load.

Dimensions: Main rotor diameter 10.20m (33ft 5in), length overall 12.10m (39ft 9in), fuselage length 10.16m (33ft 4in), height to top of rotor head 3.35m (11ft 0in). Main rotor disc area 81.7m² (879.5sq ft).

Accommodation: Designed for single pilot operation (including IFR ops). Alternative cabin layouts are for five or seven in passenger roles. Alternative medevac layouts for one stretcher, three medical attendants and the pilot, or two stretchers two attendants and pilot. Stretchers loaded through rear freight door.

Armament: None for German training aircraft.

Operators: Germany*

History: The EC 135 was designed as a replacement for Eurocopter's successful BO 105 light twin, and is developed from the BO 108 technology demonstrator. The German army is the first military customer, ordering it for advanced training.

The original MBB BO 108 was intended as a high technology helicopter demonstrator, and as such incorporated a range of high technology features including a hingeless main rotor (Sikorsky and Boeing adopted this design for their RAH-66 Comanche), all composite bearingless tail rotor, shallow transmission (allowing greater cabin height) with special vibration absorbers, composite structures, improved aerodynamics, modern avionics and EFIS instrumentation. The first BO 108 was powered by Allison 250-C20R-3 turboshafts and flew on October 15 1988.

The success of the BO 108 test program led to MBB's announcement in January 1991 that it would develop the 108 with Arrius or PW206 engines as a replacement for the BO 105, with certification planned for 1994, with deliveries in 1995.

However, the formation of Eurocopter gave the program access to Aerospatiale's Fenestron shrouded tail rotor technology. The combination of the BO 108 and the Fenestron led to the definitive EC 135 flying for the first time on February 15 1994. German certification was granted on June 14 1996.

Military EC 135s are covered by the EC 635 designation. Germany is the first customer, ordering 15 to replace Alouette IIs in the pilot training role. They will be delivered from mid 1998 to the Army Aviation Weapons Systems School in Buckeburg, and will feature NVG compatible cockpit lighting and raised skid landing gear.

Photo: A development EC 135. (Eurocopter)

Eurocopter Tiger

Countries of origin: France and Germany

Type: Anti tank and battlefield reconnaissance helicopter

Powerplants: Two 960kW (1285shp) takeoff rated MTU/Turboméca/Rolls-Royce MTR 390 turboshafts, driving a four blade main rotor and three blade tail rotor.

Performance: UHT & HAC – Max speed 269km/h (145kt), cruising speed 230km/h (124kt). Max vertical rate of climb 1023ft/min. Hovering ceiling out of ground effect 10,500ft. Endurance, operational mission 2hr 50min.

Weights: Basic empty 3300kg (7275lb), max overload takeoff 6100kg (13,448lb).

Dimensions: Main rotor diameter 13.00m (42ft 8in), fuselage length 14.00m (46ft 0in), height overall 4.32m (14ft 2in). Main rotor disc area 132.7m² (1428.8sq ft).

Accommodation: Pilot and weapons systems operator in tandem.

Armament: HAP – One 30mm Giat cannon in chin turret, four Matra Mistral AAMs and four HOT 3 anti tank missiles, or eight Trigats and four Stinger/Mistral AAMs, or combinations of rockets and missiles. HAC & UHT – Up to eight HOT 2 or Trigat anti tank missiles and four Mistrals or Stingers on two wing pylons, plus rocket and gun pods.

Operators: No production aircraft funded at time of writing.

History: Arguably the most advanced combat helicopter to be designed in Europe, the Tiger has its genesis in similar German and French army helicopter programs.

In the early 1980s the German army had begun looking at options to replace its sizeable fleet of MBB PAH-1 (BO 105) anti tank helicopters, while the French army at the same time had a very similar requirement to replace its Gazelle anti tank force. Thus the two countries signed a memorandum of understanding covering the joint development of such a helicopter in 1984.

The aim and direction of the program was subsequently reviewed, leading to an amended MoU being signed in 1987. In December that year full scale development was approved, while in late 1989 the main development contract was awarded and the name Tiger (or Tigre in French) adopted. 1989 also saw Aerospatiale and MBB form the jointly owned Eurocopter to cover development of the helicopter. (In 1992 Aerospatiale and MBB merged all their helicopter activities under the Eurocopter banner).

The Tiger is currently being developed in three versions. The HAP is the French army's escort/fire support version (called Gerfaut until 1993) with roof mounted sight, the HAC is the French anti tank version, while Germany's UHT (nee UHU) is a multirole anti tank/support helicopter (replacing the previously planned PAH-2). The U-Tiger name covers the UHT and HAC, HCP covers the HAP.

Tiger features include redundant electrical, fuel and hydraulic systems, two MTR 390 turboshafts, advanced cockpit displays and extensive use of composites.

First flight was on April 22 1993, with five development aircraft funded. Deliveries to France and Germany are planned for 2003 (HACs from 2011) and 2001 respectively. France requires about 215 Tigers, Germany 212.

Photo: The third Tiger prototype in German UHT configuration.

Eurofighter 2000

Countries of origin: Germany, Italy, Spain and the UK

Type: Advanced multirole fighter

Powerplants: Two 60.0kN (13,490lb) dry and 90.0kN (20,250lb) afterburning Eurojet EJ200 turbofans. First two development aircraft powered by two Turbo Union RB199 turbofans.

Performance: Max speed approx Mach 2.0. Time to 35,000ft up to 2min 30sec. Radius with 10min CAP over 1390km (750nm), with a 3hr CAP over 185km (100nm). Hi-lo-hi radius with external fuel tanks, three LGBs, designator and seven AAMs 1390km (750nm), lo-lo over 650km (350nm).

Weights: Empty 9999kg (22,043lb), max takeoff 21,000kg (46,297lb).

Dimensions: Wing span 10.95m (35ft 11in), length 15.96m (52ft 4in), height 5.28m (17ft 7in). Wing area 50.0m² (538.2sq ft).

Accommodation: Pilot only, or two in tandem in trainer

Armament: One 27mm Mauser cannon. 13 hardpoints can carry full range of NATO air-to-air and air-to-ground weapons.

Operators: Production contracts expected late '97 or early '98.

History: In December 1983 the air chiefs of Germany, France, Italy, Spain and the UK signed an air staff requirement for a new multirole fighter, leading to the launch of an initial feasibility study in July 1984.

In 1985 France left to develop its own, slighter smaller fighter, which resulted in the Rafale. The Eurofighter consortium was then formed in June 1986 to manage the European Fighter Aircraft (or EFA) program. Development work share was split to Germany and the UK 33% each, Italy 21% and Spain 13%. The specific concept of the EFA, a medium size (9.5 tonne) air superiority fighter with considerable air-to-ground capabilities was formalised in December 1987.

By this time BAe had flown its EAP (Experimental Aircraft Programme) technology demonstrator. The EAP was of similar overall configuration (canard delta with fly-by-wire) to the Eurofighter and the results from its five year flight test program played an important part in Eurofighter development.

In 1992 Germany's new defence minister threatened to withdraw Germany from the program unless ways were found of containing costs. Various variants of the EFA were studied, but in the end Germany decided on fewer numbers of a lower spec version of the relaunched Eurofighter EF 2000 (now just Eurofighter 2000).

Despite protracted development and controversy over its high price tag, the Eurofighter should prove to be a highly capable fighter. Features include its specifically developed EJ200 engines (developed by Rolls-Royce, MTU, Fiat Avio and ITP of Spain), ECR90 radar, an infrared search and tracking system (IRST), an advanced Defensive Aids SubSystems or DASS, (at least in British and Italian aircraft), and an advanced cockpit with helmet mounted sight and Direct Voice Input (DVI) controls (hence VTAS controls – Voice, Throttle and Stick). Future Eurofighters could feature conformal fuel tanks, thrust vectoring nozzles, electronically scanned radar and uprated engines.

The Eurofighter's first flight occurred on March 29 1994, after much delay. Britain requires 232 Eurofighters, Germany 180, Italy 121 and Spain 87. Service entry is planned for 2003.

Photo: German built Eurofighter DA5, the first with the ECR90 radar. Seven development Eurofighters are flying. (DASA)

Fairchild C-123 Provider

Country of origin: United States of America

Type: Tactical transport

Powerplants: C-123K – Two 1865kW (2500hp) Pratt & Whitney R-2800-99W Double Wasp radial piston engines driving three blade propellers and two auxiliary 12.7kN (2850lb) General Electric J85-GE-17 turbojets.

Performance: C-123K – Max speed at 10,000ft 365km/h (198kt), max cruising speed 278km/h (150kt). Takeoff run at max takeoff weight 355m (1165ft). Ferry range 5280km (2850nm), range with max payload 1665km (900nm).

Weights: C-123K – Empty 16,040kg (35,365lb), max takeoff 27,215kg (60,000lb).

Dimensions: C-123K – Wing span 33.53m (110ft 0in), length 23.93m (76ft 3in), height 10.63m (34ft 1in). Wing area 113.6m² (1223sq ft).

Accommodation: Flightcrew of two. Main cabin can accommodate up to 60 equipped troops or 50 stretcher patients and four medical attendants, or light vehicles and artillery pieces.

Armament: Usually none, although AC-123 gunship was armed with various cannons and miniguns.

Operators: El Salvador, Laos, South Korea, Thailand.

History: Widely used during the Vietnam War, the veteran Provider tactical transport still soldiers on in service, principally with Thailand and South Korea.

The Provider is unusual in that its origins lie in a glider, the Chase Aircraft XG-20. The XG-20 was an all metal design intended mainly for troop transport. One of the two prototypes was fitted with two Pratt & Whitney R-2800 Double Wasp piston radial engines as the XC-123 Avitruc to evaluate the design for assault transport.

The Avitruc flew for the first time on October 14 1949 and the type soon proved itself to the US Air Force, who, suitably impressed, ordered five pre production C-123s from Chase and 300 production C-123s (including aircraft for Saudi Arabia and Venezuela) from the Kaiser-Frazier Corporation. Kaiser-Frazier was unable to fulfil the massive order and instead Fairchild took over the contract. Fairchild refined the basic design, resulting in the C-123B Provider. Fairchild built 302 production C-123Bs between 1954 and 1958.

To improve airfield performance Fairchild fitted the Provider with two auxiliary turbojets, initially the C-123H with Fairchild J44s mounted on the wingtips. Ten C-123Hs were converted. The definitive jet augmented Provider model was the C-123K, fitted with two General Electric J85 turbojets in underwing pods. The C-123K flew for the first time on May 27 1966. In all, 183 C-123Bs were converted to jet augmented C-123K standard between 1966 and 1968.

C-123Bs and C-123Ks served widely in the Vietnam War with the US (including the AC-123 gunship) and with the Republic of South Vietnam Air Force. Several other Asian nations have operated ex USAF and RSVAF C-123Bs and C-123Ks, including Laos, the Philippines, Thailand, Taiwan and South Korea. Of those nations, Thailand, Laos and South Korea continue to operate small numbers of C-123s, while two examples survive in El Salvador.

Photo: Thailand continues to fly C-123s alongside C-47s. (Glyn Jones)

Fairchild A-10A Thunderbolt II

Country of origin: United States of America

Type: Anti armour/close air support attack aircraft

Powerplants: Two 40.3kN (9065lb) General Electric TF34-GE-100 non afterburning turbofans.

Performance: Max speed 835km/h (450kt). Max initial rate of climb 6000ft/min. Ferry range with drop tanks 3950km (2130nm), combat radius on a deep strike mission 1000km (540nm), combat radius on a close air support mission with 1hr 42min loiter 465km (250nm).

Weights: Basic empty 9770kg (21,540lb), max takeoff 22,680kg (50,000lb).

Dimensions: Wing span 17.53m (57ft 6in), length 16.26m (53ft 4in), height 4.47m (14ft 8in). Wing area 47.0m² (506.0sq ft).

Accommodation: Pilot only.

Armament: One 30mm General Electric GAU-8 Avenger seven barrel cannon mounted in the nose. 11 underwing and underfuselage hardpoints can carry a total external ordnance load of 7257kg (16,000lb), options including AGM-65 Maverick anti armour missiles, cluster bombs, laser guided bombs, conventional bombs and AIM-9s.

Operators: USA

History: Nicknamed the Warthog, the A-10 Thunderbolt II was conceived during the Vietnam War as a close support aircraft for low intensity conflicts, but grew into a dedicated anti armour platform optimised for war in western Europe.

The unsuitability of its supersonic tactical fighters in close air support roles in the Vietnam War saw the US Air Force formulate its AX specification. This called for an aircraft that could haul a heavy load of ordnance, had good endurance to loiter for long periods and could survive damage from ground fire. Originally it was envisaged that a twin turboprop design would fill the role, although the concept grew to a larger, more powerful aircraft powered by twin turbofans.

In the early 1970s designs from Northrop and Fairchild Republic were selected for a competitive fly-off, which occurred in late 1972. The A-10 (first flight April 5 1972) was selected over Northrop's YA-9, with the result that 707 production A-10A Thunderbolts were built.

The A-10's design layout was dictated by survivability. The large, low straight wing provides good agility and some shielding for the two high mounted engines. The engines themselves are separated by the fuselage so a hit to one will not necessarily damage the other, while the A-10 can fly with substantial damage to one of its twin vertical tails. The pilot is protected in a titanium armour bathtub.

The heart of the A-10's weapon system is the massive GE GAU-8 seven barrel 30mm cannon, the most powerful gun to be fitted to an aircraft in this class. This and the AGM-65 Maverick missile are the A-10's primary anti armour weapons.

Debate has surrounded the subsonic A-10's survivability in the modern battlefield, although during the Gulf War the A-10 was ideally suited to operations there where Iraqi air opposition was minimal. Over 350 remain in USAF, USAF Reserve and ANG service.

A number of A-10s have been redesignated OA-10 for the Forward Air Control role. These aircraft differ from the A-10 in designation only and carry smoke rockets and Sidewinder AAMs for self defence.

Photo: A Davis Monthan AFB, Arizona based A-10A. (Paul Merritt)

Fairchild Dornier C-26 & Metro

Country of origin: United States of America

Type: Multirole light transport

Powerplants: C-26A/B – Two 835kW (1120shp) Garrett (now AlliedSignal) TFE331-121UAR turboprops, driving four blade propellers.

Performance: C-26A/B – Max cruising speed 517km/h (280kt), economical cruising speed 467km/h (252kt). Max initial rate of climb 2370ft/min. Service ceiling 27,500ft. Range at optional MTOW 1970km (1063nm), range at standard MTOW 710km (385nm).

Weights: C-26A/B – Operating empty 4165kg (9180lb), max takeoff 6577kg (14,500lb), or optionally 7257kg (16,000lb).

Dimensions: C-26A/B – Wing span 17.37m (57ft 0in), length 18.09m (59ft 4in), height 5.08m (16ft 8in). Wing area 28.7m² (309.0sq ft).

Accommodation: Flightcrew of two. Main cabin can be configured to seat 19 passengers, or less with a VIP interior. Cabin can be configured to accept freight or stretchers.

Armament: None

Operators: Argentina, Mexico, Thailand, USA.

History: The popular Metro series of commuter airliners has found its way into military service in a variety of utility roles.

Design work on Swearingen's first complete in house design began in the late 1960s, culminating in the SA-226TC Metro's first flight on August 26 1969. The design was similar in appearance and layout to the earlier Merlins, and featured a pressurised fuselage, Garrett TPE331 turboprop engines and double slotted trailing edge flaps on the wings. It entered commercial service in 1973.

The Metro II quickly superseded the I from 1975, its improvements focusing on reducing cabin noise levels, plus changes to the flightdeck. The equivalent executive aircraft to the Metro II is the Merlin IV. Following the Metro II from 1981 was the III (by which time Fairchild had taken over Swearingen), which was certificated to a higher standard which allowed greater takeoff weights, while more efficient engines and greater wing span made the III more economical to operate. The Expediter civil freighter is based on the III.

Argentina operates three VIP equipped Merlins IVAs, and Thailand two. Sweden operated a VIP configured Merlin IVC, while a Merlin III served as the testbed for the Ericsson Erieye phased array AEW radar mounted above the aircraft's fuselage. Sweden is buying 10 Saab 340s with the Erieye radar system fitted and has sold all its Metros.

The USA is the largest military Metro customer. The first of 13 C-26As was ordered in 1988 for the US Air National Guard for use as a general transport/VIP aircraft. So far 36 C-26Bs (with TCAS, GPS and MLS) have been delivered to the Army and Air National Guard.

A single UC-26C meanwhile is fitted with an APG-66 radar (as on the F-16) and FLIR, and is used in anti drug missions. All C-26 models are based on the Metro III, but with some changes.

The current Fairchild Dornier production Metro model is the 23. It features higher takeoff weights, more powerful engines and systems improvements first introduced on the C-26. Merlin and Expediter models are also offered, while Fairchild has offered the 23 as its Multi Mission Surveillance Aircraft (MMSA) platform, fitted with a reconnaissance pod jointly developed with Lockheed Martin.

Photo: A California Air National Guard C-26A. (John Sise)

Fairchild Dornier 228

Countries of origin: Germany and India

Type: Utility transport and maritime patrol aircraft

Powerplants: 100 – Two 535kW (715shp) Garrett TPE331-5 turbo-props, driving four blade propellers. 212 – Two 560kW (776shp) TPE331-5-252Ds.

Performance: 100 – Max cruising speed 432km/h (233kt). Max initial rate of climb 2050ft/min. Service ceiling 29,600ft. Range at max cruising speed 1730km (935nm), or 1970km (1065nm) at long range cruising speed. Patrol time close to base 7hr 45min, or at 740km (400nm) from base 3hr 45min. 212 – Max cruising speed 434km/h (234kt), cruising speed 408km/h (220kt). Max initial rate of climb 1870ft. Service ceiling 28,000ft. Range with 19 passengers at max cruising speed 1037km (560nm), range with a 775kg (1710lb) payload at long range cruising speed 2445km (1320nm).

Weights: 100 – Operating empty 3235kg (7132lb), max takeoff 5700kg (12,570lb). 212 – Operating empty 3739kg (8243lb), max takeoff 6400kg (14,110lb).

Dimensions: 100 – Wing span 16.97m (55ft 7in), length 15.03m (49ft 3in), height 4.86m (15ft 9in). Wing area 32.0m² (345sq ft). 212 – Same except for length 16.56m (54ft 4in).

Accommodation: Flightcrew of two. 100 – Seating for 15. Maritime patrol configuration crew of three with a radar operator. 212 – Typical passenger seating for 19. 228-212 based 228 Cargo has a max payload of 2340kg (5159lb).

Armament: None

Operators: Germany, India, Iran, Italy, Malawi, Niger, Nigeria, Oman, Thailand.

History: The Fairchild Dornier 228 regional airliner also serves as a light military transport and in various maritime patrol configurations.

The Dornier 228 incorporates the fuselage cross section of the earlier Do 28 and 128, combined with a new supercritical wing and Garrett (now AlliedSignal) turboprops. Two fuselage length versions, the 100 and 200 were developed concurrently, the 100 offering better range, the 200 more payload. The 100 was the first to fly taking to the skies for the first time on March 28 1981, the first 200 followed on May 9 1981.

Dornier 228 developments include the 228-101 with reinforced structure and landing gear for higher weights, the corresponding 228-201 version of the -200, the 228-202 version under licence production in India with HAL (over 50 are being acquired for all three military services), and the 228-212. The -212 was the definitive Dornier production model with higher operating weights, improvements to enhance short field performance and modern avionics.

Since 1996, when Fairchild acquired Dornier, all 228 production has been undertaken by HAL (who has built the type under licence since 1991) in India.

India is by far the largest military 228 operator, with several maritime patrol configured aircraft in service with its air force and coast guard. These aircraft are fitted with a MEL Marec II search radar and linescan equipment, while the Royal Thai Navy operates 228s fitted with a Bendix 1500 radar.

Photo: Germany is one of seven military 228 operators.

FFA AS 202 Bravo

Country of origin: Switzerland

Type: Two seat basic trainer

Powerplants: AS 202/15 – One 110kW (150hp) Lycoming O-320-E2A flat four piston engine, driving a two blade fixed pitch propeller. AS 202/18A4 – One 135kW (180hp) Textron Lycoming AEIO-360-B1F fuel injected flat four driving a two blade constant speed propeller, or optionally a three blade prop.

Performance: 15 – Max cruising speed 210km/h (114kt), economical cruising speed 203km/h (110kt). Max initial rate of climb 633ft/min. Service ceiling 14,000ft. Range with max fuel and no reserves 890km (480nm). 18A4 – Max speed 240km/h (130kt), max cruising speed 226km/h (122kt), economical cruising speed 205km/h (110kt). Max initial rate of climb 800ft/min. Service ceiling 17,000ft. Range with max fuel and no reserves 1140km (615nm).

Weights: 15 – Empty equipped 630kg (1388lb), max takeoff 999kg (2202lb) for Utility, 885kg (1951lb) for Acrobatic. 18AF – Operating empty 710kg (1565lb), max takeoff 1080kg (2380lb) for Utility, 1050kg (2315lb) for Acrobatic.

Dimensions: Wing span 9.95m (31ft 12in), length 7.50m (24ft 7in), height 2.81m (9ft 3in). Wing area 13.9m² (149.2sq ft).

Accommodation: Student and instructor side by side, with room for one passenger/observer behind them.

Armament: Usually none.

Operators: Indonesia, Morocco, Oman, Uganda.

History: In service with a diverse, if small number of air arms around the world, the Bravo is a basic pilot trainer.

Design of the Bravo dates back to the late 1960s, with original design work undertaken by SIAI Marchetti of Italy as the S.202, but with production and subsequent development work the responsibility of FFA (originally established by Dornier as its Swiss subsidiary). The first prototype to fly was Swiss built, it took to the air for the first time on March 7 1969. An Italian built prototype followed soon after on May 7, while the first production standard aircraft flew on December 22 1971.

The first production model was the AS 202/15 and 34 were built through to the early 1980s. The current production model is the AS 202/18AF, which first flew in August 1974 and received certification in late 1975. This version differs from the original 15 principally in having a more powerful 135kW (180hp) engine. The AS 202/18 is operated by all the countries listed above (Iraq and Indonesia, with 48 and 40 delivered respectively, are the largest customers). A significant civil operator is the British Aerospace Flying College in Scotland which operates 11 as the Wren.

Two other models have been developed, although single examples of each have flown only. The first was the 195kW (260hp) Textron Lycoming AEIO-540 powered Bravo 26A1, which first flew in 1979. The second was the 240kW (320shp) Allison 250-B17C turbine powered Bravo 32TP which flew in 1991.

The Bravo is still offered for sale despite the fact that none have been delivered since 1989.

Photo: An AS 202/18A4 wearing Royal Air Force of Oman markings.

FMA IA-58 Pucará

Country of origin: Argentina

Type: Counter insurgency/light ground attack aircraft

Powerplants: IA-58A – Two 730kW (978shp) Turboméca Astazou XVIG turboprops, driving three blade propellers.

Performance: Max speed 500km/h (270kt), max cruising speed 480km/h (260kt), economical cruising speed 430km/h (232kt). Max initial rate of climb 3545ft/min. Service ceiling 32,800ft. Ferry range with three drop tanks 3710km (2002nm). Combat radius with a 1500kg (3307lb) warload, lo-lo-lo 225km (120nm), radius with a 1500kg (3307lb) warload, hi-lo-hi 350km (190nm). Combat radius with a 1000kg (2205lb) warload lo-lo-lo 400km (215nm), with a 1000kg (2205lb) warload hi-lo-hi 650km (350nm).

Weights: IA-58A – Empty equipped 4020kg (8862lb), max takeoff 6800kg (14,990lb).

Dimensions: IA-58A – Wing span 14.50m (47ft 7in), length 14.25m (46ft 9in), height 5.36m (17ft 7in). Wing area 30.3m^2 (326.2sq ft).

Accommodation: Pilot and observer in tandem.

Armament: IA-58A – Two 20mm Hispano HS-284 cannons and four 7.62mm Browning machine guns in the forward fuselage. One under fuselage and two underwing hardpoints can carry a total of 1500kg (3307lb) of external ordnance, including bombs and rocket pods.

Operators: Argentina, Colombia, Sri Lanka, Uruguay.

History: Made famous by its participation in the Falklands War in 1982, the Pucará was developed to meet a 1960s Argentine requirement for a counter insurgency aircraft.

Design and production responsibility fell to Argentina's government controlled Fabrica Militar de Aviones (FMA), with work culminating in the prototype's first flight on August 20 1969. This prototype was powered by two 675kW (905eshp) AiResearch TPE331 turboprops, whereas production Pucarás feature Turboméca Astazous. A second prototype, the first to be powered by Astazous, first flew in September 1970, while the first production Pucará flew in November 1974. Production deliveries did not begin until 1976.

It was also in 1976 that the Pucará had its baptism of fire against rebel guerrillas in Argentina's north west. However the Pucará is better known for its participation in the Falklands War against the British in 1982. In these actions it was less than successful, and all 24 deployed were either destroyed by ground fire or sabotaged by the SAS, or captured when Argentina was evicted from the islands. One captured example was subsequently evaluated by the RAF before it was retired to the Imperial War Museum.

The Pucará was built to be manoeuvrable, survivable and carry an effective offensive punch. However its poor showing in the Falklands meant that the type fell out of favour, and 40 of the survivors were made surplus in 1986.

Two planned Pucará variants were flown in prototype form but failed to see production. The IA-58B featured improved avionics and twin 30mm DEFA cannons, and first flew in May 1979. The single seat IA-58C had a faired over front cockpit, improved avionics and two 30mm cannons, and could carry Matra Magic AAMs and Martin Pescador ASMs. The prototype flew in December 1985.

Photo: One of 108 Pucarás built for the Argentine air force.

Fokker F27, Maritime & Troopship

Country of origin: Netherlands

Type: Tactical transport and maritime patrol aircraft

Powerplants: Maritime – Two 1770kW (2370eshp) with water methanol injection and 1505kW (2020eshp) dry Rolls-Royce Dart RDa7 Mk 536-76 turboprops, driving four blade props.

Performance: Maritime – Max speed 474km/h (256kt), cruising speed 463km/h (250kt), typical search speed range 270 to 325km/h (145 to 175kt) at 2000ft. Service ceiling 25,000ft. Max range with 30min loiter 5000km (2700nm), time on station 370km (200nm) from base 8hr, or 740km (400nm) from base 6hr, or 1205km (650nm) from base 4hr.

Weights: Maritime – Empty 12,520kg (27,600lb), max overload takeoff 21,545kg (47,500lb).

Dimensions: Maritime – Wing span 29.00m (95ft 2in), length 23.56m (77ft 4in), height 8.70m (28ft 7in). Wing area 70.0m^2 (754sq ft).

Accommodation: Maritime – Flightcrew of two. Crew complement would usually include a tactical commander/navigator, a radar operator and two observers. Troopship – Up to 46 troops, or alternatively 24 stretchers and nine medical attendants.

Armament: None, although the armed Maritime Enforcer was offered.

Operators: Algeria, Argentina, Bolivia, Finland, Ghana, Guatemala, Indonesia, Iran, Mexico, Myanmar, Pakistan, Philippines, Senegambia, Sudan, Thailand, Uruguay. Maritime – Pakistan, Spain, Thailand.

History: The Fokker F27, together with the Fairchild built F-27 and FH-227, was ordered in greater numbers than any other western built turboprop airliner, and their military derivatives serve in tactical transport and maritime patrol roles.

The Fokker F27 began life as a 1950 32 seat design study known as the P.275. A prototype first flew on November 24 1955, while a larger prototype representative of production aircraft flew in January 1957. By this stage Fokker had signed an agreement with Fairchild that would see F27s, as F-27s, built in the USA, and later the stretched FH-227.

Friendship developments included the Mk 200/F-27A with more powerful engines, the Mk 300/F-27B, the Mk 400 Combiplane and military Mk 400M Troopship tactical transport. The Troopship first flew in 1965 and features a large freight door and enlarged parachuting doors. The definitive Mk 500 airliner has a 1.50m (4ft 11in) fuselage stretch taking seating to 52, and also forms the basis for the Mk 600 quick change freight/pax aircraft.

The 400M (the Troopship name was dropped after a time) was particularly successful, and accounted for the majority of military sales with over 110 built. Other air arms acquired ex civil examples.

The most developed military variant of the ubiquitous Friendship is the maritime patrol Maritime, which provided a low cost alternative to the likes of the Atlantic and Orion. It features a Litton APS-504 search radar, bulged observation windows, a crew rest area and comprehensive navigation equipment. The armed Maritime Enforcer would also have featured sonobuoys, ESM, an infrared searcher and a MAD, although none were ordered. F27 production ceased in 1986.

Photo: A Philippines air force Fokker Maritime.

Fokker 50 & 60

Country of origin: Netherlands

Type: Multirole twin turboprop transports

Powerplants: 50 – Two 1865kW (2500shp) Pratt & Whitney Canada PW125B turboprops, driving six blade propellers. 60 Utility – Two 2050kW (2750shp) P&WC PW127Bs.

Performance: 50 – Normal cruising speed 480km/h (260kt), typical search speed 277km/h (150kt) at 2000ft. Service ceiling 25,000ft. Max radius of action with pylon tanks 3150km (1700nm). Max time on station with pylon tanks 14hr 20min. 60 Utility – Typical cruising speed 520km/h (280kt). Max operating altitude 25,000ft. Range with 50 troops 2965km (1600nm).

Weights: 50 Maritime Enforcer 2 – Operating empty 13,560kg (29,895lb), max takeoff 21,545kg (47,500lb). 60 Utility – Typical operating empty 12,500kg (27,855lb), max takeoff 21,950kg (48,390lb), or optionally 22,950kg (50,595lb).

Dimensions: 50 – Wing span 29.00m (95ft 2in), length 25.25m (82ft 10in), height 8.32m (27ft 4in). Wing area 70.0m² (753.5sq ft). Same except length 26.87m (88ft 2in).

Accommodation: 50 Utility – Seating for 40 troops. Maritime Enforcer 2 – Crew complement of two flightcrew, tactical co-ordinator, acoustic sensor operator, sensor operators and two observers. 60 Utility – Seating for up to 50 troops.

Armament: Maritime Enforcer 2 – Two fuselage and six underwing hardpoints can carry a range of armaments including mines, torpedoes, depth charges and up to four anti ship missiles such as Harpoon, Exocet, Sea Eagle or Sea Skua.

Operators: 50 – Singapore, Taiwan. 60 – Netherlands.

History: The Fokker 50 and 60 modernised developments of the basic F27 were offered in a range of military configurations.

Fokker announced development of the basic Fokker 50 airliner in November 1983. Based on the F27-500, the 50 introduced Pratt & Whitney Canada PW120 series engines with six blade props, EFIS flightdeck, small winglets, square main cabin windows and some use of composites. First flight was on December 28 1985.

In all 205 Fokker 50s were built, almost all for airlines. Nevertheless, Fokker offered numerous 50 military variants before its March 1996 financial collapse, including the unarmed Fokker 50 Maritime Mk 2 and armed Fokker 50 Maritime Enforcer Mk 2 offered with a Texas Instruments APS-134 search radar, FLIR, MAD and sonobuoys. The Enforcer can carry torpedoes, mines, and anti ship missiles such as Exocet and Harpoon. Singapore is an operator.

Other models offered included the Kingbird Mk 2 AEW variant offered with the Ericsson Erieye phased array radar mounted above the fuselage, Sentinel Mk 2 reconnaissance aircraft with either sideways looking or synthetic aperture radar and the Elint/communications Black Crow Mk 2. Finally transport versions were covered by the Utility title.

The Fokker 60 Utility (first flight November 2 1995) is a stretched version with a large cargo door whose development was launched by the Royal Netherlands Air Force. All four were delivered before Fokker ceased aircraft manufacturing.

Photo: A RNeAF Fokker 60 Utility. (Fokker)

Fokker F28 Fellowship

Country of origin: Netherlands

Type: VIP and government transport

Powerplants: Mk 3000 & 4000 – Two 44kN (9900lb) Rolls-Royce RB183-2 Spey Mk 555-15P turbofans.

Performance: Mk 3000 – Max cruising speed 843km/h (455kt), economical cruising speed 678km/h (366kt). Max cruising altitude 35,000ft. Range at high speed cruise with 65 passengers 2743km (1480nm), at long range cruise with 65 pax 3170km (1710nm). Mk 4000 – Range at high speed cruise with 85 pax 1900km (1025nm), at long range cruising speed with 85 pax 2085km (1125nm).

Weights: Mk 3000 – Operating empty 16,965kg (37,400lb), max takeoff 33,110kg (73,000lb). Mk 4000 – Operating empty 17,645kg (38,900lb), max takeoff 33,110kg (73,000lb).

Dimensions: Mk 3000 – Wing span 25.07m (82ft 3in), length 27.40m (89ft 11in), height 8.47m (27ft 10in). Wing area 79.00m² (850sq ft). Mk 4000 – Same except for length 29.61m (97ft 2in).

Accommodation: Flightcrew of two. Max passenger seating for 85 at five abreast in Mk 4000, or 65 in Mk 3000. Both marks offered with a 15-20 seat VIP interior.

Armament: None

Operators: Argentina, Colombia, Ecuador, Ghana, Indonesia, Ivory Coast, Malaysia, Netherlands, Peru, Tanzania, Togo.

History: The commercially successful F28 Fellowship was Fokker's first jet engined design. Small numbers have been acquired for military service, mainly as VIP and government transports.

Fokker began development of the F28 in 1960 after perceiving a market requirement for a jet engined and greater capacity airliner to complement its turboprop powered F27. The first of three prototypes flew for the first time on May 9 1967 and customer deliveries were made from February 24 1969.

The F28 was developed into a range of models, starting with the initial production model, the Mk 1000. The 1000 would typically seat between 55 and 65, and was powered by 44kN (9850lb) Spey Mk 555-15 turbofans. The Mk 2000 introduced a 2.21m (7ft 3in) fuselage stretch, increasing maximum seating to 79.

The longer span 5000 and 6000 were based on the 1000 and 2000 respectively, but attracted little sales interest and no 5000s and just two 6000s were built. Another version that did not come to fruition was the Mk 6600, which would have been stretched by a further 2.21m (7ft 3in), allowing for seating for 100 in a high density layout. However the F28 does form the basis for the 100 seat Tay powered Fokker 100, one of which serves in the Ivory Coast, and the smaller Fokker 70, similar in size to the F28-4000.

The final production models were the 3000 and 4000, again based on the 1000 and 2000 respectively. Both introduced a number of improvements, while the addition of two extra above wing emergency exits on the 4000 increased max seating to 85. Freight door equipped convertible versions of each model are identified by a C suffix.

Given its size and performance the F28 has been a popular choice as a VIP, Presidential and government transport, and several remain in military and quasi military service in these roles.

Photo: A Kenyan VIP Fokker 70. (Fokker)

GAF Nomad & Searchmaster

Country of origin: Australia

Type: STOL multirole light transport

Powerplants: Two 315kW (420shp) Allison 250-B17C turboprops driving three blade propellers.

Performance: N22B – Typical cruising speed 311km/h (165kt). Take-off run at max takeoff weight 225m (730ft). Max initial rate of climb 1460ft/min. Service ceiling 21,000ft. Range with standard fuel at 90% power 1350km (730nm). Searchmaster – Mission endurance at 260km/h (140kt) at 5000ft up to 8 hours.

Weights: N22B – Operating empty 2150kg (4741lb), max takeoff 3855kg (8500lb). N24A – Operating empty 2377kg (5241lb), max takeoff 4173kg (9200lb).

Dimensions: N22B – Wing span 16.52m (54ft 2in), length 12.56m (41ft 2in), height 5.52m (18ft 1.5in). Wing area 30.1m^2 (324.0sq ft). N22A – Same except length 14.36m (47ft 1in).

Accommodation: Flightcrew of one or two pilots. Seating in main cabin at two abreast for 12 (N22) or 16 (N24). Searchmaster B – Normal crew complement of one or two pilots, a tactical navigator and one or two observers.

Armament: Four underwing hardpoints can carry up to 910kg (2000lb) between them, although this capability is rarely used. Thai aircraft thought to be armed with machine guns as mini gunships.

Operators: Indonesia, Papua New Guinea, Philippines, Thailand.

History: The Nomad was developed by Australia's Government Aircraft Factory to provide the facility with work after construction of licence built Mirage III fighters was completed, and allowing it to offer a new rugged STOL utility transport suited to military and civil operators.

Developed as project N, first flight of the prototype Nomad N2 occurred on July 23 1971. A second prototype flew on December 5 that year. First deliveries of the production N22 aircraft (to the Philippines military) occurred in 1975. The N22 was followed up by the N22B with an increased max takeoff weight, this version being certificated in 1975. The military utility transport version was marketed as the Missionmaster, although most are usually just called Nomads.

The N22 also formed the basis for the Searchmaster coastal patrol aircraft. It was offered in two variants, the Searchmaster B with a nose mounted forward looking Bendix RDR 1400 search radar, and the more sophisticated Searchmaster L, with a more capable chin mounted Litton LASR (APS-504), with 360° coverage. Papua New Guinea, Indonesia and the Philippines all operate Searchmasters in the coastal patrol role.

Stretching of the N22 fuselage by 1.14m (3ft 9in) led to the N24. Aimed mainly at commuter airlines (known as the Commuterliner), this version increased passenger capacity to 16. Versions of the N24 included the Cargomaster freighter and the Medicmaster aerial ambulance. Both the Australian Army and RAAF operated N24s.

Nomad production ceased in late 1984 after 172 had been built.

By far the largest military Nomad operator was the Australian Army. However its fleet of N22Bs and N24As was permanently grounded in mid 1995 due to concerns over the type's safety and suitability.

Photo: One of the 20 ex Australian Army Nomads transferred to the Indonesian navy. (LAC Ian Hurlock, RAAF)

General Dynamics F-111 Aardvark

Country of origin: United States of America

Type: Long range strategic and tactical strike aircraft

Powerplants: F-111C – Two 82.3kN (18,500lb) with afterburning Pratt & Whitney TF30-P-103 turbofans.

Performance: F-111C – Max speed Mach 2.4 or 2550km/h (1377kt) at altitude, long range cruising speed 780km/h (420kt). Range with internal fuel over 5950km (3215nm).

Weights: F-111C – Typical empty 21,456kg (47,303lb), max takeoff 49,895kg (110,000lb).

Dimensions: F-111C – Wing span fully extended 21.33m (70ft 0in), wing span fully swept 10.35m (31ft 11in), length 22.40m (73ft 6in), height 5.22m (17ft 1in). Wing area with wings extended 51.1m^2 (550sq ft).

Accommodation: Pilot and navigator side by side.

Armament: F-111C – Weapons options include laser guided GBU-12 and GBU-10s, AGM-84 Harpoon, electro optically guided GBU-15 bombs, stand-off AGM-142 Popeye, conventional bombs, and AIM-9s.

Operators: Australia

History: Highly controversial and expensive at the time of its birth, the F-111 (officially named Aardvark at its USAF retirement in 1996) has evolved into perhaps the world's most capable strike bomber.

The F-111 was conceived in the early 1960s as the TFX, an ill-fated attempt to combine into a single aircraft the US Air Force's requirement for a new fighter-bomber and the US Navy's need for a new air defence fighter. First flight was on December 21 1964. The USN's overweight F-111B interceptor was cancelled in 1968.

The Air Force's F-111 showed considerably more promise. The F-111 was the first operational aircraft to feature swing wings and afterburning turbofans, while in a clean configuration it could cruise supersonically without afterburner. Other design features include a small internal bomb bay, a cockpit escape capsule and terrain following radar. Initially problems persisted with the complex swing wing mechanism and air inlets, but these were eventually resolved.

USAF F-111 models comprised the F-111A, the F-111E with revised air inlets, the F-111D with digital avionics (a first for a tactical fighter), the F-111F with more powerful engines and improved analog avionics, and the nuclear FB-111 strategic bomber (with longer span wings and strengthened undercarriage). In the early 1990s the FB-111s had their nuclear role removed, becoming the F-111G. The F-111F (with upgraded digital avionics and Pave Tack laser designator) was retired in July 1996, leaving just the EF-111 in USAF service.

Australia operates 22 F-111Cs which combine the engines and avionics of the F-111A with the FB-111B's heavier undercarriage and longer span wings. Four have been modified as RF-111C reconnaissance aircraft, with a similar equipment fit in the bomb bay as in the USN's F-14 TARP pod. The F-111Cs carry the Pave Tack pod and the R/F-111C fleet is undergoing a comprehensive avionics upgrade program and are unique in their ability to carry HARM and Harpoon. They are also being re-engined with 93.4kN (20,840lb) TF30-P-109s (sourced from retired USAF F-111s). An additional 15 ex USAF F-111Gs delivered from 1993 will help to extend the RAAF F-111 fleet life to 2020.

Photo: A Harpoon armed RAAF F-111C. (RAAF)

Grumman/GD EF-111 Raven

Country of origin: United States of America

Type: Electronic warfare aircraft

Powerplants: Two 82.3kN (18,500lb) with afterburning Pratt & Whitney TF30-P-3 turbofans.

Performance: Max speed 2272km/h (1226kt), max combat speed 2215km/h (1195kt), average speed in combat area 940km/h (507kt). Service ceiling 45,000ft. Combat radius 1495km (807nm). Endurance unrefuelled over 4hr.

Weights: Operating empty 25,073kg (55,275lb), max takeoff 40,347kg (88,948lb).

Dimensions: Wing span fully extended 19.20m (63ft 0in), wing span fully swept 9.74m (31ft 11in), length 23.16m (76ft 0in), height 6.10m (20ft 0in). Wing area with wings fully extended 48.8m^2 (525.0sq ft), wing area with wings swept 61.6m^2 (657.1sq ft).

Accommodation: Pilot and Electronic Warfare Officer side by side.

Armament: Usually none, although can carry two AIM-9 Sidewinders for self defence.

Operators: USA

History: The Grumman EF-111A Raven is a highly specialised electronic warfare conversion of over 40 General Dynamics F-111A strike bombers.

Grumman has considerable experience in designing, integrating and building electronic warfare aircraft, specifically the EA-6A and EA-6B Prowler variants of its Intruder for the US Navy. Thus Grumman was the logical choice as lead contractor to develop surplus F-111As as electronic warfare aircraft for the US Air Force. Development work of an EW aircraft, or Tactical Jamming System, based on the F-111 airframe began in 1972, and the US Department of Defense awarded Grumman an initial contract to build two prototypes in 1975. An aerodynamic prototype flew in late 1975, while the first production standard prototype flew in May 1977. Extensive testing ensued, and the first production conversion flew on June 26 1981. In all, the USAF took delivery of 42 EF-111 conversions.

The Raven conversion is based on the basic F-111A airframe, featuring a Tactical Jamming System based on the ALQ-99 system in the EA-6B Prowler, but with a higher degree of automation, requiring one Electronic Warfare Operator (rather than three in the Prowler).

The jamming system's antennas are housed in the System Integrated Receiver pod, the bulbous fairing on top of the fin, plus further receivers on the fin, and the two blade antennas protruding from the lower fuselage. The jamming transmitters are housed in a canoe fairing (with 10 transmitters, five exciters and six receivers) on the aircraft's underside, occupying the internal weapons bay space. A central computer processes and analyses all data received, either presenting its findings to the EWO, or carrying out automatic jamming.

The Raven's principle missions are to provide a stand-off jamming barrage to disguise incoming air raids, direct escort of strike aircraft, and battlefield jamming support. The EF-111's success in these roles in the Gulf War staved off premature retirement, although their role is due to be handed over in 1998 to joint US Navy/Air Force units flying the EA-6B Prowler.

Photo: The EF-111 is due to be retired in 1998.

Grumman S-2 Tracker

Country of origin: United States of America

Type: Maritime patrol and anti submarine patrol aircraft

Powerplants: S-2E – Two 1135kW (1525hp) Pratt & Whitney R-1820-82WA Cyclone radial piston engines driving three blade propellers. TS-2F – Two 1225kW (1645shp) AlliedSignal TPE331-15 turboprops driving five blade props.

Performance: S-2E – Max speed 425km/h (230kt), cruising speed 333km/h (180kt), patrol speed at 1500ft 240km/h (130kt). Max initial rate of climb 1390ft/min. Service ceiling 21,000ft. Ferry range 2095km (1130nm), range 1855km (1000nm). Endurance 9hr. TS-2F – Max speed 482km/h (260kt), cruising speed 467km/h (252kt). Service ceiling 24,000ft. Max range 1200km (648nm).

Weights: S-2E – Empty 8505kg (18,750lb), max takeoff 13,222kg (29,150lb). TS-2F – Empty 6278kg (13,840lb), max takeoff 13,155kg (29,000lb).

Dimensions: S-2E – Wing span 22.13m (72ft 7in), span wings folded 8.33m (27ft 4in), length 13.26m (43ft 6in), height 5.06m (16ft 7in). Wing area 46.1m^2 (496.0sq ft).

Accommodation: Normal crew complement of four comprising pilot, copilot, radar operator and MAD operator.

Armament: Internal weapons bay can hold two homing torpedoes, depth charges or mines. Six underwing pylons for bombs and rockets.

Operators: Argentina, Brazil, South Korea, Taiwan, Turkey, Uruguay.

History: The veteran S-2 Tracker still provides a number of nations with a useful maritime patrol and ASW capability.

The origins of the Tracker date back to the late 1940s when the US Navy devised a requirement to replace the hunter/killer team of Grumman TBM-3W and TBM-3S Avengers then used for anti submarine warfare. Responding to the requirement, Grumman devised its G-89, featuring a high wing, large cabin area for four crew and avionics, a search radar, extendable MAD, sonobuoys stored in the rear of each engine nacelle and an internal weapons bay. The G-89 was selected for development in June 1950, resulting in the first flight of the prototype XS2F-1 on December 4 1952. Initial production S2F Trackers entered service in February 1954. The S2F also formed the basis for the WF Tracer AEW aircraft and the TF Trader carrier onboard delivery aircraft. With the rationalisation of US designations in 1962 the S2F became the S-2, the WF the E-1 and the TF the C-1.

More than 600 Trackers were built in progressively improved variants including the S-2C with an enlarged bomb bay and the S-2D and S-2E with various equipment improvements. The S-2B was an upgrade of the S-2A, the S-2G a rebuilt S-2E. The last USN Trackers were retired from 1976.

Most surviving Trackers are S-2As and S-2Es, while Argentina and Taiwan are upgrading their aircraft with turboprops, improving performance and endurance.

A number of turboprop upgrades have flown, using either AlliedSignal TFE331s (Marsh Aviation's TFE331 program is detailed in the specs above) or Pratt & Whitney Canada PT6As. Israel's IAI offers a comprehensive S-2UP upgrade with modern systems and avionics, plus Marsh Aviation's TFE331 re-engine.

Photo: An IAI re-engined Argentine navy S-2E. (IAI)

Grumman EA-6 Prowler

Country of origin: United States of America

Type: Electronic warfare aircraft

Powerplants: EA-6B – Two 49.8kN (11,200lb) Pratt & Whitney J52-P-408 turbojets.

Performance: EA-6B – Max speed with five jammer pods 982km/h (530kt), cruising speed at optimum altitude 774km/h (418kt). Max initial rate of climb with five jammer pods 10,030ft/min. Service ceiling with five jammer pods 38,000ft. Max ferry range 3860km (2085nm), range with max external load 1770km (955nm).

Weights: EA-6B – Empty 14,320kg (31,572lb), normal takeoff from carrier in standard jammer configuration 24,705kg (54,460lb), max takeoff 29,895kg (65,000lb).

Dimensions: EA-6B – Wing span 16.15m (53ft 0in), span wings folded 7.87m (25ft 10in), length 18.24m (59ft 10in), height 4.95m (16ft 3in). Wing area 49.1m^2 (528.9sq ft).

Accommodation: Pilot and three EW officers.

Armament: EA-6B – Up to four (usually two) AGM-88A HARM anti radar missiles on four inboard (of six) underwing hardpoints.

Operators: USA

History: The Prowler is a tactical electronic warfare aircraft based on the recently retired A-6 Intruder.

The original EA-6A Intruder was developed for the US Marine Corps in the early 1960s to replace Douglas EF-10B Skynights. The EA-6A was based on the A-6A and had a crew of two. It was identifiable via its fin top bulge which housed a series of antennas, while jammers were carried in underwing pods. Of the 27 built, 15 were new build aircraft. After seeing service over Vietnam the majority of the survivors were retired in the late 1970s.

The definitive EW development of the Intruder is the EA-6B Prowler. Grumman developed the Prowler from 1966 to replace Douglas EKA-3B Skywarriors on US carrier decks. The EA-6B is based on the A-6, but with a stretched forward fuselage with a four seat cockpit for the pilot and three Electronic Warfare Officers. The other airframe mod is the bulbous fin tip antenna housing, while the jammers are carried in underwing pods. First flight was on May 25 1968, with service entry from 1971. In all, 170 were built for the USN and USMC through to 1991.

The Prowler's EW systems are collectively called the TJS (Tactical Jamming System). The TJS incorporates antennas, processing computer and the jammers, which have been progressively updated under a number of programs, with changes to software and hardware.

Update programs were: EXCAP (Expanded Capability); ICAP-1 (Improved Capability 1); ICAP-2; ICAP-2/Block 86 which gave the Prowler the ability to carry HARMs, a capability put to good use in the Gulf War; ADVCAP, or Advanced Capability; and ADVCAP/Block 91. ADVCAP aircraft feature improvements to the jamming system plus GPS, while ADVCAP Block 91 Prowlers will feature new avionics and displays.

With the pending retirement of the USAF's EF-111, the US DoD is forming five joint USN/USAF EA-6B squadrons which will be responsible for all US EW jamming missions, escorting both US Navy and US Air Force strike aircraft packages.

Photo: A Prowler of VAQ-140 over Bosnia. (Lt Craig Wevle, USN)

Grumman OV-1 Mohawk

Country of origin: United States of America

Type: Battlefield surveillance aircraft

Powerplants: OV-1D – Two 820kW (1100shp) Lycoming T53-L-15 turboprops driving three blade propellers.

Performance: OV-1D – Max speed 478km/h (258kt), max cruising speed 444km/h (240kt), economical cruising speed 334km/h (180kt). Max initial rate of climb 2350ft/min. Service ceiling 30,300ft. Takeoff distance to 50ft 268m (880ft). Ferry range with drop tanks 1980km (1068nm). Max endurance 4hr plus.

Weights: OV-1D – Empty equipped 5020kg (11,067lb), max takeoff 8722kg (19,230lb).

Dimensions: OV-1D – Wing span 14.63m (48ft 0in), length 12.50m (41ft 0in), height 3.86m (12ft 8in). Wing area 33.5m^2 (360.0sq ft).

Accommodation: Crew of two (pilot and observer) side by side.

Armament: Usually none, although guns and rocket pods have occasionally been carried on the two underwing hardpoints.

Operators: Argentina

History: The Mohawk resulted from simultaneous requirements from the US Army and US Marines for a battlefield surveillance aircraft.

The similarity of the two services' requirements – rough field STOL performance and the ability to carry a range of reconnaissance sensors – led to the creation of a joint program. The US Navy acted as program manager for the new aircraft and Grumman's G-134 design was selected for development. Nine G-134s were ordered for evaluation, and the first of these flew for the first time on April 14 1959. Initially the evaluation aircraft were designated YAO-1, but this was changed to YOV-1.

Early experience with the G-134 proved its suitability for the battlefield surveillance role, but despite this the US Marines pulled out from the program (USMC aircraft would have been designated OF-1 pre 1962). Regardless, the US Army placed contracts for what would become the OV-1A and OV-1B in 1959.

The Mohawk became the first twin turboprop powered aircraft to enter US Army service. Other notable design features include considerable crew armouring including bullet resistant glass, a mid set wing and a three tail unit (with horizontal tailplane dihedral). The side cockpit glass is bulged outwards to improve downwards visibility.

The basic OV-1A was equipped for day and night visual reconnaissance using conventional reconnaissance cameras. The OV-1B was similar except for its SLAR (side looking airborne radar) which was carried in a large pod carried under the fuselage, while it lacked optical cameras. The OV-1C was similar to the OV-1B but with an AAS-24 infrared surveillance system. The definitive OV-1D features more powerful engines, a side loading door to accept a pallet with optical (KS-80), IR (AAS-24), or SLAR (APD-7) reconnaissance sensors. Aside from new build OV-1Ds, over 110 OV-1B and OV-1C Mohawks were converted to D status. RV-1Cs and RV-1Ds were Mohawks permanently converted to electronic surveillance configuration. Other RV-1D Quick Look II aircraft were converted for Elint, while the US Army denied the existence of EV-1D Quick Look III Mohawks.

Photo: US Army Mohawks have been replaced by Raytheon Beech RC-12 Guardrails, with some of the survivors going to Argentina.

Grumman F-14A Tomcat

Country of origin: United States of America

Type: Carrier borne air defence/air superiority fighter

Powerplants: F-14A – Two 93.0kN (20,900lb) with afterburning Pratt & Whitney TF30-P-412 or -414A turbofans.

Performance: F-14A – Max speed at altitude Mach 2.4 or 2485km/h (1342kt), max speed at low level 1468km/h (792kt). Max initial rate of climb over 30,000ft/min. Service ceiling over 50,000ft. Max range with internal and external fuel 3220km (1735nm). Radius on a combat air patrol mission with six AIM-7s and four AIM-9s 1233km (665nm).

Weights: F-14A – Empty (with -414A engines) 18,190kg (40,105lb), max takeoff (with six AIM-54 Phoenix) 32,098kg (70,764lb), max overload 33,724kg (74,349lb).

Dimensions: F-14A – Wing span extended 19.54m (64ft 2in), span wings swept 11.65m (38ft 3in), length 19.10m (62ft 8in), height 4.88m (16ft 0in). Gross wing area 52.5m^2 (565.0sq ft).

Accommodation: Pilot and radar intercept officer (RIO) in tandem.

Armament: F-14A – One internal GE M61A1 Vulcan 20mm cannon. Typical intercept configuration of two AIM-54 Phoenix (the world's longest ranging air-to-air missile), two AIM-7 Sparrows and two AIM-9 Sidewinders, or combinations thereof. In ground attack configuration can carry up to 6577kg (14,500lb) of conventional bombs.

Operators: Iran, USA.

History: Arguably the most capable air defence fighter currently in service, the Tomcat emerged from the embers of the failed F-111B.

The cancellation of the overweight F-111B left the US Navy without a successor for the F-4 Phantom, which it flew primarily in the air defence role. Grumman acted as the lead contractor for the US Navy's version of General Dynamics' F-111, but had begun design studies on a new air defence fighter even before the F-111B's cancellation. One of Grumman's design concepts, the G-303, was thus selected in January 1969 to fill the gap left by the demise of the F-111B. The two crew G-303 was designed from the outset for carrier operations, although it retained many of the features of the F-111, including the powerful AWG-9 radar system and AIM-54 Phoenix compatibility, the P&W TF30 afterburning turbofans, and swing wings. Other design features included the twin tails and moveable foreplanes, or glove vanes.

The first prototype F-14 flew for the first time December 12 1970 (this aircraft subsequently crashed due to hydraulic failure), while a total of 556 production aircraft were delivered to the USN from 1972. Pre revolutionary Iran was the only Tomcat export customer, although the serviceability of the survivors of 79 delivered is questionable.

Apart from air defence and a limited ground attack capability, the Tomcat is also used for reconnaissance, carrying a Tactical Air Reconnaissance Pod System (TARPS) camera pod under the fuselage.

The F-14's TF30 turbofans proved troublesome early on, and a number of blade failures caused F-14 loses. Problems with the engines were largely overcome with the TF30-P-414A, which was adapted as standard. The re-engined F-14B and F-14D are described separately.

Photo: A US Navy F-14A of VF-213. The F-14's combination of AWG-9 radar, AIM-9, AIM-7 and AIM-54 AAMs and M61 cannon means that it can handle short to long range threats. (Dave Fraser)

Grumman F-14B & F-14D Tomcat

Country of origin: United States of America

Type: Carrier borne air defence/air superiority fighter

Powerplants: F-14D – Two 62.3kN (14,000lb) dry and 102.8kN (23,100lb) with afterburning General Electric F110-GE-400 turbofans.

Performance: F-14D – Max speed at altitude Mach 1.88 or 1997km/h (1078kt), cruising speed 764km/h (413kt). Max initial rate of climb over 30,000ft/min. Ceiling over 53,000ft. Max range with internal and external fuel approximately 2965km (1600nm). Combat radius on a CAP with four AIM-7s and four AIM-9s 1995km (1075nm).

Weights: F-14D – Empty 18,950kg (41,780lb), max takeoff 33,725kg (74,350lb).

Dimensions: F-14D – Wing span extended 19.54m (64ft 2in), span wings swept 11.65m (38ft 3in), length 19.10m (62ft 8in), height 4.88m (16ft 0in). Gross wing area 52.5m^2 (565.0sq ft).

Accommodation: Pilot and radar intercept officer (RIO) in tandem.

Armament: One GE M61A1 Vulcan 20mm cannon. Typical intercept configuration of two AIM-54 Phoenix, two AIM-7 Sparrows and two AIM-9 Sidewinders. Can carry conventional bombs. Lantirn equipped aircraft can carry various laser guided bombs.

Operators: USA

History: The Grumman F-14B and F-14D are the long planned re-engined variants of the F-14A Tomcat, although funding restrictions means they serve only in small numbers.

The TF30 turbofan has long been recognised as the F-14A's Achilles heal – not only has it suffered from a number of catastrophic blade failures, it is not considered powerful enough for the Tomcat's substantial 30 tonne plus max weight. As early as 1973 a prototype F-14 flew powered by two Pratt & Whitney F401-PW-400 turbofans as the F-14B. However this original F-14B program was cancelled due to technical and budgetary problems.

Development of a re-engined Tomcat was thus suspended until 1984 when Grumman was contracted to develop the F-14A (Plus) Interim, basically a General Electric F110-GE-400 (with extended jetpipes) powered F-14A intended as an interim aircraft until the arrival of the F-14D. The F-14A (Plus) flew for the first time in September 1986. Redesignated the F-14B, and featuring some minor avionics improvements, 38 new build F-14Bs and 32 F-14As converted to B standard were delivered from 1988.

The F-14D features two GE F110s like the F-14B, but also significant equipment changes. The primary changes are digital avionics with digital radar processing linked to the AWG-9 radar, which is redesignated APG-71, the twin IRST/TV pods under the nose, NACES ejection seats and improved radar warning receiver. Only 37 of a planned total of 127 new build F-14Ds were funded, while plans to convert the remainder of the USN's F-14A fleet to D standard were dropped due to budget cuts, with only 18 being rebuilt.

Other proposed but unfunded Tomcat variants/programs have included Quickstrike, with enhanced air-to-ground capability; the Super Tomcat-21 naval ATF alternative; Attack Super Tomcat-21 an interim A-12 replacement; and ASF-14 naval ATF alternative.

Photo: An F-14B. Tomcats are now used more widely in air-to-ground missions with the retirement of the Intruder. (Lt Lee Turner, USN)

Grumman C-2 Greyhound

Country of origin: United States of America

Type: Carrier onboard delivery aircraft

Powerplants: C-2A – Two 3665kW (4912ehp) Allison T56-A-425 turboprops, driving four blade propellers.

Performance: C-2A – Max speed 575km/h (310kt), max cruising speed 482km/h (260kt). Max initial rate of climb 2610ft/min. Service ceiling 33,500ft. Ferry range 2890km (1560nm), range with a 4535kg (10,000lb) payload over 1930km (1040nm).

Weights: C-2A – Empty 16,485kg (36,345lb), max takeoff 26,080kg (57,500lb).

Dimensions: C-2A – Wing span 24.56m (80ft 7in), span wings folded 8.94m (29ft 4in), length 17.32m (56ft 10in), height 4.84m (15ft 11in). Wing area 65.0m² (700.0sq ft).

Accommodation: Flightcrew of two. Can carry alternatively 39 passengers, or 20 stretcher patients plus medical attendants, or up to 4540kg (10,000lb) of freight.

Armament: None

Operators: USA

History: The US Navy's small fleet of Greyhounds plays a very important although unsung role in supplying the service's aircraft carriers while they are at sea.

The Greyhound is probably the last in a line of Grumman aircraft adapted for the Carrier Onboard Delivery (COD) role since WW2. Immediately after WW2 this role fell to conversions of the Avenger, while the Greyhound's immediate predecessor was the C-1 Trader, a conversion of the S-2 Tracker.

Like the COD Avengers and Traders, the Greyhound is an adaptation of an existing Grumman design, in this case the E-2 Hawkeye (described under Northrop Grumman). Unlike the earlier two aircraft, the Greyhound differs significantly from its donor airframe. The C-2 retains the Hawkeye's powerplants and wing, but features a new, much broader fuselage with an upturned tail and rear loading cargo ramp. Apart from passengers the fuselage can carry a range of cargo, including jet engines. Another change is to the tailplane, the Greyhound's unit lacks dihedral (as it does not have to contend with unusual airflows caused by the Hawkeye's radome).

Two converted Hawkeyes served as YC-2A prototypes, the first of these flew for the first time on November 18 1964. An initial batch of 17 production C-2As was built, the first of these was delivered in early 1966, the last was delivered in 1968. At that time the USN had planned to acquire a further 12 C-2s, but this order was cancelled due to budget cuts. The survivors of the 17 C-2As and two prototypes underwent a Service Life Extension Program (SLEP) from 1978.

To replace its remaining C-1 Traders and to make good C-2 attrition losses the US Navy ordered an additional 39 Greyhounds in 1982. The first of these were delivered in 1985, the last rolled off the line in 1989.

The C-2 fleet is split between three operational units while other examples are on strength with the two E-2 training units.

Photo: The Greyhound provides a vital transport link between carriers at sea and shore bases. This example is photographed at Perth in Australia. (Keith Anderson)

Gulfstream II & III, C-20 & SRA-1

Country of origin: United States of America

Type: VIP transport & reconnaissance platform (SRA-1)

Powerplants: Gulfstream II & III – Two 51.1kN (11,400lb) Rolls-Royce Spey turbofans.

Performance: GII – Max cruising speed 936km/h (505kt), economical cruising speed 796km/h (430kt). Max initial rate of climb 4350ft/min. Range with max fuel 6880km (3715nm). GIII – Max cruising speed 928km/h (501kt), economical cruising speed 818km/h (442kt). Max initial rate of climb 3800ft/min. Max operating ceiling 45,000ft. Range with eight passengers 7600km (4100nm).

Weights: GII – Operating empty 16,740kg (36,900lb), max takeoff 29,710kg (65,500lb). GIII – Empty 14,515kg (32,000lb), operating empty 17,235kg (38,000lb), max takeoff 31,615kg (69,700lb).

Dimensions: GII – Wing span 20.98m (68ft 10in), length 24.36m (79ft 11in), height 7.47m (24ft 6in). Wing area 75.2m² (809.6sq ft). GIII – Wing span 23.72m (77ft 10in), length 25.32m (83ft 1in), height 7.43m (24ft 5in). Wing area 86.8m² (41ft 4in).

Accommodation: Flightcrew of two. Main cabin seating for up to 19 in GII or 21 in GIII in a high density configuration, or eight to 12 in a typical corporate/VIP configuration. SRA-1 seats five to 10 operators depending on equipment fit.

Armament: None

Operators: Denmark, Egypt, Gabon, India, Italy, Ivory Coast, Mexico, Morocco, Saudi Arabia, USA, Venezuela.

History: The popular Gulfstream series is widely used as VIP/government transports, while a number also operate in special mission roles.

The Gulfstream II and Gulfstream III are jet powered developments of the original turboprop powered Gulfstream I. The Rolls-Royce Dart turboprop powered Grumman Gulfstream I proved to be quite successful as a large long range corporate transport, and a number have seen military service. The availability of the Rolls-Royce Spey turbofan allowed the development of a jet successor, which Grumman launched as the Gulfstream II or GII, in May 1965.

While based on the original Gulfstream I – the GII shares the same forward fuselage and cross section – there are more differences than similarities. Apart from the two Spey turbofans, the GII also has a new swept wing and T-tail. The GII's first flight was on October 2 1966.

The improved Gulfstream III followed Gulfstream American's purchase of Grumman's civil aircraft lines in 1978. The Gulfstream III first flew on December 2 1979. Changes compared with the GII include a revised wing of greater span and area with drag reducing winglets, more fuel tankage and thus range, and a 97cm (3ft 2in) fuselage stretch. Gulfstream IIBs meanwhile are GIIs retrofitted with the GIII's wing.

Production deliveries of GIIIs began in late 1980 and continued until 1986 when production ceased in preference to the Gulfstream IV.

The Gulfstream III in particular has been popular as a military VIP transport (designated C-20 in US service). Gulfstream also used the GIII as the basis of its SRA-1 (Surveillance and Reconnaissance Aircraft), which was offered in a variety of Elint, reconnaissance and maritime patrol configurations.

Photo: A Danish air force Gulfstream III. (Paul Merritt)

Gulfstream IV, C-20, SRA-4 & C-37

Country of origin: United States of America

Type: VIP & utility transport & multirole surveillance platform

Powerplants: Two 61.6kN (13,850lb) Rolls-Royce Tay Mk 611-8 turbofans.

Performance: IV – Normal cruising speed 850km/h (460kt). Max initial rate of climb 4000ft/min. Range with max payload 6730km (3633nm), range with eight pax 7820km (4220nm). IV-SP – Normal cruising speed 850km/h (460kt). Max initial rate of climb 3970ft/min. Range with max payload and reserves 6186km (3338nm), range with eight pax and reserves 7820km (4220nm). SRA-4 (maritime patrol) – Time on station 1110km (600nm) from station 6hr. Anti ship radius with two missiles, hi-lo-hi 2500km (1350nm).

Weights: IV – Empty 16,102kg (35,500lb), max takeoff 33,203kg (73,200lb). IV-SP – Same except for max takeoff 33,838kg (74,600lb).

Dimensions: Wing span 23.72m (77ft 10in), length 26.92m (88ft 4in), height 7.45m (24ft 5in). Wing area 88.3m² (950.39sq ft).

Accommodation: Flightcrew of two. Main cabin seating for between 14 and 19, plus attendant. SRA-4 – Five to 10 operators depending on configuration, or 15 stretchers plus medical attendants.

Armament: SRA-4 ASW – Two anti ship missiles on two underwing hardpoints.

Operators: Egypt, Ireland, Ivory Coast, Japan*, Netherlands, Sweden, Turkey, USA.

History: The Gulfstream IV is a significantly improved and advanced development of the earlier Spey powered Gulfstream II and III.

The most significant improvement over the earlier Gulfstream models are the Rolls-Royce Tay turbofans, which have a much lower fuel burn and dramatically lower noise emissions, despite higher thrust than the GII's and GIII's Speys. Other changes include a stretched fuselage and structurally revised wing with 30% fewer parts, greater fuel capacity (and hence range), increased span tailplane and modern EFIS displays and avionics.

Design work on the IV began in early 1983, and the first of four production prototypes made the type's first flight on September 19 1985. The improved Gulfstream IV-SP, with higher weights and improved payload range performance, replaced the IV in production.

Like earlier Gulfstreams, the GIV has been ordered for the US services. A single C-20F is in US Army use, while the USAF operates two C-20H transports. The US Navy and Marines operate C-20G Operational Support Aircraft (four and one respectively), with a convertible interior for passengers or freight, with a large freight door. Meanwhile two of Sweden's three GIVs are equipped for Elint.

Gulfstream offers the GIV for a variety of military roles, under the designation SRA-4. The SRA-4 is offered in a variety of configurations, including electronic warfare support, ASW and maritime patrol (can be armed with two anti shipping missiles), Elint and medical evacuation. Japan has ordered three maritime patrol IV-MPAs and also has utility U-4 transports in service.

The GIV forms the basis for the stretched, ultra long range BMW RR BR710 powered Gulfstream V (ff Nov 28 1995). Two (with four options) have been ordered as VIP transports for the USAF as C-37As.

Photo: A USAF C-20H. (Gulfstream)

Harbin H-5

Countries of origin: Russia and China

Type: Tactical bomber

Powerplants: Il-28 – Two 26.5kN (5950lb) Klimov VK-1A turbojets.

Performance: Il-28 – Max speed at 14,765ft 900km/h (485kt), max speed at sea level 800km/h (432kt), typical cruising speed at altitude 875km/h (472kt). Max initial rate of climb 2950ft/min. Service ceiling 40,350ft. Range at 32,810ft 2400km (1295nm), range at 3280ft 1135km (612nm).

Weights: Il-28 – Empty equipped 11,890kg (28,415lb), max takeoff 21,200kg (46,738lb).

Dimensions: Il-28 – Wing span without tip tanks 21.45m (70ft 5in), fuselage length 17.65m (57ft 11in), height 6.70m (22ft 0in). Wing area 60.8m² (654.4sq ft).

Accommodation: Crew of three – pilot under fighter style canopy, bombardier/navigator in nose and rear gunner/radio operator in tail.

Armament: Two NR-23 23mm cannons in lower forward fuselage, two NR-23 cannons in rear turret and up to 3000kg (6615lb) of bombs or two torpedoes in internal weapons bay.

Operators: H-5 – China, North Korea, Romania.

History: The Harbin H-5 is China's unlicenced copy of the Ilyushin Il-28 'Beagle' light tactical jet bomber.

Ilyushin first began design work on the Il-28 in December 1947 as a private venture. The first of three prototypes, powered by two Rolls-Royce Nenes (at the time the most powerful turbojets in the world and donated to the USSR by the UK Government during the late 1940s as 'technical aid'), flew for the first time on July 8 1948. After competitive evaluation against Tupolev's larger but similarly powered Tu-73 the Il-28 was selected for production to meet a Russian air force need for a medium sized jet bomber.

Several thousand Il-28s were built for the Soviet air force and various Warsaw Pact nations, with deliveries beginning in 1950. Over 500 were exported to China in the 1950s, while other Il-28 operators included Egypt, Indonesia, Iraq, North Korea, North Vietnam, Syria and Yemen. Small numbers were also built in Czechoslovakia as the B-228.

Il-28 variants include the basic Il-28 bomber, Il-28T torpedo bomber, reconnaissance Il-28R and the Il-28U trainer with a second cockpit in the nose (forward of the standard cockpit). Several served through to the late 1980s as target tugs and ECM platforms.

After Russia and China severed ties in the 1960s China began a program to build the Il-28 unlicenced. The Harbin Aircraft Factory was responsible for reverse engineering the Il-28 and consequently the first Chinese built 'Beagle', the H-5, first flew on September 25 1966.

H-5 production began the following year and continued into the 1980s (although late production was at a low rate primarily for attrition replacements). As many as 2000 H-5s may have been built (including HJ-5 two seaters and H-5R or HZ-5 reconnaissance platforms) for China's air force and navy. Several hundred still serve, despite their obsolescence. North Korea and Romania also operate Chinese H-5s, with the export designation B-5.

Photo: Poland was one of a number of Warsaw Pact nations to operate the Il-28. (MAP)

Hawker Hunter

Country of origin: United Kingdom

Type: Multirole fighter

Powerplant: FGA.9 – One 48.7kN (10,150lb) Rolls-Royce Avon 207 turbojet.

Performance: FGA.9 – Max speed at sea level 1150km/h (622kt), max speed at 36,000ft 1010km/h (545kt), economical cruising speed 740km/h (400kt). Max initial rate of climb 16,500ft. Time to 40,000ft 5min 30sec clean or 12min 30sec loaded. Service ceiling 50,000ft. Combat radius with two drop tanks and rockets 875km (472nm), combat radius with two 455kg/1000lb bombs and two drop tanks 352km (190nm). Max ferry range 2955km (1595nm).

Weights: FGA.9 – Empty 6610kg (14,572lb), max takeoff 11,078kg (24,422lb).

Dimensions: FGA.9 – Wing span 10.26m (33ft 8in), length 13.98m (45ft 11in), height 4.01m (13ft 2in). Wing area 32.4m² (349sq ft).

Accommodation: Pilot only, or two side by side in trainers.

Armament: Four 30mm Aden cannon in lower forward fuselage. Four underwing pylons can carry a combined total of 3355kg (7400lb) of ordnance, including rockets and bombs. Some wired for AIM-9 AAMs.

Operators: India, Lebanon, Zimbabwe.

History: Perhaps the most famous British jet fighter, the Hawker Hunter has seen four decades of frontline service and yet is still regarded as a useful ground attack platform.

The Hunter's origins lie in the Hawker P.1067 design penned by Sydney Camm to meet an RAF requirement for a replacement for the Gloster Meteor. Three P.1067 Hunter prototypes (two powered by the Rolls-Royce Avon and one by the Armstrong Siddeley Sapphire) were ordered in May 1948 for evaluation, and the first of these flew for the first time on July 20 1951.

Production Hunter F.1s were delivered from 1953, although these early aircraft suffered from a severe lack of range and engine surge when the four cannons were fired. Nevertheless, the problems with early production Hunter models were resolved in time, leaving a very capable fighter.

Early Hunter models, including the Sapphire powered F.2 and F.5, served primarily as interceptors. Most went to the RAF, although the F.4 and F.6 were the subject of some significant export orders, and were built under licence in the Netherlands and Belgium. The T.7 and T.8 were two seat side by side trainers for the RAF and RN respectively.

The definitive Hunter model, and the basis for all single seaters remaining in service, is the FGA.9, a multirole aircraft with strengthened structure and greater payload. All FGA.9s were in fact conversions of earlier aircraft, with significant operators including the RAF, India and Switzerland (whose aircraft were retired in 1994).

In 1997 Zimbabwe was the only country using the Hunter for frontline tasks, while India's Hunters are used as lead-in fighters. In the UK the Royal Navy recently retired its nine T.7 and T.8 two seaters that were with the Fleet Requirements and Direction Unit (FRADU). Chile retired its last Hunters in 1995 while Lebanon has six on strength but their status is unclear.

Photo: A Sidewinder armed Hunter FGA.9.

Hindustan Advanced Light Helicopter

Country of origin: India

Type: Troop transport/ship borne multirole helicopter

Powerplants: In first three prototypes – Two 745kW (1000shp) Turboméca TM 333-2B turboshafts, driving four blade main and tail rotors.

Performance: Max level speed 280km/h (151kt), max cruising speed 245km/h (132kt). Max initial rate of climb 1772ft/min. Service ceiling 19,680ft. Hovering ceiling in ground effect over 9840ft. Range with max fuel 800km (430nm), range with a 700kg (1543lb) payload 400km (215nm). Endurance 3hr 48min.

Weights: Army version – Empty equipped 2500kg (5511lb), max takeoff 4500kg (9920lb). Naval version – Empty equipped 2500kg (5511lb), max takeoff 5500kg (12,125lb).

Dimensions: Main rotor diameter 13.20m (43ft 4in), length overall rotors turning 15.87m (42ft 1in), fuselage length tail rotor turning 13.43m (44ft 1in), height overall tail rotor turning army version 4.98m (16ft 4in), naval version 4.91m (16ft 2in). Main rotor disc area 136.9m² (1473.0sq ft).

Accommodation: Flightcrew of two. Main cabin seating for 10 to 14, depending on configuration. Max external sling load army variant 1000kg (2205lb), naval variant 1500kg (3307lb).

Armament: Two stub wings can carry a variety of armaments, including up to four torpedoes or depth charges on naval variant, or two anti armour missiles and two rocket pods, or air-to-air missiles (land variant). Army versions can be fitted with a ventral 20mm gun pod.

Operators: India*

History: The Advanced Light Helicopter is the first indigenous helicopter of the growing Indian aircraft industry, and will be built in different versions for the Indian Army, Navy, Coast Guard and Air Force, plus civil customers.

In the early 1980s India approached Germany's MBB (now Eurocopter) to help it design and build a mid size multirole helicopter for both military and civil use. Subsequently a co-operation agreement was signed in July 1984, covering design support, development and production. Design work began in November that year, while the first flight of the first of four prototypes was on August 20 1992.

The ALH features a hingeless four blade main rotor with swept back tips and composite construction main and tail rotor blades.

The Advanced Light Helicopter will be built in two distinct military versions, one for the Indian Air Force and Army, and one for the Navy. Army and air force versions will feature skids, and will be used for a number missions including ground attack, troop transport and SAR. Naval versions will be fitted with retractable tricycle undercarriage and a folding tail boom. A civil version is also planned, powered by LHTEC CTS800s.

The Indian Government has signed a letter of intent for 300 ALHs for its military, of which 100 were covered by a firm contract signed in 1996. First deliveries are planned for 1998.

The ALH also serves as the basis for the two seat Light Attack Helicopter (LAH) design, which would feature the ALH's dynamic systems and a new fuselage. LAH development is currently unfunded.

Photo: The first prototype ALH, Z 3182. (Hindustan)

Hindustan HJT-16 Kiran

Country of origin: India

Type: Advanced trainer & light attack aircraft

Powerplant: Mk II – One 18.4kN (4130lb) HAL licence built Rolls-Royce Orpheus 701-01 turbojet.

Performance: Mk II – Max speed at sea level 704km/h (380kt), max cruising speed at 15,000ft 620km/h (335kt), economical cruising speed 417km/h (225kt). Max initial rate of climb 5250ft/min. Service ceiling 39,375ft. Range with standard fuel 615km (332nm).

Weights: Mk II – Empty equipped 2965kg (6540lb), max takeoff 4950kg (10,913lb).

Dimensions: Mk II – Wing span 10.70m (35ft 1in), length 10.25m (33ft 8in), height 3.64m (11ft 11in). Wing area 19.0m² (204.5sq ft).

Accommodation: Crew of two side by side.

Armament: Mk II – Two 7.62mm Aden guns in nose. Four underwing pylons can carry rocket pods, a single 250kg (550lb) bomb each, various practice bombs or fuel tanks.

Operators: India

History: While the last production examples were only delivered in 1989, the Hindustan Kiran (Ray of Light) was first developed in the early 1960s to replace India's sizeable fleet of two seat licence built de Havilland Vampire advanced trainers.

Design of the Kiran began at Hindustan's Bangalore facilities under the leadership of Dr V M Chatage in 1961. Dr Chatage's team came up with a design similar in some respects to the contemporary Jet Provost, as the Kiran featured a straight wing, side by side seating and a Bristol (now Rolls-Royce) Viper turbojet. The first prototype Kiran flew for the first time on September 4 1964, the second in August 1965.

A batch of 24 Kiran Mk Is was built, with the first of these delivered to the Indian Air Force from 1968. As well as the 24 pre production aircraft, 118 production Kiran Is were built, some as Kiran IAs with two underwing hardpoints for weapons training. The Kiran Mk I entered service with Indian Air Force Academy in 1973, while a small number have also been transferred to the Indian Navy.

The improved Kiran Mk II first flew on July 30 1976. Compared with the Kiran I, the Mk II introduced a more powerful Rolls-Royce Orpheus turbojet in place of the Viper, four underwing hardpoints for light ground attack/COIN work, two 7.62mm Aden guns in the forward fuselage and an improved hydraulic system.

The Mk II featured performance and payload improvements over the Kiran Mk I, but the Indian Air Force deemed it unsuitable for night flying and it had poor payload range. These findings delayed Kiran production by many years and it was not until 1983 that official development work was completed. Deliveries of the first of 61 production Kiran Mk IIs began in March 1985, with the line closing in 1989. Aside from the Indian Air Force, six Kiran Mk IIs were also delivered to the Indian Navy.

The turboprop powered Hindustan HTT-35 project to replace the Kiran (and piston powered Deepak) from the late 1990s has been suspended.

Photo: India is the only Kiran operator.

IAI Arava

Country of origin: Israel

Type: STOL utility transport

Powerplants: 201 – Two 560kW (750shp) Pratt & Whitney Canada PT6S-34 turboprops, driving three blade propellers.

Performance: 201 – Max speed 326km/h (176kt), max cruising speed 320km/h (172kt), economical cruising speed 311km/h (168kt). Max initial rate of climb 1290ft/min. Service ceiling 25,000ft. Takeoff run at MTOW 295m (960ft). Range with max payload 260km (140nm), max range with a 1585kg (3500lb) payload 1000km (540nm).

Weights: 201 – Operating empty 4000kg (8816lb), max takeoff 6804kg (15,000lb).

Dimensions: 201 – Wing span 20.96m (68ft 9in), length 13.03m (42ft 9in), height 5.21m (17ft 1in). Wing area 43.7m² (470.2sq ft).

Accommodation: Flightcrew of two. Seating for 24 passengers four abreast in 201. Configurations offered included freighter, aerial ambulance, Elint and maritime patrol.

Armament: Can be fitted with fuselage mounted 12.7mm gun pods or up to 12 rockets.

Operators: Bolivia, Cameroon, Colombia, Ecuador, El Salvador, Guatemala, Honduras, Mexico, Israel, Swaziland, Thailand, Venezuela.

History: The Arava STOL utility transport was developed to meet an Israeli requirement to replace Douglas DC-3s, but it has also proved popular with export customers in underdeveloped and rugged regions of the world.

IAI began design work on the Arava in 1966. Design objectives included STOL performance, the ability to operate from rough strips and the ability to carry 25 troops or bulky payloads. To achieve this the Arava design was of a fairly unusual configuration, featuring a barrel-like short but wide fuselage, the rear of which is hinged and swings open for easy loading and unloading; plus long span wings; twin tails (to compensate for the loss of moment arm due to the short fuselage) mounted on booms that run from the engine nacelles; and two Pratt & Whitney Canada PT6A turboprops.

The Arava first flew on November 27 1969, while a second prototype flew for the first time on May 8 1971. The initial Arava 101 was not put into production, but it formed the basis for the 101B, 102 and 201 production models. The 101B differed from the 101 in having an improved 19 seat interior and more powerful PT6A-36s. The 102 had a 20 seat passenger interior.

The 201 is the primary military version, and has sold in the most numbers. More than 70 were built, mainly for Israel and customers in Latin America. Israeli aircraft are used for a variety of roles other than transport, including maritime patrol (fitted with a search radar) and Elint. Thailand uses its Aravas for Elint/border surveillance.

The final Arava development is the 202, which is easily recognised by its large Whitcomb winglets, boundary layer fences inboard of each wingtip and slightly stretched fuselage. The winglets and boundary layer fences were offered as a kit for retrofitting to existing Aravas.

Photo: Several Latin American nations operate the Arava in transport and utility roles. (IAI)

IAI Kfir

Country of origin: Israel

Type: Multirole fighter

Powerplant: C7 – One 52.9kN (11,890lb) dry and 79.4kN (17,860lb) with afterburning IAI licence built General Electric J79-JIE turbojet.

Performance: C7 – Max speed over 2440km/h (1315kt) or Mach 2.3, max sustained speed Mach 2.0, max speed at sea level 1390km/h (750kt). Max initial rate of climb 45,930ft/min. Interception radius with two Shafrir AAMs and three drop tanks (total 3425 l/904 US gal) 775km (420nm). Radius with two 363kg/800lb and three 180kg/400lb bombs, two Shafrir AAMs and three drop tanks (total 4700 l/1241 US gal) hi-lo-hi 1185km (640nm). Ferry range with three drop tanks 2990km (1615nm).

Weights: C7 – Empty approx 7285kg (16,060lb), max takeoff 16,500kg (36,375lb).

Dimensions: C7 – Wing span 8.22m (27ft 0in), length overall 15.65m (51ft 4in), height 4.55m (14ft 11in). Wing area 34.8m² (374.6sq ft).

Accommodation: Pilot only, or two in tandem in trainer variants.

Armament: Two IAI built DEFA 30mm cannons. Five under fuselage and two underwing hardpoints can carry two AIM-9 Sidewinder, Python 3 or Shafrir 2 AAMs on outer wing stations, bombs, rockets, Shrike and Maverick ASMs, or GBU-15 laser guided bombs.

Operators: Colombia, Ecuador, Israel, Sri Lanka.

History: The Israeli developed Kfir is arguably the most potent member of the basic Dassault Mirage III/5 fighter series.

France cancelled the deliveries of paid for Mirage 5Js to Israel in 1967, leading IAI to develop and build the Nesher, an unlicensed Mirage 5 copy. After building 100 or so Neshers (some of which were subsequently sold to Argentina as the Dagger and used in the 1982 Falklands War), IAI switched to building the Kfir.

With the Kfir (Lion Cub) IAI was able to make major improvements compared with the basic Mirage, the most important of which was the use of the significantly more powerful General Electric J79 turbojet (necessitating larger intakes and dorsal airscoop, the latter for afterburner cooling), plus Israeli developed avionics (but no radar) in an extended nose. The first Kfir, a converted French built Mirage, first flew in October 1970. The first IAI built Kfir flew in September 1971.

Initial production Kfirs were delivered from April 1975, but these were soon followed by the Kfir C2, the first major production model and the first to introduce canards. Early Kfirs meanwhile were subsequently upgraded to C1 standard, fitted with small canards. Between 1985 and 1989 some were operated by the US Navy and Marines as the F-21 for aggressor training.

The C2 introduced airframe modifications to improve manoeuvrability, including larger canards, nose strakes and dogtooth wing leading edges, as well as improved avionics and a HUD. 185 C2s and two seat TC2s were built, with small numbers delivered to Ecuador and Columbia in the 1980s. Most Israeli C2s were upgraded to C7 standard during the 1980s with a modern cockpit including HOTAS controls.

Surplus Israeli Kfir C2s and C7s are now offered for export. IAI also offers the Kfir 2000 (or C10) upgrade for these aircraft, with new avionics, including the multimode radar developed for the Lavi.

Photo: An Israeli Kfir C7. (IAI)

Ilyushin Il-18, Il-20, Il-22 & Il-38

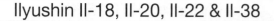

Country of origin: Russia

Type: Il-18 – VIP & general transport. Il-20 – Elint platform. Il-22 – Command Post. Il-38 – Maritime patrol and ASW aircraft

Powerplants: Il-38 – Four 3125kW (4190ehp) ZMKB Progess (Ivchenko) AI-20M turboprops, driving four blade propellers.

Performance: Il-38 – Max speed at 21,000ft 722km/h (390kt), max cruising speed at 27,000ft 610km/h (330kt), patrol speed at 2000ft 400km/h (216kt). Range with max fuel 7200km (3887nm). Patrol endurance with max fuel 12hr.

Weights: Il-38 – Empty 36,000kg (79,367lb), max takeoff 63,500kg (140,000lb).

Dimensions: Il-38 – Wing span 37.42m (122ft 9in), length overall 36.90m (129ft 10in), height 10.17m (33ft 4in). Wing area 140.0m² (1506.9sq ft).

Accommodation: Il-38 – Flightcrew of two pilots and flight engineer. Operational crew believed to be nine, which would include a tactical co-ordinator, sensor operators, MAD operator and observers.

Armament: Il-38 – Forward and aft internal weapons bays can carry homing torpedoes, sonobuoys and nuclear and conventional depth charges.

Operators: Il-18 – China, North Korea, Romania, Syria, Vietnam. Il-20 & -22 – Russia. Il-38 – India, CIS.

History: Ilyushin's Il-18 turboprop airliner played a significant role in developing the USSR's air services in the 1960s and 1970s, and has also been adopted for a variety of military roles, ranging from transport, to command post, Elint and maritime patrol.

The Il-18 was originally developed against a mid 1950s Aeroflot requirement for an economical 75 to 100 seat airliner. The Il-18 first flew on June 4 1957, and entered airline service with Aeroflot in 1959. Some 600 were built mainly for USSR and Soviet client state airlines, with a smaller number delivered for military service as VIP and general transports. Given the NATO reporting name 'Coot', a small number remain in military service.

The Il-18 airframe also serves as the basis of the Il-20 Elint/reconnaissance platform. The Il-20 ('Coot-A') was first observed in 1978 and features a variety of antennas, with a large ventral canoe presumed to contain a side looking radar. Blisters on either side of the forward fuselage are another obvious external feature.

Several Il-22 ('Coot-B') airborne command post aircraft were converted from surplus Il-18 airliners, and again feature a variety of antennas and external protuberances.

The most well known military adaptation of the Il-18 is the maritime patrol/ASW Il-38 'May'. The Il-38 is believed to have flown for the first time in 1967 and about three dozen serve with Russian naval aviation, while five were delivered to India in 1975. Details of the Il-38 are limited, but the airframe is stretched by 4m (13ft) over the Il-18 and the wings are moved forward. The tail contains a MAD, while under the forward fuselage a search radar (named 'Wet Eye' by NATO) is housed in a bulged radome. There are two internal weapons bays, one forward and one rear of the wing.

Photo: A Russian navy Il-38.

Ilyushin Il-76 & Il-78

Country of origin: Russia

Type: Strategic freighter. Il-78 – Aerial refueller

Powerplants: Four 117.7kN (26,455lb) Aviadvigatel (Soloviev) D-30KP turbofans. Il-76MF – Four 156.9kN (35,275lb) Aviadvigatel PS-90AN turbofans.

Performance: Il-76M – Max speed 850km/h (460kt), cruising speed 750 to 800km/h (405 to 432kt). Max range 6700km (3617nm), range with a 40 tonne (88,185lb) payload 5000km (2700nm). Il-76MD – Speeds same. Range with max payload 3650km (1970nm), range with 20 tonne (44,090lb) payload 7300km (3940nm). Il-76MF – Range with 40 tonne (88,185lb) payload 5200km (2805nm).

Weights: Il-76M – Max takeoff 170,000kg (374,785lb). Il-78 – Empty 98,000kg (216,050lb), max takeoff 190,000kg (418,875lb).

Dimensions: Il-76M & Il-76MF – Wing span 50.50m (165ft 8in), length 46.59m (152ft 10in), height 14.76m (48ft 5in). Wing area 300.0m² (3229.2sq ft). Il-76MF – Same except length approx 53m (174ft).

Accommodation: Il-75M & Il-76MF – Crew of seven comprising two pilots, flight engineer, navigator and radio operator, plus two freight handlers. Can carry up to 140 troops or 120 paratroops.

Armament: Il-76 – Provision for two 23mm twin barrel GSh-23L guns in the tail.

Operators: Cuba, India, Libya, North Korea, Russia, Syria, Ukraine.

History: The Ilyushin Il-76 (NATO name 'Candid') was developed as a replacement for the turboprop powered Antonov An-12 (described separately).

Il-76 development under the leadership of G V Novozhilov began in the late 1960s, resulting in the type's first flight on March 25 1971. Series production commenced in 1975.

In the now classic military freighter configuration, the Il-76 features a high mounted wing passing above the fuselage, four engines, a T-tail, rear loading ramp and freight doors. For enhanced short field performance the Il-76 features wide span triple slotted trailing edge flaps, upper surface spoilers and near full span leading edge slats, while the aircraft rides on a total of 20 low pressure tyres, the front nose unit features four wheels, the main wheel bogies having two rows of four tyres each.

Military versions developed from the basic Il-76 include the Il-76M with additional fuel and the Il-76MD with increased takeoff and payload weights and D-30KP-2s which retain their power output to higher altitudes. The stretched PS-90 powered Il-76MF first flew on August 1 1995. The A-50 AEW&C development is described under Beriev.

The Il-78 'Midas' is an air-to-air refuelling development of the Il-76, built to replace Myasischev 'Bison' tankers. The Il-78 is based on the Il-76MD and features two internal fuel tanks which can be removed, allowing the aircraft to revert to a freighter. The more developed Il-78M features three permanent tanks capable of holding up to 35 tonnes of fuel. Fuel is transferred via three hose drum units, one under each wing and one on the rear starboard fuselage, a rangefinding radar is built into the rear fuselage and the observer is located in the tail. Service entry was in 1987.

Photo: A Ukrainian air force Il-76MD transport. (Paul Merritt)

IPTN CN-235

Countries of origin: Indonesia and Spain

Type: Tactical transport and maritime patrol aircraft

Powerplants: Two 1305kW (1750shp) General Electric CT7-9C turboprops, driving four blade Hamilton Standard propellers.

Performance: CN-235 M – Max cruising speed at 15,000ft 460km/h (248kt). Max initial rate of climb 1900ft/min. Service ceiling 26,600ft. Takeoff distance to 50ft at MTOW 1290m (4235ft). Range (srs 200) with max payload 1500km (810nm), with a 3550kg (7825lb) payload 4445km (2400nm).

Weights: CN-235 M – Operating empty 8800kg (19,400lb), max takeoff 16,500kg (36,375lb).

Dimensions: CN-235 M – Wing span 25.81m (84ft 8in), length 21.40m (70ft 3in), height 8.18m (26ft 10in). Wing area 59.1m² (636.1sq ft).

Accommodation: CN-235 M – Flightcrew of two, plus typically a loadmaster. Can accommodate 48 equipped troops or 46 paratroopers. CN-235 MPA – Typical arrangement features two observer stations, two operator consoles and six passenger seats.

Armament: CN-235 MPA – Six underwing hardpoints allow the carriage of anti shipping missiles such as Exocet and Harpoon, plus two Mk 46 torpedoes.

Operators: Brunei*, Indonesia*, Malaysia*, South Korea*, UAE (Abu Dhabi).

History: CASA of Spain and Indonesia's IPTN jointly developed the CN-235 under the Airtech banner, but since 1992 both companies have developed the aircraft separately.

With initial development shared equally between the two companies, one prototype in each country was rolled out simultaneously on September 10 1983. The Spanish built prototype was the first to fly, taking to the skies for the first time on November 11 1983, while the Indonesian prototype flew for the first time on December 30 that year.

CN-235 final assembly lines are located in both Indonesia and Spain, but all other construction is not duplicated. CASA builds the centre and forward fuselage, wing centre section, inboard flaps and engine nacelles, while IPTN is responsible for the outer wings and flaps, ailerons, rear fuselage and tail.

Initial production was of the CN-235-10, subsequent and improved joint IPTN/CASA developments including the CN-235-100 and the current production -200, with more powerful engines and structural improvements respectively.

IPTN's CN-235 MPA maritime patrol aircraft is offered with a range of equipment including either a GEC-Marconi Seaspray 4000 or Texas Instruments APS-134 search radar mounted in a nose or under fuselage radome. Brunei and Indonesia are buying MPAs.

The CN-235-330 Phoenix is an improved transport which has been offered to Australia to meet a Caribou replacement requirement, with Honeywell avionics, including a MIL STD 1553B databus, INS with GPS navigation system, and the Australian developed ALR-2002 self protection electronic warfare system. It would also feature improved performance and increased weights.

Photo: An IPTN built Indonesian air force CN-235 M. (Robert Wiseman)

Kaman SH-2 Seasprite

Country of origin: United States of America

Type: Shipborne ASW, ASuW and surveillance helicopter

Powerplants: SH-2G – Two 1285kW (1723shp) General Electric T700-GE-401 turboshafts, driving four blade main and tail rotors.

Performance: SH-2G – Max speed 256km/h (138kt), normal cruising speed 222km/h (120kt). Max initial rate of climb 2500ft/min. Service ceiling 23,900ft. Hovering ceiling in ground effect 20,800ft, out of ground effect 18,000ft. Max range with two external tanks 885km (478nm). Time on station 65km (35nm) from ship with two torpedoes 1hr 30min. Max endurance with two external tanks 5hr.

Weights: SH-2G – Empty 4173kg (9200lb), MTOW 6125kg (13,500lb).

Dimensions: SH-2G – Main rotor diameter 13.41m (44ft 0in), length overall rotors turning 16.00m (52ft 6in), fuselage length 12.34m (40ft 6in), height overall rotors turning 4.62m (15ft 2in), height blades folded 4.14m (13ft 7in). Main rotor disc area 141.3m² (1521.1sq ft).

Accommodation: Crew of three, comprising pilot, copilot/tactical co-ordinator and sensor operator in US and Egyptian aircraft. Crew of two in Australian and NZ aircraft (pilot and TACCO/observer)

Armament: SH-2G – Options include one or two Mk 46 or Mk 50 torpedoes, a 7.62mm pintle mounted MG in each cabin doorway. Australian aircraft will carry Penguins, NZ aircraft AGM-65 Mavericks.

Operators: Argentina, Australia*, Egypt*, New Zealand*, USA.

History: The Seasprite was designed in response to a 1956 US Navy requirement for a long range, all weather multirole utility helicopter.

Kaman's K-20 was selected for development as the HU2K-1 (UH-2A from 1962), and it flew in prototype form on July 2 1959. The UH-2A and improved UH-2B were powered by a single General Electric T58 turboshaft, and could carry up to 11 passengers or a 1815kg (4000lb) sling load. 190 were built and used for utility transport, SAR and Vertrep. From 1968 surviving UH-2s were re-engined with two T58s.

The UH-2 was selected as the basis for an interim ASW LAMPS (Light Airborne Multi-Purpose System) helicopter in October 1970 as the SH-2D. Twenty Seasprites were converted to SH-2D standard with a Litton search radar, MAD on the starboard fuselage pylon and a removable sonobuoy launcher.

From May 1973 Kaman converted 88 Seasprites to LAMPS 2 SH-2F standard, with uprated engines, Marconi radar and towed MAD. Kaman delivered 52 new build SH-2Fs from 1981. SH-2Fs are in service with Argentina and New Zealand (pending the delivery of SH-2Gs).

The SH-2G Super Seasprite is powered by two General Electric T700s, with multi function displays and a new acoustic processor and a new tactical management system. The first YSH-2G prototype first flew on April 2 1985. Six new build SH-2Gs were delivered from 1991, alongside 18 converted from SH-2Fs. These aircraft equip two US Navy Reserve units, while similar SH-2Gs are on order with Egypt.

In 1997 the Australian and New Zealand navies selected the SH-2G to meet similar intermediate naval helicopter requirements. Australia's 11 rebuilt SH-2G(A)s will feature Litton two crew glass cockpits, Telephonics APS-143 radar, FLIR, ESM, composite rotor blades and fire the Kongsberg Penguin anti ship missile. New Zealand's four new build SH-2G(NZ)s will be similar, but fire the AGM-65 Maverick.

Photo: A USN SH-2G Super Seasprite. (Kaman)

Kamov Ka-25

Country of origin: Russia

Type: Shipborne ASW & multirole helicopter

Powerplants: Ka-25PL – Two 670kW (900shp) Glushenkov (OMKB Mars) GTD-3F turboshafts, driving two three-blade coaxial rotors.

Performance: Ka-25PL – Max speed 209km/h (113kt), normal cruising speed 193km/h (104kt). Service ceiling 11,000ft. Range with standard fuel 400km (217nm), range with external tanks 650km (350nm).

Weights: Ka-25PL – Empty 4765kg (10,505lb), max takeoff 7500kg (16,535lb).

Dimensions: Ka-25PL – Rotor diameter (each) 15.74m (51ft 8in), fuselage length 9.75m (32ft 0in), height to top of rotor head 5.37m (17ft 8in). Rotor disc area (each) 194.6m² (2095sq ft).

Accommodation: Pilot and copilot side by side. Main cabin can carry up to 12 passengers on folding seats when so equipped.

Armament: Some aircraft equipped with internal weapons bay which can contain two torpedoes or nuclear or conventional depth charges.

Operators: India, Russia, Syria, Vietnam, Yugoslavia.

History: The Kamov Ka-25 was built in large numbers for the Soviet navy and export customers as a ship based ASW and utility helicopter, but it is progressively being replaced by the Ka-32.

The Ka-25 was the end result of a 1957 Soviet navy requirement for a shipborne anti submarine warfare helicopter. In response Kamov developed the Ka-20 which flew for the first time during 1960. The Ka-20 was displayed in the 1961 Soviet Aviation Day flypast at Tushino carrying two mock air-to-surface missiles. The Ka-20 formed the basis for the production Ka-25 (NATO name 'Hormone'), 460 or so production aircraft being delivered between 1966 and 1975. In the Soviet navy the Ka-25 replaced the Mil Mi-4 as the service's primary shipborne helicopter.

The most prominent design feature of the Ka-25 is Kamov's trademark counter rotating coaxial main rotors, which do away with the need for a tail rotor, and means the tail can be kept short and thus saving space, an important consideration for naval operations. Other features include a search radar mounted beneath the nose, a downward looking electro optical sensor in the tailboom, and a MAD which can be mounted either in the fuselage or tail. The Ka-25 is usually flown unarmed, but can be fitted with an underfuselage weapons bay that can carry torpedoes and mines.

Up to 25 separate Ka-25 variants may have been built, major identified variants include the Ka-25PL 'Hormone-A', the Ka-25Ts 'Hormone-B', the Ka-25PS 'Hormone-C', and the Ka-25BShZ. The Ka-25BSh is the primary ASW variant and has largely been replaced in Russian service by the Ka-27. The Ka-25Ts was used for target acquisition and mid course guidance for ship launched missiles, with most now retired. The Ka-24PS is a dedicated search and rescue aircraft. It is stripped of all ASW equipment and can also be used for troop transport (carrying up to 12 passengers), vertrep and utility transport. Many Ka-25PSs were fitted with a searchlight and a rescue winch. The Ka-25BShZ was developed to tow minesweeping gear.

Photo: The Yugoslav navy continues to operate Ka-25s alongside Ka-28s and Mi-14s. (MAP)

Kamov Ka-27, Ka-28 & Ka-32

Country of origin: Russia

Type: ASW & multirole shipborne helicopter

Powerplants: Ka-27PL – Two 1645kW (2205shp) Klimov (Isotov) TV3-117V turboshafts driving two three-blade counter rotating coaxial main rotors.

Performance: Ka-27PL – Max speed 250km/h (135kt), max cruising speed 230km/h (124kt). Max initial rate of climb 2460ft/min. Service ceiling 16,405ft. Hovering ceiling out of ground effect 11,485ft. Ferry range with auxiliary fuel 800km (432nm). Radius of action tracking a submarine moving at up to 75km/h (40kt) at a depth of 500m (1640ft) 200km (108nm). Endurance 4hr 30min.

Weights: Ka-27PL – Basic empty 6100kg (13,338lb), operating empty 6500kg (14,330lb), max takeoff 12,600kg (27,778lb).

Dimensions: Ka-27PL – Rotor diameter (each) 15.90m (52ft 2in), length rotors folded 12.25m (40ft 2in), fuselage length 11.30m (37ft 1in), height to top of rotor head 5.40m (17ft 9in). Rotor disc area each 198.5m² (2138sq ft).

Accommodation: Ka-27PL – Normal crew complement of three, comprising pilot, tactical co-ordinator and ASW systems operator. Ka-32 – Main cabin can accommodate up to 16 passengers or freight.

Armament: Torpedoes or depth charges carried in a ventral weapons bay.

Operators: Ka-27 – Russia. Ka-28 – India, Yugoslavia.

History: The Kamov Ka-27 was developed to replace the Ka-25 in Soviet naval service, and is now the Russian navy's standard ship based ASW helicopter.

The Kamov design bureau began work on a successor for its Ka-25 in 1967, when Sergei Mikheyev became chief designer following Nikolai Kamov's death. The Soviet navy required a replacement for its Ka-25s which could not operate dunking sonar at night or in poor weather. The result was the Ka-27 (NATO name 'Helix'), an all new helicopter of similar overall dimensions to the Ka-25 and featuring Kamov's signature counter rotating coaxial main rotors. The Ka-27 flew for the first time in 1973.

The Ka-27's similar overall dimensions to the Ka-25 means it requires only the same amount of deck space to operate from as the older helicopter. However the Ka-27 features more powerful Isotov turboshafts which turn redesigned, although similar diameter rotors, giving greater performance and allowing higher weights.

The basic Ka-27PL anti submarine warfare helicopter features an under nose mounted search radar, dipping sonar and disposable sonobuoys. The Ka-27PL usually operates in 'hunter killer' teams, with one aircraft tracking the target sub, the other dropping depth charges. The Ka-28 is a downgraded export version of the Ka-27PL, while the Ka-27PS is a naval SAR helicopter with some ASW equipment deleted, an external winch and fuselage side mounted fuel tanks. The Ka-29 assault transport derivative is described separately.

The Ka-32 is the civil version of the Ka-27, and while none have been sold to military operators, some Ka-32s in Aeroflot markings have been observed operating off Russian naval vessels.

Photo: A Ka-27PL on the *Admiral Kuznetsov*. (Alex Radetski)

Kamov Ka-29 & Ka-31

Country of origin: Russia

Type: Assault transport & radar picket helicopter

Powerplants: Ka-29 – Two 1635kW (2190shp) Klimov (Isotov) TV3-117V turboshafts, driving two three-blade counter rotating coaxial main rotors.

Performance: Ka-29 – Max level speed at sea level 280km/h (151kt), cruising speed 235km/h (127kt). Max initial rate of climb 3050ft/min. Service ceiling 14,100ft. Hovering ceiling out of ground effect 12,140ft. Ferry range 740km (400nm), range with max standard fuel 460km (248nm). Combat radius with six to eight attack passes 100km (54nm).

Weights: Ka-29 – Empty 5520kg (12,170lb), max takeoff 12,600kg (27,775lb).

Dimensions: Ka-29 – Main rotor diameter (each) 15.90m (52ft 2in), length overall excluding nose probes and rotors 11.30m (37ft 1in), height to top of rotor hub 5.40m (17ft 9in). Main rotor disc area each 198.5m² (2138sq ft).

Accommodation: Crew of two. Main cabin can accommodate up to 16 combat equipped troops, or four stretcher patients and six seated patients in medevac configuration.

Armament: One 7.62mm four barrel Gatling type machine gun mounted underneath right side door. Two pylons on each stub wing can carry rocket pods, or two four-round clusters of 9M114 Shturm (AT-6 Spiral) ASMs and two rocket pods. Can carry a 30mm gun above left side stub wing.

Operators: Ka-29 – Russia. Ka-31 – India, Russia.

History: The Ka-29 development of the Ka-27 was designed specifically for use providing fire support of Russian navy amphibious landing operations.

The Ka-29 'Helix-B' was initially thought to be a non radar equipped transport version of the Ka-27, although this observation has since been proven to be untrue. The basic Ka-29 variant is the Ka-29TB attack helicopter, of which around 30 are thought to have entered Russian navy service. Service entry was in 1985.

While the Ka-29 is based on the Ka-27, there are a number of substantial changes. The Ka-29's forward fuselage is widened, with changes to the nose profile including a five piece flat windscreen and bluntened nose. Armament is carried on two stub wings with two hardpoints each, typically carrying rocket pods or air-to-surface missiles. The Ka-29 also features a small radar thought to be for missile targeting, and an electro optical sensor under the nose, thought to be a combined TV/FLIR unit.

The Ka-31 (formerly Ka-29RLD) is a radar picket development of the Ka-29 and features a large rotating E-801E Oko radar mounted beneath the fuselage. The radar folds flat against the fuselage bottom for transit flight and stowage, and extends and rotates beneath the fuselage when operated, while the undercarriage retracts upwards, so it doesn't interfere with the radar. The Ka-31 was first observed in 1988 when two were observed operating off the carrier *Admiral of the Fleet Kuznetsov* (then *Tbilsi*). Small numbers are in Russian and Indian service.

Photo: Ka-31 AEW radar picket (with radar retracted). (Alex Radetski)

Kamov Ka-50 & Ka-52

Country of origin: Russia

Type: Attack helicopter

Powerplants: Ka-50 – Two 1635kW (2190shp) Klimov TV3-117VMA turboshafts, driving two three-blade counter rotating coaxial main rotors.

Performance: Ka-50 – Max speed 310km/h (167kt). Hovering ceiling out of ground effect 13,125ft. Combat range 520km (280nm). Endurance with standard fuel 1hr 40min, endurance with auxiliary fuel 4hr.

Weights: Ka-50 – Normal takeoff 9800kg (21,605lb), max takeoff 10,800kg (23,810lb).

Dimensions: Ka-50 – Rotor diameter (each) 14.50m (47ft 7in), length overall rotors turning 16.00m (52ft 6in), height overall 4.93m (16ft 2in). Rotor disc area each 165.1m² (1777.4sq ft).

Accommodation: Pilot only in Ka-50, or crew of two in Ka-52.

Armament: One single barrel 30mm 2A42 gun on right side of the fuselage. Two hardpoints on each stub wing can carry a variety of weaponry, including up to 80 S-8 80mm rockets in four packs, or 12 Vikhr-M (AT-12) tube launched laser guided air-to-surface missiles. Other options include gun pods and AAMs.

Operators: Russia

History: The Ka-50 (or 'Hokum' in NATO parlance) is one of two attack helicopters (the other being the Mi-28) that were developed against a Russian army requirement for a new close air support helicopter.

Design work on Kamov's first helicopter for the then Soviet army began in 1977, and the first prototype Ka-50, the V.80, flew for the first time on July 27 1982. Characteristic of a Kamov helicopter, the Ka-50 features two counter rotating coaxial main rotors, which negates the need for a tail rotor and allows the construction of a simpler, more compact airframe. Unusually for an attack helicopter though, the Ka-50 is a single seater, Kamov incorporating some of the advanced autohover systems developed for its naval helicopters to reduce pilot workload. Another unique Ka-50 feature is the ejection seat – the main rotors are jettisoned before the pilot's seat is ejected. More than 35% of the Ka-50's structure by weight is of composites.

The Ka-50 was reportedly selected in preference to the Mil Mi-28 in 1986, although in early 1994 new competitive evaluation trials between the two types began. Both are in low rate low rate series production. Kamov is also developing the FLIR and NVG cockpit compatible Ka-50N.

The Russian army, concerned with the heavy workload imposed on the pilot of the Ka-50, sanctioned the development of a two seater with all weather, day and night capability, the Ka-52. The Ka-52 is unique among dedicated attack helicopters in that it seats two side by side. Approximately 85% of the airframe remains unchanged from the Ka-50. First flight was on June 25 1997.

Kamov is actively marketing the Ka-50 as the Black Shark and the Ka-52 as the Alligator on the world market and they may yet find their ways into service with Middle Eastern or African nations attracted to its relatively low purchase price.

Photo: Kamov markets the Ka-50 as the Black Shark (the Werewolf marketing name was dropped in 1996). (Bruce Malcolm)

Kawasaki C-1

Country of origin: Japan

Type: Tactical transport

Powerplants: Two 64.5kN (14,500lb) Pratt & Whitney JT8D-M-9 turbofans, licence built in Japan by Mitsubishi.

Performance: Max speed 805km/h (435kt), max cruising speed 704km/h (380kt), economical cruising speed 658km/h (355kt). Max initial rate of climb 3495ft/min. Takeoff run at MTOW 640m (2100ft). Range with max fuel and a 2200kg (4500lb) payload 3355km (1810nm), range with a 7900kg (17,415lb) payload 1295km (700nm).

Weights: Empty equipped 24,300kg (53,570lb), max takeoff 45,000kg (99,205lb).

Dimensions: Wing span 30.60m (100ft 5in), length 29.00m (95ft 2in), height 9.99m (32ft 9in). Wing area 120.5m² (1297.1sq ft).

Accommodation: Flightcrew of four, comprising two pilots, flight engineer and navigator. Can carry up to 60 equipped troops, or 45 paratroops or 36 stretchers plus medical attendants.

Armament: None

Operators: Japan

History: Japan's first large jet powered transport was developed specifically for the Japan Air Self Defence Force (JASDF) to replace an ageing fleet of Curtiss C-46 Commandos.

The JASDF formulated its C-X specification for a Japanese developed tactical transport for its C-46 replacement requirement. NAMC, a consortium of Japanese aerospace companies which had developed the YS-11 turboprop powered airliner, began work on the C-X in 1966. Kawasaki was responsible for the construction of the first three prototype XC-1 aircraft (one was a static test article) and the first of these flew for the first time on November 12 1970.

Kawasaki subsequently assumed overall responsibility for the C-1, although production remained a collaborative venture. Fuji built the outer wings, Mitsubishi the centre and rear fuselage and tail, Nihon the control surfaces and engine pods. Kawasaki built the forward fuselage and the wing centre section, as well as being responsible for final assembly and flight testing.

Just 31 C-1s were built, including prototypes and two preproduction aircraft. The first C-1 production delivery to the JASDF was in February 1974, while the last production aircraft was delivered in 1981.

The C-1 is of conventional military freighter configuration, with a T-tail, rear loading freight ramp and a high wing that does not obstruct the fuselage. Power is supplied by Mitsubishi licence built JT8D turbofans. The last five production C-1s had an additional fuel tank in the wing centre section.

The C-1 was not developed beyond its basic form and no export sales were sought. Two notable C-1 conversions though are the C-1Kai and the Asuka STOL research platform. The C-1Kai is an one-off ECM trainer and features flat bulbous nose and tail radomes, plus various antennas underneath the fuselage. The Asuka was fitted with four above wing turbofans and blown flaps.

Photo: The Japan Air Self Defence Force's sole C-1Kai ECM trainer.

Kawasaki T-4

Country of origin: Japan

Type: Two seat advanced jet trainer

Powerplants: Two 16.4kN (3680lb) Ishikawajima-Harima F3-IHI-30 turbofans.

Performance: Max speed at altitude 1038km/h (560kt), max speed at sea level 1038km/h (560kt), cruising speed 797km/h (430kt). Max initial rate of climb 10,240ft/min. Service ceiling 50,000ft. Ferry range with drop tanks 1667km (900nm), range with standard fuel 1295km (700nm).

Weights: Empty 3790kg (8356lb), max takeoff 7500kg (16,535lb).

Dimensions: Wing span 9.94m (32ft 8in), length 13.00m (42ft 8in), height 4.60m (15ft 1in). Wing area 21.0m² (226.1sq ft).

Accommodation: Student and instructor in tandem.

Armament: Usually none, although theoretically can carry up to 2000kg (4410lb) of external ordnance. Two underwing pylons designed to carry fuel tanks.

Operators: Japan

History: Very similar in overall configuration to the Alpha Jet, The T-4 is Japan's new intermediate and advanced pilot trainer, and has replaced the Fuji T-1 and Lockheed T-33 in service.

With Japan looking increasingly to its own industry to meet its requirements for military aircraft, Kawasaki headed up a design team of various Japanese aerospace companies to develop a new advanced trainer from the early 1980s. Kawasaki was selected as the prime contractor to develop the new trainer in September 1981. The T-4 was designed by a team led by Kohki Isozaki. Four XT-4 prototypes were built, and the first of these first flew on July 29 1985.

The T-4 features as much Japanese content as possible, including the engines, locally designed and built Ishikawajima-Harima turbofans. Other design features are the high mounted wing with dogtooth leading edges and a single hardpoint each for drop tanks, stepped tandem cockpits with excellent visibility from the rear seats, Japanese ejection seats and a small rear baggage compartment for liaison duties. A centreline hardpoint beneath the fuselage can carry a target towing winch, an air sampling pod or an ECM pod, reflecting the T-4's secondary utility roles.

Construction of the T-4 is a collaborative venture. Fuji constructs the rear fuselage, wings and tail unit, while Mitsubishi builds the centre fuselage including the air intakes. Fuji and Mitsubishi each have a 30% share of the T-4 construction program. Kawasaki builds the forward fuselage, as well as being responsible for final assembly and flight testing.

The Japanese Air Self Defence Force has a requirement for 200 T-4s to replace ageing Fuji T-1s and Lockheed T-33s. Of those 180 had been funded in 1997. Construction of production T-4s began in 1986 while production deliveries began in late 1988 (over 160 are in service). Aside from training units, a small number serve with operational squadrons as liaison/hack aircraft, and a small number of these wear camouflage. A developed version may be procured to replace the T-2.

Photo: This Kawasaki T-4 wears colours of the JASDF's Blue Impulse aerobatic display team. (Doug Mackay)

LAASA (FMA) IA-63 Pampa

Country of origin: Argentina

Type: Trainer and light ground attack aircraft

Powerplant: One 15.6kN (3500lb) Garrett TFE731-2-2N turbofan.

Performance: Max speed 750km/h (405kt). Max initial rate of climb 5120ft/min. Service ceiling 42,325ft. Air-to-air gunnery training mission radius with 250kg (550lb) of external ordnance 440km (237nm). Air-to-ground combat radius with 1000kg (2205lb) external load 360km (195nm). Ferry range with max internal and external fuel 1000km (1850nm). Max endurance at 555km/h (300kt) 3hr 48min.

Weights: Empty 2820kg (6220lb), max takeoff 5000kg (11,025lb).

Dimensions: Wing span 9.69m (32ft 10in), length 10.90m (35ft 10in), height 4.29m (14ft 1in). Wing area 15.6m² (168.3sq ft).

Accommodation: Student and instructor in tandem.

Armament: Four underwing and one underfuselage hardpoint can carry a combined ordnance load of 1550kg (3415lb), including 30mm DEFA cannon pod on the centreline station, and light bombs.

Operators: Argentina

History: Developed against an Argentine air force requirement for a modern armed trainer, the IA-63 Pampa is South America's only indigenous jet powered military aircraft program.

FMA (Fabrica Militar de Aviones) began development work on what would result in the Pampa in 1979, against the Argentine air force's requirement to replace its ageing Morane-Saulnier MS.760 four place jets. To design the new trainer FMA teamed with Dornier of Germany, who had gained considerable experience in developing and building jet trainers through its co-development of the Alpha Jet with Dassault. The FMA/Dornier teaming came up with seven joint designs, the selected one resembling the Alpha Jet in configuration.

Like the Alpha Jet, the IA-63 Pampa features a high wing, stepped tandem cockpits and side mounted air intakes. The Pampa differs in having a single turbofan (a Garrett, now AlliedSignal TFE731) and unswept wing and tailplane. Dornier's technical assistance also including construction of the wings and tailplanes for the first three flying prototypes and two static test airframes. The first prototype (EX-01) took to the air for the first time on October 6 1984, while the first production aircraft's first flight was in October 1987.

The Argentine air force placed firm orders for 18 Pampas, the first of which was delivered in April 1988. Delivery of those is complete, while a follow-on order for 46 is anticipated. Aside from training, the Pampas have a secondary ground attack role. They are equipped with five hardpoints and are being fitted with a HUD and an Elbit developed Weapon Delivery and Navigation System.

Development of a navalised Pampa capable of operating off the Argentine aircraft carrier *25 de Mayo* has lapsed due to a lack of funding, although Argentina's navy expressed an interest in unmodified Pampas.

The Pampa remains available for export, despite being eliminated from the USAF/USN JPATS trainer competition.

Since 1995 FMA has been under Lockheed Aircraft Argentina SA (LAASA) control.

Photo: The first Pampa prototype at Farnborough. (Jim Thorn)

Learjet 35, 36 & C-21

Country of origin: United States of America

Type: Multirole utility and VIP transport

Powerplants: Two 15.6kN (3500lb) Garrett TFE731-2-2B turbofans.

Performance: 35A/36A – Max speed 872km/h (471kt), max cruising speed 852km/h (460kt), econ cruising speed 774km/h (418kt). Max initial rate of climb 4350ft/min. Service ceiling 41,000ft. Range with four passengers and max fuel 4070km (2195nm) for 35A; 4673km (2522nm) for 36A.

Weights: 35A/36A – Empty equipped 4590kg (10,119lb), max take-off 8300kg (18,300lb).

Dimensions: 35/36 – Span over tip tanks 12.04m (39ft 6in), length 14.83m (48ft 8in), height 3.73m (12ft 3in). Wing area 23.5m^2 (253.3sq ft).

Accommodation: Flightcrew of two. Seating for up to eight in main cabin in 35 and 31, or up to six in 36A. Can carry light freight.

Armament: None

Operators: Argentina, Bolivia, Brazil, Chile, Ecuador, Finland, Japan, Mexico, Peru, Saudi Arabia, Switzerland, Thailand, USA, Venezuela.

History: The Learjet series is one of the world's best known family of business jets, and serves widely with a number of military air arms as utility and VIP transports.

The original six to eight seat turbojet powered Learjet 23 first flew on October 7 1963. It was replaced by the Lear 24 in 1966, while the Learjet 25 introduced a 1.27m (4ft 2in) fuselage stretch allowing seating for up to eight passengers. The Learjet 28 and 29 Longhorns were based on the 25 but introduced a new increased span wing with drag reducing winglets.

The Learjet 35 and 36 are larger, turbofan powered developments of the initial Learjet models. The availability of the Garrett AiResearch TFE731 turbofan in the late 1960s led to the development of the stretched Learjet 35, which first flew on August 22 1973. The Learjet 36 is similar, but sacrifices seating capacity for range. The improved 35A and 36A appeared in 1976.

Further development of the 35 and 36 resulted in the 31 which combines the 35/36's fuselage and powerplants with the wing of the Learjet 55. It has replaced the 35/36 in production.

A small number of Lear 24s and 25s survive in military service, although most military Lears are 35s and 36s. Around 200 are used for a variety of missions ranging from VIP transport, to photo survey and reconnaissance, light freight, staff transport, medevac, target towing and EW training.

The US Air Force and Air National Guard have taken delivery of a total of 85 Learjet 35As as the C-21. These are used as Operational Support Aircraft transporting priority freight and for medevac and staff transport.

Learjet also marketed a range of military developments of the 35 and 36. The PC-35A maritime patrol aircraft is offered with a search radar, ESM, FLIR, MAD and sonobuoys; the RC-35A and RC-36A are reconnaissance platforms offered with a variety of sensors; while the UC-35A is a utility transport. Japan operates four modified U-36As for target towing, EW training and anti ship missile simulation.

Photo: A USAF C-21A. (Bill Lines)

Let L 410 Turbolet

Country of origin: Czech Republic

Type: Light tactical & utility transport

Powerplants: 410 UVP-E – Two 560kW (751shp) Motorlet M 601 E turboprops, driving five blade propellers.

Performance: 410 UVP-E – Max cruising speed 380km/h (205kt), economical cruising speed 365km/h (197kt). Max initial rate of climb 1420ft/min. Service ceiling 19,700ft. Takeoff run at max takeoff weight 445m (1460ft). Range with max fuel (including wingtip tanks), a 920kg (2030lb) payload and reserves 1318km (707nm).

Weights: 410 UVP-E – Empty (without tip tanks) 4020kg (8662lb), max takeoff 6400kg (14,109lb).

Dimensions: 410 UVP-E – Wing span (with tip tanks) 19.98m (65ft 7in), length 14.42m (47ft 4in), height 5.83m (19ft 2in). Wing area 34.9m^2 (375.2sq ft).

Accommodation: Flightcrew of one or two. Standard seating for 15 at three abreast. Alternatively seats 12 paratroops and loadmaster. Can be configured for freight. Air ambulance version configured for six stretcher patients and six seated passengers, either injured or medical attendants.

Armament: None

Operators: Bulgaria, Czech Republic, Germany, Latvia, Libya, Lithuania, Russia, Slovakia, Slovenia.

History: This very successful Czech commuter was first built in response to an Aeroflot requirement for a commuter airliner, but has also seen military service with a number of Eastern European countries.

Initial design studies of the original 15 seat L 410 began in 1966. The resulting design, named the Turbolet, was conventional, but was designed with operations from unprepared strips in mind. The powerplant chosen was the all new Czech designed Walter (now Motorlet) M 601, but this engine was not developed enough to power the prototypes and so Pratt & Whitney Canada PT6A-27s were fitted in their place. First flight occurred on April 16 1969 and series production began in 1970. Initial production L 410s were also powered by the PT6A and it was not until 1973 that production aircraft featured the M 601, these being known as L 410Ms.

The L 410 was first superseded from 1979 by the L 410 UVP with a 0.47m (1ft 7in) fuselage stretch, M 601B engines and detail refinements. The UVP was in turn replaced by the UVP-E which featured a reconfigured interior to allow seating for up to 19 passengers and M 601E powerplants. The UVP-E is the current production version.

The L 410 proved to be quite popular as a commuter, and over 1000 have been built. While most of those aircraft were delivered to Aeroflot and various east European state owned airlines, others were delivered for military use as utility transports. Military duties include freight and troop transport, liaison and communications, and para-dropping.

The L 420 is an improved civil variant with more powerful M 601F engines, higher weights and improved performance, designed to meet western certification requirements. It first flew in November 1993.

Photo: A Czech Republic air force L 410. (Paul Merritt)

Lockheed T-33 Shooting Star

Country of origin: United States of America

Type: Advanced trainer, light attack, liaison aircraft & EW trainer

Powerplant: T-33A – One 24.0kN (5400lb) Allison J33-A-35 turbojet.

Performance: T-33A – Max speed 965km/h (520kt), cruising speed 732km/h (395kt). Max initial rate of climb 4870ft/min. Service ceiling 48,000ft. Ferry range with tip tanks 2050km (1105nm), range with internal fuel 1650km (890nm).

Weights: T-33A – Empty equipped 3795kg (8365lb), max takeoff 6830kg (15,060lb).

Dimensions: T-33A – Wing span 11.85m (38ft 11in), length 11.51m (37ft 9in), height 3.55m (11ft 8in). Wing area 21.8m² (234.0sq ft).

Accommodation: Two in tandem. Pilot only in RT-33.

Armament: Can be fitted with two 12.7mm (0.50in) M-3 machine guns mounted in the nose. Can carry up to 910kg (2000lb) of external armament including bombs or rockets.

Operators: Bolivia, Canada, Greece, Japan, Mexico, Pakistan, South Korea, Thailand, Turkey, Uruguay.

History: The T-33 is the most successful jet trainer in history, with more than 6000 built. More remarkable than that, significant numbers survive in service in the late 1990s, more than half a century after its first flight.

The T-33 is a development of the F-80 Shooting Star, the USAAF's first operational jet fighter. The T-33 arose from a USAF requirement for an advanced two seat jet trainer, which Lockheed was easily able to meet by stretching the F-80 and adding a second seat under a lengthened canopy. The first prototype, designated TF-80C, first flew on March 22 1948.

Subsequent Lockheed T-33 production between 1948 and 1959 amounted to 5771 aircraft. The largest T-33, or T-bird, operator was the USAF, while just under 700 modified examples were delivered to the US Navy as TV-2 SeaStars (or T-33B from 1962). Several thousand T-birds were built under the auspices of the USA's MAP (Military Assistance Program) and were delivered to friendly nations around the world.

Lockheed built variants of the T-33 included the AT-33, an armed close air support T-bird delivered to various nations under MAP, and the RT-33, a single seat variant with various reconnaissance sensors in the nose. Limited numbers of AT-33s remain in service, while Thailand and Pakistan still operate RT-33s.

Aside from Lockheed the T-33 was also built under licence in Japan by Kawasaki (210 built) and in Canada. Canadair built 656 Rolls-Royce Nene powered CL-30 Silver Stars, designated CT-133 in Canadian Forces service. Around 60 CT-133s survive in CF service, used as EW aggressors, or for various test duties. Japan meanwhile remains the largest T-33 operator, with about 100 aircraft used for training, as hacks and for various liaison tasks.

The Skyfox was a substantially reworked and modernised development of the T-33 with two Garrett TFE731 turbofans designed by Skyfox in the USA. A demonstrator flew in 1983, although no customers were found.

Photo: A Canadian CT-133. The basic P-80/T-33 family has been in military service longer than any other jet aircraft. (Paul Merritt)

Lockheed U-2

Country of origin: United States of America

Type: High altitude electronic and optical reconnaissance aircraft

Powerplant: U-2R – One 75.6kN (17,000lb) Pratt & Whitney J75-P-13B turbojet.

Performance: U-2R – Max cruising speed at 70,000ft over 690km/h (373kt). Max initial rate of climb 5000ft/min. Time to 65,000ft 35min. Operational ceiling 90,000ft. Max range over 4830km (2605nm). Max endurance 12hr.

Weights: U-2R – Empty weight without powerplant and underwing pods under 4355kg (10,000lb), operating empty approx 7030kg (15,500lb), max takeoff 18,735kg (41,300lb).

Dimensions: U-2R – Wing span 31.39m (103ft 0in), length 19.13m (62ft 9in), height 4.88m (16ft 0in). Wing area approx 92.9m² (1000sq ft).

Accommodation: Pilot only, except two in tandem in U-2RT.

Armament: None

Operators: USA

History: Perhaps the most famous spyplane in history, the U-2 remains an important part of the US' intelligence gathering capabilities.

In the early 1950s USAF reconnaissance of the USSR was performed by modified B-36 and B-47 bombers, however these aircraft were increasingly successfully intercepted by MiG-15s. Thus in 1954 the US initiated development of a purpose built spyplane which could fly at extreme altitude where it would be hopefully immune to interception. Development was entrusted to Lockheed's Skunk Works, the nature of the black program being responsible for the U-2 designation (U for utility) to hide the aircraft's true role.

The U-2 first flew in August 1955. Subsequent production comprised 48 U-2A/B/C single seaters and five two seat U-2Ds. These aircraft had outstanding high altitude performance and good endurance despite payload restrictions and they were successfully used by the USAF and CIA for a number of years. One such CIA operated aircraft, piloted by Gary Powers, gained infamy when it was shot down by a SAM while operating over the USSR in April 1960.

The early U-2s were airframe hour limited, so Lockheed developed the larger U-2R. The U-2R first flew on August 28 1967 and 12 initial production aircraft were operated by the USAF and the CIA. The U-2R features a larger airframe than earlier models, allowing the carriage of more sensors and fuel. Two seaters are designated U-2RT.

The U-2 line was reopened again in 1979, this time to build 37 new TR-1As (including two TR-1Bs and a U-2RT – both two seaters). The TR-1 was designed for tactical reconnaissance (hence the TR prefix), and combined the U-2R's airframe with the ASARS-2 battlefield surveillance radar. The TR-1s have since been redesignated U-2Rs in recognition of the fact that the two aircraft are basically identical. NASA operates three similar ER-2s.

U-2R sensors are carried in detachable noses, in the forward fuselage and in underwing pods, while some aircraft carry Senior Span satellite communications equipment for real time global data transmission in a teardrop shaped dorsal mounted pod.

From 1992 Lockheed has been re-engining the surviving U-2R fleet with a more powerful yet more efficient GE F101 turbofan.

Photo: U-2Rs are operated from Beale AFB in California. (Paul Merritt)

Lockheed C-130 Hercules

Country of origin: United States of America

Type: Tactical and multirole transport

Powerplants: C-130E – Four 3020kW (4050shp) Allison T56-A-17 turboprops, driving four blade propellers.

Performance: C-130E – Max cruising speed 592km/h (320kt), economical cruising speed 547km/h (295kt). Max initial rate of climb 1830ft/min. Service ceiling 23,000ft. Takeoff run over a 15m (50ft) obstacle 1700m (5580ft). Range with max fuel with a 9080kg (20,000lb) payload 7565km (4085nm), range with max payload 3895km (2105nm).

Weights: C-130E – Operating empty 33,064kg (72,892lb), max normal TOW 70,310kg (155,000lb), max overload TOW 79,380kg (175,000lb).

Dimensions: C-130E/H – Wing span 40.41m (132ft 7in), length 29.79m (97ft 9in), height 11.66m (38ft 3in). Wing area 162.1m² (1745.0sq ft).

Accommodation: Typical crew of five comprising two pilots, flight engineer, navigator and loadmaster. Standard layouts seat 92 troops, or 64 paratroops, or 74 stretcher patients and two medical attendants. Can carry light armoured vehicles, artillery pieces and 4WDs.

Armament: None, except on AC-130, described separately.

Operators: In service with over 60 countries including Algeria, Argentina, Australia, Brazil, Canada, Egypt, Indonesia, Israel, Japan, Morocco, Pakistan, Saudi Arabia, Taiwan, Thailand, Turkey, UK, USA.

History: With over 2200 built over four decades, the C-130 Hercules is the world's most successful and prolific postwar military transport.

The Hercules was developed against a 1951 US Air Force requirement for a new tactical transport to equip the Military Air Transport Service (MATS). The USAF ordered two YC-130 prototypes from Lockheed in July 1951 and the first of these flew for the first time on August 23 1954. The first production C-130A flew in April 1955.

The Hercules established the basic military transport configuration, with a high wing with minimal obstruction of the fuselage and a rear loading freight ramp. Other features included Allison T56 turboprops, pressurisation and limited STOL performance. Apart from the blunt, radar-less nose of early production C-130As, the Hercules' external configuration has remained largely unchanged.

The improved C-130B entered service in mid 1959. Compared with the C-130A, the B introduced more powerful engines driving four blade props, strengthened undercarriage and greater fuel capacity. In 1961 production switched to the C-130E with more powerful engines with greater hot and high performance, increased max takeoff weight, some structural strengthening and larger external fuel tanks, mounted between the engines (rather than outboard of them). Most of the USAF's fleet of 400 plus Hercules are C-130Es.

The C-130H was first introduced in 1965. Early C-130Hs featured more powerful engines, while changes introduced to the H over the following two decades included structural strengthening and updated avionics. The C-130H-30 is stretched by 4.57m (15ft), but is otherwise similar to the C-130H. C-130H production ceased in late 1996, with 690 built. Civil Hercules are designated L-100 and have been built in standard length L-100, stretched L-100-20 and further stretched L-100-30 (equivalent to the C-130H-30) versions.

Photo: A RAAF C-130H Hercules. (LACW Tracie Whiteside, RAAF)

Lockheed Martin C-130J Hercules II

Country of origin: United States of America

Type: Tactical & multirole transport

Powerplants: Four 3425kW (4590shp) Allison AE 2100D3 turboprops rated at 3693kW (4591shp), driving six blade propellers.

Performance: Max cruising speed 645km/h (348kt), economical cruising speed 628km/h (339kt). Max initial rate of climb 2100ft/min. Time to 20,000ft 14min. Max effort takeoff run 550m (1800ft), normal takeoff run 930m (3050ft). Range with a 18,155kg (40,000lb) payload 5250km (2835nm).

Weights: C-130J – Operating empty 32,615kg (71,902lb), max takeoff 70,305kg (155,000lb), max overload 79,380kg (175,000lb).

Dimensions: Wing span 40.41m (132ft 7in), length 29.79m (97ft 9in), height 11.84m (38ft 10in). Wing area 162.1m² (1745.0sq ft). C-130J-30 – Same except length 34.37m (112ft 9in), height 11.81m (38ft 9in).

Accommodation: Flightcrew of two pilots, provision for flight engineer if required. C-130J can seat 92 troops, or 64 paratroops, or 74 stretcher patients and two medical attendants.

Armament: None

Operators: Australia*, Italy*, UK*, USA*.

History: The C-130J Hercules II is the most comprehensive update of the C-130 yet, with changes to the cockpit, engines and systems.

Development of the private venture C-130J began primarily to offer the US Air Force a replacement for its ageing fleet of C-130E Hercules. The USAF was unprepared to fund the development of a new Hercules variant and so began procuring new build C-130Hs instead. This spurred Lockheed Martin to developing an improved C-130 as a private venture, aimed at both USAF and international requirements.

The C-130J and stretched C-130J-30 airframes differ little from their predecessor C-130H and C-130H-30 donors. The J features composite flaps and leading edge surfaces, and the external fuel tanks are deleted (although they can be added to extend range), but the airframe is otherwise unchanged. The engines though are new generation Allison AE 2100 turboprops, a development of the T406 turboshaft which powers the V-22 Osprey, and drive six blade, swept Dowty propellers. The J can be optionally fitted with a refuelling probe and underwing air-to-air refuelling pods.

Big changes inside the Hercules II include simplified wiring and systems and the new two crew flightdeck. The flightdeck features two HUDs, four large multifunction displays, five monochrome displays and fighter style controls on the control columns.

The first C-130J (a RAF C-130J-30/C.4) first flew after some delays on April 5 1996. Unexpected problems with stall characteristics has delayed first customer deliveries by over a year out to February 1998.

At late 1997 customers comprised the UK (12 C-130J-30s & 10 C-130Js), Australia (12 C-130J-30s with 24 options), New Zealand (eight optioned as part of Australia's order) and the USAF (16 at late '97, including some which will be converted to WC-130J weather reconnaissance configuration in service).

Photo: A stretched C-130J-30 Hercules II for the RAAF in flight. (Lockheed Martin)

Lockheed C-130 Special Missions Variants

Country of origin: United States of America

Type: Special missions adaptations of the C-130 Hercules

Powerplants: MC-130E – Four 3020kW (4050shp) Allison T56-A-7 turboprops, driving four blade propellers. AC-130H – Four 3362kW (4508shp) T56-A-15s.

Performance: MC-130E – Max speed 590km/h (318kt). Max initial rate of climb 1600ft/min. Range 3705km (2000nm). AC-130H – Max speed 612km/h (330kt), cruising speed 592km/h (320kt). Max initial rate of climb 1830ft/min. Endurance 5hr.

Weights: MC-130E – Empty 33,065kg (72,882lb), max takeoff 70,310kg (155,000lb). AC-130H – Empty 33,065kg (72,892lb), max takeoff 70,310kg (155,000lb).

Dimensions: Wing span 40.41m (132ft 7in), length 29.79m (97ft 9in), height 11.66m (38ft 3in). Wing area 162.1m² (1745.0sq ft).

Accommodation: Basic flightcrew of four.

Armament: AC-130H – Armament mounted in the left side of the fuselage comprises two M61 Vulcan 20mm cannons, two 7.62mm miniguns (not usually carried), two 40mm Bofors cannons and a 105mm Howitzer.

Operators: Special Missions – USA. KC-130 – Argentina, Brazil, Canada, Indonesia, Israel, Saudi Arabia, Singapore, Spain, UK, USA.

History: The versatility and longevity of the basic Hercules airframe is reflected in the multitude of special missions adaptations.

The USAF began modification work on a C-130A to gunship configuration in 1965. A further 17 were modified to AC-130As (equipment fit including two 7.62mm miniguns, two 20mm cannons and two 40mm Bofors cannons, plus a beacon tracker and radar), and their combat success in Vietnam led to the procurement of 11 similar AC-130Es. From 1973 the 10 survivors were upgraded to AC-130H standard with T56-A-15s, and then subsequently fitted with a 105mm Howitzer. The latest AC-130 Spectre variant is the Rockwell AC-130U with modern sensors and a 25mm GAU-12 cannon in place of the M61s.

The US Navy operates three drone carrying DC-130s, while the USAF operates the similar NC-130H. The EC-130 designation covers a number of EW Hercules adaptations. EC-130E variants include the ABCCC (Airborne Command & Control Centre); the Elint EC-130E(CL); and the EC-130E(RR) 'Rivet Rider', which apart from Comint and Sigint, can be used for TV and radio broadcasts. The EC-130H Compass Call is a stand-off jammer.

The HC-130 designation covers USAF SAR aircraft. 43 HC-130Hs were delivered with the ARD-117 Cook Aerial Tracker in a blunt radome. The HC-130N is similar but equipped for inflight refuelling (hose & drogue). New build HC-130H(N)s have modern avionics.

KC-130 is a tanker variant. The USMC is the largest operator, with KC-130Fs, KC-130Rs, KC-130Ts and stretched KC-130T-30s. Ski equipped US Navy LC-130s were used for Antarctic support operations, until replaced by USAF C-130Hs.

Finally, the USAF's MC-130 Combat Talons are used in support of special forces operations. MC-130Es are fitted with a weather/nav radar with a terrain following function in a blunt nose, Fulton STAR personnel recovery nose forks and a retractable FLIR pod. The MC-130H has a APQ-170 radar in a reprofiled nose.

Photo: A USAF AC-130H Spectre. (Paul Merritt)

LMATTS C-27J Spartan

Countries of origin: Italy and the United States of America

Type: Tactical transport

Powerplants: Two 3132kW (4200shp) Allison AE 2100D3 turboprops, driving six blade Dowty propellers.

Performance: Max cruising speed 565km/h (305kt). Range with max payload 2130km (1150nm).

Weights: Operating empty 16,500kg (36,376lb), max takeoff 30,000kg (66,138lb).

Dimensions: Wing span 28.70m (94ft 2in), length 22.70m (74ft 6in), height 9.80m (32ft 2in). Wing area 82.0m² (882.7sq ft).

Accommodation: Flightcrew of two with provision for a loadmaster. Typical accommodation for 46 fully equipped troops, or 40 fully equipped paratroops. Can carry an approx 10 tonne payload comprising light vehicles and artillery among others.

Armament: None

Operators: None ordered at the time of writing.

History: The Allison AE 2100 powered C-27J Spartan, which is being developed by LMATTS (Lockheed Martin Alenia Tactical Transport Systems), is an advanced and improved development of the Alenia G222 with significant commonality with the C-130J Hercules II.

The concept of an improved development of the G222 arose from Lockheed Martin and Alenia discussions in 1995 on industrial offsets following from Italy's then mooted purchase of C-130Js for its air force. Initially discussions focused on fitting the G222 with the C-130J's advanced EFIS cockpit displays and improved T64G variants of the G222's existing powerplant driving four blade (rather than three blade) propellers. This improved transport was dubbed the G222J.

The updated G222 concept evolved to the stage where in February 1996 Lockheed Martin and Alenia jointly launched the C-27J project (the US style C-27J designation is unofficial, but reflects that the aircraft is a C-130J style upgrade of the G222, which is in limited USAF service as the C-27A Spartan). With the new designation came the most important change to the G222, the Allison AE 2100 turboprops, driving Dowty six blade propellers.

The joint LMATTS company was formed in 1997. The C-27J's first flight is planned for 1998, with service entry possible from 2000 if customers are found. LMATTS estimates a market for over 100 C-27Js, mainly to existing C-130 customers, especially C-130J operators. The C-27J will be assembled in Italy but will feature some Lockheed Martin made components.

Apart from the C-130J's Allison engines (which output significantly more power than the G222's T64s but are 5% more fuel efficient), Dowty propellers and five colour LCD EFIS two crew flightdeck, the C-27J will also feature the C-130J's internal loading systems. Performance improvements over the G222 include higher cruising speeds and significantly improved payload range, while the C-27J will have significantly lower operating costs.

Photo: A retouched photograph showing how a C-27J would look on a takeoff run from a dirt strip. (LMATTS)

Lockheed Electra

Country of origin: United States of America

Type: Maritime patrol and transport aircraft

Powerplants: Four 2800kW (3750shp) Allison 501-D13 turboprops, driving four blade propellers.

Performance: L-188C – Max speed 720km/h (390kt), max cruising speed 652km/h (352kt), economical cruising speed 602km/h (325kt). Service ceiling 27,000ft. Range with max payload 3450km (1910nm), with max fuel 4023km (2180nm).

Weights: L-188C – Operating empty 27,895kg (61,500lb), max take-off 52,664kg (116,000lb).

Dimensions: Wing span 30.18m (99ft 0in), length 31.90m (104ft 6in), height 10.01m (32ft 10in). Wing area 120.8m² (1300sq ft).

Accommodation: Flightcrew of two pilots and flight engineer. Max payload in freighter configuration is approximately 12 tonnes (26,000lb). Seating for up to 98 in passenger configuration.

Armament: None

Operators: Argentina, Bolivia, Honduras.

History: The Electra is one of the world's first turboprop airliners and ex civil examples have found their way into limited military service with Argentina, Bolivia and Honduras.

The Lockheed L-188 Electra resulted from an American Airlines requirement for a domestic short to medium range airliner. In June 1955 Lockheed was awarded an order for 35 such aircraft. Lockheed's design, designated the L-188, featured a low wing and four turboprops. By the time the first prototype flew on December 6 1957 it had gained 144 orders. However, any optimism Lockheed would have felt about a healthy sales future would have been short lived, the onset of the jet age and two mysterious crashes soon after the Electra had entered service contributing to the order book drying up.

As an interim measure following the crashes speed restrictions were imposed on Electras while the problem was resolved. Strengthened nacelles, nacelle mountings and a stronger wing structure overcame the problems, but it was not until 1961 that the speed restrictions were lifted.

Two basic versions of the Electra were built. The L-188A was the basic production aircraft and accounted for most Electra sales. The L-188C also entered service in 1959 and had more fuel and higher weights. From 1967 Lockheed converted 41 Electras to freighters or convertible freighter/passenger aircraft, fitting a strengthened floor and a large cargo door forward of the wing on the left side. Other companies have also converted Electras to freighters. In all 170 production Electras were built.

In the early 1980s the Argentine navy acquired four L-188A Electras which it converted for maritime patrol, with the primary change being the installation of an APS-705 search radar in an underfuselage radome. Subsequently IAI has converted one of these for Elint and Sigint reconnaissance. The maritime patrol aircraft were due to replaced by ex USN P-3B Orions from late 1997.

Bolivia and Honduras are the only other current military Electra operators, with a single example in service each.

Photo: One of the Argentine navy's converted Electras.

Lockheed Martin P-3 Orion

Country of origin: United States of America

Type: Maritime patrol aircraft

Powerplants: P-3C – Four 3660kW (4910ehp) Allison T56-A-14 turboprops, driving four blade propellers.

Performance: P-3C – Max speed 760km/h (411kt), economical cruising speed 608km/h (328kt), patrol speed at 1500ft 380km/h (206kt). Service ceiling 28,300ft. Ferry range 8945km (4830nm). Mission radius with 3hr on station at 1500ft 2495km (1345nm). Max endurance with four engines 12hr 20min, with two engines running 17hr 10min.

Weights: P-3C – Empty 27,890kg (61,490lb), max normal takeoff 61,235kg (135,000lb), max permissible weight 64,610kg (142,000lb).

Dimensions: P-3B/C – Wing span 30.37m (99ft 8in), length 35.61m (116ft 10in), height 10.27m (33ft 9in). Wing area 120.8m² (1300.0sq ft).

Accommodation: Normal crew complement of 10 comprises two pilots, flight engineer and navigator on flightdeck, with a tactical co-ordinator, two acoustic sensor operators, a MAD operator and two observers/sonobuoy loaders. Has seating/bunks for a relief crew.

Armament: Internal weapons bay can carry eight torpedoes or eight depth bombs. A total of 10 underwing hardpoints can carry up to eight AGM-86 Harpoons, or 10 torpedoes, or 10 mines.

Operators: Argentina*, Australia, Chile, Greece, Japan, Netherlands, New Zealand, Norway, Pakistan, Portugal, South Korea, Spain, Thailand.

History: The Orion was developed against a 1957 US Navy requirement to replace the Lockheed P2V/SP-2 Neptune.

Lockheed's submission was based on a shortened Electra airliner and this aircraft was selected for development in April 1958. The first Orion prototype flew for the first time on November 25 1959.

Features of the Orion (which entered service in 1962) include a MAD mounted in a boom extending from the tail and an internal weapons bay forward of the wing. Initial production was of the P-3A, while the P-3B, with more powerful engines, was delivered from 1965.

The current P-3C was first introduced in 1969 and featured a new APS-115 radar, MAD and processing equipment. The P-3C was built in progressively improved Update I, II, II.5 and III forms. Australian P-3Cs feature a British AQS-901 acoustic processing suite and locally developed Barra sonobuoys.

The US Navy also employs a number of special missions developments. The VP-3 is a VIP/staff transport conversion of early P-3A/Bs, the EP-3E 'Aries' is an Elint platform, the TP-3A is a crew trainer, the UP-3A a utility transport, WP-3As perform weather reconnaissance, RP-3As are designed for oceanographic reconnaissance and NP-3As are used for trials work. Two EP-3As and three RP-3As are used for range support work, while the EP-3J is an EW trainer.

Three significant US Orion upgrades have all been cancelled or dropped for budgetary reasons – the P-7, Boeing's P-3C Update IV and the P-3H. USN Orions are instead being fitted with a new radar (APS-134). Australia is upgrading its P-3Cs to AP-3C standard with new Elta radar, MAD and processing equipment, while Lockheed Martin is now proposing the AE 2100 powered Orion 2000. Over 700 Orions have been built, including 100 under licence by Kawasaki in Japan. US production ceased in 1995, pending further orders.

Photo: A New Zealand P-3K Orion. (RNZAF)

Lockheed CP-140 Aurora & Arcturus

Country of origin: United States of America

Type: Maritime patrol aircraft

Powerplants: Four 3660kW (4910ehp) Allison T56-A-14 turboprops, driving four blade propellers.

Performance: CP-140 – Max cruising speed 732km/h (395kt). Max initial rate of climb 2980ft/min. Service ceiling 28,250ft. Ferry range 8340km (4500nm). Operational radius for an 8hr 10min patrol 1850km (1000nm).

Weights: CP-140 – Empty 27,892kg (61,491lb), max permissible load 64,610kg (142,000lb).

Dimensions: Wing span 30.37m (99ft 8in), length 35.61m (116ft 10in), height 10.27m (33ft 9in). Wing area 120.8m² (1300.0sq ft).

Accommodation: Crew complement of 11, including flightcrew of four comprising two pilots, a flight engineer and navigator.

Armament: Theoretical armament as for P-3C, including eight torpedoes or eight depth bombs in internal weapons bay. A total of 10 underwing hardpoints can carry up to eight AGM-86 Harpoons, or 10 torpedoes, or 10 mines. Can be fitted with two AIM-9 Sidewinder AAMs for self defence.

Operators: Canada

History: The CP-140 Aurora is a unique development of the Orion which combines the P-3's airframe with the electronic systems of the US Navy S-3 Viking, while the CP-140A Arcturus is a down spec Aurora optimised specifically for training and fishery patrols.

In 1976 the Canadian Armed Forces ordered the Aurora to replace the CP-107 Argus. While the resulting aircraft closely resembles the P-3 Orion externally, internal changes have made the Aurora a significantly different aircraft. The Aurora was fitted with the Texas Instruments APS-116 search radar, a Texas Instruments ASQ-501 MAD and an AYK-10 processing computer, all equipment featured on the S-3A Viking (described separately). Other equipment allows the Aurora to fly a number of secondary missions including pollution patrol, aerial survey, shipping, fishing and Arctic surveillance, and search and rescue. The Aurora also carries a crew of 11, rather than 10 on the Orion.

Canada ordered 18 Auroras and the first of these flew for the first time on March 22 1979. The last example was delivered in July 1981. They currently serve with three squadrons, two at CFB Greenwood and one at CFB Comox.

The CP-140A Arcturus is a stripped down development of the Aurora and has the twin roles of Aurora crew training (thus increasing the amount of actual patrol hours Auroras can fly, and increasing their service lives) and environmental, Arctic sovereignty and fishery patrols. The Arcturus feature no ASW equipment, but are fitted with APS-134 radar.

Canada ordered the three CP-140As in 1989. These were the last Orion family aircraft to be built at Lockheed's Burbank, California, assembly line before production was transferred to Marietta, Georgia, alongside the C-130. The final CP-140A was delivered in September 1991.

Photo: A Canadian Forces CP-140 Aurora is flying low along the edge of Vancouver's Stanley Park. (Canadian Forces)

Lockheed S-3 & ES-3 Viking

Country of origin: United States of America

Type: Carrier borne ASW aircraft

Powerplants: Two 41.3kN (9275lb) General Electric TF34-GE-2 turbofans.

Performance: S-3A – Max speed 815km/h (440kt), patrol speed at optimum altitude 295km/h (160kt). Max initial rate of climb 4200ft/min. Service ceiling 40,000ft. Max ferry range 6085km (3230nm), range with max payload 3705km (2000nm). Operational radius over 1750km (945nm). Endurance 7hr 30min.

Weights: S-3A – Empty 12,088kg (26,650lb), max takeoff 23,832kg (52,540lb).

Dimensions: Wing span 20.93m (68ft 8in), length 16.26m (53ft 4in), height 6.93m (22ft 9in). Wing area 55.6m² (598.0sq ft).

Accommodation: Crew complement of four, consisting of two pilots, a tactical co-ordinator and a sensor operator.

Armament: The internal weapons bay can house four torpedoes, or four Mk 36 Destructors, or four Mk 82 bombs, or four Mk 53 mines. Two underwing hardpoints can carry a torpedo each, or an AGM-84 Harpoon or AGM-65 Maverick each (S-3B only), or rocket pods.

Operators: USA

History: The Viking was developed to replace the S-2 Tracker and to counter increasingly difficult to detect Soviet missile submarines.

In 1967 the USN invited US manufacturers to submit designs for its consideration, with Convair, Grumman, McDonnell Douglas, North American Rockwell and Lockheed/Ling Temco Vought responding. In 1969 the USN selected Lockheed's proposal, and the first of eight service evaluation YS-3A aircraft flew for the first time on January 21 1972 (eight YS-3As were funded to expedite service entry).

Lockheed developed the Viking in co-operation with Vought, who was responsible for the design and manufacture of the aircraft's wings, tail unit, landing gear and engine nacelles. The S-3A Viking's design features a high wing, two turbofan engines, an internal weapons bay, seating for four crew, a Univac AYK-10 digital computer, Texas Instruments APS-116 search radar and a retractable FLIR pod. ASW systems comprise an extendable tail MAD boom and sonobuoys. The S-3A entered service in July 1974 and 187 were built.

Development of the improved S-3B was initiated in 1980. The S-3B gained an improved acoustic processing suite, expanded ESM coverage, better radar processing, a new sonobuoy receiver system and the ability to carry and fire the AGM-84 Harpoon anti ship missile. The first converted S-3B development aircraft flew in September 1984, and subsequently almost all S-3As were converted to S-3B configuration.

The USN also operates four US-3A Carrier Onboard Delivery (COD) aircraft, stripped of all ASW equipment. A single KS-3A dedicated tanker was evaluated, and while S-3s can buddy tank, no KS-3s were ordered.

The ES-3A 'Shadow' first flew in 1991 and is an Elint variant which replaced the EA-3B Skywarrior, which was retired in 1987. The 16 ES-3As were converted from S-3As, and feature EW equipment in a dorsal fairing, a new radome, direction finding antenna and an array of antennas beneath the fuselage.

Photos: An ES-3 Shadow of VQ-6. (Lt Cmdr Steve Zaricor, USN)

Lockheed C-141 Starlifter

Country of origin: United States of America

Type: Strategic transport

Powerplants: C-141B – Four 93.4kN (21,000lb) Pratt & Whitney TF33-P-7 turbofans.

Performance: C-141B – Max cruising speed at altitude 910km/h (492kt), economical cruising speed at altitude 795km/h (430kt). Max initial rate of climb 2920ft/min. Service ceiling 41,600ft. Takeoff distance to 50ft at MTOW 1770m (5800ft). Ferry range 10,280km (5550nm), range with max payload 4725km (2550nm).

Weights: C-141B – Operating empty 67,185kg (148,120lb), max takeoff 155,580kg (343,000lb).

Dimensions: C-141B – Wing span 48.74m (159ft 11in), length 51.29m (168ft 4in), height 11.96m (39ft 3in). Wing area 299.8m² (3228.0sq ft).

Accommodation: Flightcrew of four comprising two pilots, a flight engineer and navigator. Can be configured to seat 205 equipped troops, or 168 paratroops or 103 stretchers. Max payload 41,220kg (90,880lb). Can carry a variety of cargoes including five HMMWV 4WDs, or a single Sheridan tank, or 13 standard pallets.

Armament: None

Operators: USA

History: The C-141 Starlifter was the USA's first purpose designed jet powered strategic freighter, giving the US military the capability to airlift large amounts of equipment to a war zone in as short a time as possible.

The Starlifter was designed against Specific Operational Requirement 182 for a turbofan powered strategic freighter for the then Military Airlift Command. Lockheed was selected to develop the new airlifter ahead of Boeing, Douglas and General Dynamics. Lockheed's design took the basic cross section of the C-130 Hercules combined with swept, high mounted wings with high lift devices for good field performance and four TF33 turbofans and a rear loading ramp.

The first C-141A flew for the first time on December 17 1963 (there was no C-141 prototype). Service entry was in 1965, replacing C-124s, C-97s and interim C-135s. 285 C-141As were built through to 1968.

The Starlifter was soon used for trans Pacific transport flights to Vietnam and the type has been used in support of almost every US military deployment since. In service though it was soon found that the C-141A cargo volume would easily be filled (or bulked out) without reaching the type's maximum payload limit, thus prompting development of the stretched C-141B.

The prototype YC-141B conversion flew for the first time on March 24 1977, and through to May 1982 271 Starlifters were converted to C-141B standard. Apart from the fuselage stretch the C-141B also gained an inflight refuelling receptacle above the flightdeck.

Apart from standard transport C-141Bs, the USAF also operates 13 C-141Bs equipped for special missions support, with defensive countermeasures and a retractable FLIR pod, while four short fuselage NC-141As are used for various test duties. Raytheon E-Systems is currently upgrading C-141Bs with EFIS displays and a digital autopilot.

Photo: A USAF C-141B. (Sqn Ldr Lance Higgerson, RAAF)

Lockheed C-5 Galaxy

Country of origin: United States of America

Type: Heavylift strategic freighter

Powerplants: C-5B – Four 191.3kN (43,000lb) General Electric TF39-GE-1C turbofans.

Performance: C-5B – Max speed 920km/h (496kt), max cruising speed at 25,000ft 890 to 910km/h (460 to 480kt). Max initial rate of climb 1725ft/min. Service ceiling at 278,960kg (615,000lb) AUW 35,750ft. Takeoff distance to clear a 15m (50ft) obstacle at MTOW 2985m (9800ft). Range with max fuel 10,410km (5618nm), range with max payload 5525km (2982nm).

Weights: C-5B – Operating empty 169,643kg (374,000lb), max takeoff 379,655kg (837,000lb).

Dimensions: Wing span 67.88m (222ft 9in), length 75.54m (247ft 10in), height 19.85m (65ft 2in). Wing area 576.0m² (6200.0sq ft).

Accommodation: Crew complement of five comprising two pilots, a flight engineer and two loadmasters. Accommodation for 15 relief crew on upper deck rear of flightdeck. C-5 can accommodate up to 350 troops, with 75 on upper deck. Max payload on C-5B 118,385kg (261,000lb), can carry two M1A1 Abrams tanks, or one CH-47, or four Sheridan lights tanks and five HMMVW 4WDs, or 10 LAV 25s.

Armament: None

Operators: USA

History: The C-5 Galaxy was the world's largest aircraft for over a decade and was a remarkable engineering accomplishment.

The Galaxy was born out of the US Air Force's Cargo Experimental Heavy Logistics System (CX-HLS) requirement, which called for an enormous freighter (for the day) capable of airlifting payloads of 113,400kg (250,000lb) over 4830km (2605nm) without inflight refuelling. Boeing, McDonnell Douglas and Lockheed were awarded initial contracts for the airframe, while Pratt & Whitney and GE were awarded initial contracts to develop a suitable engine, something that would have to be substantially more powerful than anything then available.

In August 1965 GE's TF39 high bypass turbofan was selected, while Lockheed was selected as the C-5 prime contractor two months later. The Galaxy flew for the first time on June 30 1968 and entered service in December 1969, although cost overruns earned the C-5 the nickname FRED – Fantastic Ridiculous Economic Disaster.

Galaxy design features include the high wing, T-tail, rear ramp and upward lifting nose freight door, allowing roll on, roll off loading and unloading. The Galaxy also features a complex four leg main undercarriage system, designed to allow operation from semi prepared runways.

In all, 81 C-5As were delivered between 1969 and 1973 (structural problems meant 77 C-5As were rewinged in the 1980s), while the production line was reopened in the early 1980s for 50 new build C-5Bs which were delivered between 1986 and 1989. The B differs little from the C-5A except it features simplified landing gear and an improved automatic flight control system. Two Galaxies modified for satellite carriage are designated C-5C.

In early 1998 the USAF was expected to issue a RFP to upgrade the C-5's cockpit and avionics.

Photo: A Galaxy gets airborne. (Sqn Ldr Lance Higgerson, RAAF)

Lockheed L-1011 TriStar

Country of origin: United States of America

Type: Strategic freighter and tanker

Powerplants: K.1 – Three 222.4kN (50,000lb) Rolls-Royce RB211-524B or -525B4 turbofans.

Performance: K.1 – Max cruising speed 964km/h (520kt), economical cruising speed 890km/h (480kt). Max initial rate of climb 2820ft/min. Service ceiling 43,000ft. Range with max pax payload 7785km (4200nm).

Weights: K.1 – Operating empty 110,165kg (242,684lb), max takeoff 244,955kg (540,000lb).

Dimensions: K.1/KC.1/C.2 – Span 50.09m (164ft 4in), length 50.05m (164ft 3in), height 16.87m (55ft 4in). Wing area 329.0m² (3540sq ft).

Accommodation: Flightcrew of three. Total fuel capacity in K.1 136,080kg (300,000lb).

Armament: None

Operators: Jordan, Saudi Arabia, UK.

History: The TriStar was the third widebody commercial airliner to be launched and the UK has successfully adapted and modified it as a strategic tanker transport.

The L-1011 TriStar was Lockheed's last commercial airliner, and was launched in 1968 in response to an American Airlines requirement (that also resulted in the DC-10) for a large capacity medium range airliner. Lockheed initially studied a twin engined layout, but it was felt that three would be necessary to ensure it could takeoff at max weights from existing runways. Engine choice was Rolls-Royce's advanced three shaft design RB211, which after initial troubles (including bankrupting RR) eventually proved to be extremely reliable and efficient in service.

The TriStar's first flight was on November 16 1970 with service entry in 1972. The basic L-1011-1 was soon followed by a number of progressively improved models, the most significant being the shortened L-1011-500. The L-1011-500 was developed for long range missions and sacrificed seating capacity for range. The first L-1011-500 flew on October 16 1978 and entered service in May 1979. Only 50 L-1011-500s were built of a total TriStar production run of 250.

In the early 1980s the UK Ministry of Defence acquired six ex British Airways and three ex PanAm L-1011-500s for conversion into tanker transports. Marshall of Cambridge converted four of the BA aircraft to TriStar K.1s with extra fuel tanks in the cargo holds, a refuelling probe and twin retractable refuelling drogues mounted under the rear fuselage. The first K.1 conversion flew in July 1985.

Two K.1s and two additional L-1011-500s were converted to KC.1 configuration, gaining a forward freight door, structural strengthening of the main cabin door and a freight handling system allowing the carriage of palletised cargo and 35 passengers.

Two of the ex PanAm aircraft serve as C.2 troop transports without any refuelling capability, while the third is a C.2A, which is identical save for some military avionics and a new interior. All RAF TriStars have been fitted with radar warning receivers.

A single L-1011 equips Jordan's Royal Flight.

Photo: The RAF's nine TriStars equip 216 Squadron. Pictured is a K.1 without refuelling probe. (Sgt Rick Brewell RAF, UK Crown Copyright)

Lockheed SR-71

Country of origin: United States of America

Type: High speed & high altitude reconnaissance platform

Powerplants: Two 145.6kN (32,500lb) with afterburning Pratt & Whitney J58-1 continuous bleed turbojets.

Performance: SR-71A (estimated) – Max speed over Mach 3, or approximately 3220km/h (1735kt) at high altitude. Operating ceiling above 80,000ft. Approximate range at Mach 3 and 79,000ft 4830km (2605nm). Max endurance at Mach 3 1hr 30min.

Weights: SR-71A (estimated) – Empty 27,215kg (60,000lb), max takeoff 77,110kg (170,000lb).

Dimensions: Wing span 16.95m (55ft 7in), length 37.74m (107ft 5in), height 5.64m (18ft 6in).

Accommodation: Crew of two, pilot and reconnaissance systems operator in tandem in SR-71A. The SR-71B trainer seats two in tandem, with the second cockpit raised behind the first.

Armament: None

Operators: USA

History: The incredible SR-71 'Blackbird' is the pinnacle of aircraft performance, it flies faster than any other production aircraft and is able to cruise at a sustained Mach 3.0.

The SR-71 program began life in 1959 as the A-12, a CIA sponsored program to develop a high speed high flying reconnaissance platform to supplement the U-2. The A-12 was developed in complete secrecy by Lockheed's Skunk Works under the stewardship of Kelly Johnson. It flew for the first time on April 26 1962 powered by interim J75 turbojets (less than three years after program go-ahead). Some 18 A-12s were built for reconnaissance, and these aircraft could also carry the Lockheed GTD-21 drone (they were retired in 1968).

The A-12 also served as the basis for the F-12, a high speed interceptor intended for the defence of continental US airspace. Three A-12s served as YF-12A prototypes, although production of the F-12B was not funded due to cost.

The definitive SR-71 has a longer fuselage than the A-12, and first flew on December 22 1964. Thirty one SR-71s (including three SR-71B two seaters) were built, and served with the 9th Strategic Reconnaissance Wing at Beale AFB in California through to 1990.

The SR-71 was initially withdrawn from service in 1990 due to budget constraints (and rumoured introduction of the Aurora successor) and their reconnaissance role was handed to satellites. However three aircraft (including an SR-71B) were transferred to NASA for high speed research tasks.

In 1995 the SR-71 was reactivated to plug the gap in US reconnaissance capabilities left by its premature retirement. Two SR-71As (one reactivated from storage, the other transferred back from NASA) returned to USAF service in 1995, with pilot conversion training performed on NASA's SR-71B. However in late 1997 the USAF SR-71s' futures were in doubt, with the US President blocking their funding.

The secret to the SR-71's high performance lies in its aerodynamic design, titanium construction and the J58 engine installation. At high speed more thrust is produced by the suction at the intakes and from the ejector nozzles than from the engines themselves.

Photo: NASA's SR-71B two seater. (Paul Merritt)

Lockheed F-104 Starfighter

Country of origin: United States of America

Type: Multirole fighter

Powerplant: F-104ASA – One 52.8kN (11,870lb) dry and 79.6kN (17,900lb) with afterburning General Electric J79-GE-19 turbojet.

Performance: F-104ASA – Max speed at 36,000ft Mach 2.2 or 2333km/h (1260kt), max speed at sea level 1465km/h (790kt), max cruising speed at 36,000ft 980km/h (530kt). Max initial rate of climb 55,000ft/min. Service ceiling 58,000ft. Ferry range with drop tanks 2920km (1575nm), combat radius with max fuel 1247km (673nm).

Weights: F-104ASA – Empty 6760kg (14,903lb), max takeoff 14,060kg (30,995lb).

Dimensions: F-104ASA – Wing span without tip tanks 6.68m (21ft 11in), length 16.69m (54ft 9in), height 4.11m (13ft 6in). Wing area 18.2m^2 (196.1sq ft).

Accommodation: Pilot only, or two in tandem in TF-104.

Armament: F-104ASA – One 20mm T171ES Vulcan six barrel cannon. Can carry up to 3400kg (7495lb) of ordnance including AIM-9L Sidewinders, Selenia Aspide medium range AAMs, conventional bombs and rockets.

Operators: Greece, Italy.

History: The controversial Starfighter was intended as a day fighter, but grew into a capable fighter-bomber, with 2406 built.

Lockheed's Kelly Johnson and the company's Skunk Works began work on the F-104 in 1952 after evaluating the experiences of American fighter pilots in Korea. In designing the new fighter performance was considered the overriding factor, with a small size and powerful single engine allowing Mach 2 performance in an aircraft that defied the trends for greater complexity, weight and hence cost.

The resulting aircraft was quite remarkable in that it featured incredibly small, straight wings (only 10cm/4in deep at their thickest points) with blown flaps and a single J79 turbojet engine (the most advanced engine of the day) giving a max speed of Mach 2.2.

The XF-104 prototype flew for the first time on February 7 1954 powered by a Wright XJ65 (Sapphire) turbojet. Service entry was in 1958, although the USAF had transferred the survivors of its F-104A/B/C/D fleet to the Air National Guard by 1968. USAF experience with the F-104 was less than favourable, with high attrition.

The F-104 gained a new lease of life with the F-104G, which was redesigned as a fighter-bomber. The F-104G first flew on February 17 1956 and introduced a more powerful engine and a multirole nav/attack system. In what was termed the 'Sale of the Century' the F-104G was selected in 1959 by Belgium, Germany, Italy and the Netherlands for a joint production program. Germany was the largest customer, taking delivery of 750, although attrition was very high. The F-104G was also built under licence in Japan as the F-104J and in Canada as the CF-104G.

Aeritalia (now Alenia) in Italy built 246 (including 40 for Turkey) AIM-7 Sparrow capable F-104S Starfighters through to 1979. As the F-104ASA, Italian aircraft were further upgraded with FIAR Setter radar and Selenia Aspide compatibility. Around 155 survivors will remain in service until the arrival of the Eurofighter 2000.

Photo: An Italian F-104ASA. (Paul Merritt)

Lockheed Martin F-16A Fighting Falcon

Country of origin: United States of America

Type: Multirole fighter

Powerplant: F-16A – One 65.3kN (14,670lb) dry and 106.0kN (23,830lb) with afterburning Pratt & Whitney F100-PW-100 turbofan.

Performance: F-16A – Max speed at 40,000ft over Mach 2.0 or 2125km/h (1145kt), at sea level 1472km/h (795kt). Max initial rate of climb over 50,000ft/min. Service ceiling above 50,000ft. Combat radius with six 1000lb bombs, hi-lo-hi 545km (295nm).

Weights: F-16A – Operating empty 6607kg (14,567lb), max takeoff 14,968kg (33,000lb).

Dimensions: F-16A – Span with AAMs 10.00m (32ft 10in), length 15.03m (49ft 4in), height 5.01m (16ft 5in). Wing area 28.9m^2 (300.0sq ft).

Accommodation: Pilot only, except two in tandem in F-16B.

Armament: One internal M61A1 20mm cannon. Six underwing, one centreline and two wingtip hardpoints for up to 5435kg (12,000lb) of ordnance, including AIM-9 or AIM-120 AAMs (can be mounted on wingtip pylons), bombs, rockets, AGM-65 ASMs and Penguin anti ship missiles.

Operators: Belgium, Denmark, Egypt, Indonesia, Israel, Netherlands, Norway, Pakistan, Portugal, Singapore, Taiwan*, Thailand, USA, Venezuela.

History: The F-16 (or 'Viper' as it's nicknamed) was conceived as a lightweight, highly agile and relatively inexpensive multirole fighter.

The F-16 evolved from the USAF sponsored Lightweight Fighter (LWF) program to evaluate the concept of a small and manoeuvrable fighter. In April General Dynamics and Northrop were selected ahead of Boeing, LTV and Lockheed to build two prototypes each of their respective designs for a competitive fly-off. The first General Dynamics YF-16 first flew on January 20 1974, and after almost a year of evaluation against the twin engine Northrop YF-17 the type was selected for further development. The first production F-16A flew in 1978.

The F-16 was the first production fighter to feature fly-by-wire and relaxed stability. It also features wing/fuselage blending, a Westinghouse APG-66 radar, an advanced (for the time) cockpit with sidestick controller and a 30° reclined seat.

The USAF selected the F-16 for production in early 1975. Later that year Belgium, Denmark, the Netherlands and Norway jointly selected the F-16 to build under licence in Europe and replace their F-104Gs.

The inferior GE J79 turbojet powered F-16/79 was offered for export to secondary status nations until the full F100 powered F-16A was released for wider export. Production F-16As were built to Block 1, 5, 10 and 15 standard. Block 15 introduced the most noteworthy changes, including the extended horizontal stabilator and a track while scan mode for the radar. The F-16XL strike fighter with cranked delta wing was passed over by the USAF in preference to the F-15E.

The USAF also took delivery of 272 Block 15s converted to ADF (Air Defense Fighter) standard. The F-16 ADFs are air defence interceptors and feature upgraded radar, AIM-7 compatibility and a searchlight, and can be identified by their bulged fin/fuselage fairing.

Belgium, Denmark, the Netherlands and Norway are upgrading their F-16s under the MLU (mid life update) program with two colour LCDs, wide angle HUD, NVG compatible cockpit, upgraded APG-66(V2A) radar, GPS and a new modular mission computer.

Photo: A Belgium F-16A gets airborne. (Belgium SID)

Lockheed Martin F-16C Fighting Falcon

Country of origin: United States of America

Type: Multirole fighter

Powerplant: F-16C Blk 30/40 – One 122.8kN (27,600lb) with afterburning General Electric F110-GE-100 turbofan.

Performance: F-16C – Max speed at 40,000ft above Mach 2.0 or 2125km/h (1145kt), at sea level 1472km/h (795kt). Service ceiling above 50,000ft. Ferry range with drop tanks over 3890km (2100nm). Blk 40 radius with two AIM-9s, four 910kg/2000lb bombs and external fuel, hi-lo-lo-hi 630km (340nm). Blk 40 radius with two AIM-9s, two AIM-7s and external fuel with 2hr 10min CAP 370km (200nm).

Weights: F-16C Blk 30/40 – Empty 8665kg (19,100lb), max takeoff 19,190kg (42,300lb).

Dimensions: F-16C – Span with wingtip AAMs 10.00m (32ft 10in), length 15.03m (49ft 4in), height 5.01m (16ft 5in). Wing area 28.9m² (300.0sq ft).

Accommodation: Pilot only, or two in tandem in F-16D.

Armament: One internal M61A1 20mm cannon. Six underwing, one centreline and two wingtip hardpoints can carry up to 5435kg (12,000lb) of ordnance. Options include AIM-9 Sidewinder or AIM-120 AAMs (can be mounted on wingtip pylons), bombs, rockets, AGM-65 ASMs, Penguin anti ship missiles, GBU-10 and GBU-12 laser guided bombs and on Block 50D/52D AGM-88 HARMs.

Operators: Bahrain, Egypt*, Greece, Israel, Singapore*, Sth Korea*, Turkey*, USA*.

History: Various avionics, radar and cockpit changes mark the evolution of the F-16A into the more capable and heavier F-16C.

The F-16C first flew on June 19 1984. Changes to the F-16C came under the Multi Stage Improvement Program (MSIP), which aimed to increase the F-16's ground attack and all weather capabilities and introduce BVR missile compatibility. Initial production F-16C Block 25s introduced the F-16C's improved Westinghouse APG-68 radar (with increased range, more operating modes and better ECCM), an improved cockpit with a wide angle HUD, compatibility with AGM-65D and AIM-120 missiles and provision for future greater max takeoff weight. Externally the F-16C's fin base is extended forward, which made room for the since cancelled ALQ-165 jamming suite.

Subsequent F-16C/D Block Models comprise: the General Electric F110-GE-100 powered Block 30 and the PW F100-PW-220 powered Block 32; the GE powered Block 40 and PW powered Block 42 Night Falcon with upgraded APG-68(V) radar and compatibility with LANTIRN pods giving all weather navigation and attack capability with precision guided munitions; the more powerful Improved Performance Engine (IPE) F110-GE-229 Block 50 and F100-PW-220 Block 52 both with APG-68(V5); and the Block 50D and 52D with AGM-88 HARM compatibility.

The F-16N and TF-16N designations apply to 26 Block 30s modified for aggressor training for the US Navy. The two seat F-16ES (Enhanced Strike) with dorsal conformal fuel tanks was offered to Israel, while the two seat F-16U strike fighter offered to the UAE would have had a larger area wing. LM is studying a similarly winged Falcon 2000 should the JSF be cancelled. Future F-16s may also feature an electronically scanned version of the APG-68 radar. Meanwhile F-16C licence assembly continues in Sth Korea and Turkey.

Photo: An Eglin AFB test USAF F-16C with BAe ASRAAMs. (BAe)

Lockheed F-117 Nighthawk

Country of origin: United States of America

Type: Low observable precision strike fighter

Powerplants: Two 48.0kN (10,800lb) non afterburning General Electric F404-GE-F1D2 turbofans.

Performance: Max level speed 1040km/h (560kt), normal max operating speed Mach 0.9. Unrefuelled mission radius with a 2270kg (5000lb) weapon load 1055km (570nm).

Weights: Estimated empty 13,380kg (29,500lb), max takeoff 23,815kg (52,500lb).

Dimensions: Wing span 13.20m (43ft 4in), length overall 20.08m (65ft 11in), height overall 3.78m (12ft 5in). Wing area 84.8m² (913.0sq ft).

Accommodation: Pilot only.

Armament: Usually two 910kg/2000lb bombs, either BLU-109B low level laser guided bombs or GBU-10 or GBU-27 laser guided bombs, in internal weapons bay. Can also carry AGM-65 Maverick or AGM-88 HARM ASMs and AIM-9 Sidewinder AAMs. No provision for external stores carriage.

Operators: USA

History: Lockheed's 'Black Jet', the F-117 Nighthawk was designed in utmost secrecy from the ground up as a stealthy attack fighter.

Development of the F-117 traces back to the mid 1970s when the US Air Force awarded Lockheed's Advanced Development Company – the Skunk Works – a contract under the Have Blue program to develop an attack aircraft that would be very difficult to detect with radar. Two XST (Experimental Stealth Technology) Have Blue prototypes were built, and the first of these flew for the first time from Groom Lake in Nevada in December 1977. The two Have Blue demonstrators were powered by two small General Electric CJ610 turbojets and were similar in overall configuration to the ensuing F-117 except for inward canted tailplanes. Both XSTs had crashed by 1980.

Development of the operational F-117A began in November 1978 under the Senior Trend program, with the first of five preproduction F-117s flying for the first time on June 18 1981, while the first of an eventual 59 production F-117As was delivered in August 1982.

The F-117s were operated by the 4450th Tactical Group in complete secrecy at the remote Tonopah Test Range and all flights were undertaken at night. It was not until late 1988 that the veil of secrecy surrounding the F-117 was lifted when the US DoD confirmed the aircraft's existence and the type began flying daylight missions. Today they equip the 37th Fighter Wing, based at Holloman AFB, New Mexico.

The F-117 uses a range of features to defeat radar and to remain undetected, or to be detected too late. Most obvious is the Nighthawk's faceted airframe construction and the avoidance of straight lines on doors and panels, so that radar energy is reflected in all directions. The airframe is also covered in a range of radar absorbent material (RAM) coatings. The two non afterburning F404 engines' gases mix with bypass air and exit through platypus exhausts to reduce their infrared signature.

The USAF's surviving F-117s are being fitted with an upgraded navigation system and are expected to remain in service to 2015.

Photo: Nighthawks are based at Holloman AFB. (Doug Mackay)

Lockheed Martin/Boeing F-22 Raptor

Country of origin: United States of America

Type: Air dominance fighter

Powerplants: F-22A – Two 155kN (35,000lb) class Pratt & Whitney F119-PW-100 afterburning turbofans.

Performance: F-22A – Estimated max speed at sea level 1480km/h (800kt). No other figures released.

Weights: F-22A – Target empty 14,365kg (31,760lb), max takeoff approx 27,215kg (60,000lb).

Dimensions: F-22A – Wing span 13.56m (44ft 6in), length 18.92m (62ft 1in), height 5.00m (16ft 5in). Wing area 78.0m² (840.0sq ft).

Accommodation: Pilot only.

Armament: Internal long barrel GE M61A1 Vulcan 20mm cannon. Two side weapons bays can carry two AIM-9 Sidewinders each. Ventral weapons bay can carry four AIM-120A Amraams, or six AIM-120Cs, or GBU-32 JDAM PGMs. Four underwing hardpoints can carry 2270kg (5000lb) of weaponry each or fuel tanks.

Operators: USAF IOC planned for 2004.

History: The next generation Lockheed Martin/Boeing F-22 Raptor is set to become the United States' premier fighter aircraft (air dominance fighter in USAF speak) of early next century, replacing the F-15C.

The F-22 resulted from the USAF's Advanced Tactical Fighter (ATF) program to develop a replacement for the F-15 Eagle. In October 1986 the USAF selected Lockheed and Northrop to build two prototypes each of their respective ATF designs for evaluation. At the same time competing engines for the ATF from General Electric (YF120) and Pratt & Whitney (YF119) would be compared.

Lockheed teamed with General Dynamics and Boeing and their YF-22 flew for the first time on September 29 1990. The rival Northrop McDonnell Douglas YF-23 had flown on August 27. The USAF announced its selection of the P&W F119 powered F-22 in April 1991.

Currently nine F-22As development aircraft are funded, the first of which flew for the first time on September 7 1997. The USAF now plans to acquire 339 F-22s (down from 442 due to funding cuts). An initial operational capability (IOC) is planned for 2004.

The F-22 is designed to defeat all current and projected fighters in air-to-air combat (first look first kill), while it will have a secondary precision ground attack function with JDAM PGMs. The F-22 is designed to be extremely agile and incorporates low observable (stealth) technology (including RAM and serrated edges on doors and panels) as an integral part of the design. The low bypass two shaft F119 engines give the F-22 a thrust to weight ratio of 1.4 to 1 and the aircraft can cruise at supersonic speeds without afterburner (supercruise) with the exhaust exiting through two dimensional vectoring nozzles.

The avionics system integrates data from the Northrop Grumman/Texas Instruments APG-77 low probability of intercept electronically scanned radar, comms system and RWR for presentation on the HUD and four colour LCD displays. The cockpit also features a sidestick controller and the aircraft has triplex fly-by-wire flight controls.

The two seat F-22B was cancelled in mid 1996 as an economy measure, while up to 250 developed F-22 strike versions could be procured in the future to replace the F-15E and F-117.

Photo: The Raptor first flew in September 1997. (Lockheed Martin)

Lockheed Martin X-35 JSF

Country of origin: United States of America

Type: Advanced multirole fighter prototype

Powerplants: One 155kN (35,000lb) class Pratt & Whitney SE611 (F119 derivative) turbofan, plus in STOVL variant an Allison engine driven lift fan behind the cockpit.

Performance: No data publicly released at late 1997, but Lockheed Martin claims its JSF design (in CTOL form) "matches or exceeds F-16 performance levels".

Weights: No data publicly released at late 1997.

Dimensions: Wing span 10.05m (33ft 0in), width wings folded (RN & USN aircraft) 9.14m (30ft 0in), length 15.47m (50ft 9in). Wing area 42m² (450sq ft), or 50.2m² (540sq ft) for USN variant.

Accommodation: Pilot only, two seater conversion trainer planned.

Armament: Internal gun for USAF aircraft. Production aircraft armament would include AIM-9Xs, AIM-120s and JDAMs.

Operators: Planned for service with the USAF, USN, USMC & RN.

History: The X-35 is Lockheed Martin's contender for the highly ambitious, $US165bn US Joint Strike Fighter program.

The JSF resulted from the merger of the JAST program to replace USAF F-16s and USN F/A-18s and the CALF ASTOVL program to replace USMC AV-8s. The stealthy, multirole JSF is intended to be built in conventional, carrier capable and STOVL versions, using a common basic aircraft for maximum commonality to keep costs low. In December 1995 the UK became a 10% development partner in JSF, with the aim of replacing RN Sea Harriers.

By June 1996 Lockheed Martin, Boeing and McDonnell Douglas had submitted their design proposals to the JSF project office, with Boeing and Lockheed Martin then being selected to build two JSF demonstrators each (one a conventional air force variant later to be converted to carrier capable configuration, the second in STOVL form).

Lockheed Martin's X-35s and Boeing's X-32 demonstrators are scheduled to fly in 2000 for comparative evaluation, with the winning design selected in 2001. To the winner the spoils will be enormous, current planning envisages the USAF taking 2036 JSFs, the USMC 642, the USN 300 and RN 60, in addition to exports. IOC with the USAF is planned for 2007.

Lockheed Martin's X-35 effort is headquartered in Fort Worth, Texas, with its Tactical Aircraft Systems division (formerly General Dynamics), with considerable input from its famous Skunk Works division (which will build the two X-35s) and the Marietta based Lockheed Martin Aeronautical Systems (home of the F-22 Raptor). LM is also partnered with Northrop Grumman and British Aerospace.

The X-35 resembles a scaled down F-22 in broad configuration, with a mid wing, twin outward canted tailfins and internal weapons bays either side of the fuselage. LM's three JSF models will share common structural geometries, with the canopy, phased array radar, subsystems and most of the advanced avionics planned to be shared.

The carrier capable model will differ from the basic land aircraft in having a larger area wing and tail and structural strengthening for carrier ops. The STOVL variant will have an Allison designed lift fan driven by the engine and mounted behind the cockpit.

Photo: The STOVL variant of LM's JSF proposal for the USMC. (LM)

LTV (Vought) A-7 Corsair II

Country of origin: United States of America

Type: Attack aircraft

Powerplant: A-7E – One 66.7kN (15,000lb) non afterburning Allison TF41-A-2 turbofan (licence built Rolls-Royce Spey).

Performance: A-7E – Max speed 1112km/h (600kt), max speed at 5000ft 1102km/h (595kt). Ferry range with external fuel 4605km (2485nm), ferry range with max internal fuel 3670km (1980nm).

Weights: A-7E – Empty 8668kg (19,111lb), max takeoff 19,050kg (42,000lb).

Dimensions: A-7E – Wing span 11.80m (38ft 9in), span wings folded 7.24m (23ft 9in), length 14.06m (46ft 2in), height 4.90m (16ft 1in). Wing area 34.8m² (375sq ft).

Accommodation: Pilot only, or two in tandem in TA-7.

Armament: One M61A1 Vulcan 20mm cannon mounted in port side forward fuselage. Two side fuselage (AIM-9 compatible only) and six underwing hardpoints can carry a total ordnance load of over 6805kg (15,000lb). Weapon options include AIM-9 Sidewinders, bombs, laser guided bombs, AGM-65 Maverick ASMs and rockets.

Operators: Greece, Portugal, Thailand.

History: The A-7 Corsair is one of a select number of US Navy aircraft to be operated by the US Air Force, and while it is no longer in frontline US service, it flies with Greece, Portugal and Thailand.

The US Navy's 1963 VAL (light attack aircraft) specification aimed to find a 'light' attack aircraft with roughly twice the payload of the A-4 Skyhawk, for an in service date of 1967. Vought's proposal was selected ahead of those from North American, Douglas and Grumman, and seven development aircraft and 35 production A-7As were ordered on March 19 1964.

Vought's design, named Corsair II in honour of the WW2 F4U, was very similar in configuration to its F-8 Crusader fighter, however the A-7 was smaller and shorter, with fixed incidence wings, and only had subsonic performance. Power for the A-7A was supplied by a non afterburning 54.7kN (12,200lb) Pratt & Whitney TF30-P-8 turbofan. First flight was on September 27 1965, while production deliveries took place from October 1966.

It was also in 1966 that the USAF ordered its own version of the A-7 to fill a requirement for a tactical attack aircraft. The USAF's A-7D introduced the Allison TF41 turbofan, a licence built development of the Rolls-Royce Spey. The USN's developed A-7E was also powered by the TF41. The USAF's mid 1980s A-7F close air support upgrade program was cancelled.

USAF and USN Corsairs were used widely during the Vietnam War, while US Navy Corsairs were again used in anger during the Gulf War. Both these services have now retired the A-7 from frontline service.

The first Corsair II export customer was Greece, who ordered 60 A-7Hs and five TA-7Hs in the mid 1970s. The survivors can fire AGM-65 Mavericks and are used primarily for anti shipping strike. Portugal's A-7Ps are refurbished ex USN TF30 powered A-7As, and were delivered from 1981.

Finally, Thailand has acquired 18 ex USN A-7Es for service with its navy in the land based maritime strike mission.

Photo: A Maverick armed Portuguese A-7P.

McDonnell Douglas A-4 Skyhawk

Country of origin: United States of America

Type: Light attack fighter and advanced two seat trainer (TA-4J).

Powerplant: A-4M – One 50kN (11,200lb) non afterburning Pratt & Whitney J52-P-408 turbojet.

Performance: A-4M – Max speed with a 1815kg (4000lb) bomb load 1038km/h (560kt), max speed at sea level 1100km/h (595kt). Max initial rate of climb 10,300ft/min. Service ceiling 38,700ft. Ferry range 3305km (1785nm), combat radius with a 1815kg (4000lb) bomb load 545km (295nm).

Weights: A-4M – Empty 4747kg (10,465lb), normal takeoff 11,115kg (24,500lb).

Dimensions: A-4M – Wing span 8.38m (27ft 6in), length 12.27m (40ft 4in), height 4.57m (15ft 0in). Wing area 24.2m² (260.0sq ft).

Accommodation: Pilot only, or two in tandem in TA-4.

Armament: Two 20mm Colt Mk 12 cannons in wing roots. A-4M max external ordnance of 4155kg (9155lb) can be carried on one centreline and four underwing hardpoints. Weapon options include bombs, cluster bombs, AIM-9 Sidewinders, Bullpup and Maverick ASMs.

Operators: Argentina*, Indonesia, Israel, Malaysia, New Zealand, Singapore, USA.

History: Affectionately dubbed the Scooter and Heinemann's Hot Rod, the A-4 Skyhawk enjoyed a three decade 2960 unit production run.

In the early 1950s Douglas had been working on its turboprop powered A2D Skyshark to replace the piston powered AD (A-1) Skyraider, but development was terminated due to problems with the powerplant. At the same time Douglas' Ed Heinemann had been working on a compact jet powered light attack aircraft and in early 1952 the US Navy ordered this aircraft for further development. The first of nine XA4D-1 development aircraft first flew on August 14 1954. Deliveries of production A4D-1s began in September 1956.

The Skyhawk's dimensions are such that it can fit on an aircraft carrier lift without the need for folding wings. Power for initial A-4A, A-4B and A-4C Skyhawks was from a Wright J65, a licence built Armstrong Siddeley Sapphire.

The A-4C was followed into USN service by the much improved A-4E, a heavier development powered by a Pratt & Whitney J52. The final Skyhawk for the US Navy was the A-4F, characterised by its dorsal avionics hump. The ultimate production Skyhawk was the A-4M Skyhawk II, which introduced a larger canopy for better pilot vision, a more powerful J52-P-408 and a max takeoff weight double that of initial A-4As. The A-4M was developed specifically for the US Marines. The M first flew in 1970 and remained in production until 1979.

Only two seat TA-4Fs used as advanced trainers survive in US service, although the Skyhawk has been widely exported. Argentina was the first, taking delivery of A-4Ps and A-4Qs (modified A-4Bs and Cs respectively) in the mid 1960s, while it is taking delivery of Lockheed Martin refurbished ex US A-4Ms (as A-4ARs). Israel operates A-4E based A-4Hs and A-4M based A-4Ns. Malaysia operates modified ex USN A-4Es, while Singapore's A-4S is described separately. New Zealand's Kahu upgraded A-4Ks feature a HUD, HOTAS, two CRTs and APG-66 radar, and AIM-9L, AGM-65 and laser guided bomb compatibility.

Photo: A New Zealand A-4K in a trial livery. (RNZAF)

McDonnell Douglas F-4 Phantom II

Country of origin: United States of America

Type: Multirole fighter

Powerplants: F-4E – Two 52.5kN (11,810lb) dry and 79.6kN (17,900lb) with afterburning General Electric J79-GE-17A turbojets.

Performance: F-4E – Max speed at 36,000ft Mach 2.2 or 2390km/h (1290kt), cruising speed at MTOW 920km/h (495kt). Max initial rate of climb 61,400ft/min, air intercept mission rate of climb 49,800ft/min. Service ceiling 62,250ft. Ferry range 3185km (1720nm). Area intercept combat radius 1265km (683nm), defensive counter air combat radius 795km (430nm), interdiction combat radius 1145km (618nm).

Weights: F-4E – Empty 13,757kg (30,328lb), max takeoff 28,030kg (61,795lb).

Dimensions: F-4E – Wing span 11.77m (38ft 8in), length 19.20m (63ft 0in), height 5.02m (16ft 6in). Wing area 49.2m^2 (530.0sq ft).

Accommodation: Pilot and weapons system operator in tandem.

Armament: F-4E – One M61A1 20mm cannon. One centreline and four underwing hardpoints can carry 7255kg (16,000lb) of ordnance including AIM-9 AAMs, bombs, rockets and laser guided bombs. Four AIM-7s can be carried in semi recessed underfuselage stations.

Operators: Egypt, Germany, Greece, Iran, Israel, Japan, Sth Korea, Turkey.

History: The most important western fighter of the postwar period, more than 5000 F-4 Phantoms were built between 1957 and 1981.

What became the Phantom began life as a private venture, the F3H naval strike fighter, which would have been powered by Wright J65s. In 1954 the US Navy issued a letter of intent for two F3Hs for evaluation as the AH-1, to be powered by General Electric's promising J79 turbojet. Later in 1955 the AH-1 was adapted to meet a Navy requirement for a fleet defence fighter, and with suitable changes the AH-1 became the F4H Phantom II. Development go-ahead was given in May 1955. Aside from the then advanced J79s, design characteristics included the upturned outer wings and anhedral on the horizontal tail.

The first prototype XF4H-1 made the type's first flight on May 27 1958, and it demonstrated performance levels far above anything then flying. Indeed Navy Phantoms set a series of speed, altitude and time to height records in the late 1950s and early 1960s.

Initial production was of the Navy's F-4B fleet defence fighter. In 1965 the USAF took the unprecedented step of ordering a USN fighter when it ordered the F-4C. Subsequent USN and USMC F-4s comprised the F-4J, F-4N and F-4S. These models, the USAF's F-4Cs, F-4Ds and SEAD F-4Gs, and British Spey powered F-4Ks and F-4Ms have all been retired. Some F-4Ds survive with South Korea and Iran.

The definitive Phantom variant is the APQ-120 radar and gun equipped F-4E. It first flew on August 7 1965, almost 1500 were built.

About 50 Israeli F-4Es have been upgraded to Kurnass 2000 status with improved Elbit avionics and multifunction displays and Norden APG-76 radar. IAI is also updating 54 Turkish F-4Es with a structural upgrade and Elta radar. Japan's F-4EJs were built under licence by Mitsubishi and 96 are being upgraded to F-4EJ Kai standard with a Northrop Grumman APG-66J radar. Germany's Improved Combat Efficiency (ICE) upgrade to its F-4Fs adds a Hughes APG-65 radar and AIM-120 Amraam compatibility. DASA is to perform a similar upgrade for 39 Greek F-4Es.

Photo: A German ICE upgraded F-4F Phantom. (Gary Gentle)

McDonnell Douglas RF-4 Phantom II

Country of origin: United States of America

Type: Tactical reconnaissance fighter

Powerplants: RF-4C – Two 48.5kN (10,900lb) dry and 75.6kN (17,000lb) with afterburning General Electric J79-GE-15 turbojets.

Performance: RF-4C – Max speed at 40,000ft 2348km/h (1267kt), max speed at sea level 1445km/h (780kt). Max initial rate of climb 48,000ft/min. Service ceiling 59,400ft. Ferry range with external fuel 2815km (1520nm). Combat radius 1355km (730nm).

Weights: RF-4C – Empty 12,825kg (28,275lb), max takeoff 26,308kg (58,000lb).

Dimensions: RF-4C – Wing span 11.77m (38ft 8in), length 19.17m (62ft 11in), height 5.03m (16ft 6in). Wing area 49.2m^2 (530.0sq ft).

Accommodation: Pilot and reconnaissance officer in tandem.

Armament: None, although max theoretical external load is 7255kg (16,000lb). Many RF-4s wired to carry two AIM-9s for self defence.

Operators: Greece, Japan, Israel, South Korea, Spain, Turkey.

History: A number of factors made the F-4 Phantom suitable for conversion as a reconnaissance platform, including its speed (hence survivability), range and availability.

Development of the reconnaissance Phantom was done at the beckon of the US Air Force, who ordered the RF-4C in 1965 to replace its RF-101 Voodoos (also a McDonnell product). The RF-4C retained the basic airframe and systems of the F-4C fighter but introduced a lengthened nose containing an APQ-99 forward looking radar for mapping and terrain clearance plus an APQ-102 side looking radar and various optical cameras. Cameras fitted to RF-4Cs included the KS-72 and KS-87 forward looking oblique cameras, the KA-56A low altitude camera, the KA-55A high altitude panoramic camera and the 167cm (66in) focal length KS-127. Other systems fitted to the RF-4 include the ARN-101 digital navigation and reconnaissance system, infrared linescan cameras, Elint and ESM sensors.

The YRF-4C prototype first flew on August 9 1963, and production RF-4Cs were delivered from the following year. In all McDonnell built 505 RF-4C Phantoms for the USAF through to December 1973, and these have served widely including during the Vietnam and Gulf wars. Despite the type's utility, by 1995 just two Air National Guard units operated the RF-4C and the type was retired from USAF service the following year. Surplus USAF RF-4Cs were supplied to Spain in the early 1970s and to South Korea from 1988, and the recce Phantom looks set to remain in service with these nations for some years.

Similar to the RF-4C were the 46 RF-4Bs built for the US Marines from 1965. The survivors were retired in the early 1990s.

The export RF-4E was developed initially for Germany and flew for the first time in September 1970. Compared with the RF-4C, the RF-4E was based on the F-4E and did not feature some of the RF-4C's more sensitive systems. New build RF-4Es were delivered to Germany, Japan, Israel, Greece and Turkey (the latter two now also operate ex Luftwaffe RF-4Es). Israeli RF-4Es are fitted with indigenous sensors and avionics and can fire the Shafir and Python AAMs for self defence.

Photo: The last USAF ANG RF-4Cs were retired in 1996, leaving Spain the world's only RF-4C operator, with 14 on strength. (MAP)

McDonnell Douglas F-15 Eagle

Country of origin: United States of America

Type: Air superiority fighter

Powerplants: F-15C – Two 65.3kN (14,670lb) dry and 105.7kN (23,770lb) with afterburning Pratt & Whitney F100-PW-220 turbofans.

Performance: F-15C – Max level speed over Mach 2.5, or approx 2655km/h (1433kt). Max initial rate of climb over 50,000ft/min. Service ceiling 60,000ft. Ferry range with external fuel and conformal fuel tanks over 5745km (3100nm). Combat radius on an intercept mission 1965km (1060nm). Endurance with conformal fuel tanks 5hr 15min.

Weights: F-15C – Operating empty 12,793kg (28,600lb), max takeoff 30,845kg (68,000lb).

Dimensions: Wing span 13.05m (42ft 10in), length 19.43m (63ft 9in), height 5.63m (18ft 6in). Wing area 56.5m² (608.0sq ft).

Accommodation: Pilot only, or two in tandem in F-15B/D.

Armament: One M61A1 20mm cannon. Can carry total external ordnance load of 7257kg (16,000lb). Typical CAP fit of four AIM-7s on fuselage stations and two AIM-9s or AIM-120s on each wing pylon.

Operators: Israel, Japan, Saudi Arabia, USA.

History: Without doubt the pre-eminent air superiority fighter since the mid 1970s, the F-15 Eagle replaced the Phantom in US service.

Design work on a new fighter for the USAF first began in the mid 1960s, and the program gained fresh impetus later that decade when US satellites revealed the existence of the MiG-23 and MiG-25. The FX requirement took in the air combat lessons of Vietnam and called for a fighter with a thrust to weight ratio in excess of unity and that could out turn any adversary to bring its missiles to bear first.

McDonnell Douglas' design was chosen ahead of proposals from Fairchild-Republic and North American Rockwell, with the result that the first development F-15 Eagle took to the skies for the first time on July 27 1972. Design features include the specifically developed P&W F100 turbofans, the Hughes APG-63 radar, a high wing of great area and then advanced cockpit displays, including a HUD.

The F-15 entered service in January 1976, and 355 F-15As and 57 two seat F-15Bs were built. Israel was the first F-15 export customer, and its Eagles were the first to be used in combat. Production switched to the improved F-15C/D in 1979. Changes are minor but include the ability to carry the conformal fuel tanks (CFTs) on each fuselage side, uprated engines and improved radar. The C/D was exported to Israel and Saudi Arabia and Mitsubishi built 204 under licence in Japan until late 1997 as the F-15J (and DJ two seater). US F-15C/D production ceased in 1992 (622 built). The Japanese intend to upgrade 100 F-15Js with a new radar, possibly a Mitsubishi Electric active phased array unit.

Saudi and US F-15s flew extensive combat air patrols during the Gulf War in 1991, claiming 32 Iraqi aircraft without loss.

USAF F-15C/Ds were upgraded from 1985 to 1997 under the Multi Stage Improvement Program (MSIP) to feature the Hughes APG-70 radar, a colour CRT in the cockpit and AIM-120 compatibility. From 1999 164 USAF F-15C/Ds are due to be fitted with the upgraded Hughes APG-63(V)1 radar.

The F-15E strike fighter is described under Boeing.

Photo: A USAF F-15C gets airborne. (Paul Merritt)

McDonnell Douglas C-9 & DC-9

Country of origin: United States of America

Type: Multirole transport and medical evacuation aircraft

Powerplants: C-9A – Two 64.5kN (14,500lb) Pratt & Whitney JT8D-9 turbofans.

Performance: C-9A – Max speed 935km/h (505kt), typical cruising speed 810km/h (437kt). Max initial rate of climb 2900ft/min. Time to 35,000ft 25min. Service ceiling 35,820ft. Range with max payload 1690km (913nm), ferry range 4700km (2538nm).

Weights: C-9A – Basic equipped 28,235kg (62,247lb), max takeoff 48,990kg (108,000lb).

Dimensions: C-9A – Wing span 28.47m (93ft 5in), length 36.37m (119ft 4in), height 8.38m (27ft 6in). Wing area 93.0m² (1000.7sq ft).

Accommodation: Flightcrew of two. Crew on C-9A comprises two flightcrew, flight observer, senior flight nurse, nurse, senior medical technician and two medical attendants. Can carry 40 ambulatory patients or 30 stretcher patients, or combinations thereof. DC-9-30 max seating in passenger configuration for 115.

Armament: None

Operators: Italy, USA, Venezuela.

History: The DC-9 series is a highly successful (2400 built) family of twinjet airliners ranging in size from 80 to 150 seats. In its DC-9-30 form it has been adopted for military operations as an aeromedical transport (C-9A) and staff and utility transport (C-9B/C-9C).

The DC-9 was developed as a short range airliner to complement the much larger DC-8, and fill a market sector that at the time Boeing was neglecting. Development was launched on April 8 1963.

The DC-9 was an all new design, featuring rear fuselage mounted engines, a T-tail, moderately swept wings and seats for up to 80 passengers. Construction of the prototype began in July 1963 and first flight occurred on February 25 1965. Certification and service entry occurred on November 23 1965 and December 8 1965 respectively.

The DC-9 had been designed with stretched larger capacity developments in mind, and such versions of the basic DC-9-10 soon followed. The first stretch resulted in the 4.54m (14ft 11in) longer DC-9-30, which entered service in February 1967. Subsequent stretched versions are the DC-9-40, DC-9-50, JT8D-200 powered MD-80 series and the V2500 powered, 150 seat MD-90.

The DC-9-30 is the major DC-9 development adopted for military use. In August 1967 the USAF selected the DC-9-30 to meet its requirement for an off the shelf airliner suitable for development as an aeromedical transport. Designated C-9A, USAF aeromedical DC-9s are appropriately named Nightingale. The 21 C-9As delivered feature a large forward freight door, provision for a therapeutic oxygen supply and an isolated care section. In addition, the USAF acquired three DC-9-30s as C-9C VIP/staff transports.

The US Navy and Marines acquired a total of 15 freight door equipped staff/logistical transport C-9B Skytrain IIs from 1972.

Meanwhile Italy operates two DC-9-30s as VIP transports.

Photo: A US Navy C-9B staff/logistics transport. The C-9B's Skytrain II name honours that much earlier, legendary Douglas transport, the C-47/DC-3. (Keith Anderson)

MDC KC-10 Extender & DC-10

Country of origin: United States of America

Type: Strategic tanker transport

Powerplants: KC-10 – Three 233.5kN (52,500lb) General Electric F103-GE-100 (CF6-50C2) turbofans.

Performance: KC-10 – Max speed at 25,000ft 982km/h (530kt), max cruising speed at 30,000ft 908km/h (490kt), long range cruising speed 870km/h (470kt). Max initial rate of climb 2900ft/min. Range with max payload 7030km (3797nm). Max ferry range unrefuelled 18,505km (9990nm). Can transfer 90,720kg (200,000lb) of fuel 3540km (1910nm) from base.

Weights: KC-10 – Operating empty 108,890kg (240,065lb), max takeoff 267,620kg (590,000lb).

Dimensions: Wing span 47.34m (155ft 4in), length 55.35m (181ft 7in), height 17.70m (58ft 1in). Wing area 358.7m² (3861.0sq ft).

Accommodation: KC-10 – Crew complement of five, with six seats provided for a relief crew. Can be configured with 75 passenger seats. Max payload 76,845kg (169,410lb), design fuel capacity 161,510kg (356,065lb).

Armament: None

Operators: KC-10 – USA. KDC-10 – Netherlands.

History: The KC-10 Extender tanker transport is a military development of the DC-10 widebody airliner.

Development of the DC-10 airliner was launched in February 1968 with orders from American and United Airlines. The second widebody to fly (behind the 747), the DC-10 began life as a twinjet, but gained a third engine to meet the field performance American Airlines demanded. The prototype first flew on August 29 1970.

DC-10 variants include the initial production DC-10-10, the intercontinental range DC-10-30 (with extra fuel and a third main undercarriage unit) and the P&W JT9D powered DC-10-40.

In December 1977 the US Air Force selected the DC-10 as its Advanced Tanker Cargo Aircraft (ATCA), ahead of the Boeing 747. The ATCA program aimed to procure an off the shelf jet transport suitable for use as both a strategic transport and an air-to-air refueller.

Initially the USAF ordered 16 modified DC-10s as the KC-10A Extender. The first of these flew on July 12 1980. In May 1982 the total KC-10 order was increased to 60. The final KC-10 was delivered in 1988.

The KC-10 is based on the DC-10-30CF (convertible freighter) and features a large forward freight door, an air-to-air receptacle above the cockpit, a McDonnell Douglas Advanced Aerial Refuelling Boom and a hose and reel refuelling unit, both beneath the rear fuselage. In addition 20 KC-10s feature two underwing hose and reel refuelling units. As well as the basic fuel tanks, fuel is stored in seven bladder tanks in the lower cargo holds. The main deck accommodates freight and up to 75 passengers.

The only other DC-10 military operator is the Royal Netherlands Air Force, which in 1995 took delivery of the first of two ex Martinair DC-10-30CFs that KLM and McDonnell Douglas had converted with refuelling boom to KDC-10 configuration.

Photo: The Netherlands' KDC-10s feature a telerobotic refuelling system with TV cameras which provide three dimensional displays of refuelling operations to the refuelling operator. (Boeing)

MiG MAPO MiG-AT

Country of origin: Russia

Type: Two seat advanced trainer

Powerplants: Two 14.1kN (3175lb) Turboméca-SNECMA Larzac 04-R20 turbofans. Series production aircraft for Russia will have two 16.7kN (3750lb) Soyuz RD 1700s.

Performance: Estimated – Max speed at 8200ft 1000km/h (540kt), max speed at sea level 850km/h (460kt). Service ceiling 50,820ft. Ferry range approx 2600km (1405nm).

Weights: Normal takeoff 4610kg (10,155lb), MTOW 7000kg (15,420lb).

Dimensions: Wing span 10.16m (33ft 4in), length overall including nose probe 12.01m (39ft 5in), height 4.42m (14ft 6in).

Accommodation: Two in tandem. Pilot only in MiG-AS.

Armament: Six underwing and one centreline hardpoints on armed models can carry a max external load of 2000kg (4410lb), including missiles and bombs.

Operators: Russia*

History: The Mikoyan MiG-AT is one of two competitors for a Russian air force requirement for a new advanced jet trainer to replace the Czech designed L-39 Albatros.

The MiG-AT and Yak-130 were shortlisted for further development and competitive evaluation from a number of design proposals from Russian aircraft designers. In 1992 Mikoyan reached an agreement with engine manufacturer SNECMA of France that the first two prototypes would be powered by two Larzac turbofans (the Larzac powers the Alpha Jet).

The MiG-AT is of conventional configuration and features a large degree of composite construction and fly-by-wire flight controls. The wing is straight and the two engines are mounted either side of the fuselage. One early design change was the repositioning of the tailplane from the top of the fin to lower down on the tail.

If the MiG-AT is selected for the Russian trainer program it will feature Russian avionics. Regardless of the competition's outcome though Mikoyan is offering the MiG-AT for export with either Russian or French avionics. In westernised form the MiG-AT features advanced avionics and cockpit displays built by Sextant Avionique including LCD colour displays, a wide angle HUD and HOTAS controls, with all avionics connected through a MIL STD 1553B databus, allowing future integration of further western equipment and weaponry.

The first prototype first flew on March 21 1996 (following a 5min hop on March 16) and is equipped with Sextant avionics. The second prototype is equipped with Russian avionics and was due to fly in late 1997. The second prototype is built to MiG-AT-UTS standard with a ground attack capability.

The Russian air force has ordered 10 MiG-ATs for evaluation (as well as 10 Yak-130s) and these will be powered by Larzacs and feature Sextant avionics. Series production aircraft for the Russian air force though will be powered by the 16.7kN (3570lb) Soyuz RD 1700 turbofan currently under development.

A single seat attack version of the MiG-AT is also under development under the designation MiG-AS. Features could include an internal gun and radar. It will be marketed internationally.

Photo: The first MiG-AT prototype. (Paul Merritt)

Mikoyan-Gurevich MiG-15 & MiG-15UTI

Country of origin: Russia

Type: Lead-in fighter and advanced trainer

Powerplant: MiG-15UTI – One 22.2kN (5000lb) Klimov RD-45F turbojet.

Performance: MiG-15UTI – Max speed at sea level 1015km/h (549kt), max speed at 9600ft 1010km/h (547kt). Time to 16,400ft 2min 35sec, time to 32,800ft 6min 48sec. Service ceiling 48,640ft. Max range with external fuel 1425km (770nm), range with internal fuel 950km (513nm). Max endurance 2hr 30min.

Weights: MiG-15UTI – Empty 3720kg (8200lb), max takeoff 5415kg (11,938lb).

Dimensions: MiG-15UTI – Wing span 10.13m (33ft 3in), length 11.15m (36ft 7in), height 3.39m (11ft 2in). Wing area 20.6m² (221.8sq ft).

Accommodation: Pilot only in MiG-15, or two in tandem in MiG-15UTI.

Armament: None usually carried, but can be fitted with one 23mm NR-23 cannon or one 12.4mm UBK-E machine gun, or one 12.7mm A-12.7 machine gun.

Operators: MiG-15 – Albania, China, Cuba, Romania. MiG-15UTI – Albania, Angola, Congo, Guinea Republic, Mali, Romania, Vietnam, Yemen.

History: The MiG-15 shattered western beliefs of the standard of Russian aircraft design when it appeared in combat in the skies of Korea over four decades ago, while today it still survives in service in single and two seat forms.

The MiG-15 (NATO codename 'Fagot') resulted from Project S – a 1946 requirement for a new jet powered high altitude day fighter capable of speeds over 1000km/h (540kt) with a ceiling of 46,000ft. The Lavochkin, Yakovlev and Mikoyan-Gurevich design bureaus responded with fairly similar aircraft, all with swept wings and tail surfaces, a stubby fuselage with nose air intake, and, probably most important of all, a Klimov RD-45 turbojet. The RD-45 was an unlicenced copy of the Rolls-Royce Nene centrifugal turbojet and was far more advanced than contemporary Russian turbojets.

Mikoyan-Gurevich's design, the I-310, flew for the first time on December 30 1947. Following evaluation both the Mikoyan-Gurevich and Lavochkin designs were ordered into production, as the MiG-15 and La-15 respectively. Around 500 La-15s were built, compared with at least 3000 single seat MiG-15s (many under licence in Poland and Czechoslovakia).

Chinese MiG-15s were used widely in combat during the Korean War. The MiG's excellent performance came as something of a shock to the western world, although it was ably countered by experienced and well trained pilots flying North American F-86 Sabres.

Aside from the basic MiG-15, the single seater was also built in improved MiG-15bis form. MiG-15bis improvements included a more powerful engine (redesignated VK-1), lower empty weight, greater fuel capacity and some aerodynamic changes.

Finally over 5000 two seat MiG-15UTIs (or 'Midgets') were built for operational conversion and advanced training from 1949. Today several nations have MiG-15UTIs (or Chinese built FT-2s) on strength.

Photo: Soviet/Russian MiG-15UTIs were retired in the 1970s, although several third world nations continue to operate the type.

Mikoyan-Gurevich MiG-17 & Chengdu JJ-5

Country of origin: Russia

Type: Light attack fighter

Powerplant: MiG-17F – One 25.5kN (5732lb) dry and 33.1kN (7450lb) with afterburning Klimov VK-1F turbojet.

Performance: MiG-17F – Max speed at 16,400ft Mach 0.98 or 1130km/h (610kt), max speed at 32,810ft Mach 0.93 or 1071km/h (578kt). Max initial rate of climb 12,795ft/min. Service ceiling 54,460ft. Range with external fuel at 32,810ft 1470km (794nm), range with internal fuel at 32,810ft 970km (524nm).

Weights: MiG-17F – Empty equipped 3930kg (8665lb), max takeoff 6070kg (13,380lb).

Dimensions: MiG-17F – Wing span 9.63m (31ft 7in), length 11.26m (37ft 0in), height 3.80m (12ft 6in). Wing area 22.6m² (243.3sq ft).

Accommodation: Pilot only, or two in tandem in Chengdu JJ-5/FT-5.

Armament: MiG-17F – Three 23mm NR-23 cannons. Four underwing hardpoints can carry a single 250kg (550lb) bomb each, or a UV-16-57 rocket pod (with 16 x 50mm rockets) each.

Operators: MiG-17 – Algeria, Angola, Cuba, Guinea-Bissau, Guinea Republic, Madagascar, Mali, Romania, Sudan, Syria, Uganda, Vietnam. JJ-5/FT-5 – Albania, China, Sri Lanka, Sudan.

History: The MiG-17 was designed to overcome some of the performance and design shortcomings of the MiG-15.

Design work on the improved MiG-15 began in early 1949 under the designation I-330. The developed MiG-15 (Mikoyan-Gurevich's Project SI) aimed in particular to overcome the MiG-15's poor high Mach number handling characteristics (a lack of directional control limited the MiG-15's top speed to Mach 0.92). While the MiG-17 looks very similar to the MiG-15, the -17 introduced a new longer span, wider chord wing with greater sweepback angle and a redesigned tailplane. The tail is taller while the horizontal surfaces have greater sweepback.

The prototype MiG-17 first flew on February 1 1950 and the type was ordered into production in August 1951. Initial production was of the MiG-17 (NATO 'Fresco-A'), while the MiG-17F ('Fresco-C') introduced an afterburning VK-1F turbojet (still derived from the RR Nene). The MiG-17PF featured radar, the MiG-17PFU radar and four radar guided AAMs.

At least 8000 MiG-17s were built in Russia, Poland (as the Lim-6) and China (as the J-5). The MiG-17 served widely with Soviet client state air forces, initially as an interceptor and later as a light attack/close support platform armed with bombs and rockets. Several third world nations still use it for ground attack and weapons training.

The only two seat MiG-17s were built in China, as the USSR deemed the MiG-15UTI suitable for conversion training for the MiG-17 and MiG-19. The Chinese two seat MiG-17, the JJ-5, was built by Chengdu. Design changes include the two cockpits in tandem under a similar canopy as that on the MiG-15UTI and a slightly stretched fuselage. The JJ-5 first flew on May 8 1966 and Chengdu built more than 1060 through to 1986. The JJ-5 was exported widely as the FT-5 and several nations continue to operate it as an advanced trainer.

Photo: Poland retired its MiG-17s (Lim-6s) in 1992. (Alan Scoot)

Mikoyan MiG-21

Country of origin: Russia

Type: Lightweight fighter

Powerplant: MiG-21MF – One 39.1kN (8792lb) dry and 63.6kN (14,307lb) with afterburning Tumansky (now Soyuz) R-13-300 turbojet.

Performance: MiG-21MF – Max speed at 36,090ft 2230km/h (1203kt), max speed at sea level 1300km/h (703kt). Max initial rate of climb 23,620ft/min. Service ceiling (theoretical) 59,710ft. Ferry range with three drop tanks 1800km (970nm). Combat radius with four 250kg (550lb) bombs hi-lo-hi 370km (200nm), combat radius with two 250kg (550lb) bombs and external fuel hi-lo-hi 740km (400nm).

Weights: MiG-21MF – Empty 5350kg (11,795lb), max takeoff 9400kg (20,723lb).

Dimensions: MiG-21MF – Span 7.15m (23ft 6in), length inc probe 15.76m (51ft 9in), height 4.13m (13ft 6in). Wing area 23.0m² (247.5sq ft).

Accommodation: Pilot only, or two in tandem in MiG-21U/UM.

Armament: MiG-21MF – One 23mm GSh-23L cannon. Max external ordnance load of 2000kg (4410lb) on four underwing hardpoints.

Operators: Afghanistan, Algeria, Angola, Bulgaria, Cambodia, Congo, Croatia, Cuba, Hungary, India, Iraq, Laos, Mongolia, Mozambique, Nigeria, North Korea, Poland, Slovakia, Sudan, Syria, Vietnam, Yemen, Yugoslavia.

History: More MiG-21s were built (8000+), served with more nations and fought in more wars than any other jet fighter.

The MiG-21 ('Fishbed' in NATO parlance) was conceived as a lightweight day interceptor, with design emphasis on performance, simplicity, ease of construction and maintainability. Prototype MiG-21s were flown in swept wing 'Faceplate' and tailed delta forms in 1955.

The tailed delta configuration was selected for development. Consequently 40 pre production MiG-21Fs were built. Initial production was of the MiG-21F-13 ('Fishbed-C'). Primary armament was a cannon and two AA-2 'Atoll' AAMs. The MiG-21F-13 also formed the basis for the MiG-21U ('Mongol') two seater.

Further early model MiG-21s, characterised by their forward opening single piece cockpit canopies, included the gun-less MiG-21P ('Fishbed-D'), the RP-21 Sapfir radar equipped MiG-21PF and export MiG-21FL with down spec radar and less powerful engine. The MiG-21P and MiG-21PF were called 'Fishbed-E' by NATO and later subvariants featured a ventral cannon. The MiG-21PFS and PFM (both 'Fishbed-F') were similar but introduced a two piece canopy, upgraded radar and more powerful engine.

The reconnaissance MiG-21R ('Fishbed-H') was based on the MiG-21PFM and carried a centreline recce pod which could contain a variety of sensors including optical or TV cameras, infrared sensors or a Sideways Looking Airborne Radar (SLAR).

Development of fighter MiG-21s continued with the MiG-21S with a RP-22 radar and ventral gun pod. The export MiG-21M and more powerful R-13-300 powered MiG-21SM re-introduced an internal cannon. Improvement continued with the R-13-300 powered MiG-21MF ('Fishbed-J') with RP-22 radar and AAM missile capability on all four underwing hardpoints, plus the MiG-21SMT with an oversize dorsal fairing containing fuel.

Photo: A Slovakian MiG-21U.

Mikoyan MiG-21bis

Country of origin: Russia

Type: Light multirole fighter

Powerplant: One 40.2kN (9038lb) dry, 69.7kN (15,653lb) with afterburning and 97.1kN/21,825lb emergency rated Tumansky (now Soyuz) R-25-300 turbojet, with provision for two 24.5kN (5510lb) SPRD-99 rocket boosters.

Performance: Max speed at 42,650ft Mach 2.1 or 2175km/h (1177kt), max speed at sea level 1150km/h (620kt). Max initial rate of climb with two AAMs and 50% fuel 45,275ft/min. Service ceiling 57,415ft. Range at 32,800ft with one drop tank 2175km/h (1177kt). Typical combat radius 450 to 500km (245 to 270nm).

Weights: Empty 5450kg (12,015lb), max takeoff 9800kg (21,605lb).

Dimensions: Wing span 7.15m (23ft 6in), length inc probe 15.76m (51ft 9in), height 4.13m (13ft 6in). Wing area 23.0m² (247.5sq ft).

Accommodation: Pilot only.

Armament: One 23mm GSh-23 cannon. One centreline and four underwing hardpoints can carry a total ordnance load of 2000kg (4410lb). Options include four rocket pods, or two 500kg (1100lb) and two 250kg (550lb) bombs, AA-2 'Atoll' and R-60 AA-8 'Aphid' AAMs.

Operators: MiG-21bis – Afghanistan, Algeria, Angola, Croatia, Cuba, Finland, Guinea Republic, Hungary, India, Mozambique, Poland, Romania, Syria, Vietnam, Yemen, Yugoslavia.

History: The MiG-21bis was developed as a multirole fighter for the Soviet Union's Frontal Aviation and was the most important and capable MiG-21 variant. Most surviving MiG-21s are MiG-21bis.

Like earlier variants before it, the MiG-21bis introduced further improvements to the airframe, engine, avionics and weaponry. The MiG-21bis is powered by a Tumansky R-25-300 turbojet, over a third more powerful than in the original MiG-21's engine. This increase in power allowed Mikoyan to increase the MiG-21's fuel capacity in an enlarged dorsal fairing. The MiG-21bis entered Russian service in early 1972, and was allocated the NATO reporting name 'Fishbed-L'. NATO's 'Fishbed-N' designation covers later production MiG-21bis fitted with an undernose ILS antenna and improved avionics.

As well as Russian production, several hundred MiG-21s were built under licence by HAL in India between 1980 and 1987. India remains an important operator of MiG-21bis and earlier model MiG-21s with over 400 in service.

With the large numbers of MiG-21bis remaining in service the type is a logical candidate for an upgrade program. A number of MiG-21 upgrades are on offer, most notably from Mikoyan-MAPO and Israel's IAI (ironically a country that had been on the receiving end of the MiG-21 in several wars). IAI's MiG-21-2000 upgrade package is offered in varying levels of equipment, including airframe overhaul, avionics upgrade and new radar. The first upgraded MiG-21-2000 flew for the first time in May 1995.

MiG-MAPO meanwhile offers its upgraded MiG-21-93 featuring Russian avionics, a new radar and compatibility with current generation Russian AAMs. India has contracted MiG MAPO to upgrade 100 of its MiG-21s to this standard.

Photo: The Elbit/Aerostar MiG-21 Lancer upgrade for Romania features new cockpit displays, a HUD, HOTAS controls and Elta 2032 radar.

Mikoyan MiG-23

Country of origin: Russia

Type: Multirole fighter

Powerplant: MiG-23ML – One 83.8kN (18,850lb) dry and 127.5kN (28,660lb) with afterburning Tumansky (now Soyuz) R-35-300 turbojet.

Performance: MiG-23ML – Max speed with weapons Mach 2.35 or 2500km/h (1349kt). Max initial rate of climb 47,250ft/min. Service ceiling 59,055ft. Combat radius with six AAMs 1150km (620nm), combat radius with 2000kg (4410lb) of bombs 700km (378nm).

Weights: MiG-23ML – Empty 10,200kg (22,485lb), max takeoff 17,800kg (39,250lb).

Dimensions: MiG-23ML – Span wings extended 13.97m (45ft 10in), span wings swept 7.78m (25ft 6in), length overall exc probe 15.88m (52ft 1in), height 4.82m (15ft 10in). Wing area wings extended 37.3m^2 (401.5sq ft), wing area wings swept 34.2m^2 (368.1sq ft).

Accommodation: Pilot only, or two in tandem MiG-23UM and UB.

Armament: One twin barrel 23mm GSh-23 cannon. Five external hardpoints (one centreline, two underfuselage and two underwing) can carry a max external load of 2000kg (4410lb) on MiG-23ML. Typical air-to-air configuration of two R-60 (AA-8 'Aphid') and two R-23 (AA-7 'Apex') AAMs.

Operators: Afghanistan, Algeria, Belarus, Bulgaria, Cuba, Czech Republic, Ethiopia, Hungary, India, Iraq, Libya, North Korea, Poland, Romania, Russia, Sudan, Syria, Ukraine, Vietnam, Yemen.

History: From the mid 1970s and into the 1980s the MiG-23 (NATO reporting name 'Flogger') was the Soviet Union's most capable tactical fighter.

The MiG-23 was developed to replace the MiG-21, with improvements in overall performance and in particular short field performance. Two Mikoyan designed prototypes were built, the swept wing 23-01 'Faithless' and the swing wing 23-11. The 23-11 first flew on April 10 1967 and was ordered into production as the MiG-23S, fitted with the MiG-21S' RP-22 radar. Fifty were built for evaluation.

The MiG-23M ('Flogger-B') was the first model to introduce the specially designed Sapfir-23 pulse doppler radar in a larger nose radome and also featured a more powerful engine and IRST and R-23 missile compatibility. The down spec export MiG-23MS ('Flogger-E') was similar, while the export and further down spec MiG-23MF ('Flogger-B') features the RP-22 radar and smaller nose.

Subsequent fighter MiG-23s were the lightened MiG-23ML ('Flogger-G') with less fuel and no dorsal fin extension, the MiG-23P interceptor that could be automatically guided to its target by ground controllers and the MiG-23MLD ('Flogger-K') with aerodynamic changes. The MiG-23UB ('Flogger-C') meanwhile is the two seat conversion trainer.

Various MiG-23 models were also built specifically for ground attack. The first to appear was the MiG-23B with a pointy, radar-less nose and a Lyulka AL-21 turbojet. The improved MiG-23BN returned to the Tumansky turbojet. NATO called both the MiG-23B and MiG-23BN the 'Flogger-F'. Further improved MiG-23 attack variants were the MiG-23BK and MiG-23BM, both of which borrowed nav attack systems from the MiG-27.

Photo: A Czech MiG-23ML (note lack of dorsal fin). (Paul Merritt)

Mikoyan MiG-27

Country of origin: Russia

Type: Ground attack aircraft

Powerplant: MiG-27 – One 78.5kN (17,637lb) dry and 112.8kN (25,353lb) with afterburning Tumansky (now Soyuz) R-29B-300 turbojet.

Performance: MiG-27 – Max speed at 26,200ft 1885km/h (1017kt), max speed at sea level 1350km/h (728kt). Max initial rate of climb 39,370ft/min. Service ceiling 45,930ft. Combat radius with two Kh-29 ASMs and three drop tanks lo-lo-lo 540km (290nm), radius with two Kh-29s and no external fuel 225km (120nm).

Weights: MiG-27 – Empty equipped 11,910kg (26,252lb), max take-off 20,300kg (44,753lb).

Dimensions: MiG-27 – Span wings extended 13.97m (45ft 10in), span wings swept 7.78m (25ft 6in), length 17.08m (56ft 0in), height 5.00m (16ft 5in). Wing area wings extended 37.4m^2 (402.1sq ft), wings swept 34.2m^2 (367.7sq ft).

Accommodation: Pilot only.

Armament: One GSh-6-30 30mm cannon. Max external weapons load of over 4000kg (8820lb). Options include laser, TV and electro optically guided ASMs and PGMs, conventional bombs, rockets, gun and cannon pods and tactical nuclear bombs.

Operators: India, Russia, Ukraine.

History: The MiG-27 series are the strike and ground attack optimised variants of the MiG-23, and as such forms an important part of Russia's offensive inventory.

The MiG-27 designation originally applied to a range of Mikoyan design studies aimed to meet a requirement for a modern day Shturmovik that was eventually met by the Sukhoi Su-25. Instead the MiG-27 is the definitive strike/ground attack member of the 'Flogger' MiG-23/27 family.

The ground attack MiG-23s, as described in the previous entry, were regarded as interim ground attack aircraft pending the arrival of the optimised MiG-27. Compared with the MiG-23, the MiG-27 features simplified air intakes (as opposed to the F-4 style variable intake ramps of the MiG-23 optimised for high end performance) and simplified two stage afterburner nozzles. An extra external hardpoint and strengthened main undercarriage permit the carriage of over 4000kg (8820lb) of armament. Perhaps its most distinctive feature is the duckbill nose (which it shares with ground attack MiG-23s) which features a laser rangefinder and other sensors. The MiG-27 features advanced nav attack systems allowing all weather operations, and can be used in the tactical reconnaissance role carrying various recce pods.

The MiG-27 first flew in prototype form in 1972. The initial production MiG-27 was soon followed by the MiG-27K ('Flogger-D'). NATO's 'Flogger-J' designation covers the improved MiG-27D, MiG-27M and MiG-27K ('Flogger-J2') with a laser designator.

Outside the CIS India is the only MiG-27 export customer, where it has been built under licence. India calls its aircraft MiG-27M Bahadurs, although Mikoyan refers to them as MiG-27Ls.

Photo: The duckbill nose, stronger undercarriage, simpler intakes and a shorter exhaust nozzle differentiate the MiG-27 from the MiG-23. This is a Russian MiG-27D. (MAP)

Mikoyan MiG-25

Country of origin: Russia

Type: Interceptor and reconnaissance aircraft

Powerplants: MiG-25PDS – Two 109.8kN (24,690lb) with afterburning Tumansky (now Soyuz) R-15BD-300 turbojets.

Performance: MiG-25PDS – Max speed Mach 2.8 or 3000km/h (1620kt), max speed at sea level 1200km/h (647kt). Time to 65,615ft 8min 55sec. Service ceiling 67,915ft. Range with internal fuel 1730km (933nm). Endurance 2hr 5min.

Weights: MiG-25PDS – Normal takeoff with four R-40 AAMs and max internal fuel 36,720kg (80,950lb).

Dimensions: MiG-25PDS – Wing span 14.02m (46ft 0in), length 23.82m (78ft 2in), height 6.10m (20ft 0in). Wing area 61.4m² (660.9sq ft).

Accommodation: Pilot only, or two in separate cockpits in MiG-25PU.

Armament: Four underwing hardpoints can carry a total ordnance load of 4000kg (9635lb). Typical interceptor configuration of two R-40 (AA-6 'Acrid') and four R-60 (AA-8 'Aphid') AAMs, or alternatively can carry four R-40s, or two R-23s (AA-7 'Apex') and four R-73A (AA-11 'Archer') AAMs. MiG-25BM can carry four Kh-58 (AS-11 'Kilter') anti radiation missiles.

Operators: Algeria, India, Iraq, Libya, Russia, Syria.

History: The MiG-25 high altitude, high speed interceptor was initially developed to counter the Mach 3 XB-70 Valkyrie bomber under development in the US in the late 1950s and early 1960s.

Although the XB-70 program (apart from research flying) was cancelled in 1961, work on the new high speed interceptor and reconnaissance platform continued. The two main design considerations for the new aircraft were speed and high altitude performance, something that was attained at the expense of manoeuvrability. Design of the MiG-25 was also a remarkable feat, given that it had to withstand the high temperatures of high speed flight. The airframe is made mainly of nickel steel, with some titanium used in areas such as leading edges.

The first MiG-25 prototype to fly was the Ye-155R-1 reconnaissance prototype and it flew for the first time on March 6 1964. The interceptor Ye-166P-1 had its first flight that September. Under the designations Ye-266 and Ye-266M, two MiG-25s set a range of speed and altitude records, many of which remain unbroken.

Initial 'Foxbat' production was of the MiG-25P interceptor. Service entry was in 1973. Subsequent MiG-25 interceptors were the new build MiG-25PD 'Foxbat-E' with new look down shoot down radar, more powerful engines and an IRST, and the similar MiG-25PDS to which standard MiG-25Ps were rebuilt from 1979. The MiG-25PU 'Foxbat-C' two seat conversion trainer has stepped separate cockpits.

The initial reconnaissance production variant was of the MiG-25R, which was soon replaced by the MiG-25RB 'Foxbat-B', which also had a ground attack capability. Variants with different equipment were the MiG-25RBS, BSh and RBV. The MiG-25RBK is fitted with SLAR rather than optical cameras, as is the MiG-25RBF. The MiG-25RU is a two seater. Finally the MiG-25BM ('Foxbat-F') is a dedicated defence suppression platform that carries up to four Kh-58 (AS-11 'Kilter') anti radiation missiles.

Photo: A MiG-25RB.

Mikoyan MiG-31

Country of origin: Russia

Type: Interceptor

Powerplants: MiG-31 – Two 151.9kN (34,170lb) with afterburning Aviadvigatel (nee Soloviev) D-30F6 turbofans.

Performance: MiG-31 – Max speed Mach 2.83 or 3000km/h (1620kt), max speed at sea level 1500km/h (810kt), max cruising speed at altitude Mach 2.35, economical cruising speed Mach 0.85. Time to 32,800ft 7min 54sec. Service ceiling 67,600ft. Combat radius with four R-33 AAMs and max internal fuel at Mach 2.35 720km (388nm), radius with four R-33s and external fuel at Mach 0.85 1400km (755nm). Ferry range with external fuel 3300km (1780nm). Endurance with external fuel 3hr 35min.

Weights: MiG-31 – Empty 21,825kg (48,115lb), max takeoff 46,200kg (101,850lb).

Dimensions: MiG-31 – Wing span 13.46m (44ft 2in), length 22.69m (74ft 5in), height 6.15m (20ft 2in). Wing area 61.6m² (663.0sq ft).

Accommodation: Pilot and weapon systems operator in tandem.

Armament: One GSh-6-23 23mm cannon. Four R-33 (AA-9 'Amos') long range AAMs carried under the fuselage. Four underwing hardpoints (two earlier) can carry two R-40T (AA-6 'Acrid') AAMs on inner pylons and four R-60 (AA-8 'Aphid') AAMs on outboard pylons (carried two in tandem).

Operators: Russia

History: The advanced MiG-31 two seat interceptor is designed to counter low flying strike aircraft and cruise missiles.

Development of this massive interceptor began in the 1970s, although the MiG-31 was first conceived as a single tail swing wing design, and then a tailless canard delta. In the end a design based on the MiG-25 was settled upon and a development aircraft, the Ye-155MP, flew for the first time on September 16 1975. Production MiG-31 'Foxhound-A's were delivered from 1979 and 280 were built.

While the MiG-31's airframe is based on the MiG-25, it is a really a new aircraft, with several design changes and differences. Unlike the MiG-25, the MiG-31 is powered by afterburning turbofans. Its airframe construction is made up of nickel steel (50%), light alloy (33%) and titanium (16%). The MiG-31 is also the first production aircraft to feature an electronically scanned phased array radar – the SBI 16 Zalson ('Flash Dance') – which is operated from the second cockpit by the dedicated weapon systems operator. It can track up to 10 targets and engage four simultaneously. Via datalink the MiG-31 can be controlled automatically by a ground control interceptor. Other changes include a retractable inflight refuelling probe (on later production aircraft), an internal gun and tandem main undercarriage.

The improved MiG-31M has been under development since 1984 and has flown in prototype form, but has not been ordered into production. It features a new Phazotron phased array radar, retractable IRST, no gun, two centreline hardpoints, R-37 (a derivative of the R-33) and R-77 (AA-12) AAM compatibility, a massive 52 tonne max takeoff weight and three colour CRTs in the rear cockpit. One has been observed with wingtip ECM pods. Just six MiG-31Ms have been built as the program has been thwarted by a lack of funding.

Photo: Mikoyan's MiG-31 demonstrator. (Doug Mackay)

MiG MAPO MiG-29

Country of origin: Russia

Type: Tactical counter-air fighter

Powerplants: MiG-29/-29S – Two 49.4kN (11,110lb) dry and 81.4kN (18,300lb) with afterburning Klimov/Sariskov RD-33 turbofans.

Performance: MiG-29S – Max speed at altitude Mach 2.3 or 2445km/h (1320kt), max speed at sea level Mach 1.225 or 1500km/h (810kt). Max initial rate of climb 65,000ft/min. Service ceiling 59,060ft. Range with external fuel 3000km (1565nm), range with max internal fuel 1430km (772nm).

Weights: MiG-29S – Max takeoff 19,700kg (43,430lb).

Dimensions: Wing span 11.36m (37ft 3in), length inc nose probe 17.32m (56ft 10in), height 4.73m (15ft 6in). Wing area 38.0m² (409.0sq ft).

Accommodation: Pilot only, or two in tandem in MiG-29UB.

Armament: MiG-29S – One 30mm GSh-301 cannon. Six underwing hardpoints can carry a max weapons load of 3000kg (6615lb), including R-27, R-73 and R-77 AAMs, plus rockets and bombs. MiG-29SM can carry Kh-29 and Kh-31 ASMs and KAB-500 TV guided PGMs.

Operators: Bulgaria, Cuba, Germany, Hungary, India, Iran, Iraq, North Korea, Malaysia, Moldova, Peru, Poland, Romania, Slovakia, Syria, USA, Yugoslavia.

History: The highly capable MiG-29 is Russia's most important tactical fighter and has been widely exported, with over 1200 built.

Serious development of the MiG-29 began in 1974 against a Soviet air force requirement for a highly manoeuvrable lightweight fighter capable of outperforming new western fighters in dogfights and to replace a range of aircraft in Frontal Aviation service including the MiG-21, MiG-23 and Su-15. The first of 14 prototypes flew on October 6 1977, although service entry was not until 1984. Some 460 are in Russian service and several hundred have been exported.

The MiG-29 features the same overall configuration as the much larger Sukhoi Su-27 which was developed concurrently. It features excellent high angle of attack performance and low speed handling and a thrust to weight ratio greater than unity. Additionally the MiG-29 features a RP-29 pulse doppler look down shoot down radar and an IRST unit which allows it to passively detect, track and engage other aircraft, while a helmet mounted sight can cue IR guided AAMs to off boresight targets.

In addition the MiG-29 is designed for operations from primitive airfields and doors seal the main intakes to protect the engines from foreign object damage (FOD) during start-up and taxying, with air drawn from louvred intakes in the wingroots. The intake doors open on takeoff rotation.

The basic MiG-29 'Fulcrum' (and MiG-29UB two seater) was joined in production by the 'Fulcrum-C' with a larger dorsal spine containing extra fuel. The 'Fulcrum-C' was built only for Russia and forms the basis for the MiG-29S with a modified flight control system, improved Phazotron N019M radar, compatibility with the advanced Vympel R-77 (AA-12) radar guided AAM and greater weapons load. It is offered for export as the MiG-29SE (and SD export upgrade of the 'Fulcrum-A'). The MiG-29SM has greater ASM compatibility.

Photo: A Polish MiG-29 gets airborne. (Paul Merritt)

MiG MAPO MiG-29M, MiG-33 & MiG-35

Country of origin: Russia

Type: Multirole fighter

Powerplants: Two 96kN (19,355lb) with afterburning Klimov/Sariskov RD-33K turbofans.

Performance: Max speed at altitude Mach 2.35 or 2445km/h (1320kt), max speed at sea level Mach 1.06 or 1500km/h (810kt). Max initial rate of climb 64,960ft/min. Service ceiling 55,780ft. Range with external fuel 3200km (1728nm), range with max internal fuel 2000km (1080nm). Combat radius with six AAMs and external fuel 1400km (755nm), with 3000kg (6615lb) of bombs and external fuel 1200km (645nm).

Weights: Max takeoff approx 20,000kg (44,050lb).

Dimensions: Wing span 11.36m (37ft 3in), length inc probe 17.37m (57ft 0in), height 4.73m (15ft 6in). Wing area 38.0m² (409.0sq ft).

Accommodation: Pilot only.

Armament: One GSh-301 30mm cannon. Max external ordnance of 4500kg (9920lb) on eight underwing hardpoints can include R-60MK (AA-8), R-27R1 (AA-10A), R-73E (AA-11) and R-77 (AA-12) AAMs, plus laser guided Kh-25ML (AS-10 'Karen'), Kh-29L (AS-14 'Kedge') ASMs, radar homing Kh-31P/A (AS-17 'Krypton') ASMs, TV guided Kh-29T (AS-14 'Kedge') ASMs, TV guided bombs, bombs and rockets.

Operators: None

History: The MiG-29M is an advanced multirole development of the basic MiG-29.

Development of the MiG-29M dates to the mid 1980s. Six prototypes were built and the first of these flew for the first time on April 25 1986 (although powered by RD-33s rather than RD-33Ks). The first prototype powered by the definitive, more powerful RD-33K powerplants first flew in late 1989. Funding has prevented the Russian air force ordering it into production. The MiG-29ME designation would have applied to export aircraft, instead these aircraft would now be covered by the MiG-33 designation.

The MiG-29M features significant changes over the basic MiG-29. The MiG-29M has greatly increased internal fuel capacity courtesy of the bulged dorsal spine (different than that of the 'Fulcrum-C'), a smaller cannon ammunition tank and the deletion of the overwing air intakes (the MiG-29M instead features retractable meshed intake FOD doors). The MiG-29M's chaff and flare dispensers are housed in the spine rather than in the extended fins of earlier models, while the M also features redesigned leading-edge root extensions, tail, and, to a lesser extent, wing.

Internally the MiG-33 features an analog fly-by-wire flight control system and a slightly aft centre of gravity for relaxed stability, a new Phazotron N-010 Zhuk radar with vastly improved processing capabilities and new operating modes expanding air-to-ground capabilities, and a revised cockpit with two CRT displays and HOTAS controls. The MiG-29M can also fire an expanded range of advanced AAMs and ASMs.

The navalised MiG-29K was passed over in preference for a navalised development of Su-27.

MAPO-MiG has also failed to interest the Russian air force in the MiG-35 development, which would have featured a Phazotron RP-35 phased array radar, more powerful engines and thrust vectoring.

Photo: MAPO-MiG's MiG-29ME/MiG-33 demonstrator. (Alex Radetski)

Mil Mi-4 & Harbin Z-5

Country of origin: Russia

Type: Utility helicopter

Powerplant: One 1270kW (1700hp) Shvetsov ASh-82V 18 cylinder radial piston engine, driving a four blade main rotor and three blade tail rotor.

Performance: Max speed at 4920ft 210km/h (113kt), economical cruising speed 160km/h (86kt). Service ceiling 18,000ft. Hovering ceiling out of ground effect 2295ft. Range with eight passengers 400km (217km), with 11 passengers 250km (134nm).

Weights: Empty 4900kg (10,802lb), max takeoff 7800kg (17,200lb).

Dimensions: Main rotor diameter 21.00m (68ft 11in), length overall rotors turning 25.02m (82ft 1in), fuselage length 16.80m (55ft 1in), height overall 5.18m (17ft 0in). Main rotor disc area 346m² (3724sq ft).

Accommodation: Two pilots in flightdeck. Main cabin can accommodate up to 12 combat equipped troops or 1740kg (3835lb) of freight.

Armament: Some army assault Mi-4s were fitted with a fixed or movable machine gun in a ventral gondola designed to accommodate a navigator/observer. Optional weapons pylons could carry gun and rocket pods.

Operators: Mi-4 – Afghanistan, Algeria, Cuba, Mali, North Korea, Sudan, Vietnam, Yemen. Z-5 – Albania, China.

History: The Mi-4 ('Hound' to NATO) was one of Russia's first effective and useful helicopters with over 3500 built. Harbin of China built several hundred more as the Z-5 and these still form the backbone of China's helicopter force.

Development of the Mi-4 began at the direct request of Soviet Premier Josef Stalin in 1951. Hurried development resulted in the prototype Mi-4 making its first flight in August 1951, while production deliveries began the following year, initially to the state airline Aeroflot (as the passenger carrying Mi-4P). Early production Mi-4s were fitted with wooden rotor blades.

The Mi-4 is close in appearance and configuration to Sikorsky's S-55 (H-19) but larger overall and closer in weights and size to the later S-58 (described under the Westland Wessex entry). Like the S-58 the Mi-4 is powered by a radial piston engine mounted in the nose which drives the four blade main rotor via a shaft which passes between the raised cockpit and the main cabin.

The cabin can accommodate 12 fully equipped troops, while the rear fuselage is formed by two clamshell doors.

Apart from the basic troop transport Mi-4 'Hound-A' troop transport, the Mi-4 was also built in ASW 'Hound-B' form fitted with a search radar and the 'Hound-C' ECM platform. Soviet production continued until 1969.

The first Chinese built Mi-4 had its maiden flight on December 14 1959, with deliveries of Harbin built H-5s commencing in the mid 1960s. Over 500 were built through to 1979 and several hundred remain in service. The Z-6 designation applies to at least one Z-5 fitted with two Pratt & Whitney PT6T turboshafts. It flew in 1979.

Photo: Hungary was one of the more than 25 nations to have operated the Mi-4 at some stage. (MAP)

Mil Mi-6 & Mi-22

Country of origin: Russia

Type: Heavylift transport helicopter

Powerplants: Mi-6T – Two 4045kW (5425shp) Soloviev (now Aviadvigatel) D-25V (TV-2BM) turboshafts, driving a five blade main rotor and four blade tail rotor.

Performance: Mi-6T – Max speed 300km/h (162kt), max cruising speed 250km/h (135kt). Service ceiling 14,750ft. Hovering ceiling in ground effect 8200ft. Max ferry range with auxiliary fuel 1450km (780nm), range with external fuel and a 4500kg (9920lb) payload 1000km (540nm), range with a 8000kg (17,635lb) payload 620km (335nm).

Weights: Mi-6T – Empty 27,240kg (60,055lb), max takeoff for a VTO 42,500kg (93,700lb).

Dimensions: Main rotor diameter 35.00m (114ft 10in), wing span 15.30m (50ft 3in), length overall rotors turning 41.74m (137ft 0in), fuselage length exc nose gun 33.18m (108ft 11in), height overall 9.86m (32ft 4in). Main rotor disc area 962.1m² (10,356sq ft).

Accommodation: Crew of five comprising two pilots, flight engineer, navigator and radio operator. Main cabin can accommodate 65 to 90 passengers or 70 combat equipped troops or 41 stretcher patients and two medical attendants in medevac configuration. Max slung cargo load of 8000kg (17,637lb), max internal payload 12,000kg (26,450lb).

Armament: Some Mi-6s are fitted with nose 12.7mm machine gun.

Operators: Iraq, Laos, Russia, Syria, Ukraine, Vietnam.

History: At the time of its first flight the Mi-6 ('Hook') was the world's largest and fastest helicopter.

The Mi-6 was developed against a joint Soviet air force/Aeroflot requirement for a heavylift helicopter. The resulting Mi-6 is a behemoth, its 42 tonne max takeoff weight approaching that of the Lockheed Martin C-130 Hercules. The Mi-6 was also the first turboshaft powered helicopter in the USSR to reach production, and, remarkably for its size, became the first helicopter to break 300km/h (162kt).

The Mi-6 flew for the first time in late 1957 and around 800 production aircraft were built through to 1981. The basic military transport Mi-6T 'Hook-A' was joined by the civilian Mi-6P with square windows, while the type formed the basis of the civil Mi-10 flying crane.

Three specialised variants are the Mi-6VKP 'Hook-B', the Mi-22 'Hook-C' and Mi-6AYaSh 'Hook-D'. The Mi-6VKP and Mi-22 are both command support aircraft that seem to act as portable command posts. The Mi-6VKP can be identified by a U shaped antenna under the tailboom and a number of T shaped antennas around the tailboom. The Mi-22 can be distinguished by its single blade antenna on the tailboom and assortment of antennas under the fuselage. Little is known of their precise equipment or roles. The Mi-6AYaSh is another command post model fitted with what is thought to be SLAR.

While such a large helicopter may seem an anomaly in the west the lack of suitable airfields in the underdeveloped regions of Russia makes helicopters particularly useful. Indeed the Mi-6 has been superseded by an even larger helicopter, the Mi-26, although the Mi-6 still remains in widespread use.

Photo: The Mi-6's wings provide 20% of total lift in cruising flight. (MAP)

Mil Mi-26

Country of origin: Russia

Type: Heavylift helicopter

Powerplants: Mi-26 – Two 7460kW (10,000shp) ZMKB Progress (Lotarev) D-136 turboshafts, driving an eight blade main rotor and five blade tail rotor.

Performance: Mi-26 – Max speed 295km/h (160kt), typical cruising speed 255km/h (137kt). Service ceiling 15,100ft. Hovering ceiling in ground effect 14,765ft. Range with max internal fuel at max takeoff weight with reserves 800km (432nm), range with four auxiliary fuel tanks 1920km (1036nm).

Weights: Mi-26 – Empty 28,200kg (62,170lb), normal takeoff 49,600kg (109,350lb), max takeoff 56,000kg (123,450lb).

Dimensions: Mi-26 – Main rotor diameter 32.00m (105ft 0in), length overall 40.03m (131ft 4in), fuselage length 33.73m (110ft 8in), height to top of rotor head 8.15m (26ft 9in). Main rotor disc area 804.25m² (8657sq ft).

Accommodation: Flightcrew of four comprising two pilots, flight engineer and navigator, plus loadmaster. Four seat passenger compartment behind flightdeck. Main cabin accommodates freight typically (max payload 20 tonnes/44,090lb), or up to 80 combat equipped troops or in medevac role 60 stretcher patients and four or five medical attendants. Medical version comprehensively equipped with operating theatre and accommodation for stretcher patients and medical attendants.

Armament: None

Operators: India, Peru, Russia, Ukraine.

History: The largest helicopter in the world by a large margin, the Mi-26 (NATO reporting name 'Halo') has a maximum takeoff weight greater than that of the Transall C-160 and an internal freight hold close in size to that in the C-130 Hercules.

Development of the Mi-26 began in the early 1970s and resulted in a first flight on December 14 1977. The original design requirement called for a helicopter for military and civil use with a maximum takeoff weight one and a half times that of any previous helicopter. Pre production machines were built from 1980, production machines sometime after that. The first Mi-26s are understood to have become operational with the Soviet military during 1983.

Notable for its eight blade main rotor, powerful turboshaft engines, massive size, rear loading freight doors and twin internal hoists, several versions of the Mi-26 have been developed or proposed. These include the basic Mi-26 'Halo-A' freighter, the equivalent civil Mi-26T, Mi-26MS medevac version, civil Mi-26P 63 passenger airliner, Mi-26TM flying crane and Mi-26TZ fuel tanker.

The improved Mi-26M is under development and features new 10,700kW (14,350shp) ZMKB Progress D-127 turboshafts, reprofiled composite main rotor blades, improved aerodynamics, better hot and high performance, 22 tonne max payload and EFIS cockpit displays.

The Mi-26 or Mi-26M could also form the basis of a replacement for command support Mi-6s (possibly designated Mi-27).

Photo: This Mi-26T demonstrator shows to good effect the Mi-26's rear clamshell doors and freight ramp. The Mi-26 is built by Rostvertol at Rostov-on-Don. (Paul Merritt)

Mil Mi-8 & Mi-17

Country of origin: Russia

Type: Multirole transport helicopter

Powerplants: Mi-8 – Two 1255kW (1700shp) Klimov (Isotov) TV2-117A turboshafts driving a five blade main rotor and three blade tail rotor.

Performance: Mi-8 – Max speed at 3280ft 260km/h (140kt), max cruising speed 225km/h (122kt). Service ceiling 14,760ft. Hovering ceiling in ground effect 6235ft, out of ground effect 2625ft. Ferry range 1200km (650nm), range with standard fuel 465km (250nm).

Weights: Mi-8 – Empty 7600kg (16,007lb), MTOW 12,000kg (26,455lb).

Dimensions: Mi-8/-17 – Main rotor diameter 21.29m (69ft 11in), length overall rotors turning 25.24m (82ft 10in), fuselage length 18.17m (59ft 7in), height overall 5.65m (18ft 7in). Main rotor disc area 356.0m² (3823.1sq ft).

Accommodation: Mi-8 – Two pilots and loadmaster. Main cabin can accommodate 28 troops, or twelve stretcher patients.

Armament: Most variants fitted with outriggers either side of the fuselage with two hardpoints each, usually for rockets.

Operators: Mi-8 & -17 in service with at least 50 nations including Afghanistan, Angola, Belarus, Bulgaria, China, Cuba, Czech Republic, Egypt, Finland, Hungary, India, Indonesia*, Iraq, North Korea, Pakistan, Peru, Poland, Romania, Russia, Slovakia, Ukraine, Vietnam, Yemen, Yugoslavia.

History: The rugged and useful Mi-8 and Mi-17 transports have been built in more numbers (12,000+) than any other Russian helicopter.

Work on the Mi-8 began in 1960 with the aim of finding a successor for the piston engined 14 seat Mi-4 'Hound'. The resulting aircraft featured the Mi-4's dynamic systems coupled to a new fuselage and powered by a turboshaft engine. The first prototype Mi-8 ('Hip-A') flew during June 1961 and was powered by a single 2015kW (2700shp) Soloviev turboshaft, but when the Mi-8 was found to be underpowered two Isotov TV2 turboshafts and a five blade main rotor were substituted instead. The Mi-8 first flew in this configuration in August 1962.

Initial production Mi-8s including the Mi-8T are covered by the NATO designation 'Hip-C' and include the basic military transport plus civil versions with square windows. The Mi-8TB 'Hip-E' is a dedicated assault version with three (instead of two) outrigger hardpoints either side of the fuselage for rockets or 9M17 (AT-2 'Swatter') anti armour missiles, while the export Mi-8TBK 'Hip-F' was armed with 9M14M (AT-3 'Sagger') missiles.

There have been numerous Mi-8 special mission variants including the Mi-8PS 'Hip-D' radio relay/command post aircraft, the similar Mi-9 'Hip-G' with hockey stick antennas under the tailboom and fuselage, the Mi-8SMV 'Hip-J' ECM jammer, and the Mi-8PPA 'Hip-K' communications jammer with a unique antenna array either side of the fuselage (with six cross dipole antennas each).

The Mi-17 introduced uprated TV3 turboshafts and can be identified by its port side tail rotor. Covered by the Mi-8M designation in Russian service, variants include the Mi-8MT 'Hip-H' transport, improved hot and high Mi-8MTV, and the Mi-8AMT with more powerful TV3s. The Ulan-Ude built Mi-171 and Kazan built Mi-172 are export equivalents of the Mi-8AMT.

Photo: The Mi-8AMT(Sh) (developed from the Mi-8MTV). It features an electro optic sight and radar, and can be armed. (Bruce Malcolm)

Mil Mi-14

Country of origin: Russia

Type: ASW, mine countermeasures and SAR amphibious helicopter

Powerplants: Mi-14PL – Two 1397kW (1874shp) Klimov (Isotov) TV3-117MT turboshafts driving a five blade main rotor and three blade tail rotor.

Performance: Mi-14PL – Max speed 230km/h (125kt), max cruising speed 215km/h (116kt), economical cruising speed 205km/h (110kt). Max initial rate of climb 1535ft/min. Service ceiling 11,500ft. Time to 3280ft 2min 18sec. Range with max fuel 1135km (612nm). Endurance 5hr 55min.

Weights: Mi-14PL – Empty 8900kg (19,625lb), max takeoff 14,000kg (30,865lb).

Dimensions: Mi-14PL – Main rotor diameter 21.29m (69ft 11in), length overall rotors turning 25.30m (83ft 0in), fuselage length 18.38m (60ft 4in), height overall 6.93m (22ft 9in). Main rotor disc area 356.0m² (3832.1sq ft).

Accommodation: Mi-14PL has a crew of four. The Mi-14PS has a crew of three and can accommodate 10 rescued survivors in the main cabin including two on stretchers.

Armament: The Mi-14PL can carry torpedoes, bombs and depth charges in an enclosed weapons bay in the lower hull.

Operators: Bulgaria, Cuba, Libya, Poland, Romania, Russia, Syria, Yugoslavia.

History: The Mi-14 is an amphibious development of the Mi-8/Mi-17, used for a variety of maritime tasks including anti submarine warfare, search and rescue and mine countermeasures.

The Mi-8 was reported as the logical replacement for a number of Mi-4 variants in Soviet naval service, and so development began on a navalised variant in 1968. Under the preliminary designation V-14 the first Mi-14 prototype flew for the first time in 1968. This first prototype featured the TV2 turboshafts and right hand side tail rotor of the Mi-8, while production Mi-14s feature the more powerful TV3s and left hand side tail rotor later introduced on the Mi-17. The most notable feature of the Mi-14 (NATO name 'Haze') is the boat-like hull, sponsons, floatation equipment and retractable undercarriage.

The Mi-14 has been built in three basic variants. The Mi-14PL 'Haze-A' is the ASW variant and features a large undernose radome, dunking sonar, sonobuoys, an APM-60 towed MAD bird and a weapons bay which can house torpedoes, bombs and depth charges. It is designated Mi-14PW in Polish service. An improved model is designated Mi-14PLM.

The Mi-14BT 'Haze-B' is a dedicated mine countermeasures variant. The Mi-14BT was introduced into service in the early 1980s and can carry three towed sleds to counter magnetic, acoustic or contact mines. The Mi-14BT retains the nose radome but lacks the MAD bird of the Mi-14PL and has a searchlight.

Finally the search and rescue Mi-14PS 'Haze-C' features an enlarged sliding door, a retractable rescue hoist, a searchlight either side of the nose and carries 10 20-place life rafts. The cabin can accommodate 10 rescued survivors, while others can be towed in life rafts.

The Mi-14P and Mi-14GP are civilian conversions.

Photo: Former East German Mi-14BTs (including this SAR converted example) were retired after reunification. (MAP)

Mil Mi-24, Mi-25 & Mi-35

Country of origin: Russia

Type: Armed assault/attack helicopter

Powerplants: Mi-24P – Two 1635kW (2190shp) Klimov TV3-117 turboshafts driving a five blade main rotor and three blade tail rotor.

Performance: Mi-24P – Max speed 335km/h (180kt), cruising speed 270km/h (145kt), economical cruising speed 217km/h (117kt). Max initial rate of climb 2460ft/min. Service ceiling 14,750ft. Hovering ceiling out of ground effect 4920ft. Range with auxiliary fuel 1000km (540nm), range with standard internal fuel 500km (270nm). Combat radius with max military load 160km (85nm), radius with two external fuel tanks 225km (120nm), radius with four tanks 288km (155nm).

Weights: Mi-24P – Empty 8200kg (18,078lb), max takeoff 12,000kg (26,455lb).

Dimensions: Mi-24P – Main rotor diameter 17.30m (56ft 9in), length overall rotors turning 21.35m (70ft 1in), fuselage length exc gun 17.51m (57ft 5in), height to top of rotor head 3.97m (13ft 1in). Main rotor disc area 235.1m² (2530.2sq ft).

Accommodation: Weapons operator and pilot in tandem stepped cockpit. Main cabin can accommodate eight troops or four stretchers.

Armament: One 12.7mm four barrel YakB machine gun in undernose turret or twin 23mm or 30mm cannon. Two anti armour missiles on each stub wing endplate. Four underwing hardpoints for rockets and guns.

Operators: Afghanistan, Algeria, Angola, Armenia, Azerbaijan, Bulgaria, Croatia, Cuba, Czech Republic, Hungary, India, Iraq, Libya, Mozambique, Peru, Poland, Russia, Rwanda, Slovakia, Syria, Ukraine, USA, Yemen.

History: Mil's feared 'Devil's Chariot' is unique in that it is a combined armed assault/attack helicopter, although the latter is its primary role.

The Mi-24 is based on the dynamic systems of the Mi-8 transport helicopter, although almost all production aircraft featured the uprated TV3 turboshafts and port side tail rotor of the upgraded Mi-17. Design considerations were speed and firepower.

First flight of the V-24 prototype was in 1973, while production Mi-24 'Hind-A's entered service in 1973. Early production 'Hind-A's, 'Hind-B's and 'Hind-C's feature a glasshouse style cockpit for the pilot and weapons operator which offered poor visibility and protection. The Mi-24D 'Hind-D' and export Mi-25 introduced the definitive stepped and armoured cockpits, plus the four barrel 12.7mm machine gun in an undernose turret plus undernose missile guidance and electro optical pods. The similar Mi-24V 'Hind-E' (or Mi-35 for export) introduced the stubwing endplates for 9M114 (AT-6 'Spiral') anti armour missiles and a HUD for the pilot. The Mi-24VP introduced a twin barrel GSh-23L cannon on the starboard fuselage side as operational experience in Afghanistan found the original gun ineffective against some targets, while the Mi-24P 'Hind-F' (and export Mi-35P) has a twin 30mm cannon. The Mi-24RKR and Mi-24K NBC reconnaissance platforms.

Finally Mil is developing the Mi-35M, an upgraded Mi-24 featuring the Mi-28's rotors and transmission, a 23mm cannon and 9K114-9 Attacka advanced anti armour missiles, Sextant Avionique of France avionics and displays and Thomson-TTD Chlio FLIR ball.

Photo: The Czech Republic operates Mi-24Ds and Mi-24Vs. (Bruce Malcolm)

Mil Mi-28

Morane-Saulnier MS-760 Paris

Countries of

Type: Ground

Powerplants:
tric F110-GE-

Performance.

Weights: Emp

Dimensions:
overall 15.52n
(375.0sq ft).

Accommodat

Armament: (
Sidewinders o
line and four u
the radar guide
anti ship missi

Operators: Ja

History: The e
opment of the
strike, ground

Following o
Japan originall
replacement re
search and De
fighter to mee
requirements, v
the USA exerte
sourced weapc
the two countr
dropped in 198
promising on o
industrial partic

The then Ger
a Japanese dev
appointed prim
while the Gene
powerplant in [
the first of thes
was redesignat

Compared w
structed of co-c
weight), a long
Electric develop
including the int
HUD. In additio
flight control sy
refusal to releas

The JASDF o
TFS-X conversic
opment costs (c
The JDA now w
sion trainers. Fi

Photo: The first

Country of origin: Russia

Type: Two seat attack helicopter

Powerplants: Two 1545kW (2070shp) Klimov TV3-117VM turboshafts driving a five blade main rotor and four blade tail rotor.

Performance: Max speed 300km/h (162kt), max cruising speed 270km/h (145kt). Max initial rate of climb 2675ft/min. Service ceiling 19,020ft. Hovering ceiling out of ground effect 11,820ft. Ferry range with reserves 1100km (595nm), max range with standard fuel 460km (250nm). Combat radius with standard fuel, 10min loiter and reserves 200km (110nm). Endurance with max fuel 2hr.

Weights: Empty equipped 8095kg (17,845lb), max takeoff 11,660kg (25,705lb).

Dimensions: Main rotor diameter 17.20m (56ft 5in), length exc rotors 17.01m (55ft 9in), height to top of rotor head 3.82m (12ft 7in). Main rotor disc area 232.3m² (2501sq ft).

Accommodation: Navigator/weapons operator and pilot in stepped tandem cockpit with navigator in front cockpit. A rear fuselage compartment can accommodate two or three people – intended for emergency recovery of personnel only.

Armament: One NPPU-28 30mm cannon in undernose turret. Four underwing hardpoints can carry a combined ordnance load of 1920kg (4230lb). Typical configuration of two rocket pods and up to 16 9P149 Shturm C (AT-6 'Spiral') radio guided tube launched anti armour missiles.

Operators: Russia*

History: Manoeuvrable, well armed, armoured and fast, the Mi-28 is Mil's first dedicated two seat attack helicopter and is in competition with the Kamov Ka-50 to meet Russian army requirements.

Design of the Mi-28 (NATO reporting name 'Havoc') began as early as 1980 and the first of three prototypes flew for the first time on November 10 1982. Development of the basic Mi-28 is now largely complete with only a small number built for service evaluation.

The Mi-28 has tandem stepped cockpits with energy absorbing crew seats, an undernose turret containing a 30mm cannon, stubwings with two hardpoints each and twin TV3 turboshafts (the TV3 also powers the Ka-50, plus Mil's Mi-17 and Mi-24). The original three blade tail rotor unit has been replaced by a four blade X shape unit, similar to that on the AH-64 Apache. The cockpits feature ceramic and titanium armour, while the entire airframe is designed to absorb and survive small arms fire. Countermeasures are carried in the wingtip pods. The thimble nose radome contains a missile guidance radar, beneath are two fixed infrared sensors.

The Mi-28N is an improved night/all weather development featuring a mast mounted millimetre wave radar, a FLIR ball turret under the nose radome, a low light TV, night vision compatible cockpit lighting, uprated 1838kW (2465shp) for takeoff TVS-117VK turboshafts and swept main rotor tips. First flight was on April 30 1997. Production aircraft would be to Mi-28N standard.

Photo: The mast mounted sight equipped Mi-28N debuted at the 1995 Moscow Airshow but did not fly for the first time until April 1997. This aircraft was modified from the first Mi-28 prototype. (Alex Radetski)

Country of origin: France

Type: Basic trainer, light strike, fast liaison/communications and target simulation aircraft.

Powerplants: MS-760B – Two 4.74kN (1058lb) Turboméca Maboré VI turbojets.

Performance: MS-760B – Max speed at 25,000ft 695km/h (375kt), max cruising speed at 16,400ft 633km/h (342kt), economical cruising speed 550km/h (297kt). Max initial rate of climb 2460ft/min. Service ceiling 39,370ft. Max range 1740km (940nm).

Weights: MS-760B – Empty equipped 2067kg (4557lb), max takeoff 3920kg (8642lb).

Dimensions: MS-760B – Wing span 10.15m (33ft 3in), length overall 10.24m (33ft 7in), height 2.60m (8ft 6in). Wing area 18.0m² (193.7sq ft).

Accommodation: Seating for four.

Armament: For weapons training and light strike two underwing hardpoints (one under each wing) for 7.5m machine gun pods, rockets or light bombs.

Operators: Argentina, France.

History: The four seat Paris jet was designed primarily as a high speed military liaison/communications aircraft but was also offered in civil forms. A small number remain in service with the French navy and Argentine air force.

The Paris was based on Morane-Saulnier's MS-755 Flueret, a two seat jet trainer which flew in 1953. The larger MS-760 Paris features seating for four under a rearwards sliding canopy with dual controls for pilot training, a straight wing, two Turboméca Maboré turbojets (fed through air inlets in the wingroots) and a T-tail. It can be armed with four 3.5in rockets, gun pods or 50kg (110lb) bombs for weapons training missions.

The prototype Paris, designated MS-760-01, took to the air for the first time on July 29 1954. The Paris was then subsequently adopted by the French air force for communications and liaison duties. Initial production was of the 3.94kN (880lb) Maboré IIC turbojet powered MS-760A, which first flew on February 7 1958. The production total of 150 MS-760As includes 48 assembled in Argentina (by FMA).

About half of the MS-760s delivered to Argentina remain in service, upgraded to improved MS-760B standard. The MS-760B flew for the first time on December 12 1960 and introduced more powerful Maboré VI turbojets and wingtip fuel tanks. Sixty three new production MS-760Bs were built, including 48 assembled in Brazil for that country's air force. In all 219 MS-760s were manufactured. A stretched six seat development was offered for civil use.

Until recently about 30 MS-760s remained in service with the French Armée de l'Air where they were used for liaison, continuation training and target simulation, although eight survive in French navy use.

Argentina's surviving MS-760s are used by two units for weapons training, while Brazil's MS-760s have long been retired.

Photo: The French air force has retired its MS-760s, but small numbers survive with the French navy. (Armée de l'Air)

Country o

Type: Two

Powerplar
afterburnin
Royce Turb

Performan
Max initial
2595km (1

Weights: (
(28,220lb).

Dimension
17.86m (5
(14ft 3in). V

Accommoc

Armament
lower fusel
tips, plus b
four underw

Operators:

History: Th
aircraft and
advanced tr

The Japa
tractor to de
tember 196
and the resu
the Northrop
of four flying
in 1976.

The Mach
F-104J fight
Turboméca /
the TF40-IHI
control is in:
an airbrake
rate canopie
structure by

A total of !
T-2 trainers
tip missile r:
air-to-air mi
hardpoints f
search and r

A single T-
vehicle, with
nards with t
were convert
(which is des

Photo: Of the
service. (MAF

Country of origin: United States of America

Type: Two seat advanced trainer

Powerplants: Two 11.9kN (2680lb) dry and 17.1kN (3850lb) with afterburning General Electric J85-GE-5 turbojets.

Performance: Max speed at 36,000ft Mach 1.22 or 1295km/h (700kt), max cruising speed 930km/h (502kt). Max initial rate of climb 33,600ft/min. Service ceiling 53,600ft. Ferry range 1760km (950nm), typical range 1385km (747nm).

Weights: Empty 3255kg (7175lb), max takeoff 5465kg (12,050lb).

Dimensions: Wing span 7.70m (25ft 3in), length 14.14m (46ft 5in), height 3.92m (12ft 11in). Wing area 15.8m² (170.0sq ft).

Accommodation: Two in tandem.

Armament: Usually none, although Portuguese T-38s (now retired) were equipped to fire AIM-9 Sidewinder AAMs. T-38B LIFT aircraft (AT-38Bs) were equipped to carry practice bombs and rockets, plus a minigun pod.

Operators: Germany, Taiwan, Turkey, USA.

History: The supersonic Talon is the US Air Force's advanced trainer and is a development of Northrop's N-156 light fighter proposal.

Northrop began private venture development of its N-156 light fighter concept in the mid 1950s. Part of Northrop's N-156 design work was the N-156T two seater which it offered to the USAF as an advanced trainer. In 1956 the USAF ordered three N-156Ts for evaluation and the first of these YT-38s (powered by non afterburning YJ85-GE-1s) flew for the first time on April 10 1959. In all, six YT-38s were built, the final three with afterburning YJ85-GE-5s. Testing of the latter aircraft in particular was very promising, and the YT-38 was ordered into production as the T-38 Talon. Deliveries began in March 1961. Production ceased in 1972 after 1187 had been built.

The T-38A was the basic Talon production model. For a time the US Navy operated some QT-38 drones and DT-38 drone controllers and NASA flies T-38A(N)s on astronaut training duties. Finally 132 T-38As were converted to T-38B LIFT configuration, able to carry practice bombs, rockets and a minigun for weapons training. These were unofficially dubbed AT-38Bs.

The USAF expects its T-38s to remain in service until 2010 to 2015. To extend their airframe lives future USAF transport and tanker pilots now undergo advanced training on the Raytheon Beech T-1 Jayhawk rather than the T-38, while Boeing (previously McDonnell Douglas) is developing an EFIS cockpit upgrade for the aircraft.

Apart from the USAF's Air Education and Training Command, the Talon is in service with Air Combat Command and Air Mobility Command for the Companion Trainer Program. Others are used as chase aircraft for various test programs. Previous USAF T-38 operators included aggressor squadrons and the Thunderbirds.

The USAF also operates 41 German funded T-38s to train Luftwaffe pilots. Ex USAF aircraft meanwhile were supplied to Turkey and Portugal (Portugal's aircraft had an air defence role and were armed with AIM-9 Sidewinders prior to the delivery of F-16s). Finally Taiwan is leasing T-38s to make up for a shortfall in fast jet numbers pending the delivery of its F-16A/Bs which began in 1997.

Photo: A USAF Talon. (Paul Merritt)

Country of origin: United States of America

Type: Lightweight multirole fighter

Powerplants: Two 12.1kN (2720lb) dry and 18.2kN (4080lb) with afterburning General Electric J85-GE-13 turbojets.

Performance: F-5A – Max speed at 36,000ft Mach 1.4 or 1488km/h (802kt), cruising speed at 36,000ft 1030km/h (556kt). Max initial rate of climb 28,700ft/min. Service ceiling 50,500ft. Ferry range 2595km (1400nm). Combat radius with two 240kg (530lb) bombs and max fuel hi-lo-hi 990km (485nm), radius with max external bomb load (1995kg/4400lb) hi-lo-hi 315km (170nm).

Weights: F-5A – Empty equipped 3667kg (8085lb), max takeoff 9380kg (20,677lb).

Dimensions: F-5A – Wing span over tip tanks 7.87m (25ft 10in), span without tip tanks 7.70m (25ft 3in), length 14.38m (47ft 2in), height 4.01m (13ft 2in). Wing area 15.8m² (170.0sq ft).

Accommodation: Pilot only in F-5A, two in tandem in F-5B.

Armament: Two M39A2 20mm cannons. Max external weapons load of 1995kg (4400lb) including bombs, rockets and AIM-9 Sidewinders on four underwing hardpoints (AIM-9s also on wingtip stations).

Operators: Botswana, Brazil, Greece, Morocco, Norway, Philippines, Saudi Arabia, South Korea, Spain, Thailand, Turkey, Venezuela.

History: Northrop's N-156 lightweight fighter was adopted by the USA as the F-5 Freedom Fighter to supply to friendly European and Asian nations under the Military Assistance Program.

As early as 1952 Northrop designed its first lightweight jet fighter, the N-102 Fang to be powered by a single GE J79 turbojet. While the USAF rejected the Fang its interest in a lightweight fighter was aroused and in 1954 it conducted a study into the concept of a lightweight yet high performance fighter that could be supplied under MAP. This study prompted Northrop to design a new lightweight fighter to meet such a requirement, resulting in the N-156 powered by two small J85 turbojets (an engine originally developed for a decoy drone).

US official interest was initially for the two seat N-156T which became the T-38 Talon, while Northrop continued development of the single seat N-156 and a privately funded prototype flew for the first time on July 30 1959 (Mach 1 was reached on this first flight).

Because of initial USAF disinterest the first production F-5A Freedom Fighter did not fly until May 1963. The USAF operated a squadron of F-5As in Vietnam for combat evaluation (Skoshi Tiger) but it never intended to acquire the F-5 in any numbers.

However Northrop built 879 F-5As and two seat F-5Bs for over a dozen MAP customers, while Canadair built 250 (with uprated engines and an inflight refuelling probe as the CF-5A and CF-5D for Canada, NF-5A/B for the Netherlands) and CASA of Spain built 70 under licence. The RF-5A is a reconnaissance variant with four KS-92A cameras in a reprofiled nose.

Several countries have upgraded their F-5A/B fleets, including Canada, Venezuela and Norway. Canada's upgrade was the most comprehensive, with an airframe refurbishment, a HUD, advanced avionics and HOTAS controls. However, all have been retired and they have been offered for sale. Botswana purchased 13.

Photo: An F-5A of the Turkish air force's display team. (Paul Merritt)

Mitsubishi F-2

Countries of origin: Japan and the USA

Type: Ground attack & maritime strike fighter

Powerplants: One 131.7kN (29,600lb) with afterburning General Electric F110-GE-129 turbofan.

Performance: No performance figures published at time of writing.

Weights: Empty 9525kg (21,000lb), max takeoff 22,100kg (48,722lb).

Dimensions: Wing span over missile rails 11.13m (36ft 6in), length overall 15.52m (50ft 11in), height 4.96m (16ft 4in). Wing area 34.8m² (375.0sq ft).

Accommodation: Pilot only, or two in tandem in F-2B.

Armament: One M61A1 Vulcan 20mm internal cannon. AIM-9L Sidewinders or Mitsubishi AAM-3 AAMs on wingtip rails. One centreline and four underwing hardpoints for a variety of weaponry, such as the radar guided Mitsubishi ASM-1 anti ship missile, Mitsubishi ASM-2 anti ship missile and AIM-7M Sparrow AAMs.

Operators: Japan*

History: The expensive Mitsubishi F-2 is a substantial Japanese development of the Lockheed Martin F-16C to replace the F-1 for maritime strike, ground attack and counter air missions.

Following on from the success of the T-2 trainer and F-1 fighter Japan originally planned to develop an all new aircraft to meet the F-1 replacement requirement. In the early 1980s Japan's Technical Research and Development Institute had been studying designs for a new fighter to meet the Japan Air Self Defence Force's particular design requirements, which included long range and manoeuvrability. However the USA exerted considerable pressure on Japan to continue to buy US sourced weapons and to reduce the large trade imbalance between the two countries. Thus plans to develop an indigenous fighter were dropped in 1987 with the Japan Defence Agency (JDA) instead compromising on developing an existing US fighter with considerable US industrial participation.

The then General Dynamics F-16 was selected to form the basis of a Japanese developed support fighter in October 1987. Mitsubishi was appointed prime contractor for the FS-X program in November 1988 while the General Electric F110-GE-129 was selected as the FS-X's powerplant in December 1990. Four FS-X prototypes have been built, the first of these flying for the first time on October 7 1995. The FS-X was redesignated F-2 in December that year.

Compared with the F-16 the F-2 features a 25% larger wing constructed of co-cured composites (for increased strength and reduced weight), a longer fuselage, conventional cockpit canopy, a Mitsubishi Electric developed active phased array radar and Japanese avionics including the integrated electronic warfare system, LCD displays and a HUD. In addition the F-2 features a Japanese developed fly-by-wire flight control system (developed on the T-2CCV) because of the USA's refusal to release F-16 fly-by-wire software source codes.

The JASDF originally required 141 FS-Xs, including some two seat TFS-X conversion trainers, although funding cuts and spiralling development costs (over $US3bn) saw this number reduced to around 80. The JDA now wants to acquire 83 F-2A fighters and 47 F-2B conversion trainers. First deliveries are planned for 1999.

Photo: The first prototype XF-2 first flew in October 1995.

Mudry CAP 10, 20, 21 230, 231 & 232

Country of origin: France

Type: Basic trainer and aerobatics aircraft

Powerplant: CAP 10B – One 135kW (180hp) Lycoming AEIO-360-B2F fuel injected flat four piston engine, driving a two blade propeller.

Performance: CAP 10B – Max speed 270km/h (146kt), max cruising speed at 75% power 250km/h (135kt). Max initial rate of climb 1575ft/min. Service ceiling 16,400ft. Range with max fuel 1000km (540nm).

Weights: 10B – Empty equipped 550kg (1213lb), max takeoff in aerobatic category 760kg (1675lb), or 830kg (1829lb) in utility category.

Dimensions: 10B – Wing span 8.06m (26ft 5in), length 7.16m (23ft 6in), height 2.55m (8ft 5in). Wing area 10.9m² (116.8sq ft).

Accommodation: Two side by side in CAP 10, pilot only in other models.

Armament: None

Operators: CAP 10 – France, Mexico, Morocco. CAP 230 – Morocco. CAP 231 – France, Morocco. CAP 232 – France*

History: The Mudry CAP series serves as an initial flight screener/basic trainer with the French and Mexican air forces and as an aerobatic display mount for French and Moroccan teams.

The successful CAP series dates back to the Piel C.P.30 Emeraude of the early 1960s. More than 200 two seat Emeraudes (first flight 1962) were built in four different factories across Europe.

One of the companies to build the Emeraude was CAARP, a company owned by Auguste Mudry. CAARP used the basic Emeraude design as the basis for the CAP 10, which was a similar aircraft other than its 135kW (180hp) Lycoming IO-360 engine and stressing for aerobatic flight. The prototype CAP 10 first flew in August 1968. CAARP built 30 CAP 10s for the French air force before Mudry started CAP 10 production for civil orders in 1972 at his other aviation company, Avions Mudry.

The CAP 10 remains in production in 10B form with an enlarged tail. Twenty six CAP 10Bs were delivered to the French Armée de l'Air.

Other CAP 10 military operators are Morocco, the Mexican air force which took delivery of 20 for aerobatic training, and the French navy, which operates 10 for pilot screening and grading.

The CAP 20 meanwhile is a single seat development with a 150kW (200hp) AEIO-360 engine designed for civil aerobatic competition. The Armée de l'Air took delivery of six CAP 20s for its Equipe de Voltage aerobatic team.

The revised CAP 21 replaced the CAP 20 in 1981. The CAP 21 is of the same basic overall configuration to the CAP 20 but introduced a new wing and undercarriage. The following CAP 230 was heavier, stronger and powered by an uprated AEIO-540 flat six. Four were delivered to the French Equipe de Voltage team. The 230 was followed by the 231, which first flew in April 1990. Seven CAP 231s were delivered to the Moroccan air force's aerobatic display team, Marche Verte (Green March). The CAP 231 EX introduced a carbon fibre wing, while production has switched to the further improved CAP 232, which first flew in July 1994. Four French air force 231s are due to be converted to 232 standard.

Photo: A French Armée de l'Air CAP 10.

NAMC YS-11

Country of origin: Japan

Type: Utility transport, ECM trainer and Elint platform

Powerplants: YS-11A-200 – Two 2280kW (3060shp) Rolls-Royce Dart Mk 542-10K turboprops, driving four blade propellers.

Performance: -200 – Max cruising speed 470km/h (253kt), economical cruising speed 452km/h (244kt). Service ceiling 22,900ft. Range with max payload and no reserves 1090km (590nm), range with max fuel and no reserves 3215km (1736nm).

Weights: -200 – Operating empty 15,419kg (33,993lb), max takeoff 24,500kg (54,010lb).

Dimensions: Wing span 32.00m (105ft 0in), length 26.30m (86ft 4in), height 8.98m (29ft 6in). Wing area 94.8m² (1020.4sq ft).

Accommodation: Flightcrew of two. Typical seating in main cabin for 60. JMSDF YS-11M-As have seating for 48 with a rear cargo compartment. The combi YS-11A-300 was designed for freight in the forward fuselage and seating for 46 behind that.

Armament: None

Operators: Greece, Japan.

History: The NAMC YS-11 is postwar Japan's only indigenously developed airliner. Several serve with the Japanese military and the Greek air force.

The YS-11 was a product of the Nihon Aircraft Manufacturing Company, a consortium of Fuji, Kawasaki, Mitsubishi, Nippi, Shin Meiwa and Showa. NAMC formed on June 1 1959 specifically to design and develop a short to medium range airliner, with particular attention paid to meeting the requirements of Japanese domestic airlines.

Within NAMC Fuji was given responsibility for the tail unit, Kawasaki the wings and engine nacelles, Mitsubishi the forward fuselage and final assembly, Nippi the ailerons and flaps, Shin Meiwa the rear fuselage and Showa the light alloy honeycomb structural components.

The YS-11 first flew on August 30 1962. Airline service entry was in April 1965. Initial production was of the YS-11-100, while the YS-11A-200 was designed for export and had an increased max takeoff weight. The YS-11A-300 was a combi passenger/freight model, while the YS-11A-400 was a pure freighter with a forward freight door. The YS-11A-500, -600 and -700 were equivalent to the -200, -300 and -400, but with a 500kg (1100lb) greater max takeoff weight. Production ceased in February 1974 after 182 were built.

The Japan Air Self Defence Force acquired four YS-11-100s as YS-11Ps for VIP transports, a YS-11-300 combi as the YS-11PC, seven YS-11-400 freighters as YS-11Cs (one subsequently converted to a YS-11NT nav trainer), and a YS-11-200 as a YS-11FC for flight check duties. In 1976 two YS-11Cs were converted to YS-11E ECM trainers (festooned with various antennas and a large chaff/flare dispenser fairing behind the starboard wing). A third YS-11C was converted as a YS-11E(EL) in 1982 for Elint reconnaissance.

The Japanese Maritime Self Defence Force meanwhile acquired two YS-11-100s as YS-11M transports and two YS-11-400 combis as YS-11M-As. Four YS-11-200s and two YS-11-600s serve as YS-11T-A ASW crew trainers, fitted with a search radar in an underbelly radome.

Greece now operates two ex Olympic Airways YS-11s as transports.

Photo: One of Greece's YS-11s. (Greek MoD)

Nanchang CJ-5 & CJ-6/PT-6

Country of origin: China

Type: Two seat basic trainer

Powerplant: CJ-6 – One 215kW (285hp) Zhuzhou (SMPMC) HS6A nine cylinder radial piston engine, driving a two blade propeller.

Performance: CJ-6 – Max speed 297km/h (160kt), cruising speed 260km/h (160kt). Max initial rate of climb 1250ft/min. Service ceiling 20,500ft. Range with max fuel 690km (372nm). Endurance 3hr 35min.

Weights: CJ-6 – Empty 1095kg (2414lb), max takeoff 1400kg (3086lb).

Dimensions: CJ-6 – Wing span 10.22m (33ft 7in), length overall 8.46m (27ft 9in), height overall 3.25m (10ft 8in).

Accommodation: Two in tandem.

Armament: CJ-6 – None, although 10 armed CJ-6Bs built could carry light armament.

Operators: Albania, Bangladesh, China, North Korea.

History: The Nanchang CJ-6 is a Chinese development of the Yak-18 and is that country's primary basic trainer.

During the 1950s China had built the Yak-18 under licence as the CJ-5. China began development of its own version of the Yak-18/CJ-5 optimised specifically for its requirements and incorporating a number of improvements in the mid 1950s. Design work was carried out at Shenyang during the late 1950s. The first prototype flew for the first time on August 27 1958 and it was powered by a 110kW (145hp) Mikulin M-11ER engine. However the CJ-6 prototype soon proved underpowered and a re-engined aircraft powered by a 195kW (260hp) Ivchenko AI-14R first flew in July 1960.

CJ-6 design and production was subsequently transferred to Nanchang where further design changes were incorporated and a production standard CJ-6 first flew on October 15 1961. Production go-ahead was announced the following year.

Compared with the CJ-5, the CJ-6 differed in its retractable undercarriage and more powerful engine. Initial production CJ-6s were powered by the 195kW (260hp) Chinese HS6 version of the Ivchenko AI-14. The CJ-6 was superseded in production by the definitive CJ-6A in 1965. The CJ-6A introduced the 215kW (285hp) HS6A. In addition, 10 armed CJ-6Bs were built between 1964 and 1966. Interestingly the type was also considered the basis for a civil agricultural spraying aircraft, and a single prototype flew in this form as the Haiyan-A.

In all, over 2100 CJ-6s have been built, with all but 200 for the PLA-AF. It has been exported to several non-aligned nations – Bangladesh, Cambodia, North Korea, Tanzania and Zambia – where it carries the westernised PT-6A designation, except for Bangladesh, whose aircraft are designated BT-6.

The CJ-6 is easy to fly, rugged, easy to maintain and well suited to its training role. Design features include the two blade constant speed prop, dihedral on the outer wing panels and a framed glasshouse style canopy covering the two occupants and giving good all round visibility.

Photo: One of the 1800 CJ-6 trainers built. About 1500 remain in Chinese service.

Nanchang Q-5/A-5

Country of origin: China

Type: Ground attack aircraft

Powerplants: Two 25.5kN (5732lb) dry and 31.9kN (7165lb) with afterburning Shenyang WP6 turbojets.

Performance: A-5C – Max speed at 36,000ft Mach 1.12 or 1190km/h (643kt), max speed at sea level 1210km/h (653kt). Max rate of climb at 16,400ft, 16,430 to 20,275ft/min. Service ceiling 52,000ft. Range with max internal and external fuel 2000km (1080nm). Combat radius with max external stores hi-lo-hi 600km (325nm), lo-lo-lo 400km (215nm).

Weights: A-5C – Empty 6375kg (14,054lb), max takeoff 12,000kg (26,455lb).

Dimensions: A-5C – Wing span 9.70m (31ft 10in), length overall inc nose probe 16.26m (53ft 4in), length exc nose probe 15.42m (50ft 7in), height 4.52m (14ft 10in). Wing area 28.0m^2 (300.9sq ft).

Accommodation: Pilot only.

Armament: Q-5 II/A-5C – Two Norinco Type 23 23mm cannons. Ten external hardpoints for a max ordnance load of 2000kg (4410lb) including bombs, rockets, air-to-surface and air-to-air missiles. Some Chinese aircraft believed to be modified to carry a five to 20kT nuclear bomb.

Operators: Bangladesh, China, Myanmar, North Korea, Pakistan.

History: The Nanchang Q-5 (Westernised designation A-5) is a close air support/ground attack fighter developed from China's MiG-19 copy.

Development of the Q-5 (NATO reporting name 'Fantan') began in 1958, with Shenyang undertaking initial work and mock-up construction and assisting Nanchang with subsequent detail design. Construction of the prototype began in May 1960 although the Chinese Cultural Revolution intervened and the prototype program was cancelled in 1961. Between then and 1963 when development was officially reinstated a small team continued work on the aircraft. First flight was on June 4 1965 and subsequent testing revealed the need for a number of modifications. The first of two prototypes with the required modifications flew in late 1969 and production aircraft were delivered from 1970.

The Q-5 retained the Shenyang J-6's (MiG-19's) rear fuselage and powerplants but features a stretched area ruled fuselage with an internal weapons bay, side mounted air intakes, a new conical nose and larger wings with less sweepback.

Initial production was of the Q-5. The longer range Q-5 I has extra fuel in place of the internal bomb bay. Chinese navy Q-5 Is may be fitted with a radar and can carry C-801 anti ship missiles and torpedoes. The Q-5 IA gained two extra underwing hardpoints and the Q-5 II is fitted with a radar warning receiver.

The A-5C was developed for Pakistan and is based on the Q-5 I but with upgraded western avionics and compatibility with western weapons (including the AIM-9 Sidewinder). The export A-5K Kong Yun (Cloud) with Thomson-CSF laser rangefinder was cancelled in 1990.

The A-5M is also intended for export and features improved engines and Alenia avionics based on those in the AMX including a ranging radar, INS, HUD and RWR. It first flew in 1988, but none have been sold.

Photo: Note underfuselage mounted bombs on this Q-5.

Nanchang K-8 Karakorum

Country of origin: China

Type: Two seat basic/advanced trainer

Powerplant: One 16.0kN (3600lb) AlliedSignal TFE731-2A-2A turbofan.

Performance: Max speed at sea level 807km/h (435kt). Max initial rate of climb 5315ft/min. Service ceiling 42,650ft. Range with max internal fuel 1400km (755nm), range with max internal and external fuel 2250km (1215nm). Endurance with max internal fuel 3hr, endurance with max internal and external fuel 4hr 25min.

Weights: Empty equipped 2687kg (5924lb), max takeoff with external stores 4330kg (9545lb).

Dimensions: Wing span 9.63m (31ft 7in), length overall inc probe 11.60m (38ft 1in), height 4.21m (13ft 10in). Wing area 17.0m^2 (183.2sq ft).

Accommodation: Two in tandem.

Armament: One centreline and four underwing hardpoints can carry max weapons load of 945kg (2080lb). Centreline hardpoint can carry a 23mm gun pod, other weapon options include light bombs and rockets. Two outboard pylons can carry a PL-7 AAM each.

Operators: China*, Pakistan*.

History: The Karakorum is China's first locally designed jet trainer and has been developed in co-operation with Pakistan.

Development of the Karakorum, initially designated L-8, was announced at the 1987 Paris Airshow. At the time of the new trainer's launch Nanchang (or NAMC – Nanchang Aircraft Manufacturing Company) sought international partners to develop the aircraft for export. Subsequently a development and co-production deal was signed with Pakistan, which took a 25% share in the program.

When Pakistan joined the trainer project the aircraft was redesignated K-8 and named Karakorum, after the mountain range that forms part of the China/Pakistan border. Pakistan, through PAC (Pakistan Aeronautical Complex), had some design input into the K-8 and is responsible for the manufacture of the K-8's fin and tailplane. However, Pakistan decided not to establish its own K-8 assembly line.

The first of three flying Karakorum prototypes flew for the first time on November 21 1990. These were followed by 15 pre-production development aircraft, the first of which flew in 1993. Pakistan is understood to have a total requirement for up to 100 K-8s to replace T-37s – a first batch of six was delivered by late 1996. The Chinese K-8 requirement could involve several hundred airframes (it is likely to replace JJ-7s and CJ-6s).

The K-8 is of conventional design for a jet trainer, with a straight wing and tandem seating. Initial and export aircraft are powered by an AlliedSignal TFE731 turbofan with FADEC, while Chinese production aircraft (if funded) will be powered by a 16.9kN (3792lb) Progress ZMKB AI-25TL turbofan.

Other western origin equipment in the K-8 includes the two Collins CRTs in each cockpit while the crew sits on two Martin-Baker zero/zero ejection seats. Five hardpoints, one centreline and four under the wing, give the K-8 a light ground attack/weapons training capability.

Photo: An early Karakorum development aircraft. Note the sideways hinging cockpit canopy. (Gerard Frawley)

NH Industries NH 90

Countries of origin: France, Germany, Italy and the Netherlands

Type: Medium lift tactical transport and naval helicopter

Powerplants: Two 1255kW (1680shp) max continuous rated Rolls-Royce Turboméca RTM 322 turboshafts or in Italian aircraft two similarly rated GE T700-T6Es driving four blade main and tail rotors.

Performance: TTH – Dash speed at sea level 300km/h (162kt), max cruising speed at sea level 290km/h (155kt). Service ceiling 13,940ft, absolute ceiling 19,680ft. Hovering ceiling in ground effect 11,820ft, out of ground effect 9840ft. Ferry range 1205km (650nm). NFH – Time on station 110km (60nm) from base 3hr. Max endurance at 140km/h (75kt) 5hr 5min.

Weights: TTH – Empty 5400kg (11,905lb), max takeoff 10,000kg (22,045lb). NFH – Empty equipped 6430kg (14,170lb), max takeoff same.

Dimensions: Main rotor diameter 16.30m (53ft 6in), length overall rotors turning 19.50m (64ft 2in), fuselage length 15.89m (52ft 2in), height overall rotors turning 5.44m (17ft 10in). Main rotor disc area 208.7m² (2246.1sq ft).

Accommodation: TTH – One or two pilots and up to 20 combat equipped troops or a two tonne 4WD. NFH – Pilot, copilot/tacco and sensor operator, or two pilots, tacco and sensor operator.

Armament: TTH – To be fitted with area suppression and defensive armament. NFH – Anti ship missiles and torpedoes.

Operators: To be built for France, Germany, Italy and the Netherlands.

History: The NH 90 is an advanced 10 tonne class helicopter designed for battlefield transport and anti ship and ASW naval operations.

The NH 90 results from a 1985 teaming of five European nations to jointly develop a NATO Helicopter for the '90s. The UK withdrew from the program in 1987, leaving France, Germany, Italy and the Netherlands the four partners. The first prototype was rolled out at Eurocopter France's Marignane plant in September 1995 and first flew on December 18 that year.

The most significant design feature of the NH 90 is its quadruplex fly-by-wire flight control system. In addition the entire fuselage and rotor blades (with curved tips) are made of composites. The EFIS cockpit features five LCD screens.

The NH 90 will be built in two basic versions, the land TTH (tactical transport helicopter) and naval NFH (NATO Frigate Helicopter). TTH features include a rear loading ramp to allow it to carry a two tonne vehicle, ECM, NVG and FLIR compatibility and accommodation for up to 20 fully equipped troops.

The NFH is designed for autonomous anti ship, anti submarine warfare and other general naval helicopter tasks (SAR and vertrep etc). Equipment will include a search radar in an undernose radome, dipping sonar, FLIR, MAD, an EW suite and Link II datalink, plus a crew of three or four.

NH Industries' partners are Eurocopter France, Agusta, Eurocopter Deutschland and Fokker Aerostructures. National requirements at the time of writing were France 133 TTHs and 27 NFHs, Germany 205 TTHs and 38 NFHs, Italy 160 TTHs and 64 NFHs and the Netherlands 20 NFHs. Production deliveries are planned for 2003.

Photo: The second NH 90 prototype wears a navy grey colour scheme and is the first with fly-by-wire controls. (G Deulin, NH Industries)

North American T-6 Texan/Harvard

Country of origin: United States of America

Type: Advanced piston engined trainer

Powerplant: T-6G – One 410kW (550hp) Pratt & Whitney R-1340-AN-1 Wasp nine cylinder radial piston engine driving a two blade propeller.

Performance: T-6G – Max speed at 5000ft 340km/h (184kt), max cruising speed 274km/h (148kt), economical cruising speed 235km/h (127kt). Max initial rate of climb 1643ft/min. Service ceiling 24,750ft. Normal range 1400km (755nm).

Weights: T-6G – Empty 1938kg (4271lb), max takeoff 2546kg (5617lb).

Dimensions: Wing span 12.80m (42ft 0in), length 8.99m (29ft 6in), height 3.56m (11ft 9in). Wing area 23.6m² (253.7sq ft).

Accommodation: Seating for two in tandem.

Armament: Could be fitted with machine guns in the wings, a rearward firing manually operated machine gun in the rear cockpit, and with underwing bomb racks for light bombs.

Operators: Bolivia, Paraguay.

History: North American's Texan/Harvard/SNJ series was the most important Allied trainer of World War 2.

This prolific aircraft family began with the NA-16, which was similar in appearance to subsequent models but featured fixed undercarriage, open cockpits and fabric covering around the fuselage. First flight was in April 1935. The US Army Air Corp adopted the NA-16 as the BT-9 basic trainer. Similar variants included the BT-14, Canada's Yale and the retractable undercarriage BC-1 and British Harvard I. Another variant was the Australian built Wirraway, with three blade propeller, fabric covered fuselage and retractable undercarriage. The Wirraway (755 built) saw widespread use in advanced trainer, army co-operation, light bomber, dive bomber and even fighter roles (one shot down a Japanese Zero in December 1942).

The AT-6 Texan (AT = advanced trainer) was introduced in 1939 and features retractable undercarriage, a two blade prop and metal fuselage covering. The initial Texan model was the AT-6A, supplied to the US Navy as the SNJ-3 and built in Canada (by Noorduyn) as the Harvard IIB (over 2000 went to Britain). The similar AT-6C/SNJ-4/Harvard III was redesigned to eliminate high value aluminium alloys and high alloy steels, although fears of shortages of these materials proved groundless and they were reintroduced into production.

Other wartime models were the AT-6D/SNJ-5/Harvard III and the AT-6F/SNJ-6. In all 15,000 T-6s/SNJs/Harvards were built through to 1945. In addition, small numbers of single seat AT-6 based fighters were built for Peru and Siam (Thailand).

Cancar in Canada built a further 555 T-6Gs for the US and Canadian air forces between 1951 and 1954, bringing total production of all variants to approximately 20,300.

Postwar, thousands of refurbished surplus Texans (designated T-6 by the USAF from 1948) and Harvards etc served on every continent. By 1980 still more than 20 nations operated T-6s/Harvards for advanced training and light strike. South Africa had begun to replace its 50 Harvards with Pilatus PC-7 Mk II Astras from 1995 and all are now retired, while smaller numbers are operated in Bolivia and Paraguay.

Photo: An Indonesian air force historic flight T-6. (Robert Wiseman)

North American T-28 Trojan

Country of origin: United States of America

Type: Two seat advanced trainer/light attack aircraft

Powerplant: T-28D – One 1065kW (1425hp) Wright R-1820-86 Cyclone 14 cylinder radial piston engine driving a three blade propeller.

Performance: T-28D – Max speed at 10,000ft 552km/h (598kt). Max initial rate of climb 3540ft/min. Service ceiling 35,500ft. Ferry range 1705km (920nm).

Weights: T-28D – Empty equipped 2915kg (6424lb), max takeoff 3855kg (8500lb).

Dimensions: T-28D – Wing span 12.22m (40ft 1in), length 10.06m (33ft 0in), height 3.86m (12ft 8in). Wing area 24.9m² (268.0sq ft).

Accommodation: Two in tandem.

Armament: Six underwing hardpoints can carry a total weapons load of 1815kg (4000lb), including rockets, 12.7mm/0.5in machine gun pods and 500lb/230kg bombs.

Operators: South Korea, Uruguay.

History: The big T-28 Trojan was designed as a successor to the T-6 Texan/Harvard and served widely with the US Air Force and Navy and numerous South East Asian and South American air arms.

North American Aviation's NA-159 design won the US Air Force's late 1940s contest to develop a new advanced trainer to replace T-6 Texans. Like the Texan, the Trojan was powered by a large radial piston engine, but the new aircraft differed in having a tricycle undercarriage and was significantly more powerful and larger overall.

The first of two XT-28 prototypes flew for the first time on September 26 1949. Subsequently production deliveries of the first of 1194 T-28As for the US Air Force (with a 595kW/800hp Wright R-1300 driving a two blade variable pitch prop) began in January 1950. Production for the US Navy and Marine Corps comprised 489 1065kW (1425hp) Wright R-1820 powered T-28Bs with three blade props, plus 299 similarly powered T-28Cs, fitted with an arrester hook and structurally strengthened for landing on dummy aircraft carrier decks.

Total T-28 production amounted to 1984, with many Trojans delivered to South East Asian and South American nations under the auspices of the USA's Military Assistance Program.

The T-28D Trojan was produced by conversion of surplus USAF T-28As and was also supplied widely under MAP. The T-28D conversion involved re-engining with a 1065kW (1425hp) R-1820 (driving a three blade prop), six underwing hardpoints and some crew armour. T-28D conversions were performed by Fairchild (some as AT-28Ds) and North American. Sud Aviation in France converted 245 T-28As to Fennecs (desert rat), a similar standard to the T-28D and many of these served extensively in Algeria with the French air force. Meanwhile US and South Vietnamese T-28Ds saw combat in Laos and Vietnam.

In Taiwan AIDC used the T-28 as the basis for its T-CH-1 Chung Tsing advanced trainer, which was powered by a Lycoming T53 turboprop. Most have been retired from service.

Photo: Laos was one of several Asian nations to operate T-28Ds supplied under the USA's Military Assistance Program. (Steve Death)

Northrop Grumman E-2 Hawkeye

Country of origin: United States of America

Type: Carrier and land based AEW aircraft

Powerplants: E-2C – Two 3805kW (5100ehp) Allison T56-A-425 turboprops, driving four blade propellers.

Performance: E-2C – Max speed 625km/h (338kt), max cruising speed 602km/h (325kt), ferry cruising speed 480km/h (260kt). Service ceiling 37,000ft. Ferry range 2855km (1540nm). Time on station 320km (175nm) from base 4hr 25min. Endurance with max fuel 6hr 15min.

Weights: E-2C – Empty 17,860kg (39,373lb), max takeoff 24,160kg (53,267lb).

Dimensions: Wing span 24.56m (80ft 7in), length 17.60m (57ft 9in), height 5.58m (18ft 4in). Wing area 65.0m² (700.0sq ft).

Accommodation: Crew complement of five – pilot, copilot, combat information centre officer, air control operator and radar operator.

Armament: None

Operators: Egypt, France*, Japan, Singapore, Taiwan, USA.

History: The Hawkeye was developed to replace another Grumman design, the E-1 Tracer, an AEW development of the S-2 Tracker.

Grumman was announced the winner of a US Navy requirement to develop a twin turboprop AEW aircraft with a crew of five, digital processing computers and a General Electric APS-96 surveillance radar in March 1957. The resulting W2F (E-2 from 1962) Hawkeye featured the APS-96 in an above fuselage rotodome, two Allison T56 turboprops, a high wing and a wide span tailplane with considerable dihedral with four fins including two rudders (providing the necessary directional control while conforming to carrier hangar height limitations). First flight was on October 21 1960. Production E-2As (59 aircraft in all) saw widespread service in the Vietnam theatre.

From 1969 the E-2As were upgraded to E-2B standard with an improved computer and provision for inflight refuelling. Taiwan originally intended to acquire four E-2Bs which it planned to upgrade to a similar standard to the E-2C as the E-2T, but these plans were dropped in preference for acquiring four new build E-2Cs. All E-2Bs have been retired from USN service.

The definitive Hawkeye is the E-2C, which first flew in January 1970. The main new feature of the E-2C was the APS-125 radar and improved signal processing capability. The C can be identified by its large air intake ahead of the wing and has been continually updated and fitted with increasingly capable radars, in the form of the APS-138, APS-139 and now the APS-145. The APS-145 has greater resistance to jamming, better overground performance and the ability to track up to 2000 targets at one time. Other recent E-2C features include more powerful engines (as described above) and JTIDS software. The TE-2C is a trainer. Two development E-2C Hawkeye 2000s featuring a new mission computer are being evaluated by the USN.

The E-2C Hawkeye patrols at an altitude of 30,000ft and can detect and assess targets out to a range of 555km (300nm).

Over 170 Hawkeyes have been ordered, primarily for the US Navy, but also for export. Low rate production continues for the US Navy (procuring new build aircraft was found to be more cost effective than upgrading early E-2Cs) and against fresh export orders.

Photo: A Singaporean air force E-2C gets airborne. (RAAF)

Northrop T-38 Talon

Country of origin: United States of America

Type: Two seat advanced trainer

Powerplants: Two 11.9kN (2680lb) dry and 17.1kN (3850lb) with afterburning General Electric J85-GE-5 turbojets.

Performance: Max speed at 36,000ft Mach 1.22 or 1295km/h (700kt), max cruising speed 930km/h (502kt). Max initial rate of climb 33,600ft/min. Service ceiling 53,600ft. Ferry range 1760km (950nm), typical range 1385km (747nm).

Weights: Empty 3255kg (7175lb), max takeoff 5465kg (12,050lb).

Dimensions: Wing span 7.70m (25ft 3in), length 14.14m (46ft 5in), height 3.92m (12ft 11in). Wing area 15.8m² (170.0sq ft).

Accommodation: Two in tandem.

Armament: Usually none, although Portuguese T-38s (now retired) were equipped to fire AIM-9 Sidewinder AAMs. T-38B LIFT aircraft (AT-38Bs) were equipped to carry practice bombs and rockets, plus a minigun pod.

Operators: Germany, Taiwan, Turkey, USA.

History: The supersonic Talon is the US Air Force's advanced trainer and is a development of Northrop's N-156 light fighter proposal.

Northrop began private venture development of its N-156 light fighter concept in the mid 1950s. Part of Northrop's N-156 design work was the N-156T two seater which it offered to the USAF as an advanced trainer. In 1956 the USAF ordered three N-156Ts for evaluation and the first of these YT-38s (powered by non afterburning YJ85-GE-1s) flew for the first time on April 10 1959. In all, six YT-38s were built, the final three with afterburning YJ85-GE-5s. Testing of the latter aircraft in particular was very promising, and the YT-38 was ordered into production as the T-38 Talon. Deliveries began in March 1961. Production ceased in 1972 after 1187 had been built.

The T-38A was the basic Talon production model. For a time the US Navy operated some QT-38 drones and DT-38 drone controllers and NASA flies T-38A(N)s on astronaut training duties. Finally 132 T-38As were converted to T-38B LIFT configuration, able to carry practice bombs, rockets and a minigun for weapons training. These were unofficially dubbed AT-38Bs.

The USAF expects its T-38s to remain in service until 2010 to 2015. To extend their airframe lives future USAF transport and tanker pilots now undergo advanced training on the Raytheon Beech T-1 Jayhawk rather than the T-38, while Boeing (previously McDonnell Douglas) is developing an EFIS cockpit upgrade for the aircraft.

Apart from the USAF's Air Education and Training Command, the Talon is in service with Air Combat Command and Air Mobility Command for the Companion Trainer Program. Others are used as chase aircraft for various test programs. Previous USAF T-38 operators included aggressor squadrons and the Thunderbirds.

The USAF also operates 41 German funded T-38s to train Luftwaffe pilots. Ex USAF aircraft meanwhile were supplied to Turkey and Portugal (Portugal's aircraft had an air defence role and were armed with AIM-9 Sidewinders prior to the delivery of F-16s). Finally Taiwan is leasing T-38s to make up for a shortfall in fast jet numbers pending the delivery of its F-16A/Bs which began in 1997.

Photo: A USAF Talon. (Paul Merritt)

Northrop F-5A/B Freedom Fighter

Country of origin: United States of America

Type: Lightweight multirole fighter

Powerplants: Two 12.1kN (2720lb) dry and 18.2kN (4080lb) with afterburning General Electric J85-GE-13 turbojets.

Performance: F-5A – Max speed at 36,000ft Mach 1.4 or 1488km/h (802kt), cruising speed at 36,000ft 1030km/h (556kt). Max initial rate of climb 28,700ft/min. Service ceiling 50,500ft. Ferry range 2595km (1400nm). Combat radius with two 240kg (530lb) bombs and max fuel hi-lo-hi 990km (485nm), radius with max external bomb load (1995kg/4400lb) hi-lo-hi 315km (170nm).

Weights: F-5A – Empty equipped 3667kg (8085lb), max takeoff 9380kg (20,677lb).

Dimensions: F-5A – Wing span over tip tanks 7.87m (25ft 10in), span without tip tanks 7.70m (25ft 3in), length 14.38m (47ft 2in), height 4.01m (13ft 2in). Wing area 15.8m² (170.0sq ft).

Accommodation: Pilot only in F-5A, two in tandem in F-5B.

Armament: Two M39A2 20mm cannons. Max external weapons load of 1995kg (4400lb) including bombs, rockets and AIM-9 Sidewinders on four underwing hardpoints (AIM-9s also on wingtip stations).

Operators: Botswana, Brazil, Greece, Morocco, Norway, Philippines, Saudi Arabia, South Korea, Spain, Thailand, Turkey, Venezuela.

History: Northrop's N-156 lightweight fighter was adopted by the USA as the F-5 Freedom Fighter to supply to friendly European and Asian nations under the Military Assistance Program.

As early as 1952 Northrop designed its first lightweight jet fighter, the N-102 Fang to be powered by a single GE J79 turbojet. While the USAF rejected the Fang its interest in a lightweight fighter was aroused and in 1954 it conducted a study into the concept of a lightweight yet high performance fighter that could be supplied under MAP. This study prompted Northrop to design a new lightweight fighter to meet such a requirement, resulting in the N-156 powered by two small J85 turbojets (an engine originally developed for a decoy drone).

US official interest was initially for the two seat N-156T which became the T-38 Talon, while Northrop continued development of the single seat N-156 and a privately funded prototype flew for the first time on July 30 1959 (Mach 1 was reached on this first flight).

Because of initial USAF disinterest the first production F-5A Freedom Fighter did not fly until May 1963. The USAF operated a squadron of F-5As in Vietnam for combat evaluation (Skoshi Tiger) but it never intended to acquire the F-5 in any numbers.

However Northrop built 879 F-5As and two seat F-5Bs for over a dozen MAP customers, while Canadair built 250 (with uprated engines and an inflight refuelling probe as the CF-5A and CF-5D for Canada, NF-5A/B for the Netherlands) and CASA of Spain built 70 under licence. The RF-5A is a reconnaissance variant with four KS-92A cameras in a reprofiled nose.

Several countries have upgraded their F-5A/B fleets, including Canada, Venezuela and Norway. Canada's upgrade was the most comprehensive, with an airframe refurbishment, a HUD, advanced avionics and HOTAS controls. However, all have been retired and they have been offered for sale. Botswana purchased 13.

Photo: An F-5A of the Turkish air force's display team. (Paul Merritt)

Northrop F-5E/F Tiger II

Country of origin: United States of America

Type: Lightweight multirole fighter

Powerplants: Two 15.5kN (3500lb) dry and 22.4kN (5000lb) with afterburning General Electric J85-GE-21B turbojets.

Performance: F-5E – Max speed at 37,000ft Mach 1.63 or 1730km/h (935kt), cruising speed at 36,000ft 1040km/h (562kt). Max initial rate of climb 34,300ft/min. Service ceiling 51,800ft. Ferry range with max external fuel and empty tanks dropped 3720km (2010nm). Combat radius with two AIM-9s 1405km (760nm).

Weights: F-5E – Empty 4350kg (9558lb), MTOW 11,187kg (24,664lb).

Dimensions: F-5E – Wing span with tip mounted AIM-9s 8.53m (28ft 0in), length 14.45m (47ft 5in), height 4.08m (13ft 5in). Wing area 17.3m² (186.0sq ft).

Accommodation: Pilot only in F-5E, two in tandem in F-5F.

Armament: Two M39A2 20mm cannons. Up to 3195kg (7000lb) of ordnance on two wingtip, one centreline and four underwing hardpoints including AIM-9 Sidewinders, bombs, rockets, cluster bombs and ASMs (including AGM-65 Mavericks).

Operators: Bahrain, Brazil, Chile, Honduras, Indonesia, Iran, Jordan, Kenya, Malaysia, Mexico, Morocco, Saudi Arabia, Singapore, South Korea, Sudan, Switzerland, Taiwan, Thailand, Tunisia, USA, Yemen.

History: Northrop's F-5E Tiger II was selected as the USA's International Fighter Aircraft (IFA), a lightweight fighter for export.

Northrop began work on an improved F-5 as a private venture. This resulted in the first flight of a converted F-5A prototype powered by two GE J85-GE-21 turbojets in March 1969. This aircraft was submitted for the US Government's International Fighter Competition (previously Advanced International Fighter), which was managed by the USAF. To conform with government procedures for selecting and procuring a new fighter the F-5E had to be evaluated against other US fighters including versions of the Vought F-8 Crusader, Lockheed F-104 Starfighter and even the F-4 Phantom. The F-5E was officially selected in November 1970.

Compared with the F-5A, the F-5E Tiger II features more powerful engines, enlarged leading edge extensions, permanent wingtip AAM stations and more modern and more capable avionics and systems. First flight was on August 11 1972. The F-5F two seater first flew in September 1974. The RF-5E Tigereye features four KS-121A 70mm cameras in a modified nose section.

The F-5E was extremely popular and over 1300 (including two seater F-5Fs) were built. Licence production was undertaken in Taiwan, South Korea and Switzerland, while large numbers have seen USAF and USN service as DACT aggressors. Several companies now offer F-5 upgrades, including IAI which upgraded Chilean aircraft with a new Elta M-2032 radar, avionics, HUD and HOTAS, and Northrop Grumman who offers a staged upgrade with similar features.

The ultimate expression of the F-5 line was the F-5G, or F-20 Tigershark, powered by a GE F404 and fitted with a modified APG-66 radar. It was offered for sale in the early 1980s but the relaxation of availability restrictions for the F-16 damaged its sales prospects and the program was subsequently cancelled.

Photo: A Singaporean RF-5E Tigereye. (Doug Mackay)

Northrop Grumman B-2 Spirit

Country of origin: United States of America

Type: Low observables strategic bomber

Powerplants: Four 77.0kN (17,300lb) General Electric F118-GE-110 turbofans.

Performance: Max speed at sea level approx 915km/h (495kt). Service ceiling 50,000ft. Range with eight AGM-129s and eight B83 bombs (total weapons weight 16,920kg/37,300lb) hi-hi-hi 11,665km (6300nm), hi-lo-hi with 1850km (1000nm) flown at low level 8150km (4400nm). Range with eight AGM-129s and eight B61s (total weapons weight 10,885kg/24,000lb) hi-hi-hi 12,225km (6600nm), hi-lo-hi with 1850km (1000nm) flown at low level 8335km (4500nm).

Weights: Empty 69,717kg (153,700lb), normal takeoff 152,635kg (336,500lb), max takeoff 170,550kg (376,000lb).

Dimensions: Wing span 52.43m (172ft 0in), length 21.03m (69ft 0in), height 5.18m (17ft 0in).

Accommodation: Crew of two with provision for a third member.

Armament: Two Boeing rotary launcher assemblies (RLAs), one in each bomb bay, can carry a total of 16 AGM-129 ACMs, or 16 B61 tactical/strategic or B83 strategic freefall nuclear bombs, or 80 Mk 82 bombs, or 16 JDAMs, or 16 GAMs, or 16 Mk 84 bombs.

Operators: USA

History: Highly controversial for its more than $US45bn development and production costs, the B-2 Spirit strategic penetration stealth bomber was designed from the outset to be almost invisible to radar

Concept work on a new strategic bomber incorporating low observables or stealth technology was already underway in 1977 when the Rockwell B-1A was cancelled. The resulting Advanced Technology Bomber (ATB) program was launched in 1978, and a Northrop design (with Boeing as principal subcontractor) was selected over a rival concept from Lockheed/Rockwell in June 1981. Work on the aircraft continued under complete secrecy and only the existence of the program and that the aircraft was a flying wing had been officially recognised until the B-2 was rolled out in November 1988. First flight was on July 17 1989.

The USAF originally planned to acquire 133 B-2s, although the aircraft's cost and the end of the Cold War has seen this figure reduced to 21, including the refurbished AV-1 development prototype.

The B-2 is unlike anything before it. Its flying wing design harks back to Northrop's revolutionary postwar XB-35 and XB-49, and features a double W trailing edge with eight flying control services. The flying wing design has an inherently low radar cross section, and the airframe is largely constructed of graphite/epoxy, which forms a honeycomb radar absorbent structure. Exterior surfaces are designed to minimise radar returns and heat radiation. Other features include four GE F118-GE-110 turbofans (modified non afterburning GE F110s), fly-by-wire flight controls, two side by side internal weapons bays, a Hughes APQ-181 low probability of intercept radar (for terrain following and last minute target position updates) behind two dielectric panels beneath the nose, a 81 to 90 tonne internal fuel capacity and seating for two crew on ejection seats side by side.

Photo: B-2 production is due to end in 1998, but all aircraft will not be upgraded to full Block 30 standard until 2000. (Boeing)

Northrop Grumman E-8 Joint STARS

Country of origin: United States of America

Type: Long range battlefield reconnaissance platform

Powerplants: E-8C – Four 80.1kN (18,000lb) Pratt & Whitney JT8D-3B turbofans.

Performance: E-8C – Max speed 1010km/h (545kt), max cruising speed 974km/h (525kt), long range cruising speed 885km/h (478kt). Service ceiling 42,000ft. Endurance with internal fuel 11hr, endurance with one inflight refuelling 20hr.

Weights: E-8C – Empty 77,565kg (171,000lb), max takeoff 152,407kg (336,000lb).

Dimensions: Wing span 44.42m (145ft 9in), length 44.61m (152ft 11in), height 12.95m (42ft 6in). Wing area 283.4m² (3050.0sq ft).

Accommodation: Two pilots and flight engineer. E-8A fitted with consoles for 10 operators. E-8C fitted with 18 operator consoles, one of which is for navigation/self defence.

Armament: None

Operators: USA*

History: The Northrop Grumman developed E-8 Joint STARS is a Joint Strategic Target Attack Radar System, a long range battlefield surveillance platform fitted with a side looking radar.

Grumman was awarded a full scale development Joint STARS contract, covering the conversion of two Boeing 707 airliners to serve as prototypes, in September 1985. The first of these prototypes first flew in converted E-8A configuration on December 22 1988. Originally the USAF planned to acquire 22 new build E-8B production aircraft, powered by F108 turbofans (CFM56s), and one green airframe was built (and flown in 1990) before the US instead opted to convert second hand Boeing 707 airliners into E-8Cs. The two E-8A prototypes will be upgraded to E-8C standard to serve alongside 13 production E-8C conversions. The first E-8C production aircraft first flew in March 1994, although it will used as a permanent testbed. The E-8Cs will be operated by the USAF on behalf of the US Army, with first deliveries in 1996.

The heart of the E-8 is the Norden APY-3 side looking phased array multimode radar, which is housed in a canoe fairing beneath the forward fuselage. In synthetic aperture radar mode the APY-3 can image targets up to 175km distant and can survey one million km² in one eight hour sortie. Pulse doppler modes gather moving target information allowing the operators to track moving vehicles and convoys.

Joint STARS provides ground commanders with a complete overview of the battlefield and can also be used for specific target reconnaissance and for individual targeting functions. E-8 gathered information is relayed to mobile ground stations (with operator stations similar to those onboard the aircraft) via datalink, allowing individual ground commanders to access specific information they require.

The two E-8As were hastily deployed to the Gulf War in 1991 where they flew 49 operational missions, providing invaluable information to ground commanders and proving the Joint STARS concept in a real war environment. Joint STARS were also used operationally over Bosnia between December 1995 and January 1997

Photo: The production E-8C Joint STARS are operated by the 93rd Air Control Wing based at Robins AFB, Georgia. (Doug Mackay)

Pacific Aerospace CT-4 Airtrainer

Country of origin: New Zealand

Type: Two/three seat light basic trainer

Powerplant: CT-4A – One 155kW (210hp) Teledyne Continental IO-360-D fuel injected flat six piston engine, driving a two blade propeller. CT-4B – One 155kW (210hp) IO-360-HB9.

Performance: CT-4A – Max speed 290km/h (157kt), cruising speed 240km/h (130kt), long range cruising speed 235km/h (127kt). Max initial rate of climb 1345ft/min. Range at long range cruising speed 1300km (700nm). CT-4B – Max speed 267km/h (144kt), cruising speed 260km/h (140kt). Max initial rate of climb 1250ft/min. Range with max fuel at normal cruising speed 1110km (600nm).

Weights: CT-4A – Empty 690kg (1520lb), max takeoff 1088kg (2400lb). CT-4B – Max takeoff 1202kg (2650lb).

Dimensions: Wing span 7.92m (26ft 0in), length 7.06m (23ft 2in), height 2.59m (8ft 6in). Wing area 12.0m² (129.0sq ft).

Accommodation: Two side by side, with optional third seat behind.

Armament: None

Operators: New Zealand, Thailand.

History: Affectionately dubbed the Plastic Parrot, the CT-4 Airtrainer is a two seat basic trainer.

The CT-4 is developed from the Australian Victa Airtourer, a light two seat GA aircraft. The Airtourer was designed in 1953 by Henry Millicer, then chief aerodynamicist at Australia's Government Aircraft Factory. Victa had developed a larger four place Aircruiser, but development work was not continued with and instead the production rights for the Aircruiser were purchased by Aero Engine Services Ltd (or AESL) of New Zealand in 1974, which by then already had the rights to the Airtourer series. AESL made a number of changes to the basic Aircruiser design, including a new clamshell canopy, structural strengthening for aerobatic work and stick controls, making it suitable for military basic training.

The first such CT-4A Airtrainer flew on February 23 1972. Primary customers were the Australian (51 aircraft), New Zealand (24) and Thai (26) air forces. Production by NZAI (New Zealand Aircraft Industries), as AESL had become, continued until 1977.

In 1991 Pacific Aerospace Corporation (the successor to NZAI) resumed production of the CT-4B against an order from the then BAe/Ansett Flying College in Tamworth, Australia. Using these aircraft the college provides flight screening and basic training for Australian and Papua New Guinea military pilots under contract. Australia's CT-4As were retired in early 1993. Five CT-4Bs were also built for the Royal Thai Air Force, while that service's surviving CT-4As have been rewinged to extend their service lives.

Three other CT-4 developments have been offered but have not been ordered into production. The turboprop Allison 250 powered CT-4C flew on January 21 1991, and a retractable version, the CT-4CR, was proposed. The 225kW (300hp) IO-540 powered CT-4E was aimed at the US Air Force's Enhanced Flight Screening competition (won by the Slingsby Firefly). CT-4 production has ceased, but the aircraft could be returned to production if new orders are found.

Photo: A New Zealand Airtrainer in the new yellow training livery the RNZAF is adopting for its CT-4s. (RNZAF)

Panavia Tornado IDS & ECR

Countries of origin: Germany, Italy and UK

Type: Strike/ground attack aircraft

Powerplants: IDS (from 1983) – Two 40.5kN (9100lb) dry (downrated to 38.5kN/8650lb for RAF aircraft) and 71.5kN (16,075lb) with afterburning Turbo-Union RB199-34R Mk 103 turbofans.

Performance: IDS – Max speed Mach 2.2 (Mach 1.3 for RAF aircraft), max speed with external stores Mach 0.92 or 1112km/h (600kt). Time to 30,000ft less than 2min. Combat radius with a heavy weapon load hi-lo-lo-hi 1390km (750nm). Ferry range approx 3890km (2100nm).

Weights: IDS – Basic empty approx 13,890kg (30,620lb), max takeoff approx 27,950kg (61,620lb).

Dimensions: Span wings extended 13.91m (45ft 8in), span wings swept 8.60m (28ft 3in), length 16.72m (54ft 10in), height 5.95m (19ft 6in). Wing area (25° sweepback) 26.6m² (286.3sq ft).

Accommodation: Pilot and weapons system operator/navigator.

Armament: Two IWKA-Mauser 27mm cannons. Max external load over 9000kg (19,840lb), including AIM-9s, bombs, laser guided bombs, ALARM (RAF) and HARM (ECR) anti radiation missiles, WE177B (RAF) and B61 (Luftwaffe) nuclear bombs, JP 233 (RAF) and MW-1 (Luftwaffe) area denial weapons, Sea Eagle (GR.1B) and Kormoran (Marineflieger) anti ship missiles.

Operators: Germany, Italy, Saudi Arabia, UK.

History: A veteran of combat over Iraq, the Tornado is western Europe's most important strike aircraft.

The Tornado resulted from a late 1960s feasibility study conducted by Belgium, Canada, Germany, Italy, the Netherlands and the UK (Belgium, Canada and the Netherlands subsequently withdrew). Panavia was formed in March 1969 to develop and build the aircraft, dubbed the MRCA (Multi Role Combat Aircraft), with formal development beginning in mid 1970.

The first of nine prototypes flew for the first time on August 14 1974, production aircraft were delivered from July 1980. Orders stand at 828 with the last due to be delivered to Saudi Arabia in 1998.

The Tornado features variable geometry wings, two Turbo-Union RB199 engines (developed specifically by a consortium of Rolls-Royce, MTU and FiatAvio), a Texas Instruments radar with terrain following and ground mapping, fly-by-wire and a Ferranti built digital INS.

UK aircraft are designated GR.1 and feature a laser rangefinder in an undernose pod, while their intakes have been fixed and engines downrated. Twelve GR.1As are used for reconnaissance and are fitted with a BAe SLIR (side looking infrared) and Vinten IR linescan. The 24 converted GR.1Bs are used for maritime strike and can carry up to five Sea Eagle anti ship missiles. The GR.4 upgrade (involving 142 GR.1s) will comprise a new HUD, undernose FLIR, new avionics and ECM. First redeliveries are due from 1998.

Italy and Germany are upgrading their IDS aircraft under the MDI (Mid Life Improvement) program with FLIR, ECM and new avionics.

The Tornado ECR (Electronic Combat Reconnaissance) for Germany and Italy is a dedicated Suppression of Enemy Air Defence (SEAD) variant of the IDS fitted with a Emitter Location System (ELS) and can fire the AGM-88 HARM. The ECR's guns are deleted.

Photo: An Italian air force Tornado IDS.

Panavia Tornado ADV

Countries of origin: Germany, Italy and UK

Type: Air defence fighter/interceptor

Powerplants: F.3 – Two 40.5kN (9100lb) dry and 73.5kN (16,520lb) with afterburning Turbo-Union RB199-34R Mk 104 turbofans.

Performance: F.3 – Max speed Mach 2.2. Operational ceiling approx 70,000ft. Combat radius supersonic 555km (300nm), subsonic over 1850km (1000nm). CAP endurance 555 to 740km (300 to 400nm) from base with time for interception and 10min combat, 2hr.

Weights: F.3 – Operating empty approx 14,500kg (31,970lb), max takeoff 27,895kg (61,700lb).

Dimensions: Span wings spread 13.91m (45ft 8in), span wings swept 8.60m (28ft 3in), length 18.68m (61ft 4in), height 5.95m (19ft 6in). Wing area (25° sweepback) 26.6m² (286.3sq ft).

Accommodation: Pilot and radar operator in tandem.

Armament: One IKMA-Mauser 27mm cannon. Four underfuselage Skyflash AAMs and two AIM-9L Sidewinders on each underwing pylon. Italian F.3s modified to carry Alenia Aspide AAMs under fuselage.

Operators: Italy, Saudi Arabia, UK.

History: An air-to-air Tornado model had always been envisioned in early planning, and a feasibility study of an air defence variant was first conducted in 1968.

The Tornado was subsequently selected to meet the UK's 1971 requirement for an air defence fighter armed with BAe's Skyflash medium range air-to-air missile and fitted with an advanced radar. Formal development of the Tornado ADV or Air Defence Variant, as the Tornado fighter was designated, was authorised in March 1976.

The first of three Tornado ADV prototypes flew for the first time on October 27 1979, while the first production Tornado F.2 first flew in March 1984.

Compared with the Tornado IDS, the ADV features a 1.36m (4ft 6in) fuselage stretch, allowing the underfuselage carriage of four Skyflash missiles in semi recessed stations, while also increasing internal fuel capacity to 7143 litres. The ADV features the GEC-Marconi AI.24 Foxhunter radar, which was designed to track up to 20 targets while scanning, with a search range out to 185km (100nm). Development of the Foxhunter however was troubled and early production Tornado F.2s and F.3s were fitted with Foxhunters completed to X and Y standards, not meeting the full RAF requirement. AA standard Foxhunters fully meeting the RAF requirement were installed in production aircraft since 1989, while all radars were now being upgraded to much improved 2G standard with a new data processor.

The RAF ordered 173 Tornado ADVs, the first 18 of which were delivered in interim F.2 standard with less powerful Mk 103 engines, while the definitive F.3 features the RB199 Mk 104. F.2s have been retired from service. F.3s are being fitted with JTIDS and about 100 are being modified to carry ASRAAM and AIM-120 missiles.

Saudi Arabia is the only Tornado ADV export customer, with 24 delivered from 1989. Saudi and RAF Tornados flew combat air patrols during the Gulf War, but without seeing combat. Meanwhile Italy has leased 24 RAF Tornado F.3s (modified to fire the Alenia Aspide) to bolster its fighter force pending the delivery of the Eurofighter.

Photo: RAF F.3s. (Sgt Rick Brewell RAF, UK Crown Copyright)

Pilatus PC-6 Porter & Turbo-Porter

Country of origin: Switzerland

Type: STOL utility transport

Powerplant: PC-6/B2-H4 – One 410kW (550shp) flat rated Pratt & Whitney Canada PT6A-27 turboprop driving a three blade propeller.

Performance: PC-6/B2-H4 (Utility version) – Economical cruising speed 213mk/h (115kt). Max initial rate of climb 940ft/min. Max operating altitude 25,000ft. Takeoff run at sea level 127m (415ft). Range with max payload at economical cruising speed and no reserves 730km (395nm), range with max internal fuel 925km (500nm), with external fuel 1610km (870nm).

Weights: PC-6/B2-H4 – Empty equipped 1270kg (2800lb), max takeoff 2800kg (6173lb).

Dimensions: PC-6/B2-H4 – Wing span 15.87m (52ft 1in), length 10.90m (35ft 9in), height tail down 3.20m (10ft 6in). Wing area 30.2m² (324.5sq ft).

Accommodation: Pilot and passenger on flightdeck, with max seating for nine in main cabin. Standard seating for six in main cabin. Alternative layouts include two stretchers and three medical attendants, or 10 paratroops.

Armament: Usually none. Thai AU-23s armed with one XM-197 cannon and two pod mounted 7.62mm machine guns, plus rockets and bombs.

Operators: Austria, Bolivia, Chad, Ecuador, France, Mexico, Myanmar, Peru, Switzerland, Thailand, UAE (Dubai), USA, Yugoslavia.

History: Highly regarded for their exceptional STOL performance and low speed handling, the Pilatus Porter and Turbo-Porter STOL utilities are used for a number of utility tasks ranging from paradropping, to liaison, reconnaissance and light transport.

The Porter flew for the first time on May 4 1959. The first production aircraft built, delivered from 1960, were powered by the six cylinder Lycoming GSO-480 piston engine, but it was not long after that a turboprop powered development flew. The first PC-6/A Turbo-Porter flew in May 1961, powered by a 390kW (523shp) Turboméca Astazou II turboprop. The majority of PC-6s built however are PC-6/Bs, powered by the ubiquitous Pratt & Whitney Canada PT6A. PC-6/Cs are powered by a 310kW (575shp) Garrett TPE331 and were first delivered in 1965.

The PC-6/B was first delivered from 1964, and remains in production today. Initial models were powered by the 410kW (550shp) PT6A-6 or -20. The PC-6/B2-H2 was first flown in 1970 and introduced the PT6A-27 and an increased maximum takeoff weight. Current production is of the PC-6/B2-H4 with a further increase in max takeoff weight, larger dorsal fin fillet, revised wingtips, strengthened airframe structure and improved undercarriage.

Fairchild in the USA manufactured the PC-6 under licence as the Heli-Porter. Included in US production was the AU-23 Peacemaker, an armed COIN variant initially ordered by the US Army for evaluation against the Helio Courier. The 15 evaluation AU-23As were subsequently delivered to the Royal Thai Air Force, plus 20 new production aircraft. About 22 are still in RTAF service.

The US Army's two PC-6s are designated UV-20 Chiricahuas.

Photo: A Swiss PC-6 Turbo-Porter. Note the balloon tyres and long span wing. (Swiss MoD)

Pilatus PC-7 Turbo-Trainer

Country of origin: Switzerland

Type: Two seat trainer

Powerplant: One 485kW (650shp) flat rated to 410kW (550shp) Pratt & Whitney Canada PT6A-25A turboprop, driving a three blade prop.

Performance: Aerobatic category – Max cruising speed 412km/h (222kt), economical cruising speed 317km/h (171kt). Max initial rate of climb 2150ft/min. Service ceiling 33,000ft, max operating altitude 25,000ft. Max range at cruise power and reserves 1200km (647nm). Utility category – Max cruising speed 364km/h (196kt), economical cruising speed 305km/h (165kt). Max initial rate of climb 1290ft/min. Max range at cruise power with reserves 2630km (1420nm).

Weights: Basic empty 1330kg (2932lb), max takeoff aerobatic category 1900kg (4188lb), max takeoff utility category 2700kg (5952lb).

Dimensions: Wing span 10.40m (34ft 1in), length 9.78m (32ft 1in), height 3.21m (10ft 6in). Wing area 16.6m² (179.0sq ft).

Accommodation: Two in tandem.

Armament: Usually none.

Operators: Angola, Austria, Bolivia, Botswana, Brunei*, Chad, Chile, France, Guatemala, Iran, Malaysia, Mexico, Myanmar, Netherlands, South Africa*, Surinam, Switzerland, UAE (Abu Dhabi), Uruguay.

History: The PC-7 Turbo-Trainer basic trainer is Pilatus' most successful military aircraft program.

The PC-7 is based on the earlier Pilatus P-3, a two seat basic trainer developed for the Swiss air force to replace North American T-6s. A total of 78 P-3s was built for Switzerland and Brazil in the mid 1950s. The P-3 was powered by a 195kW (260hp) Lycoming GO-435 flat six piston engine. All have been retired.

The first PC-7s were converted P-3s and the first prototype flew on April 12 1966. A series of P-3-05 preproduction aircraft were built, however it was not until August 18 1978 that the first production aircraft flew. In that time the PC-7 underwent significant structural redesign (in conjunction with Dornier) to arrive at its current production form. Deliveries of production aircraft (to Myanmar, then Burma) began in December 1978.

Through the early 1980s the PC-7 attracted large orders from a number of air forces. Other than Switzerland, the PC-7 is in service with the air arms of the Netherlands, Abu Dhabi, Bolivia, Iran, Malaysia, Mexico and Myanmar. Optional Martin-Baker ejection seats were offered from 1985.

The basic PC-7 has now been joined by the PC-7 Mk II, which Pilatus developed specifically to meet a South African Air Force requirement to replace T-6 Harvards. The Mk II has been substantially revised and features the PC-9's airframe and a more powerful 520kW (700shp) PT6A-25 engine driving a four blade prop. South Africa has ordered 60, which it has named Astra, with significant local industrial participation including assembly. The first PC-7 Mk II flew for the first time on September 28 1992. Production of kits for assembly by Atlas began in early 1994. Max cruising speed is 463km/h (250kt), range with internal fuel 1425km (770nm) and max takeoff weight is 3200kg (7054lb). Brunei has ordered four.

Photo: The PC-7 Mk II externally closely resembles the more powerful PC-9. (Pilatus)

Pilatus PC-9

Country of origin: Switzerland

Type: Two seat advanced trainer

Powerplant: PC-9 – One 855kW (1150shp) Pratt & Whitney PT6A-62 turboprop (flat rated to 710kW/950shp) driving a four blade propeller

Performance: PC-9 – Max speed at 20,000ft 555km/h (300kt), max speed at sea level 500km/h (270kt). Max initial rate of climb 4090ft/min. Max operating altitude 25,000ft, service ceiling 35,000ft. Max range at cruise power with reserves 1640km (887nm). Endurance at typical mission power settings, two 1hr sorties plus reserves.

Weights: PC-9 – Basic empty 1685kg (3715lb), max aerobatic category takeoff 2250kg (4960lb), max utility category takeoff 3200kg (7055lb).

Dimensions: PC-9 – Wing span 10.19m (33ft 5in), length 10.18m (33ft 5in), height 3.26m (10ft 8in). Wing area 16.3m² (175.3sq ft).

Accommodation: Two in tandem.

Armament: Usually none.

Operators: PC-9 – Angola, Australia, Croatia, Cyprus, Iraq, Myanmar, Saudi Arabia, Slovenia, Switzerland, Thailand.

History: Pilatus' PC-9 is a more powerful and higher performing turboprop trainer based on the PC-7. Intended for basic and advanced training, the PC-9 was also the successful contender for the USAF/USN's JPATS program.

Design work on the PC-9 began in 1982. Aerodynamic features of the PC-9 were test flown on a modified PC-7 in 1982/3, while the first of two preproduction PC-9s had its first flight on May 7 1984. Aerobatic category Swiss civil certification was granted in September 1985.

The PC-9 retains 9% structural commonality with the earlier PC-7. Key differences are the more powerful Pratt & Whitney PT6A-62 turboprop driving a four blade prop (when the PC-9 was first in development some reports suggested it would be powered by a Garrett TFE331), stepped tandem cockpits with ejection seats and an airbrake under the centre fuselage.

Major PC-9 operators are Australia, Iraq, Saudi Arabia and Thailand. Australia ordered 67 PC-9/As to replace CT-4 Airtrainers and Macchi MB-326s for basic and advanced training. All but the first two were assembled in Australia by Hawker de Havilland and all feature low pressure tyres (as on the PC-7) for grass strip operations and Bendix EFIS displays. Saudi Arabia's 30 PC-9s were sold through British Aerospace as part of a comprehensive arms deal, while Thailand's 20 PC-9s have augmented RFB Fantrainers. In Germany a civil firm operates 10 PC-9Bs equipped for target towing under contract to the Luftwaffe. In all sales of the PC-9 exceed 200.

In June 1995 a modified version of the PC-9 was selected to meet the US Air Force and Navy's Joint Primary Aircraft Training System program, which aimed to find a successor for the USAF's T-37s and the USN's T-34s. The T-6 Texan II (previously Beech Mk II) will be built by Raytheon Beech in Kansas and features a new two piece canopy for increased bird strike protection, an upgraded engine, single point refuelling and zero zero ejection seats. This aircraft is fully described under its own entry.

Photo: An Australian PC-9/A. (LAC Pete Battye, RAAF)

Pilatus PC-12 Eagle

Country of origin: Switzerland

Type: Special missions and light utility transport

Powerplant: One 895kW (1200shp) Pratt & Whitney Canada PT6A-67B turboprop, driving a four blade constant speed Hartzell propeller.

Performance: PC-12 – Max cruising speed 500km/h (270kt), economical cruising speed 430km/h (232kt). Initial rate of climb 2040ft/min. Service ceiling 25,000ft. Range at economical cruising speed with reserves 2965km (1600nm). Eagle – Max cruising speed 463km/h (250kt). Max range at 30,000ft and 370km/h (200kt) 3080km (1635nm). Endurance 5hr plus.

Weights: PC-12 – Empty 2386kg (5260lb), max takeoff 4000kg (8818lb). Eagle – Empty 2900kg (6393lb), max takeoff 4500kg (9920lb).

Dimensions: PC-12 – Wing span 16.08m (52ft 9in), length 14.38m (47ft 2in), height 4.26m (14ft 0in). Wing area 25.8m² (277.8sq ft). Eagle – Same except wing span 16.11m (52ft 10in)

Accommodation: PC-12 – Flightcrew of one or two pilots. Max seating for nine in commuter airliner configuration. Corporate/executive transport configurations typically seat six. Combi passenger/freight version seats four passengers in main cabin plus freight pallet. Eagle – Has two work stations in main cabin.

Armament: None

Operators: South Africa*

History: The latest in a line of single engined PT6 powered Pilatus products, the PC-12 is a new generation utility aimed at fulfilling commuter, executive and freight transport missions. Although designed primarily for private customers, Pilatus is also offering it for military and police work in the PC-12 Eagle special missions form.

Pilatus announced it was developing a new single engine multi purpose transport at the National Business Aircraft Association's annual convention in October 1989. First flight of the first of two prototypes occurred on May 31 1991. This aircraft then entered a flight test program that originally envisaged achieving Swiss certification in mid 1993, with first deliveries later that year. However the development program was delayed somewhat when Pilatus redesigned the wing to feature winglets to meet performance guarantees. The improvements were successful, but the delays meant that the PC-12 was not certificated until mid 1994, with first deliveries following soon after.

The PC-12 is offered in standard nine passenger combi form and in a six seat executive configuration. The South African Air Force has ordered one basic PC-12 for utility work.

The PC-12 Eagle is a special missions variant, pitched at military and government requirements. It is offered with two workstations in the main cabin and a ventral pannier that can carry a range of sensors, such as a FLIR, search radar, synthetic aperture radar and infrared linescan. The Eagle also has revised wingtips and could be fitted with self protection equipment such as chaff/flare dispensers and a missile approach warning system.

Photo: The first of two Pilatus PC-12 Eagle demonstrators. Note the ventral pannier with ball turret FLIR. (Pilatus)

Pilatus Britten-Norman Islander/Defender

Country of origin: United Kingdom

Type: STOL utility transport

Powerplants: BN-2B-20 – Two 225kW (300hp) Textron Lycoming IO-540K1B5 flat six piston engines, driving two blade props.

Performance: BN-2B-20 – Max speed 280km/h (151kt), max cruising speed 264km/h (142kt), economical cruising speed 245km/h (132kt). Max initial rate of climb 1130ft/min. Service ceiling 17,200ft. Takeoff run at sea level 352m (1155ft). Range at economical cruising speed with standard fuel 1136km (613nm), with optional fuel 1965km (1061nm).

Weights: BN-2B-20 – Empty equipped 1925kg (4244lb), max takeoff 2993kg (6600lb).

Dimensions: Wing span 14.94m (49ft 0in), length 10.86m (35ft 8in), height 4.18m (13ft 9in). Wing area 30.2m² (325.0sq ft).

Accommodation: Flightcrew of one or two, with seating for eight in main cabin.

Armament: Defender fitted with four underwing hardpoints for bombs, rockets and gun pods.

Operators: Angola, Belgium, Belize, Botswana, Cyprus, Guyana, Haiti, India, Jamaica, Madagascar, Mauritania, Panama, Philippines, Rwanda, Seychelles, South Africa, Surinam, Turkey, UAE (Abu Dhabi & Dubai), UK, Venezuela, Zaire, Zimbabwe.

History: More than 1200 Islanders, Defenders and Turbine Islander/Defenders have been built for civil and military customers.

The BN-2 Islander was Britten-Norman's second original design, work on which began during 1963. Design emphasis was on producing a rugged and durable aircraft that had good field performance and operating economics and was easy to maintain. One unusual feature was that there was no centre aisle between seats in the main cabin, instead there were three doors along each side of the fuselage for passenger boarding. The prototype BN-2 Islander (powered by two 155kW/210hp Continental IO-360s) first flew on June 13 1965.

The first production machines were powered by 195kW (260hp) Lycoming O-540s and were simply designated the BN-2, the first flew in 1967. Since then it has been built in improved BN-2A and BN-2B forms, the BN-2B still remaining in production with Pilatus Britten-Norman. The military specific Defender differs little from the Islander except for its four underwing hardpoints.

The BN-2T Turbine Islander/Defender is powered by two Allison 250 turboprops, and flew for the first time in August 1980. The BN-2T is not in as wide scale service as its piston powered brothers, but has spawned a range of military special mission derivatives.

The maritime patrol ASW/ASV Islander flew in demonstrator form in 1984, but was not built. The CASTOR Islander battlefield surveillance platform was intended for the British Army while the MASTOR is similar. Various AEW Defenders have also been marketed including the current MSSA (Multi Sensor Surveillance Aircraft) or BN-2T-4R, fitted with an APG-66 radar in a bulbous radome, plus FLIR and GPS.

The Defender 4000 features the larger wing of the Islander's three engined brother, the Trislander, plus an enlarged nose for a search radar, more powerful engines and increased weights. It first flew in August 1994.

Photo: A Belgium piston powered Islander. (Belgium SID)

PZL Mielec TS-11 Iskra

Country or origin: Poland

Type: Two seat advanced trainer

Powerplant: One 9.81kN (2205lb) IL SO-1/SO-3 turbojet.

Performance: Max speed at 16,400ft 720km/h (390kt), cruising speed 600km/h (324kt). Max initial rate of climb 2915ft/min. Service ceiling 36,100ft. Range with max fuel 1460km (790nm), standard range 1250km (675nm).

Weights: Empty 2560kg (5645lb), max takeoff 3840kg (8465lb).

Dimensions: Wing span 10.06m (33ft 0in), length 11.17m (36ft 8in), height 3.50m (11ft 6in). Wing area 17.5m² (188.4sq ft).

Accommodation: Two in tandem, or pilot only in Iskra-Bis C.

Armament: One 23mm internal cannon in forward starboard fuselage. Four underwing hardpoints (two on Iskra-Bis A) can carry a max external ordnance of 400kg (882lb), mainly practice weapons.

Operators: India, Poland.

History: The TS-11 Iskra (or Spark) jet trainer was ordered into production for the Polish air force despite losing a Warsaw Pact competition for an advanced trainer to the Czech Aero L-29 Delfin.

The TS-11 and L-29 (and the Yak-30) were designed against a late 1950s requirement for a standardised basic jet trainer to be adopted by Warsaw Pact nations. The XL-29 Delfin prototype flew for the first time on April 5 1959, while the first Iskra first flew some months later on February 5 1960. Subsequent evaluation saw the L-29 selected for production for the USSR and most other Warsaw Pact nations, however, Poland, in the interests of maintaining its aviation industry, elected instead to procure the Iskra. The Iskra entered production in 1963 and the first production aircraft were handed over to the Polish air force the following year.

The Iskra features a straight, mid mounted wing, tandem seating with lightweight ejection seats and the rear seat slightly raised, a Polish developed SO-1 or SO-3 turbojet, a 23mm internal gun and four underwing hardpoints (except on early production examples) for practice armament. The tailplane is mounted on a boom to keep the control surfaces clear of the engine's exhaust.

Early production Iskras were powered by the interim 7.65kN (1720lb) H-10 Polish designed turbojet, pending the availability of the more powerful SO-1 (designed by the Instytut Lotnictwa/Aviation Institute and built by PZL Rzeszów). Some Iskras are powered by the improved but similarly rated SO-3.

Initial production was of the Iskra-Bis A with the two underwing hardpoints, while the Iskra-Bis B has four. The Iskra-Bis D weapons trainer is basically similar, and 50 were delivered to India in 1975 and the survivors still serve. The Iskra-Bis C or Iskra 200 was a single seater optimised for light ground attack, although it was only built in small numbers. The Iskra-Bis DF is a two seat reconnaissance and combat trainer, while the upgraded TS-11R (six delivered from late 1991) is used by the Polish navy for reconnaissance

Large numbers of TS-11s remain in Polish service although they are due to be replaced by the I-22 Iryda. Likewise India's TS-11s remain in service, although they are also due to be replaced.

Photo: A line-up of Iskras from the Polish air force's aerobatic display team. (Paul Merritt)

PZL Mielec I-22, M-93 & M-95 Iryda

Country of origin: Poland

Type: Two seat advanced trainer/ground attack aircraft

Powerplants: M-93K – Two 14.7kN (3305lb) PZL-5 turbojets.

Performance: M-93K – Max speed at altitude 950km/h (513kt). Max initial rate of climb 8268ft/min. Service ceiling 44,940ft. Time to 16,400ft 2min 30sec. Combat radius with max external stores at 1640ft 250km (135nm).

Weights: M-93K – Empty equipped 4650kg (10,251lb), max takeoff clean 6700kg (14,771lb), max takeoff 8700kg (19,180lb).

Dimensions: M-93 – Wing span 9.60m (31ft 6in), length 13.22m (43ft 5in), height 4.30m (14ft 1in). Wing area 19.9m² (214.4sq ft).

Accommodation: Two in tandem, or pilot only in proposed M-97.

Armament: M-93K – Ventral gun pack contains a 23mm GSz-23L twin barrel gun. Four underwing hardpoints can be fitted with total external load of 1800kg (3968lb), including AAMs, rockets and bombs.

Operators: Poland*

History: The Iryda was developed to replace the TS-11 Iskra and Lim-6 (MiG-17) in Polish air force service as an advanced weapons trainer and a light ground attack aircraft.

Poland elected not to adopt the L-39 Albatros as its new advanced trainer and instead launched development of the indigenous Iryda in 1977. Five PZL-5 turbojet powered prototypes were built and the first of these first flew on March 3 1985 (although this aircraft crashed in 1987).

Poland requires about 50 Irydas which will be used for advanced training, ground attack and reconnaissance training. The first pre production Iryda flew in 1992 and was subsequently delivered to the Polish air force that October.

The basic I-22 Iryda features stepped tandem cockpits, twin Polish designed and built PZL-5 turbojets mounted either side of the fuselage and a high mounted wing with four underwing hardpoints. The Iryda is designed to accept more powerful engines and greater weapons load in future developments, and to be easy to maintain and repair.

Apart from the basic I-22 PZL Mielec has developed and proposed a number of Iryda variants. The M-93 Iryda has been re-engined to overcome some shortcomings of the PZL-5 turbojet. The M-93K is powered by two 14.7kN (3305lb) Instytut Lotnictwa K-12 turbojets, and is the initial Iryda production model.

The M-93R is a proposed two seat reconnaissance variant, the M-93M a proposed maritime attack and naval reconnaissance development. Meanwhile the M-93V is powered by two 14.7kN (3305lb) Rolls-Royce Viper 545 turbojets and is intended primarily for export. The prototype was displayed at the 1995 Paris Airshow.

The proposed M-95 would have mildly swept wings, six underwing hardpoints, a choice of uprated powerplants comprising Vipers, Larzac 04-V3s or K-15s, and an advanced nav attack system.

Finally the M-97 Iryda and M-99 Orkan (Eagle) are proposed single seat ground attack developments. Both would have wingtip AAM stations, the M-99 could have Adour or Slovak DV-2 turbofans.

Photo: The Viper powered M-93V. (PZL Mielec)

PZL Swidnik (Mil) Mi-2

Countries of origin: Poland and Russia

Type: Light utility helicopter

Powerplants: Two 300kW (400shp) Isotov designed Polish built GTD-350 turboshafts, driving a three blade main rotor and two blade tail rotor.

Performance: Max cruising speed 200km/h (108kt), long range cruising speed 190km/h (102kt). Max initial rate of climb 885ft/min. Service ceiling 13,125ft. Hovering ceiling in ground effect 6560ft, out of ground effect 3280ft. Range with max payload and reserves 170km (91nm), range with max fuel 440km (237nm), range with optional fuel 580km (313nm).

Weights: Basic operating 2365kg (5213lb), max takeoff 3550kg (7825lb).

Dimensions: Main rotor diameter 14.50m (47ft 7in), length overall 17.42m (57ft 2in), fuselage length 11.40m (37ft 5in), height to top of rotor head 3.75m (12ft 4in). Main rotor disc area 166.4m² (1791.1sq ft).

Accommodation: Two pilots or one pilot and passenger on flightdeck, and main cabin seating for seven in passenger configuration. Ambulance configurations can accommodate four stretchers and one medical attendant or two stretchers and two attendants. Can carry 700kg (1540lb) of internal freight.

Armament: Mi-2URP – Four 9M14M Malyutka (AT-3 'Sagger') anti armour missiles (with four more in cargo compartment). Mi-2US – One port fuselage side mounted 23mm NS-23m cannon, two 7.62mm gun pods either side of fuselage and two 7.62mm pintle mounted guns in rear cabin. Mi-2URN – As Mi-2US plus two rocket pods.

Operators: Bulgaria, Cuba, Czech Republic, Ghana, Hungary, Iraq, Latvia, Libya, Nicaragua, Poland, Romania, Russia, Slovakia, Syria, Ukraine.

History: Poland's most massed produced helicopter was originally developed in Russia by Mil. More than 5200 have been built since the mid 1960s.

Mil originally designed the light utility Mi-2 (NATO reporting name 'Hoplite') in Russia during the early 1960s, resulting in a first flight in September 1961. In January 1964 an agreement between the USSR and Poland transferred development and production to the latter country, which commenced in 1965. The Mi-2 has evolved since that time and it remains in very low rate production today.

Swidnik has developed a diverse number of Mi-2 variants apart from the basic civil Mi-2. The Mi-2T is the basic military transport variant, while the Mi-2RM is a naval version. Three armed Mi-2s are the combat support/reconnaissance Mi-2URN, anti tank Mi-2URP and Mi-2US gunship. Their respective armament fits are described above.

The Kania (or Kitty Hawk) is a substantial upgrade of the basic Mi-2, and features Allison 250-C20B turboshafts, western avionics, composite main and tail rotor blades and US FAR Pt 29 certification. Developed in co-operation with Allison, the Kania first flew on June 3 1979 and US certification was granted in February 1986. The Kania is in limited production while existing Mi-2s can be upgraded to Kania standard.

Photo: A Czech Mi-2T transport. (MAP)

PZL Swidnik W-3 Sokol

Country of origin: Poland

Type: Multirole utility helicopter

Powerplants: Two 670kW (900shp) takeoff rated WSK-PZL Rzeszów PZL-10W (polish built Mars TVD-10) turboshafts, driving a four blade main rotor and three blade tail rotor.

Performance: W-3A – Max cruising speed 243km/h (131kt). Max initial rate of climb 2008ft/min. Hovering ceiling in ground effect 9200ft, out of ground effect 6220ft. Service ceiling 19,680ft. Range with standard fuel 680km (367nm).

Weights: W-3A – Empty 3300kg (7275lb), operating empty 3850kg (8488lb), max takeoff 6400kg (14,110lb).

Dimensions: W-3A – Main rotor diameter 15.70m (51ft 6in), length overall rotors turning 18.79m (61ft 8in), fuselage length 14.21m (46ft 8in), height overall 5.14m (16ft 10in), height to top of rotor mast 4.20m (13ft 10in). Main rotor disc area 193.6m² (2083.8sq ft).

Accommodation: Two pilots or pilot and flight engineer or passenger on flightdeck. Main cabin seating for 12 in passenger configuration, or three medical attendants and eight rescued survivors in SAR Anaconda version, or four stretchers and medical attendants in ambulance configuration, one stretcher and medical attendants in critical care EMS version. Can carry a 2100kg (4630lb) sling load.

Armament: W-3U – Trialled with an undernose GSh-23L 23mm gun and four hardpoints on outriggers for rockets, Grot anti armour missiles and two 9M32M 'Strela' AAMs.

Operators: Czech Republic, Myanmar, Poland*.

History: The multi purpose W-3 Sokol, or Falcon, is the first helicopter to be fully designed and built in Poland.

Developed during the mid 1970s, the Sokol made its first flight on November 16 1979. Following a fairly protracted development program, low rate production of the Sokol commenced during 1985, since when about 110 have been built. The collapse of communism has allowed PZL Swidnik to broaden its sales base and market the Sokol internationally.

The Sokol is of conventional design and construction, with its two PZL-10W turboshafts are based on the Russian designed TVD-10B turboprops. Composites are used in the tail and main rotor blades.

Sokol variants are many and include the improved W-3A Sokol which was awarded US civil certification in May 1993. Apart from the initial civil/military W-3 transport, military variants include the W-3RM Anakonda offshore search and rescue development in Polish navy service with a watertight cabin, external winch and inflatable flotation bags; the armed W-3U Salamandra with a roof mounted sight with TV and FLIR and four weapon stations on fuselage outriggers (since shelved); and the similar armed W-3W but without the sight.

The W-3WB Huzar flew in demonstrator form and was based on the W-3W but with Denel weapons and systems as developed for the Rooivalk. Development was suspended when the Polish military failed to support it. It has been replaced by the S-1W which is under development.

Other W-3 variants to have been proposed include the stretched 14 seat W-3 Sokol-Long and the W-3U-1 Alligator naval ASW variant.

Photo: A W-3RM Anakonda. (Grzegorz Holdanowicz, PZL Swidnik)

PZL Warszawa-Okecie Orlik

Country of origin: Poland

Type: Two seat basic/advanced trainer

Powerplant: PZL-130TC-1 – One 560kW (750shp) Walter M 601 E turboprop driving a five blade propeller. TC – One 710kW (950shp) Pratt & Whitney Canada PT6A-62.

Performance: PZL-130TC-1 – Max speed at 19,685ft 500km/h (270kt), max speed at sea level 454km/h (245kt). Max initial rate of climb 2620ft/min. Service ceiling 33,000ft. Range with max fuel 970km (523nm). TC – Max speed at 19,685ft 560km/h (302kt), max speed at sea level 510km/h (274kt). Max initial rate of climb 4055ft/min. Service ceiling 33,000ft. Range with max fuel 930km (500nm), range with two external tanks 2300km (1242nm).

Weights: PZL-130-TC-1 – Empty 1600kg (3527lb), max takeoff 2700kg (5952lb). TC – Empty 1450kg (3197lb), max takeoff same.

Dimensions: Wing span 9.00m (29ft 6in), length 9.00m (29ft 6in), height 3.53m (11ft 7in). Wing area 13.0m² (139.9sq ft).

Accommodation: Two in tandem.

Armament: Six underwing hardpoints (stressed for 160kg/353lb each) for bombs, rockets and 'Strela' air-to-air missiles.

Operators: Poland*

History: The PZL-130 Orlik (Spotted Eagle) was designed as the aircraft centrepiece of the Polish air force's System 130 pilot training program.

System 130 called for a new trainer aircraft, aircraft diagnostics equipment and an aircraft simulator. Design work on the aircraft began in 1983 under the leadership of Andrej Frydrychewicz. The Orlik trainer originally began life powered by the Russian radial piston Vedneyev M14. Otherwise though it was similar to contemporary trainers with tandem seating (with the second seat slightly raised) and retractable undercarriage. First flight was on October 12 1984.

The piston powered PZL-130 was hamstrung by supply problems with the Vedneyev engine and PZL Warszawa-Okecie was forced to look at alternative powerplants. In 1988 a preproduction Orlik made its first flight powered by a Polish Kalisz KS-8A but this aircraft soon proved underpowered and development of a piston powered Orlik was abandoned in 1990.

Development of a turboprop powered Orlik, or Turbo Orlik, dates to 1984 when PZL looked at powering the Orlik with a Pratt & Whitney Canada PT6. A so powered Orlik development aircraft had its first flight on July 13 1986. Subsequent Motorlet M 601 powered and PT6A-25 powered Turbo Orlik development aircraft were designated PZL-130TM and PZL-130T respectively.

The Polish air force ordered 48 M 601 powered Turbo Orliks (the Turbo prefix was subsequently dropped) as the PZL-130TB and deliveries against this order are continuing. These aircraft are now being built to improved PZL-130TC-1 standard with Martin-Baker zero-zero ejection seats and GPS, while early production TBs were upgraded to TC-1 configuration. The PT6A-62 powered PZL-130TC is aimed primarily at export markets and features Bendix/King avionics and a HUD. The PZL-130TC-2 is similar save for its less powerful 560kW (750shp) PT6A-25C.

Photo: A production PZL-130TC-1 Orlik. (PZL Warszawa-Okecie)

Raytheon Beech King Air

Country of origin: United States of America

Type: Utility, VIP, Elint, ESM, Sigint and maritime patrol aircraft

Powerplants: B200T – Two 635kW (850shp) Pratt & Whitney Canada PT6A-42 turboprops, driving three blade propellers.

Performance: Maritime Patrol B200T – Max cruising speed 490km/h (265kt) at 4990kg (11,000lb) AUW, typical patrolling speed 260km/h (140kt). Range with max fuel, patrolling at 420km/h (227kt) with reserves 3315km (1790nm). Typical endurance at 260km/h (140kt) patrolling speed with reserves 6hr 35min. Max time on station with wingtip fuel tanks fitted 9hr.

Weights: B200T – Empty 3745kg (8255lb), max takeoff 5670kg (12,500lb), max takeoff restricted category 6805kg (15,000lb).

Dimensions: Wing span over tip tanks 17.25m (56ft 7in), wing span 16.61m (54ft 6in), length 13.34m (43ft 9in), height 4.57m (15ft 0in). Wing area 28.2m² (303.0sq ft).

Accommodation: Flightcrew of two. Main cabin seating for up to eight in King Air 90 family, 13 in 100, 200, 300 and 350 series.

Armament: None

Operators: 90 series – Includes Bolivia, Chile, Japan, Mexico, Peru, USA, Venezuela. 200 series – Includes Argentina, Australia, Bolivia, Colombia, Ecuador, Greece, Guatemala, Ireland, Israel, Japan, Libya, Morocco, Peru, Sweden, Thailand, USA, Venezuela. RC-12 – USA. B200T – Algeria, Malaysia, Peru, Puerto Rico, Uruguay.

History: A highly successful family of light corporate aircraft in civilian life, Beech's King Air series has also been adopted for a diverse range of military tasks, ranging from transport to Elint gathering.

The King Air series began life as a turboprop powered development of the piston engined Queen Air (itself developed from the civil Twin Bonanza) which today is in limited military service. The initial 90 series King Air differed from the Queen Air primarily in having two Pratt & Whitney Canada PT6 turboprops and pressurisation. First flown in January 1964 it remains in military service with a number of nations. US military developments of the 90 King Air include the US Army's unpressurised U-21 Ute and the RU-21 Elint aircraft, and the US Navy's T-44 Pegasus trainer.

Beech stretched the King Air 90 in 1969 to come up with the King Air 100, but the by far the most important military King Airs are based on the 200. The Super King Air 200 used the stretched 100's fuselage, combined with a T-tail and first flew in October 1972. Most Super King Airs are used as transports (designated C-12 in US service).

A small number of Maritime Patrol B200Ts are in military service, fitted with a search radar, bubble observation windows and wings that can be fitted with tip tanks. Optional B200T equipment includes ESM, GPS, FLIR, sonobuoys and processor and a tactical navigation computer.

The US Army's RC-12 Guardrail meanwhile has been developed in a number of progressively improved developments, and is used for intercepting enemy radio transmissions.

Military developments of the Super King Air 300 and stretched 350 series are also on offer.

Photo: The Australian Army operates a small number of leased, civil registered Super King Air 200s. (Robert Wiseman)

Raytheon Beech T-1A Jayhawk & T-400

Country of origin: United States of America

Type: Tanker and transport aircrew trainer

Powerplants: Two 12.9kN (2900lb) P&WC JT15D-5 turbofans.

Performance: Max level speed 867km/h (468kt) at 27,000ft, typical cruising speed at 12,500ft 835km/h (450kt), long range cruising speed 725km/h (392kt). Service ceiling 41,000ft. Range with max fuel and four passengers at long range cruising speed 3575km (1930nm).

Weights: Operating empty 4589kg (10,115lb), max takeoff 7157kg (15,780kg).

Dimensions: Wing span 13.25m (43ft 6in), length 14.75m (48ft 5in), height 4.24m (13ft 11in). Wing area 22.4m² (241.4sq ft).

Accommodation: T-1A – Student pilot and instructor side by side on flightdeck, with observer seated behind them on a jump seat. Main cabin can accommodate four passengers or waiting students.

Armament: None

Operators: T-1 – USA. T-400 – Japan.

History: The Jayhawk is an off-the-shelf development of the Beechjet 400A business jet acquired to meet a US Air Force requirement for a Tanker Transport/Training System (TTTS) aircraft.

The TTTS requirement was formulated as part of the US Air Force's Specialized Undergraduate Pilot Training system which is designed to make USAF pilot training more efficient and to ease strain on the Northrop T-38 Talon fleet. The TTTS requirement was issued in the late 1980s, with the USAF considering proposals from British Aerospace, Learjet, Cessna and Beech. In February 1991 the USAF ordered the first 28 of an eventual 180 Beechjet 400A based T-1A Jayhawks. The first was delivered in January 1992 and an initial operating capability (IOC) was achieved in January 1993. The final Jayhawk was delivered to the USAF on July 23 1997. Pilots training on the T-1 will go on to fly transports such as the C-17, C-141, C-5, KC-10 and KC-135.

The Beechjet 400 design began life as the Mitsubishi MU-300 Diamond, which first flew in August 1978. The improved Diamond 2 production aircraft flew in June 1984, but only 11 production aircraft were built before Beech acquired the manufacturing and development rights. Beech replaced the Diamond 2's JT15D-4s with -5s, improved the interior, moved production to the USA and renamed the aircraft the Beechjet 400.

The improved Beechjet 400A, on which the T-1 is based, first flew in September 1989 and introduced a number of improvements including EFIS. Beech also increased the weights and repositioned the rear fuselage fuel tank to increase cabin volume.

The T-1 differs from the 400A in having fewer cabin windows, the avionics relocated from the nose to the cabin, greater fuel capacity, single point refuelling, TACAN, reinforced windscreen protection against birdstrikes and strengthening of the wing carry through structure and engine pylons to handle increased low-level flight stresses.

The Japanese Air Self Defence Force also selected the Beechjet as the basis for a transport aircrew trainer, designated the T-400. Nine T-400s are fitted with the optional thrust reversers, plus long range inertial navigation and direction finding systems.

Photo: A USAF T-1A Jayhawk. (Fernando Serna, USAF)

Raytheon Beech T-6A Texan II

Countries of origin: United States of America and Switzerland

Type: Two seat advanced trainer

Powerplant: T-6A – One 1274kW (1708shp) Pratt & Whitney Canada PT6A-68 turboprop (flat rated to 820kW/1200shp) driving a four blade propeller.

Performance: T-6A – Max speed above 555km/h (300kt). Initial rate of climb over 4500ft/min. Certificated ceiling 35,000ft. Max range over 1665km (900nm).

Weights: T-6A – Max takeoff 2858kg (6300lb).

Dimensions: T-6A – Wing span of 10.18m (33ft 5in), length 10.16m (33ft 4in), height 3.25m (10ft 7in).

Accommodation: Two in tandem.

Armament: None

Operators: USA*

History: The Raytheon Beech T-6A Texan II was the winner of the USAF's and USN's JPATS advanced trainer competition and is a reworked development of Pilatus' successful PC-9.

In 1991 the JPATS (Joint Primary Aircraft Training System) program was formed to find a replacement for USAF T-37s and the US Navy's T-34 Turbo Mentors, aiming to reduce costs through commonality and procuring an off the shelf design (which necessarily meant a foreign aircraft as no US manufacturers build trainers). For various reasons the program was delayed, meaning the Request For Proposals (RFP) deadline was not until March 1994, despite the seemingly straightforward nature of the requirement.

Seven jets and turboprops vied for the lucrative contract, all non US designs bar one (the Cessna 526) with their manufacturers teamed with US aerospace companies. On June 22 1995 the Beech Pilatus PC-9 Mk II development of the PC-9 was selected.

Earlier in support of its JPATS contest work, Beech (now part of Raytheon) modified two Pilatus built PC-9s. Beech then built two production prototypes (respective first flights Dec '92 and July '93), the second of which was the closest to full production standard and was used for USAF and USN evaluation flying.

The T-6 Texan II designation (honouring the original North American T-6 Texan) was officially bestowed on the PC-9 Mk II on June 2 1997, by which time construction of the first production T-6 was underway (first flight was expected by late 1997). First deliveries of production aircraft for the USAF are planned for late 1998. IOC with the USAF is planned for 2001 at Randolph AFB Texas, while IOC with the USN, at NAS Whiting Field, Florida, is planned for 2003.

Despite the name Texan, T-6s will be built at Raytheon's Wichita, Kansas, facilities, with the production rate rising to 43 per year by 2004. In all, the USAF will take delivery of 372 T-6As through to 2011, while deliveries of the USN's 339 T-6As will wind up in 2017.

Compared to the basic PC-9, the T-6 features many improvements, with 90% of the structure redesigned and strengthened, a more powerful PT6A-68 with a Power Management Unit for linear power delivery (for easier student transition to jets), a higher max takeoff weight, EFIS, zero-zero Martin-Baker ejection seats, and a revised shape cockpit canopy thickened for improved birdstrike protection.

Photo: The second Beech built prototype T-6A Texan II. (Raytheon)

Raytheon Hawker 800/BAe 125 & Dominie

Countries of origin: United Kingdom and United States of America

Type: VIP transport, navigation trainer (Dominie) and SAR aircraft

Powerplants: 700 – Two 16.6kN (3700lb) Garrett TFE731-3-RH turbofans. 800 – Two 19.1kN (4300lb) TFE731-5R-1Hs.

Performance: 700 – Max cruising speed 808km/h (436kt), economical cruising speed 723km/h (390kt). Service ceiling 41,000ft. Range with max payload 4725km (2500nm). 800 – Max cruising speed 845km/h (456kt), economical cruising speed 741km/h (400kt). Max initial rate of climb 3100ft/min. Service ceiling 43,000ft. Range with max payload 5318km (2870nm), range with max fuel 5560km (3000nm).

Weights: 700 – Empty 5826kg (12,845lb), max takeoff 11,567kg (25,500lb). 800 – Empty 6676kg (14,720lb), max takeoff 12,430kg (27,400lb).

Dimensions: 700 – Wing span 14.33m (47ft 0in), length 15.46m (50ft 9in), height 5.36m (17ft 7in). Wing area 32.8m² (353.0sq ft). 800 – Wing span 15.66m (51ft 5in), length 15.60m (51ft 2in), height 5.36m (17ft 7in). Wing area 34.8m² (374.0sq ft).

Accommodation: Flightcrew of two. Typical seating for nine in VIP layout, or max seating for 14. Dominie crew complement of two pilots, instructor and three students.

Armament: None

Operators: Botswana, Brazil, Japan, Malawi, Saudi Arabia, UK.

History: The Hawker 800 is one of the latest versions and names for the longest running corporate jet production run in history. Limited numbers serve as VIP transports and the basic type forms the basis for the RAF's Dominie navigation trainer.

What is now the Hawker 800 started life as the de Havilland DH.125, which flew for the first time on August 13 1962. For a time named the Jet Dragon, initial production was of the Series 1 and improved Series 1A and 1B.

The similar Series 2 meanwhile was the basis for the Dominie T.1, the Royal Air Force's standard navigator trainer since 1966. Twenty Dominies were built, while from 1993 11 were updated with modern systems to make the aircraft more representative of current frontline aircraft. Subsequent Viper powered 125 models were the Series 3; Series 4, or Series 400 when de Havilland merged into Hawker Siddeley; and the Series 600 with a stretched fuselage and seating for eight.

The much improved British Aerospace 125-700 with new fuel efficient Garrett turbofans flew for the first time in 1976. The 700 remained in production until replaced by the 125-800 in the early 1980s. The 125-800 first flew in May 1983 and introduced aerodynamic changes including a reprofiled nose and windscreen; a larger ventral fuel tank, more powerful engines and a redesigned interior.

The 125-800 became the Raytheon Hawker 800 from mid 1993 when Raytheon purchased BAe's Corporate Jets division. Production was transferred to the US between 1995 and 1997. Raytheon delivered the first of 34 required SAR equipped Hawker 800s (U-125) to the Japan Air Self Defence Force from 1995 (deliveries should continue through to 2004). These aircraft feature a search radar, FLIR and observation windows.

Photo: One of 11 RAF Dominie T.1 navigation trainers. (Paul Merritt)

Rockwell T-2 Buckeye

Rockwell OV-10 Bronco

Country of origin: United States of America

Type: Two seat carrier capable advanced trainer

Powerplants: T-2C – Two 13.1kN (2950lb) General Electric J85-GE-4 turbojets.

Performance: T-2C – Max speed 840km/h (470kt). Max initial rate of climb 6200ft/min. Service ceiling 40,415ft. Range 1685km (910nm).

Weights: T-2C – Empty 3680kg (8115lb), max takeoff 5977kg (13,179lb).

Dimensions: T-2C – Span over tip tanks 11.62m (38ft 2in), length 11.67m (38ft 4in), height 4.51m (14ft 10in). Wing area 23.7m² (255.0sq ft).

Accommodation: Two in tandem.

Armament: T-2C – Usually none, but has two underwing hardpoints for practice bombs, rockets and gun pods. T-2D/T-2E – Six underwing hardpoints can carry a total ordnance load of 1588kg (3500lb) for rockets and bombs.

Operators: Greece, USA, Venezuela.

History: The T-2 Buckeye advanced trainer has been responsible for training and carrier qualifying countless thousands of US Navy fast jet pilots since the early 1960s.

In 1956 the US Navy issued its requirement for a new jet powered trainer able to train pilots once they had some basic tuition on the T-34 through to advanced training, weapons and combat training and carrier qualification. Later in 1956 North American Aviation, a company which had already made thousands of SNJ and T-28 Trojan trainers (plus the FJ Fury fighter) for the US Navy was selected to develop its NA-249 design proposal and an initial order for 26 production T2J-1s was placed.

The NA-249/T2J-1 design featured a single 15.1kN (3400lb) Westinghouse J34-WE-36 turbojet fed by two undernose intakes, plus tandem seating, a mid mounted straight wing with tip tanks and an arrester hook for carrier operations/training.

The first T2J-1 had its maiden flight on January 31 1958, there being no prototype. Some 217 T2J-1 (T-2A from 1962) Buckeyes were built, the first entered service in July 1959. In 1960 two T2J-1s were converted to YT2J-2 standard powered by two 13.4kN (3000lb) Pratt & Whitney J60-P-6 turbojets. The first of these flew on August 30 1962 as the YT-2B, while the first production T-2B had its first flight on May 21 1966. The 97 production T-2Bs were delivered to the USN from 1966.

The definitive US Navy Buckeye is the T-2C. The T-2C is powered by two General Electric J85 turbojets (the J85 also powers the F-5), and first flew in 1968. The T-2C was delivered between 1968 and 1976, replacing surviving T-2As and T-2Bs in service. The T-2C itself is now being replaced by the T-45 Goshawk. Small numbers of T-2B and T-2Cs were converted to DT-2 drone controllers.

The Buckeye found export customers in Greece and Venezuela. Venezuela ordered 12 T-2Ds (with some avionics changes and no carrier gear) in 1972. A subsequent batch of 12 T-2Ds featured six underwing hardpoints. Greece's T-2E are essentially similar, with the six underwing hardpoints. Forty were delivered from 1976.

In all, 550 Buckeyes were built through to 1976.

Photo: A Greek air force T-2E. (MAP)

Country of origin: United States of America

Type: Light attack/COIN and FAC aircraft

Powerplants: OV-10A – Two 535kW (715ehp) Garrett T76-G-416/417 turboprops, driving three blade propellers.

Performance: OV-10A – Max speed 452km/h (244kt). Max initial rate of climb 2650ft/min. Service ceiling 24,000ft. Takeoff run at normal takeoff weight 225m (740ft). Combat radius with max external ordnance 367km (198nm). Ferry range with external fuel 2300km (1240nm).

Weights: OV-10A – Empty equipped 3160kg (6970lb), max takeoff 6552kg (14,444lb).

Dimensions: OV-10A – Wing span 12.19m (40ft 0in), length 12.67m (41ft 7in), height 4.62m (15ft 2in). Wing area 27.0m² (291.0sq ft).

Accommodation: Two in tandem, plus two stretchers and a medical attendant or five troops in rear fuselage.

Armament: Four 7.62mm machine guns in underfuselage sponsons. Two underwing, one centreline and four under sponson hardpoints for light bombs, rockets and gun pods.

Operators: Indonesia, Morocco, Philippines, Thailand, Venezuela.

History: The OV-10 resulted from the US Marines sponsored Light Armed Reconnaissance Aircraft (LARA) program to find a multirole utility aircraft that could perform recce and light attack missions.

North American's NA-300 design was selected in August 1964. Seven YOV-10A prototypes were ordered for evaluation and the first of these first flew on July 16 1965.

The OV-10 has a unique configuration with two crew in tandem under a large canopy, room in the rear fuselage for five troops or two stretchers, a high wing and twin tailbooms extending from the engine nacelles. Power is from two Garret T76s (one YOV-10 was powered by two T74s/PT6s). Sponsons extending either side of the fuselage house four 7.62mm guns and feature hardpoints for a variety of weaponry.

Production OV-10As were delivered to the USAF, Navy and Marines, and many saw operational service in Vietnam where they were used for forward air control (FAC) and light attack.

The OV-10B designation applies to six Broncos delivered to Germany from 1970 for target towing. A further 18 OV-10B(Z)s for Germany were fitted with an above wing mounted J85 auxiliary turbojet. All have been retired.

The Royal Thai Air Force continues to operate the survivors of 32 OV-10Cs delivered from 1971, while Venezuela took delivery of 16 OV-10Es (and later ex USAF OV-10As). The OV-10C and OV-10E are similar to the OV-10A.

Seventeen OV-10As were converted to OV-10D standard over 1979/80 for the US Marines, the result of the US Navy sponsored OV-10D NOGS (Night Observation/Gunship System) program to give the Bronco an all weather capability. Now retired, the OV-10Ds featured an undernose turret containing a FLIR, laser designator and automatic video tracker, plus uprated engines and extra underwing hardpoints. The OV-10D saw service during the Gulf War and could be armed with a 20mm M197 three barrel cannon in place of the 7.62mm guns.

Photo: Venezuela operates OV-10Es (pictured) and ex USAF OV-10As.

Rockwell B-1B Lancer

Country of origin: United States of America

Type: Strategic bomber

Powerplants: Four 64.9kN (14,600lb) dry and 136.9kN (30,780lb) with afterburning General Electric F101-GE-102 turbofans.

Performance: Max speed at altitude Mach 1.25 or 1324km/h (715kt), penetration speed at 200ft over 965km/h (520kt). Service ceiling over 50,000ft. Range with standard fuel approx 12,000km (6475nm).

Weights: Empty equipped 87,090kg (192,000lb), max takeoff 216,365kg (477,000lb).

Dimensions: Wing span fully extended 41.67m (136ft 9in), span wings swept 23.84m (78ft 3in), length 44.81m (147ft 0in), height 10.36m (34ft 10in). Wing area approx 181m² (1950sq ft).

Accommodation: Crew of four comprising pilot, copilot, offensive systems operator (OSO) and defensive systems operator (DSO).

Armament: Max internal payload of 34,020kg (75,000lb) in three internal weapons bays. Weapons include B-61 and B-83 thermonuclear bombs or on rotary launchers up to 8 AGM-86B ALCMs, 24 AGM-69A short range attack missiles (SRAM-As), 12 B-28, 28 B-61 or 28 B-93 free fall nuclear bombs. Can carry up to 84 500lb/225kg Mk 82 conventional bombs and CBU-87, -89 & -97 cluster bombs, and is being upgraded to carry JDAMs, JSOWs and JASSMs.

Operators: USA

History: The USA's most numerically important strategic bomber, the B-1 has had to endure criticisms of its high cost, cancellation, a 20 year gestation period and operational serviceability problems.

The B-1 resulted from the USAF's Advanced Manned Strategic Aircraft (AMSA – or, as it became known, America's Most Studied Airplane) program of 1965 to find a low altitude penetration nuclear bomber to replace the B-52. A North American Rockwell design was eventually selected for further development in 1970 from competing designs from Boeing and General Dynamics.

The first of four B-1A prototypes first flew on December 23 1974. However in 1977 new US President Carter cancelled planned B-1A production (SAC hoped to acquire 250) but test flying continued.

The B-1 was resurrected in 1981 when Ronald Reagan was installed as US President and 100 improved production B-1s, designated B-1B, were ordered. Compared with the B-1A the B-1B (ff Oct 18 '84) features improved avionics and systems, incorporation of some low observable features such as RAM coatings, strengthened landing gear, optional weapons bay fuel tanks, external underfuselage hardpoints for fuel and weapons, ejection seats rather than a crew escape capsule, fixed, rather than variable air inlets (limiting top speed to Mach 1.25 rather than the B-1A's Mach 2.3) with ducting masking the engines from radar. The B-1B's offensive systems are based around the APG-164 radar (based on the APG-66) for navigation and terrain following, with a low observable phased array antenna. The core of the defensive systems is the Eaton ALQ-161 upgradable ECM suite.

All 100 production B-1B Lancers had been delivered by April 1988. An upgrade program is currently underway to equip the Lancer with precision conventional weapons, principally the JDAM, plus the ALE-50 Towed Decoy System (TDS). Completion is due in 2002.

Photo: The B-1B Lancer. (Paul Merritt)

Saab 105

Country of origin: Sweden

Type: Two seat basic/advanced trainer, liaison and light attack aircraft

Powerplants: Sk 60B – Two 7.3kN (1638lb) Turboméca Aubisique turbofans. Sk 60W – Two 8.1kN (1812lb) class Williams Rolls FJ44-1C (RMIS) turbofans.

Performance: Sk 60B – Max speed at 20,000ft 765km/h (413kt), max speed at sea level 720km/h (388kt), max cruising speed 685km/h (370kt). Max initial rate of climb 3445ft/min. Time to 29,530ft 15min. Service ceiling 39,370ft. Ferry range 1780km (960nm), standard range 1400km (755nm). Sk 60W – Max speed 790km/h (426kt). Service ceiling 36,080ft. Range on internal fuel 2500km (1350nm).

Weights: Sk 60B – Empty 2510kg (5535lb), MTOW 4500kg (9920lb). Sk 60W – Empty 2782kg (6134lb), MTOW 4832kg (10,654lb).

Dimensions: Wing span 9.50m (31ft 2in), length 10.50m (34ft 5in), height 2.70m (8ft 10in). Wing area 16.3m² (175.5sq ft).

Accommodation: Two side by side in all models except Sk 60D, which has seating for four on fixed (non ejection) seats.

Armament: Sk 60B – Six underwing hardpoints can carry a total ordnance load of 800kg (1764lb), including rockets and bombs. Saab 105Ös can carry a 2000kg (4410lb) ordnance load.

Operators: Austria, Sweden.

History: The light attack, liaison and advanced jet trainer Saab 105 began life as a private venture.

Saab designed the 105 to be capable of a number of different missions as diverse as ground attack, reconnaissance, basic and advanced pilot training, liaison, target towing and even air ambulance. The first of two Saab 105 prototypes made its first flight on June 29 1963, while the following year the Swedish air force ordered 130 production aircraft (later 150) as the Sk 60. The first production Sk 60 flew in August 1965.

The Sk 60A trainer entered service in 1966. These aircraft were delivered unarmed but were later retrofitted to carry hardpoints for weapons, allowing a secondary wartime ground attack role. The Sk 60B meanwhile is primarily tasked with weapons training and ground attack. The Sk 60C has a Fairchild KB-18 reconnaissance camera in the nose, but also retains a secondary ground attack capability. The Sk 60D and four seat Sk 60E (with the two ejection seats replaced by four fixed seats) are used for liaison and check rides.

Through 1998 96 Swedish Sk 60s are being re-engined with Williams Rolls FJ44 turbofans to Sk 60W standard. The prototype conversion first flew in October 1995. Benefits include lower fuel consumption and maintenance costs and improved reliability.

The only Saab 105 export customer was Austria, who ordered 40 Saab 105Ös. The 105Ö is based on the General Electric J85 turbojet powered Saab 105XT, which first flew on April 29 1967. The Saab 105XT was intended for export and apart from the more powerful engines has improved avionics, greater internal fuel capacity and a strengthened wing allowing an increased external ordnance load. For many years the 105Ös were tasked with air defence until the arrival of Austria's Drakens.

Photo: An Austrian Saab 105Ö. (Austrian Armed Forces)

Saab 32 Lansen

Country of origin: Sweden

Type: EW trainer/aggressor and target tug

Powerplant: J 32B – One 68.1kN (15,190lb) Svenska Flygmotor licence built Rolls-Royce Avon RM6A turbojet.

Performance: J 32B – Max speed Mach 0.93 or 1100km/h (594kt). Max initial rate of climb 19,700ft/min. Service ceiling 52,500ft. Range with external fuel 2000km (1080nm).

Weights: J 32B – Empty 7990kg (17,600lb), max takeoff 13,530kg (29,800lb).

Dimensions: Wing span 13.00m (42ft 8in), length 14.94m (49ft 1in), height 4.65m (15ft 3in). Wing area 37.4m² (402.6sq ft).

Accommodation: Two in tandem.

Armament: J 32B – Four 30mm Aden cannons in forward lower nose. Four underwing hardpoints latterly used for EW jammer pods etc, originally designed for Sidewinder AAMs, rockets, bombs and ASMs. A 32 had a max external load of 1360kg (3000lb) and four 20mm cannons.

Operators: Sweden

History: Sweden's Lansen (Lance) was a highly capable all weather fighter, reconnaissance and ground attack aircraft. Until 1997 it was used an electronic warfare trainer and aggressor and as a target tug.

The Lansen was developed to replace the earlier twin piston powered Saab 18. From the outset it was developed in three separate versions to perform all weather fighter (J 32B), all weather ground attack (A 32A) and reconnaissance (S 32C). Development first began in 1948. The Lansen began life first as a twin powered by two de Havilland Ghosts, while a subsequent design, the P1150, would have been powered by a single Swedish developed STAL Dovern turbojet, before development of the Dovern was dropped because of cost and timescale issues. Instead the P1150 gained a Rolls-Royce Avon and became the Saab 32 Lansen. First flight was on November 3 1952. In all 450 production Lansens were built from 1954 through to 1960.

Aerodynamically the Lansen is straightforward, simple and clean, and it can reach a max speed of Mach 1.12 in a shallow dive, despite a modest thrust to weight ratio. Power is from a Swedish licence built Avon and the rear fuselage is detachable to allow easy access to the engine. In the nose of the A 32A and J 32B were four cannons, while the A 32A had an Ericsson mapping radar, the J 32B had a S6 fire control radar for lead pursuit interception. The S 32C had various reconnaissance sensors in the nose, such as cameras and radar.

The last Lansens to remain in service were versions of the J 32B, which was the most powerful and heavy of the Lansen variants. The J 32E conversions carried various radar and radio/communications jammers in the nose and in underwing pods and chaff dispensers. They were used to provide a realistic electronic warfare environment for military exercises, while unmodified J 32Bs served as crew trainers. Finally five converted J 32Ds were used to tow VM-6 aerial targets.

In 1997 all operational Lansens (of F16M) were retired, with a handful kept in flying reserve and used for testing and other duties.

Photo: A J 32E Lansen EW aggressor/trainer. (Paul Merritt)

Saab 35 Draken

Country of origin: Sweden

Type: Multirole fighter

Powerplants: 35XD – One 56.9kN (12,790lb) dry and 78.5kN (17,650lb) with afterburning Volvo Flygmotor RM6C turbojet (licence built Rolls-Royce Avon 300).

Performance: 35XD – Max speed Mach 2 or approx 2125km/h (1145kt). Max initial rate of climb 34,450ft/min. Time to 36,000ft 2min 36sec, time to 49,200ft 5min 0sec. Radius with internal fuel only, hi-lo-hi 635km (345nm), with two 100lb/455kg bombs and two drop tanks hi-lo-hi 1005km (540nm). Ferry range with max internal and external fuel 3250km (1755nm).

Weights: 35XD – Empty 8250kg (18,188lb), max takeoff 16,000kg (35,275lb). J 35J – MTOW 12,500kg (27,557lb).

Dimensions: Wing span 9.40m (30ft 10in), length 15.35m (50ft 4in), height 3.89m (12ft 9in). Wing area 49.2m² (529.6sq ft).

Accommodation: Pilot only, or two in tandem in Sk 35C and TF-35.

Armament: One or two 30mm Aden cannons (one in each wing). Nine external stores stations can carry 454kg (1000lb) each, weapons include Bofors rockets, 1000lb/455kg and 500lb/225kg bombs, Rb 24 Sidewinder (licence built AIM-9P) and Rb 27 Falcon (licence built AIM-4) AAMs.

Operators: Austria, Finland, Sweden.

History: The remarkable Draken (Dragon) was developed against a demanding 1949 Swedish air force requirement to develop an advanced high performance interceptor to replace the Saab J 29 Tunnan.

Among that requirement's specifications was speed 50% greater than any other fighter then entering service. Saab's design team led by Erik Bratt used a unique double delta wing, giving Mach 2 performance and shorter airfield takeoff lengths than contemporaries such as the Mirage III and F-104. The double delta wing configuration was successfully test flown on the Saab 201 research aircraft before the first of three Draken prototypes (powered by an Avon 200) flew for the first time on October 25 1955.

Initial production RM6B powered J 35A fighters were delivered to the Swedish air force from 1960. New build and converted J 35Bs featured Saab's S7 fire control radar and a lengthened rear fuselage, while the J35D was powered by an improved and uprated RM6C turbojet. The final Swedish fighter Draken, the J 35F, introduced a Hughes weapon system comprising a pulse doppler radar, automatic fire control system and Falcon AAMs. The J 35F-II has a Hughes infrared sensor. Sixty six J 35Fs have been upgraded to J 35J standard for service through to the end of the 1990s, when they are due to be replaced by the JAS 39 Gripen.

Aside from the J 35 fighters the Swedish air force acquired reconnaissance S 35Es with a nose containing five cameras and the Sk 35 two seat conversion trainer.

The export 35X was sold to Denmark (the 35XD as the F-35 fighter, reconnaissance R-35 and two seat TF-35) and Finland which bought 12 J 35XS and later ex Swedish J 35Fs. Finally Austria's J 35ÖEs are rebuilt ex Swedish air force J 35Ds (24 were delivered from 1988).

Photo: Swedish Drakens are due to be retired in 1999. (Saab)

Saab 37 Viggen

Country of origin: Sweden

Type: Multirole fighter

Powerplant: JA 37 – One 72.1kN (16,203lb) dry and 125kN (28,108lb) with afterburning Volvo Flygmotor RM8B turbofan.

Performance: JA 37 – Max speed above Mach 2, or more than 2125km/h (1145kt), max speed at 330ft Mach 1.2. Time to 32,800ft less than 1min 42sec. Takeoff run approx 400m (1310ft). AJ 37 – Tactical radius with external ordnance hi-lo-hi over 1000km (540nm).

Weights: Clean takeoff approx 15,000kg (33,070lb), takeoff with normal armament 17,000kg (37,478lb).

Dimensions: Wing span 10.60m (34ft 9in), length overall inc probe 16.40m (53ft 10in), fuselage length 15.58m (51ft 2in), height 5.90m (19ft 4in). Wing area 46.0m^2 (495.1sq ft).

Accommodation: Pilot only, or two in separate cockpits in Sk 37.

Armament: JA 37 – One 30mm Oerlikon KCA cannon in permanent underfuselage pack. Four underwing and three under fuselage hardpoints for Rb 74 Sidewinders, Rb 71 Sky Flashes on each inboard wing pylon, plus rockets. AJ 37 – Weapons include Saab Rb 15F anti ship and Rb 75 Maverick missiles, Rb 27/28 Falcon and Rb 74 Sidewinder AAMs, rockets and bombs.

Operators: Sweden

History: The Viggen (Thunderbolt) currently forms the bulk of Sweden's front line fighter strength.

The Viggen was developed as the airborne component of Sweden's System 37 air defence network and to replace the Saab Lansen. Design work of a new single engine fighter began in the early 1960s and considerations included Mach 2 at altitude, supersonic flight at low level and unprecedented STOL performance. To meet these requirements Saab utilised the then unconventional canard delta configuration. First flight was on February 8 1967.

The canards or foreplanes are fixed but have trailing edge flaps. The wing arrangement not only gives good agility but also excellent takeoff performance, allowing operations from damaged runways or sections of freeways. Power is from a modified Volvo Flygmotor RM8 licence built Pratt & Whitney JT8D with afterburning. Tandem main undercarriage and thrust reversal allows short, non flare landings.

Initial production was of the AJ 37 Viggen (first delivered in June 1971) optimised for ground attack but with a secondary interception role. 110 were built and they featured an Ericsson PS-37/A radar, Saab digital nav/attack computer and a HUD. The SF 37 (26 built) and SH 37 (26 built) are reconnaissance variants, the SH 37 with radar is optimised for maritime reconnaissance with a secondary maritime strike role. The Sk 37 (18 built) is a two seater.

Final production was of the JA 37 interceptor with an Ericsson PS-46/A multimode, doppler, look down/shoot down radar, Sky Flash and Sidewinder missile armament, an uprated RM8B engine and new avionics. The last of 149 built was delivered in June 1990.

About 100 AJ, SH and SF 37s have been modified to multirole AJS 37 standard with expanded weaponry and some new avionics, while 60 JA 37s are being upgraded under a MLU with PS-46/A radar, improved avionics and cockpit displays, and AIM-120 compatibility.

Photo: A JA 37 Viggen. (Paul Merritt)

Saab JAS 39 Gripen

Country of origin: Sweden

Type: Lightweight multirole fighter

Powerplant: One 54.0kN (12,140lb) dry and 80.5kN (18,100lb) with afterburning Volvo Aero Corporation RM12 turbofan (licence built General Electric F404-GE-400).

Performance: Supersonic at all altitudes. Takeoff and landing strip length approx 800m (2625ft). Range not published.

Weights: Operating empty 6622kg (14,600lb), max takeoff approx 13,000kg (28,660lb).

Dimensions: Wing span 8.40m (27ft 7in), length overall 14.10m (46ft 3in), height 4.50m (14ft 9in).

Accommodation: Pilot only, two in tandem in JAS 39B.

Armament: One 27mm Mauser BK27 cannon. Wingtip stations for Rb 74 (AIM-9) AAMs. One centreline and four underwing hardpoints for rockets, DWS 39 cluster bomb dispensers, Rb 75 (AGM-65) ASMs, RBS 15 anti ship missiles, bombs, AIM-120 or Matra Mica AAMs.

Operators: Sweden*

History: Saab's sixth jet fighter, the Gripen (Griffin) is perhaps the most advanced and capable single seat fighter currently in service.

The Gripen was developed to replace the Royal Swedish Air Force's Viggens and remaining Drakens. Definition studies of the new fighter began in 1980, while government program approval and development funding (including for five prototypes and 30 production aircraft) was approved in 1982. Meanwhile in 1981 the IG JAS (Industry Group JAS) teaming of Saab, Volvo Aero Corporation, Ericsson and FFV Aerotech had been formed to develop and build the new aircraft.

From the outset it was recognised that the growing cost of new fighters meant that the new aircraft would be smaller than the Viggen and that it would be powered by a single engine. The General Electric F404 turbofan was selected for local development and construction, while other design features include the canard delta configuration (for manoeuvrability and to meet the strict short field requirements), lateral instability with fly-by-wire, an Ericsson/GMAv PS-05/A pulse doppler multimode look down/shoot down radar with multiple target track while scan and ground mapping capabilities, and a modern cockpit with three multifunction displays, a wide angle HUD and HOTAS controls. Thirty percent of the Gripen by weight is of composites (including the wing boxes, canards and fin), while the aircraft is designed to be easily maintained in the field.

The first prototype Gripen made its first flight on December 9 1988 but crashed the following February due to fly-by-wire software problems. The second prototype Gripen first flew in May 1990. The first production Gripen delivery was in June 1993 and 204 are on order. The first Swedish air force Gripen squadron was declared operational in 1997, while deliveries are due to continue to 2007.

Apart from the basic JAS 39A fighter, the Gripen is built in JAS 39B two seater form which first flew on November 22 1996. Unlike the Viggen, Saab is able to aggressively offer the Gripen for export and in 1995 signed an international marketing agreement with British Aerospace. Export Gripens would be fully NATO interoperable and feature inflight refuelling.

Photo: Gripens are now being delivered with low vis markings. (Saab)

Saab Safari & Supporter & PAC Mushshak

Country of origin: Sweden

Type: Two seat basic trainer

Powerplant: MFI-17 – One 150kW (200hp) Lycoming IO-360-A1B6 flat four piston engine, driving a two blade propeller.

Performance: MFI-17 – Max speed 236km/h (127kt), cruising speed 208km/h (112kt). Max initial rate of climb 807ft/min. Service ceiling 13,450ft. Endurance 5hr 10min.

Weights: MFI-17 – Empty equipped 646kg (1424lb), max takeoff 1200kg (2646lb).

Dimensions: MFI-17 – Wing span 8.85m (29ft 1in), length 7.00m (23ft 0in), height 2.60m (8ft 7in). Wing area 11.9m² (128.1sq ft).

Accommodation: Standard seating for two side by side, with optional rear facing seat behind them.

Armament: Mushshak – Six underwing hardpoints, inner two stressed for 150kg (330lb) each, outer four for 100kg (220lb), for rocket and gun pods and Bofors Bantam anti tank missiles.

Operators: Safari – Norway. Supporter – Denmark, Zambia. Mushshak – Iran, Oman, Pakistan, Syria.

History: The MFI-15 Safari and MFI-17 Supporter resulted from Saab's adaptation of the MFI-9 Junior/Minicom for basic training for civil and military operators.

The original two seat tricycle undercarriage Malmo (of Sweden) MFI-9 flew for the first time on October 10 1958. MBB of Germany acquired production rights to the MFI-9 which it built locally as the Bo 208 Junior (first flight in 1962). In all over 250 75kW (100hp) Rolls-Royce Continental O-200 powered MFI-9s and Bo 208s were built through to the late 1960s, mostly for civil customers.

In 1968 Saab began work on its MFI-15, based on the MFI-9 but with some design changes. Foremost of the changes in the Saab built MFI-15 prototype was the 120kW (160hp) Lycoming IO-320 piston engine. Like the MFI-9/Bo 208 though the MFI-15 retained the unusual braced, mid mounted and slightly forward swept wing and rearward hinging canopy, offering good all round vision. The prototype Saab MFI-15's maiden flight was on July 11 1969. Following testing the MFI-15 gained a more powerful IO-360, while the horizontal tail was relocated to clear it of damage of thrown up debris. First flight in this modified form was in February 1971.

Sold as the MFI-15 Safari, most went to civil customers, however Sierra Leone and Norway took delivery of Safaris for military pilot training. To improve the Safari's military market appeal, Saab developed the MFI-17 Supporter, fitted with six underwing hardpoints for light and practice weaponry, giving it weapons training and light COIN capabilities. First flight was on July 6 1972. Important customers were Denmark (designated T-17) and Zambia. Production ended in the late 1970s after about 250 Safaris and Supporters had been built. Most were for civil customers.

Pakistan meanwhile has taken delivery of 18 Saab built Supporters, while 92 have been assembled locally by PAC from knocked down kits and a further 149 were built locally by PAC. It is named Mushshak (Proficient) in Pakistani service.

Photo: A Norwegian MFI-15 Safari. Norway uses its Safaris for pilot screening. (MAP)

Saab 340 & Argus

Country of origin: Sweden

Type: VIP transport (Tp 100) and AEW platform (Argus)

Powerplants: 340B – Two 1305kW (1750shp) General Electric CT7-9B turboprops driving four blade propellers.

Performance: 340B – Max cruising speed at 15,000ft 523km/h (282kt), long range cruising speed at 25,000ft 467km/h (252kt). Max initial rate of climb 2000ft/min. Service ceiling 31,000ft. Range with 35 passengers and reserves at max cruising speed 1490km (805nm), at long range cruising speed 1735km (935nm).

Weights: 340B – Operating empty 8140kg (17,945lb), max takeoff 13,155kg (29,000lb).

Dimensions: Wing span 21.44m (70ft 4in), length 19.73m (64ft 9in), height 6.97m (22ft 11in). Wing area 41.8m² (450sq ft).

Accommodation: Flightcrew of two. Main cabin seats up to 37 in passenger configuration. Tp 100 configured for VIPs. AEW S 100B has three multifunction workstations in main cabin.

Armament: None

Operators: Sweden*

History: Saab's largest commercial aircraft sales success, the Saab 340 has been adapted for military service as a VIP transport and as an AEW platform as the S 100B Argus.

In 1979 Saab (who wanted to diversify out of military aviation) and Fairchild reached an agreement to conduct joint feasibility and development studies on a 30 to 40 seat commuter. The resulting SF340 design was modern if conventional and powered by two General Electric CT7 turboprops (a commercial development of the T700 turboshaft which powers Sikorsky's H-60 series of helicopters). Within the 65%/35% Saab-Fairchild partnership Saab was responsible for the fuselage, fin and final assembly, while Fairchild was responsible for the wings, engine nacelles and empennage.

The first of three SF340 prototypes flew for the first time on January 25 1983. Saab assumed total program responsibility on November 1 that year and the SF340 designation was subsequently changed to 340A.

The first improved development of the Saab 340 is the 340B with more powerful engines improving hot and high performance, while other changes include a higher max takeoff weight and better range. First delivery was in September 1989. The latest development of the 340 is the further improved 340B*Plus*. Saab will cease regional airliner production in 1999.

The only 340 military operator is Sweden. A single VIP configured Saab 340B was delivered to the Royal Swedish Air Force's Royal Flight in 1990 as the Tp 100.

Sweden meanwhile has adopted the 340B for airborne early warning and control as the S 100B Argus. Six (including the prototype, which first flew in 1994) are on order, fitted with an Ericsson PS-890 Erieye side looking phased array radar mounted above the fuselage. The Erieye has a range of 300km (190nm) against fighter sized targets, including against clutter, and also has a sea surveillance mode. The Argus can be fitted with three multifunction workstations, while commands and information can be transmitted to and from ground stations via datalink. Delivery to the Swedish air force began in 1997.

Photo: The prototype S 100B Argus. (Saab)

Samsung - Lockheed Martin KTX-2

Countries of origin: South Korea and the United States of America

Type: Advanced/lead-in fighter trainer and light fighter

Powerplants: One 71kN (16,000lb) class afterburning General Electric F404 turbofan.

Performance: Max speed Mach 1.4. Max initial rate of climb 27,000ft/min. Service ceiling 45,000ft.

Weights: Max takeoff 8600kg (18,960lb).

Dimensions: Wing span 9.1m (29ft 10in), length 12.8m (42ft 0in), height 4.4m (14ft 5in).

Accommodation: Two in tandem.

Armament: An internal 20mm gun. Two wingtip, one centreline, and four underwing hardpoints for a variety of weaponry including AIM-9 Sidewinder AAMs and AGM-65 Maverick ASMs (wingtip stations can carry AAMs only), rockets and bombs.

Operators: South Korea*

History: The KTX-2 is being developed jointly by Samsung and Lockheed Martin as a supersonic advanced trainer/lead-in fighter trainer, initially to meet a South Korean requirement, but will also be marketed internationally.

Initial design of the KTX-2 goes back to 1992. Samsung was assisted with preliminary design work by Lockheed as part of offset work arising from Korea's F-16 purchase. By mid 1995 the basic design had been finalised (one early design configuration envisaged a mid mounted wing and twin tail configuration).

However the KTX-2 program had to bide its time for the next two years while the Korean Government decided whether or not to proceed with the project. Finally on July 3 1997 Korea elected to go ahead with the KTX-2 project (in favour of a rival offering from Daewoo with DASA's proposed AT2000). Subsequently Samsung signed a co-operation agreement with Lockheed Martin covering joint development of the aircraft.

The South Korean Government will fund 70% of the KTX-2 program's $US2bn pricetag and has ordered 94 for the RoKAF. Samsung will fund 17% and Lockheed Martin the remaining 13%. As well as further Korean air force orders, Samsung and Lockheed Martin forecast a world market for the aircraft of 600 to 700 units (including to replace the popular Northrop F-5 light fighter).

Full scale KTX-2 development was due to get underway in late 1997. First flight is planned for 2001 with RoKAF deliveries continuing until 2009. All production aircraft will be built at Samsung's modern Sachon plant (where Samsung builds F-16Cs under licence).

The KTX-2 will feature seating for two in tandem, a shoulder mounted wing with wingtip AAM stations, a 71kN (16,000lb) class afterburning GE F404 turbofan and fly-by-wire flight controls. Lockheed Martin is responsible for developing the KTX-2's avionics system, flight control system and wings at its Fort Worth facilities. The KTX-2's cockpit displays will feature similar symbology and switchology as LM's F-16, F-22 and JSF fighters.

Fighter versions of the KTX-2 could be fitted with radar.

Photo: The KTX-2 is due to fly in 2001.

Schweizer/Hughes 269, TH-55 Osage & 300

Country of origin: United States of America

Type: Training and light utility helicopter

Powerplant: 300C – One 140kW (190hp) Textron Lycoming HIO-360-D1A fuel injected flat four derated from 170kW (225hp) driving a three blade main rotor and two blade tail rotor.

Performance: 300C – Max cruising speed 153km/h (82kt), economical cruising speed 124km/h (67kt). Max initial rate of climb 750ft/min. Hovering ceiling in ground effect 5900ft, out of ground effect 2750ft. Service ceiling 10,200ft. Range with max fuel and no reserves 360km (195nm). Max endurance 3hr 24min.

Weights: 300C – Empty 474kg (1046lb), max takeoff 930kg (2050lb), or 975kg (2150lb) with an external sling load.

Dimensions: Main rotor diameter 8.18m (26ft 10in), length overall 9.40m (30ft 10in), fuselage length 6.80m (22ft 0in), height to top of rotor head 2.66m (8ft 9in). Main rotor disc area 52.5m^2 (565.5sq ft).

Accommodation: 300C – Typical seating for three (two in 269). Can lift a 475kg (1050lb) payload in an external sling load.

Armament: Usually none.

Operators: Greece, Nigeria, Spain, Sweden, Thailand, Turkey.

History: With over 3000 built by two manufacturers over three decades, the Hughes/Schweizer 260/TH-55/300 series is one of the most successful two/three seat light helicopter families built.

Development of this versatile helicopter dates back to the mid 1950s when Hughes flew the two seat Model 269 for the first time in October 1956. The basic design sparked US Army interest and five were ordered as the YHO-2-HU for evaluation in the scout and observation roles. Deliveries of commercial equivalent Model 269As began in 1961.

The 269A program received a huge boost when Hughes won a US Army contract for a light helicopter primary trainer. Eventually a total of 792 was built as the TH-55A Osage and more than 60,000 US Army helicopter pilots learned to fly in the type. The Osage has been replaced in US Army service by the Bell TH-67 Creek, but TH-55s survive in service with a number of nations including Spain (as the HE.20), Sweden (as the Hkp 5B) and Japan, where Kawasaki built 38 TH-55Js (essentially similar to the TH-55A) under licence.

The three seat, slightly larger 269B, which Hughes marketed as the Hughes 300, first flew in 1964. The 300 was followed from 1969 by the improved 300C, which introduced a more powerful 140kW (190hp) Lycoming HIO-360 engine and increased diameter main rotor, giving an increase in payload of 45%, plus overall performance improvements. The 300C (or 269C) flew in August 1969 and remains in production to this day, essentially unchanged.

Since 1983 the 300C has been built by Schweizer in the USA. Schweizer built the 300C initially under licence for Hughes, and then acquired all rights to the helicopter in 1986. Under Schweizer's stewardship more than 250 minor improvements have been made to the 300C, but the basic design has been left unchanged.

Both Schweizer and Hughes have delivered 300s to military customers, while the 300C was also built in small numbers under licence in Italy by Breda Nardi as the NH-300C.

Photo: A TH-55 Osage in US Army markings.

SEPECAT Jaguar

Countries of Origin: France and UK

Type: Ground attack aircraft

Powerplants: GR.1A – Two 23.7kN (5320lb) dry and 35.8kN (8040lb) with afterburning Rolls-Royce/Turboméca Adour Mk 104 turbofans.

Performance: GR.1A – Max speed Mach 1.6 or 1700km/h (917kt), max speed at sea level Mach 1.1 or 1350km/h (730kt). Time to 30,000ft 1min 30sec. Service ceiling 45,930ft. Combat radius hi-lo-hi with internal fuel 850km (460nm), or lo-lo-lo 537km (290nm). Combat radius with external fuel hi-lo-hi 1408km (760nm), lo-lo-lo 917km (495nm). Ferry range with external fuel 3525km (1902nm).

Weights: GR.1A – Empty equipped 7700kg (16,975lb), max takeoff 15,700kg (34,612lb).

Dimensions: GR.1A – Wing span 8.69m (28ft 6in), length inc probe 16.83m (55ft 3in), length exc probe 15.52m (50ft 11in), height 4.89m (16ft 1in). Wing area 24.2m² (260.3sq ft).

Accommodation: Pilot only, or two in tandem in Jaguar/T.2.

Armament: GR.1B – Two 30mm Aden cannons. Two above wing (for AAMs only), four underwing and one centreline hardpoint for 4540kg (10,000lb) of ordnance, including bombs and rockets.

Operators: Ecuador, France, India, Nigeria, Oman, UK.

History: The world's first binational military aircraft program began as a trainer but evolved into a highly capable ground attack aircraft.

The Jaguar was the result of a joint British/French requirement for an advanced jet trainer, the British originally requiring a supersonic jet trainer, the French wanting a subsonic, cheap to build trainer/attack aircraft with good field performance. To build such a demanding aircraft the SEPECAT (Société Européenéde Production de l'Avion de Ecole de Combat et Appui Tactique) teaming of Breguet (design leader) and BAC was established in 1966, while Rolls-Royce and Turboméca teamed to develop the Adour engine.

The first of eight prototypes flew for the first time on September 8 1968. Service deliveries began to the French in 1973 and the British in 1974, by which time the Jaguar was viewed solely as a ground attack platform and both the Hawk and Alpha Jet had been launched.

The 200 Jaguars delivered to the RAF comprised 165 GR.1 (Jaguar S) single seaters and 35 two seat T.2s (Jaguar B). The GR.1s (since upgraded to GR.1A standard with Adour Mk 104s) feature an advanced nav/attack system and laser rangefinder in a chisel shaped nose. Britain is currently upgrading its Jaguars to GR.3 (and T.4) standard with TIALD pod compatibility, a helmet mounted sight, improved ECM, a towed decoy system, new LCD screen in the cockpit and up to 25% more powerful Adour Mk 106 turbofans.

France took delivery of 160 single seaters (Jaguar As) and 40 trainers (Jaguar Es). French Jaguar Es were delivered with a less advanced nav/attack system and twin DEFA cannons. Half were delivered with an undernose laser rangefinder and 30 can carry the ATLIS laser designator pod for the AS.30L laser guided missile.

The Jaguar International was exported with some success. It was marketed and built by BAe, and was based on the GR.1. India is the largest customer, where it is built under licence. Some are fitted with an Agave radar and can fire Sea Eagle anti ship missiles.

Photo: An RAF Jaguar GR.1A. (Sgt Rick Brewell, UK Crown Copyright)

Shenyang J-6/F-6

Countries of origin: Russia and China

Type: Interceptor/ground attack fighter

Powerplants: J-6 – Two 24.5kN (5730lb) dry and 31.9kN (7165lb) with afterburning Liming Wopen-6 (Tumansky R-9BF-811) turbojets.

Performance: J-6 – Max speed Mach 1.45 or 1540km/h (831kt), cruising speed 950km/h (512kt). Max initial rate of climb over 30,000ft/min. Service ceiling 58,725ft. Combat radius with external fuel 685km (370nm). Normal range 1390km (750nm), ferry range with external fuel 2200km (1187nm).

Weights: J-6 – Empty approx 5760kg (12,700lb), max takeoff approx 10,000kg (22,045lb).

Dimensions: J-6 – Wing span 9.20m (30ft 2in), length inc probe 14.90m (48ft 11in), length exc probe 12.60m (41ft 4in), height 3.88m (12ft 9in). Wing area 25.0m² (269.1sq ft).

Accommodation: Pilot only, or two in tandem in JJ-6/FT-6.

Armament: Three 30mm NR-30 cannon (one in each wing root and one in lower forward fuselage). Four underwing hardpoints for 500kg (1100lb) of external ordnance including AAMs (AIM-9 Sidewinders on Pakistani aircraft), rockets and bombs.

Operators: Albania, Bangladesh, China, Egypt, North Korea, Pakistan, Tanzania, Zambia.

History: The Shenyang J-6 is a Chinese built development of the 1950s MiG-19 and numerically is still the most important combat aircraft in Chinese military service.

The MiG-19 (NATO reporting name 'Farmer') was designed as an interceptor and flew for the first time on January 5 1954. Capable of supersonic speeds in level flight, 2500 were built (including in Czechoslovakia) in several variants including the radar equipped MiG-19P. It was not exported widely and all are believed to have been retired from service (except perhaps Cuba).

China selected the basic MiG-19 for licence manufacture in the late 1950s. Russia supplied production diagrams for the MiG-19P to the Shenyang Aircraft Factory and the first Chinese assembled MiG-19 flew for the first time on December 17 1958, while the first Chinese built MiG-19 flew the following September.

Shenyang and initially Nanchang were assigned to build the MiG-19 (from 1961 the basic MiG-19S 'Farmer-C' dayfighter), however China's political and cultural instability during much of the 1960s meant that production was sporadic and quality often poor.

From the 1970s stability returned and new Chinese developments appeared, foremost being the JJ-6 tandem two seat trainer (there being no two seat MiG-19). The JZ-6 is a high altitude reconnaissance variant while the J-6III had a variable shock cone in the nose and was often misidentified as the J-6Xin and as having a radar. A J-6 variant that was radar equipped was the J-6A or J-6IV. The J-6C meanwhile is similar to the basic J-6 except for repositioned brake parachute.

As the F-6 (and two seat FT-6) the J-6 was exported widely and production lasted into the 1980s. Total J-6/F-6 production is estimated at 3000.

Photo: A Pakistani F-6. Note the large wing fences. About 100 F-6s remain in Pakistani service.

Shenyang J-8

Country of origin: China

Type: Interceptor

Powerplants: J-8 II – Two 42.7kN (9590lb) dry and 65.9kN (14,815lb) with afterburning Liyang (Guizhou) WP13A II turbojets.

Performance: Max speed at 36,000ft 2338km/h (1262kt). Max initial rate of climb 39,370ft/min. Service ceiling 66,275ft. Ferry range 2200km (1190nm). Combat radius 800km (432nm).

Weights: J-8 II – Empty 9820kg (21,649lb), max takeoff 17,800kg (39,242lb).

Dimensions: J-8 II – Wing span 9.34m (30ft 8in), length 21.59m (70ft 10in), height 5.41m (17ft 9in). Wing area 42.2m² (454.3sq ft).

Accommodation: Pilot only.

Armament: One 23mm Type 23-2 cannon in underfuselage blister fairing. One centreline and six underwing hardpoints for PL-2B infrared guided AAMs, PL-7 medium range semi active radar guided AAMs, unguided air-to-air rockets, air-to-ground rockets and bombs.

Operators: China

History: China's J-8 and J-8 II interceptors have suffered from protracted and fitful development.

The J-8 (NATO reporting name 'Finback') resulted from a 1964 requirement for a new interceptor with improved performance compared to the MiG-21. The resulting aircraft was similar in overall configuration to the MiG-21, being a tailed delta with a nose air intake, ranging radar in the intake centrebody and a single piece forward opening canopy, but much larger and powered by two engines.

The first of two prototypes flew for the first time on July 5 1969, despite China's Cultural Revolution then underway. Because of the Cultural Revolution initial production was not authorised until 1979. Only small numbers of J-8s were built, although around 100 improved J-8 Is were delivered from the mid 1980s. The J-8 I featured a Sichuan SR-4 radar in an enlarged intake centrebody, conferring some all weather capability, plus some aerodynamic changes. First flight was on April 24 1981.

Development of the much improved and revised J-8 II began in 1981 and the first flight took place on June 12 1984. The J-8 II introduced lateral air intakes (similar in configuration to the MiG-23's) and a nose mounted radar and features a ventral folding fin which extends after takeoff and conventional two piece canopy, and has a secondary ground attack role. About 30 have been built and low rate batch production continues. It has been offered for export as the F-8 II.

The Peace Pearl program to fit the J-8 II with US avionics (integrated by Grumman) including the APG-66 radar and US ejection seat, HUD and INS, as well as a bubble canopy with a frameless windscreen was suspended following the 1989 Tienanmen Square massacre. Two J-8 IIs had been delivered to Grumman in the US for conversion but were returned unmodified to China in 1993.

Shenyang is currently working on the F-8 IIM which is intended for export. It features more powerful 68.7kN (15,432lb) WP13B turbojets, a Russian Phazotron Zhuk-8 II pulse Doppler radar and a modernised cockpit with a HUD, HOTAS controls, a multifunction display and INS and GPS navigation. First flight was on March 31 1996.

Photo: The export F-8 II. (Peter Ricketts)

ShinMaywa US-1/SS-2

Country of origin: Japan

Type: Search and rescue amphibian

Powerplants: US-1A – Four 2605kW (3493ehp) Ishikawajima licence built General Electric T46-IHI-10J turboprops, driving three blade propellers.

Performance: US-1A – Max speed 522km/h (281kt), cruising speed at 10,000ft 426km/h (230kt). Max initial rate of climb, AUW 36,000kg (79,365lb) 2340ft/min. Service ceiling 28,400ft. Max range at 425km/h (230kt) cruising speed 3815km (2060nm).

Weights: US-1A – Empty 23,300kg (51,367lb), empty equipped 25,500kg (56,218lb), max takeoff from water 43,000kg (94,800lb), max takeoff from land 45,000kg (99,200lb).

Dimensions: Wing span 33.15m (108ft 9in), length 33.46m (109ft 9in), height 9.95m (32ft 8in). Wing area 135.8m² (1462.0sq ft).

Accommodation: Flightcrew of two pilots, flight engineer and navigator/radio operator (in main cabin). Main cabin can seat 20 seated survivors or 12 stretcher patients, plus two medical attendants, or alternatively up to 69 passengers.

Armament: None

Operators: Japan

History: An anomaly among modern aircraft, the US-1 is a large four engine amphibian which re-entered production in the early 1990s.

The search and rescue US-1 is a development of the earlier PS-1 flying boat ASW/maritime patrol aircraft. The first Shin Miewa (ShinMaywa from 1992, Kawanishi up to 1949) PX-S prototype flew for the first time on October 5 1967, while in all, 23 production PS-1s (SS-2s to Shin Meiwa) were delivered to the Japanese Maritime Self Defence Force. Power was from four licence built General Electric T64 turboprops, and the PS-1 was equipped with sonobuoys, a MAD and search radar, and could carry mines, torpedoes and rockets. An auxiliary gas turbine (a GE T58) provided high pressure air for boundary layer control over the flaps, rudder and elevators, allowing the PS-1 to fly at very low speeds and reducing takeoff runs. The last PS-1 was retired from JMSDF service in 1989.

The US-1 (ShinMaywa designation SS-2A) was based closely on the PS-1 and differed mainly in its internal fit and permanent retractable undercarriage. First flight, from water, was on October 16 1974, while the US-1's first flight from land was in December that year. Initially 13 US-1s were built (for the JMSDF), while in 1992 production restarted against a single order and a second new US-1 was ordered in 1993.

All US-1s have been upgraded to US-1A standard with more powerful T64-IHI-10J engines replacing the original T64-IHI-10s. A single US-1 was evaluated as a firebomber, fitted with a tank system developed by Comair of Canada.

ShinMaywa is now working on the much improved US-1A Kai. The US-1A Kai will likely feature new engines – 3350kW (4500shp) Allison AE2100Js with Dowty six blade propellers offering up to 93km/h (50kt) higher cruising speed – possibly a new composite construction wing, fly-by-wire flight controls and glass cockpit, pressurisation, a redesigned empennage and a Thomson-CSF Ocean Master search radar. First flight could be in 2002/03.

Photo: The US-1 amphibian.

Shorts Skyvan

Country of origin: United Kingdom

Type: Light STOL utility transport

Powerplants: Srs 3 – Two 535kW (715shp) Garrett TPE331-2-201A turboprops, driving three blade propellers.

Performance: 3M – Max cruising speed 324km/h (175kt), normal cruising speed 311km/h (168kt), economical cruising speed 278km/h (150kt). Max initial rate of climb 1530ft/min. Service ceiling 22,500ft. Takeoff run at MTOW 238m (780ft). Range with max fuel 1075km (582nm), range with a 2270kg (5000lb) payload 385km (208nm).

Weights: 3M – Operating empty (in utility configuration) 3355kg (7400lb), max takeoff 6577kg (14,500lb).

Dimensions: 3M – Wing span 19.79m (64ft 11in), length 12.21m (40ft 1in), or 12.60m (41ft 4in) with weather radar, height 4.60m (15ft 1in). Wing area 35.1m² (378sq ft).

Accommodation: Flightcrew of one or two. Seating for up to 22 combat equipped troops, or 16 paratroopers or 12 stretcher patients.

Armament: None

Operators: Austria, Botswana, Ghana, Mauritania, Mexico, Nepal, Oman, Yemen.

History: The box like and rugged Shorts Skyvan STOL utility transport dates back to the civil postwar Miles Aerovan project.

Development of the Skyvan, or SC.7, began in 1959 when Shorts decided to design a small multirole transport with a square sided fuselage to accommodate oversize loads and good STOL performance. The new design incorporated the results of Miles' research into high aspect ratio wings, with Shorts adopting the Aerovan's wing design for the SC.7. The SC.7 first flew in Series 1 prototype form powered by two Continental 290kW (390hp) GTSIO-520 piston engines on January 17 1963.

Unlike the prototype, initial production aircraft were powered by 545kW (730shp) Turboméca Astazou XII turboprops. The original piston powered Series 1 prototype was the first Astazou powered Skyvan to fly (with 390kW/520shp Astazou IIs), in October 1963. The re-engined prototype was designated the Series 1A, while early Astazou powered production aircraft were designated Series 2.

Early on in the SC.7's production run Shorts decided to switch the powerplant choice to 535kW (715shp) Garrett TPE331-201s, resulting in the definitive Series 3 (first flight December 15 1967). Many of the early build Series 2 Skyvans were also converted to Garrett power.

The basic civil Series 3 and the higher takeoff weight Series 3A Skyvans perform a number of utility missions including passenger transport, ambulance, aerial survey and freight work, while the Skyliner was a commuter airliner version.

The definitive military Skyvans are the Series 3M and the higher max takeoff weight 3M-200 with a rear loading freight ramp. The Skyvan proved reasonably popular with third world military customers for operations in undeveloped areas. Almost 60 of the 150 or so Skyvans built were for military customers and many remain in service.

Photo: The Skyvan's roomy fuselage and good STOL performance endear it for military transport missions. (Austrian Armed Forces)

Shorts 330 & C-23 Sherpa

Country of origin: United Kingdom

Type: Utility transport

Powerplants: C-23A – Two 895kW (1120shp) Pratt & Whitney Canada T101-CP-100 (PT6A-45R) turboprops, driving five blade propellers.

Performance: C-23A – Max cruising speed 352km/h (190kt), economical cruising speed 291km/h (157kt). Max initial rate of climb 1180ft/min. Service ceiling 20,000ft. Takeoff run at MTOW 560m (1840ft). Range with a 2270kg (5000lb) payload 1240km (670nm), range with a 3175kg (7000lb) payload 362km (195nm).

Weights: C-23A – Empty equipped 6680kg (14,727lb), max takeoff 11,565kg (25,500lb).

Dimensions: Wing span 22.76m (74ft 8in), length 17.69m (58ft 1in), height 4.95m (16ft 3in). Wing area 42.1m² (453sq ft).

Accommodation: Flightcrew of two. Typical passenger seating configuration for 30. In combi freight/passenger configuration can house freight in the forward fuselage and 18 passengers in the rear.

Armament: None

Operators: Thailand, USA.

History: The Shorts 330 is a stretched and enlarged development of the modestly successful SC.7 Skyvan.

Beginning life designated the SD3-30, the 330 retained the Skyvan's overall configuration, including the slab sided fuselage cross section, supercritical braced, above fuselage mounted wing design (extended by 2.97m/9ft 9in) and twin tails. Compared with the Skyvan the fuselage is stretched by 3.78m (12ft 5in), allowing seating for 10 extra passengers. Improved performance over the fairly slow Skyvan is courtesy of the two Pratt & Whitney PT6A turboprops driving five blade props, a more streamlined nose and retractable undercarriage. More than 60% greater fuel capacity boosts range significantly over the Skyvan.

An engineering prototype of the 330 flew for the first time on August 22 1974, while a production prototype flew on July 8 1975. The first true production aircraft flew that December.

Initial Shorts 330s were powered by PT6A-45As and -45Bs and are known as 330-100s, while definitive 330s feature more powerful PT6A-45s. Known as 330-200s they also feature a number of detail improvements, while equipment previously available as options were made standard. The 330 also forms the basis for the larger 36 seat Shorts 360, which also features more powerful PT6A-65R (or -67R) engines and a conventional single tail.

The 330 has seen only limited military service. Thailand's Army took delivery of two Shorts 330-UTs with rear loading freight ramp. The US Air Force ordered 18 similar C-23A Sherpas (lacking side windows) for transport service between its European bases and they operated between 1984 and 1990. Ten C-23Bs (with cabin windows) were delivered to the US Army National Guard and are used in various support and utility transport roles. In addition 28 ex airline Shorts 360s have been converted to C-23B+ configuration for the US Army National Guard. The conversion involves fitting a rear loading freight ramp and twin tails, plus new avionics. The last conversion was completed in early 1997.

Photo: A USAF C-23A Sherpa. (Bombardier)

Sikorsky SH-3 Sea King & S-61R

Country of origin: United States of America

Type: ASW, SAR and utility maritime helicopter

Powerplants: SH-3H – Two 1045kW (1400shp) General Electric T58-GE-10 turboshafts driving five blade main and tail rotors.

Performance: SH-3H – Max speed 267km/h (144kt), economical cruising speed 219km/h (118kt). Max initial rate of climb 2200ft/min. Service ceiling 14,700ft. Hovering ceiling in ground effect 10,500ft, out of ground effect 8200ft. Range 1005km (542nm).

Weights: SH-3H – Empty 5600kg (12,530lb), max takeoff 9525kg (21,000lb).

Dimensions: Main rotor diameter 18.90m (62ft 0in), length overall rotors turning 22.15m (72ft 8in), fuselage length 16.69m (54ft 9in), height overall 5.13m (16ft 10in). Main rotor disc area 280.5m² (3109sq ft).

Accommodation: Crew of four, optional seating for 15 in main cabin.

Armament: Max external ordnance of 380kg (840lb), typically comprising two torpedoes.

Operators: SH-3 – Argentina, Denmark, Italy, Japan, Malaysia, Peru, Spain, USA. AS-61R/S-61R/HH-3 – Iraq, Italy, Malaysia.

History: For many years the Sea King formed the backbone of the US Navy's ASW helicopter force. While largely replaced by the SH-60 in US service, many other nations rely on the Sea King for ASW, SAR and various maritime utility duties.

The Sikorsky HSS-2 (S-61) Sea King was the end result of a US Navy requirement for a single helicopter that could both detect/track and attack submarines. Sikorsky was awarded the contract to develop such an aircraft in 1957 and the first YHSS-2 prototype made its maiden flight on March 11 1959. At that time the Sea King represented a significant advance on anything before it, featuring twin turboshafts (GE T58s) mounted above the voluminous main cabin which had space to accommodate bulky ASW gear, plus dunking sonar and radar. Other features were a boat hull for amphibious operations and five blade main and tail rotors.

Initial production was of the SH-3A (HSS-2 pre 1962) and 245 were built, while 73 SH-3Ds had improved sonar and radar and uprated engines. Subsequently over 100 SH-3As were converted to SAR/transport SH-3G form, with ASW gear deleted. The SH-3H (116 converted) was modified for service from aircraft carriers for inner zone ASW, plane guard and surface surveillance and targeting. Most have been replaced by SH-60Fs. Other US conversions were the UH-3A utility transport, VH-3A/D VIP transport and SAR HH-3A.

Mitsubishi (SH-3A/D/H), Agusta (SH-3D) and Westland (its Rolls-Royce Gnome powered variants are described separately) all built the Sea King under licence.

The stretched S-61R or CH-3C was developed specifically for the USAF and had a stretched fuselage with a rear loading freight ramp. As the HH-3E 'Jolly Green Giant' it gained fame rescuing downed aircrew in Vietnam. All USAF CH/HH-3s have been retired, as have all the US Coast Guard's HH-3F Pelicans. Agusta licence built 35 AS-61Rs for SAR and combat rescue and these remain in use.

Photo: One of more than 30 stretched AS-61R Pelicans in service with the Italian air force.

Sikorsky CH-53 Sea Stallion

Country of origin: United States of America

Type: Medium/heavylift helicopter

Powerplants: MH-53J – Two 2935kW (3935shp) General Electric T64-GE-7A turboshafts driving a six blade main rotor and four blade tail rotor.

Performance: MH-53J – Max speed at sea level 315km/h (170kt), cruising speed 278km/h (150kt). Max initial rate of climb 2180ft/min. Service ceiling 20,400ft. Hovering ceiling in ground effect 11,700ft, out of ground effect 6500ft. Range 868km (468nm).

Weights: MH-53J – Empty 10,691kg (23,569lb), max takeoff 19,050kg (42,000lb).

Dimensions: Main rotor diameter 22.02m (72ft 3in), length overall rotors turning 26.90m (88ft 3in), fuselage length 20.47m (67ft 2in), height overall rotors turning 7.60m (24ft 11in), height to top of rotor head 5.22m (17ft 2in). Main rotor disc area 380.9m² (4099.8sq ft).

Accommodation: Flightcrew of three. Seating in main cabin for 55 equipped troops or 24 stretcher patients and four medical attendants.

Armament: MH-53J – Can be fitted with 12.7mm machine guns and 7.62mm miniguns.

Operators: Germany, Israel, USA.

History: The CH-53 Sea Stallion was the result of a US Marine Corps requirement for a heavylift helicopter for troop transport to replace Sikorsky's CH-37C.

Sikorsky used its CH-54 Tarhe (S-64 Skycrane) as the basis to meet the Marines' 1960 requirement for a new heavylift assault transport. The resulting S-65 used the CH-54's dynamic systems coupled with an all new fuselage, including a watertight hull giving an emergency water landing capability and rear loading freight ramp.

Two prototypes were ordered in August 1962, the first of which flew for the first time on October 14 1964. Production deliveries of CH-53As to the Marine Corps commenced in 1966 and by 1967 it was being used operationally in Vietnam. CH-53A standard Sea Stallions were exported to Austria (two, both sold to Israel in 1980), Germany (112 CH-53Gs, most licence built in Germany) and Israel (45). Israel is upgrading its aircraft with new avionics as the CH-53 Yasur 2000. The USMC's CH-53D has uprated engines and automatic blade folding.

The US Air Force ordered its first combat rescue variants of the CH-53 in 1966. Eight initial HH-53Bs were followed by 44 HH-53Cs with external fuel tanks and an inflight refuelling probe. Some of these were later converted to HH-53H Pave Low III configuration with terrain following radar, doppler and INS navigation, GPS, nose turret mounted FLIR, and then to MH-53H standard with a night vision goggle compatible cockpit for insertion/extraction missions.

From 1986 39 H-53s were upgraded to MH-53J Pave Low III Enhanced standard. Equipment fit includes terrain following radar, FLIR, GPS, inflight refuelling probe, secure communications, titanium armour, jammers, flare and chaff dispensers, NVG compatible cockpit, searchlight and external hoist. Due to remain in service until 2010 the survivors have undergone a life extension program.

The US Navy's RH-53D minesweepers have been replaced by MH-53E Sea Dragons. Six were delivered to pre revolutionary Iran.

Photo: A USAF MH-53J Pave Low III Enhanced. (Paul Merritt)

Sikorsky Super Stallion & Sea Dragon

Country of origin: United States of America

Type: CH-53E – Heavylift assault transport. MH-53E – Mine sweeper

Powerplants: CH-53E – Three 3265kW (4380shp) General Electric T64-GE-416 turboshafts, driving a seven blade main rotor and four blade tail rotor.

Performance: CH-53E – Max speed at sea level 315km/h (170kt), cruising speed at sea level 278km/h (150kt). Max initial rate of climb (with a 11,340kg/25,000lb payload) 2500ft/min. Service ceiling 18,500ft. Hovering ceiling in ground effect 11,550ft, out of ground effect 9500ft. Operational radius with 9070kg (20,000lb) external payload 925km (500nm), with a 14,515kg (32,000lb) external payload 93km (50nm). Ferry range 2075km (1120nm).

Weights: CH-53E – Empty 15,072kg (33,338lb), max takeoff 31,640kg (69,750lb), max takeoff with external sling load 33,340kg (73,500lb).

Dimensions: CH-53E – Main rotor diameter 24.08m (79ft 0in), length overall rotors turning 30.19m (99ft 1in), fuselage length 22.35m (73ft 4in), height overall rotors turning 8.97m (29ft 5in), height to top of rotor head 5.32m (17ft 6in). Main rotor disc area 455.4m² (4901.4sq ft).

Accommodation: Flightcrew of three. Accommodation in main cabin for 55 equipped troops or light artillery pieces or vehicles.

Armament: Usually none but has been trialled with AIM-9s for self defence.

Operators: CH-53E – USA. MH-53E – Japan, USA.

History: The CH-53E (S-80) Super Stallion is a three engined development of the Sea Stallion, with greatly improved lifting capabilities.

The Super Stallion resulted from a US Marine Corps' need for a helicopter with much greater lifting abilities than the already impressive CH-53 able to operate from its amphibious assault ships. Sikorsky met the requirement by adding a third engine and uprated transmission to the CH-53, resulting in the CH-53E (S-80). The third engine (all GE T64-GE-415s) was mounted near the main rotor mast on the aircraft's port side. Other changes to the CH-53E were a lengthened fuselage and enlarged fuselage sponsons housing extra fuel, a removable inflight refuelling probe and a seven blade main rotor.

The first YCH-53E prototype flew for the first time on March 1 1974 (this aircraft was subsequently destroyed during a ground running test). The second YCH-53E was the first to feature the revised tail (the vertical tail is canted 20 degrees to port, while the horizontal tail is braced). Delivered from June 1981, around 175 CH-53Es have been funded for the USMC and US Navy. The Marines use them primarily for lifting heavy weapons and equipment (including recovering downed aircraft) alongside CH-53Ds, while the USN's are used for ship supply. Various CH-53E upgrades have been proposed, but these have generally been thwarted by a lack of funding. Low rate CH-53E production continues.

The MH-53E Sea Dragon mine countermeasures helicopter was developed for the US Navy to replace RH-53Ds. Identifiable by their extra large composite construction sponsons which house extra fuel, the MH-53Es tow a hydrofoil sled carrying mechanical, acoustic and magnetic sensors for mine detection. Eleven similar S-80M-1s (without the inflight refuelling probe) were exported to Japan from 1989.

Photo: A USMC CH-53E in flight. (Sikorsky)

Sikorsky S-76/H-76 Eagle

Country of origin: United States of America

Type: Utility helicopter

Powerplants: H-76 – Two 660kW (885shp) max continuous rated Pratt & Whitney Canada PT6B-36A turboshafts driving four blade main and tail rotors.

Performance: H-76 – Max speed 287km/h (155kt), cruising speed 270km/h (145kt). Max initial rate of climb 1650ft/min. Max operating altitude 15,000ft. Range at 257km/h (140kt) cruising speed with no reserves 650km (350nm).

Weights: H-76 – Basic empty 2545kg (5610lb), max takeoff 5170kg (11,400lb).

Dimensions: Main rotor diameter 13.41m (44ft 0in), length overall 16.00m (52ft 6in), fuselage length 13.21m (43ft 4in), height overall 4.41m (14ft 6in). Main rotor disc area 141.3m² (1520.5sq ft).

Accommodation: Flightcrew of two. Accommodation for 10 equipped troops. VIP configurations seat six or eight. Medevac configured aircraft can accommodate three stretchers and two medical attendants.

Armament: AUH-76 – Can be fitted with pintle mounted machine guns in main doorways, plus rockets, gun and cannon pods, Hellfire and TOW anti armour missiles and Stinger AAMs. H-76N – Torpedoes and Sea Skua anti ship missiles.

Operators: Honduras, Philippines, Spain, Thailand.

History: Unique among Sikorsky's current helicopter line, the S-76 was designed for civilian use and then adapted for military service, rather than the other way around.

Sikorsky developed the mid sized S-76 to diversify its product lineup away from military work. The S-76 was designed to perform a diverse range of roles including oil rig support and executive transport. Sikorsky began development work on the S-76 (for a time named Spirit) in the mid 1970s and used technologies and knowledge gained from the military H-60/S-70 program. The resulting design featured two Allison 250-C30S turboshafts and a wide cabin with seating for 12. First flight was on March 13 1977.

Civil models comprise the S-76A; the S-76 Mark II (introduced in March 1982) with more powerful Allison engines and numerous detail refinements; the twin Pratt & Whitney Canada PT6T powered S-76B; the S-76C, powered by two Turboméca Arriel 1S1 engines; the S-76A+ – undelivered S-76As subsequently fitted and delivered with Arriel engines and S-76As converted to Arriel power; and the S-76C+ with more powerful Arriel 2S1 engines.

More than 400 S-76s have been built, but almost all of them have been for civil customers. The Philippines (12 AUH-76s and five S-76 Mk IIs) and Spain (eight S-76Cs designated HE.24 and used for IFR helicopter pilot training) are current operators, while Jordan took delivery of 18 for SAR and VIP transport, but has since sold the survivors.

The H-76 Eagle is the dedicated military variant developed from the S-76B. The AUH-76 is a cannon, rocket and missile armed gunship, while the navalised S-76N can be fitted with search radar and armed with torpedoes and anti ship missiles. Thailand has ordered six for its navy (but without radar and unarmed).

Photo: Thailand is taking delivery of six S-76Ns. (Royal Thai Navy)

Sikorsky UH-60/S-70A Black Hawk

Country of origin: United States

Type: Medium lift helicopter

Powerplants: UH-60A – Two 1150kW (1560shp) General Electric T700-GE-700 turboshafts, driving four blade main and tail rotors.

Performance: UH-60A – Max speed at sea level 296km/h (160kt), max cruising speed 257km/h (140kt). Max vertical rate of climb from 4000ft 411ft/min. Service ceiling 19,000ft. Hovering ceiling out of ground effect 10,400ft. Range with max internal fuel 592km (319nm), range with four external fuel tanks 2220km (1200nm).

Weights: UH-60A – Empty 5118kg (11,284lb), max takeoff 9185kg (20,500lb).

Dimensions: UH-60A – Main rotor diameter 16.36m (53ft 8in), length overall rotors turning 19.76m (64ft 10in), fuselage length 15.26m (50ft 1in), height overall rotors turning 5.13m (16ft 10in), height to top of rotor head 3.76m (12ft 4in). Main rotor disc area 210.1m² (2262sq ft).

Accommodation: Flightcrew of two with gunner/crew chief behind them. Accommodation in main cabin for 11 equipped troops, or 14 in a high density configuration, or alternatively six stretcher patients.

Armament: Two pintle mounts for machine guns or miniguns, one either side in forward cabin. Four hardpoints on detachable external stores support system (ESSS) usually for fuel but, as on AH-60, can carry Hellfire anti armour missiles and rockets.

Operators: Argentina, Australia, Bahrain, Brazil, Brunei, China, Colombia, Egypt, Israel, Japan, Jordan, Malaysia*, Mexico, Morocco, Philippines, Saudi Arabia, South Korea*, Taiwan, Turkey*, USA.

History: The UH-60 is the US Army's standard troop transport helicopter, and has been adopted for a number of special mission roles.

The Black Hawk was developed to replace the Bell UH-1 Iroquois, meeting the US Army's 1972 Utility Tactical Transport Aircraft System (UTTAS) requirement. Three YUH-60A prototypes (first flight October 17 1974) were successfully evaluated against prototype Boeing Vertol YUH-61s. The first production UH-60 Black Hawk flew for the first time in October 1978, with first deliveries in 1979.

The basic Black Hawk features twin General Electric T700 turboshafts which bestow excellent speed and hot and high performance and lifting capabilities, the large cabin was designed to accommodate an 11 man squad while the whole aircraft was designed with crash survivability in mind. Basic US Army Black Hawk transport models are the UH-60A and improved UH-60L (with more powerful engines to combat increased weight, first flight 1988). Other US models include the EH-60A ECM jammer; FLIR equipped special missions MH-60A, MH-60L and definitive MH-60K with terrain following radar and inflight refuelling probe; medevac UH-60Q Dustoff; Hellfire and rocket armed AH-60L 'Direct Action Penetrator'; and the command and control UH-60V, currently under development. The US Air Force operates about 100 MH-60Gs, now HH-60G combat rescue Black Hawks. The US Marine Corps operates nine VIP VH-60N White Hawks.

The CH-60 has been developed to meet a USN requirement for a Combat SAR and vertrep helicopter. First flying on October 6 1997, the USN requires 250. It combines the airframe of the UH-60 with the SH-60's automatic flight control system, blade and tail folding mechanisms.

Photo: A USAF MH-60K with TFR and refuelling probe. (Doug Mackay)

Sikorsky SH-60/S-70B Seahawk

Country of origin: United States of America

Type: Shipborne ASW helicopter

Powerplants: SH-60B – Two 1415kW (1900shp) General Electric T700-GE-401 turboshafts, driving four blade main and tail rotors.

Performance: SH-60B – Dash speed at 5000ft 235km/h (126kt). Max vertical rate of climb at sea level 700ft/min. Operational radius with 3hr loiter 93km (50nm), or for a 1hr loiter 278km (150nm).

Weights: SH-60B – Empty for ASW mission 6190kg (13,648lb), max takeoff 9925kg (21,884lb).

Dimensions: SH-60B – Main rotor diameter 16.36m (53ft 8in), length overall rotors turning 19.76m (64ft 10in), fuselage length 15.26m (50ft 1in), height overall rotors turning 5.18m (17ft 10in), height to top of rotor head 3.79m (12ft 6in). Main rotor disc area 210.1m² (2262sq ft).

Accommodation: Pilot and airborne tactical officer in cockpit, sensor operator station in main cabin.

Armament: Two Mk 46 or Mk 50 torpedoes or AGM-119 Penguin anti ship missiles, plus pintle mounted machine guns.

Operators: Australia, Greece, Japan, Spain, Taiwan, Thailand*, Turkey*, USA.

History: The Seahawk is the US Navy's standard shipborne anti submarine warfare helicopter.

Sikorsky based its proposal to meet the US Navy's LAMPS (light airborne multipurpose system) Mk III program for a new ASW helicopter on the UH-60 Black Hawk airframe. Sikorsky's bid was selected ahead of a rival proposal from Boeing Vertol. The prototype YSH-60B first flew on December 12 1979.

The SH-60 features navalised General Electric T700 turboshafts, a repositioned tailwheel with twin wheels, lateral pylons for torpedoes or external fuel tanks, an external winch and a sensor station in the main cabin. The SH-60B Seahawk is operated off US Navy frigates, destroyers and cruisers, and is fitted with an undernose mounted APS-124 search radar and a 25 tube sonobuoy launcher on the port side of the fuselage and carries a towed MAD. Primary armament is Mk 46 torpedoes and more latterly Mk 50 torpedoes and AGM-119 Penguin anti ship missiles.

The SH-60F is the USN's CV Inner Zone ASW helicopter and provides close-in ASW protection for USN aircraft carrier battle groups. It features a dunking sonar, FLIR and ESM, while the search radar is deleted. Eighty one were delivered to replace SH-3H Sea Kings, while Taiwan has 10 similar S-70C(M)-1 Thunderhawks.

Seahawks have been exported to Australia (S-70B-2, with Thomson Thorn Super Searcher radar and integrated Rockwell Collins avionics), Greece (S-70B-6, a hybrid SH-60B/F), Japan (SH-60J) and Spain (HS.23).

Other SH-60 variants include the USN's minigun armed HH-60H Rescue Hawk used for strike rescue (recovery of downed aircrew) and SEAL commando insertion/extraction, the US Coast Guard's HH-60J Jayhawk and the USN's SH-60R. The US Navy plans to remanufacture all its SH-60Bs and SH-60Fs to a common SH-60R standard (with dipping sonar, APS-147 radar, laser ranger and colour displays). IOC for the SH-60R is planned for 2002.

Photo: A SH-60F of the USN's HS-5 Squadron. (Jim Vidrine, USN)

Sikorsky S-92

Country of origin: United States of America

Type: Medium lift transport helicopter

Powerplants: S-92IU – Two 1415kW (1900shp) takeoff rated General Electric CT7-8 turboshafts, driving four blade main and tail rotors.

Performance: S-92IU – Max cruising speed 287km/h (155kt), economical cruising speed 260km/h (140kt). Hovering ceiling in ground effect 12,700ft, out of ground effect 8300ft. Range 890km (480nm).

Weights: S-92IU – Max takeoff 10,930kg (24,100lb), max takeoff with sling load 12,020kg (26,500lb). Civil S-92C empty weight 6743kg (14,866lb).

Dimensions: Main rotor diameter 17.71m (56ft 4in), length overall rotors turning 20.85m (68ft 5in), fuselage length 17.32m (56ft 10in), height overall 6.45m (21ft 2in). Main rotor disc area 231.6m² (2492.4sq ft).

Accommodation: Flightcrew of two. Accommodation in main cabin for 22 combat equipped troops.

Armament: None announced.

Operators: None at the time of writing. Sikorsky estimates a market for 5000 civil and military helicopters in S-92 class between 2000 and 2019.

History: The S-92 is a new medium lift helicopter using dynamic components from the H-60/S-70 series.

Development of the S-92 was first announced in 1992 when Sikorsky unveiled a mockup of the new helicopter. In 1993 however Sikorsky postponed launching the S-92 due to the international helicopter market downturn and instead began searching for international risk sharing partners. By 1995 Sikorsky had formed its Team S-92 partners and formally launched the S-92 at the 1995 Paris Airshow.

Sikorsky will initially build five development S-92s. The first to fly will be a civil S-92C, with first flight scheduled for 1998. Three S-92Cs (named Helibus) and two military/international utility S-92IU development aircraft are planned.

The S-92 will combine the dynamic systems of the H-60/S-70 series with a larger cabin. Components based on those from the H-60 series include the rotor head, transmission and powerplants. Otherwise the S-92 will be all new with all composite wide chord and drooped tip rotor blades (40% of the aircraft will be of composite construction). The main cabin is wider and longer than the H-60's and features a rear loading freight ramp, while the cockpit will feature four liquid crystal displays, with provision for a fifth.

Team S-92 members include risk sharing partners Mitsubishi Heavy Industries (7.5%, responsible for the main cabin), Gamesa of Spain (7% – cabin interior and transmission housing) and China's Jingdezhen Helicopter Group (2% – tail pylon and tailplane), while Taiwan Aerospace (6.5% – flightdeck) and Embraer (4% – sponsons and fuel system) are fixed price suppliers/partners. Russia's leading helicopter designer Mil is also a program participant.

S-92 rollout is planned for January 1998, with first flight expected later that year from Sikorsky's West Palm Beach, Florida, Development Flight Centre. Civil certification is anticipated in 2000.

Photo: The S-92 mockup as unveiled in 1992. (Sikorsky)

Singapore Aerospace Super Skyhawk

Countries of origin: USA and Singapore

Type: Light ground attack aircraft

Powerplant: One 48.4kN (10,800lb) General Electric F404-GE-100D non afterburning turbofan.

Performance: Max speed at sea level 1128km/h (609kt), max cruising speed at 30,000ft 825km/h (445kt), economical cruising speed at 35,000ft 785km/h (424kt). Max initial rate of climb 10,913ft/min. Combat ceiling 40,000ft. Range with max payload 1160km (625nm), range with internal and external fuel 3790km (2045nm).

Weights: Operating empty 4650kg (10,250lb), max takeoff 10,205kg (22,500lb).

Dimensions: Wing span 8.38m (27ft 6in), length 12.72m (41ft 9in), height 4.57m (15ft 0in). Wing area 24.1m² (259.8sq ft).

Accommodation: Pilot only, or two in tandem, separate cockpits in TA-4SU.

Armament: One centreline and four underwing hardpoints for rockets, bombs, AIM-9 Sidewinder AAMs, AGM-65 Maverick ASMs and gun pods.

Operators: Singapore

History: Singapore's program to upgrade the A-4 with a non afterburning F404 turbofan and modern avionics has resulted in perhaps the ultimate Skyhawk variant.

Singapore joined the ranks of McDonnell Douglas A-4 Skyhawk operators in 1970 when the first of 40 refurbished ex USN A-4Bs were delivered (as the A-4S). Lockheed upgraded the first eight aircraft, the remainder were modified in Singapore by Singapore Aerospace. The upgrade to A-4S standard involved installing a more powerful Wright J65-W-20 turbojet, spoilers and new nav attack system. The two seat TA-4S Skyhawk conversion is unique in its installation of separate tandem cockpits. Further ex US Navy Skyhawks were delivered (16 A-4Bs in 1983 and 70 A-4Cs in 1980) and while most of these were broken down for spares, enough were converted to A-4S standard to allow the formation of an additional squadron.

In 1984 Singapore elected to further upgrade its Skyhawks to extend their service lives rather than replace them. Phase one of Singapore Aerospace's two phase Super Skyhawk program was developed with Grumman and General Electric assistance and involved installing a non afterburning General Electric F404-GE-100D turbofan, plus strengthening to accommodate the new and heavier engine and modification to the air intakes. The 27% more powerful F404 results in a 15% higher dash speed, a 35% greater climb rate, and 40% better level acceleration, plus enhanced takeoff performance and sustained turn rate. The first F404 powered Skyhawk flew for the first time on September 19 1986, with production conversions of 52 A-4S Skyhawks to GE powered A-4SU standard completed in 1989.

The separate phase two of the program was the Ferranti (now part of GEC-Marconi) developed avionics upgrade. Features of the avionics upgrade includes a MIL STD 1553B databus, head-up display, a multifunction display, mission computer and ring laser gyro INS.

The first Republic of Singapore Air Force Super Skyhawk squadron became operational in 1992.

Photo: Super Skyhawks are operated by Singapore's 142, 143 and 145 Squadrons. (Paul Merritt)

Slingsby T67/T-3A Firefly

Country of origin: United Kingdom

Type: Two seat basic trainer

Powerplant: T-3A – One 195kW (260hp) Textron Lycoming AEIO-540-D4A5 flat six piston engine driving a three blade propeller.

Performance: T67C – Max speed at sea level 280km/h (152kt), max cruising speed (75% power) 260km/h (140kt). Max initial rate of climb 1380ft/min. Range with max fuel at 65% power 755km (410nm).

Weights: T-3A – Empty 807kg (1780lb), max takeoff 1145kg (2525lb).

Dimensions: T-3A – Wing span 10.59m (34ft 9in), length 7.57m (24ft 10in), height 2.36m (7ft 9in). Wing area 12.6m² (136.0sq ft).

Accommodation: Seating for two side by side.

Armament: None

Operators: Belize, USA.

History: The Firefly two seat basic trainer has been adopted by the USAF as the T-3A for flight screening duties.

The Firefly is a development of the Fournier RF-6B which first flew in March 1974. Forty five were built (powered by a 75kW/100hp Rolls-Royce Continental O-200 flat four) through to the early 1980s. In 1980 Fournier flew a more powerful development of the RF-6B, the 87kW (116hp) Lycoming O-235 powered RF-6B-120. It was this aircraft that formed the basis for Slingsby's T67 Firefly.

Prior to purchasing the manufacturing and development rights for the French Fournier RF-6B two seat aerobatic basic trainer in 1981, Slingsby Aviation specialised in sailplane construction and composite materials. Slingsby initially built nine T67As, which were basically RF-6B-120s, before placing into production its own development of the type, the T67B.

The T67B was the result of a fairly thorough redevelopment of the T67A. The main difference was that the T67B was made almost entirely from glassfibre reinforced plastics (GFRPs), Slingsby drawing on its extensive experience in that field. The benefits of GFRP include better resistance to fatigue, less weight and less drag.

The definitive civil version of the Firefly is the T67C. The T67C is similar to the T67B except for its more powerful 120kW (160hp) Textron Lycoming O-320 engine. Variants of the T67C are the T67C1 with standard fuselage fuel tankage and one piece canopy, the T67C2 with a two piece canopy and the T67C3 with wing tanks and three piece canopy.

The basic military Firefly is the T67M Mk II, which first flew in December 1982. Many are used for initial military pilot training and screening with civil firms under contract (including in the Netherlands, Canada and the UK's Joint Elementary TS). T67Ms have aerobatic engines and two blade constant speed props, among other changes, compared with the T67C. The T67M200 has a 150kW (200hp) AEIO-360.

In addition 113 T67M260s (powered by a 195kW/260hp AEIO-540) were ordered by the US Air Force as the T-3A Firefly. The Firefly was selected to meet the USAF's Enhanced Flight Screener contract to replace Cessna T-41 Mescaleros. Northrop Grumman assembled the 113 T-3As in Texas and they were delivered between early 1994 and late 1995.

Photo: USAF training on the T-3A began in 1994. (F Serna, USAF)

Soko Galeb & Jastreb

Country of origin: Bosnia-Herzegovina

Type: Two seat trainer (Galeb) and light strike fighter (Jastreb)

Powerplant: G2-A – One 11.1kN (2500lb) Rolls-Royce Viper Mk 22-6 turbojet.

Performance: G2-A – Max speed at 20,350ft 812km/h (438kt), max speed at sea level 755km/h (408kt), max cruising speed at 19,685ft 730km/h (395kt). Max initial rate of climb 4500ft/min. Time to 19,685ft 5min 30sec. Service ceiling 39,375ft. Max range with tip tanks full at 29,520ft (9000ft) 1240km (670nm). Max endurance at 23,000ft 2hr 30min.

Weights: G2-A – Empty equipped 2620kg (5775lb), max takeoff (strike version) 4300kg (9840lb).

Dimensions: G2-A – Wing span over tip tanks 11.62m (38ft 2in), length overall 10.34m (33ft 11in), height overall 3.28m (10ft 9in). Wing area 19.4m² (209.1sq ft).

Accommodation: Two in tandem in Galeb, pilot only in Jastreb.

Armament: G2-A – Two 12.7mm machine guns in nose. Underwing hardpoints for two 50kg (110lb) or 100kg (220lb) bombs and four rockets. J-1 – Three 12.7mm machine guns in nose. Eight underwing hardpoints, inner most for light bombs, outer hardpoints for single rockets.

Operators: Libya, Yugoslavia, Zambia.

History: The Galeb (Seagull) two seat advanced trainer and subsequent Jastreb (Hawk) single seat attack fighter were Soko's first products.

Yugoslavia's VTI (Aeronautical Technical Institute) began design work on the G2-A Galeb began in 1957. The first flight of the first of two prototypes was in May 1961. Production began in 1963, making it the first indigenous jet to be built in that country. Production lasted through to the early 1980s.

The Galeb is similar to the contemporary Aermacchi MB-326 in configuration and both are powered by a single Rolls-Royce Viper turbojet. The Galeb features a straight wing with tip tanks, Folland Type 1-B lightweight ejector seats, sideways hinging canopy transparencies and underwing hardpoints for light bombs and rockets. In all, around 270 Galebs were built for the Yugoslav air force, Libya, which took delivery of 120, and Zambia (six).

The J-1 Jastreb is a single seat ground attack development of the Galeb. Changes include a more powerful engine, structural strengthening, extra hardpoints for rockets and three, instead of two, 12.7mm guns in the nose. The RJ-1 is a reconnaissance variant, with a fuselage camera and one in each wingtip. Approximately 250 to 300 Jastrebs were built, including 30 or so RJ-1s, plus around 30 two seat JT-1 trainers (basically the Galeb with the Jastreb's strengthening, extra hardpoints and weaponry and more powerful engine). First flight was in 1974, with deliveries from 1975. In addition 20 J-1Es and RJ-1Es were delivered to the Zambian air force in 1971, about half of which remain operational.

Both Galebs and Jastrebs saw service during Yugoslavia's civil war with Serbian forces.

Photo: The Galeb is used for advanced and weapons training with the Yugoslav air force.

Soko Super Galeb

Country of origin: Bosnia-Herzegovina

Type: Advanced trainer and light attack aircraft

Powerplants: G-4 – One 17.8kN (4000lb) Rolls-Royce Viper Mk 632-46 turbojet.

Performance: G-4 – Max speed at 32,800ft Mach 0.81, max speed at 13,120ft 910km/h (490kt), max cruising speed at 19,700ft 845km/h (455kt), economical cruising speed at 19,700ft 550km/h (297kt). Max initial rate of climb 6100ft/min. Service ceiling 42,160ft. Range with max internal fuel at 36,090ft 1900km (1025nm), range with max external and internal fuel 2500km (1350nm). Range with gun pod and four BL-755 cluster bombs 1300km (700nm).

Weights: G-4 – Empty equipped 3172kg (6993lb), max takeoff 6300kg (13,890lb).

Dimensions: G-4 – Wing span 9.88m (32ft 5in), length overall 12.25m (40ft 2in), fuselage length 11.02m (36ft 2in), height 4.30m (14ft 0in). Wing area 19.5m² (209.9sq ft).

Accommodation: Two in tandem.

Armament: Removable ventral gun pod contains a GSh-23L twin barrel cannon. Four underwing hardpoints can carry 1280kg (2820lb) of bombs, cluster bombs and rockets. G-4M has wingtip rails for R-60 (AA-8 'Aphid') AAMs and can also carry AGM-65 Mavericks on outboard hardpoints.

Operators: Croatia, Myanmar, Yugoslavia.

History: The Super Galeb advanced trainer was developed to replace the Galeb and Lockheed T-33 in Yugoslav service and has a secondary ground attack mission.

Design of the new trainer began in 1973 and was undertaken by VTI, the then Yugoslavia's Aeronautical Technical Institute (which also designed the Novi Avion MiG-21 replacement light fighter which was cancelled in 1992). Prototype construction began in 1975 while first flight was on July 17 1978. The prototype and six pre series Super Galebs were designated G-4 PPP.

The Super Galeb is of conventional design and configuration for an advanced trainer. Features include its swept wing with four underwing hardpoints, stepped cockpits, a Rolls-Royce Viper turbojet and anhedral on the all moving tailplane. The basic version is designated G-4. The improved G-4M would have featured advanced avionics including a HUD and multifunction displays, a greater payload and wingtip rails for AAMs. The G-4M was designed to take over some of the weapons training syllabus of front line combat aircraft. First flight was planned for 1992 but development was abandoned due to the Yugoslav civil war.

About 135 Super Galebs were built for the Yugoslav air force (production aircraft entered service in 1985), while Myanmar took delivery of 12 in the early 1990s. In 1992 during the Yugoslav civil war the Soko plant at Mostar, within Bosnia, was abandoned (including several incomplete aircraft) while Mostar was occupied by Serbian forces. The Super Galeb jigs were transferred to UTVA within the new Yugoslav state (Serbia and Montenegro), however Super Galeb production did not resume.

Photo: Super Galebs were used for light ground attack during Yugoslavia's civil war. Croatia armed its aircraft with AAMs and AGM-65 Maverick ASMs. (Les Bushell)

Soko Orao & Avioane IAR-93

Countries of origin: Bosnia-Herzegovina and Romania

Type: Ground attack aircraft

Powerplants: IAR-93B – Two 17.8kN (4000lb) dry and 22.2kN (5000lb) with afterburning Turbomecanica/Orao licence built Rolls-Royce Viper Mk 633-47 turbojets.

Performance: IAR-93B – Max speed at sea level 1085km/h (585kt), max cruising speed at 15,240ft 1090km/h (587kt). Max initial rate of climb 12,800ft. Service ceiling 44,625ft. Radius with four rocket launchers and 5min over target lo-lo-lo 260km (140nm), radius with two rocket launchers, six 100kg (220lb) bombs and one drop tank, with 10min over target, hi-lo-hi 450km (243nm), radius with four 250kg (550lb) bombs and one drop tank with 5min over target hi-hi-hi 530km (285nm).

Weights: IAR-93B – Empty equipped 5750kg (12,675lb), max takeoff 10,900kg (24,030lb).

Dimensions: Wing span 9.30m (30ft 6in), length overall inc probe 14.90m (48ft 11in), two seater length overall inc probe 15.38m (50ft 6in), height 4.52m (14ft 10in). Wing area 26.0m² (279.9sq ft).

Accommodation: Pilot only, or two in tandem in two seaters.

Armament: IAR-93 – One GSh-23L 23mm twin barrel cannon in lower forward fuselage. One centreline and four underwing hardpoints can carry a max external stores load of 1500kg (3305lb), for rockets, bombs and AAMs (up to eight on twin launchers on each underwing hardpoint).

Operators: Croatia, Romania, Yugoslavia.

History: The J-22 Orao (Eagle) and IAR-93 were the results of a joint collaboration between the aircraft industries of the former Yugoslavia and Romania to meet requirements for a ground attack fighter.

A joint team of Romanian and Yugoslav designers began work on the J-22/IAR-93 in 1970 under the project name Yurom. Planning called for the new aircraft to be built in single seat ground attack and two seat advanced trainer/conversion trainer versions, with service entry around 1977. Both countries built single seat prototypes which both made their first flights on October 31 1974, similarly two two-seaters, one built in each country, had their maiden flights on January 29 1977. After 30 pre series prototypes were built (15 in each country), series production began in Romania (with IAv Craiova, now Avioane) in 1979 and with Soko in Yugoslavia in 1980.

Romanian IAR-93s and Yugoslav Oraos are generally similar. Romanian production models comprised the initial non afterburning single and two seat IAR-93A (26 single seat and 10 two seaters built), and the single and two seater IAR-93B with afterburning engines (first flight 1985, 165 built).

Yugoslav Orao variants are the non afterburning Orao 1 (17 built), which was considered underpowered and was relegated to reconnaissance duties as the IJ-22 (two two-seaters were designated INJ-22), the NJ-22 production two seat reconnaissance variant (35 built, some with afterburning) and the J-22 Orao production single seater (most with afterburning). Soko built 75 J-22s at Mostar in Bosnia until 1992 when the factory was abandoned and the J-22 jigs were transferred to UTVA within the new Yugoslav state.

Photo: Note deployed airbrakes on this Yugoslav Orao. (MAP)

Sukhoi Su-17/-20/-22

Country of origin: Russia

Type: Ground attack/strike fighter

Powerplant: Su-22M4 – One 76.5kN (17,200lb) dry and 110.3kN (24,800lb) with afterburning Lyulka AL-21F-3 turbojet.

Performance: Su-22M4 – Max speed Mach 1.74 or 1850km/h (1000kt). Max speed at sea level Mach 1.1 or 1350km/h (730kt), or with external stores Mach 1.02 or 1250km/h (675kt). Max initial rate of climb 45,275ft/min. Service ceiling 49,865ft. Range with external fuel at altitude 2550km (1375nm), at low level 1400km (755nm).

Weights: Su-22M4 – Empty equipped 10,767kg (23,737lb), max takeoff 19,400kg (42,770lb).

Dimensions: Wing span extended 13.68m (44ft 11in), span wings swept 10.03m (32ft 11in), length inc probes 19.03m (62ft 5in), fuselage length 15.87m (52ft 1in), height 5.13m (16ft 10in). Wing area wings extended 38.5sq² (414.3sq ft), wings swept 34.9m² (375.1sq ft).

Accommodation: Pilot only, or two in tandem in Su-17U/Su-22U.

Armament: Two 30mm NR-30 guns, one in each wing root. Nine hardpoints for 4000kg (8820lb) of armament including bombs, gun pods, rockets, two R-13M, R-60 or R-73A AAMs, Kh-25ML, Kh-27, Kh-29 and Kh-58 ASMs.

Operators: Afghanistan, Algeria, Angola, Bulgaria, Czech Republic, Hungary, Iraq, Libya, Peru, Poland, Russia, Slovakia, Syria, Ukraine, Vietnam, Yemen.

History: The swing wing Su-17 was the result of efforts to improve the Su-7 'Fitter-A's payload range and takeoff performance.

The prototype for the Su-17, designated S-22I or Su-7IG (Izmenyaemaya Geometriya – variable geometry) and designated by NATO 'Fitter-B', flew for the first time on August 2 1966 (each wing pivots midway along its length, outboard of a large wing fence). Similar Lyulka AL-7 powered 'improved Fitter-B' pre series Su-17s were noted in service in the early 1970s.

Initial production was of the Su-17M 'Fitter-C' with ranging radar, a 110.3kN (24,800lb) AL-21F-3 turbojet and a new nav/attack system. It was exported as the Su-20. In addition small numbers of reconnaissance pod carrying Su-17Rs and Su-20Rs were built.

The improved Su-17M2 and shorter fuselage Su-17M2D (both 'Fitter-D') were built from 1974 and introduced a slightly cut down nose for better pilot visibility, a fixed intake centrebody carrying a laser rangefinder and a doppler radar in an undernose pod. The 'Fitter-D' was exported as the Tumansky R-29 powered Su-22 'Fitter-F'.

A two seat development of the Su-17M2 is the Tumansky R-29 powered Su-22U 'Fitter-E'.

Lyulka powered two seater Su-17UM3 'Fitter-G' conversion trainers and single seat Su-17M3 'Fitter-Hs' have a deeper spine and modified tail, the Su-17M3 also has an internal doppler radar. Respective export variants are the Tumansky or Lyulka powered Su-22UM-3K 'Fitter-G' and Tumansky or Lyulka powered Su-22M3 'Fitter-J'. The Lyulka powered Su-17M4 and export Su-22M4 (both 'Fitter-K') have a dorsal air inlet for cooling and were delivered from 1980.

Sukhoi now offers the Su-22M5 upgrade in conjunction with Sextant Avionique, with changes including a HUD, HOTAS, twin MFDs, FLIR, new radar and mission computer offered.

Photo: A Czech Su-22M4 'Fitter-K'. (Paul Merritt)

Sukhoi Su-24

Country of origin: Russia

Type: Long range strike fighter

Powerplants: Su-24M – Two 75.0kN (16,864lb) dry and 109.8kN (24,690lb) with afterburning Saturn/Lyulka AL-21F-3A turbojets.

Performance: Su-24M – Max speed Mach 1.35, max speed at low level with six FAB-500 bombs 1200km/h (648kt). Service ceiling 36,090ft. Ferry range with external fuel 2500km (1350nm). Combat radius with six FAB-500 bombs 410km (220nm).

Weights: Su-24M – Empty equipped 22,300kg (49,163lb), max takeoff 39,570kg (87,235lb).

Dimensions: Su-24M – Wing span extended 17.64m (57ft 11in), span wings swept 10.37m (34ft 0in), length inc probe 24.60m (80ft 8in), height 6.19m (20ft 4in). Wing area wings extended 55.2m² (593.8sq ft), wing area wings swept 51.0m² (549.2sq ft).

Accommodation: Pilot and weapon systems operator side by side.

Armament: One 23mm gun. Nine external stores stations for TN-1000 and TN-1200 nuclear weapons, or four TV or laser guided bombs, or Kh-23 (AS-7 'Kerry'), Kh-25ML (AS-10 'Karen'), Kh-58 (AS-11 'Kilter'), Kh-25MP (AS-12 'Kegler'), Kh-59 (AS-13 'Kingbolt'), Kh-29 (AS-14 'Kedge') and Kh-31 (AS-17 'Krypton') ASMs, two R-60 (AA-8 'Aphid') AAMs for self defence, rockets and conventional bombs.

Operators: Algeria, Iran, Iraq, Libya, Russia, Syria, Ukraine.

History: The formidable Su-24 (NATO reporting name 'Fencer') strike fighter was developed to replace Il-28 and Yak-28 medium bombers.

Sukhoi originally planned to meet the new bomber requirement with its delta wing T-6 with four RD-36-35 auxiliary lift jets to improve takeoff performance. A T-6-1 prototype first flew in July 2 1967, but the jet lift configuration was abandoned in favour of using swing wings to achieve the desired field performance. Thus a variable geometry T-6-2IG prototype flew for the first time on January 17 1970. The T-6-2IG was adopted for production as the Su-24 and more than 900 have been built.

The basic Su-24 was built in three variants, which NATO designated 'Fencer-A', 'Fencer-B' and 'Fencer-C'. The 'Fencer-A' first flew in late 1971 but served only in small numbers with a trials unit. The 'Fencer-B' was the first major production variant while the 'Fencer-C' had improved avionics.

The improved Su-24M 'Fencer-D' is the major production strike/bomber development. It is believed to have a terrain following radar (rather than terrain avoiding radar), a retractable inflight refuelling probe, a longer nose for new avionics including a Kaira laser/TV weapons guidance system, wing root fences (on Russian aircraft only) and a single nose probe. The export version is the Su-24MK.

The Su-24MR 'Fencer-E' reconnaissance variant has a Shtik side looking radar in a shortened nose (with dielectric panels), infrared and TV sensors, a panoramic camera in the nose and an oblique camera in the lower fuselage (and no wing root fences). The Su-24MR can also carry various reconnaissance and Elint pods.

The final Su-24 variant is the EW, jammer and Sigint Su-24MP 'Fencer-F', developed to replace the Yak-28PPP. Only 12 are thought to have been built.

Photo: An Su-24 'Fencer-B'.

Sukhoi Su-25

Country of origin: Russia

Type: Close support/ground attack aircraft

Powerplants: Two 44.2kN (9920lb) Soyuz/Tumansky R-195 turbojets.

Performance: Su-25TM – Max speed at sea level 950km/h (512kt), max cruising speed at 650ft 700km/h (378kt), economical cruising speed 650km/h (350kt). Max initial rate of climb 11,415ft/min. Service ceiling 32,800ft. Combat radius with a 2000kg (4410lb) weapon load at altitude 630km (340nm), at low level 400km (215nm). Ferry range 2250km (1215nm).

Weights: Su-25TM – Max takeoff 20,500kg (45,195lb).

Dimensions: Su-25TM – Wing span 14.52m (47ft 8in), length overall 15.35m (50ft 5in), height 5.20m (17ft 1in). Wing area 31.1m² (324.0sq ft).

Accommodation: Pilot only, or two in tandem in Su-25UB.

Armament: Su-25T – One NNPU-8M 30mm gun. Ten underwing hardpoints for laser guided rockets, bombs, Vikhr M anti armour tube launched missiles, laser guided Kh-25ML (AS-10 'Karen') and Kh-29L (AS-14 'Kedge') ASMs, KAB-500 laser guided bombs and Kh-58 (AS-11 'Kilter') anti radiation missiles, and R-27, R-77 and R-73 AAMs.

Operators: Afghanistan, Angola, Bulgaria, Czech Republic, Iraq, North Korea, Slovakia, Russia, Ukraine.

History: The Su-25 ('Frogfoot' to NATO) was designed specifically for close air support missions in support of ground forces.

Su-25 development began in 1968, although it wasn't until February 22 1975 that a prototype, designated T-8-1, first flew. This prototype was powered by twin Tumansky RD-9Bs, (non afterburning developments of the MiG-19's engines). Between then and 1984 when the first Soviet Su-25 units were declared operational, the Su-25 underwent a number of detail modifications and engine changes.

A unit of Su-25s, initially pre production aircraft, saw combat in Afghanistan where experience resulted in a number of modifications including bolt on chaff/flare dispensers, engine exhaust IR signature suppressors and titanium shielding between the engines.

The Su-25 features titanium cockpit armouring and wingtip pod airbrakes. The Su-25's engines can run on kerosene, diesel or petrol if necessary while the aircraft can self deploy its own ground support and maintenance equipment in four underwing pods.

The basic Su-25 and export Su-25K (both 'Frogfoot-A') account for most Su-25 production. The Su-25UB and export Su-25UBK (both 'Frogfoot-B') are two seat conversion trainers with a ground attack capability. The Su-25UT, later Su-28 (both also 'Frogfoot-B'), was offered as a dedicated advanced trainer. Ten carrier capable two seat Su-25UTGs (with arrester hook and strengthened undercarriage) were built for carrier trials while 10 similar Su-25UBPs were ordered, but may have been cancelled. Su-25BMs are single seater target tugs.

The Su-25TM (Su-39 to Sukhoi) is a dedicated anti tank variant based on the two seaters but with the rear cockpit faired over for additional fuel and avionics including a new nav system, plus chaff/flare dispenser in the base of the tail and a laser rangefinder and TV camera in the nose for target tracking. Only pre series Su-25TMs have been built, but Sukhoi is upgrading existing Russian AF Su-25s to Su-25TM standard.

Photo: A Czech air force Su-25K. (Paul Merritt)

Sukhoi Su-27, Su-30 & Su-33

Country of origin: Russia

Type: Air superiority/multirole/carrier based fighter

Powerplants: Su-27P – Two 79.4kN (17,857lb) dry and 122.6kN (27,557lb) with afterburning Saturn/Lyulka AL-31F turbofans.

Performance: Su-27P – Max speed at altitude Mach 2.35 or 2500km/h (1350kt), max speed at sea level Mach 1.1 or 1345km/h (725kt). Max initial rate of climb 60,040ft/min. Service ceiling 59,055ft. Range with max fuel 3680km (1985nm). Intercept radius with four AAMs 1500km (810nm).

Weights: Su-27P – Empty 16,380kg (36,110lb), max takeoff 33,000kg (72,750lb).

Dimensions: Su-27P – Span 14.70m (48ft 3in), length exc probe 21.94m (72ft 0in), height 5.93m (19ft 6in). Wing area 62.0m² (667.4sq ft).

Accommodation: Pilot only, or two in tandem in Su-27UB and Su-30.

Armament: Su-27P – One GSh-301 30mm gun. Ten hardpoints for up to 10 AAMs comprising semi active radar guided R-27Rs (AA-10A 'Alamo-A'), IR guided R-27Ts (AA-10B 'Alamo-B'), semi active radar guided R-27ERs (AA-10C 'Alamo-C'), IR guided R-27ETs (AA-10D 'Alamo-D'), R-73s (AA-11 'Archer') and R-60s (AA-8 'Aphid').

Operators: China, India*, Indonesia*, Russia, Ukraine, Vietnam.

History: The Su-27 'Flanker' is a formidable fighter, boasting long range without external tanks, a large missile armament, modern radar and sensors and superb manoeuvrability.

The Su-27 was designed as a manoeuvrable all weather interceptor and bomber escort with a secondary ground attack capability. Development work began in 1969 under the leadership of Pavel Sukhoi, resulting in the first flight of a prototype designated T-10-1 (and powered by two AL-21F-3 turbojets) on May 20 1977. Designated 'Flanker-A' by NATO, the T-10-1 and subsequent T-10 prototypes exhibited serious control problems and so the aircraft was considerably redesigned, resulting in the T-10S-1. The T-10S-1 first flew on April 20 1981 and closely resembled production Su-27s.

Su-27 design features include the blended wing/fuselage design, widely separated AL-31 turbofans, all moving tailplanes, a large F-15 style airbrake, leading edge slats, an IRST and laser rangefinder set which allows passive target detection and engagement, fly-by-wire, HUD and Zhuk look down/shoot down and track while scan radar.

The Su-27P 'Flanker-B' is a single seat air defence fighter; the Su-27S has wingtip EW pods and multirole tasking and can carry a 4000kg (8820lb) bomb load (available for export as the Su-27SK); the similar Su-27SMK has two extra hardpoints; while the Su-27UB 'Flanker-C' is the two seat operational trainer. A modified Su-27, designated P-42, set a series of time to height world records.

The two seat Su-30 air defence fighter is designed for up to 10 hour missions and can provide targeting information for other Su-27s by datalink. The Su-30M and export Su-30MK are multirole variants, the latter ordered by India and Indonesia.

The Russian navy has over 20 carrier capable Su-33 'Flanker-D' air defence fighters for its conventional carrier *Kuznetsov*. First flown in Su-27K prototype form, features include folding wings, canards, strengthened undercarriage, refuelling probe and arrester hook.

Photo: An Su-33 on the carrier *Kuznetsov*. (Alex Radetski)

Country of origin: Russia

Type: Multirole fighter

Powerplants: Su-35 – Two 125.5kN (28,218lb) with afterburning Saturn/Lyulka AL-35F turbofans. Su-37 –Two 142.2kN (31,970lb) AL-37FUs.

Performance: Su-35 – Max speed Mach 2.35 or 2500km/h (1350kt), max speed at sea level Mach 1.14 or 1400km/h (755kt). Service ceiling 59,055ft. Range with max internal fuel over 4000km (2160nm), range with inflight refuelling over 6500km (3510nm). Su-37 – Similar but range with internal fuel 3300km (1780nm).

Weights: Su-35 – Empty 17,000kg (37,479lb), max takeoff 34,000kg (74,956lb). Su-37 – Max takeoff same.

Dimensions: Su-35 & Su-37 – Wing span over wingtip ECM pods 15.16m (49ft 9in), length 22.20m (72ft 10in), height 6.36m (20ft 10in). Wing area 62.0m² (667.4sq ft).

Accommodation: Pilot only.

Armament: Su-35 – One GSh-30 30mm gun. Twelve external hardpoints can carry 8000kg (17,655lb) of weapons, including R-27, R-40, R-60, R-73A and R-77 AAMs, Kh-25ML, Kh-25MP, Kh-29, Kh-31 and Kh-59 ASMs, S-25 IR and laser guided rockets, and laser guided GBU-500 and GBU-1500 laser guided bombs and GBU-500T and -1500T TV guided bombs. Su-37 – Same options plus R-37 and KS-172 AAMs and anti radiation Kh-15P and Kh-65S ASMs.

Operators: Russia*

History: Development of advanced Su-27s variants began in the mid 1980s.

A development Su-27 fitted with canards flew for the first time in May 1985, while the first prototype for what would become the Su-35, the T-10S-70, first flew on June 28 1988. For a time the improved Su-27 was designated Su-27M, it has since been redesignated Su-35.

Changes over the basic Su-27 are numerous. Canard foreplanes were added while power is from two upgraded Saturn AL-35F (or AL-31MF) turbofans. Flight control is provided by a digital fly-by-wire system with quadruplex redundancy (the Su-27's fly-by-wire system is analog). The reprofiled nose houses a multimode Phazotron N011 Zhuk 27 radar (with a larger diameter, flat plate antenna) which has a search range of 100km (55nm), can track 24 targets simultaneously and has terrain following/avoidance. The tailcone houses a rearwards facing Ryazan radar. A new IRST set has been repositioned on the nose. The EFIS cockpit features three colour CRTs and a HUD. Other features are a retractable inflight refuelling probe, taller squared off fins each containing an auxiliary fuel tank and twin nosewheels. Some have been noted with large ECM wingtip pods.

The Su-37 first flew in 1996 and is a further improvement of the Su-35 with two dimensional thrust vectoring nozzles operated through the fly-by-wire flight control system. Other Su-37 features include a Zhuk-PH phased array radar and an improved cockpit with sidestick controller and four Sextant LCD multifunction displays.

The Russian air force had hoped to introduce the Su-35 into service in the late 1990s, although these plans may have been overtaken by the availability of the Su-37.

Photo: The thrust vectoring Su-37. (Paul Merritt)

Country of origin: Russia

Type: Long range strike aircraft

Powerplants: Su-34 – Two 74.5kN (16,755lb) dry and 122.6kN (27,577lb) with afterburning Saturn/Lyulka AL-35F turbofans.

Performance: Su-34 – Max speed at 36,000ft Mach 1.8 or 1900km/h (1025kt), max speed at sea level Mach 1.14 or 1400km/h (755kt). Range with max internal fuel 4000km (2160nm).

Weights: Su-34 – Max takeoff 44,360kg (97,800lb).

Dimensions: Wing span 14.70m (48ft 3in), length 25.20m (82ft 8in), height 6.20m (20ft 4in). Wing area 62.0m² (667.4sq ft).

Accommodation: Pilot and weapon systems operator side by side.

Armament: One 30mm GSh-301 gun in forward starboard fuselage. Two wingtip stations for self defence AAMs. Six underwing, plus centreline and under intake hardpoints for full range of Russian precision guided bombs and missiles, anti radiation missiles, anti ship missiles, rockets and conventional bombs.

Operators: Russia*

History: The Su-34 is a two seat (side by side, rather than tandem) development of the Su-27 fighter intended for long range strike, replacing older types such as the Su-17, MiG-27 and Su-24, while the Su-32FN is a shore based maritime strike fighter.

When the Su-34 first appeared in 1991 confusion surrounded its intended role, with the first prototype, '42', variously identified as an aircraft carrier trainer designated Su-27KU (Korabelnii Uchebno or shipborne trainer) and a strike fighter as the Su-27IB (Istrebitel Bombardirovschik or fighter-bomber). It may well have been that the two seat side by side 'Flanker' was originally designed for carrier training for Su-33 pilots, but instead was adopted for strike. The Su-27IB first flew in April 1990.

However it is now clear that two distinct variants of the aircraft have been developed, the air force Su-34 (based on the Su-27IB) and the Su-32FN, a shore based long range maritime strike fighter intended to replace Russian naval aviation Su-24s. It is unclear if the Su-32FN will make it into frontline service.

Features of the Su-34 (aside from side by side seating) include twin nosewheels and tandem main undercarriage units, canards, AL-35F turbofans, a Leninetz phased array multifunction radar with terrain following/avoidance (the Su-34 had a rearwards facing radar in the tailcone, as on the Su-35), a retractable inflight refuelling probe, broader chord tailfins, multifunction displays in the cockpit and modern avionics. Access to the cockpit is via an integral ladder aft of the nosewheel, while behind the two crew seats in the humped fuselage is a small galley and toilet. The crew sit on Z-36 zero/zero ejection seats and the cockpit is protected by titanium armour.

The Su-32FN is similar but features a maritime search radar, sonobuoy launcher, MAD, laser rangefinder, wingtip ECM pods and seven LCD screen EFIS cockpit.

The Su-34 may enter Russian air force service as early as 1998, and, if funding permits, replace Su-17s, MiG-27s and early Su-24s.

Photo: An Su-32FN. (Paul Merritt)

Sukhoi S-37

Country of origin: Russia

Type: Fighter technology demonstrator

Powerplants: Two 152kN (34,200lb) with afterburning Aviadvigatel D-30F6 turbofans. May latter be fitted with two 196kN (44,000lb) with afterburning and thrust vectoring Saturn AL-31F turbofans.

Performance: Max speed at 30,000ft 2200km/h (1190kt), max speed at sea level 1400km/h (756km/h). Service ceiling 59,000ft. Basic range 3300km (1782nm).

Weights: Normal takeoff 25,670kg (56,590lb), max takeoff 34,000kg (74,690lb).

Dimensions: Wing span 16.7m (54.7ft), length 22.6m (74ft), height 6.4m (21ft).

Accommodation: Pilot only

Armament: None in the prototype. A production version would carry air-to-air and air-to-ground weapons in internal weapons bays and on external pylons.

Operators: Experimental aircraft, not in operational service.

History: The S-37 is an experimental fighter technology demonstrator built to validate and gain experience with various technology advances (particularly the forward swept wings) which could be incorporated into a fifth generation Sukhoi fighter.

The S-37 was initially known as the S-32 and initial reports of the program's existence surfaced in early 1996 when it appeared the aircraft was intended to be a fifth generation fighter, rather than a technology demonstrator.

The S-32 first flew on September 25 1997 (two weeks after the F-22's first flight), with greater details and photographs made public shortly after. The most obvious feature of the new Sukhoi is its forward swept wing, which is made of composite materials to give the necessary structural strength. Benefits of forward sweep include improved manoeuvrability at subsonic speeds, enhanced controllability at high angles of attack, reduced takeoff and landing rolls (also resulting in improved range) and a reduced forward hemisphere radar signature (the S-37 may also be fitted with radar absorbent material).

As well as the forward swept wings, the S-37's flying and control surfaces include canards, conventional horizontal tails and slightly outward canted twin vertical tails.

Power for the S-37 is provided by twin Aviadvigatel D-30F6 turbofans, generating 152kN (34,200lb) with afterburner (the D-30FR also powers the MiG-31). Later on the S-37 may be fitted with 196kN (44,000lb) Saturn AL-41F turbofans. The S-37's inlet are fixed, while air scoops on the wings' leading edge extend to provide the engines with additional airflow at low speeds.

The S-37's canopy and cockpit are from the Su-27, the landing gear from the Su-27K.

Sukhoi hopes to develop the S-37 into an operational fighter for the Russian air force, but significant obstacles would have to overcome for this to become reality, including funding difficulties and MiG MAPO's rival 1-42.

Photo: The S-37 prototype flew for the first time on September 25 1997. (Sukhoi)

Transall C-160

Countries of origin: France and Germany

Type: Tactical transport

Powerplants: Two 4550kW (6100ehp) Rolls-Royce Tyne RTy.20 Mk 22 turboprops driving four blade propellers.

Performance: Max speed 513km/h (277kt). Max initial rate of climb 1300ft/min. Service ceiling at 45,000kg (99,210lb) AUW 27,000ft. Takeoff run 715m (2345ft). Range with 8 tonne (17,640lb) payload and reserves 5095km (2750nm), range with a 16 tonne (35,275lb) payload and reserves 1853km (1000nm). Max ferry range with centre section wing fuel tank 8850km (4780nm).

Weights: Min operating empty 28,000kg (61,730lb), typical operating empty 29,000kg (63,935lb), max takeoff 51,000kg (112,435lb).

Dimensions: Wing span 40.00m (13ft 3in), length exc probe 32.40m (106ft 4in), height 11.65m (38ft 3in). Wing area 160.1m² (1722sq ft).

Accommodation: Flightcrew of three. Main cabin can seat up to 93 equipped troops, or 61 to 68 paratroops, or 62 stretcher patients and four medical attendants, or armoured vehicles, artillery and 4WD vehicles and trucks. Can airdrop an 8 tonne load.

Armament: None

Operators: France, Germany, Indonesia, Turkey.

History: The Transall C-160 tactical transport forms the backbone of the transport fleets of the German and French air forces.

Germany and France formed Transall Allianz in January 1959 to design and build a tactical transport for each countries' air force, plus for export. Germany and France participated in the program on a 50/50 basis, with program partners comprising Germany's MBB and VFW and France's Aerospatiale. Design features settled upon included a high wing, voluminous fuselage, rear loading freight door and two Rolls-Royce Tyne turboprops.

First flight occurred on February 25 1963. Production lines were established in France (at Toulouse) and Germany and aircraft were delivered from 1967 for the air forces of Germany (110 C-160Ds), France (50 C-160Fs) and South Africa (9 C-160Zs, now retired). Turkey took delivery of 20 C-160Ts, all ex German aircraft.

Transall production initially ceased in 1972, but a French requirement saw a further 33 C-160s (including four for an Indonesian civil operator now operated by the air force) built between 1981 and 1985. These new aircraft are designated C-160NG (Nouvelle Generation) and feature a fixed inflight refuelling probe. Ten C-160NGs have a secondary tanker role and are fitted with a hose drum unit in the port undercarriage sponson. Five more C-160NGs are plumbed to be converted to tankers.

Two C-160NGs were converted as Sigint platforms before delivery as the C-160 GABRIEL or C-160G. Features include wingtip pods, a blister fairing on the rear port fuselage, a large retractable dome under the forward fuselage and various antennas around the fuselage. Four other French C-160s, designated the C-160H ASTARTE, carry a Rockwell Collins TACAMO VLF radio for submarine communications.

France and Germany are upgrading their C-160s to extend their service lives, French C-160s are being fitted with HUDs and four screen EFIS.

Photo: A German Transall C-160D in UN markings. (Luftwaffe)

Tupolev Tu-16 & Xian H-6

Country of origin: Russia

Type: Multirole bomber, EW & reconnaissance aircraft

Powerplants: Tu-16K-11-16 – Two 93.2kN (20,945lb) Mikulin AM-3M-500 turbojets.

Performance: Tu-16K-11-16 – Max speed at 19,685ft 1050km/h (565kt), cruising speed 850km/h (460kt). Service ceiling 49,200ft. Range with a 3000kg (6615lb) weapon load 7200km (4475nm).

Weights: Tu-16K-11-16 – Empty equipped 37,200kg (82,012lb), max takeoff 75,800kg (167,110lb).

Dimensions: Tu-16K-11-16 – Wing span 32.99m (108ft 3in), length 34.80m (114ft 2in), height 10.36m (34ft 0in). Wing area 164.7m² (1772.3sq ft).

Accommodation: Normal crew of four, comprising two pilots side by side on flightdeck, navigator/bombardier in nose, and tail gunner, plus two observation stations (blisters either side of rear fuselage).

Armament: Defensive armament comprises six 23mm cannons, two in tail, two in forward dorsal turret and two in rear ventral turret. Normal conventional bomb load of 3000kg (6600lb). Stand-off missiles include a Kh-26 (AS-6 'Kingfish') anti ship missile (with conventional or nuclear warhead) carried on port underwing hardpoint, or the Kh-10 (AS-2 'Kipper') anti ship missile semi recessed in bomb bay.

Operators: H-6 – China. Tu-16 – Russia, Ukraine.

History: One of Russia's first effective jet bombers, the Tupolev Tu-16 has enjoyed a frontline service career matched by few other types.

The Tu-16 was made possible by the development of the Mikulin AM-3 turbojet, which also powered the four engined Myasishchev M-4 'Bison'. A prototype designated Tu-88 and powered by AM-3A turbojets flew for the first time on April 27 1952. A second, considerably lightened prototype flew later that year and the type was subsequently selected for production ahead of the rival Ilyushin Il-46.

Early production Tu-16s covered by NATO's 'Badger-A' designation include the Tu-16A nuclear bomber, torpedo armed naval Tu-16T and the Tu-16N tanker for other Tu-16s (using the unique wingtip to wingtip method). Of the 'Badger-A's, only Tu-16Ms survive in service, although over 100 Chinese built Xian H-6s remain in service.

The first anti ship missile launching Tu-16 was the Kh-1 (AS-1 'Kennel') firing Tu-16KS-1 'Badger-B' with retractable radome (now retired). The Tu-16K-10 'Badger-C' is identifiable by its large, flat nose radome housing the I-band 'Puff Ball' radar and carried a single Kh-10S (AS-2 'Kipper') missile semi recessed under the fuselage (modified to Tu-16K-10-26 'Badger-C Mod' standard it could carry a single Kh-26/AS-6 'Kingfish'). The similar Tu-16K-11-16 'Badger-G' was developed to carry the 320km (170nm) range Mach 1.2 Kh-11/ Kh-15 (AS-5 'Kelt'). 'Badger-G's modified to fire the Kh-26 are designated Tu-16K-26 'Badger-G Mod'.

Many of the 1800 plus Tu-16s built were converted to Elint/ reconnaissance platforms. The Tu-16Ye is an elint conversion of 'Badger-C's, the Tu-16P 'Badger-H' and Tupolev Tu-16P 'Badger-J' are ECM jammers, while the Tu-16R 'Badger-E, F and K' are optical reconnaissance variants. The Tu-16RM 'Badger-D' is a radar equipped maritime reconnaissance aircraft.

Photo: A late 1970s photo of a Tu-16R intercepted by a US Navy F-4.

Tupolev Tu-95 & Tu-142

Country of origin: Russia

Type: Strategic bomber (Tu-95) and maritime patrol platform (Tu-142)

Powerplants: Tu-95MS – Four 11,035kW (14,795ehp) KKBM Kuznetsov NK-12MV turboprops, driving eight blade counter rotating propellers.

Performance: Tu-95MS – Max speed at 25,000ft 925km/h (500kt), at sea level 650km/h (350kt), cruising speed 710km/h (385kt). Ceiling 39,370ft. Radius with a 11,340kg (25,000lb) payload 6400km (3455nm).

Weights: Tu-95MS – Empty 120,000kg (264,550lb), max takeoff 187,000kg (412,258lb).

Dimensions: Tu-95MS – Wing span 50.04m (164ft 2in), length 49.13m (161ft 2in), height 13.30m (43ft 8in). Wing area 289.9m² (3120sq ft).

Accommodation: Seven crew – two pilots, comms operator, nav/ defensive systems operator, flight engineer, navigator and tail gunner.

Armament: Tu-95MS – Up to six Kh-55 (AS-15A 'Kent') cruise missiles on a rotary launcher in the bomb bay.

Operators: Tu-95 – Russia, Ukraine. Tu-142 – India, Russia.

History: The massive Tu-95 was first developed in the early 1950s when the turboprop offered the best compromise between speed and range.

The Tu-95 (NATO reporting name 'Bear') was developed around the 8950kW (12,000shp) Kuznetsov NK-12 turboprop and the fuselage cross section originally introduced on the Tu-4 'Bull', the USSR's unlicenced copy of the B-29 Superfortress. The engines deliver their power through eight blade counter rotating propellers, while the wings, unique for a propeller driven aircraft, are swept. The Tu-95's unique powerplant/airframe combination gives it a top speed over Mach 0.8, while its massive internal fuel capacity and the relative efficiency of the turboprops gives intercontinental range.

The prototype Tu-95 flew for the first time on November 12 1952. Initial production was of the Tu-95M 'Bear-A' high altitude freefall nuclear bomber (now withdrawn from use). Some were converted as Tu-95U crew trainers. Tu-95Ms were converted to Kh-20 (AS-3 'Kangaroo') cruise missile launching Tu-95K-20 'Bear-B' standard with a nose mounted radar. The Tu-95KD was similar but had an inflight refuelling probe. The similar Tu-95KM 'Bear-C' (thought to be new build aircraft) had an inflight refuelling probe, Elint antennas and some reconnaissance sensors. The Tu-95K-22 'Bear-G' had a revised radome profile and carried two Kh-22 (AS-4 'Kitchen') missiles, one under each wing root. The final bomber variant was the Tu-95MS 'Bear-H', developed specifically to carry the Kh-55 (AS-15A 'Kent') and based on the Tu-142's airframe, and was built from 1983.

Surplus Tu-95M bombers were converted to maritime reconnaissance Tu-95RT 'Bear-D' and Tu-95MR 'Bear-E' configurations. The Tu-95RT has an undernose radome and was used for missile mid course guidance and reconnaissance duties, while the Tu-95MR has various cameras in the bomb bay.

The Tu-142 is a dedicated ASW platform developed from the Tu-95. The Tu-142 'Bear-F' features a slight fuselage stretch and a maritime search radar in a ventral radome. It carries sonobuoys, torpedoes and mines. The later Tu-142M 'Bear-F Mod 2' introduced a Magnetic Anomoly Detector (MAD) on top of the tail. The Tu-142MR 'Bear-J' is used as a submarine communications relay.

Photo: A Tu-142M 'Bear-F Mod 2'. (Paul Merritt)

Tupolev Tu-22

Country of origin: Russia

Type: Strategic bomber/electronic warfare aircraft

Powerplants: Tu-22K – Two 123.5kN (27,560lb) dry and 163.0kN (36,375lb) with afterburning Dobrynin RD-7M-2 turbojets.

Performance: Tu-22K – Max speed at 39,350ft Mach 1.52 or 1610km/h (970kt), max speed at sea level 890km/h (480kt). Service ceiling 43,635ft. Combat radius hi-lo-hi with a 400km (215nm) full throttle dash 2200km (1190nm). Ferry range with internal fuel 4900km (2645nm).

Weights: Tu-22K – Empty 38,100kg (83,995lb), normal loaded 85,000kg (187,390lb), max rocket assisted takeoff 94,000kg (207,230lb).

Dimensions: Tu-22K – Wing span 23.50m (77ft 0in), length 42.60m (139ft 9in), height 10.67m (35ft 0in). Wing area 162.0m² (1744sq ft).

Accommodation: Crew of three in tandem, with navigator/systems operator system forward of pilot in lower forward nose.

Armament: One NR-23 23mm gun in tail for self defence. Weapons bay can hold 8 tonnes (17,600lb) of bombs. Tu-22K can alternatively carry a single Kh-22 (AS-4 'Kitchen') supersonic cruise missile semi recessed in the weapons bay.

Operators: Libya, Iraq, Russia, Ukraine.

History: The Tu-22 was Russia's first successful attempt at fielding a supersonic bomber.

The Tu-22 ('Blinder' in NATO parlance) dates from a 1955 study to build a supersonic bomber capable of penetrating then modern air defences and carrying a payload similar to the subsonic Tu-16. The new aircraft (Tupolev's own designation was Tu-105) flew for the first time in September 1959 (piloted by Yu I Alasheyev). The Tu-22 remained unknown in the west until two years later at the Tushino Aviation Day flypast when 10 Tu-22s (one with an Kh-22/AS-4 'Kitchen' cruise missile) made a flypast.

The Tu-22's most unusual feature is the position of the engines at the base of the fin, which had the dual benefits of leaving the fuselage free for fuel (and without the need for long inlet ducts) and giving the two engines (mounted side by side) largely undisturbed airflow. The lips of the intakes move forward for takeoff creating a gap through which extra air is drawn. The slender, area ruled fuselage houses a bombing/navigation radar in the nose, a crew of three with the navigator in the lower forward fuselage with the pilot and radio operator/gunner in tandem behind him, an internal weapons bay, 45,000 litres internal fuel capacity and a 23mm defensive gun in the tail. The large swept wing features pods into which the main undercarriage units retract into.

Approximately 250 Tu-22s were built. Initial production was of the Tu-22 'Blinder-A' conventional and nuclear bomber. About 150 Tu-22s were Kh-22 cruise missile firing Tu-22K 'Blinder-C's with an enlarged radome for the 2.8m diameter multimode radar. The Tu-22U 'Blinder-D' trainer had a raised second cockpit aft of the normal cockpit, while about 60 of the Tu-22R and -22RD 'Blinder-C's were built, fitted with a range of reconnaissance sensors. Most surviving Tu-22s in Russian service have been converted as Tu-22PD 'Blinder-E' EW jammers.

Photo: Two Tu-22s soon after takeoff.

Tupolev Tu-22M

Country of origin: Russia

Type: Strategic and maritime strike/reconnaissance bomber

Powerplants: Tu-22M-3 – Two 245.2kN (55,115lb) with afterburning Kuznetsov/KKBM NK-25 turbofans.

Performance: Tu-22M-3 – Max speed at high altitude Mach 1.88 or 2000km/h (1080kt), max speed at low level Mach 0.86 or 1050km/h (567kt), normal cruising speed at altitude 900km/h (485kt). Service ceiling 43,635ft. Supersonic combat radius with a 12,000kg (26,455lb) weapons load 1500 to 1850km (810 to 1000nm). Subsonic combat radius with max weapons load hi-hi-hi 2200km (1190nm). Subsonic combat radius with 12,000kg (26,455lb) bomb load lo-lo-lo 1500 to 1665km (810 to 900nm), or hi-lo-hi 2410km (1300nm).

Weights: Tu-22M-3 – Empty 54,000kg (119,050lb), max takeoff 124,000kg (273,370lb), rocket assisted takeoff 126,400kg (278,660lb).

Dimensions: Tu-22M-3 – Wing span wings extended 34.28m (112ft 6in), span wings swept 23.30m (76ft 6in), length overall 42.46m (139ft 4in), height 11.05m (36ft 3in). Wing area wings extended 183.6m² (1976.1sq ft), wing area wings swept 175.8m² (1892.4sq ft).

Accommodation: Crew of four with pilot and copilot side by side, with navigator and weapons systems operator behind them.

Armament: One GSh-23 twin barrel 23mm cannon in the tail. Can carry 24,000kg (52,910lb) of conventional bombs or mines in bomb bay, or six Kh-15P (AS-16 'Kickback') ASMs on a rotary launcher in bomb bay and four underwing, or three Kh-22 (AS-4 'Kitchen') ASMs, one semi recessed under fuselage and one on each underwing hardpoint.

Operators: Russia, Ukraine.

History: The Tu-22M was conceived as a swing wing conversion of the Tu-22 but evolved into essentially an all new aircraft.

Tupolev first looked at fitting the Tu-22 with swing wings in 1961. Wind tunnel tests revealed that fitting the Tu-22 with swing wings and a minimum of other changes would almost double combat radius while halving field length. Design work on this aircraft, designated Tu-22M, began in 1962, however Tupolev took the opportunity to substantially redesign the basic Tu-22 to even further improve performance. Apart from the swing wings the other key change was the powerplants, two Kuznetsov NK-20 afterburning turbofans mounted in the rear of the fuselage. The engines were fed by two F-4 style intakes with variable splitter plates. The nose was redesigned, while new six wheel main undercarriage units retracted into the fuselage.

The first Tu-22M-0 prototype, a much converted Tu-22, first flew on August 30 1964, although the west did not identify the new bomber until September 1969. The NATO reporting name 'Backfire-A' was subsequently adopted. Production was of the further redesigned Tu-22M-2 (with a new nav/attack radar) and did not begin until 1972.

About 200 Tu-22M-2 'Backfire-Bs' were built before production switched to the Tu-22M-3, which first flew in 1980. The Tu-22M-3 is powered by two increased thrust NK-25 turbofans fed by new wedge shaped air inlets, and introduced a new multimode radar in a reprofiled nose and has an increased max takeoff weight. The Tu-22MR is an ECM or EW aircraft, with about 10 in service.

Almost 500 Tu-22Ms of all models have been built.

Photo: A Tu-22M-3. Note the bomb racks. (Paul Merritt)

Tupolev Tu-160

Country of origin: Russia

Type: Strategic bomber

Powerplants: Four 137.3kN (30,865lb) dry and 245.2kN (55,115lb) with afterburning Samara/Trud NK-231 turbofans.

Performance: Max speed at 40,000ft Mach 2.05 or 2220km/h (1200kt), cruising speed at 45,000ft 960km/h (518kt). Max initial rate of climb 13,780ft/min. Service ceiling 49,200ft. Radius of action at Mach 1.3 2000km (1080nm). Max unrefuelled range 12,300km (6640nm).

Weights: Empty 110,000kg (242,505lb), max takeoff 275,000kg (606,260lb).

Dimensions: Wing span wings extended 55.70m (182ft 9in), wing span wings swept 35.60m (116ft 9in), length 54.10m (177ft 6in), height 13.10m (43ft 0in). Wing area wings extended 360.0m² (3875sq ft).

Accommodation: Crew of four, with two pilots side by side and with navigator/bombardier and electronic systems operator behind them.

Armament: Max weapon load 40,000kg (88,185lb), comprising freefall bombs or ASMs in two internal bomb bays. One rotary launcher can be carried in each bay to carry six Kh-55MS (AS-15 'Kent') ALCMs or 12 Kh-15P (AS-16 'Kickback') SRAMs. No defensive armament.

Operators: Russia, Ukraine.

History: The massive Tu-160 ('Blackjack' to NATO) is the heaviest and most powerful bomber ever built and was developed as a direct counter to the Rockwell B-1A.

Tupolev began design work under the leadership of V I Blizruk of its all new 'Aircraft 70', a direct response to the B-1, in 1973. Although the B-1A was cancelled in 1977, design and development work on the new bomber continued, resulting in a first flight on December 19 1981, about a month after it was first spotted by a US spy satellite. Production of 100 Tu-160s was authorised in 1985 although only about 30 were built before the line closed in 1992.

The Tu-160 is similar in overall configuration to the B-1, but is much larger overall and has a number of different features. The four NK-231 afterburning turbofans are the most powerful engines fitted to a combat aircraft and are mounted in pairs under the inner fixed wings. The variable geometry air inlets are designed for speed (Mach 1 at low level, over Mach 2 at altitude). The Tu-160 has a retractable inflight refuelling probe although it is rarely used due to the aircraft's massive 130 tonne internal fuel capacity.

The variable geometry wings have full span leading edge slats and double slotted trailing edge flaps, while the airframe is free of any protuberances (except for a small video camera window for the pilots). The nav/attack radar is believed to have a terrain following function, while the Tu-160 has a comprehensive ECM jamming system. The four crew sit on their own ejection seats and the pilots have fighter style sticks. The Tu-160 has a fly-by-wire flight control system.

About a dozen Tu-160s are in Russia (some are not airworthy) and 19 in the Ukraine, with an initial 10 of these due to be transferred to Russian control.

The Tu-160SK is a commercial variant being offered as a launch vehicle for the Burlak-Diana satellite launching rocket.

Photo: The Tu-160 is designed for high and low level penetration.

Tupolev Tu-134

Country of origin: Russia

Type: VIP transport

Powerplants: Tu-134 – Two 64.9kN (14,490lb) Soloviev D-30 turbofans. Tu-134A – Two 66.7kN (14,990lb) Soloviev D-30 Srs IIs.

Performance: Tu-134 – Max cruising speed 900km/h (485kt), economical cruising speed 750km/h (405kt). Normal operating ceiling 39,730ft. Range with 7000kg (15,420lb) payload and reserves 2400km (1295nm), with 3000kg (6600lb) payload 3500km (1890nm). Tu-134A – Max cruising speed 900km/h (485kt), long range cruising speed 750km/h (405kt). Range with 5000kg (11,025lb) payload and reserves 3020km (1630nm).

Weights: Tu-134 – Operating empty 27,500kg (60,627lb), max takeoff 44,500kg (98,105lb). Tu-134A – Operating empty 29,050kg (64,045lb), max takeoff 47,000kg (103,600lb).

Dimensions: Tu-134 – Wing span 29.00m (95ft 2in), length 34.35m (112ft 8in), height 9.02m (29ft 7in). Wing area 127.3m² (1370.3sq ft). Tu-134A – Same except length 37.05m (121ft 7in), height 9.14m (30ft 0in).

Accommodation: Two pilots and a navigator. Tu-134 seats 72, Tu-134A seats up to 84. Most military Tu-134s are fitted with a VIP interior.

Armament: None

Operators: Bulgaria, Czech Republic, Poland, Russia.

History: For many years the Tupolev Tu-134 (700 built) was the standard short haul jet airliner in the USSR and eastern Europe. Today small numbers are in military service as VIP transports.

The Tupolev design bureau was responsible for the Soviet Union's first jet powered airliner, the Tu-104 (which was based on the Tu-16 bomber), and the Tu-104's smaller brother the Tu-124. Both of these short range jetliners had a number of performance and technology shortfalls however, and the Tu-134 was developed to address these problems. Initially the Tu-134 was based fairly closely on the Tu-124, and for a time was designated the Tu-124A. However the decision was instead taken to change the aircraft's overall configuration to feature rear fuselage mounted engines and T-tail.

Flight testing of the Tu-134 began during 1962, with six development aircraft being built. Production began in 1964 although it was not until September 1967 that Aeroflot launched full commercial services.

Initial production was of the standard fuselage length Tu-134. The stretched Tu-134A entered Aeroflot service in the second half of 1970 and could seat up to 76 passengers in a single class. Tu-134A features include a 2.10m (6ft 11in) fuselage stretch, a reprofiled nose, more powerful D-30 engines and an APU. Other versions are the Tu-134B with a forward facing position for the third crew member between and behind the pilots, the Tu-134B-1 which has a revised interior to seat up to 90 passengers without a galley, and the Tu-134B-3 which can seat 96 with full galley and toilet facilities.

Apart from converted Tu-134s serving in a military VIP role, Russia operates a small number converted as bomber trainers. The Tu-134BSh is a bombardier trainer and features the Tu-22M's radar in the nose. The Tu-134UBL meanwhile is a Tu-160 crew trainer with the 'Blackjack's avionics and radar in a Tu-160 shaped nose.

Photo: A Czech air force VIP Tu-134A. (Paul Merritt)

Tupolev Tu-154

Country of origin: Russia

Type: Medium range airliner

Powerplants: Tu-154 – Three 93.9kN (20,950lb) Kuznetsov NK-8-2 turbofans. Tu-154M – Three 104kN (23,380lb) Aviadvigatel (Soloviev) D-30KU-154-II turbofans.

Performance: Tu-154 – Max cruising speed 975km/h (527kt), economical cruising speed 900km/h (486kt), long range cruising speed 850km/h (460kt). Range with max payload and reserves 3460km (1870nm), range with max fuel and 13,650kg (31,100lb) payload 5280km (2850nm). Tu-154M – Max cruising speed 950km/h (513kt). Range with max payload 3900km (2105nm), range with max fuel and 5450kg (12,015lb) payload 6600km (3563nm).

Weights: Tu-154 – Operating empty 43,500kg (95,900lb), max takeoff 90,000kg (198,415lb). Tu-154M – Basic operating empty 55,300kg (121,915lb), max takeoff 100,000kg (220,460lb).

Dimensions: Wing span 37.55m (123ft 3in), length 47.90m (157ft 2in), height 11.40m (37ft 5in). Wing area 201.5m² (2169sq ft).

Accommodation: Flightcrew of three or four. Typical single class seating for 158 to 164 at six abreast, or 167 in a high density layout for Tu-154; Tu-154M seats a maximum of 180. Most military Tu-154s have been converted with a VIP interior.

Armament: None

Operators: Czech Republic, Germany, North Korea, Poland, Russia.

History: The Tu-154 is Tupolev's sixth commercial airliner design and is currently in widespread civil use in Russia as a medium range airliner. Small numbers of the 900 built are in military service, mainly used as VIP transports.

The Tu-154 was developed to replace the turbojet powered Tupolev Tu-104, plus the An-10 and Il-18 turboprops. Design criteria in replacing these three relatively diverse aircraft included the ability to operate from gravel or packed earth airfields, the need to fly at high altitudes above most Soviet Union air traffic, and good field performance. In meeting these aims the initial Tu-154 design featured three Kuznetsov (now KKBM) NK-8 turbofans, triple bogey main undercarriage units which retract into wing pods and a rear engine T-tail configuration.

The Tu-154's first flight occurred on October 4 1968. Regular commercial service began in February 1972. Three Kuznetsov powered variants of the Tu-154 were built, the initial Tu-154, the improved Tu-154A with more powerful engines and a higher max takeoff weight and the Tu-154B with a further increased max takeoff weight. Tu-154S is a freighter version of the Tu-154B.

Current production is of the Tu-154M, which first flew in 1982. The major change introduced on the M was the far more economical, quieter and reliable Soloviev (now Aviadvigatel) turbofans. The Tu-154M2 is a proposed twin variant powered by two Perm PS90A turbofans.

Most Tu-154s in military service are used for VIP transport, while Germany has converted one with various sensors for Open Skies treaty verification flights.

Photo: A German Tu-154M. One of Germany's two Tu-154s was involved in a mid air collision with a USAF C-141 off the African coast during 1997. (Paul Merritt)

Vickers VC10

Country of origin: United Kingdom

Type: Strategic transport and tanker transport

Powerplants: C.1 – Four 97.0kN (21,800lb) Rolls-Royce Conway RCo.43 Mk 301 turbofans.

Performance: C.1 – Max cruising speed 935km/h (505kt) at 31,000ft, economical cruising speed 885km/h (478kt). Max initial rate of climb 3050ft/min. Service ceiling 42,000ft. Range with max payload 6275km (3385nm).

Weights: C.1 – Empty 66,225kg (146,000lb), max takeoff 146,510kg (323,000lb). K.2 – Max takeoff 142,000kg (313,056lb). K.3 – Max takeoff 151,900kg (334,882lb).

Dimensions: C.1 & K.2 – Wing span 44.55m (146ft 2in), length excluding probe 48.38m (158ft 8in), height 12.04m (39ft 6in). Wing area 272.4m² (2932sq ft). K.3 – Same except length excl probe 52.32m (171ft 8in).

Accommodation: C.1 – Flightcrew of two pilots and flight engineer. Seating for up to 150 in main cabin, or alternatively 76 stretchers and six medical attendants. K.2 – Practical max fuel weight 74,000kg (163,142lb). K.3 – Practical max fuel weight 80,000kg (176,370lb).

Armament: None

Operators: UK

History: The VC10 forms the backbone of the Royal Air Force's tanker/transport fleet.

Work on the VC10 dates back to 1956. Design of the VC10 was mainly against a BOAC (the British long haul international airline) requirement for a jet airliner capable of serving its routes to Africa, the Far East and Australasia, and thus dictated the requirement for good airfield and hot and high performance. BOAC officially selected the VC10 in May 1957, and ordered 35 of the type on January 14 1958.

The VC10 had its first flight on June 29 1962. Features of the basic design included four rear mounted Rolls-Royce Conway turbofans, T-tail and an advanced wing with complex high lift features. Awarded civil certification in April 1964, the VC10 at the time was the largest aircraft to enter production in western Europe.

The VC10 was also selected by the Royal Air Force to meet its 1960 requirement for a strategic transport for the then Transport Command and 14 were ordered as VC10 C.1s. These aircraft differed from standard airliner VC10s in having uprated Conways, a refuelling probe, a large freight door, extra fuel in the fin and rear facing passenger seats. The first flight of an RAF C.1 was in November 1965 and deliveries began early the following year. VC10 C.1s remain in RAF service, and they are being fitted with two underwing refuelling pods as C.1(K)s, giving them a secondary tanker role.

The first VC10 tankers though were delivered from 1984. Five VC10s and four stretched Super VC10s, all ex airliners, were converted to dedicated tankers, involving fitting fuel tanks on the main deck, closed circuit TV to monitor tanking operations, two underwing refuelling pods and a rear fuselage mounted refuelling unit. The VC10 tankers are designated K.2, the Super VC10s K.3. The K.4 designation applies to five additional Super VC10s converted to tankers in the late 1980s. The K.4s do not feature main deck fuel tanks.

Photo: The RAF operates 27 VC10s. (Alan MacDonald)

Vought F-8 Crusader

Country of origin: United States of America

Type: Carrier borne fighter

Powerplant: F-8E(FN) – One 47.6kN (10,700lb) dry and 80.1kN (18,000lb) with afterburning Pratt & Whitney J57-P-20A turbojet.

Performance: F-8E(FN) – Max speed at 36,000ft 1827km/h (986kt), cruising speed at 40,000ft 900km/h (485kt). Max initial rate of climb 21,000ft/min. Service ceiling approx 58,000ft. Ferry range 2250km (1215nm). Combat radius 965km (520nm).

Weights: F-8E(FN) – Empty 9038kg (19,925lb), max takeoff 15,420kg (34,000lb).

Dimensions: F-8E(FN) – Wing span 10.87m (35ft 8in), length 16.61m (54ft 6in), height 4.80m (15ft 9in). Wing area 32.5m² (350.0sq ft).

Accommodation: Pilot only.

Armament: F-8E(FN) – Four Colt Mk 12 20mm cannons. Two underwing and four fuselage side hardpoints for AIM-9 Sidewinder or Matra Magic or R 530 AAMs.

Operators: France

History: The F-8 Crusader was the US Navy's first supersonic day interceptor and its last single engine, single crew fighter.

The Crusader resulted from Vought's proposal to meet a 1952 US Navy requirement for a supersonic fighter but with a landing speed below 185km/h (100kt) and powered by a Pratt & Whitney J57 turbojet. Vought's design was selected for development ahead of the North American Super Fury, a navalised F-100. The prototype of the new fighter, designated XF8U-1, flew for the first time on March 25 1955.

The F8U Crusader's most unusual feature was its high mounted variable incidence wing, which rotated to a high angle of attack for takeoff to increase lift and for landing to increase drag and to give the pilot better forward vision. The F8U also featured folding wings, all moving horizontal tails, four 20mm cannons, a fire control radar and supersonic performance in level flight.

In all, 1259 Crusaders were built through to 1965. Initial production was of the F8U-1 (F-8A from 1962), followed by the more powerful F8U-1E (F-8B), the reconnaissance F8U-1P (RF-8A), the F8U-2 (F-8C) with four fuselage side missile rails and a more powerful engine and the all weather F8U-2N (F-8D). The final production model was the multirole F8U-2NE or F-8E, with an APQ-94 fire control radar and a weapons load of 2265kg (5000lb), including Bullpup ASMs. Rebuilds to extend many F-8s' service lives saw F-8Ds become F-8Hs, F-8Es become F-8Js, F-8Cs become F-8Ks, and F-8Bs upgraded as F-8Ls.

Apart from the Philippines, France has been the only country outside the US to operate the Crusader. The French navy ordered 42 F-8E(FN)s for its carriers *Foch* and *Clemenceau*. The F-8E(FN) differs from the basic F-8E in having blown flaps and other high lift devices to allow it to operate off the smaller French carriers. The surviving F-8E(FN)s (the only Crusaders remaining in service) are due to be replaced by Rafale Ms from 2000.

The F-8E(FN) is an agile dogfighter but lacks a long range missile capability, thus limiting its effectiveness in the naval air defence role.

Photo: Note the raised wing and deployed flaps and slats of this French Crusader on its landing run. The last Crusader is due to be retired by 2002. (Paul Merritt)

Westland Wasp

Country of origin: United Kingdom

Type: Naval utility helicopter

Powerplant: One 785kW (1050shp) derated to 530kW (710shp) Rolls-Royce (Bristol Siddeley) Nimbus Mk 503 turboshaft driving a four blade main rotor and two blade tail rotor.

Performance: Max speed at sea level 193km/h (104kt), max and economical cruising speed 180km/h (96kt). Max initial rate of climb 1440ft/min. Hovering ceiling in ground effect 12,500ft, out of ground effect 8800ft. Max range with standard fuel 488km (263nm), range with four passengers 435km (235nm).

Weights: Empty 1565kg (3452lb), max takeoff 2495kg (5500lb).

Dimensions: Main rotor diameter 9.83m (32ft 3in), length overall rotors turning 12.29m (30ft 4in), fuselage length 9.24m (30ft 4in), height overall tail rotor turning 3.56m (11ft 8in), height to top of rotor head 2.72m (8ft 11in). Main rotor disc area 75.9m² (816.9sq ft).

Accommodation: Operational crew of three, or up to four passengers.

Armament: Two Mk 44 torpedoes or a single Mk 46 torpedo, or depth charges, or two Aerospatiale AS 12 wire guided anti ship missiles if fitted with a roof mounted sight.

Operators: Indonesia, Malaysia, New Zealand.

History: The Westland Wasp is a specialised maritime development of the Scout utility and anti tank helicopter operated by the British Army for many years.

The helicopter that eventually evolved into the Wasp started life as a Saunders Roe design before that company merged with Westland. That original design was the P.531 which Saunders Roe began design work on in 1956. The first of two prototype P.531s flew for the first time on July 20 1958.

The new turboshaft powered helicopter attracted the interest of the British Army Air Corps and a pre production batch of P.531-2 Mk 2s was ordered for evaluation, which occurred from October 1960. The British Army's initial order for what would become 150 Scout AH.1s was placed in October 1960. The AH.1 could be armed with up to four AS 11 anti tank missiles and a number saw operational service in the Falklands War.

The last Scouts were retired from British Army service in 1994, leaving a single example with the Empire Test Pilot School the only Scout in military service. Two Scouts were exported to the Royal Australian Navy and three to Jordan but these are no longer in service.

Soon after its merger with Saunders Roe, Westland began work on a naval P.531 development. The Royal Navy ordered two such naval P.531s, which it designated Sea Scout HAS.1, for trials. The Sea Scout name was subsequently changed to Wasp before the first Wasp/Sea Scout flew for the first time on October 28 1962. The Wasp differs from the Scout primarily in that it has wheels rather than skids. It lacks sensors of its own but can carry up to two torpedoes.

In all, 133 Wasps were built, comprising 98 for the Royal Navy and 35 for export to Brazil, the Netherlands, New Zealand and South Africa. Current operators are Indonesia (with ex Netherlands aircraft), Malaysia (ex RN aircraft) and New Zealand (new build and ex RN aircraft).

Photo: New Zealand's Wasps will be retired in 1998, replaced by SH-2F Seasprites. (Doug Mackay)

Westland Wessex

Countries of origin: USA and UK

Type: Utility transport/SAR helicopter

Powerplants: HC.2 – Two 1005kW (1350shp) Rolls-Royce (Bristol Siddeley) Gnome Mk 110/111 turboshafts, driving a four blade main rotor and four blade tail rotor.

Performance: HC.2 – Max speed at sea level 212km/h (115kt), max cruising speed 195km/h (105kt). Max initial rate of climb 1650ft/min. Hovering ceiling out of ground effect 4000ft. Ferry range with auxiliary fuel 1040km (560nm). Range with standard fuel 770km (415nm).

Weights: HC.2 – Operating empty 3767kg (8304lb), max takeoff 6123kg (13,500lb).

Dimensions: HC.2 – Main rotor diameter 17.07m (56ft 0in), length overall rotors turning 20.04m (65ft 9in), fuselage length 14.74m (48ft 5in), height overall 4.93m (16ft 2in), height to top of rotor head 4.39m (14ft 5in). Main rotor disc area 228.1m² (2643.0sq ft).

Accommodation: Two pilots on flightdeck with up to 16 equipped troops in main cabin. In medevac configuration can be fitted for eight stretcher patients, two seated patients and a medical attendant.

Armament: None usually.

Operators: UK, Uruguay.

History: The Wessex is a re-engined and re-engineered development of Sikorsky's S-58, developed initially for the Royal Navy as an ASW platform.

The Sikorsky S-58 arose from a 1951 US Navy requirement for an ASW helicopter. The Wright R-1820 radial piston engine powered S-58 flew for the first time on March 8 1952 and was adopted by the US Navy as the HSS-1 Seabat (or SH-34G from 1962). Other S-58 variants include the US Army's CH-34 Choctaw and the US Marine Corp's UH-34 Seahorse. All piston powered S-58s have now been retired from military service, although small numbers of twin Pratt & Whitney Canada PT6T turboshaft S-58T conversions serve in Thailand and Indonesia.

UK interest in the S-58 came about when the Royal Navy cancelled development of the twin Napier Gazelle turboshaft powered Bristol 191 in 1956. The 191 was being developed to meet an ASW helicopter requirement but instead the RN opted for the development of a single Napier powered development of the S-58 to meet its requirement. A Westland re-engined Napier powered S-58 flew for the first time on May 17 1957, and the type was ordered into production as the Wessex HAS.1 (with dunking sonar and armed with torpedoes).

Retired Wessex variants include the HAS.1, more powerful HAS.3 with a new automatic flight control system, the Royal Marines' HU.1 troop transport and the RAF's HC.5, a transport conversion of RN HAS.1/HAS.3s.

The RAF's major Wessex variant is the HC.2, which differs significantly from the Royal Navy's Wessexes in that it is powered by two Bristol Siddeley Gnome turboshafts joined through a combining gearbox. About 15 HC.2s still serve with the RAF for search and rescue and utility transport, while HC.2s exported to Brunei (as the Mk 54), Iran (Mk 52) and Ghana (Mk 53) have all been retired. Uruguay is the only other current Wessex operator.

Photo: A RAF 32 (The Royal) Squadron VIP Wessex HCC.4. (Paul Merritt)

Westland Sea King & Commando

Country of origin: USA and UK

Type: ASW, SAR and utility transport helicopter

Powerplants: HC.4 – Two 1240kW (1660shp) Rolls-Royce Gnome H.1400-1T turboshafts, driving a five blade main rotor and six blade tail rotor.

Performance: HC.4 – Cruising speed at sea level 245km/h (132kt). Max initial rate of climb 2030ft/min. Max vertical rate of climb 808ft/min. Hovering ceiling in ground effect 6500ft, out of ground effect 4700ft. Ferry range with auxiliary fuel 1740km (940nm). Range with max payload (28 troops) 395km (215nm).

Weights: HC.4 – Typical operating empty 5620kg (12,390lb), max takeoff 9752kg (21,500lb).

Dimensions: Main rotor diameter 18.90m (62ft 0in), length overall rotors turning 22.15m (72ft 8in), fuselage length 17.02m (55ft 10in), height overall rotors turning 5.13m (16ft 10in), height to top of rotor head 4.72m (15ft 6in). Main rotor disc area 280.6m² (3020.3sq ft).

Accommodation: Two pilots with normal seating in main cabin for up to 28 in Commando. Normal Sea King crew of four (two pilots, radar operator and sonar operator).

Armament: Commando – Door mounted machine guns, can be fitted with sponsons for rockets. Sea King – Up to four torpedoes.

Operators: Sea King – Australia, Belgium, Germany, India, Norway, Pakistan, UK. Commando – Egypt, Qatar.

History: Despite appearances, Westland's Sea King and Commando are very different aircraft from Sikorsky's SH-3 Sea King.

Westland developed its own Sea King development in response to a Royal Navy requirement for an advanced long endurance ASW helicopter to replace the Wessex. Changes over the SH-3 were numerous and included Rolls-Royce Gnome turboshafts and British avionics and ASW systems, including the search radar, dunking sonar and processing equipment. First flight was on May 7 1969.

Initial Westland production was of the Sea King HAS.1 – 56 were delivered to the Royal Navy followed by 21 improved HAS.2s (plus 37 conversions) with uprated engines, six blade tail rotors and air intake deflectors/filters. From 1980 30 improved Sea King HAS.5s with a Sea Searcher radar and ESM were delivered, while the final RN ASW Sea King is the HAS.6 (six new build and 69 conversions delivered from 1990). They feature improved processing and ESM. ASW Sea Kings have also been delivered to Australia, India and Pakistan. The current export standard is the Advanced Sea King with uprated engines.

The Royal Navy also operates Sea King AEW.2s with an EMI Searchwater radar mounted in a swivel radome on the starboard side of the fuselage. Development was spurred by the Falklands War. They are being upgraded with Searchwater 2000 radar to AEW.7s.

Search and rescue Sea Kings include the RN's HAR.5 and the RAF's HAR.3 and HAR.3A. Germany, Belgium and Norway also operate SAR Westland Sea Kings.

Finally the Westland Commando is a troop transport/assault development with seating for 28 troops and no ASW gear or floats. It was sold to Egypt and Qatar (three with full Sea King systems), while the Royal Navy operates the similar Sea King HC.4 for the Royal Marines.

Photo: An upgraded Australian navy Sea King Mk 50A. (Nick Sayer)

Westland Lynx AH.1, AH.7 & AH.9

Country of origin: United Kingdom

Type: Battlefield transport and anti tank helicopter

Powerplants: AH.9 – Two 845kW (1135shp) Rolls-Royce Gem 42-1 turboshafts, driving four blade main and tail rotors.

Performance: AH.9 – Max continuous cruising speed 255km/h (138kt), max endurance cruising speed 130km/h (70kt). Max initial rate of climb approx 2480ft/min. Hovering ceiling out of ground effect 10,600ft. Range 685km (370nm).

Weights: AH.9 – Operating empty in troop transport configuration 3495kg (7707lb), max takeoff 5125kg (11,300lb).

Dimensions: AH.9 – Main rotor disc diameter 12.80m (42ft 0in), length overall rotors turning 15.24m (50ft 0in), length rotors folded 13.24m (53ft 5in), height overall rotors turning 3.73m (12ft 3in). Main rotor disc area 128.7m² (1385.4sq ft).

Accommodation: Max seating for pilot and 12 equipped troops, or six stretcher patients and a medical attendant in medevac layout.

Armament: Eight TOW anti tank missiles in two fuselage side launchers in anti tank configuration. Can also be fitted with pintle mounted machine guns and 20mm cannon on fuselage sides.

Operators: UK

History: Westland's Lynx is well regarded for its exceptional agility and good speed. Land based versions serve widely with the British Army for troop transport and anti armour missions.

The origins of the Lynx lie in the Westland WG.13, one of three helicopter designs covered by the February 1967 British/French helicopter coproduction agreement which also included the Gazelle and Puma. Unlike the Gazelle and Puma, which are of French design with some Westland production content, the Lynx is entirely of Westland design with Aerospatiale (now Eurocopter) responsible for 30% of production (including the forged titanium rotor hub for the four blade semi rigid main rotor, which is the key to the Lynx's agility). Other Lynx features are its digital flight control system and all weather avionics.

The first of 13 Lynx prototypes flew for the first time on March 21 1971. The Lynx was originally intended as a ship borne ASW/anti surface warfare helicopter for the British and French navies, but its large cabin and excellent performance attracted British Army interest for troop transport and anti tank missions to replace Scouts.

The British Army's first Lynx model was the AH.1, which first flew in 1977. Of the 113 AH.1s built 103 were upgraded to AH.7 standard with improved systems and an IR suppressor on the exhaust, while the tail rotor is made from composites and rotates in the opposite direction to reduce noise.

The latest British Army Lynx model is the AH.9, which is equivalent to the export Battlefield Lynx (none ordered). The AH.9 features wheeled undercarriage rather than skids, no TOW capability, composite construction main rotor blades with swept tips and an increased max takeoff weight. Sixteen new build AH.9s were ordered plus seven conversions. Five have been outfitted as command posts.

The British Army plans to upgrade its AH.7s and AH.9s to a common equipment standard with a 1553B databus, GPS/INS/Doppler navigation and improved defensive aids.

Photo: The Lynx AH.9 has wheeled undercarriage. (Westland)

Westland Lynx – Naval Models

Country of origin: United Kingdom

Type: Shipborne ASW, ASuW, SAR and utility helicopter

Powerplants: HAS.8 – Two 845kW (1135shp) Rolls-Royce Gem 42-1 turboshafts, driving four blade main and tail rotors.

Performance: HAS.8 – Max continuous cruising speed 232km/h (125kt), max endurance cruising speed 130km/h (70kt). Max initial rate of climb approx 2170ft/min. Hovering ceiling out of ground effect 8450ft. Max range approx 595km (320nm). Combat radius with four Sea Skua anti ship missiles 275km (148nm). Radius of action for a 140min ASW patrol with one torpedo 37km (20nm). Surveillance mission endurance 140km (75nm) from ship 245min.

Weights: HAS.8 – Basic empty 3290kg (7255lb), max takeoff 5125kg (11,300lb).

Dimensions: HAS.8 – Main rotor disc diameter 12.80m (42ft 0in), length overall rotors turning 15.24m (50ft 0in), length with main rotor blades and tail folded 10.85m (35ft 7in), height overall rotors turning 3.67m (12ft 1in). Main rotor disc area 128.7m² (1385.4sq ft).

Accommodation: Crew of two or three.

Armament: Two Mk 44, Mk 46, A244S or Stingray torpedoes, or two Mk 11 depth charges in ASW configuration. For anti ship missions up to four Sea Skua anti ship missiles. French Lynx can fire up to four AS 12 wire guided missiles.

Operators: Brazil, Denmark, France, Germany, Netherlands, Nigeria, Norway, Portugal, South Korea, UK.

History: Naval Lynx variants form an important part of the inventories of several NATO navies, primarily performing ASW and ASuW missions.

When the 1967 Anglo/French helicopter production deal was signed covering the Lynx (originally WG.13), Gazelle and Puma, the Lynx had been planned from the outset as a ship based ASW/ASuW helicopter and it was not until later that land based variants for the British Army (described separately) were developed. The first Lynx prototype flew for the first time on March 21 1971, while the first production Lynx HAS.2 for the Royal Navy had its maiden flight in February 1976. All naval Lynx feature wheeled undercarriage, an advanced automatic flight control system and a folding tail and main rotor.

Features of the RN's Lynx HAS.2 include a Ferranti Seaspray search radar and dunking sonar. France's HAS.2(FN) is similar but has a OMERA-Segid search radar. The RN's HAS.3 has uprated RR Gem 42-1 turboshafts and a modified GEC-Marconi Seaspray radar. Most export Lynx are of similar standard to the HAS.2/HAS.3.

The most advanced naval Lynx variant is the HAS.8, which features composite main rotor blades with swept tips, uprated engines, a nose mounted GEC Sea Owl thermal imager and improved ESM and processing equipment. A rear mounted MAD and 360° coverage Sea Spray radar were planned, but dropped due to a lack of funds. Forty five RN Lynx HAS.3s are being upgraded to HAS.8 standard with conversion work due to be completed in 2001.

Naval Lynx are now being offered in three versions – the basic Series 100 equivalent to the HAS.8 but with 360° radar, the Series 200 with LHTEC CTS800 engines, and the Series 300 with CTS800s and a two crew, six screen EFIS cockpit.

Photo: A Brazilian Lynx Mk 21 (Series 100). (Westland)

Yakovlev/Aermacchi Yak-130

Country of origin: Russia

Type: Two seat advanced trainer and ground attack aircraft

Powerplants: Two 21.6kN (4850lb) Povazske Stojàrne/Klimov RD-35M turbofans.

Performance: Estimated – Max speed Mach 0.92, max speed at sea level 1000km/h (540kt). Time to 35,000ft 4min 12sec. Service ceiling 41,000ft. Max ferry range with internal fuel 2220km/h (1200nm).

Weights: Production aircraft – Normal takeoff 5400kg (11,905lb), max takeoff 9000kg (19,841lb).

Dimensions: Production aircraft – Wing span 10.40m (34ft 11in), length 11.24m (36ft 11in), height 4.76m (15ft 8in). Wing area 23.5m^2 (253.0sq ft).

Accommodation: Two in tandem.

Armament: Seven hardpoints can carry up to 3000kg (6605lb) of weapons of both Russian and western origin, such as R-27 AAMs, GSh-23, GSh-30, DEFA or Aden cannon pods, rockets, bombs, laser guided bombs and ASMs such as AGM-65 Mavericks or Kh-25s.

Operators: Russia*

History: The Yak-130 is one of two contenders for the Russian air force's advanced trainer requirement and is being offered for export in conjunction with Aermacchi.

The Yak-130 is in competition with the Mikoyan MiG-AT to meet the Russian air force's requirement to replace approximately 1000 Aero L-29 and L-39 jet trainers. The Russian air force will acquire about 200 of the winning design for basic, advanced, weapons and combat training.

Design work on the Yak-130 began in 1987. In 1993 Yakovlev signed a collaborative agreement with Aermacchi covering design and marketing. Aermacchi has had considerable input into refining the basic Yak-130 design including 5000 hours of windtunnel testing of various configurations and 3000 hours of rig testing of the Yak-130's fly-by-wire system. The first prototype Yak-130 publicly rolled out in May 1995, with first flight on April 25 1996. Production aircraft will be slightly smaller than the prototype.

Features of the basic Yak-130 include twin RD-35 turbofans (origi-nally designed in the Ukraine, now built in Slovakia but with some Russian design input) which gives the trainer a 0.8 thrust to weight ratio and a healthy climb rate. Aerodynamic features include winglets, leading edge slats and LEXs, permitting flight up to 35° angle of attack to be flown.

The baseline aircraft features modern Russian avionics built around a western standard Mil Std 1553 databus (which allows easy integra-tion of western avionics and weapons), a HUD in the front cockpit and two colour LCD displays in each cockpit. The Yak-130's fly-by-wire system may later be programmed so that the aircraft's flight envelope can be gradually increased as the student pilot becomes more proficient.

Aside from the basic Yak-130, other variants have been proposed including a single seat light fighter and a carrier capable trainer.

All production Yak-130s will be built in Russia. Yakovlev is responsi-ble for marketing within the CIS, Aermacchi for the rest of the world. Ten are being built for Russian air force evaluation.

Photo: The first Yak-130 prototype. (Paul Merritt)

THE 1998/99 WORLD AIRPOWER GUIDE
The inventories of the world's air arms

Australia operates a fleet of five Boeing 707-320s, four of which are equipped for probe and drogue F/A-18 refuelling as illustrated here. Note the extended TV camera pod underneath the 707's rear fuselage. (RAAF)

AFGHANISTAN
Air Force
25+ MiG-23. 60+ MiG-21. 25+ MiG-17. 50+ Su-17/20/22. 12 Su-25. 13 MiG-15UTI. 24 L-39C. 22 L-29. 15+ Yak-11/Yak-18. 6 An-32. 15 An-26. 1 An-24. 12 An-12. 6 Il-14. 1 Il-18. 12+ An-2. 30+ Mi-24. 45 Mi-8/17. Operational status of some of these aircraft unknown.

ALBANIA
Air Force
10 F-7. 60 F-6. 16 F-5/FT-5. 13 F-2. 10 FT-2. 10 CJ-5. 6 Yak-11. 4 Il-14M. 10 Y-5. 11 Harbin Z-5. Operational status of some of these aircraft unknown.

ALGERIA
Air Force
30+ MiG-25/R/U. 65 MiG-23B/E/BN/U. 75+ MiG-21MF/bis/U. 40 MiG-17. 10 Su-24. 32 Su-20. 12 Su-7BM/U. 10 L-39ZA. 21 CM 170. 3 MiG-15UTI. 19 Zlin 142. 6 T-34C. 6 An-12. 3 Il-76. 16 C-130H/H-30. 3 F27 400/600. 3 Gulfstream III. 2 Falcon 900. 2 Super King Air 200T. 30 Mi-24. 50 Mi-8/17. 3 SA 330. 3 Alouette III.

ANGOLA
Air Force
19 MiG-23. 15 MiG-21MF/bis. 8 MiG-17. 15 Su-22. 9 Su-25. 4 PC-7/9. 1 F27MPA. 2 EMB-111A. 6 MiG-21U. 3 MiG-15UTI. 5 Yak-11. 3 Cessna 172. 2 L-100-20. 10 An-26. 6 CASA 212. 6 BN-2A. 4 An-2. 5 Do 27. 1 707. 29 Mi-25/Mi-35. 24 Mi-8/-17. 5 SA 365M. 6 SA 342M. 5 SA 341. 14 SA 316. 30 IAR 316. Operational status of some of these aircraft unknown.

ARGENTINA
Air Force
19 Mirage IIIC/B. 14 Mirage IIIE/D. 9 Mirage 5. 21 Dagger A/B. 5 Canberra B.62/T.64. 12 A-4P. 36 A-4AR (A-4M/OA-4M). 75 IA-58A. 32 T-34A. 27 EMB-312. 14 IA-63. 27 MS-760B. 2 PA-24. 3 PA-34. 3 PA-28R. 2 KC-130H. 11 C-130E/H. 1 L-100-30. 5 707-320B/C. 13 F27 400/600. 5 F28-1000/1000C. 9 C-47. 7 DHC-6-200. 15 IA-50. 1 Sabreliner 75A. 5 Learjet 35A. 1 PA-31. 12 Commander 560. 25 Cessna A182J. 2 CH-47C. 5 Bell 212. 2 UH-1D/H. 22 Hughes 369/500D. 4 SA 315B.
Naval Aviation
12 Super Etendard. 5 A-4Q. 5 MB-339A. 4 MB-326GB. 12 EMB-326. 10 T-34C. 3 P-3B*. 7 S-2E/A. 6 L-188. 3 F28-3000. 9 Super King Air 200. 5 Queenair B80. 2 PC-6B. 9 SH-3D/H. 6 SH-2F. 4 AS 555. 4 Agusta A 109A. 6 Alouette III.
Coastguard
5 C-212. 1 AS 332B. 1 SA 330H. 6 HB 350B. 2 Hughes 500.

ARMENIA
Small number of Mi-8s and Mi-24s believed operational.

AUSTRALIA
Air Force
32 F-111C/G. 4 RF-111C. 71 F/A-18A/B. 3 P-3A*. 19 P-3C. 33 Hawk 127*. 28 MB-326H. 65 PC-9. 12 C-130J-30*. 24 C-130E/H. 5 707-320C. 14 DHC-4. 5 Falcon 900. 7 HS.748. 4 C-47. 2 Super King Air 200.
Navy Fleet Air Arm
16 S-70B-2. 11 SH-2G(A)*. 7 Sea King 50/50A. 6 AS 350BA. 3 Bell 206B-1. 2 HS.748EW.
Army Aviation Corps
36 S-70A-9. 25 UH-1H. 24 Bell 206B-1. 17 AS 350BA. 1 DHC-6-300. 4 Super King Air 200.

AUSTRIA
Air Force
24 J35ÖE. 29 Saab 105ÖE. 16 PC-7. 5 O-1E. 11 Cessna L-19. 2 Skyvan 3M. 12 PC-6. 23 AB 212. 21 AB 204B. 11 AB 206A. 11 OH-58B. 24 Alouette III.

AZERBAIJAN
Some MiG-21s and Mi-24s thought to be operational.

BAHAMAS
Air Force
1 Cessna 421C. 1 Cessna 404.

Army Aviation
23 OV-1. 6 Cessna T-41. 5 Cessna T-207. 2 Cessna U-17. 1 C-212. 3 Aeritalia G222. 2 DHC-6. 1 Sabreliner 75A. 1 Citation II. 3 Merlin III. 3 Merlin IV. 1 Queenair B-80. 20 AS 532. 3 AS 332B. 2 SA 330L. 1 Bell 212. 4 Bell 205A1. 22 Bell UH-1H. 5 Agusta A 109A. 5 SA 315B. 8 UH-12ET.

BAHRAIN
Air Force
12 F-16C/D. 11 F-5E/F. 14 AH-1E. 3 BO 105. 2 BO 105ASW. 1 S-70A. 2 Hughes 369D.

BANGLADESH
Air Force
11 F-6/FT-6. 14 F-7M. 9 MiG-21MF. 2 MiG-15UTI. 14 CM 170. 46 CJ-6. 4 Cessna 152. 6 Cessna 337. 3 An-26/An-24. 8 Mi-8. 11 Bell 212. 2 Bell 206L.

BELGUIM
Air Force
88 F-16A/B. 31 Alpha Jet E. 10 CM 170. 34 SF.260M. 11 C-130H. 3 HS.748. 2 A310*. 2 727QC. 5 Merlin III. 2 Falcon 20. 1 Falcon 900. 5 Sea King.
Naval Aviation
3 Alouette III.
Army Aviation
10 BN-2. 46 Agusta A-109HA/HO. 32 Alouette II.

BENIN
Air Force
2 An-26. 2 C-47. 2 Dornier 128-2. 2 An-2. 1 Commander 500B. 2 AS 350B. 1 Alouette II. 1 Kamov Ka-26.

BOLIVIA
Air Force
25+ AT-33A/N. 22 PC-7. 4 AT-6G. 3 SF.260C. 14 T-23 Uirapuru/Tangara. 12 Cessna 152. 9 Cessna 172K/T-41D. 8 C-130A/H/L-100-30. 5 F27-400. 3 CV-440. 1 Basler Turbo 67. 1 IAI-201. 1 C-212. 15 PC-6B. 1 L-188C. 2 Sabreliner 60/65A. 2 Learjet 25/35A. 4 King Air F90/200/200C. 1 Commander 690. 4 Cessna 402B/404/421B. 19 Cessna 185.

8 Cessna 206. 2 Cessna 210. 1 Cessna 310. 2 Bell 212. 19 UH-1H. 10 Hughes 500M. 15 SA 3158/HB 315.
Army Aviation
2 C-212. 1 King Air 200. 1 OV-10.
Naval Aviation
1 Cessna 206. 1 Cessna 402.

BOTSWANA
Air Force
6 BAC 167 Strikemaster. 7 PC-7. 10 BN-2A. 2 CN-235. 2 Skyvan 3M. 1 BAe 125-800. 2 Cessna 152. 5 Bell 412. 2 AS 350.

BRAZIL
Air Force
16 Mirage IIIEBR/DBR. 47 F-5. 8 F-5B/F. 79 AMX/AMX-T*. 177 EMB-326. 124 EMB-312. 100 EMB-312 ALX*. 122 T-25 Universal. 65 T-23 Uirapuru. 8 EMB-145*. 11 S-2A/E. 21 EMB-111A. 4 707-320C. 2 KC-130H. 7 C-130E/H. 3 RC-130E. 17 DHC-5A. 11 HS.748. 127 EMB-110. 2 737-200. 12 HS.125. 9 Learjet 36A. 10 EMB-120. 7 EMB-121. 33 EMB-810C. 9 Caravan 1. 94 U-27A/L-42/U-42. 7 AS 332M. 57 UH-1D/H. 6 Bell 206A/B. 4 Hughes OH-6A. 29 HB 350B Esquilo. 10 AS 355F.
Naval Aviation
10 SH-3D. 5 Lynx 21/23. 9 Super Lynx. 5 AS 332F. 15 Bell 206B. 20 HB 350B/AS 355F-2 Esquilo*.
Army Aviation
4 UH-60*. 19 AS 550 Fennec. 16 HB 350-1 Esquilo. 36 AS 365K.

BRUNEI
Air Force
2 SF.260W. 4 PC-7. 10 C-212. 4 UH-60L*. 6 S-70C/UH-60. 1 Bell 214ST. 6 BO 105CB/CBS. 2 Bell 206B.

BULGARIA
Air Force
22 MiG-29A/UB. 45 MiG-23BN/MF. 9 MiG-23UM. 18 MiG-21M. 6 MiG-21RF. 17 MiG-21U/UM. 20 Su-22M/U. 39 Su-25K/U. 37 L-39. 83 L-29. 8 An-24/An-26. 1 An-30. 5 L 410UVP-E. 2 Tu-134. 1 Yak-40. 43 Mi-24. 26 Mi-8/17. 14 Mi-2.
Naval Aviation
6 Mi-14PL. 2 Ka-25BSH.

BURKINA FASO
Air Force
1 Commander 500B. 3 Mi-8. 2 SA 365N. 1 SA 316B.

BURUNDI
Army Aviation
5 SF.260W. 4 SF.260TP. 3 SF.260C. 3 Cessna 150. 1 Dornier Do 27Q. 2 SA 342L. 3 SA 316B.

CAMBODIA
Air Force
19 MiG-21PF. 4 MiG-21UM. 5 Shenyang F-6. 6 L-39. 3 Mi-24. 2 An-24RV. 8 Mi-8/17. Operational status of some of these aircraft unknown.

CAMEROON
Air Force
4 Alpha Jet. 9 CM 170. 3 C-130H. 4 DHC-5D. 9 DHC-4A. 1 IAI-201. 2 Dornier 128D-6. 1 PA-23. 1 707. 2 AS 332L. 1 SA 365N. 3 SA 319B. 1 SA 318C. 3 Bell 206L-3. 4 SA 342L.

CANADA
Air Command
60 CF-18A/B Hornet. 18 CP-140 Aurora. 3 CP-140A Arcturus. 139 CT-114 Tutor. 58 CT-133. 5 CC-137 (707). 5 CC-150 (A310). 30 CC-130E/H Hercules. 14 CC-115 Buffalo. 6 CC/CT-142 Dash 8. 7 CC-138 Twin Otter. 15 CC-144 Challenger. 13 CH-113A Labrador (CH-46). 8 CH-118 Iroquois. 30 CH-124A/B Sea King. 109 CH-146 Griffon (Bell 412)*. 61 CH-136 Kiowa. 3 CH-135 Twin Huey.

CAPE VERDE
Air Force
1 Dornier 228. 1 EMB-110.

CENTRAL AFRICAN REPUBLIC
Air Force
1 C-337. 2 BN-2. 1 Rallye 235. 1 AS 350 Ecureuil.

CHAD
Air Force
2 PC-7. 2 SF.260W. 2 C-130H. 2 PC-6B. 5 Reims-Cessna FTB-337. 1 An-2. 2 Alouette II.

CHILE
Air Force
14 Mirage 50C/50CN. 2 Mirage 50DC/IIIB. 20 Mirage VBA/BD. 15 F-5E/F. 2 Canberra PR.9.

28 A-37B. 20 A-36. 16 T-36. 21 T-37B/C. 78 T-35A/B Pillan. 8 Cessna T-41D. 5 T-25 Universal. 18 PA-28. 3 707-320B/C. 1 IAI Phalcon. 3 UP-3A . 4 C-130H2 2 Y-7. 4 C-47. 15 DHC-6 100/200. 9 Beech 99A. 1 King Air 100. 1 Super King Air 200CT. 2 Learjet 35A. 8 Twin Bonanza. 6 Extra 300. 3 0-1. 1 AS 332. 11 UH-1D/H. 1 Bell 212. 6 SA 315B. 6+ BO 105CB.
Naval Aviation
6 EMB-111. 1 Falcon 20. 10 PC-7. 3 EMB-110CN. 3 C-212. 6 AS 332F. 6 BO 105. 6 Bell 206. 6 AS 532C*. 8 P-3A.
Army Aviation
16 R172K. 2 CN-235M. 6 C-212A. 1 PA-31. 3 Cessna 337G. 1 Citation III. 1 Falcon 200. 1 AS 332B. 10 SA 330F/L. 2 UH-1H. 2 Bell 206B. 12 SA 315B. 15 Enstrom 280FX. 5 MD 530F.

CHINA
Air Force
125+ H-6 (Tu-16). 100 H-5 (Il-28). 550+ Q-5. 50 Su-27SK. 400+ J-8/J-8II*. 600+ J-7. 2500+ J-6. 525 J-5. 350+ J-4. 8 SA 342L-1. 1500+ CJ-6. 2 Tu-154. 22 Y-7/An-24. 12 Y-14/An-26. 8 An-30. 7 Il-18. 25 Y-8 (An-12). 17 Harbin Y-11/Y-12. 30+ Li-2. 50+ Il-12. 300 Y-5. 14 SA 321. 22 S-70C-II. 50+ Mi-8/17. 350+ Z-5/Z-6 (Mi-4). 20 Z-9 (Dauphin). 18 Trident 1E/2E. 2 CL-601. 6 AS 332.
Naval Aviation
150+ H-5 (Il-28). 5 SH-5. 12+ Be-6. 325+ J-6. 100+ J-5. 100+ Q-5. 2 Y-7. 9 Li-2. 24+ Y-5. 6+ Z-5. 3+ Z-9.

COLOMBIA
Air Force
12 Kfir C7/TC7. 12 Mirage VCOA/VCOD. 14 A-37B/OA-37B. 12 T-37C. 3 IA 58A. 14 EMB-312. 20 T-34A/B. 31 T-41D. 7 C-130B/H-30. 1 707-320C. 4 DC-6. 2 C-47. 1 C-117. 2 IAI-201. 2 C-212. 2 EMB-110P. 1 F28-1000. 1 Citation II. 3 U-6A. 1 Super King Air C90. 1 PA-31. 1 Cessna 441. 1 Cessna 310. 1 Cessna 210. 2 Bell 412. 14 Bell 212. 13 UH-60A. 19 UH-1B/H. 11 Hughes 500. 7 Enstrom F-28F.
Naval Aviation
1 PA-31. 3 Commander 500. 4 PA-28 Cherokee. 4 BO 105CB.

CONGO
Air Force
12 MiG-21. 9 MiG-17F. 1 MiG-15UTI. 6 An-24/An-26. 1 N.2501F Noratlas. 1 727. 2 SA 318. 2 SA 316. Operational status of some of these aircraft unknown.

COSTA RICA
Civil Guard
3 Cessna 337. 4 Soloy 206. 1 PA-23. 1 PA-34. 1 Commander 680. 1 Cherokee Six. 3 Hughes 269C/500E.

(left) Several nations have used Hercules transports to support scientific research stations and missions in Antarctica, Chile among them. This is one of four Chilean air force C-130H Hercules. (Chilean air force)

COTE D'IVOIRE
Air Force
5 Alpha Jet. 4 Beech F33C. 1 Fokker 100. 1 Gulfstream IV. 1 Gulfstream III. 1 Cessna 421. 1 Cessna 401. 1 SA 330H. 1 SA 365C. 1 SA 319.

CROATIA
Air Force
30 MiG-21bis/MF. 2 Orao. 5 Super Galeb. 3 An-26. 3 An-2. 2 CL-601. 1 Gulfstream III. 1 Dornier Do 28. 10 Mi-24. 30 Mi-8. 12 SA 342. 6 Bell UH-1/212. 1 Bell 205. 2 Hughes 500.

CUBA
Air Force
36 MiG-29. 18 MiG-23M. 32 MiG-23BN. 2 MiG-23U. 100 MiG-21F/MF/PFMA. 77 MiG-21bis. 18 MiG-21U. 29 MiG-19SF. 18+ MiG-17. 10+ MiG-15bis. 15 MiG-15UTI. 20 L-39C. 20 Zlin Z 326. 4 An-24. 21 An-26. 2 An-32. 12+ Il-14. 3 Yak-40. 30 An-2. 19 Mi-24. 10 Mi-14. 48 Mi-8/Mi-17. 20 Mi-4. 5 Mi-2.

CYPRUS
National Guard
2 PC-9. 1 BN-2B. 3 SA 342L-1. 2 Hughes 500. 2 Bell 206B.

CZECH REPUBLIC
Air Force
23 MiG-23ML/UB. 39 MiG-21. 17 Su-22M-4/UM. 19 Su-25BK/UBK. 72 L-159*. 29 L-39. 16 L-29. 8 Zlin Z 142. 26 An-24/An-26. 12 L-410M/T/UVP. 1 Tu-154. 25 Mi-24. 25 Mi-8/17. 10 Mi-2.

DENMARK
Air Force
69 F-16A/B. 3 C-130H. 3 Gulfstream III. 8 Sikorsky S-61A. 27 T-17 Supporter.
Naval Aviation
7 Lynx.
Army Aviation
12 Hughes 500M. 12 AS 550.

DJIBOUTI
Air Force
2 C-212. 1 Cessna U206G. 1 Socata 235GT. 3 AS 355F. 1 AS 350.

DOMINICAN REPUBLIC
Air Force
8 A-37B. 5 O-2A. 10 T-34B. 3 C-47. 2 Aero Commander 680. 3 Queenair 80. 2 PA-31. 1 Cessna 210. 5 T-41D. 9 Bell 205A/UH-1H. 3 Alouette II/III. 1 Hughes 369. 1 SA 365C.

ECUADOR
Air Force
14 Mirage F1JE/JB. 14 IAI Kfir C2/TC2. 8 Jaguar International S/B. 12 Strikemaster. 7 A-37B. 17 T-34C. 12 SF-260ME. 11 T-41D/ Cessna 172F. 7 Cessna 150L. 2 C-130H/ L-100-30. 2 DHC-5D. 4 HS.748-2A. 5 DHC-6-300. 3 Sabreliner 40R/60/75. 1 King Air E90. 5 AS 332. 1 SA 330. 4 UH-1H. 1 Bell 212. 3 SA 315B. 6 SA 316B.
Naval Aviation
3 T-34C. 1 CN-235M. 1 Citation I. 1 Super King Air 200. 4 Cessna 337. 1 Cessna 320. 4 Bell 206B.

Finland's air force has begun taking delivery of 64 Boeing F/A-18C/D Hornets, most assembled locally by Valmet. The F/A-18 deliveries have already allowed Finland to retire its MiG-21s, with the Saab Drakens soon to follow suit. (Boeing)

Army Aviation
2 DHC-5D. 1 CN-235M. 4 IAI-201. 3 PC-6B. 1 Sabreliner 40R. 1 Learjet 24D. 2 King Air 100/200. 3 Cessna 172. 1 Cessna 185. 1 Cessna 206. 13 SA 342K/L. 6 AS 332B. 5 SA 330. 1 Bell 214B. 1 UH-1. 4 AS 350B. 3 SA 315B.

EGYPT
Air Force
25 F-4E. 40 F-16A/B. 107 F-16C/D*. 19 Mirage 2000C/B. 70 Mirage 5D/E/E2. 11 Mirage 5SDR/SDD. 168 F-7/MiG-21. 40 F-6/FT-6. 40 Alpha Jet. 6 Beech 1900. 3 Boeing 707. 21 C-130H. 9 DHC-5D. 4 Gulfstream III/IV. 1 Super King Air. 3 Falcon 20. 40 L-29. 45 L-39. 24 L-59E. 36 Al-Gumhuria. 53 EMB-312. 74 SA 342K/L/M. 15 CH-47C. 27 Commando. 39 Mi-8. 2 UH-60A. 17 Hiller UH-12E. 24 AH-64A. 5 Sea King. 5 E-2C.

EL SALVADOR
Air Force
8 Ouragan. 10 A-37B. 5 CM 170. 13 O-2A. 6 AC-47. 1 T-41A. 3 IAI-201. 1 DC-6. 2 C-123K. 8 C-47/Turbo-67. 3 Cessna 180/ 185. 12 Dornier Do 28. 2 Rallye 235GS. 1 Hughes 300C. 60 UH-1H/N. 6 Hughes 500/ 500M.

ERITREA
6 MB-339C.

ETHIOPIA
Air Force
16 MiG-23BN. 15 MiG-21MF. 15 L-390ZO. 4 An-12. 1 Yak-40. 16 Mi-24. 21 Mi-8. 2 Mi-14.
Army Aviation
2 DHC-6. 2 UH-1H.

FINLAND
Air Force
64 F/A-18C/D*. 31 Saab 35S/FS. 9 Saab 35BS/CS. 54 Hawk 51/51A. 28 L-70. 3 Fokker F27. 3 Learjet 35. 6 PA-31-350 Cheiftain. 9 L-90. 8 PA-28 Arrow II/IV.
Army Aviation
7 Mi-8. 2 Hughes 500D.

FRANCE
Air Force
5 Mirage IV-P. 10 Mirage F1C/C-200. 40 Mirage F1CR-200. 40 Mirage F1CT. 10 Mirage F1B. 115 Mirage 2000C/B. 45* Mirage 2000D. 65 Mirage 2000N. 78 Jaguar A/E. 4 E-3F. 112 Alpha Jet E. 92 Epsilon. 49 EMB-312. 7 CAP 10/230. 12 C-135FR. 2 A310-300. 5 DC-8-55/62CF/72. 67 C-160/ C-160NG. 6 C-160NG (command post/ECM). 14 C-130H/H-30. 8 CN-235M*. 23 Nord 262 Fregate. 10 DHC-6. 11 Falcon 20. 6 Falcon 50/900. 24 EMB-121. 10 Jodel D 140E. 5 PC-7. 7 AS 332C/L. 29 SA 330B/H. 43 AS 355F-1/N Ecureuil/Fennec. 11 Alouette II/III.
Naval Aviation
19 F-8E(N). 53 Super Etendard. 20 Etendard IVP/MP. 24 Alizé. 31 Atlantic I. 42 Atlantique ATL2. 5 Falcon 20H. 14 Nord 262. 16 CM 175. 8 MS-760. 10 CAP 10B. 15 Rallye 100S/ 100ST. 8 Falcon 10/10MER. 16 EMB-121. 12 PA-31. 2 Robin HR 100. 17 SA 321. 37 Lynx HAS.2(FN)/HAS.4 (FN). 4 SA 365F. 22 AS 350B*. 34 Alouette III/III ASW. 8 Alouette II.
Army Aviation
132 SA 330B/H. 24 AS 332M. 156 SA 341M/ F. 30 SA 342L1. 155 SA 342M. 10 AS 555. 56 SE 3160. 125 SE 3130/SA 318C. 2 Cessna F406. 2 Socata TBM 700. 5 Pilatus PC-6.

GABON
Air Force
9 Mirage V. 1 C-130H. 2 L-100-30. 1 EMB-110P. 1 EMB-111A. 2 NAMC YS-11A. 3 SA 330C/H. 5 SA 342L. 1 SA 316/319.
Presidential Guard
6 CM 170. 4 T-34C-1. 1 ATR 42F. 1 EMB-110P. 1 Falcon 900. 1 Gulfstream III. 1 SA 332L.

GERMANY
Air Force
147 F-4F. 238 Tornado IDS. 35 Tornado ECR. 23 MiG-29A/UB. 84 C-160. 5 A310. 2 707-320. 1 Tu-154M. 7 CL-601. 3 VFW 614. 4 L 410UVP. 100 UH-1D. 3 Mi-8T/S. US based training units operate 10 F-4F, 10 T-38 and 35 T-37B.
Naval Aviation
53 Tornado IDS. 18 Atlantic 1. 2 228. 22 Sea King 41. 17 Sea Lynx 88.
Army Aviation
107 CH-53G. 175 UH-1D. 205 Bo 105P. 96 BO 105M. 42 Alouette II.

For an aircraft that started life as an advanced trainer, the Jaguar is a very capable ground attack platform for its principle operators France (pictured) and the UK. Both countries plan to replace their Jags sometime next decade, with Rafales and Eurofighters respectively. This example is taking on fuel from a French KC-135 which has a drogue refuelling basket attached to its boom. (Armée de l'Air)

GHANA
Air Force
4 MB-326K. 2 MB-339A. 11 L-29. 10 Bulldog 122/122A. 5 Fokker F27. 1 F28-3000. 1 C-212. 6 Skyvan 3M. 2 Bell 212. 4 SA 319. 2 Mi-2.

GREECE
Air Force
76 F-4E. 25 RF-4E. 38 Mirage 2000EG/BG. 80 F-16C/D*. 54 A-7H/TA-7H. 48 A-7E/TA-7C. 92 F-104G/TF-104G. 89 F-5A/RF-5A/F-5B/NF-5A/NF-5B. 30 Mirage F1CG. 14 C-130B/H. 2 NAMC YS-11A. 10 C-47. 16 CL-215. 10 Do 28. 47 T-33A. 19 Cessna T-41A. 31 T-37B/C. 36 T-2E. 23 G-164 Agcat. 27 PZL Dromader. 15 AB 205A. 2 AB 206A. 5 Bell 47G. 20 Nardi-Hughes 500. 3 Bell 212.
Army Aviation
24 UH-60*. 20 AH-64A. 10 CH-47C. 99 UH-1/AB-205A. 15 AB 206A. 1 Agusta A 109A. 26 Nardi-Hughes 300C. 5 Bell 47G. 20 Cessna U-17A (185). 1 King Air 200. 2 Commander 680.
Naval Aviation
5 S-70B. 12 AB 212ASW. 4 Alouette III.

(right) A Hungarian two seat MiG-29UB moments before touchdown. Hungary is one of the three initial former Warsaw Pact nations which have been invited to join NATO, and wants to replace its MiG-23s and MiG-21s with a modern western fighter such as the Gripen or F/A-18. (Paul Merritt)

GUATEMALA
Air Force
10 A-37B. 10 PC-7. 6 IAI-201. 6 C-47. 1 DC-6B. 3 F27. 8 Cessna 172/180/182. 5 Cessna 185/206. 1 Super King Air 200. 9 Bell 412/212. 10 UH-1D/H. 3 Bell 206L.

GUINEA REPUBLIC
Air Force
7 MiG-21. 4 MiG-17F. 2 MiG-15UTI. 3 L-29. 5 Yak-18. 2 An-12. 3 An-14. 1 SA 342K. 1 SA 330. 1 IAR 330. 1 SA 316B. 4 Mi-4.

GUINEA-BISSAU
Air Force
3 MiG-17F. 1 MiG-15UTI. 1 SA 318. 2 SA 319.

GUYANA
Air Corps
1 BN-2A. 1 Bell 412. 1 Bell 206B.

HAITI
Air Corps
8 0-2/337. 5 SF.260TP. 1 F33. 4 172/150. 3 C-47. 1 DHC-6-200. 1 BN-2A. 2 DHC-2. 1 Cessna 402. Operational status of some of these aircraft unknown.

HONDURAS
Air Force
12 F-5E/F. 10 A-37B. 4 C-101B. 10 EMB-312. 6 T-41D. 2 C-130A. 6 C-47. 1 L-188A. 1 PA-31. 4 Cessna 180/185. 9 UH-1B/H. 9 412SP. 1 S-76.

HUNGARY
Air Force
28 MiG-29A/UB. 9/2 MiG-23MF/UB. 54 MiG-21. 11 Su-22M. 19 L-39ZO. 9 An-26. 4 Zlin 43. 32 Mi-24D/V. 7 Mi-17/P. 35 Mi-8. 7 Mi-17/PP. 20 Mi-2.

ICELAND
Coast Guard
1 F27-200. 1 AS 332L1. 1 AS 365N. 1 AS 350B.

INDIA
Air Force
40 Su-30MKI*. 66 MiG-29. 120 MiG-27M. 8 MiG-25R/U. 80 MiG-23MF/BN. 244 MiG-21. 35 Mirage 2000H/TH. 110 Jaguar. 18 Hunter T.66. 13 Canberra B(I).58/PR.57/T.54. 110 HPT-32. 170 Kiran 1/2. 38 TS-11. 2 Gulfstream III. 2 Learjet 29. 2 707-320C. 24 Il-76MD. 105 An-32. 60 HS.748. 2 737-200. 42 Dornier 228. 98 Mi-8/Mi-17. 32 Mi-24/Mi-35. 10 Mi-26. 160+ Chetak. 100 Cheetah.
Naval Aviation
20 Sea Harrier FRS.51. 4 Harrier T.60. 12 Kiran 1/2. 8 HPT-32. 6 BN-2A. 8 Tu-142M. 5 Il-38. 7 Alizé. 30 Dornier 228. 11 Sea King 42/42A. 26 Sea King 42B/C. 3 Ka-31*. 8 Ka-27 Helix. 5 Ka-25. 26 Chetak. 4 Hughes 269B.
Coast Guard
2 F27. 36 Dornier 228*. 6 Chetak.

INDONESIA
Air Force
12 Su-30MK*. 11 F-16A/B. 12 F-5E/F. 27 A-4E/TA-4H. 12 OV-10F. 14 Hawk 53. 26 Hawk 200*. 14 Hawk 100. 23 T-34C. 39 AS 202. 3 737-2X9. 2 KC-130B. 19 C-130B/H/H-30. 1 L-100-30. 7 F27-400M. 1 F28-1000. 1 Skyvan 3M. 10 NC 212. 1 707-320C. 32 CN-235. 5 DHC-5. 7 401/402. 11 T-41D. 20 MD3*. 13 NAS 332. 11 AS 330.

2 Bell 204B. 12 NBO 105C/CB. 12 S-58T. 12 Hughes 500C.

Naval Aviation

38 Nomad. 6 PA-38. 6 CN-235. 18 NC-212*. 4 Commander 100. 10 NAS 332L. 4 NBO 105C. 9 Wasp HAS.1.

Army Aviation

4 NC-212. 2 C-47. 1 BN-2A. 2 Cessna 310. 2 Commander 680. 18 PZL Wilga 32. 8 Mi-17*. 28 NB-412. 12 Bell 205A-1. 15 NBO 105. 10 Hughes 300C.

IRAN

Air Force

35 F-4D/E/RF-4E. 25 F-14A. 35 MiG-29. 24 Su-24. 44 F-5E/F. 50 F7. 9 T-33A. 25 EMB-312. 35 PC-7. 18 Beech F-33A/C. 25 Mushshak. 9 747. 2 An-72T-200. 50 C-130E/H. 18 F27. 4 Dornier 228. 2 Jetstar 2. 13 Falcon 20. 2 Aero Commander 690. 14 PC-6B. 44 Cessna 185/180/150. 35 CH-47. 70 AH-1J. 55 AB 214A. 50 AB 205. 10 AB 212.

Naval Aviation

4 F27-400M/600. 4 Falcon 20E. 7 Commander 500/690. 2 RH-53D. 7 AB 212AS. 15 AB 205. 10 AB 206.

Army Aviation

4 F27 400M/600. 4 Falcon 20E. 6 Commander 500/690. 10 Cessna O-2A. 6 Cessna 310. 23 Cessna 185. 11 AH-1J. 62 CH-47. 230 AB 214A. 12 AB 212. 21 AB 205A-1. 88 AB 206A/B. Operational status of some of these aircraft unknown.

IRAQ

Air Force

4 Tu-22. 1 Tu-16. 20 MiG-25. 15 MiG-29. 40 MiG-23MF/ML. 38 MiG-23/MiG-27. 150 MiG-21MF/bis/U/F-7. 55 Su-20/22. 8 Su-24. 28 Su-25. 39 Mirage F1EQ/BQ. 20 L-29. 26 L-39. 5 An-12. 10 SA 321. 20 SA 330. 49 SA 342L. 30 Alouette III. 40 Bell 214ST. 5 AS-61TS. 19 BK 117A/B. 70 BO 105C. 28 Mi-24/Mi-25. 90 Mi-8/Mi-17. 15 Mi-6. 2 Adnan AEW. Operational status of some of these aircraft unknown.

IRELAND

Air Corps

6 CM 170. 7 SF.260. 6 FR172/K. 2 CN-235N. 1 Super King Air 200. 1 Gulfstream IV. 5 AS 365N. 8 SA 316B. 2 SA 342L.

Iran took delivery of 79 F-14As before the fall of the Shah in 1979, with about 25 survivors believed to remain partially serviceable. (Northrop Grumman)

ISRAEL

Air Force

140 F-4E/RF-4E. 74 F-15A/B/C/D. 25 F-15I*. 120 F-16A/B. 130 F-16C/D. 140 Kfir C2/C7. 127 A-4N. 80 CM 170. 35 PA-18 Super Cub. 9 747-200. 13 707-320. 19 IAI-201. 3 KC-130H. 13 C-130H. 4 Super King Air 200. 10 RU-21A/RC-12D King Air. 16 Queenair B80. 7 Do 28. 3 Seascan. 21 Cessna U206C. 42 AH-64A. 40 AH-1G/1S. 33 500MG. 41 CH-53. 60 Bell 212. 40 AB 206/206L. 2 HH-65A Dauphin. 15 Bell 205. 57 UH-1D.

ITALY

Air Force

24 Tornado ADV. 93 Tornado IDS. 135 F-104S. 20 TF-104G. 136 AMX*. 94 MB-339A. 15 MB-339CD*. 38 SF.260AM. 18 Atlantic. 4 707-320. 18 C-130J*. 12 C-130H. 31 G222. 4 G222VS/RM. 2 DC-9-32. 2 Gulfstream III. 4 Falcon 50. 10 PD-808RM/ECM. 2 P-166M. 6 P-166DL-3. 37 S.208M. 32 AS-61R (HH-3F). 2 SH-3D-TS. 35 AB 212/412. 50 NH-500E.

Naval Aviation

16 AV-8B*. 2 TAV-8B. 16 EH 101*. 36 SH-3D/H. 64 AB 212ASW.

Army Aviation

60 A 129*. 26 CH-47C. 16 AB 412. 24 AB 212. 93 AB 205A. 6 AB 204B. 23 A 109EOA. 4 A 109A. 134 AB 206A. 21 AB 47G/OH-13H. 8 Dornier 228-200. 40 SM 1019. 3 O-1E.

JAMAICA

Air Force

1 BN-2A. 1 King Air 100. 2 Cessna 210M. 3 Bell 205. 3 Bell 212. 4 Bell 206B.

JAPAN

Air Self Defence Force

111 F-4EJ. 25 RF-4E/EJ. 190 F-15J/DJ. 62 F-1. 13 E-2C. 62 T-2. 158 T-4. 11 T-33. 54 Fuji T-1A/B. 50 Fuji T-3. 28 C-1. 15 C-130H. 13 YS-11. 2 747-400. 5 BAe 125-800. 2 Gulfstream IV. 3 Queenair A65. 21 MU-2J/S. 15 CH-47J. 24 KV-107. 15 UH-60J. 9 T-400.

Naval Aviation

100 P-3C. 4 EP-3C/NP-3C. 10 US-1/1A. 10 NAMC YS-11T/M. 34 King Air TC-90/UC-90. 23 Fuji T-5 (KM-2D). 33 Fuji KM-2. 4 Learjet 36A. 10 MH-53E. 9 S-61A. 49 SH-3A/B. 51 SH-60J. 11 UH-60J. 12 OH-6D/J.

Army Aviation

16 MU-2. 2 Super King Air 350*. 85 AH-1F*. 38 CH-47J*. 11 KV-107-II. 3 AS 332L. 142 UH-1B/H*. 195 OH-6D/J.

JORDAN

Air Force

24 F-16A/B. 31 Mirage F1B/C/E. 56 F-5E/F. 13 C-101CC. 11 Bulldog 125/125A. 5 C-130H. 2 C-130B. 2 C-212. 1 TriStar 500. 21 AH-1F. 3 S-70A. 10 AS 332M-1. 3 BO 105.

KENYA

Air Force

10 F-5E/F. 9 Hawk 52. 1 Strikemaster 87. 12 Shorts Tucano 51. 7 Bulldog 103/127. 6 DHC-5D. 3 Dash 8-100. 1 PA-31-350. 20 SA 330/IAR-330. 28 Hughes 500MD/ME. 17 Hughes 500MD/M. 1 BO 105S. 1 SA 342K.

KUWAIT

Air Force

40 F/A-18C/D. 12 Hawk 64. 16 Shorts Tucano. 1 737. 2 L-100-30. 4 AS 332AF. 5 SA 330H. 13 SA 342K.

LAOS

Air Force

40+ MiG-21PF. 7 C-47/AC-47. 3 C-123K. 7 An-24/An-26. 11 An-2. 2 Yak-40. 1 Mi-6. 9 Mi-8. 3 Sikorsky UH-34D Choctaw. Operational status of some of these aircraft unknown.

LATVIA

Air Force

4 An-2. 8 Mi-2. 2 L 410.

Indonesian F-16s wearing the colours of the Elang Biru (Blue Falcons) aerobatic display team at the Indonesia Airshow '96. Indonesia's plans to buy a second batch of F-16s were blocked by the US Congress, and instead the country has ordered Sukhoi Su-30s. (Robert Wiseman)

NATO co-operation. A French Mirage F1 takes on fuel from a USAF KC-135R, while a HARM armed German Tornado ECR awaits its turn. The three aircraft were participating in a NATO IFOR mission over Bosnia. (DASA)

LEBANON
Air Force
3 Hunter F.70/T.66C. 5 CM 170. 5 Bulldog 126. 9 SA 330L. 7 SA 342L. 1 Shrike Commander. 2 Alouette II. 12 Alouette III.

LESOTHO
Air Wing
2 C-212. 1 Cessna 182Q. 3 Bell 412. 2 BO 105CBS. 1 Bell 47G.

LIBERIA
Army Aviation
2 DHC-4. 4 IAI-101B. 1 Cessna Caravan 1. 4 Cessna 337G. 1 Cessna 185. 3 Cessna 172.

LIBYA
Air Force
61 MiG-25/U. 130 MiG-23/BN/U. 69 MiG-21bis. 50 Su-20/-22BM. 6 Su-24MK. 6 Tu-22. 28 Mirage F1A/E/B. 6 Mirage F1BD. 80 Mirage 5. 80 G-2A Galeb. 150 L-39. 20 SF.260W. 20 Il-76. 12 C-130H/L-100-30/L-100-20. 14 An-26. 16 G-222. 15 L 410UVP. 20 Mi-2. 65 Mi-24/Mi-35. 34 Mi-8/-17.
Army Aviation
10 O-1E. 13 CH-47C. 5 AB 206A. 40 SA 342. 10 Alouette III. 7 AB 47G.
Naval Aviation
5 SA 321. 24 Mi-14PL.

LITHUANIA
Air Force
4 L-39. 2 L 410. 22 An-2. 3 An-26. 3 Mi-8.
National Defence Force
2 An-2. 1 Yak-18T. 21 Yak-52. 1 Yak-55. 1 PA-38A. 1 W-35A. 14 L-13. 3 Yak-16M. 2 Yak-12. 2 Jantar-Standart.

MACEDONIA (FYROM)
Defence Force
4 Mi-17.

MADAGASCAR
Air Force
8 MiG-21FL. 4 MiG-17F. 4 An-26. 2 C-212. 3 BN-2A. 1 PA-23. 1 Cessna 310R. 1 Cessna F337. 4 Cessna 172. 6 Mi-8.

MALAWI
Army Air Force
2 C-47. 2 Dornier 228. 4 Dornier Do 28D. 1 HS.125-800. 3 SA 330F. 1 AS 532. 5 AS 350.

MALAYSIA
Air Force
18 MiG-29SE. 8 F/A-18D. 15 F-5E/F. 2 RF-5E. 26 Hawk 100/200. 10 MB-339A. 38 PC-7. 6 C-130H-MP. 8 C-130H. 11 DHC-4A. 4 King Air 200. 1 F28-1000. 1 Falcon 900. 9 Cessna 402B. 34 S-61A Nuri/AS-61N. 2 S-70A*. 1 Agusta A 109C. 13 Alouette III.
Naval Aviation
6 Wasp HAS.1.

MALI REPUBLIC
Air Force
9 MiG-21. 5 MiG-17F. 1 MiG-15UTI. 6 L-29. 2 Yak-18. 4 Yak-11. 2 An-26. 2 An-24. 2 An-2. 1 Mi-8. 2 Mi-4.

MALTA
Armed Forces
5 Cessna L-19. 3 AB 47G. 1 Bell 47G. 1 AB 206. 2 NH.500M. 3 Alouette III.

MAURITANIA
Air Force
6 BN-2A. 4 Cessna 337G. 2 PA-31 Cheyenne II. 2 DHC-5D. 1 Skyvan 3M. 1 Caravelle. 1 Gulfstream II. 1 Broussard. 1 AL-60. 4 Hughes 500M.

MAURITIUS
Air Arm
1 Dornier 228-101. 1 BN-2T.

MEXICO
Air Force
10 F-5E/F. 26 AT-33A. 73 PC-7. 30 F33C/F-33F. 10 Musketeer. 15 CAP 10B. 9 C-130A. 3 C-47. 3 C-118 (DC-6). 12 IAI-201. 2 Skyvan. 3 727-100. 2 737-200. 1 757. 1 Jetstar 8. 2 Gulfstream III. 1 Citation I. 2 Sabreliner 60/75A. 5 King Air 90. 4 C-26. 2 Merlin IV. 14 Commander 500S. 25 Bell 212. 1 Bell 205A-1. 25 MD 530F. 18 Bell 206. 5

AS 332L. 3 SA 350F. 4 UH-60. 4 PC-6. 14 Stearman PT-17. 10 Maule MXT-7-180. 6 Maule M-T-235
Naval Aviation
4 An-30. 8 C-212-200. 10 F-33C Bonanza. 9 Tonatiuh. 6 Cessna 152. 1 DHC-5D. 1 FH-227. 1 Learjet 24D. 1 King Air 90. 1 Commander 695. 2 Cessna 402. 10 B55 Baron. 1 Cessna 337G. 6 Cessna 152. 11 BO 105C/CB. 3 Alouette III. 3 MD 500E.

MOLDOLVA
Armed Forces
6 MiG-29. 8 Mi-8.

MONGOLIA
Air Force
37 MiG-21. 11 MiG-17F. 3 MiG-15UT1. 13 Yak-18. 7 An-24/An-26. 38 An-2. 3 PZL-104. 11 Mi-8.

MOROCCO
Air Force
20 F-16A/B. 29 Mirage F1CH/EH. 20 F-5E/F. 12 F-5A/B. 1 RF-5A. 4 OV-10A. 22 Alpha Jet. 22 CM 170. 12 T-34C. 10 AS 202A. 9 CAP 10B/230/231. 15 C-130H. 2 KC-130. 3 Boeing 707. 7 CN-235M. 3 Do 28D. 4 Falcon 20. 1 Falcon 50. 2 Gulfstream II/III. 2 Citation V. 10 King Air A100/200C. 6 Broussard. 7 CH-47. 27 SA 330C. 44 AB 205A/212. 18 AB 206A/B. 24 SA 342L. 4 SA 319.

MOZAMBIQUE
Air Force
40 MiG-21. 5 An-26. 2 C-212. 1 Cessna 172. 2 Cessna 152. 3 PA-32. 4 Mi-24. 5 Mi-8.

MYANMAR (BURMA)
Armed Forces
36 F-7M/F-6*. 20 Super Galeb G-4. 7 PC-9. 15 PC-7. 4 F27/FH-227. 2 C-212. 7 PC-6B. 1 Citation II. 5 Cessna 180. 12 Bell 205A-1. 7 HH-43B Huskie. 12 W-3 Sokol*. 10 SE 3160. Operational status of some of these aircraft unknown.

NATO
E-3 Component
18 E-3A. 3 707-320.

NEPAL
Air Force
1 HS.748. 4 Skyvan 3M. 1 DHC-6-300. 1 AS 332L. 2 SA 330C/G. 4 SA 316B.

NETHERLANDS
Air Force
163 F-16A/B. 13 PC-7. 2 KDC-10-30. 2 C-130H-30. 4 Fokker 60. 2 Fokker 50. 2 F27 Maritime. 27 BO 105C. 49 Alouette III. 3 AB 412SP. 6 CH-47D*. 7 CH-47C. 17 Cougar Mk2*. 12 AH-64A. 30 AH-64D*.
Naval Aviation
13 P-3C. 1 Super King Air 200. 22 SH-14D Lynx.

NEW ZEALAND
Air Force
19 A-4K/TA-4K. 17 MB-339CB. 15 CT-4B Airtrainer. 6 P-3K. 5 C-130H. 2 727-100C. 4 Andover C.1. 13 UH-1H. 5 SH-2G*. 4 SH-2F. 5 Wasp HAS 1. 5 Bell 47GB-2.

NICARAGUA
Air Force
4 L-39Z. 5 SF.260W. 3 Cessna 337. 4 An-26. 2 C-212A. 4 C-47. 5 An-2. 2 Commander 500/680. 11 Cessna 180/U-17/T-41. 19 Mi-8/Mi-17. 4 Mi-2. 2 Alouette III.

NIGER
Defence Force
1 C-130H. 1 An-26. 1 737-200. 1 Do 28D. 1 Dornier 228.

NIGERIA
Air Force
15 Jaguar SN/BN. 18 MiG-21. 4 MiG-21UTI. 19 Alpha Jet. 22 L-39MS. 12 MB-339AN. 8 C-130H/H-30. 5 G222. 3 Dornier 228. 17 Dornier 128-6. 2 SA 330. 4 AS 332. 15 BO 105C. 14 Hughes 300C.
Naval Aviation
2 Lynx Mk 89.

NORTH KOREA
Air Force
30 MiG-29. 60 MiG-23. 155 MiG-21PF/ PFMA. 10 MiG-21U. 40 A-5. 120 F-6. 30 Su-7BMK. 22 Su-25. 80 Harbin H-5 (Il-28). 35 FT-2. 15 L-39. 100+ CJ-5/CJ-6. 12 Yak-11. 200+ Y-5. 12 An-24. 5 Il-14. 4 Il-18D. 3 Tu-154B. 1 Il-62M. 80 Hughes 300/ 500. 40 Mi-8/Mi-4.

NORWAY
Air Force
58 F-16A/B. 15 F-5A/B. 6 P-3C/N. 6 C-130H. 3 DHC-6 100/200. 16 Saab MFI-15 Safari. 12 Sea King Mk 43. 18 Bell 412SP. 5 Lynx 86.

OMAN
Air Force
22 Jaguar S/B. 16 Hawk 200/100. 13 Strikemaster 82/82A. 6 BN-2A. 3 C-130H. 15 Skyvan 3M. 3 BAC One-Eleven 475. 7 Mushshak. 4 AS 202. 5 Bell 214B/214ST. 20 AB 205A. 3 AB 212.

PAKISTAN
Air Force
38 F-16A/B. 94 F-7M/P. 53 A-5. 99 F-6/ FT-6. 16 Mirage IIIEP. 15 Mirage IIIRP/DP. 50 Mirage IIIO. 62 Mirage 5. 23 FT-5. 6 FT-2. 10 T-33A. 4 RT-33A. 55 T-37B. 88 Mushshak. 6 K-8 Karakorum*. 3 P-3C. 4 Atlantic 1. 4 707-320. 12 C-130B/E/L-100-20. 1 F27. 1 Falcon 20E. 2 Travelair. 1 Commander 680. 1 Twin Bonanza. 2 PA-34. 4 Cessna 172N. 1 SA 330J. 4 HH-43B Huskie. 12 Alouette III. 7 SA 315B.
Naval Aviation
2 F27. 6 Sea King 45. 3 Lynx. 1 Maritime Defender. 4 Alouette III.
Army Aviation Corps
108 Mushshak. 40 O-1E. 2 Commander 840/ SMA. 1 Cessna 421. 20 AH-1S. 35 SA 330J. 10 Mi-8. 15 Bell 205/UH-1H. 10 Bell 206. 22 Alouette III. 12 Bell 47G.

PANAMA
National Air Service
6 T-35D Pillan. 2 C-212. 1 CN-235. 1 BN-2A. 1 Piper Seneca I. 9 UH-1B/H. 6 Bell 212/UH-1N.

PAPUA NEW GUINEA
Defence Force
2 CN-235. 4 N22 Nomad. 4 UH-1H.

PARAGUAY
Air Force
12 F-5E*. 9 EMB-326. 12 AT-6G Texan. 5 EMB-312. 15 T-35D Pillan. 5 T-25 Universal. 8 T-23 Uirapuru. 4 C-212. 1 Convair C-131D. 7 C-47. 1 DHC-6. 1 Cessna 421. 1 Cessna 337. 1 Cessna U-17. 1 DHC-3. 3 UH-1B. 3 HB 350B. 1 UH-12. 4 Bell 47G.

PERU
Air Force
12 Mirage 2000P/DP. 12 MiG-29*. 52 Su-20/ 22M/U. 30 Mirage V. 11 Canberra. 2 Canberra T.54. 25 A-37B. 13 MB-339AP. 28 EMB-312. 14 T-41D. 4 Cessna 150F. 1 707-320C. 8 L-100-20/C-130A. 21 An-32. 13 DHC-5A. 6 DHC-6. 2 DC-8-62CF. 1 FH-227. 5 Y-12. 1 EMB-120. 1 F28-1000. 1 Falcon 20F. 4 Learjet 25B/36A. 3 King Air 90. 13 Queenair. 1 PA-31T. 1 Cessna 421. 12 PC-6B. 5 Cessna U206/185. 9 Mi-24. 44 Mi-8/17. 2 Bell 412HP. 11 Bell 212. 5 Bell 214ST. 12 UH-1H. 24 BO 105C/L. 11 Bell 206B. 12 Bell 47G. 3 AS 350B. 2 Alouette III.
Naval Aviation
12 F27G. 3 EMB-110. 6 T-34C. 2 An-32. 4 C-47. 6 Super King Air 200. 6 SH-3H. 5 AB 212ASW. 6 UH-1D. 2 Alouette III. 8 Bell 206B.
Army Aviation
3 An-32. 1 Queenair. 1 Cessna 337. 8 Cessna U-17A/150/206. 40+ Mi-8/-17. 6 Alouette III. 7 SA 315B/Alouette II. 9 Enstrom F28F. 6 Bell 47G.

PHILIPPINES
Air Force
10 F-5A/B. 23 OV-10. 19 S.211. 36 SF.260M/W. 6 Cessna T-41D. 1 F27 Maritime. 10 C-130H/L-100-20. 3 F27. 1 F28. 12 N22 Nomad. 1 S-70A. 4 Bell 214. 61 UH-1H. 5 Bell 205A-1. 10 Sikorsky S-76. 22 MD 520 Defender.
Naval Aviation
9 BN-2A. 2 BO 105C.

POLAND
Air Force
22 MiG-29A/UB. 36 MiG-23MF/UM. 100+ MiG-21PFM/M/MF. 40+ MiG-21bis. 30 MiG-21R/RF. 20 MiG-21UM/US. 99 Su-22. 12 Su-20MK. 50 I-22*. 150 TS-11. 47 PZL-130*. 1 An-12B. 10 An-26. 2 An-28. 25 An-2. 2 Tu-154M. 10 Yak-40. 5 Mi-8. 100 Mi-2. 15 W-3*.
Naval Aviation
18 TS-11. 4 An-28. 4 An-2. 13 Mi-14PL/PS. 6 Mi-2. 6 W-3.
Army Aviation
31 Mi-24. 38 Mi-8/17. 111 Mi-2. 16 W-3W.

PORTUGAL
Air Force
20 F-16A/B. 20 A-7P/TA-7P. 39 Alpha Jet. 16 Epsilon. 11 Cessna FTB337G. 24 C-212. 2 C-130H-30. 4 C-130H. 6 P-3P. 4 Falcon 20/ 50. 16 SA 316 Alouette III. 10 SA 330C.
Naval Aviation
5 Lynx Mk 95.

QATAR
Air Force
12 Mirage 2000-5*. 6 Mirage F1. 6 Alpha Jet. 6 AS 332F. 12 Commando 2A/2C/3. 6 AS 332F. 14 SA 342L. 2 SA 341G.

ROMANIA
Air Force
12 MiG-29A/UB. 33 MiG-23MF/UM. 115 MiG-21. 135 IAR-93A/B. 14 H-5R (Il-28). 33 L-39. 6 MiG-17F. 13 MiG-15bis/UTI. 30 L-29. 50 IAR-99. 40 IAR-823. 28 Yak-18. 10 IAR-28M. 16 An-24/An-26. 3 An-30. 2 Il-18. 1 Tu-154. 2 Boeing 707-320. 4 C-130B. 3 BN-2A. 10 An-2. 90 IAR-330. 7 Mi-8. 6 Mi-2. 99 IAR 316. 12 IAR 317.
Naval Aviation
6 Mi-4PL. 6 IAR 316.

RUSSIA
Air Force
20 Tu-160. 130 Tu-22M. 90 Tu-22. 88 Tu-95. 135 Su-27. 430 MiG-29. 150 MiG-25. 400 MiG-23. 55 MiG-31. ? Su-30*. ? Su-35/-37*. 12 Su-34*. 445 Su-24. 170 Su-17. 179 Su-25. 600 MiG-27. ? L-20. 1000+ L-39.

Qatar is the latest Mirage 2000 customer, and began taking delivery of the 12 2000-5s it has on order in 1997. (Dassault)

A Slovakian MiG-29 launches into the air with afterburners alight. Slovakia operates 15 MiG-29s alongside MiG-21s. (Bruce Malcolm)

300 Il-76. 10 Il-78M. ? An-12. ? An-26. 50 An-32. ? An-70*. 20 An-72. 26 An-124. Tu-134, Tu-154 and Il-62 used in small numbers for VIP transport.

Air Defence Force
300+ Su-27. 320 MiG-31. 200 MiG-25PD. 600+ MiG-23P/MiG-23PLD. 15 A-50. 10 Tu-126. Unknown number of An-12 and An-24 transports.

Naval Aviation
160 Tu-22M. 70 Tu-95/142. 65 Tu-16. 20 Tu-22R. 20 Su-33. 50 Su-25. 95 Su-24. 35 Su-17. 35 MiG-29. 40 MiG-27. 35 Il-38. 25 Be-12. 20 A-40 Albatross*. Approx 500 helicopters including 88 Mi-14, 130+ Ka-25, Ka-27, 50 Ka-29.

Army Aviation
10 Ka-50. 2400+ Mi-8/Mi-17. 1200+ Mi-24. 265 Mi-6. 35 Mi-26. ? Mi-28FN. 500 Mi-2. 20 An-2.

Border Guards
? Mi-24. 6 An-72P. 15* SM-92 Finist.

Strategic Missile Forces
Several hundred transport & support aircraft.

RWANDA
Air Force
2 Mi-24.

SAUDI ARABIA
Air Force
72 F-15S*. 92 F-15C/D. 24 Tornado ADV. 93 Tornado IDS*. 60 F-5E/F. 10 RF-5E. 14 F-5B. 5 E-3A. 8 KE-3A. 30 Hawk. 30 PC-9. 35 BAC Strikemaster 80/80A. 17 Cessna 172G/H/M. 2 Jetstream 31. 8 KC-130H. 48 C-130E/H. 2 VC-130H. 4 CN-235. 1 747SP. 2 707-320. 1 737-200. 1 TriStar. 4 BAe 146. 1 Gulfstream III. 4 HS 125-800. 2 JetStar 8. 3 Learjet 25/35A. 1 Super King Air 200. 1 Cessna 310. 17 KV-107-II. 3 AS 61A. 49 AB 205A/212. 26 AB 206A.

Army Aviation
12 AH-64A. 21 S-70A/UH-60L. 12 AS 532A2*. 6 SA 365N. 15 Bell 406CS.

Naval Aviation
24 AS 565. 12 AS 332.

SENEGAMBIA
Air Force
4 CM 170. 3 Rallye 235. 4 Rallye 160ST/235A. 6 F27-400M. 1 727-200. 1 EMB-111P. 2 Broussard. 1 PA-23 Aztec. 2 SA 330F. 1 SA 341H. 2 SA 318C.

SEYCHELLES
Coast Guard – Air Wing
1 BN-2A. 1 Caravan II. 1 Cessna 152.

SINGAPORE
Air Force
18 F-16C/D* 6 F-16A/B. 43 F-5E/F. 6 RF-5E. 70 A-4S/SU. 15 TA-4S/S-1 4 Fokker 50 Enforcer 2. 4 E-2C. 6 CH-47D*. 4 C-130H. 2 C-130H-30. 4 C-130B. 6 Skyvan 3M. 21 AS 332B/M. 24 UH-1B 16 UH-1H. 20 AS 550C-2/U-2. 29 S.211. 26 SF.260M/W.

SLOVAKIA
Air Force
15 MiG-29A/UB. 35 MiG-21MF. 8 MiG-21R. 14 MiG-21US/UM. 12 Su-25K/UBK. 20 Su-22M-4/U. 19 Mi-24. 26 Mi-8/17. 16 Mi-2. 9 L 410M/T/UVP. 20 L-39. 15 L-29. 4 An-24/26. 1 An-12. 1 Tu-154B.

SLOVENIA
Air Force
7 PC-9. 3 Bell 412ER. 1 A 109A 3 Zlin 242L. 3 UTVA 75. 1 Let L 410VP-E.

SOMALIA
Aeronautical Corps
Nominal strength includes MiG-21s, Shenyang F-6s and Hunters, but they are unlikely to be operational.

SOUTH AFRICA
Air Force
18 Mirage F1AZ. 16 Cheetah C. 14 Cheetah D. 19 Atlas Impala II. 30 Impala I. 5 707-320. 5 C-130B 5 C-130E*. 31 C-47/Turbo Dak. 1 Falcon 900. 2 Falcon 50. 5 HS.125-400B. 3 BN-2A. 5 Super King Air 200. 22 Cessna 185. 11 Cessna 208. 2 Citation II. 4 C-212. 1 CN-235. 60 PC-7 Mk II. 1 SA 365. 50 Oryx. 16 CSH-2*. 9 BK 117A-1/3. 58 Alouette III.

SOUTH KOREA
Air Force
64 F-4D. 59 F-4E. 18 RF-4C. 120 F-16C/D*. 39 F-16A/B. 20 Hawk 60. 197 F-5E/F. 47 F-5A/B. 94 KTX-2*. 27 A-37B. 38 T-33A. 42 T-37C. 20 T-28D. 20 T-41B. 11 Cessna O-2A. 20 CN-235*. 10 C-130H-30. 14 C-123J/K. 9 C-46F. 10 C-54D. 1 C-118A. 2 HS.748. 1 737-300. 2 Commander 520/560F. 5 DHC-2 Beaver. 26 O-1A/E. 3 AS 332L. 3 Bell 412. 7 Bell 212/UH-1N. 5 UH-1D/H.

Army Aviation
49 AH-1J/S/F. 17 CH-47D*. 81 UH-60P*. 62 UH-1B/H. 245 MD 500. 5 Kawasaki KH-4 (Bell 47G). 11 DHC-2 Beaver. 13 O-1A.

Naval Aviation
8 P-3C. 24 S-2A/E. 12 Lynx 99. 29 MD 500M/ASW. 12 Alouette III. 2 Bell 206B.

SPAIN
Air Force
14 RF-4C. 69 EF-18A/B. 24 F/A-18A*. 61 Mirage F-1C/E/B. 31 F-5A/B/RF. 7 P-3A/B. 3 F27 Maritime. 74 C-101B. 37 T-35C. 5 B55 Baron. 3 707-320. 5 KC-130H. 7 C-130H/H-30. 20 CN-235. 74 C-212. 15 CL-215T. 3 Falcon 20. 1 Falcon 50. 2 Falcon 900. 15 Hughes 269C/TH-55. 8 Sikorsky S-76. 5 SA 330. 16 AS 332. 2 Cessna Citation IV.

Naval Aviation
8 EAV-8B Plus. 10 EAV-8B. 3 Citation II. 11 SH-3H. 6 SH-60B. 10 AB 212. 10 Hughes 500M.

Army Aviation
48 UH-1H. 69 BO 105. 6 AB 212. 18 AS 332. 18 CH-47. 11 OH-58A.

SRI LANKA
Air Force
5 Kfir C2. 1 Kfir TC2. 4 F-7. 1 FT-7. 2 FT-5. 5 SF.260TP. 5 SF.260W. 1 Cessna 421. 1 Cessna 150. 1 King Air 200. 3 HS.748. 1 An-32. 6 Y-12. 1 Y-8. 6 Mi-24. 12 Bell 212. 2 Bell 412. 3 Bell 206B. 4 IA 58. 11 Mi-17. Numbers may have been affected by ongoing guerilla activity.

SUDAN
Air Force
12 F-7. 9 F-5E/F. 3 MiG-23. 8 MiG-21PF. 16 F-6. 7 F-5/FT-5. 3 Jet Provost 55. 3 Strikemaster. 4 MiG-15UTI. 4 MiG-21U. 5 C-130H. 5 An-24. 3 DHC-5D. 5 C-212. 1 F27-100. 6 EMB-110P. 1 Falcon 20.1 Falcon 50. 8 IAR 330 Puma. 11 AB 412. 2 Mi-24. 5 Mi-8. 4 Mi-4.

SURINAM
Air Force
1 PC-7. 3 BN-2B 1 Cessna 172. 1 Cessna 310. 1 Bell 205. 1 Alouette III.

SWEDEN
Air Force
204 JAS 39*. 133 JA 37. 26 AJS/AJ 37. 32 SF/SH 37. 50 J 35J. 2 Sk 35C. 6 S 100B. 107 Sk 60. 60 Sk 61 (Bulldog). 8 C-130E/H. 2 Tp 86 Sabreliner. 1 Tp 100 (Saab 340). 3 Tp 101 (King Air). 10 AS 332M-1. 3 Gulfstream IV. 12 Saab 340/FSR 890.

Naval Aviation
1 C-212. 3 PA-31. 14 BV 107/KV-107. 10 AB 206B.

Army Air Corps

16 AB 204B. 20 BO 105CB. 18 AB 206A. 25 Hughes 300C.

SWITZERLAND
Air Force

34 F/A-18C/D*. 101 F-5E/F. 45 Mirage III/S/ RS. 19 Hawk 60. 38 PC-7. 12 PC-9. 1 Falcon 50. 1 Learjet 36. 18 PC-6B. 2 Dornier Do 27. 15 AS 332M-1. 72 Alouette III.

SYRIA
Air Force

20 MiG-29/UB. 35 MiG-25/25R/25U. 80 MiG-23ML/MS. 50 MiG-23BN/UM. 210 MiG-21. 20 Su-24MK. 100 Su-20/22BKL. 90 L-39. 40 Flamingo. 4 Il-76T. 4 An-26. 2 An-24. 6 Il-14. 4 Il-18B. 6 Yak-40. 2 Falcon 20. 2 PA-31. 50 Mi-24. 110 Mi-8/17. 8 Mi-2. 56 SA 342.

Naval Aviation

2 Mi-14. 5 Ka-25.

TAIWAN
Air Force

130 A-1 Ching-Kuo*. 150 F-16A/B*. 60 Mirage 2000-5*. 304 F-5E/G. 36 F-5A/B. 21 T-38A. 60 AT-3/3B. 43 T-34C. 44 T-CH-1B. 4 E-2B. 12 C-130H. 40 C-119G Packet. 10 C-123. 1 DC-6B. 9 C-47. 11 Beech 1900C-1. 5 720B/727-100. 14 S-70C. 58 UH-1H. 30 TH-67*. 6 OH-6A. 10 Bell 47G/OH-13.

Army Aviation

3 BV-234 Chinook. 60 UH-1H. 8 AH-1W. 7 CH-34 Choctaw. 13 O-1.

Naval Aviation

32 S-2E/F. 20 S-70B. 11 MD 500MD/ASW.

TANZANIA
Defence Force

11 J-7. 10 J-6. 3 J-5. 2 MiG-15UTI. 5 PA-28. 4 DHC-5D. 3 HS.748. 1 Y-7. 2 Cessna 404. 7 Cessna 310. 1 Cessna 206. 2 F28. 1 BAe 125-700B. 4 AB 205B. 6 Bell 206.

THAILAND
Air Force

8 F/A-18C/D*. 36 F-16A/B. 38 F-5E/F. 1 RF-5A. 19 OV-10C. 3 AC-47. 22 AU-23. 4 T-33A. 3 RT-33A. 3 T-37B/C. 30 Fantrainer 400/600. 24 PC-9. 11 SF.260MT. 12 CT-4A. 7 C-130H. 5 C-130H-30. 6 G222. 2 CN-235. 3 C-123K. 8 HS.748. 15 C-47. 3 CASA C-212. 19 N22B. 3 IAI-201. 1 A310-300. 1 737-300. 2 Learjet 35A. 3 Merlin IVA. 7 Cessna T-41D. 28 Cessna O-1. 12 H-36 Dimona. 12 S-58T. 19 Bell UH-1H. 7 Bell 412. 5 Bell 212. 3 AS 332L2.

Naval Aviation

18 A-7E/TA-7E. 8 AV-8S. 2 TAV-8S. 2 P-3T. 1 UP-3T. 7 S-2F/US-2C. 3 F27 Maritime. 2 F27 400M. 6 Dornier 228. 2 CL-215. 11 Summit Sentry O-2-337. 5 N24A Searchmaster. 4 U-17A/B. 4 O-1A/E. 6 S-70B. 6 S-76N. 8 214ST. 5 212ASW. 4 UH-1H.

Army Aviation

2 C-212. 1 Jetstream 41. 2 Shorts 330UTT. 2 Beech 1900C. 2 King Air 200. 1 Beech 99. 10 T-41A. 60 O-1. 25 Maule. 10 Cessna U-17. 8 Cessna U-27A. 4 AH-1F. 3 CH-47C. 5 CH-47D. 56 Bell 212. 68 UH-1/D/H. 10 Bell 206A/B. 48 Schweizer TH-300.

Thai navy A-7Es and TA-7Es. Between them, Thailand's navy and air force operates F-16s, F-5s, A-7s and AV-8s. (Royal Thai Navy)

TOGO
Air Force

5 Alpha Jet. 4 EMB-326G. 3 Epsilon. 4 CM 170. 2 DHC-5D. 1 707-320B. 1 F28-3000. 2 Beech 58 Baron. 2 Reims-Cessna F337. 1 Dornier Do 27A-4. 1 AS 332L. 1 SA 330. 2 SA 315B. 1 SA 319.

TONGA
Air Wing

1 Beech 18.

TUNISIA
Air Force

15 F-5E/F. 10 MB-326B/K/L. 18 SF.260C/W. 2 C-130H. 12 L-59T*. 2 SIAI Marchetti S.208A. 15 AB-205A. 4 UH-1N/H. 5 SA 341. 6 SA 313. 6 AS 350B. 1 AS 365. 3 SA 316.

TURKEY
Air Force

144 F-4E. 40 RF-4E. 240 F-16C/D. 120 F-5A/B. 33 S-2A/E. 70 T-38A. 34 T-33A. 62 T-37B/C. 40 SF.260D. 7 KC-135R*. 13 C-130B/E. 19 C-160. 40+ C-47. 30 CN-235M. 1 Gulfstream IV. 3 Viscount 700. 4 Citation II. 2 BN-2A. 50+ UH-1H. 5 UH-19.

Army Aviation

40 Citabria 150S. 15 T-42A Baron. 19 Do 28D. 1 DHC-2. 28+ Bell 206. 50+ O-1. 10+ PA-18 Super Cub. 12 AH-1W. 185+ AB 205A/UH-1H. 20 AB 204B. 3 Bell 212. 20

AS 532UL. 39 AB 206A*. 30 Hughes 300C. 15+ AB 47G. 92 S-70A*. 28 AB 212/205/204.

Naval Aviation

16 AB 212ASW. 3 AB 204AS.

UGANDA
Army Air Force

4 MiG-17F. 1 AS 202 Bravo. 1 L-100. 1 Gulfstream II. 3 L-39. 5 SF.260. 2 Mi-8. 4 AB 412. 3 Bell 212/412. 3 AB 206.

UKRAINE
Air Force

19 Tu-160. 29 Tu-22M. 70 Tu-22. 28 Tu-95. 60 Su-27. 62 MiG-29. 205 Su-24. 35 Su-25. 40 Su-17. 30 Il-78M. 170 Il-76. Plus An-26 and other transport types as well as helicopters including 40 Mi-6, 40 Mi-14, 20 Mi-26.

UNITED ARAB EMIRATES
Abu Dhabi

35 Mirage 2000E/R/D. 29 Mirage VAD/RAD/ DAD. 18 Hawk 100. 16 Hawk 63. 23 PC-7. 4 C-130H. 5 DHC-5D. 4 C-212. 1 BN-2A. 10 AS 332F/L. 11 SA 330. 1 AS 350. 20 AH-64. 11 SA 342. 7 Alouette III. 1 AB-206B.

Dubai

3 MB-326KD 2 MB-326LD. 5 MB-339A. 8 Hawk 61. 5 SF.260TP. 2 L-100-30. 1 G222. 1 BN-2T. 2 PC-6B. 1 Cessna 182. 4 Bell 212 4 Bell 214B. 6 Bell 205A. 5 206B/AB-206A. 1 Bell 206L. 6 BO 105S.

Turkey's substantial fleet of almost 200 Phantoms includes about 40 RF-4Es. (MAP)

A 13 Squadron RAF Tornado GR.1 over the Yorkshire moors. Note the practice bomblets carried under the fuselage. (Sgt Rick Brewell RAF, UK Crown Copyright)

Sharjah Air Wing
1 Shorts 330. 3 Skyvan 3M. 2 BK 117. 3 Bell 206.

UNITED KINGDOM
Air Force
164 Tornado GR.1/GR.1A/GR.1B. 120 Tornado F.3. 52 Jaguar GR.1/T.2. 68 Harrier GR.7/T.10. 92 Hawk T.1/T.1A. 26 Nimrod MR.2. 2 Nimrod MR.1P. 7 Sentry AEW.1. 9 Canberra PR.9/T.4/PR.7. 9 TriStar K.1/KC.1/K.2./C.2/C.2A 14 VC10 K.2/K.3/K.4. 13 VC10 C.1/C.1K. 25 Hercules C.4/C.5*. 58 Hercules C.1/C.2/C.3. 3 BAe 146 C.2. 8 HS.125 CC.2/CC.3. 116 Bulldog T.1. 11 Dominie T.1. 10 Jetstream T.1. 66 Tucano T.1. 14 Chinook HC.2/HC.3. 35 Chinook HC.1/2. 22 Merlin HC.3*. 37 Puma HC.1. 25 Sea King HAR.3/3A. 15 Wessex HC.2. 9 Griffin HT.1. 38 Squirrel HT.1/HT.2. 35 Gazelle HT.3/HCC 4.
Navy Fleet Air Arm
26 Sea Harrier F/A.2. 7 Harrier T.4/T.8. 6 Hawk T.1. 12 Jetstream T.2/3. 60 Sea King HAS 5/6. 9 Sea King AEW.2. 33 Sea King HC.4. 58 Lynx HAS.3/8. 6 Lynx AH.7. 9 Gazelle AH.1. 17 Gazelle HT.2/3.
Army Air Corps
67 WAH-64D*. 100 Lynx AH.1/7. 24 Lynx AH.9. 164 Gazelle AH.1. 7 Islander AL.1. 21 Chipmunk T.10. 4 A 109A.

USA
Air Force
21 B-2A*. 81 B-1B. 85 B-52H. 620 F-15/F-15E. 810 F-16. 53 F-117. 21 MiG-29. 223 A-10/OA-10. 21 AC-130. 2 SR-71. 35 U-2R/TU-2R. 19 RC-135. 81 C-5A/B. 2 VC-25. 140 C-17*. 59 KC-10. 154 C-141/NC-141. 5 C-137. 4 C-32A*. 6 C-135. 253 KC-135. 23 C-9. 16 C-130J*. 200 C-130E/H. 10 C-27. 76 C-21. 3 C-23. 36 C-12. 4 E-4. 32 E-3. 4 EC-18. 20 E-8*. 1 EC-137. 16 EC-135. 22 EC-130. 2 E-9. 55 MC-130. 4 NC-130. 2 OC-135. 2 NKC-135. 450 T-38/AT-38. 420 T-37. 160 T-1A. 112 T-3. 1 T-39. 10 T-43/CT-43. 2 UV-18. 70 HH-1/UH-1. 49 HH-53/MH-53. 45 HH-60. 13 MH-60.
Air Force Reserve
9 B-52H. 73 F-16A/B/C/D. 51 A/OA-10. 32 C-5A. 46 C-141B. 72 KC-135E/R. 141 C-130E/H. 23 HH-60G.
Air National Guard
14 B-1B. 116 F-15. 631 F-16. 101 A-10. 13 C-5. 3 C-22. 18 C-141. 242 C-130. 4 C-21. 40 C-26. 224 KC-135. 2 T-43. 18 HH-60.
Navy
225 F-14A. 79 F-14B. 49 F-14D. 545 F/A-18. 11 F-16N. 3 TF-16N. 37 F-5E/F. 128 EA-6B. 254 P-3C. 130 S-3A/B. 17 C-130F/T. 9 KC-130. 7 LC-130F/R. 5 VP-3A. 6 C-20D/G.

7 CT-39E/G. 2 C-28A. 38 C-2A. 29 C-9. 94 E-2C. 16 E-6A. 1 EC-24A. 10 EP-3E/J. 16 ES-3A. 3 DC-130A. 10 UP-3A/B. 5 US-3A. 85 U-21A. 2 U-6A. 62 UC-12B/F/M. 4 RC-12F/M. 1 RP-3A. 30 T-45A. 125 TA-4J. 133 T-2C. 319 T-34C. 8 T-38A. 11 TP-3A. 2 TC-130G/Q. 1 T-39D. 57 T-44A. 4 TC-4C. 1 TE-2C. 39 CH-53E. 28 CH-46D. 17 CH-46E. 43 HH-1N. 43 HH-46D. 24 HH-60H. 45 MH-53E. 4 OH-58A. 6 OH-6B. 3 OV-10A. 19 RH-53D. 23 SH-2G. 52 SH-3D/G/H. 236 SH-60B/F. 95 TH-57B/C. 50 UH-3A/H. 13 UH-46D. 3 UH-60A. 4 VH-3A. This listing does not include stored, experimental, evaluation or test aircraft.
Marine Corps
216 F/A-18A/B/C/D. 72 F/A-18D Night Attack. 13 F-5E/F. 166 AV-8B. 26 AV-8B/TAV-8B. 20 EA-6B. 2 C-9B. 60 KC-130F/R/T. 8 KC-130F/R/T. 1 C-20G. 18 UC-12B/F. 155 AH-1W. 38 CH-53D. 112 CH-53E. 20 CH-53D/E. 224 CH-46E. 3 CT-39A/D/G. 108 UH-1N. 11 VH-3D. 8 VH-60N.
Army Aviation
458 AH-64A. 430 AH-1E/F/G/P/S. 307 OH-58D. 224 OH-58A/C. 40 AH-6C/G/MH-6B/E/H. 211 CH-47D. 904 UH-60A/L. 67 EH-60A. 50 MH-60. 317 UH-1H/V. 157 TH-67A*. 2 F27-400. 3 UC-35. 45 C-12. 42 RC-12D/H/K. 4 U-21. 2 UV-20.
Army National Guard & Army Reserve
192 AH-64A. 347 AH-1E/F/G/P/S. 229 OH-58A/C. 373 UH-60. 84 C-12. 4 C-20. 3 C-21. 43 C-23. 3 RC-12. 4 UC-35.

URAGUAY
Air Force
11 A-37B. 7 T-33A. 5 IA-58B. 3 C-130B. 4 EMB-110. 3 C-212. 1 F27. 8 Queenair. 5 U-17. 11 T-34A/B. 5 T-41D. 5 PC-7U. 2 Cessna 182. 2 Bell 212. 3 UH-1H.
Naval Aviation
4 S-2A/G. 1 Super King Air 200T. 2 T-28S Fennec (Trojan). 2 T-34B. 2 T-34C. 1 PA-34-200T. 1 Cessna 182 Skylane. 2 PA-18. 3 Wessex 60. 2 Bell 47G.

VENEZUELA
Air Force
24 F-16A/B. 15 Mirage 50EV/DV. 18 CF-5A/D. 6 NF-5A. 22 OV-10E. 19 T-2D. 30 EMB-312. 13 T-34A. 1 707-320C. 1 737-200. 1 DC-9-15. 5 C-130H. 8 G222. 3 Gulfstream II/III/IV. 3 Falcon 20D. 2 Learjet 24D. 4 Citation I/II. 4 Super King Air 200. 7 Queenair. 1 PA-31 Navajo. 2 Beech TravelAir. 11 Cessna 182N. 8 AS 332M-1. 8 412/214ST. 1 212. 15 UH-1D. 15 Alouette III.
Naval Aviation
1 Dash 7. 4 C-212-200AS. 1 King Air 90. 1 Cessna 402C. 2 Cessna 310R. 1 PA-23. 12 AB 212ASW.
Army Aviation
5 IAI-201. 1 Super King Air 200. 1 King Air 90. 1 Queenair. 1 BN-2A. 4 172/182. 4 AS-61A. 7 UH-1H/205A. 2 206B/L. 6 A 109A.
National Guard
6 IAI-201. 1 King Air 200. 1 King Air 90. 2 Queen Air. 2 BN-2. 1 Cessna 402C. 1 Baron. 2 Cessna 337. 1 Cessna 206. 11 AS 355. 1 214ST. 5 206. 1 206L. 5 A 109.

US Navy Grumman F-14s of VF-31 'The Tomcatters' on the flightline at NAS Oceana, Virginia Beach. (John Sise)

(right) Zimbabwe uses its Hawk 60s for advanced training, interception (note the Sidewinder) and ground attack. (BAe)

VIETNAM
Army Air Force
12 Su-27. 8 MiG-23ML/UM. 18 F-5A/B/E/RF-5A. 150 MiG-21PF/bis. 77 MiG-17F. 73 Su-22BKL. 30 Su-17. 5 A-37B. 12 Be-12. 15 MiG-15UTI. 25 L-39. 33 Yak-11/18. 5 C-130A/B. 40 An-26. 9 An-24. 12 Il-14. 2 Il-18. 24 Li-2/C-47. 20 An-2. 11 Yak-40. 30 Mi-24. 16 Ka-25. 66 Mi-8. 10 Mi-6. 36 Mi-4.

YEMEN
Air Force
22 MiG-23BN. 29 MiG-21. 14 F-5E/B. 44 MiG-17F. 57 Su-22BKL/M-2/U. 4 MiG-15UTI. 18 Yak-11. 2 C-130H. 1 An-12B. 13 An-24/26. 8 Il-14. 14 Mi-24. 56 Mi-8. 6 AB 212. 2 AB 204B. 5 Mi-4. 6 AB 206B.

FEDERAL REPUBLIC OF YUGOSLAVIA
Air Force
13 MiG-29A/B. 60 MiG-21. 26 J-1. 45 G-4M. 65 J-22. 12 An-12. 6 An-26. 9 Il-14. 4 Il-18. 6 Yak-40. 2 707-320C. 2 Falcon 50. 14 PC-6. 35 UTVA-75. 44 Mi-8/-17. 65 SA 342. 5 Ka-25. 3 Ka-28. 14 Mi-14.

ZAIRE
Air Force
6 MB-326K. 9 MB-326GB. 20 F337. 9 SF.260MZ. 4 C-130H. 3 DHC-5D. 6 C-47. 1 BN-2A. 1 MU-2J. 11 Cessna 310R. 12 Cessna 150. 1 AS 332. 9 SA 330. 7 Alouette III. 6 Bell 47G. Operational status of some of these aircraft unknown.

ZAMBIA
Air Force
12 MiG-21MF. 2 MiG-21U. 12 F-6. 2 FT-5. 16 MB-326GB. 12 G-2. 8 SF.260MZ. 4 C-47. 4 An-26. 2 DC-6B. 3 DHC-4. 4 DHC-5D. 7 Do 28. 1 HS.748. 3 Yak-40. 12 Mi-8. 9 AB 205A/AB 212. 12 AB 47G. Operational status of some of these aircraft unknown.

ZIMBABWE
Air Force
12 F-7. 1 FT-7. 6 Hunter FGA.9. 11 Hawk 60/60A. 15 Reims-Cessna C337G. 23 SF.260M/W/TP. 12 C-212. 5 BN-2A. 2 AS 532UL. 8 AB 412. 2 AB 205. 25 SA 319.

GLOSSARY OF TERMS AND ACRONYMS

AAA – Anti aircraft artillery.

AAC – Army Air Corps (UK).

AAM – Air-to-air missile.

ABM – Anti ballistic missile. A missile capable of destroying hostile ballistic missiles or their payloads before they impact on their target.

ACC – Air Combat Command (USAF).

ACM – Air combat manoeuvring.

ACMI – Air combat manoeuvring instrumentation.

ACMR – Air combat manoeuvring range.

ADF – Australian Defence Force.

ADIZ – Air defence identification zone.

AEW – Airborne early warning.

AEW&C – Airborne early warning and control.

AF – Air force.

AFB – Air force base (US).

AFMC – Air Force Materiel Command (USAF).

ALBM – Air launched ballistic missile.

ALCM – Air launched cruise missile.

AMC – Air Mobility Command (USAF).

Amraam – Advanced medium range air-to-air missile, the Hughes AIM-120.

ANG – Air National Guard (USA).

APU – Auxiliary power unit.

ARM – Anti Radiation missile.

ASM – Air-to-surface missile.

ASPJ – Airborne self protection jammer.

Asraam – Advanced short range air-to-air missile. An IR guided missile under development by BAe.

AST – Air staff target.

ASTOVL – Advanced short takeoff and vertical landing

ASV – Anti surface vessel.

ASW – Anti submarine warfare. All measures designed to reduce or nullify the effectiveness of hostile submarines.

ASuW – Anti surface warfare.

ATBM – Anti tactical ballistic missile.

AUW – All up weight.

AWACS – Airborne Warning and Control System. In particular refers to Boeing E-3 Sentry.

BAe – British Aerospace.

BVR – Beyond visual range.

C2 – Command and control.

C3 – Command, control and communications.

C3I – Command, control, communications and intelligence.

CAF – Canadian Armed Forces, now Canadian Forces.

CAP – Combat air patrol.

CAS – Close air support.

CDU – Control display unit.

CEA – Circular error average.

CEP – Circular Error Probable. A measure of the accuracy of missiles or bombs, the CEP is the radius of a circle in which half the shots are statistically likely to fall.

CF – Canadian Forces.

CFE – Conventional Forces Europe.

CIWS – Close-In Weapon System (US).

COIN – Counter insurgency.

CRT – Cathode ray tube.

CV – Attack aircraft carrier, conventionally powered (US).

CVN – Attack aircraft carrier, nuclear powered (US).

DA – Dalnyaya Aviatsiya, Long Range Aviation, Russian AF command in charge of strategic bombers.

DEW – Distant early warning (US).

DFC – Distinguished Flying Cross: air force decoration.

DGPS – Differential GPS.

DoD – Department of Defence.

DVI – Direct Voice Input.

ECCM – Electronic counter countermeasures. A form of electronic warfare designed to overcome enemy use of ECM and thus continue to make effective use of the electromagnetic spectrum.

ECM – Electronic countermeasures. A form of electronic warfare designed totally or partially to prevent effective use by the enemy of part of the electromagnetic spectrum.

ECR – Electronic combat reconnaissance, SEAD Panavia Tornado variant.

EFIS – Electronic flight instrument system.

ELINT – Electronic intelligence. Intelligence derived from enemy electronic transmissions other than telecommunications (ie radar).

Endurance – The length of time an aircraft's fuel load will permit it to remain airborne.

ESM – Electronic support measures.

EW – Electronic warfare • Early warning.

FA – Frontal Aviation, Russian AF command in charge of tactical fighters.

FAA – Fleet Air Arm (UK, Aus) • Fuerza Aerea Argentina, Argentine AF.

FAB – Forca Aera Brasileira, Brazilian AF.

FAC – Forward air control/forward air controller • Fuerza Aerea de Chile, Chilean AF • Fuerza Aerea Colombiana, Colombian AF.

FAE – Fuel air explosives • Fuerza Aerea Ecuatoriana, Ecuadorian AF.

FBW – Fly-by-wire (electronic signalling of flight controls).

fire and forget missile – AAM or ASM with self guiding capability.

FLIR – Forward looking infrared.

fly-by-wire – Flight-control system with electric signalling.

FMS – Foreign military sale (US).

g – Force of gravity.

GAM – GPS-Aided Munition. Mk 82 bombs with a GPS guidaince tail kit, developed for the B-2.

GCA – Ground controlled approach. An instrument approach procedure provided by a ground controller on the basis of radar displays. The aircraft is 'talked down' to within sight of the runway when weather conditions would otherwise preclude a safe landing. This predates ILS.

GCI – Ground-controlled intercept.

GE – General Electric.

GPS – Global positioning system. A worldwide system by which the user can derive his position by receiving signals from navigation Satellites.

HF – High frequency: 3 to 30 MHz.

HOTAS – Hands on throttle and stick.

HOTCC – Hands on throttle, collective and cyclic.

hp – horsepower

hr – Hour/s

HUD – Head-up display.

HUDWAC – HUD weapon aiming computer.

HUDWASS – HUD weapon aiming subsystem.

IADS – Integrated air defence system.

IAS – Indicated airspeed shown on the airspeed indicator, when corrected for instrument error.

... ...mental ballistic missile. Land based missile with range ... 5600km (3000nm).

IFF – Identification friend or foe.

IGE – In ground effect.

ILS – Instrument landing system.

Imp – Imperial (UK).

INS – Inertial navigation system. A navigation system in which displacement from the point of departure is determined by measuring the acceleration exerted upon a gyroscopically stabilised platform by vehicle movement.

IOC – Initial operational capability. Date when a weapon system can be considered capable of being used by troops even though not fully developed and troops not fully trained (US).

IR – Infrared.

IRAN – Inspect and Repair As Necessary.

IRBM – Intermediate range ballistic missile. Land based missile with range of 2780km (1500nm) to 5600km (3000nm).

IRCM – Infrared countermeasure.

ISA – International Standard Atmosphere.

IRS – Inertial reference system.

IRST – Infrared search and track.

JASDF – Japan Air Self Defence Force.

JAST – Joint Advanced Strike Technology.

JDAM – Joint Direct Attack Munition. INS and GPS guidance kits for conventional bombs. Mk 84 with JDAM is GBU-31.

JGSDF – Japan Ground Self Defence Force.

JMSDF – Japan Maritime Self Defence Force.

Joint-STAR – Joint Surveillance Target Attack Radar System, as in Northrop Grumman E-8.

JSOW – Joint Stand-Off Weapon. Currently being developed in GPS/INS guided AGM-154 form.

JSF – Joint Strike Fighter (USA), replaced JAST. A current program to find a multirole fighter for the USAF, USN, USMC and RN.

JTIDS – Joint Tactical Information Distribution System.

KCAS – Calibrated airspeed in knots.

kg – Kilogram/s.

KIAS – Knots indicated airspeed.

km – Kilometre.

km/h – Kilometres per hour.

kN – KiloNewton (1000 Newtons, 1 Newton = 0.2248lb of force).

Knot – Aviation and maritime unit of velocity. 1 knot = 1 nautical mile per hour.

KT – Kiloton. Explosive yield equivalent in effect to 1000 tons of TNT.

Kt/kt – Knot/s

KTAS – True airspeed in knots.

kW – KiloWatt. SI measure of power.

LAMPS – Light airborne multi purpose system (US).

LANTIRN – Low altitude targeting infrared for night.

LABS – Low Altitude Bombing System.

LAPES – Low Altitude Parachute Extraction System.

lb – Pounds, either of mass or thrust.

LCD – Liquid crystal display.

LF – Low frequency: 30 to 300 kHz.

LGB – Laser guided bomb.

LO – Low observables, ie stealth.

LRMP – Long range maritime patrol aircraft.

LZ – Landing zone.

Mach number, M – Ratio of true airspeed to speed of sound in surrounding air (which varies as square root of absolute temperature). In standard conditions, the speed of sound (Mach 1) is 1223km/h (661kt) at sea level and 1063km/h (575kt) at 36,000ft.

MAC – Military Airlift Command, now AMC (USAF).

MAD – Magnetic Anomaly Detector. ASW equipment designed to detect disturbances in the Earth's magnetic field.

MAP – Military Assistance Program (USA).

MAW – Marine Air Wing (USMC).

MCM – Mine countermeasures.

MFD – Multi Function Display.

min – Minute/s.

MLU – Mid life update.

MoD – Ministry of Defence.

MPA – Maritime patrol aircraft.

MR – Maritime reconnaissance.

MRBM – Medium range ballistic missile. Land based missile with range of 1100km (600nm) to 2780km (1500nm).

MSIP – Multi Stage Improvement Program (US).

MTOW – Maximum takeoff weight.

NAS – Naval air station.

NASA – National Aeronautics & Space Administration (US).

NATO – North Atlantic Treaty Organisation. Current members are Belgium, Canada, Denmark, France, Germany, Greece, Iceland, Luxembourg, Netherlands, Norway, Portugal, Spain, Turkey, UK, USA.

Nautical mile – Unit of measurement of distance. 1nm is one minute of great circle of the earth, standardised at 6080ft (1853m) but actually varying with latitude from 6046ft to 6108ft (1842 to 1861m).

nav/attack system – One offering either pilot guidance or direct command of aircraft to ensure accurate navigation and weapon delivery against surface target.

nm – Nautical mile.

OCU – Operational Conversion Unit.

OGE – Out of ground effect; supported by lifting rotor(s) in free air with no land surface in proximity.

OTH-B – Over-the-Horizon Backscatter Radar. This transmits signals that extend beyond the line-of-sight along the ground. Range is of the order of 2900km (1570nm).

OTHR – Over-the-horizon radar.

OTHT – Over the horizon targeting.

PACAF – Pacific Air Force (USAF).

Passive – Not itself emitting. Usually used when describing detection devices which do not use electro-magnetic emissions to operate. They cannot be detected in the way that 'active' devices can.

Payload – Weapon and/or cargo capacity of an aircraft or missile.

PGM – Precision guided munition.

PID – Passive identification device.

PNGDF – Papua New Guinea Defence Force.

PVO – Protivo-Vozdushnoy Oborony, Air Defence Force, the independent Russian military service equipped with interceptors and SAMs.

R&D – Research and development.

RAAF – Royal Australian Air Force.

RAAWS – Radar altimeter and altitude warning system.

RAF – Royal Air Force (UK).

RAM – Radar absorbing material.

RAN – Royal Australian Navy.

RAST – Recovery assist, secure and (deck) traverse system.

RATO – Rocket assisted takeoff.

RCS – Radar cross section.

Recce – Reconnaissance.

RMAF – Royal Malaysian Air Force.

RN – Royal Navy (UK).

RNeAF – Royal Netherlands Air Force.

RNZAF – Royal New Zealand Air Force.

ROE – Rules of Engagement.

RoKAF – Republic of Korea Air Force (Sth Korea).

RPV – Remotely piloted vehicle.

RR – Rolls-Royce.

RSAF – Republic of Singapore Air Force • Royal Saudi AF.

RWR – Radar warning receiver.

SAAF – South African Air Force.

SAC – Strategic Air Command (USAF, merged into ACC).

SAM – Surface-to-air missile.

SAR – Search and rescue.

SEAD – Suppression of enemy air defences.

SENSO – Sensor operator.

SLAR – Side looking airborne radar.

Sigint – Signals intelligence.

Smart – Device possessing precision guidance. Normally used to describe ASMs and bombs with terminal guidance to differentiate them from iron or gravity bombs.

Sonobuoy – A small sonar device dropped by aircraft into the sea. The device floats for several hours and transmits information to the aircraft above. It then sinks automatically to prevent retrieval by a hostile agency.

SSM – Surface-to-surface missile.

SRAM & SRAM II – Cancelled Short Range Attack Missiles (nuclear) for the B-2 Spirit.

Stealth – Stealth (or low observables) technology is used to render aircraft or satellites invisible or near invisible to visual, radar or infrared detection. The Northrop Grumman B-2 Spirit and the Lockheed F-117 Nighthawk are stealth aircraft.

STO – Short takeoff

STOL – Short takeoff and landing.

STOVL – Short Takeoff Vertical Landing.

TAC – Tactical Air Command (USAF, now merged into ACC).

TACAMO – Take Charge And Move Out.

TACAN – Tactical Aid to Navigation. Military UHF navaid.

TACCO – Tactical coordinator.

TANS – Tactical Air Navigation System.

TBO – Time Between Overhauls.

TFR – Terrain following radar.

TIALD – Target Identification Airborne Laser Designation.

TNI-AU – Tentara Nasional Indonesia-Angkatan Udara, Indonesian AF.

TOW – Tube launched, Optically tracked, Wire guided. Anti armour missile.

TSSAM – Tri Service Stand-Off Attack Missile. Cancelled stealthy stand-off weapon.

UAV – Unmanned aerial vehicle.

UHF – Ultra-high frequency: 300MHz to 3GHz.

UN – United Nations.

USAF – United States Air Force.

USAFE – US Air Forces in Europe.

USMC – United States Marine Corps.

USN – United States Navy.

VHF – Very high frequency: 3 to 300MHz.

V/STOL – Vertical or short takeoff and landing.

VTAS – Voice, throttle and stick.

VTOL – Vertical takeoff and landing.

VVS RF – Voenno-Vozdushniye Sily Rossiskoi Federatsii, the Russian Federation Air Force.

WSO – Weapon system operator (occasionally weapon systems officer).

zero-zero seat – Ejection seat qualified for operation at zero height, zero airspeed; ie pilot can safely eject from parked aircraft.

INDEX

Workbook

News Reporting and Writing

Melvin Mencher

Professor Emeritus, Columbia University

Workbook

Ninth Edition

News Reporting and Writing

Melvin Mencher
Professor Emeritus, Columbia University

Boston   Burr Ridge, IL   Dubuque, IA   Madison, WI   New York   San Francisco   St. Louis
Bangkok   Bogotá   Caracas   Kuala Lumpur   Lisbon   London   Madrid   Mexico City
Milan   Montreal   New Delhi   Santiago   Seoul   Singapore   Sydney   Taipei   Toronto

McGraw-Hill Higher Education
*A Division of The **McGraw-Hill** Companies*

Workbook for use with
NEWS REPORTING AND WRITING

1 2 3 4 5 6 7 8 9 0 QPD/QPD 9 0 9 8 7 6 5 4 3 2

ISBN 0-07-249195-7

http://www.mhhe.com

Contents

Preface

This *Workbook* provides material for you to sharpen your journalistic skills and to broaden the background essential for the practice of journalism. The material covers the wide range of journalism. You are asked to cover speeches, write obituaries, and report accidents and fires.

Six types of work are offered:

Exercises: All the facts are supplied. The exercises can be done in class or at home.

Assignments: You are asked to observe events, interview sources, provide background.

Projects: Two types are offered, one for reporting events on campus, the other for reporting in your city. Some projects involve team reporting.

Home Assignments: Writing that can be done on your own time.

Class Discussion: Media topics.

Skill Drill: Short answer quizzes.

You will write stories in a variety of styles—newspaper, broadcast, online news service. Each of the writing tasks is identified by a *slug,* one or two words that describe the story. Put the slug at the top of your story under your name. Some of the slugs in the *Workbook* have an identifying icon that describes the nature of the work:

 indicates you are to conduct a survey or poll.

 indicates the assignment is based on material in the textbook *News Reporting and Writing.*

 indicates you are to write for an online news service, www.freenews.com.

Unless otherwise indicated, the Exercises are set in our city of Freeport. A map of Freeport, two city directories and a source list are included at the back of the *Workbook.*

How to Use the Freeport Map, City Directories and Source List

1. An exercise may refer to the superintendent of schools without naming the official. Your story should include his name, which you can find by consulting the **Freeport Source List** under *Freeport School Officials.* You'll find his name is Herbert Gilkeyson.
2. You may be told in an exercise that Anne Downey was injured in an automobile accident. Because addresses are an essential part of a person's full identification, you would consult the **Freeport Directory** to find her address, 165 Vincent St.

3. Your instructor may give you an exercise about a fire located at State Highway 166 and U.S. 81 and ask you how you would handle the assignment if you were on deadline. You would, of course, call the fire department for information. You would also want an on-the-scene account if it were a big fire. Because you could not take the time to go there, you might call people who live nearby. Using the **Freeport Map** and the **Freeport Cross Directory,** you can locate someone to call.

Consulting the map, you would find the intersection is at the southern edge of town and that Hunter Avenue is the city continuation of U.S. 81. The map shows that a place known as Three Corners Junction is in the vicinity.

You would use the **Freeport Cross Directory** to find an address on Hunter Avenue. The first entry, 4700 Hunter Ave., lists a Three Corners Cafe. You would call the Cafe to find someone who can describe the fire for you while another reporter and a photographer are on the way.

PART ONE

The Reporter at Work

1 On the Job

Wayne Miller

'How fast was he going?'

Introduction

Journalists say that before they begin writing they think a story through to decide what they will write. They review the material that they have gathered and draft a writing plan. This helps them know how to begin a story and how they will end it. The writing plan may consist of a short written outline, or it may be a mental picture of the story. Some writers number their notes in the order in which the material is to be placed in the story. Adopt whatever approach works best for you. Not all writing plans work out. Sometimes, a rewrite is necessary.

Editing Your Copy

Before handing in their work, writers correct errors they may have made in grammar, punctuation, spelling and word usage. They check to see that their copy conforms to the stylebook for abbreviations, capitalizations and the like. Names, addresses and titles are double-checked for accuracy in the directories. Stories are always given a final read before they are handed in.

On the next page are the copy editor's marks you can use if you pencil-edit your work.

Exercises I

A. Kliff

A 22-year-old man was chared with reclessly driving last night after a high-speed chase from Pleasant Valley road, up

albright Avenue to the driveway of his home.

The man, Paul A. Kliff, 22, of 29 Tudor St., was to be arranged on district court today.

Police said a Police Cruiser gave chase when the suspect's auto was seen speeding on Valley Rd. When it was stopped

finally in the driveway at Tudor St., police said, Kliff removed himself of his auto and began to struggle with officers as a crowd

of people gathered.

capitalize	U.S. district court judge Frank	District Court Judge
transpose / insert word	J. Broyles will hear arguments oral Monday	oral arguments / Monday
delete word and close up	on a suit Monday filed by a woman	suit filed
correction	who wants to build a new MontAssori	Montessori
new paragraph	School in east Freeport. Jane	
lowercase / separate	Fraker Levine, President of a	president / of a
insert apostrophe / insert comma	childrens group filed suit last week	children's / group, filed
delete letter and close up	alledging that city officials illegally	alleging
separate / bring together	revoked a building permit she said s he	revoked a / she
spell out	obtained last July from the (CHA) for	City Housing Authority
abbreviate	the school at 301 Oregon (Avenue.)	Ave.
abbreviate	In January, the (City Housing Authority)	CHA
use figures	said it had (eleven) objections but	11
retain / addition	decided to issue anyway. (stet) the permit	to / the permit

Copy Editing Marks

B. Dumped

Michael Canzian, deputy A. G., charged today that the states' menatl institutions are being used as "dumping grounds for senior citzens and alcoholocs."

Canzian estimaed that it costs the state approximately $15,000 a year for each mental patient now "incarcerated" in State institutions over the state. He said the attorney generl's affice has filed suit against sveral hospitals to call attention to the situation. He hopes that the suits will go to trial in the spring of next year.

"Too many people whose only problem is ther age have been sent to mental homes", he said in a talk to the Golden Years Club at its clubhouse at 56 Forester Road.

C. Spring

A menu of wet snow, slush and rain—gurnished with glum and fog—was dished up to Maryland residents today as the state struggled to switch from winter to Spring.

Whereas most of the state was doused with rain, northwestern areas recieved not-unsubstantial amounts of snow. The record for the sudden return to winter was May 9, of 1977, when the regeion recieved eleven inches, an event that caused power failures and alot of traffic problems throughout the state.

State police said there was no major traffic problems state-wise. Sanding crews took care of the slush and ice that piled up on highways police said.

D. Trees

The planing of trees on long-barren city streets will be slowed considerably this year because the amount of federal funds available for the work of planting is much less than last year, when almost 3,000 street trees were planted throughout the city.

City Forester John T. Voboril said he hopes to plant about 1,000 trees this year, but he said he is not sure that enough money will be available to reach that goal of 1000 tree plantings.

Because of this uncertainty, Voboril said he has temporarily halted work on a survey to ascertain which streets are most in need of new trees.

Last year the city used a $400 thousand dollar public works grant from the Federal Government to pay for about 2,000 trees, and planted about 1,000 more with funds provided by the Mayor's office of Community Development (MOCD).

But the Federal Government is not offering public works grants this year. So the city has to rely solely on its community development fund for tree plantings.

Voboril said he requested $200,000 from the development office for street trees, enough for about 1,000 plantings. But has not been told yet whether he will get this amount.

E. Various

1.   "You can not flaunt the will of the people", Gov. Janet Kocieniewski warned the state legislator today. Last week, she said, the democrats hung themselves when they vetoed her welfare program. In her last press conference, the governors face turned livid in response to reporters questions. She pointed out she became nauseous when she read reports that her administration was running a gauntlet of public criticism, "we are doing a good job," she said, adding that she is confident her staff is performing good.
2.   The university accepted the bid of Haight & Sons Co. for the construction of a new facility to store atheletic equipment. The sight will be near the gym.
3.   For desert, he not only ate the pie but also 2 bowlfuls of Jello.
4.   Polce said J. Frank Pounder, 38, is wanted for the murder of Mr. and Mrs. Arthur B. Harris. The Harris's were found dead yesterday in the bedroom of their home, 123 Western Avenue. A large amount of money, between $2–$3000 dollars was taken, police said, in giving robbery as a possible motive for the mishap.
5.   From the group of fifty who took the test, there were only three who received As, the professor said. They included Arthur b. Able, J. Frank Rodgers, and Roberta Redford.

Skill Drill I: Spelling (1)

The 50 words that follow are among the most frequently misspelled. Without checking the dictionary, circle the correct spelling. Put a mark next to the words whose spelling you would usually check in a dictionary.

_____	1. (a) municipal	(b) municiple		_____	26. (a) belief	(b) beleif
_____	2. (a) cemetery	(b) cemetary		_____	27. (a) privilege	(b) priviledge
_____	3. (a) indispensable	(b) indispensible		_____	28. (a) predjudice	(b) prejudice
_____	4. (a) occurrence	(b) occurence		_____	29. (a) their	(b) thier
_____	5. (a) villain	(b) villian		_____	30. (a) grammer	(b) grammar
_____	6. (a) exhillirate	(b) exhilarate		_____	31. (a) accommodate	(b) accomodate
_____	7. (a) irresistible	(b) irresistable		_____	32. (a) barberous	(b) barbarous
_____	8. (a) consensus	(b) concensus		_____	33. (a) athelete	(b) athlete
_____	9. (a) committment	(b) commitment		_____	34. (a) preceed	(b) precede
_____	10. (a) nuclear	(b) nuculear		_____	35. (a) arguement	(b) argument
_____	11. (a) pronunciation	(b) pronounciation		_____	36. (a) harrass	(b) harass
_____	12. (a) existance	(b) existence		_____	37. (a) repetition	(b) repitition
_____	13. (a) illiterate	(b) iliterate		_____	38. (a) definately	(b) definitely
_____	14. (a) liaison	(b) liason		_____	39. (a) disasterous	(b) disastrous
_____	15. (a) nineth	(b) ninth		_____	40. (a) exagerate	(b) exaggerate
_____	16. (a) dissention	(b) dissension		_____	41. (a) achievement	(b) acheivement
_____	17. (a) develement	(b) development		_____	42. (a) vaccum	(b) vacuum
_____	18. (a) desireable	(b) desirable		_____	43. (a) apparent	(b) apparant
_____	19. (a) occasion	(b) occassion		_____	44. (a) conscience	(b) concience
_____	20. (a) nickle	(b) nickel		_____	45. (a) dependant	(b) dependent
_____	21. (a) alot	(b) a lot		_____	46. (a) forty	(b) fourty
_____	22. (a) referring	(b) refering		_____	47. (a) embarrass	(b) embarass
_____	23. (a) seperate	(b) separate		_____	48. (a) interpetation	(b) interpretation
_____	24. (a) similar	(b) similir		_____	49. (a) assistant	(b) assisstant
_____	25. (d) receive	(b) recieve		_____	50. (a) allotted	(b) alotted

Skill Drill II: Grammar, Punctuation and Style

Each of these sentences contains a writing error of some kind. Rewrite each sentence to eliminate the error in grammar, spelling, punctuation, style or usage.

A. Grammar

1. Leaping on his back, the horse galloped into the circus ring to applause.
2. The cook found he had no salt, he immediately stalked out of the kitchen.
3. Oil is it's leading export.
4. All departments lost business last year. Except furnishings and hardware.
5. He shot at the fleeing man. Hoping to hit him in the leg.
6. He said he was feeling alright but was still a little dizzy from the trip.
7. He looked up at the planes. Straining to see the biplane he had been told was performing.
8. The plane went into a spin. Which thrilled everyone.
9. Its too late to help, he said.
10. Everyone hoped they could help.
11. The team played as though they wanted to win.
12. Before typing his story, the notes were arranged.

B. Punctuation

1. The two men each of whom had a hat pulled over his eyes entered the store.
2. To confuse them the owner busied himself at the rear.
3. He asked "What do you want?"
4. "Nothing." the taller one answered.
5. The childrens', mens', and womens' departments lost money last year.

4

6. He took James's books and ran.
7. He asked who's book it is.
8. "Why do you want to know," he asked?
9. The question—which was shot out like a bullet, left him dazed.
10. He enjoyed daydreaming, but some people thought him a little "strange."

C. Style, Word Usage

1. Clarity is a major principal in good writing, he said.
2. To weak writers, the proper words are often illusive.
3. Nevertheless, even weak writers like to be complemented on their work.
4. One of the marks of a weak writer is a lose style.
5. She ordered a box of monogrammed stationary.
6. Police discovered the convict's horde of bonds in a cellar.
7. Some products domineer the marketplace.
8. Milton's percentage of Anglo-Saxon words was 81, with 90 for Shakespeare, and the King James Bible runs around 94 percent.
9. This doesn't mean a writer has to consultate the dictionary.
10. Just avert jargon and colloquialisms.
11. This is excellent advise that effects us all.
12. The media is often blamed for establishing writing criteria that is copied without thinking by the public.
13. Less errors in newspapers would be helpful.
14. However, no one should imply all newspapers print poor writing.
15. Scarcely never do you see outrageously bad writing like you do in freshman compositions.
16. The true facts are sometimes difficult to face.
17. Too much writing is discursively digressive and is wordy and verbose.
18. As a freshman, I could always anticipate my instructor to literally cover my compositions with indecipherable red marks.
19. At that point in time, I thought I could write.
20. At this point, I know I can't.
21. He has his facts wrong.
22. Five bandits convinced a Brink's armed guard to open his truck door.
23. A cement block building was destroyed.
24. Three persons died in the mishap.
25. Its no fun trying to write but not knowing how.

Skill Drill III: Abused and Misused Words

Samuel Johnson, the 18th-century lexicographer and author, was riding in a closed carriage with several other passengers on a hot, dusty and long trip. As the afternoon wore on, one of the passengers, an estimable middle-aged woman, was obviously disturbed by the odor arising from the corner where Johnson was sitting. In those days, bathing was infrequent, and Johnson's personal hygiene was minimal. Finally, unable to hold back, the woman turned to Johnson. "Sir, you smell," she said.

"No madam," Johnson said. "You smell. I stink."

Benjamin Disraeli, a British prime minister in the 19th century, was asked to define the difference between a misfortune and a calamity. Without hesitation, Disraeli plucked the name of his political rival William Gladstone from memory and replied: "If, for instance, Mr. Gladstone were to fall into the river, that would be a misfortune. But if anyone were to pull him out, that would be a calamity."

Few reporters have to make these fine distinctions. Nevertheless, the precise use of language is an essential tool of the good reporter. Here are word-couples often confused and misused. Use them properly in sentences:

1. affect/effect
2. allusion/illusion
3. angry/mad
4. bring/take
5. complement/compliment
6. council/counsel
7. emigrate/immigrate
8. flaunt/flout
9. farther/further
10. fewer/less
11. imply/infer
12. lay/lie
13. lend/loan
14. principal/principle
15. rebut/refute

Developing the Story Idea

In the following exercises, first list the elements in the material you will want to include in your story. Next, number them in order of importance. Then write the lead based on the element or elements you considered first in importance. Finally, write the rest of the story. You may have to use the Freeport directories at the back of the *Workbook* to add names or addresses to your story.

Exercises II

A. Memorial

The mayor's press secretary, Leon Roper, calls to tell you that a softball game will be played on the Horace Mann High School athletic field Sunday at 2 p.m. between teams composed of city employees and members of the local chamber of commerce. No admission will be charged, but contributions will be solicited for the Chris Hatfield Memorial Fund. Hatfield was the city manager for three years and died last August of Hodgkin's disease at the age of 31. The fund goes toward cancer research. Cliff Guzman, the president of the chamber, will pitch for his team, and Albert Heffner, the city budget director, will throw curves for the city team.

B. Merit

Pamela Elman, 18, 3732 Palisades Ave., a senior at Dwight D. Eisenhower High School, won a National Merit Scholarship: $3,000. Will attend the University of Texas (Austin), as a premed student. The only one to win from this city; 3,500 in country. (Information from Bernard A. Meyers, principal.) Your newspaper's files have a story dated last year in which Meyers announces she is one of six students to have all A's in their first three years of high school work. In her freshman and sophomore years, she was confined to a bed while undergoing treatment for spinal birth injury and took courses by special telephone. She has been in a wheelchair since then.

C. Planning

The secretary of the city Zoning and Planning Board, Betty Forde, telephones to say that the regular board meeting scheduled for tomorrow night is called off because of the death this morning of the wife of the chairman, Philip Nicholson. The meeting, set for 8 o'clock in the city council chambers, will be held next Tuesday at 8 p.m. instead. Her name is Alice Nicholson. She was 42 and died of cancer.

D. Wind

Police report: High winds last night damaged residences and businesses on State Highway 166 near Clovia. The winds were estimated at 80 miles an hour at their height, and they touched down for about two minutes at 11 p.m. Most of the damage, totaling $15,000, was to outbuildings. Largest single damage, about $5,000, was to the Crossroads Grocery at Three Corners Junction, where all the glass was blown out and merchandise shaken from shelves. Two gas pumps shattered and a storage building flattened. No injuries.

E. Zoo

Information from Cyrus Tucek, the director of the zoo: The Newman Municipal Zoo has purchased two animals, a 6,000 pound female African elephant and a burro. After becoming accustomed to their surroundings, the animals will be put on exhibit. The elephant is named Baby and was obtained from the Brookfield Zoo in Chicago. The burro, which will be added to the Children's Zoo, is from the H. Gage Ranch in northern New Mexico and will be named by children who use the zoo. Suggested names will be put on a bulletin board and the children will vote. Names put up by zoo workers are Pancho, Rodney, Eeyore, Captain B, Secretariat, Taco, Chico, Cyrus, Mr. Cronkite and Cyrano.

Tucek also said the zoo is considering the use of birth control methods to keep its tiger population down. The female tigers have been producing litters of three to five cubs every 10 months, he said, and the zoo has no room for them. Nor will other zoos accept the young tigers. "They're full up, too, and are using a time-release contraceptive implanted under the skin for females and vasectomies for males.

"Lions, tigers and leopards are disappearing in the wild and proliferating in zoos and wildlife parks so fast there's no room for them," Tucek said.

F. District Attorney

Paul Robinson, the district attorney, calls to say he will give a talk at a National Conference of Prosecutors convention in Chicago on July 23 where about 1,500 district attorneys will meet. His talk will be about the career-criminal tracking system that he says he has begun to use in Freeport. The system is designed to identify the frequent offender on arrest. An assistant district attorney is immediately assigned to the case and follows it, beginning with arraignment. "The purpose is to avoid plea bargaining with the resultant lenient sentences and probation for these offenders," he says. Robinson says the latest data show that career criminals commit 61 percent of all homicides, 76 percent of all rapes, 73 percent of all robberies and 65 percent of all aggravated assaults.

G. Laundromat

Police report: Jerome Pardee, 20, 1874 Ogden St. in Freeport, arrested and charged with public drunkenness. Found naked in a laundromat at 402 Newell St. at 11 p.m. yesterday, Pardee told police that he planned to put his clothes back on as soon as the dryer was finished with them. Police had to wait 30 minutes for the cycle to finish before they could take him in.

H. Weather

The weather bureau said temperatures over the past 24 hours ranged from 25 at 5 a.m. to 40, the high, at 2 p.m. This was the third straight day of unseasonably cold weather. This morning's temperature of 25 was the lowest for this time of year in 15 years. The all-time low for the date was in 1880, 15 degrees. The all-time high was 69 in 1991. The forecast for today is for lows in the 40s, highs in the 50s and an end to the sudden cold snap.

I. Fire

The Freeport fire department reports two small fires overnight: a storeroom blaze at the IGA at 135 Kentucky Ave., 10:30 p.m., cause unknown, damage $450 in canned goods; a fire in a car in a garage at 630 Orcutt Ave., 11 p.m., cigarette ignited papers on car seat, $1,200 damage to the car. Dennis Held, car owner who lives at Orcutt address, treated for minor burns at Community Hospital and discharged. Wife saw smoke and pulled him from car. He had fallen asleep listening to a baseball game.

J. Parade

The county volunteer fireman's association calls: It will hold its annual Kiddies Day Parade next Sunday, beginning at 1 p.m. at Massachusetts Avenue and Albany Street and running down Massachusetts through Freeport's business section to the grounds of the First Congregational Church, where judges will make awards for funniest costume, prettiest costume, smallest pet and best float. On display at the church grounds will be the new pumper purchased last month. Last year, 200 children from three to eight years took part. Mayor Sam Parnass will lead the parade, carrying his 1-year-old daughter, Candy.

K. Ombudsman

Call from the governor's office: Bruce Stroh, a former local high school basketball player who was sentenced to 15 years in the state penitentiary for armed robbery 10 years ago, has been appointed state ombudsman for prisoners in state institutions. Gov. Janet Kocieniewski made the announcement today from the state capitol. "Stroh will investigate prisoner complaints and report directly to the governor. This is a new system that is designed to make us more responsive to the needs of inmates," the governor said. Stroh was paroled five years ago and has worked as a probation officer in Freeport.

L. Recital

Telephone call from the Freeport parent association secretary and notes from the switchboard operator: Artur Rothstein, a French concert pianist, has donated his services for a recital in the music wing of the Horace Mann School, Friday, 8 p.m. Tickets are $5. The concert will include Chopin's mazurkas and études, Beethoven's piano version of music from *The Magic Flute* and several works of Franz Liszt. Proceeds will go toward the purchase of a high-fidelity system for the music department.

M. Tourism

Thomas Everingham of the Freeport Chamber of Commerce calls: "We have made a study of the city's commerce and industry and we have found that tourism is one of the three major sources of income for the city. So we've decided on a promotional program to start at the end of next month aimed at attracting tourists. We're going to canvass the business community to see what it is willing to invest in this effort. Our goal is to raise $125,000 for the publicity program. Our budget for promotion has always ranged around $25,000. So this is a major undertaking. Everyone benefits when people stop in Freeport for a few days.

"We have formed a committee to head the fund drive. It consists of Elizabeth Bennett, president of the National Security Bank here; William Sharman, dean of students at Mallory College; Bert Gentle, head of the Hotel and Restaurant Workers Union; Herbert Blitzer, dean of the journalism program at Mallory.

"Our first step is to decide whether to make the fund drive completely voluntary or to set a charge to be added to the Chamber's membership fees, or a combination of both."

Exercises III

These stories will be longer than the preceding stories. Handle them in the same way. If you find more than one theme, again select only the most important of the elements for the lead. Put the others in order of importance and base the body of the story on your priority list.

A. Bus

Here is a news release from Jack Nagel, who is the press officer for the state Public Utilities Commission:

The People's Bus Line, Inc., 1320 Torrence Ave., Freeport, owner George W. Hulbert, has filed with the state Public Utilities Commission today a request for permission to operate a route into the downtown area from outlying communities, state PUC chairman Michael McKirdy announced today.

Hulbert seeks state approval to operate an unscheduled Monday through Friday service and asserts in his application that "domestic workers needing to reach downtown for trains to the suburbs where they work are not being served by present bus lines." Protests or supporting witnesses will be heard 28 days from the date of the application, at 3 p.m., in the state Executive Office Building.

Hulbert submitted with his request a petition bearing 65 signatures of local residents. The petition has a preamble reading: "We the undersigned find it costly to reach commuter lines from our section of the community and support the request of George W. Hulbert for unscheduled bus service in our area."

Write 200 words for *The Freeport News*.

B. Missing

It is 60 minutes to deadline, and the police reporter of *The Freeport News* calls in the following notes for you. Write a story:

Billy Joe Appel, 4, 1133 Madison St., was located at 12:30 p.m. at the home of Mrs. Bernice McCoy, 320 Manley St., a friend of Alice Kragler, 16, the babysitter. He disappeared from the Appel home around 9 o'clock last night when the babysitter said she fell asleep looking at TV. He is the son of Alan and Roberta Appel.

Police said that after questioning Miss Kragler this morning, she admitted she had wanted "to get even with the Appels for not letting me have my boyfriend visit me when I was babysitting with Billy Joe."

She said she called her friend, Mrs. McCoy, 20, and asked her to come and pick up the kid because she had to return home for an emergency and would pick him up in an hour. When McCoy heard the news about the missing child on the radio last night she said she was too frightened to do anything.

The Appels say they are happy to have their child back and are not going to file charges against Kragler.

Quote from Mrs. Appel: "Alice is a good girl. She just got upset. Those things happen. She loves Billy Joe and would never let anything happen to him."

The police say a full report will be turned over to juvenile authorities since there was a violation of the law. Kragler lives with her divorced mother, Bertha. About 20 volunteers turned out last night to search for the child in the woods near the Appel home where the parents thought he might be wandering.

1. Write 250 words for *The Freeport News,* a morning newspaper.
2. Write 100 to 150 words for *The Freeport News* online news service, www.freenews.com. The service presents a 7 p.m. news roundup of the day's major stories.

C. Longo

An official of the B.C. Krebs Manufacturing Co. of Freeport calls to tell you of the death from a heart attack in San José, Costa Rica, yesterday of Frank Longo, former personnel manager of the local company, which employs 250. He has prepared the following, which he dictates to you and which you should use as the basis for a story:

Longo was visiting his sister, Mrs. Rose Quintana, who lives in San José and is his only survivor. Longo was 88 and lived at 465 Lief St.

He went to work for the firm as a teen-ager after immigrating from Italy. Employed as a janitor, he worked up to inventory clerk within two years. As a clerk, he noticed the painstaking and cumbersome way in which inventory was kept and he devised an automatic system that was so successful it was copied by other large firms and eventually became the established procedure. Business textbooks referred to it as the Longo System, and it was in use until the introduction of the computerized inventory system.

Longo never had any formal education that we know of, but he was an omnivorous reader and donated books and funds to the local public library, which he called his high school, college and graduate school. He was made personnel manager at the age of 45 and completely changed the company's hiring system so that it became color-, sex- and age-blind two years later. He retired at 75.

He adds that the company telephoned Quintana at noon to offer assistance. Longo will be buried there tomorrow. She said her brother had been a prudent investor and had an estate of $1.5 million. He left $250,000 to her and the rest to the local public library system.

D. Outage

On a routine check of the sheriff's office 15 minutes before deadline, you are given the following information by the dispatcher:

We got a call from one of our patrol cars about half an hour ago that a car hit a power pole northwest of Freeport and people in the new housing subdivision out there were without electricity for about 45 minutes. I don't know any more than that. Oh, yes—no one was hurt in the accident.

You call the local office of the power and light company and the public information officer tells you:

We have just returned service. It was out from 1:02 to 1:40 p.m. It affected Arden Hills, where we have 250 meters, all residences. All of them were out.

Write a brief story based on the information. (Arden Hills is a new subdivision. It was completed last year.)

E. Elephant

Cyrus Tucek, the director of the Freeport's Newman Zoo, calls to say that they believe Baby, their new acquisition, is pregnant. He says that officials at Baby's previous home encouraged a match between her and Zoltan, a bull elephant, and that the local zoo knew of the nuptials. "Two for the price of one was our hope," Tucek says. "A more positive diagnosis will be available in a month or two. Too bad Daddy can't be here."

F. Goals

A well-known British journalist and critic who appears on television (BBC) is giving the major address at the annual state convention of the Daily Newspaper Association, which is held in conjunction with Newspaper Day at Mallory College. The speaker is Jeffrey St. George. His topic is "Goals for Journalism Education." He will speak at 8 o'clock tonight. Here are some excerpts supplied by the campus press office from the text of his talk which you should use for a story of 300 to 350 words.

Your experiences in this country with public events and public officials have served to develop a sense of responsibility and maturity in your press that is, I believe, unmatched anywhere in the world. This is a positive development for educators who prepare men and women for the media. Let us try to set out some goals for the journalism educator so that he or she may respond to these responsibilities.

Clearly, a professional education must give the student skills and a sense of craft. But it is not enough to prepare the student only for the first job. The education must be sufficiently broad and deep so that the underpinnings of a creative and positive life are established. There must be established a commitment to the contemplative as well as the active life, for skills without understanding become as automatic as the water pump. . . .

I do not mean to imply that these aims are visionary. Journalism education in your country is clearly moving in this direction. I should only wish to reinforce the movement. I would suggest a few questions any educator might ask of the program of study he or she is adopting:

Will the curriculum or the course do the following?
_____ Will it give the student a sense of purpose and broaden his or her knowledge?
_____ Will it deepen his or her interest in ideas, give him or her sufficient materials to think about?
_____ Will it free the imagination and develop initiative?
Finally, the question whose answer might be the most important of all of these for the journalism student:
_____ Will it develop a free and open mind, a journalist free of the biases of the society so that he or she can act independently, intelligently and spontaneously?

In closing, let me emphasize that I do not share the disdain of some educators for the real needs of the editor for young reporters who can spell the words of their mother tongue correctly and who can use a comma and a period with precision. But I do believe that this can hardly be the goal of journalism education. Nor, for that matter, can the education be narrowly conceived as instruction in the technology and the forms and practices of current journalism, which is only a step beyond the rules of grammar, punctuation and spelling. All are essential, of course. To use the words of one of my countrymen, Alfred North Whitehead, "The major aim of education should be an understanding of the insistent present. To do this one must know a great deal of the world and must understand the past in order to know the present."

Photo, Ladies Professional Golf Association
The first to do it—Sandra Haynie's hole in one at the Woodside Club.

G. Golfers

You are on the sports desk of the *The Freeport News* when a call comes in from a journalism student the *News* hired to cover the state Women's Amateur Golf Meet at the Woodside Club in which several local women are entered.

She dictates the following:

Here's a rundown of first-round play by local women. I also have their local addresses and ages:

Mrs. Heidi Levy, 39, 54 Maplewood Ave., shot an 83.
Mrs. Anne Downey, 42, 165 Vincent St., 87.
Mrs. B. Kroeger, 32, 880 Augusta Ave., 77.
Mary Ellen Flynn, 18, Roth Road, 77.
Sally Grubbs, 17, Smith Farms, 71.

Sally shot a hole-in-one on the seventh hole, and I went over to interview her after her first round. It was the only hole-in-one today, and they say it is the first one on this course by a woman in 30 years since a visiting pro, Sandra Haynie, first did it on the same seventh 30 years ago. Sally is only the second to do it.

Sally is a senior at Eisenhower High and is going to go to the University of Missouri. Her mother and father were here and they were pleased as punch. Her dad, Oscar Grubbs, said he gave her a putter when she was three and he says "she never stopped swinging it." She sank it with a four iron on the 145-yard par-three hole.

Says Sally: "The ball hit on the front of the green just to the right and the ball rolled smoothly into the cup. It looked good when I hit it, right on the line, but I never thought it would go in."

"It's my first since I was seven and played on a kiddie course. My 9-year-old sister, Kay, was here today and she brings me good luck."

Sally didn't compete at all last year. This is her first big tourney. The leaders: Terry Pauli, 70; Carol Trucco, 71; Sally Grubbs, 71; Carolyn Oshiro, 72; Janet Bakinski, 73; Maureen Gerson, 75; Tamara Cort, 75; Joan Bodnar, 75; Diane Stark, 76; Tess Walters, 76.

The concluding round will be played tomorrow.

Write a 300-word story for the newspaper and a condensed version for www.freenews.com.

H. Wedding

You are the courthouse reporter for an Albuquerque newspaper. One morning you come across this suit among a dozen on file in the courthouse. Write 150 to 200 words. (Mr. and Mrs. Lopez live at 712 Silver Ave., SW.)

```
STATE OF NEW MEXICO                          COUNTY OF BERNALILLO

          IN THE SECOND JUDICIAL DISTRICT COURT


   TOBIAS LOPEZ and
   CAROLYN LOPEZ,
   his wife,

          Plaintiffs,

     -vs-

                                        No._____578749_____
   MRS. L. DURRANCE and
   THE WOMEN'S CLUB, INC.,
                                        FILED IN MY OFFICE THIS
          Defendants.
                                             AUG 12


                        COMPLAINT
                                        Solomon Gallegos
                                        CLERK DISTRICT COURT
```

(Continued on next page.)

Plaintiffs state:

I

That on or about July 8 Plaintiffs entered into a leased contract with Defendants for the purpose of leasing premises known as Women's Club Hall at 22 Gold Avenue, SW, for a wedding celebration to take place between the hours of 8:00 p.m. and 12:00 p.m., on July 25.

II

That rental was paid therefor and accepted by Defendants.

III

That as a result of said agreement, Plaintiffs invited over 200 parties for said wedding celebration, relied upon said agreement therefor, made large and elaborate preparation, including the hiring of musical entertainment therefor, and planned a honeymoon trip immediately after the culmination of said celebration, all with knowledge to invitees and said Defendants.

IV

That on July 25 at the hour of 8:00 p.m. Plaintiffs, together with approximately 200 invitees, and their orchestra, attempted to enter said premises as per their contract and were met by another party of approximately 100 people who advised Plaintiffs and their invitees that said hall was being used by them and that Plaintiffs and their invitees could not use said hall for the purpose for which Defendants promised.

V

That the entire wedding celebration was ruined, all to the deep and everlasting and irreparable humiliation suffered by Plaintiffs and their invitees.

VI

That as a result of the ruination of said celebration, the humiliation suffered by Plaintiffs, the gross embarrassment to their reputation, Plaintiffs were forced to postpone perhaps indefinitely their honeymoon trip, Plaintiff CAROLYN LOPEZ suffered deep and excruciating shock to her nervous system, the extent of which is unknown to Plaintiffs.

WEREFORE, Plaintiffs pray for judgment against Defendants, and each of them, in the sum of Five Thousand ($5,000.00) Dollars plus costs herein lawfully expended.

Assignments

Some of these assignments ask for specific information that will form the basis of your story. Others give starting points only.

A. Charity

List all the fund drives in your community. Include the dates of the next campaign, the goal, last year's goal and the actual amount raised.

Interview the executive director of one of the organizations for a story. Any new techniques to be used? Any general comments on generosity or parsimony of the community? Any national or local factors involved in the amounts set as the goal or actually raised?

If the city has a United Fund that collects for all local charities, write about its next fund drive; summarize the most recent campaign, using exact totals and comments.

B. Merit Folo

Locate the names of several National Merit Scholars from local high schools over the past 5 to 10 years. Call their principals, and try to learn where the scholars are now and how they have done in college and thereafter. If a Merit Scholar is available locally, interview him or her.

C. Acquisition

Visit a local or nearby museum and interview the curator or director on new acquisitions. Has he or she been able to obtain what the museum has wanted? Is the museum interested in specializing in a particular area? How much money is available for acquisitions? Is it sufficient? What is the source of the funds? Is there a plan to try to increase funds? If the museum has priorities other than acquisitions, ask about them.

D. Tippers

Are local residents and visitors good tippers? Interview hotel bellhops, waiters and waitresses, barbers, taxi drivers and others. What is considered a good tip? Who are the best tippers: men, women; young, middle-aged or elderly; local people, out-of-towners or foreigners? Are students good tippers?

E. Meetings

For practice in covering spontaneous events, cover a meeting of one or more of the following:

1. City council or commission.
2. Service club speaker (Lions, Kiwanis, etc.).
3. Planning, zoning commission.
4. County commission, board of supervisors.

F. Sabbatical

A college admissions consultant suggests that high school graduates take a year off before going to college. "If you're older, you do better," he says. "You don't fall down drunk and waste your time." What is the experience at your college? Do older students do better? Interview faculty members and administrators.

Campus Projects

A. Plans

What do college seniors plan to do after graduation? Interview students about their plans for work, travel, graduate study. Will those who plan to work be doing so in the area of their major? Where are the travelers bound? Ask those who intend to continue their education why they selected their field for graduate study. Are some planning marriage soon after they graduate? What are the work or study plans of people planning to marry?

B. Involvement

A survey of more than 330,000 college freshmen conducted by the Higher Education Research Institute at UCLA found among the freshman class the lowest interest and involvement in politics in three decades. Fewer than a third said that "keeping up with political affairs" is an important goal for them. Thirty years before, two-thirds said it was important for them.

Other surveys have found an annual decline in concern for the environment, racial understanding and community action programs as well as a lessening interest in political issues. Paul Rogat Loeb, an associate scholar at the Center for Ethical Leadership in Seattle, describes this campus spirit as "less indifference and more learned helplessness—the feeling that students can't change the world, so why try?"

The political leadership, Loeb says, carries considerable responsibility for this cynicism. President Clinton talked populism, he says, but courted "wealthy donors." The Bush administration talked "compassionate conservatism" but gave "relentless service to the most powerful economic interests."

 Design a survey for your school to determine students' "involvement factor." Try to find reasons for your findings.

C. Great Speeches

What are the five best speeches delivered in the country's history? Interview members of various departments on campus. Among those most often mentioned are Lincoln's Gettysburg address and Martin Luther King's "Free at Last" speech in Alabama. Quote from the speeches to illustrate the points your sources make.

Community Projects

A. Career

What do high school seniors want to do after they graduate? What affects their plans—finances, parents' wishes, high school studies and grades, friends' decisions?

B. Prayer

One of the most angrily debated subjects in the country is whether prayers should be allowed in public schools. The American Center for Law and Justice states that there is legal ground for states challenging court rulings against school prayer. But the American Civil Liberties Union says federal courts generally have ruled that prayer in public school is unconstitutional. Have efforts been made to include religious activity in local schools?

Home Assignments

Underline or circle the most important fact in the following material—the one you think best sums up the event and is of greatest reader or listener interest.

Then write a lead based on the underlined or circled material.

I. Important

A. Dispute

1. The Queens Mountain Rescue Squad and the Queens Mountain police chief have been in a controversy for a week.
2. Chief Lloyd Earl had ordered police officers not to stop traffic at intersections to let ambulances through.
3. The squad, made up of volunteer rescue workers, felt the chief interfered with its work.
4. The rescue squad complained to Mayor Henry Joyner and to the Queens Mountain Board of Commissioners.
5. At an executive session of the board with the mayor last night, the chief resigned.

B. Taxes

1. Next year's proposed Gaston County budget calls for expenditures of $54.8 million.
2. This is $2.1 million more than the current budget.
3. Revenue collections will be about $1.4 million short of the expenditures next year.
4. David Hunscher, the county manager, supplied this information to the county board of commissioners last night in presenting his proposed budget.
5. Hunscher says that he made many cuts in budget requests from department heads and it will be difficult to make more.
6. The probability, he said, is that taxes will have to be raised.

C. Mail

1. T. J. Ellingson, an assistant United States postmaster general, issued a statement at a news conference today.
2. He said that the costs of running the postal service are constantly increasing.
3. "Further attempts must be made to cut costs," he said.
4. "One of the plans under consideration is twice-weekly home mail delivery and thrice-weekly deliveries to business."
5. "Nothing is definite yet pending further examinations of the options," he said.

D. Shooting

1. Mrs. Bernice Joyce, 32, of 44 Broadway, was arrested this morning at the home of her mother.
2. She was taken to criminal court and charged with shooting her husband, Coleman, last night during an argument.
3. The two had quarreled over her plans to divorce him.
4. He had been staying at a hotel and returned to the house to try to persuade her to drop the divorce.
5. A fight ensued during which he was shot.
6. He is in critical condition at Fairlawn Hospital.
7. The charge is attempted homicide.

E. Drive

1. Sara F. Glasser, president of the local chapter of the American Civil Liberties Union, announces a new membership drive.
2. The chapter usually solicits members by mail and telephone.
3. Next month, the drive will be made on a person-to-person basis to gain 50 new members.
4. Members and volunteers will be asked to invite friends to their homes to acquaint them with the ACLU.
5. "The chapter hopes to increase its membership to replace those who have dropped out and moved away," she said.
6. "If we cannot do so, we must discontinue the chapter," she said.

F. Gas

1. The supply of natural gas to Wisconsin has been going down for the past five years.
2. The state Public Service Commission has warned natural gas customers that the situation will steadily worsen.
3. Today, the Wisconsin Gas Co. announced it is halting all further commercial and industrial gas hookups.
4. It also announced it is submitting a plan to the PSC to reduce gas deliveries to some present customers during temporary shortages.
5. The utility will continue to serve its 356,000 customers in central and eastern Wisconsin.
6. The cutbacks were necessary, the firm says, because of continued natural gas shortages and an anticipated further reduction in available supplies next year.

G. Tennis

1. The annual Freeport Tennis Clinic will be held Aug. 21 to 24 at Mallory College.
2. The clinic will feature exhibitions and instruction.
3. This is the 12th annual clinic, sponsored by six Freeport civic clubs.
4. Chris Evert Lloyd, holder of a number of tennis titles, will play Aug. 23 at 2 p.m.
5. Lloyd will play local tennis pro Marty Friedman in a singles match and then will team up with Friedman to play a mixed doubles match against Mr. and Mrs. James Wigglesworth, the state mixed-doubles champions.
6. Friedman made the announcement today.

H. Bicycle Trip

1. Two students are going by bicycle from Boston to Seattle this summer.
2. The University of Rochester announced the project in a news release.
3. Edward A. Nelson and Kenneth Hardigan, third-year students in the university medical school, will make the trip.
4. The project is designed to test the body's ability to adapt to intensive training, the university release states.
5. "Information gained from the cross-country ride is expected to provide data of value to physiology in general and to sports medicine in particular," the release states.
6. Nelson, of Kent, Conn., will be the test subject and Hardigan, of Boston, will accompany him.
7. Nelson will be tested before and after the trip, and along the way he will conduct frequent self-tests.

S
in on

V

B. S

F
tende
job. F
the p:
Univ

tl

c

a

a
tl

N
I
a

tl
s

I
local

i(
v

y

1.
2.

Ver

Exe

Poet

y
ary cr
in thi
centl}
riod i
the p(

T
have

v

h
b

"High grades are no longer an adequate index of a student's knowledge or ability," says Paul J. Korshin of the English faculty at the University of Pennsylvania. He cites the incident of a state college student with a 2.1 grade average who falsified his transcript and was admitted to Yale where he earned a 3.0 average.

How have grade averages changed over the years at your school? What are the criteria that the graduate schools use for admission?

D. Road Rage

The American Automobile Association reports that "an alarming number of people are being hurt or killed over traffic offenses." The AAA study found more than 10,000 incidents over the past six years in which drivers or passengers attacked each other. More than 200 died in these attacks over perceived infractions—another driver not signaling, cutting off, tailgating, obscene finger gestures.

Talk to local traffic authorities about the situation.

Campus Project

Books

What books are required reading for freshmen in their English courses? The list changes with the times. For example: Women writers were rarely included in the reading lists until 25 or 30 years ago. In more recent years, authors from Africa and Asia have been included. Have any such changes occurred on reading lists used by the English Department?

Community Projects

A. H.S. Grads

A college degree is within reach of the richest quarter of the population, with about 80 percent of those from families with incomes greater than $65,000 earning degrees. But the graduation rate is 8 percent for those from families in the poorest population group, those with incomes of less than $23,000.

Interview high school seniors about their college plans. Does their family income play a role in whether they decide to go to college? Are there other factors that influence their decision?

B. Dump

The computer is an office necessity. But it has also become a dangerous component of landfills. More than 300 million computers have wound their way to landfills where the billion pounds of lead leach into the ground. Only one of sixteen computers is recycled. But some organizations are battling to have computer makers see to it that their products are recycled. Localize this.

Home Assignment

Components

Clip stories from campus and local newspapers that illustrate:

1. The two kinds of attribution:
   (a) **Statements** that are attributed to a source.
   (b) **Information** about events not witnessed by the reporter that is attributed to a source.
2. A trial balloon (see Chapter 2 in textbook for a description of the term) and a media-event or pseudo-event. What do you think the motives of the source are?
3. Unfairness that falls into these categories:
   (a) **Slanting:** Using material that is favorable to a person or a policy and ignoring contradictory, relevant information.
   (b) **Distorting:** Using material inaccurately with the intention to mislead.
   (c) **Quoting out of context:** Using quoted material to make a point the original material did not intend.
   (d) **Name-calling:** Using words that have an unpopular or unfavorable connotation.
   For number 3 you may use any material you have heard or read—books, magazines, television, advertising, editorials, columns.
4. The use of human interest to make a technical or complex story more interesting and easier to understand. Also, find an example of a story that could profit from the introduction of human interest. What kinds of people, or which specific individuals, would you interview for the story?

Class Discussion

A. Direct

Clip from your college and community newspapers local stories that are based on direct observation and second- and third-hand sources. Explain your classification and indicate whether the reporter could have observed the event directly but settled for another person's account. Did the reporter fail to attribute information not obtained directly? If so, why do you think there was no attribution?

B. Press Freedom

Freedom House conducts an annual survey of print and broadcast media to determine whether their host countries allow freedom of the press. Only one person in five lives in a country with a free press, the survey has determined.

In a recent survey, the countries with completely free media were Canada, Germany and the United States. Those with the most controlled press were China, Indonesia, Egypt, Turkey, Singapore and Malaysia.

What constitutes a free press, and what makes up a controlled press?

Skill Drill: Guidelines

Each of the following items violates at least one basic guideline for writing news stories. The guidelines are:

Accuracy in detail and expression.
Attribution of all statements and information to reliable sources.
Verification of assertions, charges.
Balance and fairness.
Brevity.
Human interest in stories when possible.
News point stressed.

Identify the errors. When possible, make corrections or indicate what should be done.

A. Salary

He said his take-home pay from his salary of $400 a week as an elevator operator was slightly more than $300 a week. His weekly deductions included: social security, $16; federal taxes, $46; state taxes, $21; and series EE government bonds, $25. (Paragraph in story.)

B. Fine

He was fined $25 last year for loitering near the theater. But this felony conviction did not deter him from his task. (Paragraph in story.)

C. Resignation

Jenkins announced his resignation yesterday. He is quitting the force because of its authoritarian structure and the dictatorial attitude of Chief McCabe. (Paragraph in story.)

D. Shots

A city plan, proposed by municipal health authorities today, would inoculate all unleashed animals and take them to the local pound where they would be given anti-rabies shots and returned to their owners after a $15 fine is paid. (Lead.)

E. Success

Lee capped his successful 1975 season with the Red Sox by helping his teammates win the World Series against the Cincinnati Reds, Peralta said in his talk to the Boosters' Club. (Paragraph in story.)

F. Talk

The local chapter of the Public Relations Society said today José Lopez García, director of an advertising agency in Mexico City, will address its meeting Oct. 20 at 8 p.m. in the Chamber of Commerce boardroom.

Mr. García is on a tour of this country to gather ideas for the Mexican public relations industry. (Short item.)

G. Noise

A special airport-sound study committee, set up at the local airfield, issued its report, Marshall Peat, airport manager, reported today.

The study was set up to determine whether there would be any problems if the undeveloped land to the northeast of the field were developed for use as a housing project.

The report stated that noise and the possibility of accidents make this area unfit for housing.

"That should kill the housing proposal of Mitchell & Co.," Peat said. More than 250 acres are involved. Half the residents of the area said they intend to move if they can find housing. (Story.)

H. New Age

"A new age of pot is dawning," said Albert Goldman in his talk to the Rotary Club this afternoon.

Goldman, a writer, said marijuana will replace liquor and tobacco as the new middle-class social habit. Already, he said, it is used by almost all age and social groups. Because it has no known ill effects, Goldman said, it is safer than the habit-forming alcohol and cigarettes. (Story.)

I. Adoption

Robert G. Dowle was named head of the Interfaith Children's Agency today at the annual meeting of the board.

The agency arranges for the adoption of local youngsters through the various religious groups and the city social services department.

Dowle said he was pleased by the appointment, particularly because he was placed in the home of his adoptive parents, Mr. and Mrs. Albert Dowle, in the first year of the agency's operation in 1937. (Story.)

J. Tour

During his travels, he dropped off in Iceland, the world's largest island. He toured the interior, which is covered with an enormous sheet of ice. He said the island was discovered by Eric the Red almost 1,000 years ago. (Part of story.)

PART THREE

Writing the Story

3 What Is News?

Mike Roemer

**Passionate protests
make news.**

Introduction

News is the timely account of events of importance and significance. The closer the event—psychologically or physically—the greater its news value. News value is enhanced by the involvement in events of people who are well-known. We also make news out of strange and unusual situations. News values are not absolute. Decisions on what is to be used and how it is to be used depend on considerations such as the nature of the news medium and its audience and the role that the individual station or newspaper has established for itself in the community.

Exercises

A. Craftsman

You are working on the news desk of the newspaper in Flagstaff, Ariz., and you receive this press release in the mail. Rewrite it in less than 100 words for your newspaper.

DETROIT—Youths from Medford, Ore., and Arlington, Va., were the top winners today in the $38,000 Fisher Craftsman's Guild Scholarship Awards for Model Car Designs.

Eighteen awards were made.

Tom H. Semple, 19, Medford, Ore., won a $5,000 university scholarship for taking first place in the 16–20 age group with his original one-twelfth scale model of a black sports coupe.

Winner of a similar scholarship in the competition for boys between 11 and 15 years old was Richard R. John, 15, Arlington, Va. His entry was a blue and aqua hardtop sports car.

The awards will be made at a special luncheon for the winners, Nov. 15.

Each year hundreds of youths enter the competition for awards totaling $117,000, including the scholarships. The contest is sponsored by Fisher Body Division for General Motors. Runner-up in the senior division was Michael B. Antonick, Mount Vernon, Ohio, while John M. D'Mura, 13, Flagstaff, Ariz., took second place honors in the junior competition. Each received a $4,000 scholarship.

The other awardees:

Third Place ($3,000 scholarships): Richard L. Beck, 20, Louisville, Ky., senior division; Melvin G. Gable, 14, Ypsilanti, Mich., junior division.

Fourth place ($2,000 scholarships): Michael S. Reese, 16, Houston, Tex., senior division; Harry F. Mahe Jr., 15, Brooklyn, N.Y., junior division.

B. Poet

You are covering the county courthouse and a court employee tells you that District Court Judge Harvey Smith has handed down a decision in rhyme and that it might make a good story. You check and find he has indeed written a poem consisting of 15 stanzas.

The decision was made in an appeal of a municipal court decision in Ridgefield Park in which Eugene T. Bohelska was fined $300 on his conviction for using profanity on the telephone, a violation of state law. Bohelska was also convicted of driving an improperly registered vehicle, although he contended he was driving someone else's car and should not have been held responsible. He appealed his conviction on the profanity charge, which grew out of an incident with the court clerk.

The incident began when, after two delays in his municipal court hearing on the driving charge, Bohelska called the court to ask for another delay. He said he was ill with a fever. The clerk refused to make a postponement and he allegedly cursed her. The clerk, Geraldine Mucella, then filed charges.

Here are the key stanzas from the judge's long poem:

DECISION:
Vulgar words transmitted by phone
Are not enough when standing alone
To land said caller in a jail cell
Where, for six months, he's required to dwell;
For while such words may cause some resentment
Their use is protected by the First Amendment.
Tempers then flared 'til it sounded the same
As a Rangers–Flyers hockey game.
"F--- you, go f--- yourself" Eugene blurted
Though use of that word should be averted.
Before the sentence was even completed
He wished that the expletive had been deleted.
You say things couldn't possibly worsen?
Well the clerk of the court was a female person.
Next day the cop in the hat rang the bell and waited.
Eugene opened the door, his fever had abated.
He knew that he now would be printed and booked.
Figured his goose was practically cooked.
They went to the station and straight to the jail.
He stayed there 'til mother posted his bail.
Title Two A, Chapter One Seventy, Section Twenty-nine (three)
Is the charge for which posting of bail set him free.
It provides that when using the telephone
Mere profanity standing alone
Even if stated in friendship or jest
Is a criminal act, hence the arrest.
The Ridgefield Park docket was busy that night
Traffic, this case and a big bar room fight.
Judge George A. Browne, if I may opine
Talks a lot like the late Gertrude Stein.
Justice was dispensed at a good rapid pace.
Next thing you know they called Eugene's case.
There were few facts disputed, no witnesses lied.
The question was "How would the law be applied?"

Judge George A. Browne made his position quite clear
He said that his clerk was shell pink of ear.
The words Eugene used were obscene and profane
And it caused her anguish and much mental pain.
For that telephone call with the curses and hollers
The fine imposed was three hundred dollars.
The lawyer protested and fought on with zeal
So now we turn to Eugene's appeal.
Can you swear if you hit your thumb with a hammer
Without risk of spending six months in the slammer?
When the bank computer errs and bounces your check
Is your language confined to aw gees and oh hecks?
Does the law require you to stand mute
While a cigarette burns a hole in your suit?
Is it reasonable to remain calm and composed
If the photograph shows your horse has been nosed?
Statutory attempts to regulate pure bluster
Can't pass what is called constitutional muster.
Use of vulgar words that may cause resentment
Is protected by the First Amendment.
There must be a danger of breach of the peace
For this near sacred right ever to cease.
This was no obscene call from a sick deranged stranger.
Of a breach of the peace there was no possible danger.
Eugene hurled an expletive in sheer exasperation
And that isn't a crime anywhere in this nation.
The cop in the hat and Judge George A. Browne
Will read this opinion and grumble and frown.
They may ring me up just to holler and curse
But I still can't affirm. I have to reverse.

1. Write a 300-word story for tomorrow's *Freeport News*.
2. Write a news item for tonight's News at 7 on Channel 7.
3. Write 150 words for tonight's www.freenews.com.

C. Center

The Freeport Zoning and Planning Board last night completed a hearing on the proposal of the Salvation Army for a community center at 740 Springfield St. A decision is expected at the next meeting, Jan. 20.

At the hearing:

The Army proposes to build a two-story center at a cost of $500,000. The Army was promised the new location as part of a land swap in a downtown urban renewal project whose planning was completed two years ago.

The present center is three blocks away. That land is part of a proposed mall.

Merchants at 740 and 742 Springfield oppose the board's granting approval. The owners are Frank Chaffee, Frank's Deli; Margaret Williams, Mayfair Fabrics; Thomas Ashkinaze, Ashkinaze's Men's Styles; and Bernzar Berents, B&D Butchers.

They ask the board not to get rid of going businesses that pay taxes. "We cannot find anything in the area," Berents said. He's the spokesman. "It would be tragic to eliminate going concerns."

The Army spokeswoman, Major Barbara Geddings, said, "We will have to eliminate our youth program at a time when the city's juvenile delinquency rate is growing. This is a part of the city where young people are without parks, without recreation of any kind, if we close our center."

Berents also told the board, which must approve a zoning change before the community center can be built: "We are taxpayers, contributing to the city treasury. What sense does it make to remove us from the city tax base and in our place put a tax-exempt operation? You are finding out that downtown businesses are fleeing every week and your tax base is eroding."

Asked by Harry Kempe, a member of the board, whether the merchants have investigated moving to the mall, Berents said that the merchants have done so but have not been assured of a date when the mall will be completed.

"We can't just close up and wait," Berents said. "For all we know, the mall won't be built for another two years. What will we do in the meantime? Go on welfare?"

Write 250 to 300 words for *The Freeport News.*

Assignments

A. Restricted

Librarians are placing books that might be stolen or mutilated on restricted reserve. Years ago, the restricted section consisted of works that were considered bawdy or licentious: James Joyce's *Ulysses* and the works of Henry Miller, Havelock Ellis and the Marquis de Sade. During the 1960s the locks came off and students could find de Sade's *120 Days of Sodom* on the open shelves.

Their place on the closed shelves was taken by valuable books that brought a high price on the used and rare book markets. Also, engravings were a target: Thieves would razor out the Winslow Homer engravings in old copies of *Harper's Weekly,* for example.

In the 1990s, another group made it to the closed shelves, books deemed politically incorrect and thus likely to be mutilated. Salman Rushdie's *Satanic Verses* was isolated. De Sade's works went back in the cupboard because they depict "violence against women," as one group put it.

Interview the head librarian on the campus and in the community. What books are on the restricted shelves? (Obtain authors' names and book titles.) Why?

B. Canines

Interview an official at the local American Society for the Prevention of Cruelty to Animals or dog shelter for a story on the dog population and its characteristics.

Do most people own mutts? What is the favorite breed? Is there a licensing regulation or leash law; if so, how is it obeyed and how is it enforced?

C. Vox Populi

How strong is the voice of the people in your community? Interview the editor of the editorial page of the local newspaper and the station managers of local broadcast stations. How many letters and telephone calls do they receive a day, a week? What are the subjects that move people to write or call? Select a recent local issue—have there been any letters or calls about it?

D. Emergency

Visit the emergency clinic of a local hospital. Are the doctors and nurses overwhelmed? Why? How many patients do they see on a shift? Is there a peak—weekends, late evenings? What are the most common ailments? Who uses the clinic? Are there any proposals to alter the clinic's services?

E. Shoplifting

Is shoplifting a problem for local merchants? If so, how do they cope with it? Is the situation better or worse than 10 or 15 years ago? Why? Are most shoplifters in one age group, of one sex? Do merchants prosecute? Consult the police and the district attorney's office to determine whether any shoplifters have gone to court; if so, learn what has happened to them. What is the usual charge (misdemeanor, felony) lodged against a shoplifter?

F. Fans

Interview members of one of the local teams—college or professional—about local fans. Are the fans enthusiastic, tolerant of losses, fair-weather followers? Is the team treated better on the road? Does the attitude of fans affect play? How?

Obtain attendance figures: total, season ticket holders. Up or down?

Do winning and losing affect attendance?

Do not settle for the usual quotes, but try to dig into the actual feelings of the athletes.

Campus Project

Diet

Interview students who live off-campus about their eating habits. Try to have them recall their meals for the last two or three days. Set these findings against your background information and what the campus dietitian or a local nutritionist says is a healthy diet.

If you want to take this a step further, differentiate among students who eat at home, those who live in a cooperative arrangement and those who are on their own. Are there significant differences in their diets? Do eating habits differ between men and women?

Community Projects

A. Eating

In the last 25 years, consumers have made a major shift in their food consumption. Beef and eggs are consumed less often, poultry and fish more frequently. Fruits and vegetables are a major part of the diet, as are whole grains. The U.S. Department of Agriculture reports these changes in food consumption:

Fruits: up 125 percent
Low-fat milk and yogurt: up 202 percent
Whole grains: up 245 percent
Fish: up 39 percent
Red meat: up 5 percent
Chicken: up 105 percent
Broccoli: up 770 percent
Green vegetables: up 169 percent

Make a survey of local residents and their eating habits. Talk to shoppers in groceries and supermarkets, men shopping after business. Have shoppers changed their family's and their diets in response to concerns about cholesterol, heart disease, overweight, hypertension? Is there a difference in the dietary practices among age groups, between men and women?

B. Outdoors

What do people do when they have spare time? A survey found that most take to the road. People were asked to list their favorite outdoor recreations, and they responded:

Driving for pleasure	40 percent
Swimming	35
Picnicking	33
Fishing	26
Bicycling	21
Running, jogging	19
Hiking, wildlife viewing	18
Camping (tent at campground)	16
Photography	15
Bird watching	14
Backpacking	13
Golf	11
Motorboating	10

Less than 10 percent responded, in order: tennis, recreational vehicle camping, hunting, target shooting, motorcycling, water skiing, canoeing and kayaking, downhill skiing, horseback riding, mountain biking, off-road vehicle driving.

List these recreational subjects and let people check their preferences. Compare your findings locally with these national results.

Hauling in a muskie on the French River.

C. Clergy

Searches for ministers, priests and rabbis to meet the needs of churches and synagogues have come up empty in many communities. The pool of candidates has shrunk as fewer choose a religious career, and even among those who do, many select a career outside the pulpit. The shortage is felt most severely in rural and inner-city churches. Five years ago, said the head of a seminary, his graduates would wait months for an offer. Today, he continued, there are three job offers for every graduate. What is the situation in your area?

Home Assignment

Technical

Leaf through a technical journal to find an article that could be of general interest if rewritten. Rewrite it for a newspaper, magazine or radio broadcast. Hold the rewrite to 300 words. Some suggestions: *American Journal of Nursing, American Journal of Psychology, American Journal of Sociology, Journal of the American Medical Association, Journalism Quarterly, Lancet, Nature, Science, Public Opinion Quarterly, Foreign Affairs.*

Class Discussion

Front-Page Play

Select newspaper stories that have been given front-page play primarily because of impact or significance, timeliness, prominence, proximity, conflict, the bizarre, currency, or necessity. Identify the stories as such. Do you agree with the newspaper selection and the comparative play of the stories?

Jean Pierre Rivest, *The Gazette*

A basic tool: the telephone directory.

Introduction

The news writer uses a variety of reference materials and tools to gather information and to ensure the story's accuracy and thoroughness. Among these are the computer, the telephone and city directories, a dictionary, and a handbook of grammar. Names and addresses are always double-checked, allegations and charges verified whenever possible, and all mathematical calculations are checked for errors. The writer's rule is: When in doubt, check it out. The computer has become a basic tool for gathering information. It is also useful in sorting large quantities of material for stories and has made possible large-scale investigative projects.

Exercises

A. Priorities

Social scientists at Mallory College took a poll of student opinions last semester and the results were released today. The results were compared with a similar poll taken 30 years ago. Professor Margot Adler, head of the Department of Sociology, announced the results. In both polls, 600 students were questioned.

In addition to the information that follows, she says that 30 years ago 32 percent of those polled were interested in a political revolution; the figure last semester was 23 percent. Thirty years ago, 32 percent of those polled felt a religious commitment was important; last semester, the figure was 38 percent. One area remained unchanged: the importance of love relationships. The figure was 92 percent for both years.

Administrators have used the polls for clues about student attitudes and dissatisfaction. Write 350 to 450 words. (See *NRW Plus,* **Appendix B, Public Opinion Polling Checklist.**)

Column A refers to the poll taken 30 years ago, B to last semester's poll.

Personal Priorities

	Important		Unimportant	
	A	**B**	**A**	**B**
High grades	48%	89%	47%	11%
Social service	49%	75%	44%	24%
Sports	47%	65%	50%	35%
Personal pleasures	85%	95%	12%	5%
Professional preparation	63%	81%	33%	19%
Entrepreneurship	18%	43%	73%	57%
Satisfying employment	68%	85%	27%	15%

4 **The Tools of the Trade**

Expectations of Mallory

	Expected		Actually Found	
	A	B	A	B
Great teachers	58%	57%	17%	16%
Opportunity to become more humane	20%	12%	19%	10%
Prestige in outside world	26%	35%	21%	31%

Contributes to Overall Learning

	Contributes		Does Not Contribute	
	A	B	A	B
Bull sessions	79%	60%	16%	19%
Personal contact with faculty	53%	37%	36%	44%

Sources of Frustration at Mallory

	Frustrated		Satisfied	
	A	B	A	B
Immutability of system	53%	67%	9%	5%
Living arrangements	36%	26%	52%	59%
Personal grades	30%	34%	45%	45%
Competitive atmosphere	35%	59%	21%	20%
Financial aid	22%	34%	31%	26%
Extracurricular	15%	11%	60%	84%

B. Growth

The news office at Mallory College has released some figures in its annual report for the current academic year and for 10 years ago:

	Now	10 Years Ago
Students	1,608	1,435
Faculty	118	105
Holding doctorates	86	52
Buildings	40	33
Volumes in library	325,000	245,000
Annual operating budget	$9,709,000	$4,695,000
Endowment		
Book value	$25,937,156	$11,770,500
Market value	$28,732,939	$14,888,675
Investment in plant	$17,348,159	$11,274,100
Total assets	$47,882,299	$25,711,500
Faculty salary scales		
Instructor	$31,350–34,500	$21,000–24,000
Assistant professor	$33,870–37,650	$22,000–27,350
Associate professor	$39,250–49,460	$23,500–30,450
Professor	$51,800–72,750	$31,250–46,150
Student aid		
Number assisted	460	348
Total awards	$1,179,000	$650,000

The college president, Ruth Pitts Renaldi, described the report's findings as "a decade of progress," according to the press release accompanying the data. The release goes on, quoting Renaldi:

> In every category, there is marked improvement. We have finally, through the addition of our science center, been able to improve our offerings in the physical sciences. Our library has grown considerably.
>
> But it would be dangerous to rest on this growth. We are faced with ever-increasing demands on our plant. Our faculty salaries are not competitive with other small, high-quality liberal arts schools. We need more money for student aid to match our tuition increase from $12,500 10 years ago to $20,000 today.
>
> I think that our first priority will have to be to raise funds for a library addition. I foresee a fund drive of $4,500,000.
>
> This will be one of our major construction projects. . . .

Your editor suggests that, in addition to using some of the data, you make calculations of your own to derive relevant information. Write 350 words for *The Freeport News* and 150 words for www.freenews.com.

C. Projection

In 1984, the consumption of soft drinks exceeded the consumption of water for the first time. The growth in soft drink consumption has not let up since. During the 1980s and 1990s, coffee consumption steadily declined, beer and milk consumption were slightly down and consumption of fruit juice slowly climbed. Here are some projected figures for U.S. per capita annual consumption of beverages in **gallons** released today by the Associated Beverage Industry:

	In Two Years
Soft drinks	65
Water	41
Coffee	21
Beer	20
Milk	19
Fruit juice	15
Other	19

Soft drink bottlers released the following current consumption **percentages:**

	Current Year Percentage Consumption
Soft drinks	25
Water	19
Coffee	11
Beer	12
Milk	15
Fruit juice	6
Other	12

Write 250 to 350 words.

Assignments

A. Checks

Find out where the following information may be obtained and then do so and write tight stories—no more than 200 words each—with the information.

1. What was the per capita federal aid to your state last year, and how does it compare with the highest and lowest state rates of per capita aid and the median for the nation?
2. What is the birth rate for your city and state, compared with previous years?
3. What was the amount of financial aid to students last year—total and per student, in the institution as a whole and by schools?

4. What is the income of families by race in your city and state?
5. What were the expense account expenditures by the mayor and members of the mayor's staff over the past month, the past six months, the past year?

B. High-Low

Here are some figures that are used by those who make quality-of-life determinations. These figures are five years old. Bring them up to date. Find the figures for your state and place them in relationship to the other data.

Write an article on your findings.

	High/Best	**Low/Worst**
1. Crime		
Violent crime rate	North Dakota (67)	Florida (854)
Murder rate	New Hampshire (1.5)	Louisiana (10.7)
Rape rate	New Jersey (17.3)	Alaska (83.5)
Aggravated assault rate	North Dakota (34.1)	South Carolina (651)
2. Economics		
Average annual pay	Connecticut ($42,653)	Montana ($23,253)
Per capita personal income	Connecticut ($39,300)	Mississippi ($20,688)
Household income (median)	Alaska ($51,046)	Arkansas ($28,398)
3. Education		
Average teacher salaries	Connecticut ($51,584)	South Dakota ($28,552)
Public high school graduation rate	Nebraska (91.9%)	Louisiana (51.5%)
Per capita state and local school expenditures	Alaska ($2,007)	Hawaii ($796)
Per capita state and local higher education expenditures	Delaware ($678)	Florida ($259)
Books in public libraries per capita	Vermont (5.4)	Tennessee (1.6)
4. Health		
Persons not covered by health insurance	Rhode Island (6.9%)	New Mexico (25.8%)
Low birth weight by percent of births	Vermont (0.1%)	California (10.5%)
Percent of mothers receiving late or no prenatal care	Rhode Island (1.5%)	New Mexico (8.5%)
Infant mortality rate	New Hampshire (4.4)	Alabama (10.2)
White	New Hampshire (4.2)	North Dakota (8.2)
Black	Massachusetts (8.3)	Arizona (20.0)
Motor vehicle deaths per 100,000 population	Maine (8.2)	Arkansas (28.9)
Suicide	Rhode Island (7.3)	Nevada (24.5)
5. Voting		
Percent of eligible population voting	Minnesota (60.0)	Tennessee (23.7)

C. Distractions

Education authorities say that student performance has fallen off because children spend too much time watching television and playing computer games. The National Assessment of Educational Progress checked the reading proficiency of fourth graders and found that children who read at home every day scored 223, whereas those who watched television six or more hours a day and rarely read at home scored 198. Those who watched TV one hour a day scored 220.

Interview campus and local educators about the latest findings and their comments about them.

D. SAT

If your admissions office uses the Scholastic Aptitude Test or similar national tests in admitting freshmen, what weight is given to these tests? A number of colleges and universities contend that these tests do not indicate the variety of competences they seek in entering students. Some of these schools have dropped the SAT and similar tests as a requirement for applicants. What is being done at your school?

Campus Projects

A. Weight

More than half of all female college students are overly concerned about their weight, health officials report, and 20 percent of them have severe eating disorders. Thousands suffer from anorexia and bulimia.

By age 13, 53 percent of the girls surveyed in a national report said they were unhappy with their bodies. This unhappiness lasts through college, studies show.

A study of 682 women enrolled in a Midwestern university showed two-thirds of them admitted being so concerned about their body image they resorted to unhealthy behavior to control their weight. Laurie Mintz, a psychologist at the University of Southern California who did the study, said 17 percent reported taking appetite control pills, 10 percent used self-induced vomiting or laxatives to control weight and many engaged "in other unhealthy behavior such as chronic dieting and meal skipping."

The data, she said, suggest a widespread, damaging effect of American society's "pervasive preoccupation" with female weight and appearance. She said that advertisers for clothes and other commodities "often set up an unattainable body image for women by hiring adolescent models and dressing them up to look older."

A generation ago, a fashion model weighed 8 percent less than the average woman; today, models weigh 23 percent less. The average model, actress or dancer is thinner than 95 percent of the female population.

Devise a plan for a study on your campus that will result in a story about women and weight. For additional background, use a database.

B. Spending

What does it cost students to attend your college or university, and how do they raise the money? Make a survey and obtain plenty of anecdotal information. Include in the cost side of the ledger tuition, room and board, entertainment, travel, payment of debts, laundry, etc.

On the income side include savings, jobs, loans, grants and scholarships, assistance from home, etc.

Reach some general conclusions: Do students have to skimp to get by? Do they consider entertainment (movies, tapes, video equipment) part of their necessities? What have they had to eliminate? Do they find they will be able to graduate without taking an extended period away from school to earn money?

Community Projects

A. Bodies

Every year, 150,000 women die from complications associated with anorexia and bulimia. The National Association of Anorexia Nervosa and Associated Disorders says 7 million American women suffer from the two diseases associated with the female desire to be thin.

A survey of 33,000 women by *Glamour* magazine shows that women value being thin more than they value success or love.

"More women than ever before are dissatisfied with their bodies." This is the beginning of a story in a Midwestern newspaper that covers surveys of American women "varying in age, occupation, marital status, race, ethnic background and social class."

A story in *The Wall Street Journal* reports that many "outwardly healthy teen-agers think of these drugs (appetite suppressants) as a standard way to diet. An astonishing 49% of teen-age girls responding to a recent survey by *Sassy* magazine reported using diet pills, while 13% of the magazine's young readers have tried laxatives or diuretics for weight loss."

These pills are "neither effective nor safe," says the *Journal* story, but they are easily available and their use continues despite articles about their dangers.

The New York Times reports that "poor body image is the most common cause of depression among adolescent girls," and a survey of 10-year-old girls shows that a majority reported being afraid of becoming too fat.

Among adult women, complaints center on anxiety over specific body parts. One physician said women view their bodies as "an enemy." Surveys have found:

- One out of two women diets most of her life.
- Two out of three have mixed or depressed feelings looking at their nude bodies in the mirror.
- Fewer than half agreed with the statement, "I like my looks the way they are."
- Almost half said they would consider cosmetic surgery.

Using this information, and any other you may obtain through a database search, devise a survey of girls, teen-agers and women in the community on the subject of body image and diet.

C. Rates

1. If the stat
   year.
2. The pow
   the new rate
   a _____ perc
3. He said l
   deposits, or
4. The city
   but some of
   payments o
5. Police sa
   Roxboroug

D. Math Tes

After you

1. The me
   long is the

   $\left\{ \right.$

   a. 236
   b. 264
   c. 270
2. A stere
   needed to
   a. 1
   b. 4
   c. 2
3. The ci
   spent on
   a. $2
   b. $2
   c. $4
   d. $4
   e. $3

B. Regulations

What are the regulations regarding smoking in your city for restaurants, bars, workplaces, schools, sports areas? Some cities have these regulations:

Restaurants: Smoking prohibited except in a separately enclosed, separately ventilated smoking room not to exceed 25 percent of the seating area.
Workplaces: Smoking prohibited except in a separately enclosed, separately ventilated smoking room.
Schools: Prohibited on all school property, K–12. For post-secondary schools, smoking is allowed only in a separately enclosed, separately ventilated room.
Indoor sports areas: Only in separately enclosed, separately ventilated smoking room not to exceed 25 percent of the area.

Do health authorities consider the regulations in your community sufficient to prevent the dangers of second-hand tobacco smoke? What do the political leaders think; what have they done?

What about the local jail? Many cities forbid smoking, as do state prisons in Oregon, Texas, Utah and Maryland. Seven other states permit inmates to smoke in restricted areas only.

Home Assignment

A. Readers

Research by newspapers indicates that young people do not read newspapers as avidly as their grandparents. Select 10 or more students and find out whether they read a newspaper regularly. Don't accept a yes without checking by asking about a story or two in the day's newspaper front page.

B. Polls

What polling techniques are the least and the most reliable? Why?

Class Discussion

Figures

Arthur M. Ross, a former federal commissioner of labor statistics, made these points, among others, in an article, "The Data Game," in *The Washington Monthly*:

If you are measuring the number of cows in Nevada, nothing more is reported or implied than what has been counted: 6,000,000 cows. A cow exists in a state of nature and is directly observable. But suppose you administer an intelligence test to a group of children. The test is one thing, a mechanical instrument; intelligence is something else altogether, an abstraction devised by psychologists. While the scores of a test can be calculated, that which is measured remains an abstraction. Educators have been learning the painful lesson that great care must be used in drawing inferences from one to another.

When government officials call for statistics, they seldom want anything as palpable as the cows of Nevada. They want measures of inflation, or poverty, or hard-core unemployment, or criminal activity, or American prestige abroad, or the progress of the Vietnam war. These are man-made concepts, *socially defined*. It is man who invents the categories; it is man who decides to characterize them in terms of one or two measurable dimensions. But as in the case of I.Q. tests, the people who read government statistics—the press, the public, and the officials—are prone to regard partial or statistical truths as objective realities.

Thus shadow is confused with substance. Essentially this is how public officials deceive themselves with statistics of impeccable quality. The officials are vulnerable because they are searching desperately for ways to clarify and simplify the protean problems of government. Statistics enable them to do this at the cost of heroic oversimplification: one or two dimensions, which happen to be measurable, serve to symbolize an elusive, many-sided phenomenon.

The trouble is that the unmeasured, or unmeasurable, aspects of a problem may be vastly more important than those which have been, or can be, measured. And even with measurements that are known to reflect on the core of a problem, the rate of change in the United States has become so swift that "good" statistics, intelligently used in decision-making, may be rendered irrelevant or obsolete by the time action results from an official's decision. . . .

Charles Murray

Dollars fail
average rent doe
like and smells li
street outside the
stroll after night

How can journ

Skill Drill I: Re

Which referen

1. The name of
2. Background
3. The name of
4. The Nationa
5. Background
6. A good quot
7. An explanat
8. The names o
9. The names o
10. The vote for
11. The occupat
12. The states a
13. Details abou
14. The content
15. The highwa

Skill Drill II:

Arithmetic is
porter who can d
this useful tool m
porters often hav
did the computin

A. Percentage

1. The numbe
2. In the city,
   year the total
3. His weight
4. The facult
5. The averas
   are _____ per

B. Fractions

1. During the
   month to 4.
2. About ___
   165 failed.
3. _____ tim
   were 1,390,
4. The Unite
5. If any mo
   15,270 felon

---

5 The Lead

John Shearer

The lead's right on target.

Introduction

Because the lead is the first part of the story the reader sees or the listener hears, it must be crafted with particular care. Generally, it is short—25 to 35 words—and captures the most important or interesting aspect of the event being described. The lead follows the subject-verb-object sentence pattern for quick comprehension. The two types of leads are the direct lead, which is used for breaking news events, and the delayed lead, which is used for feature stories. Increasingly, the delayed lead, with its emphasis on an interesting incident or anecdote, is being used on straight news stories.

Exercises

A. Dickens

This story appears in the Mallory College newspaper:

Charles Dickens is often thought of as a creative giant whose novels are required reading in high school (*A Tale of Two Cities*) and in college (*Bleak House* or *Hard Times*). He is less often understood as a radical reformer with a social purpose who put his zeal not only into his novels but also into journalism.

Professor Merle Rubens, of the English Department at Mallory College, has just completed and has had accepted for publication by the Mallory College University Press his book, *Dickens: The Crusader*.

In his book, Professor Rubens says that Dickens' crusades included campaigns against the workhouse, which mistreated and starved paupers, and the working conditions in factories. Dickens wrote many articles about the deaths and mutilations in factories and the attempts by manufacturers to defy the laws designed to protect workers. "He pointed out that there were many fewer thefts, murders and other crimes than there were deaths from factory accidents," Professor Rubens said.

In the pages of his weekly magazine *Household Words,* Dickens said of public health in London that it "was the tragedy of 'Hamlet' with nothing in it but the gravedigger." He campaigned for clean air, water fit to drink and sewers for the poor in the slums, the English professor said.

Dickens also lauded the Ragged Schools, which consisted of volunteers who gave the poor children free instruction. There were no government-supported public schools then.

"There is no one like him today, this whirlwind of energy, decency and genius. He oversaw charities and devised slum-clearing projects that included cheap housing for the poor with libraries, playgrounds and schools nearby," Professor Rubens says in the introduction to his book, which he says took five years to research and write.

"Dickens," he said, "was one of society's great activists—a tough-minded, hard-headed man who worked for reform in his novels, his journalism, his personal life."

1. You are on the AP state wire rewrite desk and will put 150 words on the wire.
2. You are in charge of the online www.freenews.com and decide to put this story out for your readers.
3. You work for Channel 7 in Freeport and have still photos of copies of *Household Words.* Write a one-minute item.
4. Write the story for *The Freeport News.* 150

B. Jobs

Here are some recent figures from the Bureau of Labor Statistics on the groups of workers with the highest rates of on-the-job fatalities. The rate is on the basis of the number of fatalities per 100,000 workers in the category:

Commercial fishermen	106
Loggers	102
Airplane pilots	94
Metalworkers	65
Taxi drivers	47
Construction laborers	39
Roofers	30
Electrical workers	29
Truck drivers	25
Farm workers	24

First, use the computer or another aid to make a bar graph. Then write leads for the following:

1. The Associated Press.
2. A newspaper published in Oregon.
3. A newsletter for airplane pilots.
4. A TV or radio station in Anchorage.
5. An all-news radio station in New York City.

Assignments

A. Unsafe

Some cars are safer than others. Find out which are prone to rollovers, which have the highest death and injury figures in accidents. The Insurance Institute for Highway Safety keeps figures and six years ago reported the death rate in the smallest cars on the market was more than double the rate in standard-sized cars, 3 deaths per 10,000 registered cars for the smallest, 1.3 for the larger models.

Bring these figures up to date and include figures on deaths and injuries for SUVs. What drives people to purchase cars that are not as safe as standard models?

Write a Sunday feature.

B. Investment

What do investment authorities advise their clients to buy these days? What are they saying are good ways to put money away that may appreciate considerably and that combine safety and good return? High return usually involves some risks; what are they?

Compare investments such as mutual and other funds, U.S. Savings Bonds, treasury notes and bonds, municipal bonds and stocks.

C. PWC

The personal watercraft, colloquially known as the Jet Ski, is a point of contention wherever people take to the water. Some object to the noise, some to the carefree antics of their users. Recently, objections have centered on the PWC as a hazard to safety.

During a recent year, more than 2,500 PWC accidents led to 84 deaths. The result: Some states have decided to require drivers to be 16 years old. Some states require an instruction course. Connecticut requires a 10-hour course, New Jersey an 8-hour course.

What is the situation in your state? Are PWC operators licensed; is there a minimum age; are courses required; what is the safety-accident record?

Campus Projects

A. Marriage

About a fifth of all women surveyed say they do not plan to marry. What do women students on the campus say of their marital plans? The Census Bureau says that of women in their peak childbearing age (18–34), most plan on two children. The figures:

No children—10 percent
One child—13 percent
Two children—47 percent
Three or more—30 percent

What size family do women on your campus plan and why? How many of the women you survey plan on careers after graduation? How will those who plan careers and marriage blend the two?

B. Online Classes

What is your school doing about:

1. Distance education—the opening of classes to students off campus through online classes? If offered, can on-campus students take such classes?
2. If such courses exist, what do students who take them think of them as compared with the standard classroom setting?

These are much-debated subjects. Some say the idea of having students take courses at home without personal instruction denies students social interaction with other students and personal direction by a faculty member. In response, some educators say that where classes consist of more than 100 students, it makes little difference. Also, there are considerable cost savings in online teaching when tuition is inexorably rising to meet costs of traditional teaching.

C. Shortchanged

Many undergraduate courses are taught by graduate students with little or no teaching experience, and many courses consist of lectures in large auditoriums. These are two of the charges leveled against large universities. Consult Web sources for a 350-word story on the alleged shortcomings of undergraduate education and some of the suggested remedies. Do any of these apply to your school? If so, localize your story with ample background.

Community Projects

A. Broken

What doesn't work in town? What do people complain about: traffic lights, potholes, traffic jams, poor city services, crowded schools, lack of certain kinds of stores, high prices, lack of opportunities for young people? See whether the complaints form a pattern.

B. Differences

The lines that separate religions are no longer only those that differentiate Catholics, Protestants, Jews and Moslems. Religion is also divided by lines within religious traditions.

Some Catholics believe in the infallibility of the Pope, but others do not. Several Protestant groups consider the Bible absolutely authoritative, whereas others do not accept its literal meaning. Among Jews, the Orthodox have far stricter rules than those who belong to Reform synagogues.

In your community, select a religious group and describe its agreements and differences with other groups in the same denomination. Write for the newspaper's religious column or for a broadcast feature.

Home Assignment

Leads

Clip from a recent newspaper five local stories for a study of their leads.

1. Classify them as direct or delayed leads.
2. Are they all denotative leads, or is there an interpretative lead among the five?
3. Do any of the five stories back into the lead, or is the lead buried?
4. Make a readability study of the leads from the guides in the textbook.

Class Discussion

A. Second Day

Here is the beginning of a story in the regional morning daily newspaper in your area:

The Freeport Chamber of Commerce announced last night that it will launch an investigation into complaints that merchants along U.S. 81 are gouging tourists.

The chamber's board of directors approved the inquiry after a four-hour closed-door discussion that was marked by heated debate. The vote was 8–7, Fred Graham, secretary of the Chamber said.

The matter was forwarded to the chamber by the U.S. Highway Users Assn., which said its members had complained of "outrageous prices, discourteous service, and unsanitary conditions" along U.S. 81 approaching and in Freeport. . . .

Make a list of story ideas for a folo in the local afternoon newspaper. Give specifics for those you would contact.

U.S. 81 begins at the southwest corner of the city near Three Corners Junction, enters on Hunter Avenue, goes up Vermont Avenue to Concord Street and then turns northeast on Oregon Avenue and exits the city. (See **Freeport City Map**.)

B. Purpose

In his essay "Why I Write," George Orwell says there are:

". . . four great motives for writing, at any rate for writing prose. They exist in different degrees in every writer, and in any one writer the proportions will vary from time to time, according to the atmosphere in which he is living. They are:

1. Sheer egoism. Desire to seem clever, to be talked about, to be remembered after death, to get your own back on grownups who snubbed you in childhood, etc., etc. It is humbug to pretend that this is not a motive, and a strong one. . . .

2. Aesthetic enthusiasm. Perception of beauty in the external world, or, on the other hand, in words and their right arrangement. Pleasure in the impact of one sound on another, in the firmness of good prose or the rhythm of a good story. Desire to share an experience which one feels is valuable and ought not to be missed. . . .

3. Historical impulse. Desire to see things as they are, to find out true facts and store them up for the use of posterity.

4. Political purpose—using the word *political* in the widest possible sense. Desire to push the world in a certain direction, to alter other people's idea of the kind of society that they should strive after. Once again, no book is genuinely free from political bias. The opinion that art should have nothing to do with politics is itself a political attitude."

Orwell said that when he sits down to write it is "because there is some lie that I want to expose, some fact to which I want to draw attention, and my initial concern is to get a hearing. But I could not do the work of writing a book, or even a long magazine article, if it were not also an aesthetic experience. . . ."

Do you think Orwell's motives apply to journalism and journalists? Where do you find yourself in his list? Or have you still another motive?

Skill Drill I: Lead Choice

Indicate whether a direct or a delayed lead would be appropriate for these events:

1. Adoption of the city budget. _____
2. Announcement of a performance next month of *Trial by Jury* by the local Gilbert and Sullivan Society. _____
3. Introduction of calculators into grade school arithmetic classes. _____
4. Election of officers of the county medical society. _____
5. Award of fellowship to a faculty member. _____
6. Arrival of Barnum & Bailey Circus in town. _____
7. Preparations of Doina Melinte for metric-mile race in Olympics. _____
8. Teaching innovations by modern language department. _____
9. Total employment in the United States for past year. _____
10. Background of candidate for U.S. Senate. _____
11. Approval by FCC of interstate telephone rate increase. _____
12. Jury verdict. _____
13. Survey of consumer complaints on automobile repairs. _____
14. Arrest of Utah congressman on charge of soliciting for prostitution. _____
15. Curtis Strange's dropping out of college to become golf pro. _____

Skill Drill II: Simplifying

Some editors demand short leads, under 30 words whenever possible. This requires reporters to stress single-element and summary leads in their stories. Rewrite the following leads, making them single-element or summary with fewer than 30 words.

1. The city planning department plans to make repairs this coming summer on Ogden, Concord and Vincent Streets at an estimated cost of $18,000, $22,000 and $78,000, respectively, it was announced by City Engineer O. M. Shelton.

2. After a three-day search, police today reported the arrest of Eileen McCoy, 19, in a Chicago bus depot on a charge of arson in connection with the fire that left Kmart Eastview a burned-out hulk last week at an estimated loss of $2 million.

3. The state purchasing agent will open bids Dec. 10 for the purchase of electronic equipment for the state university, including calculators for the mathematics department, audiovisual projectors and tape recorders for the modern language department, and installation of an all-electronic newsroom for the school of journalism. The newsroom installation is expected to cost at least $250,000 and will enable students to write and edit copy without typewriters or pencils.

4. A last-quarter scoring spree by Connie Hawkins, the newly arrived forward, enabled the Bullets to erase a seemingly insurmountable 22-point halftime lead by the Warriors in a come-from-behind win, 88-87.

5. "The defendant's crime may not have caused physical harm, but the hardship he inflicted on those who trusted him with their savings cannot be ignored," said District Judge Marvin Hurley yesterday in sentencing Norris Josephson to a minimum of five years in the state penitentiary on a fraudulent investment scheme that bilked local residents of more than a half million dollars.

6. The weather bureau today offered little hope to corn and wheat growers across a wide belt of Minnesota with a prediction of no rain for the next week to relieve the month-long drought that has cut crops by an estimated 5 percent to date.

7. F.W. Walkenhorst, a university regent, said at a meeting of the regents today that the teaching staff at the state university works an average of fewer than 20 hours a week and that, unless this is remedied by a larger course load, the state legislature could not be expected to approve the university's current budget request.

8. The Crested Butte Dam burst last night and a wall of water 12 feet high swept through small towns, farms and ranches in eastern Idaho leaving an unknown number of dead and injured and millions of dollars in destruction.

9. In a talk last night to the local press club, Russell Cooper, a political reporter based in Washington, D.C., said that the traditional role of the political reporter has been superseded by modern advertising techniques, which allow a candidate to project the image the candidate desires in "the picture-hungry, simplicity-oriented media that are unwilling or unable to deal with complexities."

10. The use of publicly employed teachers in religious schools has come under constitutional challenge in a suit filed in federal court here today by the National Coalition for Public Education and Religious Liberty (PEARL). The organization contends that the United States Commission on Education has violated the Constitution by ignoring Supreme Court rulings barring the assignment of public school teachers to religious schools during regular school hours.

City Engineer, O. M. Shelton, announced that up to $118,000 worth of repairs are to be done on Ogden, Concord, and Vincent streets.

6 Story Structure

Michel du Cille

Putting the story elements in order.

Introduction

The news story moves logically and smoothly from the lead through the body of the story to the ending. Each part of this structure serves a distinct purpose:

• **Lead:** Gives the reader the crux of the story. It is written to invite the reader into the story.

• **Body:** Amplifies the lead with supporting documentation; includes secondary material.

• **Ending:** Carries the least important material. For features, it provides the punch line or kicker and sometimes is used to summarize the material in the story.

Exercises

Write 150 words at most for each.

A. Opening

Information called in by the campus correspondent:

The Mallory College Food Cooperative opened with flying banners and rock music yesterday. Provost Thomas Palmer and a college alum, Louis Truett, '54, founder and president of the ShopRite supermarket chain, were on hand to send off the manager, David Green, and his staff of a dozen students in their program to bring students a low-cost campus grocery. The school turned over a basement room in the F.L. McCoy dormitory to the student entrepreneurs after Green complained that students were paying exorbitant prices for basics in town.

B. Lobby

Call from Mildred Cahan:

The Freeport League of Women Voters will send a 10-person delegation to the state capitol, leaving 8 a.m., Monday, to talk to members of the state legislature about a minimum wage bill, introduced last month and now in the Senate Labor Committee, that would exempt several types of workers from the state minimum wage law. To be exempted: hotel, restaurant and laundry workers, hospital aides, domestic workers, nonclassified municipal and state clerical workers. The local league last week endorsed the stand of the state organization opposing the bill. Mildred Cahan, chairwoman of the local chapter, said, "The bill clearly is aimed at the low-income female worker who now barely makes $6 an hour, a wage enabling her to bob up and down in a sea of poverty."

C. Trip

Peter Hay, BPOE secretary, press release:

The Freeport Elks Club announces that 42 of its members and their wives have signed up for a trip this summer to Russia, and 16 will be going to China. The Russian contingent leaves July 15 for 2 weeks: the Chinese group leaves Aug. 15 for 15 days. One couple, Mr. and Mrs. Dale L. Himmelstein, will make both trips. "These will be our 21st and 22nd countries since Dale retired three years ago," Mrs. Himmelstein says. He was a clerk at United Airlines in Freeport for 30 years "and never left the state until his retirement," she adds.

Assignments

A. Trail (1)

Reporters talk about following the "paper trail" of a person they are checking or investigating. They obtain documents about the person that include birth certificate, court records, divorce filing and school documents. First, make a list of documents you think would make up part of the paper trail; then, see which of these is available to the public.

B. Trail (2)

Make a paper trail on someone in the community: a politician, school official, lawyer, physician, police official, businessperson.

C. Admissions

A rash of fabricated applications for admissions has hit colleges in recent years, and some schools have reviewed their admissions process. Students who submitted excellent essays were discovered to have had low grades in high school English. Some applicants falsified membership in student organizations. Transfer students doctored their grades, and some did not submit all SAT test scores despite being required to do so.

"We're all vulnerable," said the dean of admissions at the University of Pennsylvania. "The system is based on trust. There are no metal detectors in this business."

Has your school's admission office had trouble with admissions and, if so, how has it handled the problem?

Campus Projects

A. Tatters

A study by the Carnegie Foundation for the Advancement of Teaching said the campus has been the scene of a breakdown in civility and that traditional academic and social values on campus have been undermined.

It also found that many students were unprepared for college work and that, while on campus, most did only enough studying "to get by."

Racial and other tensions have undermined a sense of community in academic life, the foundation found. "The idyllic visions that are routinely portrayed in college promotional materials often mask disturbing realities of student life," said Ernest L. Boyer, president of the foundation, in the prologue to the study.

The study found that "words are used not as the key to understanding but as weapons of assault. . . . Equally disturbing is the fact that abusive language is revealed most strikingly in racial, ethnic and sexual slurs."

The problems were most acute at large institutions, where more than 60 percent of the students said sexual harassment was a problem and half complained of "racial intimidation and harassment." At smaller liberal arts colleges, the study found the percentages were 30 and 15 percent, respectively.

The foundation criticized the academic system that encourages faculty members to pursue research at the expense of teaching. "Faculty, because of their reward system, are often not able to spend time with students, especially undergraduates," the foundation reported. "Teaching frequently is not well rewarded, especially for young teachers seeking tenure. . . ." The report stated that young instructors find "it's much safer to present a paper at the national convention than it is to spend time with undergraduates back home."

It also reported that 23 percent of the students spent more than 16 hours a week studying outside the classroom, down from 33 percent in 1985.

Organize a campus study that includes students, admissions officers, nontenured and tenured faculty members and administrators. Paint a portrait of campus life.

B. Alumni

Find out when alumni are having a reunion on campus and interview them. First, design a set of questions that include the benefits and liabilities of their college education, the changes they see on the campus and in themselves, their advice to students in various fields of study.

Community Projects

A. Polite

How polite are people in your city? Some cities have the reputation of being cold and indifferent, and others are known for warmth and courtesy. New York City is considered by residents and visitors alike to be harsh and rude. Cheyenne, Wyo., says Marjabelle Young-Stewart, who runs etiquette classes for executives, is the most polite city in the country.

Young-Stewart, who has been compiling lists of the country's most polite cities for 15 years, says the Wyoming city encourages residents to greet visitors with a friendly "howdy," and out-of-towners are given tongue-in-cheek parking tickets that state that hanging is the usual punishment for such infractions.

Among the other cities she lists as polite are Charleston, S.C.; Portland, Ore.; Seattle; Mobile; Pensacola, Fla.; San Diego; Denver; Pittsburgh; Washington, D.C.

Washington? One of her clients, Young-Stewart said, told her, "When they hold someone up there they say, 'Excuse me, but can I have your wallet?' "

Conduct a politeness study of your community.

B. Concern

What's bothering people in town? Here is a list of problems most commonly cited in many polls. Draw up a survey plan and write a story that blends data with comments by individuals:

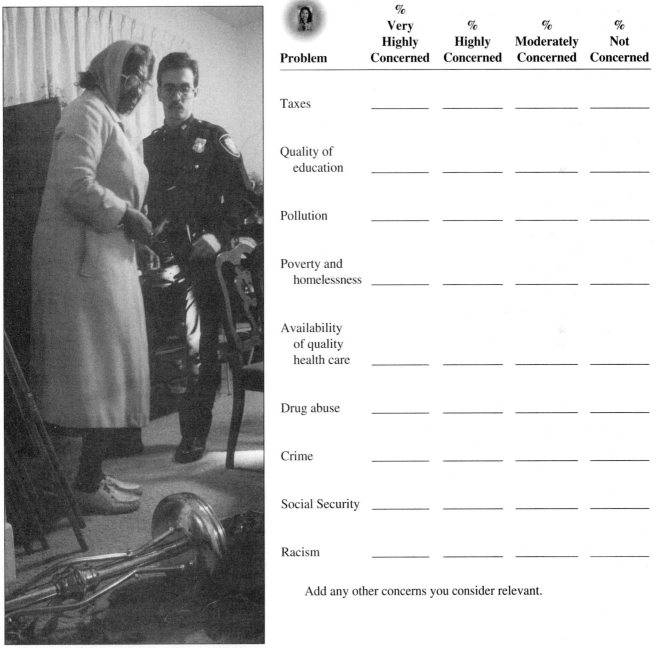

Problem	% Very Highly Concerned	% Highly Concerned	% Moderately Concerned	% Not Concerned
Taxes	_____	_____	_____	_____
Quality of education	_____	_____	_____	_____
Pollution	_____	_____	_____	_____
Poverty and homelessness	_____	_____	_____	_____
Availability of quality health care	_____	_____	_____	_____
Drug abuse	_____	_____	_____	_____
Crime	_____	_____	_____	_____
Social Security	_____	_____	_____	_____
Racism	_____	_____	_____	_____

Add any other concerns you consider relevant.

Rodger Mallison, *Fort Worth Star-Telegram*
Home burglary—one of 2.5 million a year.

Home Assignment

A. Cemetery

The news story structure is:

Lead that contains the most important fact or facts.

Body that contains:
- Material that amplifies and buttresses the lead.
- Background information.
- Secondary facts or information.

Clip a local news story from the most recent issue of the newspaper you read and break it down into its basic structure. Here is an example of how you might do it with the use of a lettering system.

The city zoning board yesterday approved the construction of a 10-foot-high chain-link fence around the Temple B'nai Shalom cemetery to keep out vandals.	Lead—A
But the board denied the congregation's request for a barbed wire at the top of the fence because the cemetery, at 1282 Airport Road, is in a residential zone.	Amplification of lead—A_1
"The fence is not worth anything to us without the barbed wire," William Gamm, a lawyer for the congregation, said last night.	Amplification of lead—A_2
Mr. Gamm said that young people are using the cemetery as a shortcut to the GoldMart Shopping Center at 1300 Airport Road and that unless an impenetrable fence is erected graves will be desecrated.	Amplification of lead—A_3
The temple made its request for the fence last month following the discovery by members of the congregation of several overturned grave markers.	Background
In other actions, the zoning board acted on the following requests:	Secondary material
Barry Tobin, 112 Bismark St., use of first and second floors as massage parlor—postponed.	Secondary fact—B
Raymond Feeney, 167 Kentucky Ave., remove one-story rear addition and erect three-story rear addition—approved.	Secondary fact—C
Daniel Snead, 481 Yale Ave., use of first floor as private club—disapproved.	Secondary fact—D

B. Comparison

Contrast stories that use the inverted pyramid and the storytelling form. What conclusions can you draw about why each form was used for the stories you selected?

Class Discussion

Bids

Analyze this story, using the sample analysis of *A. Cemetery* as a model:

Apparent low bids totaling $216,000 were submitted today for the renovation of the former Scott Building, 526 Broadway, for use by the local police and traffic engineering departments as a garage.

The bids were referred by the city purchasing agent to the city engineer for review.

A total of 41 bids were received for four separate contracts involved in the renovation. The city council had appropriated $350,000 for the renovation project. The city has already spent $423,000 for the purchase of the property.

The board also received bids for the purchase of 15 police vehicles, for the purchase of two pickup trucks for the water department and for the paving of a portion of Elm Street.

Apparent low bidders for the garage renovation, the amount bid and the number of bidders for each contract were:

—General construction: Hesch Construction Corp., of Albany, $111,958, 13 bidders.
—Heating and ventilation: Brown Plumbing and Heating, Inc., of Clovia, $44,492, 10 bidders.

—Plumbing: J.N. Hunsley Co., of Piedmont, $33,332, eight bidders.
—Electrical work: McCall Electric Co., of Albany, $25,980, 10 bidders.

Freeport Dodge, Inc., the sole bidder in each instance, was awarded three contracts to provide 15 police vehicles for a total cost of $120,237.

Freeport Dodge offered the apparent low bid of $15,400 each for two pickup trucks. The only other bid of $19,554 was from Simpson Motors Co.

Wrightson Industries Inc., of Freeport, submitted the apparent low bid of $67,986 for the improvement of 1,500 feet of Madison Street. The council had appropriated $120,000 for the job. There were five other bidders.

In a final action, E.W. Grimes Co., of Freeport, was awarded $15,605 for fireproofing the city-owned Mohawk Brush Building on Blue Ridge Road.

Skill Drill: Necessities

Every story may be said to demand certain necessary information. It is the reporter's task to include the information in the story. List the information that would be required in the following stories:

A. Royalty

The election of the high school homecoming king and queen.

Jeff W. Henderson

B. Fatal

A traffic accident in which a person died.

C. Lieutenant

Promotion of a local serviceman.

D. Project

Announcement of a new construction project.

E. Blaze

A fire that destroys a building in town.

F. New

Appointment of a new teacher, clergyman, city official.

G. Game

The result of a football or basketball game.

H. Verdict

The verdict in a trial.

I. Death

The obituary of a former city official.

J. Clinic

Proposed closing of a neighborhood public health clinic.

K. Zone

Request for a change in zoning classification from residential to commercial.

L. Crime

The annual citywide crime report.

M. Split

A divorce filing.

N. Damage

Suit alleging $250,000 damages for injuries in an auto accident.

O. Meters

Introduction of an ordinance to get rid of parking meters downtown.

7 The Writer's Art

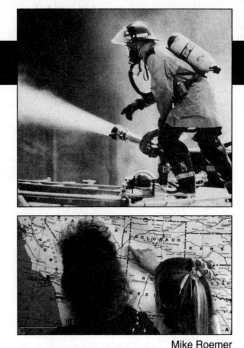

Introduction

The well-written story is clear and convincing. Quotes, anecdotes and actions involve the reader and listener in the event. Their use and the inclusion of specific details serve to convince the reader and viewer that the account is truthful. To keep the reader glued to the piece, sentences are short, an everyday vocabulary is used and transitions are used to keep the separate elements and themes tightly structured. The well-written story has a tone, pace and a rhythm that match the nature of the event. Writers read widely to learn the writing trade, and they are not reluctant to rewrite their work.

Mike Roemer

The event dictates the pace of the piece.

Exercises

A. Pap Test

The city health department has released a study on preventive medicine in Freeport and your editor instructs you to write a series on the findings. One of the articles will concern what Jane Jacobson, director of the department, describes as "a dangerous situation for Freeport women who do not have routine Pap tests."

Here and on the next page are two key graphs from the Freeport study you should use in your article of 250 words.

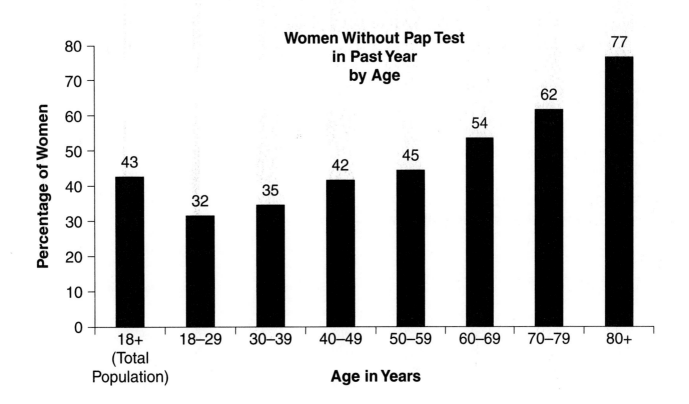

Women Without Pap Test in Past Year by Age

Percentage of Women vs. Age in Years:
- 18+ (Total Population): 43
- 18–29: 32
- 30–39: 35
- 40–49: 42
- 50–59: 45
- 60–69: 54
- 70–79: 62
- 80+: 77

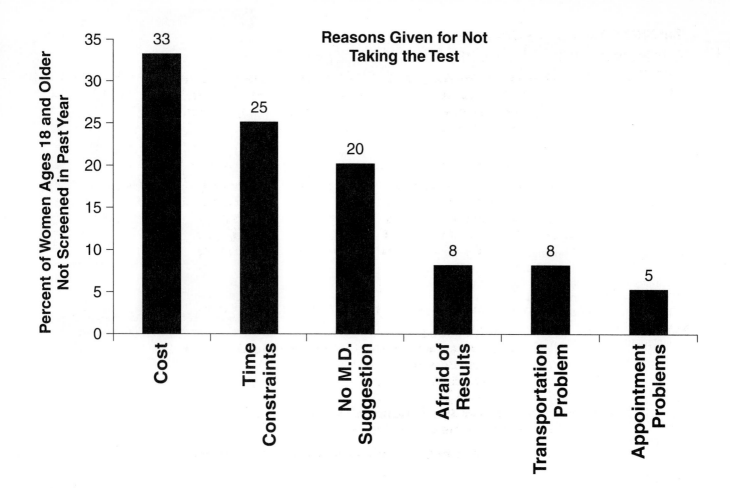

Reasons Given for Not Taking the Test

Percent of Women Ages 18 and Older Not Screened in Past Year

Cost	Time Constraints	No M.D. Suggestion	Afraid of Results	Transportation Problem	Appointment Problems
33	25	20	8	8	5

B. Consequences

Trustees of Mallory College have been considering a 27.5 percent increase in tuition to $25,500 a year. But some members of the faculty have objected that the increase would prevent too many students from applying. The Sociology Department made a study that concluded: "Any significant tuition increase would shut our doors to the disadvantaged and the different." It issued a graph (see right) that the department head, Margot Adler, said "is evidence of the problems we already face, problems that would worsen with the adoption of the proposed increase. We find most black and Hispanic students are in the low parental income group."

The trustees meet next Tuesday. Your editor wants a 250-word story that uses the material in the graph.

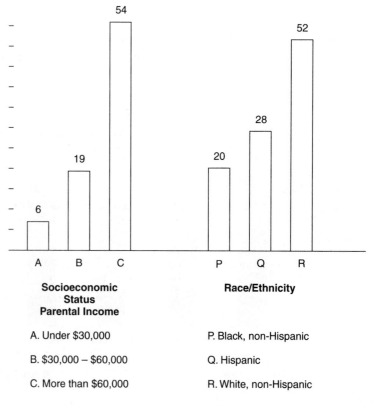

Percentage of students enrolled five years ago as freshmen who received bachelor's degrees last year.

A	B	C	P	Q	R
6	19	54	20	28	52

Socioeconomic Status Parental Income

Race/Ethnicity

A. Under $30,000

B. $30,000 – $60,000

C. More than $60,000

P. Black, non-Hispanic

Q. Hispanic

R. White, non-Hispanic

Assignments

A. Inflation

The senior research scientist at the College Board, Howard Everson, made the following observation about grades and SAT scores:

> Between 1987 and 1994, the percentage of students reporting "A" grade averages rose from 28 to 32 percent, but their average SAT scores fell 6 to 15 points. Overall, average grades were lowest in mathematics and natural science, and highest in arts/music and social science/history.

Interview campus sources: Is Everson's finding still relevant that grade inflation persists in high schools?

B. Librarian

Among the 850,000 high school students who took the Scholastic Aptitude Test, fewer than 300 indicated that they intended to study library science in college. That's a tiny fraction of 1 percent and by far the smallest intended college major. Why? Interview librarians on campus and in town.

C. Camera

Interview the head of a local photography club or organization. Discuss recent developments in photography such as the digital camera. What seems to interest photographers who, in the past, seemed to prefer the grab shot, candid pictures taken with the 35-mm camera? Is there any tendency to salon or scenic photography, toward larger cameras? What do they think of photo enhancement?

D. Architecture

Have a local architect or a member of the art or architecture department accompany you on a walking tour of the city center for an assessment of the architectural value of the buildings there.

E. Jailed

Visit a city jail and ask the person in charge for an inventory of crime. That is, for what offenses are the men and women behind bars? Does this vary with the day of the week, time of month, part of year? Are totals from the past week or the past month significantly different from previous periods?

F. Deposits

Obtain from local banks, or other reliable sources, total amounts in savings and checking (time and demand) accounts for the last period for which new figures are available—quarter, half-year or annual. Is there a marked change from previous periods? What is the significance of these figures? What do they usually reflect? Note the Christmas Club totals.

G. Grades

Is there a correlation between the Scholastic Aptitude Test (SAT) or American College Test (ACT) scores of entering students and their success in your school? The subject is frequently studied on campuses. Compare with national data and other schools, if your source has such information. (At the University of New Mexico, of 2,147 students entering with ACT scores of 15 and under, 388 graduated; of 1,649 students entering with ACT scores of 26 and above, 1,237 graduated.)

H. Health Stats

Interview local health authorities and examine statistics to identify some of the major health problems in the city.

Campus Projects

A. Cheating (1)

College authorities report that cheating is increasing on the campus. Instructors say they are finding more cases of plagiarism than ever before. A journalism instructor tells this story:

> I assigned students to select a well-known person to interview, and this student handed me a well-written piece. The trouble is he didn't know the man had died three years ago. I went to NEXIS and found that he picked up an interview story from a Chicago newspaper, then apparently didn't look further.

The student was dismissed from the program.

Student newspapers at the Naval Academy and MIT report unprecedented cheating. A study by Donald McCabe of the Rutgers University business faculty of 6,000 students found that two-thirds of the students admitted cheating. His follow-up study of 18,000 students concluded 9 of 10 students admitted cheating at least once.

Cheating varies from putting notes on handkerchiefs to stealing examinations before they are given. It includes providing false footnotes on a paper, using fraternity and Internet papers for a course, submitting papers written by another.

How does your school define cheating, and what is its frequency on your campus? What preventive measures are used, and what punishment is meted out to offenders?

B. Recruit

Make an inventory of your college or university's recruiting efforts. Examine its efforts to recruit bright high school students, athletes, students with special abilities (musicians, artists, actors) and faculty members.

Scholars: Is anyone in the admissions office assigned to reach out to bright students? How? Is there a special fund for such recruiting? What inducements are offered these students: scholarships, special placement, jobs? How does the school describe the kind of student it is looking for? Is there alumni participation in this area of recruiting? Do any particular high schools have a reputation for graduating bright students?

Interview administrators, students, faculty members and high school college placement officers. Dig for particulars, examples, specifics.

Athletes: What kind of recruiting is done for intercollegiate athletics? Do coaches make trips to high schools? What is the budget for this? What sports are emphasized in recruiting athletes? What inducements are offered these athletes: special classes for remedial work, special eating facilities, athletic dormitory, scholarships? Describe these in detail.

What is the contribution of alumni and booster clubs in financial assistance and recruiting? How is this formalized? Do local merchants contribute? Has the school been involved in any problems with the NCAA? Explain.

In both areas, make sure to interview those involved: students who have been recruited, administrators, faculty members, people in the community.

C. Interfaith

The rate of interfaith marriages has steadily increased over the past 25 years. About 40 percent of the Catholics who marry each year do so outside their faith. The 1973 figure was 23 percent. Among Jews, the percentage of interfaith marriages went from 30 percent in 1970 to 52 percent in a recent year.

How much of a factor is religion in campus dating? Ask students and chaplains assigned to student religious organizations.

Community Projects

A. Bottlenecks

Make a traffic inventory of the community. Do commuters complain of delays? Are there dangerous intersections, poorly marked corners, pockmarked streets?

Interview commuters; listen to radio traffic reports for trouble spots and talk to those who gather information for the traffic reports. Talk to school safety patrol personnel, city street department employees and their superiors. Interview police, sheriff's officers and highway patrol officers who deal with traffic. Have the city highway or traffic engineer conduct a tour of known trouble spots.

Obtain the master plan for road repair, reconstruction, rerouting and new construction.

B. Adoption

Black children represent a disproportionate share of the children who are available for adoption. But long-established practices of social workers and adoption agencies follow racial, ethnic and religious lines, even in states that prohibit such restrictions.

What is the situation in your community? How many children of what race are available for adoption, and what is the practice about placing them? Are there white families that have adopted nonwhite children, and if so what was their experience?

Home Assignment

A. Fog

One way to check the readability of a story is to use the following formula:

1. Find the average number of words per sentence by counting the words in each sentence and dividing by the number of sentences. Use seven or eight sentences.
2. Add to the average sentence length the number of three-syllable words. Don't count easy words.
3. Multiply by 0.4.

The result will give you the grade level of the material.

The seven sentences and five three-syllable words I just used make for a sixth-grade reading level.

Test the daily newspaper you read and at least one of the magazines you read for their reading levels. Write a brief assessment of each, and indicate whether the material is written so that readers of the publication can understand it.

Background: About 25 million adults read below the fifth-grade level. Half the high school seniors cannot read at grade level. *The Washington Post* news columns tested at 14.5, *New York Times* at 12.6 and *USA Today* at 10.6.

B. Principles

The textbook describes the four principles of good writing. Apply them to an article from your local newspaper.

Class Discussion

Syracuse

Here is a handout from a sports publicity office. List all the clichés and trite expressions. Rewrite.

SYRACUSE, N.Y.—Syracuse University has 10 sophomore newcomers who may play more than a little football, but four of the young men could climb well up the ladder of success by December.

The athletes in question are halfback Ernie Davis, and Ken Ericson, center Bob Stem and quarterback Dave Sarette. The authority is Orange head coach Floyd (Ben) Schwartzwalder.

Top man among the rookie group is Ernie Davis, the fleet 6-2, 205-pound speedster from Elmira, N.Y., who was a world-beater with the SU frosh last fall and an All-American in high school. As the expression goes, Davis has all the tools.

"Ernie is our top prospect, no question about that," offers Schwartzwalder. "He'll be in our starting lineup against Kansas this Saturday and he's going to become a great football player. I'd like to have about 10 more like Ernie."

Ericson, a 6-2, 190-pound end from Weymouth, Mass., became an even more important factor in Schwartzwalder's plans last week when knee injuries sidelined starting left end Dave Baker and slowed up reserve flanker Tom Gilburg.

Ericson got a chance to scrimmage with the Syracuse starting team, due to the mishaps, and was very impressive. He is regarded as an outstanding pass receiver.

Stem, a fire-plug 5-11, 195-pound pivot from Phillipsburg, N.J., has improved by leaps and bounds and is pressing veterans Dave Applehof and Al Bemiller at center. Bob has drawn raves for his line-backing.

Skill Drill: Tightening the Lead

Reporters usually try to make their leads as short as possible. Here are some leads that contain unnecessary attribution, redundancies, opinions of the reporter, excess wordage, unimportant quotes, unnecessarily specific information. Use the subject-verb-object sentence structure for most of the leads.

A. Pollute

In looking for pollution along the city's lakeshore, investigators for the state Environmental Protection Commission said today they have discovered what they described as "high levels of beach and waterfront pollution."

B. Contract

The city today awarded a contract to Polly Plumbing Inc., of Roanoke, for the construction of 35 "necessary houses," also known as outhouses, along the state's roads and highways. The successful low bid by the firm was $89,565.

C. Year-End

The office of the police department today released year-end crime figures for the city that show homicides were down from 139 the previous year to 124 last year, but all other types of violent crime increased, 896 to 1,086.

D. Women

In a talk entitled "Whither Women," Hortense Hillerbrandt, an assistant state attorney general, and vice president of the caucus, told some 450 delegates to the annual convention of the Women's Caucus meeting here not to "put aside family responsibilities when you hang up the apron."

E. Kids

Benjamin Brown, the well-known child psychologist and author, said today in a speech to state educators that his studies and those of others indicate young children spend more time in front of TV sets than in bed asleep.

F. Fatal

Two cars collided at the intersection of Elm and Johnson Streets last night at 10:45 p.m. and took the lives of a local couple, Herbert and Helen Oliver, 56 Fairmont Blvd., and injured the passengers in the second car, Dwight Tanner and Beatrice Honer, both of Topeka.

G. Retire

When the church bells strike 12 noon tomorrow, the Rev. Frederick Malabee, who has retired, will walk down the main isle of St. John's for the last time as the church's pastor. He has presided over 542 Sunday services without missing one since he came here more than 10 years ago.

H. Concert

The community concert of the Philadelphia Symphony Orchestra, which had been scheduled for tomorrow evening at 8 p.m., has been indefinitely postponed because of the sudden illness of the conductor, Mrs. Ellen Klein, secretary of the concert association, said today.

I. Aspirin

Although we do not know much about why it works wonders, the most common household medicine, aspirin, has added stroke prevention to its powers, a report by a team of researchers at the Southwestern Community Hospital reported today. One or two aspirin a day is the recommended dosage.

J. Tax

Good news for taxpayers: Rep. Harmon C. Connally, of Texas, told members of the local Lions Club at their luncheon today at the Belmont Motel that big federal spending programs will face tough sledding in Congress next session.

8 Features, Long Stories and Series

Bob Thayer, *The Providence Journal*

A teen's dreams make for a good feature.

Introduction

• **Features.** Written to entertain. When people are involved, the writer lets the personalities carry the story. People are made to talk, act and interact.

• **Long stories.** Structured to keep the reader committed to staying with the story to the end. Sidebars are used to keep story length within readable bounds.

• **Series.** Written when the subject is too complex for a single story. Each part makes a specific point.

These story types rely for effectiveness on revealing details, meaningful quotes, and incidents that symbolize the thrust of the event or personality.

Features

Exercises I

A. Opening React

A Freeport merchant, Russell Rothkrug, owner of Russ's Market, which is across the street from the Mallory College campus, calls your city editor with a complaint. The editor turns the call over to you. He says it is a complaint about the new campus grocery store whose opening was recently described in the newspaper. (See Chapter 6, **Exercises, A. *Opening.***)

"No, it's not the story I don't like," says Rothkrug. "It's the college encouraging the kids to compete with private merchants. We have to operate at a profit, but these kids don't have families to support or rent to pay. I think it's unfair."

You ask if his business has been affected.

"Sure it has. Since that store opened 10 days ago, my business has fallen off about 20 percent."

Has he done anything?

"Yeah, I called the provost, Thomas Palmer, and complained, but all he would say is that he would look into it. He wasn't very encouraging."

You check with another merchant near the campus, Aaron Elston, owner of A-1 Shopping Center, and he says that he, too, has been disturbed, but that he has not yet noticed any appreciable downturn.

"Maybe 10 percent. But I am worried what it may be like when word spreads around the campus. They certainly don't have any costs, like hiring a guard here to keep those college kids from stealing everything off the shelves.

"They won't do that to the campus store. Well, maybe they will. Maybe those junior businessmen will learn what it's like to be a small merchant. Oh, the worries and the taxes and the rip-offs and the lousy quality of goods. You know, now that I think of it, I hope they stick around for a while. Those kids who talk so much about how private enterprise is exploitative may learn something.

"Tell that kid running the store I'll be happy to give him the name of my doctor. He has some good stuff for the nerves."

Write a story of 250 words for *The Freeport News* or Channel 7.

B. Waiter

A Freeport woman, Mrs. Arthur Katzen, telephones the newsroom to say she wants to describe a pleasant experience she had in New York City on a recent trip. She had read a piece in your newspaper about a honeymooning couple whose luggage was stolen by a taxi driver on their arrival in New York. She says:

> I was staying at the Waldorf Astoria this weekend and had breakfast in the Peacock Alley. I left what I thought was a $1 tip. During the day I noticed that I was short of money and couldn't figure out why.
>
> The next morning I went back for breakfast in the Peacock Alley. A waiter came over to me and handed me a $20 bill. He said I'd left it as a tip.
>
> So you see, not everyone there is a thief. He was such a pleasant young man. I gave him a reward of $5 for returning the $20.

Write a brief story.

C. Santa

It is three days before Christmas and you are sent to Stranger's department store to interview a Santa Claus on his experiences. The Santa Claus is Alfred York, 43, of 15 Templeton Ave., who had been a shipping clerk in a warehouse until last month.

> I got tired of hauling 80-pound crates around and when I saw the ad for a Santa Claus I figured lifting three-year-old kids would be a lot easier.
>
> I have four of my own, a little older now, but I could pick one up with each hand when they were little. I like kids, too. I mean, they give you a fresh way of looking at the world. They are so innocent, most of them, that is. But you can't believe some of them.
>
> They not only want everything they can think of, but they let you know if they don't get it there's going to be hell to pay. The other day I had this kid who whispered in my ear what he wanted, and then said to me, "And if I don't get it, you old bastard, I'm going to kick your ass."
>
> I used to hear that language in the Army. Maybe I hear a couple like that a day. Some of them don't know that their language is unusual. They hear it all day long and they think it's as normal as please and thank you.
>
> I wish all kids could have the innocence of youth that I had. But they grow up with violence, hookers on streetcorners, porno films everywhere. That's progress.
>
> Most of the boys still ask for basketballs, helmets and guns, and the girls want dolls and other feminine things. I guess liberation hasn't seeped down to the younger generation.

York is 6'2", weighs 195, needs a little padding around the stomach. He sits in a high chair in the toy department on the third floor and usually has a line of four or five children waiting to talk to him. Each child is given a minute or two. He continues:

> Most of them are decent kids. If their parents could hear what they ask for they might be ashamed of themselves—some for pampering the heck out of their children and spoiling them, some for having such narrow goals for themselves and their children. Many of these kids just want love, and they'll ask me if I can tell their parents to be kind to them. One little boy said to me, "Santa, I want peace and love for everyone, that's all I want."

Write a story of 300 words. Write 150 words for (www.freenews.com.)

D. No Baby

You are looking at some old clips and your eye catches a story about Baby, an African elephant in the local zoo whose pregnancy was reported by the zoo director, Cyrus Tucek, five months ago. You wonder how Baby is faring and you call the zoo.

Tucek is not there but his assistant, Bayard Parker, fills you in with a few words.

"She isn't," he tells you.

"Isn't what?" you ask.

"Pregnant," he replies.

"What happened?" you ask.

"False pregnancy, I guess," he says.

Sensing that Parker is a man of few words, but hoping to draw him out, you say you never heard of such a thing.

"Well, you have now," he says.

"How's she doing generally?" you ask.

"OK."

"When did you find out about Baby's false pregnancy?"

"Two days ago."

"When will Mr. Tucek be back?"

"Two weeks."

You decide you can't wait that long. Anyway, you see that you have the basic information, and you decide to write a short story.

Assignments I

A. IRS

The FBI says that most threats and almost half of all assaults on federal workers are directed at employees of the Internal Revenue Service. Interview an IRS worker and find out what his or her life is like. 350 words.

B. Pets

Write a short feature on one of these topics:

1. What are some of the pets students keep on campus? Are there restrictions?
2. Snakes and monkeys are supposedly bad risks for those seeking exotic pets. Why? What are the best bets for someone who wants an offbeat pet at home?
3. Breeds of dogs ebb and flow in popularity. Cocker spaniels were the favorites a couple of decades ago and then German shepherds, poodles and a variety of small dogs. What's the latest favorite? How expensive are these animals?
4. Is raising saltwater fish in the home aquarium as expensive and difficult as it once was? How popular is this hobby?
5. The lure of the cat, to some, is that it is mysterious. Unlike dogs, cats usually cannot be trained. Is this why people keep cats? Interview cat lovers.
6. Do people keep birds as pets? Canaries used to be popular but are no longer. Why? Can exotic birds be kept in the average home?

C. Lunch Box

What do manual workers eat for lunch? Go to construction sites where workers take lunch boxes and see what is inside. Write 300 words.

D. Dining

A third to a half of all meals are supposedly eaten outside the home. Interview family heads and single people about their dining habits. Why do they prefer to eat out? Write 350 words.

E. Genealogy

Interview local genealogists who help people do the research that enables them to find their roots.

F. Portrait

Write profiles of no more than 350 words on the following people:

1. A couple recently celebrating their 50th wedding anniversary.
2. A person born on February 29.
3. A fry cook at a fast-food outlet.
4. A maid in a local motel.
5. A rookie police officer. The police officer with the longest service record. An officer who works with juvenile offenders, with rape victims.
6. A disc jockey on an all-night radio program.
7. The winner of an award for academic achievement: National Merit Scholar, Westinghouse prize, Phi Beta Kappa, etc.
8. An athlete recruited from a distant city or country.
9. The night clerk in a local hotel or motel.
10. A faculty member recently returned from a trip abroad.

G. Holiday

Write a precede with as much local material as possible on one of these observances: New Year's Day, Chinese New Year, Lincoln's Birthday, St. Valentine's Day, Washington's Birthday, Ash Wednesday, Purim, St. Patrick's Day, Palm Sunday, Ramadan, first day of Passover, Good Friday, Easter, May Day, Memorial Day, Kwanzaa, Pentecost, Flag Day, Independence Day, Labor Day, Martin Luther King's Birthday, first day of Rosh Hashana, Yom Kippur, Columbus Day, Halloween, All Saints' Day, Veterans Day, Thanksgiving, first Sunday of Advent, first day of Hanukkah, Christmas.

Also, check your local ethnic, religious and racial groups for any special observances, parades, services. Write 300 to 350 words.

Long Stories and Series

Exercise II

Museum

You are sent to interview Thomas Chamberlain, who has recently joined the staff of the Chicago Art Institute as an assistant to the director. He is visiting colleges and universities around the country to learn about new techniques in the management of art museums. He is 29, has graduate degrees (M.A. and Ph.D.) from Brown University and his B.A. from the University of New Mexico. He was born in Grand Junction, Colo., is married, has no children.

Your editor wants a piece for the Sunday Leisure section on his opinions about museums. Chamberlain has been abroad on a study tour of museums and is just about finished with his U.S. tour, the editor says, and should have strong opinions about art. You interview him and you find he does have such opinions. Here are some quotes:

One of the key questions in art museum work today is whether to maintain the museum for the discerning person or to reach out to the masses. That may be a crude way to put it, but if you go to some museums you will see what I mean. In some, children are everywhere. Hordes of them. Sitting, bored out of their skulls, in front of a Rembrandt while some poor soul lectures these seven-year-olds on his use of somber colors.

The art student, or the person who wants to look at the genius of a Rembrandt that day, simply hasn't a chance to contemplate the work. Nor can he or she find quiet refuge anywhere in the museum most days.

But let's look at the other side. Museums are public institutions—many of them anyway. People are entitled to make use of what their money is paying for. More important, isn't the function of art in a democracy to uplift people, to take them from their daily pursuits of money, prestige, power, material possessions and the like?

Why shouldn't Rembrandt be for them? Why shouldn't his genius, his incredible humanity reach all of us? That outreach was the belief of Thomas Hoving at the Met in New York, and it was one of the many reasons for his stormy tenure there.

Ah, but that's only the beginning, and you people are going to have to face the problem here when your local art museum board or curator or director makes policy. By emphasizing the museum as "art accessible to all," do you take a small but definite step toward the majority culture of entertainment? Do you start to entice the crowds in with tricks; do you spiffy up the exhibits; do you somehow make your artists "relevant"?

Is there something to be said for high culture, that it should be kept from popular culture's lowering hand? Everything today in art and culture has become marketable, even the museum. The bottom line is all-important. Move in that direction in high art and it becomes lowbrow.

You interrupt Chamberlain and ask him what his own feelings are about the subject. Should the local art museum—any art museum, for that matter—be administered for those who seek education, inspiration, edification or should it consciously reach out with programs, tours for children, large-scale exhibits and the like?

What worries me is that when you reach out for the many you end up with a leveling process, and although the low may come up, the high goes down. Exhibits are geared for the person who has never heard a Mozart quintet or seen an El Greco. I know this sounds old-fashioned, even undemocratic. I like what Robert Brustein, the theater critic, says about how the traditional lines between culture and show business broke down. "Something happened in the Fifties," Brustein says, "something symbolized by the marriage of Arthur Miller and Marilyn Monroe. . . ."

Everyone wants culture with a capital C delivered in easy and digestible bites. Well, why not put the "Polish Rider" on the back of a cereal box? Or have a Renoir doll in every nursery? That doll would really sell, and it would take culture into every little girl's playroom.

Great works of art should not be inaccessible to people. But they cannot be mass marketed with the idea that they are as easily reached as some situation comedy on television. Hard work is involved in reaching out to the artist. Effort that makes the understanding all the more enjoyable.

Read *The Great Gatsby* or *Wuthering Heights* slowly. The language, the emotion open up to you. You cannot get it on television or in the movies—not the splendor of the creation, the beauty of the language and the depth of meaning. Those books are to be read, reread, to have people stop in the middle of a paragraph and look up and wonder. The same with art.

You should certainly have all the guidance and help you need to meet the artist on his or her terms. But finally, it's as they say in football—or is it basketball?—it's one on one. You and the artist. And the museum should make that confrontation possible.

Use the schools, use the lecture halls for education in art. But keep museums for those confronting the artist's work.

Write 750 to 900 words. Include background from research and interviews with members of the fine arts department, museum specialists.

Assignments II

A. Diseases

Draw or obtain a map of your city by health district. Chart changes in each district by cause of death for the past year, the year before and other years. Can you find any correlations between income and the mortality rates? Any other correlations? Pay special attention to infant mortality and to deaths from pneumonia and influenza, AIDS, drugs, diabetes, tuberculosis, cirrhosis of the liver, homicide. These usually are associated with socioeconomic factors. Write a long piece or plan a series.

B. Catholic

Interest in the papacy and the changes in the Roman Catholic Church have grown since the pontificate of John XXIII in 1958. A historian, J. M. Cameron, wrote:

> Papal authority is today scrutinized in a new way. The authority of authorities is less compelling and less evidently justifiable than it used to be . . . that particular authorities stand in need of justification, that no claims on their part are to be taken as self-justifying, as we might think the authority of a musician or an actor is justified in the performance, these things are accepted, even by theologians.
>
> In the past 15 years Roman Catholic theologians have become increasingly nervous over their performances, especially where the question of authority has been touched upon. . . .

Since the pontificate of John Paul II in 1978, some observers of the church see a countermovement to preserve the power of the church with its own followers and in countries that have enacted laws that directly violate some of the church's sacrosanct teachings. They saw John Paul II as a conservative force, unyielding in the face of liberalizing efforts by U.S. and Western European bishops. His refusal to recognize the state of Israel—church policy for more than 15 years—and his welcome to Austrian President Kurt Waldheim, a former Nazi whom many nations shunned, were seen as impediments to ecumenism. Other church observers see John Paul II as a tireless crusader for values under attack from a modernism that compromises morality. They also praise him for specific acts of generosity and, in the case of the church's persecution of Jews, repentance.

Some say the church's turn from Vatican II and toward more conservative values, a turn away from what some describe as the American virtues of democracy and pluralism, a toleration of differences, began in 1968 with the encyclical *Humanae Vitae*. In it, Pope Paul VI solemnly reaffirmed the church's condemnation of "artificial birth control." This, said many outside the church and some liberals inside it, was a historic mistake.

As the critics of the encyclical predicted, in Europe and North America the prohibition is ignored. Birthrates reveal that Catholics use contraception as frequently as non-Catholics.

This rejection, say students of the church, also indicates a rejection of the authority of the papacy and it has weakened the doctrine of papal infallibility. (The doctrine is relatively new in the church's history; it was issued by the First Vatican Council in 1870.)

One church observer, James Carroll, a former Paulist priest, says, "The increased willingness of Catholics to trust their own consciences, even in grave violation of official teaching, represents the long overdue beginning of a new era in the life of the church, one that builds on earlier, unrealized impulses. . . ."

John Miller, a British neurologist who was a member of the Papal Commission on Birth Control of Pope John XXIII, said that around 85 percent of Catholics use some form of artificial birth control and do not think it is morally wrong to do so. He argues that this high number of practicing Catholics who do not abide by the church's instructions leads to questions by Catholics about the church's credibility on larger matters of faith.

But Pope John Paul II has not retreated from his strong position on many social issues, particularly on abortion.

In his encyclical *Evangelium Vitae* in 1995, the pope called on Catholics to resist laws that violate the "original inalienable right to life." He said that despite legislation that permits abortion and euthanasia, there is "no obligation in conscience to obey such laws. Instead, there is a grave and clear obligation to oppose them by conscientious objection."

He warned of a "profound crisis of culture" that is the result of exalting individual freedom at the expense of personal responsibility. This freedom has created, the pope said, "a veritable structure of sin."

For women who have had abortions, the pope offered hope for redemption: "The wound in your heart may not yet have healed. Certainly what happened was and remains terribly wrong. But do not give into discouragement and do not lose hope."

The pope's message was offered at a time, the Vatican reported, that 40 million abortions are performed around the world each year. An aide commented, "This is a pope who wants to say 'no' to aspects of what is known as modernity. It doesn't upset him in the least to be against society."

To remove legal protection from life at any stage, even by majority vote, the pope wrote, introduces moral relativism that undermines democracy.

Conor Cruise O'Brien, a former U.N. official and international commentator, wrote in his book *Passion and Cunning and Other Essays* that John Paul's purpose is to rehabilitate the doctrinal authority of the papacy and revert to pre-Vatican II moral dogma. Although in public the pope appears to endorse Vatican II, O'Brien concludes, he is in reality reasserting the conservative doctrines of Vatican I.

Margaret O'Brien Steinfels, the editor of *Commonweal* magazine, a liberal Catholic publication, describes the Roman Catholic Church as moving "very slowly and very carefully. Twice in this century it has acted in an uncharacteristically bold manner. The first instance was Pope John XXIII's decision to convene the Second Vatican Council in 1962—the first such council in nearly 100 years. The second bold move was the election in 1978 of a non-Italian Pope, Karol Cardinal Wojtyla. . . ." At first, she writes, people admired his work in the church, such as his rapprochement with Jews, the repenting of Catholic anti-Semitism. But with the years many have come to "disagree sharply with policies he has aggressively pursued."

She writes that the Pope's "remedies for a church in crisis have been to recentralize authority, restrict episcopal collegiality, apply conservative litmus tests in the appointment of bishops, impose restraints on theologians." He seems, she continues, "willfully blind to some of the church's most pressing issues, including the priest shortage and the much-ignored ban on artificial contraception."

For a long Sunday feature or a two- or three-part series, write about the changes in the Roman Catholic Church and the direction in which it seems headed in the areas of doctrine, the celibate clergy, women priests, abortion, birth control and other issues. Use local and campus authorities and consult reference works and databases for background.

Campus Projects

A. Educated

What are the most important books ever written? Interview members of the faculty, department heads, deans and distinguished professors for a list of books they think a person must read before he or she can be described as an educated person.

Compile a list of no more than 10 of the most frequently mentioned books and then visit the college library and the local public library to see whether they are available and how frequently they circulate.

You might ask your sources about the most recent additions to their lists.

Finally, survey students and try to determine how many of the books they have read.

This can be a two-part series: (1) the list of books and (2) the students' reading.

B. Gamblers

Compulsive gambling is defined as "an impulse-control disorder" by the American Psychiatric Association, and it is reported to be growing. Among youths, the disorder is higher than most had thought. A recent study found it affects 1 in 25 youths.

Interview students on your campus. Do many gamble on football and basketball games, regularly go to casinos or gamble in other ways? Differentiate between occasional betting and compulsive gambling in your 350-word article. Include the difficulty or ease with which college gamblers can wager. A recent police raid at Columbia University, for example, found that a fraternity house was the center for campus gamblers with bookies living in the house.

Community Project

A. Schoolhouse

What is this generation of primary-grade schoolchildren being taught? Go into classrooms in the community to find out whether there are new techniques in teaching reading, writing and arithmetic. Are children made aware of pollution and other threats to the environment and of the dangers of drugs, smoking, alcohol and AIDS?

What is unchanged from their parents' and grandparents' days as students?

B. Kwanzaa

Kwanzaa, usually celebrated between December 26 and January 1, was designed to connect African Americans to their African heritage. It has become popular on campuses and in some communities. For a feature of 350 to 500 words, find out what the plans are on your campus and in the community for Kwanzaa this year. Find out about the participation of churches and other organizations, and include descriptions of the activities. Also, incorporate some of the history of this relatively new celebration.

C. Prisoners

Many states used their prisoners to improve and build state roads. The prisoners were also leased to private businesses for work in brickyards, sawmills, turpentine farms, phosphate pits and coal mines. Sometimes the prisoners were chained together in what was known as a chain gang. Do a historical feature about the treatment of state prison inmates, comparing their treatment in the past with today.

The Library of Congress

65

Home Assignments

A. Formula

Select an article from a magazine and apply "The Magazine-Story Formula" described in Chapter 8 to the article.

B. Slave Trade

A group from Freeport plans to travel to Gambia and Senegal next month to visit areas in which their ancestors lived. In the itinerary is a visit to Gorée Island in Senegal that was one of the major shipping points in Europe's trans-Atlantic slave trade. For three centuries, Africans were taken to Gorée for shipment, some branded like cattle, the rebellious chained to a 17-pound weight or placed in neck and leg chains. Families taken to Gorée were broken up; the mother may have been shipped to South America, a child to America, the father to the Antilles.

In the American slave trade, run mostly by traders from Massachusetts and Rhode Island, ships left American ports with rum and returned with shiploads of slaves. A male slave sold in the Southern states brought 60 English pounds by mid-18th century, and slave importation was so profitable that two-thirds of the ships sailing from Rhode Island ports were engaged in the slave trade. By 1770, 450,000 slaves were at work in the colonies.

Matthew Bennington Rogers, 985 Millbank Rd., who will lead the tour, said the tour is an attempt to establish "a connection with our past, our past as Africans."

"When Nelson Mandela went to Gorée after his release from prison," Rogers said, "he sat in an isolation cell used to punish rebellious slaves. He was there for five minutes and emerged shaken and red-eyed. He understood."

Pope John II also visited and apologized for the slave trade and asked forgiveness for those who had participated in the trade, including Catholic missionaries, who accepted the situation.

With background material, write 300 to 400 words.

Bharati Sadasivam

The first slaves were taken from Gorée in 1536, and the slave trade continued until 1848.

Class Discussion

A. Top Five

In every reporter's experience there are stories that should be covered but somehow never are. Most of the time, the stories go unreported because there are insufficient resources to dig into them. For a class project, select three to five subjects, on or off campus, that should be but have not been covered. How would you turn the ideas into journalism? Why did you select these stories? Your story ideas should be added to those of the other students, and then the list should be reduced to five stories. You can select one of the five to write, or the whole class can decide on which one has the highest priority and do that one. Write 350 to 500 words.

B. Entrapment

The tabloid newspaper *Globe* paid a woman to invite TV sports announcer Frank Gifford to a Manhattan hotel room for a liaison and published photos of him embracing the woman. The tabloid hid a video camera in the room.

An editor of the rival *National Enquirer* said: "It's one thing to catch a celebrity cheating and another to induce or entrap them. Without the *Globe,* there would be no story here. I'm in the tabloid industry, and this is way over the top. It's downright cruel."

The *Globe* editorial director replied: "The issue is not what we did; the issue is what Frank Gifford did. . . . If we did something that someone would consider close to entrapment, I'd say so do the police every day in catching criminals. We caught a moral criminal."

What do you think of the *Globe*'s journalistic feat?

Skill Drill: Spelling (2)

In each of the three-word sets below, choose the word that is NOT spelled correctly. Note that "all correct" or "all wrong" are also options.

1. (a) fiery (b) judgement (c) exceed (d) all correct (e) all wrong
2. (a) desireable (b) recieve (c) truely (d) all correct (e) all wrong
3. (a) siege (b) sheik (c) disappearance (d) all correct (e) all wrong
4. (a) cemetery (b) calendar (c) valuable (d) all correct (e) all wrong
5. (a) describe (b) proffession (c) awkward (d) all correct (e) all wrong
6. (a) alot (b) rythm (c) marvellous (d) all correct (e) all wrong
7. (a) category (b) picnicking (c) forty (d) all correct (e) all wrong
8. (a) liesure (b) usable (c) assassin (d) all correct (e) all wrong
9. (a) religious (b) pursue (c) dilemna (d) all correct (e) all wrong
10. (a) harrass (b) Fahrenheit (c) tomatoes (d) all correct (e) all wrong
11. (a) suprise (b) analysis (c) sheriff (d) all correct (e) all wrong
12. (a) souvenir (b) beginner (c) bureaucrat (d) all correct (e) all wrong
13. (a) yeild (b) committed (c) attendance (d) all correct (e) all wrong
14. (a) support (b) connoisseur (c) fulfill (d) all correct (e) all wrong
15. (a) acknowledgment (b) developement (c) advertising (d) all correct (e) all wrong

Broadcast Newswriting

Judith Siewert

Readying for the 6 p.m. newscast

Introduction

Broadcast copy is written for comprehension at its first and only hearing. To accomplish this, the writer uses simple language and short sentences that consist of a single idea and conform to the subject-verb-object structure. The present tense is used whenever possible to give the listener a sense of the immediacy of the report. Action verbs are preferred, adjectives and adverbs avoided. Attribution is placed at the beginning of the sentence so the listener knows the source of the information. The active voice is preferred to the passive. For complex stories, introductory phrases and sentences may be used.

Exercises I

Rewrite for radio the following stories taken from the news wires of the AP and UPI. Keep the copy under 100 words.

A. Solitary

SAGINAW, Mich. (AP)—Unruly students will again be placed in solitary confinement, in a decision by the Carrollton School District that is being protested by some parents and a school board member.

Under the program, names of students who misbehave are written on a chalkboard. After the fourth incident, students may be confined to one of three rooms—one 9 by 12 feet and two others 6 by 9 feet—for a six-and-a-half-hour school day, with two restroom breaks and with lunch brought in.

David Pawley, a high school principal, said 21 of the school's 486 students had gone into solitary confinement since the policy went into effect at the beginning of the school year. The infractions covered by the policy include talking out of turn, walking around the classroom without permission and forgetting books for class.

The policy was scrapped last month after several parents complained. But the school board, in a 6–1 vote Monday, decided to reinstate it.

B. Edison

NEW YORK (AP)—In a ruling that could affect scores of other cases, a civil jury in the Bronx has found Consolidated Edison Co. guilty of gross negligence in connection with last year's city blackout.

The jury of one woman and five men returned a damage award of $40,500 to a chain of supermarkets Wednesday after deliberating three hours following an eight-day trial in state Supreme Court.

Con Edison, which had won all other blackout damage decisions in higher courts, said it would immediately appeal the decision.

The latest ruling differs from earlier ones in that it is the first involving a commercial establishment and also in that a different section of the law was argued in this case.

The award went to Pageant Food Co., Inc., a chain of seven supermarkets. The company had sought $75,000, alleging spoilage and loss of business due to the blackout, which darkened the city for more than 24 hours in July.

In what had been considered the most significant ruling on the matter to date, a three-judge appeals panel found last December that Con Edison could not be held liable for damages incurred by residential customers during the blackout.

The judges threw out seven damage awards ranging from $45 to $972 that had been granted by a lower court.

The judges noted in that ruling that the lower court judge had incorrectly overruled a state Public Service Commission regulation that exempts Con Edison from ordinary negligence claims.

But the appeals panel ruled that Con Edison could be found liable if gross negligence was demonstrated.

A Bronx jury found the utility guilty of gross negligence following the trial.

Con Edison spokesman Irv Levine said the company was confident the state exemption clause would be upheld in this case on appeal, as it has been on the previous occasions involving residential customers.

In the case of a finding of gross negligence, Con Edison claims its tariff exempts damage claims when service is interrupted "from causes beyond its control."

Scores of other cases against Con Edison are pending in state Supreme Court throughout the city and parts of Westchester County. The only action thus far on those suits has been the denial of class-action status for them, thereby forcing individual firms to file their own suits.

—AP-NY-05-09 23:20 EDT

C. Twins

CINCINNATI (UPI)—On Aug. 19, 1939, a 14-year-old unwed girl gave birth to identical twin boys in Piqua, Ohio.

A few weeks later, the twins were put up for adoption and taken in by different families—the Ernest Springer family in Piqua, and the Jess Lewis family in Lima, Ohio, 45 miles away.

Apparently through bureaucratic misinformation, neither family knew at the time that their adopted son had a twin brother.

About a year later, the Lewis family discovered through final adoption papers their adopted son had a twin, but they couldn't find out who had adopted him.

So, the twins grew up in different homes 45 miles away, not knowing the other, and went on to lead separate adult lives.

But the Lewis twin, who learned from his adoptive family that he had a brother, kept searching for his look-alike.

Finally, 63 years after birth, he found probate court records that led him to his brother, now living in Dayton, Ohio.

When the twins got together, they discovered some amazing coincidences about their separate lives.

The Springer family named their adopted son "Jim." The Lewis family named their adopted son "Jim."

Both boys had had pet dogs. Both named their dogs "Toy."

After school, both took law enforcement training. Both enjoyed similar hobbies: blueprinting, drafting and carpentry.

Jim Lewis had been married three times, Jim Springer twice. Both their first wives were named "Linda." Both their second wives were named "Betty." Both named their first sons "James Allan."

University of Minnesota researchers who specialize in studying twins recently examined the two for a week to study similarities and differences in twins who had grown up separately. Similarities were the rule.

"They found out that our brainwaves and heartbeat patterns are the same," Springer said. "Our handwriting is similar. We have virtually identical fingerprints. Our eye and ear structures are exactly the same, which is the real test of twins.

"And," he added, "the results of all the tests we took looked like one person had taken the same tests twice."

—UPI 05-10 01:09 AED

D. Lakes

ORLANDO, Fla. (AP)—The 82 lakes that give Orlando its picture-card look will die without the infusion of millions of dollars and stringent drainage and pollution-control ordinances, a consulting group says.

The lakes, which get their water from rainfall and runoff, are victims of pollution washed from the city's growing expanse of roofs, driveways,

parking lots and streets, according to a report released this week by the firm of Dyer, Riddle, Mills & Precourt.

Every lake in Orlando "has been degraded by storm-water and other pollutants to the extent that favorable conditions exist for excessive aquatic weed growth, large-scale algae blooms, possible fish kills and loss of recreational use," the report said.

Exercises II

Here are some news stories that are to be tightened up for an evening television newscast. Allow each story 20 seconds.

A. Heart

CHICAGO (UPI)—Some smokers think that after they have been diagnosed with heart disease, it's too late to give up the cigarettes that caused their disease.

"It's never too late," counters Dr. Ronald Vliestra, author of a study published today in a special anti-smoking issue of the Journal of the American Medical Association.

Vliestra, a cardiologist with the Mayo Clinic, reported that heart disease patients who refuse to quit smoking are nearly twice as likely to die of heart attacks as those who kick the habit. He said the study should have a major impact on how much emphasis physicians place on quitting smoking as part of the treatment of heart disease.

"The issue for physicians is made a lot more clear," he said in a telephone interview. "This is in contrast to the situation with lung cancer, where once the cancer which is related to the cigarette smoking has been caused, it's too late to give up (smoking). The same is not true for coronary heart disease—it's not too late."

Vliestra and his colleagues at the University of Washington in Seattle studied the smoking behavior and survival of 4,165 smokers who had been diagnosed as having coronary heart disease, a blockage of arteries to the heart.

The five-year survival rate for the 1,490 patients who quit smoking was 85 percent, compared to a 78 percent survival rate for smokers. Patients who never smoked had an 87 percent survival rate.

The difference in mortality was almost entirely attributable to differences in the heart attack rates between the two groups, the researchers said, with 7.9 percent of the smokers dying from heart attacks compared to only 4.4 percent of the quitters.

But despite this finding and earlier similar studies, 57 percent of the smokers in the study continued to smoke even after being diagnosed with heart disease.

"A consistently effective method of enabling patients with coronary artery disease to quit smoking would have a major impact on health care," the researchers concluded.

B. Cyanide

NASHVILLE, Tenn.—Tests revealed cyanide in a Tylenol capsule found near the body of a man who died from the poison, but the cyanide was different than the kind that killed a New York woman this month, officials said today.

"Nothing was found that indicates any connection between the Nashville death and that of Diane Elsroth," who died Feb. 8 after swallowing a cyanide-laced Tylenol, Food and Drug Administration commissioner Frank E. Young said.

Young said the FDA's Cincinnati lab had determined that the lone Extra-Strength Tylenol capsule found Sunday under the deathbed of Timothy Green, 32, contained 91 percent sodium cyanide.

"This is a different kind of cyanide from the potassium cyanide found in the capsules associated" with Elsroth's death or the deaths of seven people in the Chicago area in 1982, he said.

Young also said the cyanide in the Nashville capsule is different from any used in the laboratories of Johnson & Johnson, manufacturer of Tylenol, and that the FDA has "no evidence that this is not an isolated incident."

The capsule and a Tylenol container were found Sunday under the bed where Green's body lay. The FDA tested the capsule, and the container was released to the FBI and sent to Washington for analysis.

Green, a bachelor who moved to Nashville about a year ago to become a songwriter and join a Jehovah's Witness congregation, was poisoned by cyanide. Police said they don't know if his death was suicide, murder or an accident.

Medical Examiner Charles Harlan said Green ingested 20 times a lethal dose of cyanide, and an autopsy found no evidence of the active ingredient in Extra-Strength Tylenol—acetaminophen—in Green's body.

That could mean Green "did not take a Tylenol, or the Tylenol could have been removed from the capsule and replaced with cyanide," Harlan said.

Green had been dead for four or five days, police said.

C. Children

HOFFMAN ESTATES, Ill. (AP)—Six of ten children in a family for whom police had started a Christmas collection died in a fire that engulfed their home in this Chicago suburb, authorities said Sunday.

A teen-age brother of the victims escaped the blaze and had to be restrained by firefighters when he tried to re-enter the house to help his brother and sisters.

In Southfield, Mich., a brief, smoky fire killed six elderly residents of a hospice and rehabilitation center Sunday and forced the evacuation of about 30 people, some of them bedridden, according to authorities in that Detroit suburb.

The house here was engulfed in flames and smoke when firefighters and police arrived late Saturday, police Sgt. Robert Syre said.

"From what I understand, when they got there, the heat was so intense that they couldn't do anything and everything just started to break apart," he said. "This is the worst fire in our history. I've been here 15 years and I would have heard of something worse."

"There was fire coming out of the living room window. Smoke was coming out of everywhere," said neighbor Charles Durec.

The victims, five sisters and a brother ranging in age from 8 to 15, were among 10 children living in the home with their divorced mother, Patricia Krawczyk, who had recently suffered a heart attack, Syre said.

"They were having a hard time. You know how it is with 10 kids," Syre said. Officers in the police de-partment, where one of the Krawczyk youngsters had worked for two summers, had recently begun a Christmas collection for the family.

The mother and three children were not home at the time of the blaze, police and a neighbor said.

The eldest son, Kevin, 18, was awakened by a smoke detector and yelled "Fire!" then kicked his way out a window to escape, Syre said. Police had to restrain him from trying to get back into the burning house, he said.

"They were good kids," said Durec, who added that the family had lived in the house for about six years.

Syre said it appeared the blaze may have started near a fireplace adjacent to a garage. He said it had not been determined if the fireplace had been used in Saturday night's freezing temperatures.

D. Sting

WASHINGTON (AP)—Using free Washington Redskins tickets as bait, authorities arrested 100 fugitives who showed up Sunday at a pregame brunch where police and federal marshals posed as waiters and served warrants.

U.S. marshals called it the largest mass arrest of fugitives in recent memory.

"It was like an assembly line," said Herbert M. Rutherford III, U.S. marshal for the District of Columbia. "It was party time, and they fell for it, hook, line and sinker."

"This ain't fair, this just ain't fair," said one prisoner who was led in handcuffs from one of two large buses that carried the prisoners to a local jail.

"They said they was takin' us to a football game, and that's wrong," said another man. "That's false advertising."

U.S. marshals, working with the Metropolitan Police Department, sent out invitations to 3,000 wanted persons. The invitations said that as a promotion for a new sports television station, Flagship International Sports Television, they were winners of two free tickets to the National Football League game Sunday between the Redskins and the Bengals.

The invitation said 10 of the "lucky winners" would receive season tickets to the Redskins' games and that a grand prize drawing would be held for an all-expenses paid trip to the upcoming Super Bowl.

The initials for the TV enterprise, F.I.S.T., also stand for the Fugitive Investigative Strike Team, a special U.S. Marshals force.

About 100 fugitives responded to the invitation and appeared at the D.C. Convention Center for the special brunch. The building was decorated with signs saying, "Let's party" and "Let's all be there."

Some of the fugitives showed up wearing the bright burgundy and gold wool Redskins hats as well as Redskins buttons, while others were attired in suits and ties for the pregame feast.

One marshal was dressed in a large yellow chicken suit with oversized red boots while another turned up as an Indian chief complete with large headdress.

Other marshals wearing tuxedos handed small name stickers to each of the fugitives.

Buses that were to take them to the game, however, took them to the police department's central cellblock several blocks away instead.

"When we verified their identity, we escorted them in small groups to a party room, where officers moved in from concealed positions and placed them under arrest," said Stanley Morris, head of the U.S. Marshals Service.

The sting netted 100 fugitives by 11 A.M., marshals said.

Arrested were two people wanted for murder, five for robbery, 15 for assault, six for burglary, 19 for bond or bail violations, 18 for narcotics violations, officials said. Others were arrested on charges of rape, arson and forgery. Two of those arrested were on the D.C. police department's 10 most wanted list.

A similar scam in Hartford, Conn., last November invited people to attend a luncheon with pop singer Boy George. Fifteen were picked up by a limousine and arrested. Marshals said they used job offers as the bait to arrest about 90 people in Brooklyn last year.

"Redskin tickets are valuable. And when you're trying to get a person, you play on their greed," said Toby Roche, chief deputy U.S. marshal for Washington, who coordinated the operation.

The cost of the project was estimated to be $22,100, or about $225 dollars per arrest.

One man who got into the Convention Center before apparently being spooked by the circumstances was arrested on the street, still wearing his "Hello, my name is . . ." sticker.

Assignments

A. Hope

Prepare a feature of at least three minutes on the dreams and aspirations of children in grade school. Obtain permission to interview in school, or seek out youngsters after class. Talk to them without their parents or other adults listening in, and try to conduct your interviews one-on-one, not in a group of youngsters. Discuss their plans for school, jobs, marriage, family. Let them take the interview where they will.

B. Parents

Prepare a companion feature to **A. Hope** by interviewing parents of grade-school children on the same subjects. Do they believe their children will have the opportunities children require to develop their dreams and aspirations? If not, what are the obstacles?

C. Overlooked

Is there some aspect of local history that should be recognized but has been overlooked? In Malden, W.Va., for example, a cabin and nearby church associated with Booker T. Washington was rebuilt with the help of students from St. Cloud University in St. Cloud, Minn.

Washington, son of a slave, became a renowned educator and the founder of Tuskegee Institute. He moved to Malden after Emancipation. Washington worked in the mines by day and taught himself to read in the African Zion Baptist Church at night, the church students rebuilt.

Is there some site, building or area that needs similar attention? Do a broadcast feature on the situation.

D. Ceremonial

Many groups celebrate important stages in a person's life, from birth to death. Christians have baptismal celebrations, and Jewish boys are circumcised in a ceremony shortly after birth known as the *bris*. Confirmation is an important occasion in the lives of Catholic boys and girls.

The passage to adulthood for Mexican girls, which is celebrated with lavish parties in many Mexican-American communities, is known as the *quinceañera*. Navajo, Apache and other Native American tribes also celebrate the beginning of adult life.

Among Jews, the bar and bat mitzvah mark the beginning of religious duty and responsibility.

Sweet 16 parties are common, and in some cities there are lavish coming-out parties for young women described as *debutantes.*

Later in life, couples who have been married for 50 years sometimes ask a priest or minister to conduct another church wedding ceremony.

Do a feature on one of these celebrations that has occurred in your community.

E. Breakdown

The Centers for Disease Control and Prevention has issued these infant mortality figures by race and ethnicity of mothers for last year:

Japanese	3.5
Cuban	3.6
Chinese	4.0
Mexican	5.6
White	6.0
Filipino	6.2
Puerto Rican	7.8
American Indian	9.3
Hawaiian	10.0
Black	13.8

Prepare a broadcast documentary about these figures by discussing them with experts in the field of maternal and child health.

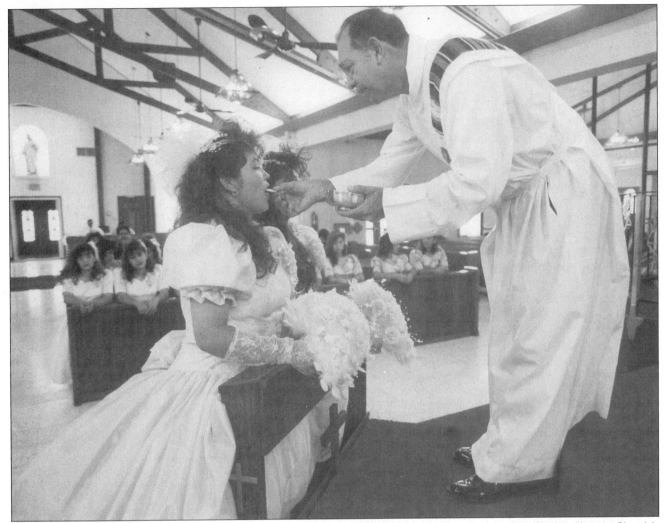

Betty Tichich, *Houston Chronicle*

At the Quinceañera

Campus Projects

A. Wired

College quarters are electronic marvels. Television and stereo sets abound. Computers are as common as chairs and tables. How much time do students spend watching TV, listening to their CDs, surfing the Internet, making contacts in chat rooms, playing computer games? What do faculty members think of the time being devoted to nonacademic activities?

Prepare a script for a five-minute documentary.

B. Population

A national organization, Zero Population Growth, has initiated a campaign to urge "lawmakers to make a contract with future generations by adopting measures that encourage a sustainable balance of people, resources and the environment." It predicts that, unless efforts are made to curb world population growth, today's population of 5.7 billion could become 19.2 billion at the end of the 21st century. The group urges:

• Universal access to a full range of reproductive health care services.
• Stronger environmental protection and an end to government subsidies that promote wasteful consumption.
• U.S. policies that reduce global migration pressures.
• A comprehensive and compassionate national adolescent pregnancy prevention program.
• Education, employment and training to improve women's status.
• School-based programs that raise awareness of population and environmental issues.
• Increased funding for international population and sustainable development programs.

Interview authorities on the campus to find out what they think of the goals of the campaign, how feasible population control is politically, who the proponents and opponents of the campaign would be.

Community Project

A. At Risk

A study by the Centers for Disease Control and Prevention found "a substantial proportion of students engage in behaviors that place them at risk for HIV infection." By their senior year, 29 percent of high school seniors have had four or more sex partners, and less than half of the students are protecting themselves against AIDS and other sexually transmitted diseases, the CDC reported.

In fact, says the federal agency, condom use falls off as students advance in high school.

"The best way to explain it to kids is that it's like playing Russian roulette and not knowing how many live bullets are in the chambers," says Dr. Lloyd Kolbe, director of the CDC's Division of Adolescent and School Health. "If you pull the trigger once it can cause you to become infected."

Male high school students are more likely than female students to be sexually active, 27 percent to 12 percent. By age 19, 54 percent of females have experienced sexual intercourse. A similar study 20 years ago among females 15 to 19 found 29 percent had engaged in sexual intercourse.

The New Jersey Governor's Advisory Council on AIDS recommended that condoms be made available to all students beginning in the ninth grade. It also recommended that a sexual education program be statewide and mandatory. "HIV/AIDS education should *not* be left entirely up to local school boards," the Council stated. For a documentary or a series of programs, gather information locally on AIDS education programs and blend this in with any data you gather about sexual activities of high school students.

B. Adoptions

How many children in your community are eligible for adoption? How does this compare with preceding years? What are the barriers to adoption? Are children placed only in homes that match their race and religion?

C. Care

How much attention does your community pay to the well-being of its children? Here are some measures to use in comparing it with similar cities:

Health—Infant mortality rate; children's diseases.
Education—Dropout rates; test scores; college-bound percentages; graduation rates.
Crime—Juvenile facilities; rehabilitation programs.
Community support—Recreational facilities; child care for working parents.

Home Assignment

A. Tips

Of the 32 "Top Tips of the Trade" listed in the textbook, list five you find you need to be reminded of as you do broadcast writing.

B. Choices

Select three *Workbook* exercises that you have written in newspaper style. Rewrite for radio, giving no more than 100 words to each item. Compare the two versions: Are all the facts given in the broadcast account? What was eliminated and why? Is there some validity to the observation that broadcast news is a headline service?

Class Discussion

A. Time

Time each item on a half-hour evening TV newscast. Make a log of subject matter, the placement of items in the newscast and the amount of time given each item.

Then compare the space given these items in the next day's newspaper.

Also, compare the play in the newspaper with the placement on the TV newscast. Was the lead item on the newscast given major play by the newspaper?

With whose decisions on time-space and play do you find you agree? Why?

B. Wasteland Revisited

Here are excerpts from an article by Newton Minow, who as chairman of the Federal Communications Commission in the early '60s described television as a "vast wasteland." This article, "How Vast the Wasteland Now?" was written 35 years after he made that assessment:

One evening as I watched, with my remote control in hand, I flipped through the channels and saw a man loading his gun on one channel, a different man aiming a gun on a second, and another man shooting a gun on a third. And if you don't believe me, try it yourself. I think the most troubling change over the past 30 years is the rise in the quantity and quality of violence on television. In 1961 I worried that my children would not benefit much from television, but now I worry that my grandchildren will actually be harmed by it. One recent study shows that by the time a child is 18 he has seen 25,000 murders on television. In 1961 they didn't make PG-13 movies, much less NC-17. Now a 6-year-old can watch them on cable. . . .

In the last 30 years, the television marketplace has become a severely distorting influence in at least four important public areas. We have failed 1) to use television for education; 2) to use television for children; 3) to finance public television properly; and 4) to use television properly in political campaigns. . . .

. . . Bob Keeshan, our Captain Kangaroo for life, has seen how television for children all over the world is designed to be part of the nurturing and educational system. But "in America," he says, "television is not a tool for nurturing. It is a tool for selling."

. . . Studies of political campaigns show that the average block of uninterrupted speech by a presidential candidate on network newscasts was 9.8 seconds; in 1968 it was 42.3 seconds. As Walter Cronkite observed, this means that "issues can be avoided rather than confronted." And David Halberstam adds, "Once the politicians begin to talk in such brief bites . . . they begin to think in them."

A United States senator must now raise $12,000 to $16,000 every week to pay for a political campaign, mostly to buy time for television commercials. A recent United Nations study revealed that only two countries, Norway and Sri Lanka (in addition to the United States), do not provide free airtime to their political parties. If we are to preserve the democratic process without corrupting, unhealthy influences, we must find a bipartisan way to provide free time for our candidates and stop them from getting deeply in hock to special interests in order to pay for television commercials.

Do you agree with this assessment? Why?

C. TV News

Neil Postman, head of the Communication Arts Department at New York University, says that television news is "fatally hampered" by television's need to keep people entertained. When people turn on the set, they are waiting to be entertained, whatever the program, even when it is news.

Do you agree? Watch the evening news for a few days. Can you detect techniques and content used to keep the audience glued to the set?

D. Responsibility

Here are some comments by Patricia Dean, of the broadcasting department of the Medill School of Journalism at Northwestern University. Do you agree with her?

We found [in a content analysis of 10 local TV markets] that almost 30 percent of the time spent on local TV news was devoted to crime and court stories. Ten percent was devoted to reporting calamities and natural disasters. Government and politics accounted for little more than 15 percent. Two critical areas were almost nonexistent. Education stories totaled a mere 2 percent. Race relations totaled 1.2 percent.

Consultants tell us we should report stories the viewers care about. . . . How can they care if they don't know about it? They don't care because we give them no reason to care. This is our job as journalists.

Every station is under tremendous pressure to keep costs as low as possible. Breaking news that is crime- and crisis-driven is cheap to cover and easy to cover. Murders, fires and traffic accidents require little background research.

As a profession, we cannot afford to throw up our hands saying there is nothing we can do. We cannot afford to blame the consultants, the accountants and business owners. Journalists must take responsibility and take back the decision-making process.

PART FOUR

Reporting Principles

 10 | **Digging for Information**

**The right questions =
useful replies.**

Introduction

The reporter's task is to make the story come as close to the truth of the event as his or her reporting and writing skills allow. In reporting, the deeper journalists dig, the closer they come to the underlying truth, which is often covered by layers of material constructed from self-serving sources. Perspective on the event is best served through the observations of several sources; the single-source story can cause trouble. Background, causes and consequences are an important part of the account, and when reporters are allowed to provide interpretation, this, too, helps give a rounded picture of the event.

Exercises

A. Scores

The Freeport schools superintendent has released the following information about the SAT tests taken by students in city high schools this year. Use the material as the basis of a news story of 150 words for www.freenews.com tonight and a 300-word news story for tomorrow's *Freeport News*.

Income	Number of SAT Takers	% Male/Female	SAT-V Mean	SAT-M Mean
Less than $10,000	51	38/62	350	416
$10,000–$20,000	75	42/58	377	435
$20,000–$30,000	132	44/56	402	454
$30,000–$40,000	150	46/54	416	469
$40,000–$50,000	188	48/52	429	482
$50,000–$60,000	202	49/51	437	492
$60,000–$70,000	213	49/51	446	502
$70,000 or more	249	50/50	469	531

Schools superintendent Herbert Gilkeyson said in a news release accompanying the scores:

It is clear from these scores that we have serious work to do. I am pleased by the improvement in the math scores, generally up 5 to 10 points in all income levels. But I am dismayed by the low verbal scores, down the same numbers. Clearly, low-income students are spending study time working to help support families. The problem lies deep in our socio-economic problems.

B. Tourism Folo

The Freeport Chamber of Commerce issued a report today on the fund drive to raise $125,000 to publicize the town. Here is the report:

Display stand for visitors

The drive has a month to go, but $75,500 has already been raised and the Chamber set into motion plans for attracting visitors.

One of the first steps was to order five display stands, one of which has already been set up in the downtown city parking lot.

Titled, "How to find the best things in Freeport," the large sign contains a map of the city linked to major attractions.

Visitors are directed to the Chamber offices if they want a copy of the map and the guide.

"The other four stands will be placed at strategic spots in the city where travelers are likely to congregate," said Thomas Everingham, public relations director of the Chamber. "The idea came from our committee that is heading the fund drive and it was enthusiastically supported by the membership. We decided to go ahead now, rather than wait for the drive to be completed. The tourist season is underway and we wanted to show people that it's worthwhile to stay an extra day or two to see everything we have to offer."

Assignments

A. Issue

Select an issue of national, regional or local significance that is before the U.S. Senate or House of Representatives and write to one or more of the senators or the congressperson from your area asking for his or her opinion on the matter.

Your letter should include specific questions. Base the questions on research, and include this background material in the article you write.

B. Barometers

Interview city officials and businesspeople about data they use to measure the community's economic health. Some of these figures include bank clearings, sales tax receipts, building permits, unemployment payments. Obtain the most recent data.

What do these figures tell you about present economic conditions?

C. Feet

A San Diego podiatrist, Brian A. Rothbart, is quoted in a wire service story from that city as saying that, although long distance runners may have the cardiovascular fitness of teen-agers, they have the feet of old men. "Runners are putting more stress on their feet in one year than the average person does in 10 years," he said. "I can look at a runner who is 20 and who is in superb condition, except for his feet, which are those of a 60-year-old." He suggests runners practice on sawdust tracks, sand or grass. Concrete can be a foot killer, he said. Athletes may suffer mild to serious injuries of the foot, he said.

Interview joggers about their foot problems. Interview the runners at the local college or university about their foot problems. How do they practice? Is there a team podiatrist? What is the track coach's attitude?

D. Payroll

Make a study of the number of people on public payrolls, city, county or state, whichever is most accessible to you. How many are there now compared with last year and five years ago?

How many are appointive, civil service or merit system employees? What is the total cost of public employees in salaries, retirement, other benefits?

Obtain comments from the heads of various bureaus, departments and agencies whose payrolls have increased or decreased the most sharply. What are the reasons?

E. Sterile

The president of the California Veterinary Medical Association, Dr. Dan R. Evans, advocates birth control for animals, a wire service story datelined Escondido, Calif., reports. He says there is an overpopulation of dogs and cats, and the result is that each year more and more animals are destroyed by humane societies. He says researchers are working on a sterilization drug, necessary because most people cannot pay to have their pets neutered.

Do a local follow-up. Does your city or county veterinary group have a voluntary sterilization program, as Dr. Evans says his county does? Is there a pet overpopulation in your area? Consult the humane society, the dog shelter, police, veterinaries, citizens. How many pets are destroyed each year? The exact figures are available, if you can dig them out.

F. Foreign

Sunday editions of newspapers and the editorial pages of the regular editions often carry long interpretative pieces. Prepare such a piece of 750 to 1,000 words on one of the following subjects in the field of international affairs:

1. Africa: hope or despair?
2. The continuing revolution in Mexico: real or spurious?
3. China: changes over the past decade.
4. The Palestinian battle for a homeland.
5. The perils of overpopulation: a case study—India. (Or any country of your choice.)
6. Can the two Canadas coexist? (This refers to the continuing strife between French- and English-speaking Canadians.)

Consult the library and Internet sources. If these governments have offices in your community or if there are faculty members or local residents from these countries, interview them.

G. Carols

The holding of Christmas assemblies, including the singing of carols, in the public schools; prayers at athletic contests; the posting of the Ten Commandments in classrooms; the beginning of the school day with a prayer—these are some of the activities the American Civil Liberties Union and other groups have attacked as violating the constitutional separation of church and state. Write an interpretative story of 750 words on the current policy of the local school system and blend in background from a database search or use of the *Reader's Guide* and/or *The New York Times Index.*

H. Interpret

Gather material and write an interpretative story on one of these subjects:

1. The need to protect the identity of juvenile offenders.
2. The necessity to hold the line on salary increases for city workers.
3. The establishment of a required core curriculum for all candidates for the bachelor's degree to include a year of college mathematics, three years of a foreign language, one year of a physical science, three years of humanities.
4. The end to subsidies of athletes in the major sports and a more equitable distribution of funds to all college sports.
5. Elimination of compulsory schooling at age 14 or 16.
6. The pros and cons of the strong mayor system for local government.
7. A reassessment of local residential and commercial properties to bring them into a more balanced relationship.
8. The debate over the place of multiculturalism in the curriculum.

Campus Projects

A. Evaluation

More than four of five colleges and universities (86 percent) use student evaluations to measure teaching effectiveness. In some schools, they are a major, and sometimes the only, source of faculty performance evaluation. But Peter Seldin, professor of management at Pace University in Pleasantville, N.Y., contends that student ratings should never be the sole determinant of teaching effectiveness.

Seldin recommends a wider approach that includes evidence of student learning, observations of teaching by colleagues and reviews of instructional material.

Also, he recommends that the evaluation form have 20 to 30 questions on teaching behavior, including:

*   Are tests and papers graded and returned promptly?
*   Is the instructor well prepared?

Some instructors contend that student evaluations force them to engage in grade inflation. A student given a poor grade may retaliate with a negative evaluation, they say.

Interview faculty members, administrators and students about the effectiveness of student evaluations. How does your administration use the results of the evaluations?

B. Admissions

Colleges and universities have been changing their requirements for admission to accommodate some groups. Traditionally, colleges have used academic records—high school grades, scores on the ACT and SAT tests, ranking in the senior class, letters from teachers—as the major criteria for admission.

Exceptions have been made for the sons and daughters of alumni, athletes and those with special talents, such as musicians. In the last two decades, the doors have been widened through affirmative action to accept members of racial and ethnic groups that have traditionally not attended college.

Investigate the changes in your school's admission policies. Look at admission guidelines. Have they led to changes in the student population?

Has the change in admission policies affected academic work and the curriculum? Has the school added remedial courses for the less-prepared students?

Have students in minority groups found that the school meets their needs?

The admissions office keeps records on how students in various categories fare in college. Obtain dropout and graduation rates for students in minority groups, students with high and low SAT or ACT scores, athletes, etc.

Has there been any controversy about admission standards in the last few years? How has your school adjusted to recent legal decisions about affirmative action?

Community Projects

A. Aged

How is your community meeting the special needs of the aged? Identify the problems; then see whether solutions have been found. For example, a growing number of the aged use walkers and small vehicles to get around. They have trouble negotiating curbs, and many cities have rebuilt curbs at intersections to eliminate the rise.

Is there a housing project for the aged, a recreation center, food programs for the shut-ins? Learn what the city, church groups and civic organizations are doing for this growing segment of the population.

B. Gay-Lesbian

A study by the U.S. Department of Health and Human Services found that gay and lesbian adolescents make up almost a third of all teen-age suicides. One of the reasons, counselors say, is the anti-gay atmosphere in high schools. Although racial and religious slurs are no longer acceptable, anti-gay comments are part of the school culture.

At some schools, gay students are advised to stay in the closet. A Boston high school teacher said, "They'd get killed if they came out. At our school, male students get harassed just for being in drama or chorus."

But at other schools, administrators are trying to open the closet. At the Phillips Exeter private school in New Hampshire, a gay/straight alliance was formed, and gay and lesbian students are permitted to hold dances. A number of other private schools have similar organizations. Much of the effort to open up high schools has come from gay teachers.

Opposition is powerful. A minister in Mattapan, Mass., the Rev. Earl W. Jackson, advocates firing gay and lesbian teachers who are open about their sexual orientation.

"We are not going to let anyone stand up and say, 'I'm lesbian,' " he said.

In Washington and Oregon, anti-gay initiatives have been aimed at introducing legislation that would prohibit gays and lesbians from teaching. Although the situation is easing for gay students at boarding schools, gays and lesbians say little progress has been made in public high schools. Examine the situation in your local high schools. Has the board of education taken any steps to include treatment of gay issues in the curriculum; are there any gay/straight clubs in any high schools? Interview gay and lesbian students about their experiences in school.

You might post a notice about your interest in talking to these students, after you obtain permission from the school.

C. Big Dough

At the kickoff of his campaign for the Republican presidential nomination, Senator Phil Gramm of Texas announced, "I have the most reliable friend that you can have in American politics, and that is ready money." Information about political donations to candidates in your state is available to the public. For a recent election, check the names and affiliations of donors. Interview some donors; find out their reasons for donating. Interview political leaders and faculty members about how effective money is in elections.

Home Assignments

A. Layers

1. Clip examples of Layer I, II and III stories in your newspaper.
2. Do you think the Layer I stories could have been better handled, or were there obvious factors that made it unnecessary or impossible for the reporters to dig deeper?
3. Do any of the Layer II and Layer III stories contain opinions and judgments of the reporters? Are they legitimate? Explain.

B. Featured Women

Your editor has decided to run a monthly feature about distinguished American women. The news peg will be the anniversary of some important date in her career. The editor hands you a list he has started. "This is the beginning. Give me 250 to 350 words on one of these women, or someone you have selected," he tells you.

Ethel Barrymore, 8/16/1879–6/18/1959
Mary Beard, 8/5/1876–8/14/1958
Mary McLeod Bethune, 7/10/1875–5/18/1955
Rachel Carson, 5/27/1907–4/14/1964
Carrie Chapman Catt, 1/9/1859–3/9/1947
Dorothy Day, 11/9/1897–11/29/1980
Emily Dickinson, 12/10/1830–5/15/1886
Dorothea Dix, 4/4/1802–7/18/1887
Isadora Duncan, 5/27/1878–9/14/1927
Mary Baker Eddy, 7/16/1821–12/3/1910
Margaret Fuller, 5/23/1810–7/19/1850
Sarah Hale, 10/24/1788–4/30/1879

Alice Hamilton, 2/27/1869–9/22/1970
Julia Ward Howe, 5/27/1819–10/17/1910
Helen Keller, 6/27/1880–6/1/1968
Dorothea Lange, 5/26/1895–10/11/1965
Margaret Mead, 12/16/1901–11/15/1978
Edna St. Vincent Millay, 2/22/1892–10/19/1950
Frances Perkins, 4/10/1880–5/14/1965
Bessie Smith, 4/15/1894–9/26/1937
Gertrude Stein, 2/3/1874–7/27/1946
Harriet Beecher Stowe, 6/14/1811–7/1/1896
Harriet Tubman, c. 1821–3/10/13
Edith Wharton, 1/24/1862–8/11/1937

Class Discussion

A. Pseudo-Events

There are several names given to events that are planned or planted for press coverage. They have been called *staged-events, orchestrated-events, media-happenings* or *media-events* and *pseudo-events*. They have in common the intent of the planner to entice press coverage for the benefit of the planner or the person or group represented.

1. Find an example of such an event.
2. Assess the way the reporter handled it. Did the reporter simply pass on information from the source, or was there independent reportorial checking and backgrounding?
3. One study indicates that in some newspapers as much as 80 percent of the stories originate with sources and are untouched by reporters. That is, reporters serve merely a stenographic function. Can you make an educated guess about the content of your local newspaper? Does it have a reputation for its staff-originated stories, as differentiated from source-originated stories?

B. New News

Rolling Stone magazine says that the "Old News is pooped, confused and broke," and in its place the New News is evolving, "a heady concoction, part Hollywood film and TV, part pop music and pop art, mixed with popular culture and celebrity magazines, tabloid telecasts, cable and home video."

The New News, says the magazine, sets the subjects of conversation and will establish the country's social and political agenda.

In response, the television journalist Bill Moyers says:

> People want to know what is happening to them, and what they can do about it. Listening to America you realize that millions of Americans are not apathetic. They will respond to a press that stimulates the community without pandering to it, that inspires people to embrace their responsibilities without lecturing or hectoring them, that engages their better natures without sugarcoating ugly realities or patronizing their foibles.

In which direction do you think journalism is heading?

11 Making Sound Observations

Spencer Tulis,
The Leader-Herald, Gloversville, N.Y.

The joy of victory . . . and empty stands.

Introduction

The public relies on the reporter's eyes and ears for an understanding of events and their meaning. Reporters station themselves at key surveillance points—called *beats*—in order to observe the important events that unfold. They have sufficient background to understand the events they cover, and they have a solid grasp of their beats so that they are able to ask the questions that elicit relevant information. The journalist understands that he or she can never completely reflect the truth of the event but is not deterred from seeking to move as close to truth as possible.

Exercises

A. Newsstand

The circulation manager of your newspaper tells you that a newsstand operator is in his office with a "crazy story about how some sanitation workers carted off his newsstand and its contents." He suggests you talk to the man, Rosario Marvello. You go downstairs, and Marvello says that the men swept down on him yesterday and, without a word, leveled his stand.

"I've been there for 12 years," he says, "trying to make a living to support my family. And now I have nothing."

You sense a story and suggest he show you his location. You go with him to Albany and Massachusetts and, sure enough, his stand is gone. You note it was on the northwestern corner.

You call the Freeport Sanitation Department and a public affairs officer tells you that the commissioner, William Applegate, is out of town but that the stand was torn down because it violated the city code by (1) obstructing pedestrian traffic, (2) being too far from the building line, (3) not conforming to the architectural code. He says you can't quote him, just the department.

Marvello, who is 62, says six men took 15 minutes to do the job and all he could do was stand by and watch. He says he is thinking of hiring a lawyer but hasn't much money.

"That's not a way to get rich," he says. "I make enough to get by week by week, and that's it."

You call around and learn that the City Planning Department is conducting a study of the design and location of newsstands. A source in the department tells you on a not-for-attribution basis that the department wants to cut down on the number of newsstands and limit their locations. "It's all hush-hush, but word got out and somehow these guys at Sanitation jumped the gun. The idea is to get him out of there."

1. Write a story for today's newspaper with the information you have; 300 words.
2. Marvello's plight now has been on television and people are calling the mayor, who issues the following press release.

    Write a second-day story with the new information; 350 words.

The City of Freeport   *Office of the Mayor*

For Release: Immediate

Statement by Mayor Sam Parnass

I was upset to learn that a newsstand operated by Rosario Marvello was demolished in error by the Sanitation Department. This should not have happened.

Everyone makes mistakes, including those of us in government. The important thing is to right those mistakes. I have ordered that the newsstand be rebuilt or replaced and turned over to Mr. Marvello immediately without cost to him. The work has already begun and it will be on the same site he has had for 12 years.

Deputy Mayor Stan Brezen talked with Ruth Marvello, expressing the city's regrets about this unfortunate incident and assuring her that any property taken by the Sanitation Department would be returned or the department's community funds would pay for any property destroyed.

While we are restoring Mr. Marvello's business, it is important to remember that the Department of City Planning and an interagency task force are engaged in a long-term study of the rules for location and design of newsstands. Our aim is to rationalize decision making on this issue so that the distribution of newspapers and magazines flourishes while legitimate community concerns, chiefly about impediments to pedestrian flow on the sidewalks, are addressed.

In a reaction to preliminary recommendations, publishers, editorial commentators and columnists have suggested that the city wants to eliminate newsstands. Nothing could be further from the truth. Newsstands are an essential part of the city and provide valuable service to people.

It is absolutely not our intention to diminish the sale of newspapers. On the contrary, we believe more news and editorial coverage of matters of public interest benefits the city and its people.

At the end of this process, it is my hope that we will have developed sensible criteria that encourage the creation of attractive newsstands in busy locations that people in neighborhoods around the city will welcome.

It is conceivable that at some future date Mr. Marvello will be asked to move, but if that happens it will be part of a citywide reorganization plan. It will not be as the result of a demolition raid.

B. Provost

St. Mary's University has appointed a new provost, Stanley Stiga, 42, who was a professor of chemistry at Michigan State University. The announcement was made today by university president, N. Francis Simms. You attend a news conference at which the announcement is made. In answers to questions, Stiga advances this list of actions he intends to initiate:

- Greater emphasis on research by the faculty. "We must make this university stand out, and the way to accomplish this is through research and publication of the research of our faculty. I will be stressing to all department heads that advancement depends on such activity."
- A fund for tutoring all students having difficulty in a course. "Our task is to teach students, and some learn slower than others or can see better with direction from someone with another perspective."
- More self-government among students. "A student judicial council could take over all disciplinary matters outside of the academic area. College students are just a few years away from taking on responsibilities in the real world. Why not train them here? In fact, you might say that I look at college students as adults. The days of in loco parentis are gone."
- A meaningful advisory system. Every student should have a student advisor in the freshman year as well as a faculty advisor. "We want to be able to anticipate any problems. When a student is having trouble in class, in a dormitory or with parents or a friend, we want to be able to be in a position to offer help. Students sometimes are better able to help than faculty members."
- Coeducational housing should extend to most of the campus. "Again, this is part of the business of treating college students as adults. At Colby, the fraternities began to show an interest in such living arrangements, and one did welcome several women as residents. No one should be forced to live in a coeducational facility. Indeed, some students are much happier and productive in a single-sex housing facility. But the option should be there. This is the reality of life students will face. Anyway, the arguments in its favor are well known, and the issue now is hardly earthshaking."

Write 300 words.

Assignments

A. Bidding

Newspapers report the bidding on major contracts awarded by the city, county or state. These contracts include large construction projects such as schools, office buildings and jails; highway construction; improvements such as sewers, street lighting and sidewalks.

Here are the items usually included in a story on bid openings for public works projects:

Bid Openings Checklist

- Low bidder (or apparent low bidder).
- Amount of bid.
- Character of project.
- Engineer's estimates.
- Next-lowest bid, or all other bids and bidders.
- Experience of low bidder; previous contracts; reputation.

- Open or closed shop (particularly in industrial regions).
- Date for award.
- Starting date for construction.
- Source of funding for project.
- Date, location of bid opening.

Here is the beginning of a bid-opening story by Mike Hiltzik that appeared in the *Courier-Express* of Buffalo, N.Y.:

Two area construction firms were apparent low bidders Monday on an estimated $9.8 million in sewer construction contracts in Amherst, with combined bids 40 percent lower than the engineer's estimates.

The firms, Cimato Bros., Inc., of 165 Hartford Road, Amherst, and Wm. W. Kimmins and Sons, Inc., of 1300 Military Road, Kenmore, submitted bids lower than those of eight other firms, including two from out-of-state. They were on three contracts to construct an interceptor sewer along a former railroad right-of-way—known as the "Peanut Line"—that cuts across the town from east to west.

The project is part of a more than $30 million phase of the town's massive $136 million sewer plant project, one of the largest public works projects in Erie County.

The Cimato firm was apparent low bidder on two of three contracts. On one, for construction of the interceptor from Campbell Boulevard to Hopkins Road, the firm bid $1,974,655, as against the $2,902,557 estimate provided by Amherst's consulting engineer firm of Nussbaumer and Clarke, Inc.

Attend a bid opening for a local project or obtain information about such an opening and write a news story.

B. Family

Each year, the Department of Labor announces the annual poverty level. This is the line separating poverty and subsistence. The poverty level 10 years ago was about $16,000 for an urban family of four. What is it today? Just what does this figure mean in terms of what the department considers essentials for a family of four: food, clothing, shelter, entertainment and the like?

C. Subsidy

A study by the Consortium on Financing Higher Education has found that a group of private colleges is using revenue from tuition to subsidize scholarships for poor students. The study of 31 prestigious schools found that an average of 20 percent of tuition (which averaged $19,110) goes to help less affluent students. The subsidies ranged from 43.7 percent at Mount Holyoke to 1 percent at Princeton, which is low, say officials there, because the university has a $450 million endowment devoted to scholarships.

What is the situation at your school? Does it have a formal plan to help students from low-income homes?

D. Unobtrusive

There are many opportunities to carry out unobtrusive observations. Try to find an inconspicuous spot in a restaurant, a laundromat, a bus, a park where mothers walk or sun their babies, a ball game, a hotel lobby, a department store, a tourist attraction, a fishing pier, a driving range, a bird walk or a hike. The possibilities are unlimited. Take notes carefully or use your memory. Do a piece that could be part of a series: "What Freeport Residents Are Talking About" or "The Talk of the Town." If there is a solid news story in what you overhear, follow that up also.

Campus Project

A. Live In (1)

The Live In, described in the textbook, usually takes about 10 hours of observation. Select someone on campus willing to let you spend some time with him or her, and over the next few weeks do your reporting. The work will be in the nature of a long feature story or a series.

Here are some possible subjects: a disabled student; an older man or woman trying to balance studies with a job and family responsibilities; a student preparing for a role in a campus production; an athlete balancing practice and studies; a science student carrying out an experiment for a graduate degree; an instructor preparing for a dissertation defense; an admissions officer deciding on the next freshman class; the provost or budget officer preparing next year's budget; the campus official responsible for fund raising preparing to launch a new fund drive; a foreign student adjusting to the campus; a new instructor coping with his/her first classes; an instructor preparing materials for a tenure committee; an alumni officer putting together a class reunion; a student balancing jobs and classes; sorority or fraternity members screening potential new members; the organization of a new campus group—gay and lesbian, minority, political, etc.

B. Notification

Should parents be notified when their college son or daughter abuses drugs or alcohol?

Yes: Parents can play a crucial role in helping cope with the problem. Since parents pay for their children's education, they are entitled to know when something goes wrong. If parents are held liable for the actions of their children, then they ought to know when the children violate the law.

No: Notification violates the students' right to privacy. Not all students have a relationship with their parents that is positive and thus notification is meaningless. Complexities arise: Should married students, international students, graduate students be treated differently?

Conduct a survey on campus among different groups—students, faculty members, administrators. Write 350 to 500 words.

Community Projects

A. Live In (2)

Some suggestions: working people—a letter carrier, police officer, postal worker, ambulance driver, bus driver, long-distance truck driver, grade school teacher, public defender preparing a case, welfare or social worker, public health nurse, doctor, dentist, judge. A newly retired man or woman, a man or woman on probation, a local journalist, librarian, foster mother or father, any member of a family on welfare, a die-hard fan.

Usually, the Live In works best when the reporter becomes involved in an ongoing situation that engages the subject. For example, a Live In with a judge could involve the reporter's watching the judge try a case or observing the judge reach a decision on a sentence after conviction. Show the person in action.

B. Votes

Make a voting record checklist for your state's representatives and senators. First, determine key votes over the past year (or two). Then find out how your representatives and senators voted on these issues. Third, make up a checklist.

You can decide on key issues by interviewing political science instructors, local political leaders and various interest groups such as educators, bank officials, chamber of commerce personnel, etc.

Make sure to prepare a tight summary of the issues so the reader can see what the vote was about. Not all issues were voted on by both houses, so you probably will have two groups of issues, one for the House, one for the Senate.

C. Pharmacists

The organization Pharmacists for Life International has lobbied state legislatures and state pharmacy associations to adopt regulations that allow pharmacists to refuse to fill prescriptions for contraceptives and abortifacients and to refuse to refer patients to other pharmacists. The group has been active in California, Louisiana, Kentucky, Wisconsin, New Jersey and in South Dakota the legislature passed an anti-choice bill. What is the situation in your state?

Home Assignment

A. Observe

Gustave Flaubert advised the young Guy de Maupassant to observe one person in a group so closely that the significant details and individual characteristics of that person would clearly separate him or her from other police officers, teachers, passers-by.

Try this with a class member. Observe physical characteristics, listen to the person's speech, watch his or her actions.

Do not name the person in your description. See how quickly other students can identify your subject. Or try it with a faculty member or administrator known to classmates.

B. Scenario

Select a subject or event and outline how you would go about writing a story based on:

1. Unobtrusive observation.
2. Participant observation.

Class Discussion

Interests

Compile a list of the special interests and the demographics of local people that influence coverage and play in local newspapers and broadcast stations. For example, in a region whose economy is based on farming, the media would emphasize crop reports, market prices for produce and animals, weather, government price supports and state and federal legislation on farm issues.

Note any large numbers of religious, ethnic or national groups and give examples of coverage of interest to those groups.

12 Building and Using Background

Mary Beth Meehan,
Providence Journal-Bulletin

**Knowing diverse cultures
makes for good stories.**

Introduction

Without an understanding of the subject of the beat and the particular story being covered, the reporter is handcuffed. General knowledge helps the journalist understand the context of the event. Specific information guides the reporter to the newsworthiness of the event. Reporters are always at work adding to their storehouses of knowledge and information bank. This is accomplished through wide and diverse reading—from newspapers and magazines to novels and nonfiction—and diverse experience. The good reporter is open to ideas that contradict his or her beliefs and convictions.

Exercises

Essays

The public relations office of the Freeport school system calls to announce the winners of the Peter Gallagher Memorial Day Essay Contest. They are:

1st: Beatrice Skinner, 17, Eisenhower H.S., daughter of Mr. and Mrs. Vernon Skinner.
2nd: Michael Nelley, 18, Southside H.S., son of Margaret Nelley.
3rd: Gretchen Young, 16, Horace Mann H.S., daughter of William Young.

The announcement is made by Rodney Addison, chairman of the city board of education. The 1st prize is a $100 government bond; 2nd, $50 bond; 3rd, $25 bond. Each high school in the city sends what it considers to be the best essays submitted for the contest. The judges were Samuel Ward, head of the English department at Mallory College; Billy Jo Barber, juvenile fiction writer; F.W. Stern, coordinator of high school English in the city school system.

You call Addison in hopes of getting some kind of angle on the story. You wonder how many entries there were and what the quality of the writing was.

Addison tells you:

There were only a dozen entries, the smallest number since the contest started in 1971 to honor young Gallagher, a local high school graduate of great talent who died in the Vietnam War. You know, his classmates started the prize then and they have kept it funded ever since. When we started, we would get maybe 30 or 40 fine essays.

Professor Ward tells you:

Except for the winners, the essays were dull, poorly written and had a paucity of ideas. Received ideas, you might call them. You wonder what the younger generation has on its mind, if anything. You don't expect any startling revelations, but you hope to see young minds trying to handle subjects important to them in a fresh way.

Barber says:

I graduated from the local school system only 20 years ago, but if these essays are an example of the best, I think something funny has been going on down there in the classes. The three winners were clearly outstanding, and then nothing. I think we're developing a meritocracy based on literacy. If you can read, write and think these days, the world is yours. But maybe the world belongs to the visual generation. Still, who is going to read manuals to repair our cars and TV sets, or will there just be deliverymen who show up with a replacement for the set when the wire is disconnected or a new car when the muffler conks out?

You begin to think that these quotes are going to make what you thought would be a routine story into a good feature, perhaps even a page 1 story. You talk it over with the city editor, and he encourages you to keep going, to try to interview some of the winners, too.

"We'll make this into a Sunday feature. Let the parents know what their charming children are learning in this school system," he says.

You call the school office back and ask for the titles of the winning essays. They are:

> 1st: "Humanity's Hope—World Government."
> 2nd: "Life on an Island!"
> 3rd: "Meaningless Competition."

Then you call Skinner and ask what she wrote about. She replies:

> Ever since the discovery of atomic energy, we've had the power to destroy ourselves. A world government movement started then, but it disappeared in the Cold War because of the rise of nationalism, for example, among the Third World countries. The United Nations tried, but it has no teeth. I did a lot of research on world government as a hope for human survival.
> I hope to go into government myself. I consider that as much a public service as being a doctor.

Write a feature for *The Freeport News;* Channel 7; www.freenews.com.

Assignments

A. B Copy

B copy consists mostly of background culled from clippings. When newspapers expect an event to occur, such as the death of a prominent person who is critically ill, B copy will be prepared ahead of time so that, should the event occur close to deadline, the story can be used quickly with only the addition of the lead. Prepare B copy for one of the following situations:

1. The death of the president of your college or university.
2. The confirmation of the attorney general of the state as a justice of the U.S. Supreme Court.
3. The retirement of the senior U.S. senator for health reasons, to be formally announced in Washington in two days.
4. The appointment of the chairman of the board of Du Pont Co., of Delaware, as distinguished professor for one year at your college or university.

B. Degrees

The following figures represent the percentages of the given ethnic groups that hold bachelor's degrees or higher:

White	21.5
Black	11.4
Hispanic	9.2
Asian/Pacific Islander	36.6
American Indian	9.3

Conduct interviews with educational authorities and consult appropriate references for an article that explains the wide variations in these figures.

C. Periodicals

Select a subject area from the following subject list: business, computers, home construction and repair, journalism, music, psychology, religion, international affairs. Gather from library resources the titles of five major periodicals that specialize in the subject.

D. Commentary

Select an article from one of the library's publications on journalism or current events and summarize the article in 250 words. Then comment on the article in 250 words.

E. Smoker

The American Cancer Society sponsors the Great American Smokeout each year. The Society asks smokers to use this day to quit or at least to reduce their nicotine use.

1. When will it be this year? Are organizations in the community planning any special activities for the Smokeout?
2. Interview a smoker. How has he or she tried to stop smoking? What methods have been used, and how successful have they been?
3. Interview someone who has stopped smoking. How did he or she succeed?

Campus Projects

A. Unwed

Each year, about 400,000 unwed teen-age women have children and most decide to raise the children themselves. Some experts oppose this because, they say, the stress leads to neglect in these households, and poverty takes a firm foothold. But other observers, to quote Francis A.J. Ianni, who has studied thousands of American adolescents, see it as a measure of both the increased "acceptability of single motherhood" and an inclination for "pregnant teens to avoid marriages that have little chance of success."

Interview members of the sociology, psychology and other faculties who may have some expertise in this area for their observations about the phenomenon. Obtain national and local data for background.

B. Tension

The Carnegie Foundation reports that one-fourth of university and college presidents say that racial tension is a moderate to major campus problem. The National Institute Against Prejudice and Violence of Baltimore estimates that one in four minority students experiences a physical or psychological attack motivated by prejudice.

Make a reading of the racial situation on your campus.

Community Project

Deadbeat Dads

Many men walk away from court-ordered child-support payments, and little is done to make them conform to the orders. Some men owe $15,000 and more, and state governments report they are collecting on less than 20 percent of 13 million cases. The case rate is growing by tens of thousands a month.

Examine the situation in your area. Obtain the names of women who have tried to collect child-support funds without success and interview them. What are they doing to try to collect?

Some states have enacted tough child-support laws that allow officials to attach to child support everything from lottery winnings of parents behind in payments to settlements in court suits. Federal and state income tax refunds have been intercepted in some states.

In New Jersey, which has some of the toughest child-support laws in the country, the state can withhold child-support payments from paychecks, and the state notifies credit agencies about parents who are delinquent.

Look over your state's laws and see whether they are sufficiently effective. Talk to lawyers for women owed payments to see how successful they have been and whether they think your state needs tougher laws.

You can make a database search for background.

Home Assignment

Background (1)

The textbook describes two types of background knowledge a reporter should possess. Give examples of the two a reporter needs to cover:

1. A city council discussion of next year's budget.
2. The state high school basketball tournament.
3. A murder trial.
4. A fire at a downtown hotel.
5. An interview with a major rap artist.

Class Discussion

A. Educated Journalists

In the end, the educated city room betrayed its promise. When the quick but unschooled working-class reporters were displaced and the well-educated took over the work, that social dislocation might have been justifiable if the news media were going to serve democracy more effectively, if the educated reporters were using their professional skills to enhance citizens' ability to cope with power in a more complicated world. The educated reporters instead secured a comfortable place for themselves among the other governing elites. The transformation looks more like a nasty episode of social usurpation, a power shift freighted with class privilege.

If the promise was not fulfilled, then what was the point of turning a craft into a profession? Aside from personal glory, what was really gained from all the journalists with college degrees, if they decline to use their skills to challenge power on behalf of their readers? Those of us who prospered from the transformation of the city room are burdened with those questions and naturally reluctant to face them. Educated journalists, it turns out, are strong on the facts and weak on the truth.

—William Grieder (*Who Will Tell the People;* New York: Simon & Schuster, 1992)

What do you think of Grieder's analysis?

B. Interject

Here is a paragraph from a *New York Times* story by Christopher S. Wren:

Because it is in Iraq's interest to provide documents, Mr. Aziz said, "the Special Commission should not insist and request something that does not exist." In the past, inspectors repeatedly found documents with details of biological and chemical weapons production that Iraqi officials had insisted did not exist.

How would you describe the second sentence in this paragraph? What is its purpose? Is this a legitimate interjection?

Skill Drill I: Famous Works

Who wrote, painted, composed or otherwise created or devised the following?

1. *The Republic*
2. *The Iliad*
3. *Measure for Measure*
4. *War and Peace*
5. *Ulysses* (Novel)
6. "Under Milk Wood"
7. *The Waste Land*
8. "A Hard Day's Night"
9. *A Doll's House*
10. *Kubla Khan*
11. *Miss Lonelyhearts*
12. *The Aeneid*
13. *The Catcher in the Rye*
14. *Lord of the Rings*
15. *Citizen Kane*
16. *The Brothers Karamazov*
17. *Uncle Tom's Cabin*
18. *The Magic Flute*
19. *La Traviata*
20. *La Dolce Vita*
21. *The Night of the Iguana*
22. *The Return of the Native*
23. *The Decline of the West*
24. *The Great Gatsby*
25. *The Magic Mountain*
26. *Pride and Prejudice*
27. *The Gulag Archipelago*
28. *The Sound and the Fury*
29. *The Sun Also Rises*
30. *Sister Carrie*
31. *The Cherry Orchard*
32. *Candide*
33. *The Scarlet Letter*
34. *Wuthering Heights*
35. *The Mikado*
36. *Bartleby, the Scrivener*
37. *Winesburg, Ohio*
38. *Leaves of Grass*
39. *On the Origin of Species*
40. *Bleak House*
41. *Of Human Bondage*
42. *The Turn of the Screw*
43. "Blowin' in the Wind"
44. "To His Coy Mistress"
45. *Through the Looking Glass*
46. *Don Quixote*
47. *Madame Bovary*
48. *Mona Lisa*
49. *Guernica*
50. *Birth of a Nation*
51. *Mein Kampf*
52. "Love Me Tender"
53. *Ten Little Indians*
54. "La Belle Dame sans Merci"
55. *Invisible Man*
56. *Tom Jones*
57. *Richard III*
58. *My Antonia*

59. *The Emperor Jones*
60. *Walden*
61. The Model T
62. *The Interpretation of Dreams*
63. *The Education of Henry Adams*
64. *Die Meistersinger*
65. *Sonnets from the Portuguese*
66. *Faust*
67. "The Gettysburg Address"
68. *Annie Hall*
69. *Das Kapital*
70. The steam engine
71. *Swan Lake*
72. *The Metamorphosis*
73. "First Epistle to Corinthians"
74. *Orlando*
75. "Swann's Way"
76. *The Shame of the Cities*
77. "Essay Concerning Human Understanding"
78. *Germinal*
79. "The 95 Theses"
80. *Black Boy*
81. "The Trout Quintet"
82. *Silent Spring*
83. *The City of God*
84. *Le Sacre du Printemps*
85. *Discourse on Method*
86. *Death in the Afternoon*
87. *Time* Magazine
88. The cotton gin
89. *Pygmalion*
90. *A Streetcar Named Desire*
91. *Point Counter Point*
92. *Coming of Age in Samoa*
93. "Mrs. Robinson"
94. *The Grapes of Wrath*
95. "The Sermon on the Mount"
96. "Letter from Birmingham City Jail"
97. *The Jungle*
98. *Jane Eyre*
99. *The Wealth of Nations*
100. *Fidelio*

Skill Drill II: What Every Reporter Should Know

1. The difference between robbery and burglary.
2. The decisions of the U.S. Supreme Court in *Plessy v. Ferguson* and *Brown v. Board of Education, Topeka.*
3. The source of funding for most public school systems.
4. What happens during an arraignment.
5. The difference between a stock and a bond.
6. What to do when a relative of the deceased requests that flowers not be sent to the funeral home.
7. Who succeeded Richard M. Nixon to the presidency.
8. What happened at Gettysburg.
9. The federal minimum wage.
10. The function of a grand jury.
11. The difference between a progressive and a regressive tax.
12. What the Electoral College does.
13. What a zoning variance is.
14. How many people serve in Congress, and how often they are elected.
15. The difference between gross and net income.

Jack Rendulich, *Duluth News-Tribune*
Getting close to the source.

Introduction

A time-honored journalism adage states: A reporter can be no better than his or her sources. Reporters depend on their sources for background, tips and corroborating information. The reporter looks for the best-qualified human sources. Reporters have techniques for testing their sources' reliability, and when a source fails the test, that source is dropped. The journalist also uses a variety of physical sources that include records and documents. An understanding of how systems work points the reporter to useful physical sources.

Exercise

Alcohol (1)

This graph was used by Margot Adler, chairwoman of the sociology department at Mallory College, this afternoon for her talk "Women and Alcohol" at a tri-state conference of colleges and universities on the Mallory College campus. The conference, which began yesterday and concludes this evening, was called by the Mallory College president after disturbances at Mallory and other campuses following attempts to curb what college authorities at Mallory described as "excessive and under-age drinking." The conference was titled "How to Cope with Campus Drinking."

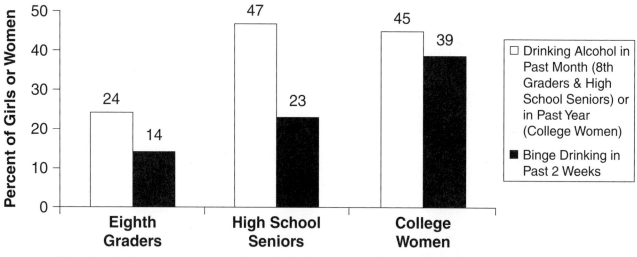

Alcohol Consumption by Adolescent Girls and College Women

Binge drinking is defined for eighth-graders and high school seniors as five or more drinks in a row at least once in the prior two-week period. For college women, binge drinking is defined as four or more drinks in a row at least once in the prior two-week period.

Here are excerpts from Adler's talk, which your editor wants reported in a story of 350 words or more, including background material such as the bar graph.

This graph shows figures about alcohol consumption by girls and young women. My studies indicate an increase in binge drinking by eighth graders of at least 20 percent and an increase of at least 15 percent in drinking by high school seniors and college women over the past five years. This is nothing short of phenomenal.

We have very little idea of why this is happening, why women are engaging in this dangerous, sometimes lethal, activity. And we have no idea of how to curb campus drinking. I am sure the figures will continue to increase. What was once an exclusively men's activity now has been joined by women, and we are all alarmed at the consequences.

Students seem to be taking their social life far more seriously than their academic life. Perhaps it is because most of them begin partying early. Life on TV is just one long party, and they've been ingesting TV from the cradle. Perhaps it is because they never knew hard times and have not understood that education is the route to a good job. They believe that jobs fall out of the sky and will shower on them.

We are now doing some research to find the answers. The most obvious answer is peer pressure. Everyone wants to party, and when we party we drink. All of us. But students drink until they drop.

Our college students believe that partying and drinking are an entitlement, that whatever their age they have the right to drink, and that no one has any business denying them that right. Our task is to find causes, but it also is to make clear at the outset—at their admission to the campus—the rules and regulations regarding drinking. We certainly cannot rely on their common sense.

Assignments

A. Government

Take any branch of local government and write a public service piece on how a department or an agency within that branch functions.

1. **Executive:** mayor's office; city manager; departments and bureaus. You might pick the head of a department and show the work done, the pressures on the executive, the rewards and frustrations. You may select a midlevel person from among the civil servants whose activities keep city government functioning.
2. **Legislative:** city council or city commission. You can focus on the body as a whole or on an individual. If the former, you might examine its changing functions through the years, its accomplishments and failures. If you select an individual, you might follow a particular piece of legislation under consideration by the council and watch the person reach a decision on the matter.
3. **Judicial:** court system, judges, prosecutors, legal aid. Is the system functioning well? If so, describe the people who make it work. If not, why not, and what will have to be done? If you focus on the individual, show that person at work.

B. Statistics

Consult the appropriate references to find out the following about your state and nearby states and see whether your state ranks high or low in these categories. Find out why your state ranks where it does by interviewing authorities. Write 350 words.

1. Physicians, dentists and nurses.
2. Motor vehicle deaths.
3. Average salary of public elementary and secondary school teachers.
4. Years of school completed, by race.
5. Median family income.
6. Life insurance in force.
7. Infant mortality rate.
8. Crime rate: homicide, robbery.
9. Suicide.
10. Infectious diseases: tuberculosis, syphilis, measles, mumps.

C. Requirements

A national panel recommended better science education in the schools in response to studies in the 1990s that showed American students consistently score below European and Asian students. The panel suggested science education begin in the elementary grades. It stated, for example, that fourth-graders should know that the sun appears to make the same trek every day but that its path gradually changes during the four seasons. Similar findings and recommendations have been made about the study of mathematics.

Most high schools require only two years of science and two years of mathematics for high school graduation. Among those that require three years of each for all students are Florida, Georgia, Hawaii, Louisiana and Pennsylvania. To graduate with academic honors, students in Indiana and Florida are required to take four years of science and mathematics.

What is the situation in your city's high schools? Are grade and high schools emphasizing science and math? Does the state have any requirements in these study areas?

Campus Projects

A. Gender

Examine the status of female faculty members on your campus. What percentage of the total faculty are women? What percentage do they make up of the ranks—instructor, assistant professor, associate professor, professor? Examine their salary levels and compare with those of their male counterparts.

Break down the totals into various schools and departments on the campus.

Interview male and female faculty members for their comments on the situation, and talk to department heads and deans.

B. Ranking

Several guidebooks rate and rank colleges and universities. *America's Best Colleges,* published by *U.S. News & World Report* is the best selling of the guidebooks. It ranks 1,422 accredited four-year schools, and although many college administrators criticize the methods used to gain information for the rankings, the guidebook and others are used by high school graduates and their parents in selecting schools to attend.

Consult the various guidebooks to see where your college or university ranks. Also, examine guides and accreditation groups for information about the graduate schools and programs offered at your university.

Then ask administrators and faculty members for their comments. Round up the material for a broadcast or print feature of 500 words.

C. Alcohol (2)

A study by the Harvard School of Public Health concludes that heavy drinking on college campuses did not decline in the 1990s despite programs to combat binge drinking. At the end of the decade, 22.7 percent of students reported they were "frequent binge drinkers," defined as five or more consecutive drinks for men and four for women on three or more occasions in a two-week period; 21.4 percent declared themselves "occasional binge drinkers," defined as one or two binges in two weeks. The remaining students defined themselves as nonbinge drinkers (36.6 percent) and abstainers (19.2 percent).

Conduct a survey to see how students on your campus fare in this four-part breakdown.

Community Project

Sweet Stuff

A study of grocery and supermarket shelves has shown that children's cereals, which contain about 45 percent sugar, are displayed at eye level to attract children whereas so-called adult cereals, which contain about 10 percent sugar, are placed higher.

The Center for Science in the Public Trust, lists percentages of sugar found in various cereals:

Cereal	Maker	% Sugar
Ghostbusters	Ralston	64
Apple Jacks	Kellogg	49
Froot Loops	Kellogg	45
Cap'n Crunch	Quaker	42
Cocoa Pebbles	Post	42
Trix	General Mills	42
Corn Pops	Kellogg	42
Cocoa Puffs	General Mills	39
Lucky Charms	General Mills	39
Frosted Flakes	Kellogg	39

Bob Thayer, *The Journal-Bulletin*

He shopped and he shopped, and then he dropped.

Check local grocery and supermarket shelves to see where children's breakfast cereal is kept. Talk to the store manager to see whether this is a standard practice. Examine the packaging of these cereals and compare it with so-called adult cereal packaging.

Ask nutritionists about the sugar percentages listed for children's cereals. What is an acceptable sugar level and what is wrong with the high levels? Did you notice any other sweets at a child's grab level?

Home Assignments

A. Source Test

What tests of reliability would you apply to:

1. Human sources.
2. Online sources.

B. Suffrage

The right to vote is considered one of the foundations of a democracy. Yet, this right was given only to white male property owners by most states after the American Revolution. There was nothing in the Constitution that guaranteed women this right, and this disenfranchisement spurred a long period of activism by women.

Some states did extend the right to women who owned property, but despite the work of women like Susan B. Anthony and others, the resistance was powerful well into the 20th century.

When Carrie Chapman Catt became president of the National American Woman Suffrage Association in 1900 for four years and then again in 1915, she reorganized it and emphasized work in the states to influence state legislatures to adopt women's suffrage, a tactic that moved from state to state with success.

Finally, in August 1920, Tennessee became the 36th state to ratify a suffrage amendment to the Constitution, and the Nineteenth Amendment was adopted. Catt had persuaded the Tennessee legislature to act.

No! No! No! to the Suffragettes
Organized resistance to the women's vote was common throughout the country.

Find out your state's action, or inaction, on women's suffrage and prepare a broadcast or magazine feature that tells the story. Use as a peg some date in the history and aim your story's use at the anniversary of that date.

Class Discussion

Lists

Compile a list of the major news sources in your community and on your campus. Each list should contain a minimum of a dozen names that will include not only the obvious sources—mayor, police chief, university president and deans—but the so-called movers and shakers in the community and on the campus.

Skill Drill: What's Next?

1. You hear a rumor that the Democratic State Committee is planning an important meeting next week at the Freeport Motor Lodge and that it may speak out about presidential candidates. You have two hours to deadline. You call the lodge and ask for next week's events, but the desk clerk finds no party meeting on the calendar. You ask for the manager, and he replies that she is not in. Where is she? "At home, next door," he says, and in answer to your request for her name and phone number, he says he's too busy and hangs up. What do you do?
2. The manager of the Freeport Kiwanis Club, John F. Berlin, is in Atlanta attending a national convention. A source calls and says he died of a heart attack there this morning. How will you get information for a local story?
3. The Freeport Civic Society's president, Lawrence Berry, says the group will meet next month to add to the list of "objectionable" books it drew up last year. Your editor tells you he wants you to do a precede on the activities of such groups and the response to their activities. Where do you start looking?
4. You hear on the police radio that a man is holding his infant daughter outside an apartment building window on Springfield Street and is threatening to drop her. You do not have time to go there before your noon local news broadcast. The police are giving you only the barest details. How do you gather more information?

Interviewing Principles

An interview for a profile.

Introduction

Journalists rely for most of their information on interviews with sources. The two types of interviews are:

News interview: Material is gathered from sources to explain and to document the event a reporter is covering. Sometimes the source is used for explanatory background. The focus is the event.

Profile: The individual is the focus of the story.

Effective interviews follow the reporter's careful preparations. The reporter has a good grasp of the event or situation for the news interview. For the profile, the reporter has checked the individual's background and recent activities.

Exercise

Cars

The office of financial aid at St. Mary's University calls and says it has a release of great importance. You go there and C.L. Braverman, the director of the office, says there is a new policy on the use of cars by students receiving aid. He tells you:

We've had nothing but trouble with cars here. Students ask us for help and when we get a financial statement from them, we find they have a new Chevy or a Porsche.

How can we justify aid to students whose college money goes not for tuition, room, board or books, but for car payments and oil and gas?

We now have $250,000 a year for aid and about twice that amount in low-interest loans. Last year, 220 of the 600 freshmen sought help. Well, that averages to a little more than $1,000 a student for scholarships; and we estimate costs per year are $25,000, minimum.

Then we'd hear about these students with cars. The system was not equitable.

He describes the new policy, adopted unanimously by the student aid committee:

The following regulation, to take effect next fall, pertaining to the use of motor vehicles by financial-aid recipients, reflects the concern of the committee that limited aid resources might be awarded to students who would utilize these funds for the maintenance of a vehicle for personal convenience, rather than for educational expenses. The regulation, however, is designed to give financial aid recipients the opportunity to have at their disposal a motor vehicle if they are willing to experience a reduction in gift scholarship.

The regulation is as follows:

Students receiving financial aid may have a motor vehicle at their disposal while attending college provided they register the vehicle or vehicles in their names at the Buildings and Grounds office, and provided that they accept a reduction in their financial aid at a rate of $200 per semester per vehicle.

Failure to register a vehicle may result in the loss of all financial aid and/or revocation of the privilege of college vehicle registration and/or operating privileges and suspension from college.

Any attempt, plan, device, combination or conspiracy, such as registering a vehicle in another's name, arranging a temporary sale, parking a vehicle off campus, designed to circumvent or that results in the circumvention of the above regulation may result in the loss of all financial aid and/or revocation of the privilege of college vehicle registration and/or operating privileges and suspension from college for all others involved in the combination or conspiracy.

The Director of Financial Aid may grant exemption from the above for financial-aid recipients who (1) have necessary employment off campus requiring the use of a personal vehicle; (2) have academic assignment, such as the off-campus Teaching Practicum; (3) have physical disability; or (4) are commuters who reside at their homes with no other available transportation.

Write 250 to 300 words.

Assignments

In the following assignments, several questions are suggested. These should not limit you. Nor should they necessarily be the thrust of the interview. All interviews should be preceded by research. Remember: Always ask the source to give specific answers and to illustrate with an anecdote or an example some of the points being made. Good interviews let us see and hear the person—use descriptions and quotations.

A. Prospects

Interview two or three of the major automobile dealers in town about prospects for the coming year and sales during the past year. Any significant changes in purchasing patterns? Any models that are locally popular? Have the proportions of new and used vehicles sold changed in recent years?

B. Postal

What is the life of a postal worker like—what are its rewards, discouragements? Why did the person go into the work? Would he or she advise young people to become a postal worker? Any interesting experiences while delivering the mail? Was he or she affected by the anthrax scare after the terror bombings in 2001?

C. Behavior

Interview the dean of students about changing patterns in student behavior and in teaching:

1. Are students more mature?
2. Has racial tension increased/decreased among students?
3. Is there less concern by administrators over student off-campus behavior?
4. Is there any sentiment on campus for a more demanding curriculum?
5. Is there an indication of grade inflation, and, if so, what is being done about it?

D. Religion

Interview religious leaders in the community for a roundup on changes in number and types of members, attendance at services and Sunday school, shifts in doctrine or policies of the parent church. Is the church attracting young members?

E. Accountant

Most people presume the life of an accountant is tedious and boring. Interview a local accountant about his or her work.

F. Music

Interview the leader of one of the local music groups. What kind of music do people prefer these days? Is this a shift from past preferences? Do people prefer listening, dancing or both? Is the audience growing? Are there any all-female groups, female lead musicians?

G. Union

Attitudes toward unions and union leaders rise and dip with the times. Lately, unions have been losing membership. Interview the head of a local union and ask for his or her assessment of public sentiment. Has this made the work of the union easier, more difficult? What is the history of a local union: when founded, membership totals, accomplishments, failures? What are its immediate and long-range goals?

H. Donations

Interview the campus official who is in charge of raising money from private sources. How successful has the past year, half year or quarter been? What is the money being used for? Any plans for future fund drives for special purposes? Who, what are the big givers? Any change in giving patterns over the past few years?

I. Lawyer

One of the problems criminal defendants with modest income face is their inability to hire a lawyer. Legal commentators say most lawyers turn away from trial law, preferring the more lucrative practice of corporate or business law. Locate a trial lawyer and discuss his or her work, its rewards, its liabilities.

J. Law Students

Check the opinions and intentions of students in a law school or seniors in prelaw about the desirability of careers as trial lawyers. If a student is planning such a career, why? Those who say no, why not? Focus on two students, each representing different choices.

K. GP

The general practitioner in medicine seems to be a rare species among professionals. Locate one and interview him or her. What are the rewards for such an arduous life? What does the doctor think of the future of general practice? Will it be overwhelmed by the trend toward medical specialties?

L. Med Students

Interview several medical students about their career plans. Do any plan a small-town or general practice? Do their aspirations bear out the fear that the general practitioner and the small-town doctor will disappear? If so, do the students think that this is bad? What new fields of medicine do they see opening up for them in the future?

M. Cars React

What is done, if anything, on your campus to students who own cars and receive financial aid? Are there any limitations on their activities; any proposals for limitations? Do any regents, trustees or workers in the financial aid office think there should be? Interview those who are involved in making financial aid policies.

N. Suspension React

Interview school officials on the policies for suspension, hearings and appeal in use in the local public school system. Have they changed in recent years? What is the school administration's reaction to the policies? Teachers' reactions? Obtain data.

O. Styles

Short skirts are back, says a headline of a trade newspaper. Interview local clothing merchants for the latest style trends in men's and women's clothing. Where will hems be next year at this time? Are stubby or pointed toes back for men's shoes? Is formal dress making a comeback?

P. Divorce Rate

Class project: Here are the number of divorces per 1,000 population in the United States:

1962: 2.2	1983: 5.0	1990: 4.7	1998: 4.2
1969: 3.2	1985: 5.0	1991: 4.6	
1979: 5.3	1987: 4.8	1996: 4.3	

Check the figures for your state and bring all the figures up-to-date. Interview religious leaders, sociologists, psychiatrists, psychologists, marriage counselors and young married couples to find out why the number of divorces is increasing or declining in your state. (Figures are from the Bureau of the Census, www.census.gov/.)

Q. Protection

As a result of the spate of school shootings, what changes, if any, have been made in local high schools' security procedures? Interview a school superintendent and some high school principals.

Campus Projects

A. Racial

Make a study of the racial composition of the faculty and the administration and staff on your campus. How have these changed in the past decade?

Colleges and universities are making a determined effort to hire minority faculty members, but a major impediment is the scarcity of blacks, Hispanics and Native Americans with advanced degrees in a number of fields. Half the Ph.D. degrees received by blacks in a recent year, for example, were in education, and almost none were received in mathematics, astronomy, physics and allied scientific areas.

Interview faculty members, administrators, staff employees. Obtain data for your campus, and with material from a database search or other research, blend the local and national figures.

B. Incidents

Campus incidents of bigotry have increased in recent years. Black groups report increased harassment of students and the Anti-Defamation League says anti-Semitic campus incidents are up more than 150 percent in the past decade. Anti-Semitic acts have occurred at the University of Miami, Texas A & M, San Francisco State University and Howard University and at Bates, Colby and Bowdoin Colleges.

What is the situation on your campus? Has your campus been involved in any incidents in recent years? If there have been any acts of racism, religious persecution or homophobia, what has been the administration's reaction? How would you describe the campus attitude toward minority groups? Would a poll ascertain that attitude?

Material about homophobic incidents on campus is available from GLAAD, the Gay and Lesbian Alliance Against Defamation (8455 Beverly Blvd. Ste. 305, Los Angeles, CA 90048-9886, www.glaad.org/latest.html). Anti-Semitism is tracked by the Anti-Defamation League (823 U.N. Plaza, New York, NY 10017, 212/490-2525, www.adl.org). Local and regional chapters of the National Association for the Advancement of Colored People (NAACP) can provide information about racist incidents.

Distribution of hate literature would not fall under the category of bias crime. Nor would the uttering of slurs. However, many colleges and universities have rules about biased behavior. Some university codes about hate speech have been altered because of court challenges of their constitutionality. Does your campus have a speech code; has it been revised?

C. Professors

A Duke University professor describes faculty members as "a strange mixture of ambition, competitiveness and social awkwardness . . . University professors are often the types of people who like to work alone for many hours a day. . . . We are not, as a group, very capable of interacting with other people, nor are we usually hired for our ability to work as part of a team. . . ."

Interview a cross section of faculty members to see whether this portrait is accurate. Is there any difference in the responses of members of different disciplines?

Community Projects

A. Arms

Almost half of all American adults (46 percent) keep a gun in their homes, a poll has revealed. Make a determination of local gun ownership. In your survey, differentiate among hunting guns, target guns and revolvers kept for protection.

Ask if anyone has had to use a gun of any type in self-defense. Check local police to see whether guns in the home have been responsible for accidents or deaths. What do the police think of home ownership of guns for protective purposes? How do your representatives and senators stand on gun-control legislation? What are the city and state laws on the possession of guns? Has the National Rifle Association donated funds to your legislative or congressional representatives, and have they issued any statements explaining their votes on legislation?

B. Toys

Body piercing and tattooing, leg warmers and purple hair. Fads come and go for teen-agers and college students. But what about the younger generation? The Cabbage Patch Kid, the rage of 1984, disappeared fairly quickly. The Beanie Babies soared and sank. Is G.I. Joe still popular? (He goes way back.) And what about Barbie and Ken? And the Sing and Snore Ernie dolls, once so popular they caused an underground market that made the $30 doll into a $300 item. Are they still hot?

Interview local merchants about the toys and dolls on their shelves. What's this year's hot item? What are the perennial best sellers? Do they still stock Tickle Me Elmo and the Mighty Morphin Power Rangers? What was their biggest bust, their best seller?

Home Assignment

A. Scapegoat

Your editor gives you a press release from the mayor's office about a parade along Massachusetts Avenue sponsored by the Jewish Community Council. The parade is in response to the coming appearance, next Monday, in Freeport of Louis Farrakhan, head of the Nation of Islam, who is to speak at 8 p.m. in the Civic Auditorium.

Write a 350-word story that includes the mayor's release, background on Farrakhan and the following statement by Arthur Hoch, director of the Jewish Community Relations Council:

> We hope that all Freeport residents will join us in this parade tomorrow at 1 p.m. to show that Freeport does not approve the kind of religious hatred espoused by Mr. Farrakhan. In his attempt to scapegoat one religious group for the misfortunes of another group, he is espousing the bigotry he says he seeks to eliminate. We, too, know the consequences of such scapegoating. He has every right to speak, but we do not have to listen. We shall be at the Auditorium with material about Mr. Farrakhan.
>
> Freeport citizens should know that Mr. Farrakhan has attacked Judaism as "a gutter religion," and he has rewritten history to make Jews slave traders.
>
> No one disputes the real grievances of blacks and other minorities in this country, but Mr. Farrakhan serves no good purpose in espousing hatred and bigotry among the people he says he is trying to help.

The City of Freeport   *Office of the Mayor*

For Immediate Release

Statement by Mayor Sam Parnass
on Anti-Semitism March and Rally

> Tomorrow the Jewish Community Council is holding an important march and rally to protest anti-Semitism. I add my voice to the chorus in once again condemning this odious form of bigotry.
>
> People of good will everywhere must work to eliminate anti-Semitism, racism and prejudice whenever and wherever they occur—be it on our streets, in our workplaces, from the pulpits of houses of worship, from classroom lecterns or from the offices of political officials in America or abroad. I will continue to criticize all acts of anti-Semitism and hatred—from off-color jokes to drawings of swastikas and the desecration of cemeteries.
>
> I hope everyone will join me in seeking passage of the hate crimes legislation now pending in the state legislature. The bill will put the force of law behind the voices of morality and justice. I know that silence is never acceptable in the face of acts of prejudice, and thus I have lent my voice for decades to the fight against prejudice: in combating the oppression of Jews in the Soviet Union, in protesting in 1975 the enactment of the Zionism equals racism resolution at the United Nations, in criticizing the comments of Louis Farrakhan at Madison Square Garden in 1985 and in memorializing the victims of the Holocaust in 1985 at Dachau. As the mayor of a city with a large Jewish population, my voice will continue to be heard and I will continue to do everything necessary to ensure that our Jewish residents, and all Freeport residents, can lead happy and productive lives free of crime and incidents of hatred. I will take part in the parade.
>
> African-American veterans of the then-segregated U.S. Armed Forces in World War II were recently reunited with Jewish Holocaust survivors whom they had liberated in 1945 from the Nazi death camps of Buchenwald and Dachau. They shared the common pain of having been victims of discrimination and of having witnessed and survived the result of horrific hatred. They shed tears and renewed bonds of friendship in a pledge to combat prejudice.
>
> Let all of us, of every color and every faith, draw inspiration from their example and unite to fight anti-Semitism, racism and hatred today and everyday.

B. Questions

You are to interview one of the following for a profile. Devise open-ended and closed-ended questions for your subject.

1. A candidate for Congress.
2. A new journalism instructor on the faculty.
3. The newly elected captain of the college football team.
4. The police chief on crime trends in the city.
5. A local car dealer on sales forecasts, new models.

Class Discussion

Profile

If you were assigned to interview the following people for profiles, how would you prepare for the interview, and what specific questions would you ask?

1. A new member of the English department.
2. A candidate for the city council.
3. The newly elected president of the League of Women Voters.
4. A local businessman who has been appointed to a newly authorized state Reorganization Commission to study the possibility of fewer elective offices and greater centralization of administration.
5. An organizer for a union of campus clerical workers.

15 Interviewing Practices

Roy Karten, *City & State*

Listen to the words, watch the gestures.

Introduction

Successful interviews depend on incisive questions, accurate observations and a comfortable relationship between the reporter and the source. Occasionally, the reporter will adopt a personality to be more effective in establishing this relationship: friend, confidante, authority figure. Generally, the reporter keeps a low profile in the interview. Regardless of what the source says, no matter how much the source's opinions and comments may irk the reporter, the reporter maintains a neutral mask. Questions are kept short and relevant to the topic, although there may be a prior warming-up period.

Exercises

A. Criticism

You are told that Frederick Cole, a retired editor of newspapers in Florida, California and Michigan, is in the city to serve as an adviser to the local newspaper, which plans to revamp its makeup and coverage and to go online. Your editor tells you that Cole has strong feelings about journalism education and he tells you to interview Cole for a 350- to 450-word piece.

Cole is 73, never went to college, was a successful city hall, legislative and White House reporter by the time he was 30 and then became city editor of *The Chicago Sun.* He went on to the *Houston Chronicle* and then the *San Francisco Examiner,* and he was executive editor of a group of newspapers in the Chicago area, the Atlas Newspapers, since absorbed by the other newspapers in the area. He retired a year ago. He had a reputation as a tough editor.

Your editor tells you that it would be a good idea to find out as much as you can about journalism education before seeing Cole, and you first make a list of material you want to dig up in references: the number of students now enrolled in journalism schools and their majors (advertising, broadcast, communication, news-editorial, public relations); the number enrolled in past years; the number of accredited schools; recent articles about journalism education.

You next make up a list of questions for Cole. You have heard that he thinks journalism students are not well-prepared for their jobs. You list questions along those lines.

You then interview Cole at his hotel. He is white-haired, has a ruddy complexion, is thin and of medium height, is wearing a blue suit. He has a strong grip when you shake hands and he often smiles, as if to reassure you that he is not really the orge he is made out to be.

> I still think of myself as an editor, and I talk that way. Can't get the business out of my system. I was a copy boy when I was 16 and I never graduated from high school. But in my days, eighth grade was terminal. A high school boy studied Latin, algebra and read the plays of Shakespeare.
>
> Anyway, the newsroom was an education. We had sports reporters who knew the archaeology of Greece, and city editors who could recite French poetry. Not many. But enough to tell a kid that there was more to this business than fires and murders. I learned it all.
>
> I'm not sure that youngsters take to learning the way we did, and this is showing up in the young men and women who come into the newsroom as beginners. Editors and educators have a common objective: We want to strive for optimum quality in our newspaper. And to do that we need each other.
>
> What we need to do is candidly appraise the weaknesses of today's journalism education—and then do something about it.
>
> Too many applicants lack a working knowledge of the English language. Some can't spell.
>
> Half of the aspirants who come into my office think a board of supervisors is plural. And they see nothing wrong with a sentence such as "The Chamber of Commerce will hold their annual meeting tomorrow night."
>
> Many of them can't type 30 words a minute. Their spelling is atrocious. I've found that fewer than half of them can spell such commonly used words as *accommodate, commitment* and *judgment.*

They are still being taught that a good lead includes the Five W's and an H. There's little evidence they ever were taught that a reader's degree of understanding drops off dramatically for each word over 20 in a sentence.

We're getting too many hopefuls who lack a background in economics, literature, philosophy, sociology and the natural sciences. They know little of local government. And they can't even report to the office on time.

Are the applicants we're getting imaginative? They think they are because, when using words of attribution, they come up with every word they can think of but the one that usually is the best to use: *said.*

That's not the kind of creative thinking we're looking for. We want young reporters who have enough imagination to go after the stories that are not usually done and to write them with a style and flair that will excite our readers.

And none of them can cope with the pressure of deadlines. When they must write fast, they tie up.

Sure, we expect a lot because we don't label our stories—written by a beginner, intermediate or advanced reporter. Our readers pay for a professionally done product.

How important is spelling to today's editors? We wouldn't even consider hiring a reporter who couldn't pass our spelling test. If he can't spell, we don't care how many prizes he won in college.

My advice to journalism educators is:

- You should be turning out graduates who want jobs in the general practice of journalism rather than specialization. That will come later.
- If students can't dig, write or spell, counsel them—or flunk them out. You'll be doing them a favor, for we don't want them.

Maybe it's time to be more demanding about applicants for the journalism major. I'd make all students who want to study journalism take spelling, punctuation and grammar tests as well as force them to write a story from a set of facts so that we can see whether they can use the right word in the right place.

Many students are going to be terribly disappointed because they simply are in the wrong field. Journalism requires an outlook, a mental discipline, a curiosity and, above all, a willingness to work hard day and night.

B. Galloway

You have been sent to interview a reporter, Joseph L. Galloway Jr., who will be speaking tomorrow night to journalism students at the local college. You have been given his background and have quotes from your interview. Galloway is well-built and of medium height, has close-cropped hair. Write 400 words.

Background

Joseph L. Galloway Jr. became a UPI correspondent in 1961. Before going to Moscow as a bureau manager, he was manager for Southeast Asia with headquarters in Singapore. He also has served in New Delhi, Jakarta and Tokyo. Before going to Asia, he worked for UPI in Kansas City and Topeka, Kansas.

He was a combat correspondent in Vietnam, about which he has written a book, and was nominated for the Pulitzer Prize for his war coverage in 1965. He was among the last American correspondents in Saigon before it fell to the North Vietnamese in 1975.

He was born Nov. 13, 1941, in Bryan, Tex., and attended Victoria College in his native state. He now works for *U.S. News & World Report.* His quotes:

Given the time and material, a person who has learned the basics of bricklaying can build a grand cathedral. Without those basics his structures will turn out to be hollow and dangerous shells.

It is no different for the reporter.

A good police-beat reporter can cover the White House, and perhaps more of them should.

The basics for the reporter from station house to White House are accuracy and fairness—honest information honestly conveyed.

The reporter owes a lifelong debt to his editor, his readers and, above all, to himself. The ledger on that debt is updated and balanced every time he touches a keyboard or a microphone.

He owes all parties the debt of full, fair, balanced coverage of a story which he should approach with personal interest, personal knowledge and a personal commitment to the truth.

There are no routine stories, only stories that have been covered routinely.

Beginning reporters are traditionally "broken in" with a tour of writing obituaries, considered a small, ho-hum, back-row operation of no seeming consequence.

What nonsense. What an opportunity.

The obits are probably read by more people with greater attention to detail than any other section of a newspaper. Nowhere else is error or omission more likely to be noticed.

A good reporter gives each obit careful, accurate handling and searches in the stack for the one or two that can be brought to life.

"Veteran of WWII," the funeral-home sheet says. Did he make the D-Day landing on the beaches of Normandy? "Taught junior high English for 43 years." Find some former pupils who can still quote entire pages of Longfellow because somehow she made it live and sing for them.

Look around. See who's likely to go before long and interview him. Few people can resist the opportunity to tell of their life and times. The good reporter finds them, listens to them, and learns from them.

Whatever the assignment, look for the people, listen to their stories, study them—and in your copy let them move, speak, act naturally. Put no high-flown words in mouths that never spoke them. You write of real people, not puppets to be yanked around from paragraph to paragraph, and you owe them their reality.

Check your facts. The more startling the claim, statement or allegation, the more attention should be given to double or triple-checking for error or misinterpretation.

A good reporter is a student all his life. Each new assignment demands a crash course in the theory and practice of yet another profession or system. From station house to courthouse to state house or White House, you have to find out what the official sitting in the chair knows, and you cannot recognize the truth from a position of blind ignorance.

Reporting involves long hours of listening to those who do know the ins and outs of the story, digging in the morgue files, filling up another shelf in the bookcase at home.

Then there is always the continuing study of your job as a reporter and writer whose challenging subject is the changing and unchanging conditions of mankind. For that study, you must read.

The prescription "to read" by itself does not convey what I mean.

If in this electronic era you are not accustomed to it, then you must train yourself to gulp down the printed word with the true thirst of someone who has covered the last 15 miles of Death Valley on his belly.

Read for your life.

Read every newspaper that comes under your eye for style, for content, for ideas, for pleasure. And the books, my God, the books. The world of modern publishing has a 500-year head start on you and it is pulling further ahead every year.

Never mind your transcript or your résumé. Let me see your bookshelves at home and your library card.

In a long career, a reporter's assignments may change radically and often, or he may spend his lifetime on a single beat in one town. That is a matter of personal choice, opportunity and chance. What never changes is the basic debt owed and the only way to settle it.

I served my apprenticeship on a small Texas daily, sitting at the left hand of a fine, conscientious reporter who handled the city government beat. He had been there for years then and today—years later—he is still there. In amazement, I heard him turn down job offers from big city dailies. He knew and encouraged my own ambitions, but his ambition was simply to continue providing honest, informative coverage of his beat.

His explanation:

"You may go and cover the great capitals of the world and the great conflicts, and that's an important job. But unless the people of this town, and all the other towns like it, know and understand the workings of their own city hall, how can you expect them to understand what is happening 6,000 miles away? Unless there's someone doing my job right, your job is hopeless."

Assignments

A. Applicants

Interview the editors of local broadcast stations and newspapers to see what they think of applicants for reporting jobs. Use some of the material from **Exercises, A. Criticism** and **B. Galloway** in this chapter as the basis of questions. Are there many applicants, more than in past years? How are they weeded out? If tests are given, how have the applicants fared?

B. Ratings

Schools and departments of colleges and universities are accredited by various agencies called accrediting groups or accrediting agencies. Some organizations or individuals also rank professional schools. Dig out accreditation reports (which often cite areas for improvement) and ratings for your college or university. Interview students within the departments and schools, the deans or directors, faculty members and others for comments on the latest report.

C. Dates

Valentine's Day brings out some strange stories in newspapers. One that is often plucked from the city editor's file sends out reporters to ask people, "What was your worst-ever date? What happened?" Try the questions on a few men and women.

D. Fantasies

What do people eat when they want to indulge themselves? Some nominees: ice cream, candy, pie. Separate men and women and see whether there is a difference in selections.

E. Class Based

A speaker on your campus has said that admissions and scholarships should not be given on a racial basis but on a class basis in order to foster diversity on the campus. In his talk, he made the following point:

> It makes no sense to use an affirmative-action program that is based on race, for that will give us the sons of doctors and accountants simply because of race, but deny admission to the white daughter of a coal miner or the white son of a single mother working in a supermarket as a bagger.
>
> We are supposed to be furthering multicultural contacts on the campus with the racially based admission and scholarship policy. But the reality on many campuses is that blacks and Hispanics, and even Native Americans, have been allowed to self-segregate in dormitories of their own. They eat with their own, and usually congregate in classes devoted to studies of their own culture.

What is the situation on your campus regarding the admission of minorities and scholarships for minority students? What is the extent of self-segregation on your campus? What do administrators and faculty members think of shifting from race-based admissions and to class-based assistance?

F. Shakespeare

A growing number of colleges and universities are dropping requirements for English majors that they study the traditional English writers, Shakespeare, Milton and Chaucer. A study by the nonprofit educational organization the National Alumni Forum found that two-thirds of 67 schools surveyed had dropped such requirements. In their place, the forum found, such courses as "Melodrama and Soap Opera" (Duke University), "The Gangster Film" (Georgetown) and "20th Century American Boxing Fiction and Film" (Dartmouth College).

"It's happened because English teachers don't want to teach Shakespeare and Chaucer any more," said Jerry L. Martin, president of the Forum. "They want to teach pop culture courses because that's what the students want."

In response, the chairman of the English Department at Dartmouth said, "We musn't deify Shakespeare."

Of the 67 colleges and universities surveyed by the Forum, only 23 required their students majoring in English to take the Shakespeare course. Several schools, among them Amherst and the University of Michigan, report it is possible for an English major to avoid reading a single play or sonnet by Shakespeare.

What is the situation at your school, and what do members of the English department think of this trend?

Campus Projects

A. Dating

Among black college students, there were 785,000 women and 495,000 men enrolled during a recent year. This presents a series of problems, and one is dating. "Some black women who are seniors say they have gone four years without a date," writes Emily Nelson in an article in *The New York Times.* "Black women will not ever have the luxury of limiting themselves to black men if they want a partner," says Audrey B. Chapman, a family therapist at the Howard University Counseling Service. "The numbers don't support that."

What is the situation on your campus? Interview students. Are there similar problems among other ethnic or racial groups?

B. Icons

Here is a list of women who have been described as female icons in various fields. How many of these women can students on your campus identify, and what adjective or descriptive term would they use in saying what these women mean to them? Write 300 to 400 words.

Madeline Albright	Aretha Franklin	Carole Lombard	Ida Tarbell
Naomi Campbell	Judy Garland	Golda Meir	Elizabeth Taylor
Doris Day	Indira Ghandi	Jackie Onassis	Mother Theresa
Amelia Earhart	Helen Keller	Rosa Parks	Oprah Winfrey
Dale Evans	Dorothea Lange	Eleanor Roosevelt	Virginia Woolf

C. Surfers

Students at a large midwestern university were surveyed about the time they spend at their computers in non-academic activities. Almost half the students said they devote more than three hours a day surfing the Web, playing games, chatting. Some students said their activity constituted an addiction that imperiled their studies, and a few indicated they were failing because of the time they lost in these activities.

Draw up a survey for your campus to find out what students do with their time away from classes. Is surfing and playing computer games a major time consumer? Seek out specific rather than general replies about just what students do—the games they play, the correspondence they maintain, the groups they are involved with.

Community Projects

A. Satisfaction

The Regional Plan Association asked residents of five metropolitan areas how satisfied they were with the quality of life in their communities. Their findings in percentages:

Area	Very Satisfied	Somewhat Satisfied	Dissatisfied
New York	35	48	17
Atlanta	49	42	9
Dallas/Fort Worth	47	40	13
Los Angeles	43	43	14
Seattle	52	42	6

Residents were also asked if they would stay in the area, if they were not sure whether they would stay or move or if they would move if possible:

Area	Would Stay	Not Sure	Would Move
New York	54	4	42
Atlanta	61	4	35
Dallas/Fort Worth	61	3	36
Los Angeles	57	2	41
Seattle	66	3	31

Also, the residents of these areas were asked what they most liked or disliked about their communities. They were given a list that included taxes, crime, schools, job opportunities, affordable housing, clean air and water, public transportation, race relations.

Devise and conduct a poll of your own in your community and compare the findings with those shown here.

B. Inhale

Teen-age smoking is increasing. Ten years ago, 700,000 teen-agers a year took up smoking. Today, the figure is 1.2 million. Two-thirds of new smokers are under the age of 18.

Michael Ericksen, director of the Centers Office on Smoking and Health, says:

> Over the past decade, adult smoking has declined by about 20%, while teenage smoking has actually increased. It's alarming that, despite a decade of unprecedented attention to the health dangers of smoking, there are more teenagers smoking now than there were ten years ago. Tobacco Industry opposition has hindered our ability to use the three most powerful weapons we have to reduce adolescent smoking, namely eliminating advertising, increasing price and enforcing access laws.

Conduct a survey among high school seniors to see what percentage smoke. When did they start smoking and what influenced their taking up smoking? Were they able to buy cigarettes despite the law against sales to minors? Explore the causes and ask whether they know the consequences of smoking. Obtain the latest figures from the CDC on teen smoking.

C. Teen Topics

A poll taken by *The New York Times* and CBS News found the following about teen-agers:

Weekday hours watching TV	3.9
Weekday hours at home computer	2.5
Weekday hours spent online	1.9
Have own car	14%
Have own telephone	17%
Have beeper or pager	18%
Have TV in their rooms	66%
Have part-time job	49%
Have ridden in a car driven recklessly by another teen-ager this year	
Ages 13–15	22%
Ages 16–17	58%
Firearm in the household	
Northeast	28%
Midwest	41%
South	43%
West	35%

Conduct a survey of your local high schools and compare figures. Write 450 words.

Home Assignment

Roles

Which of the roles described in the textbook would you adopt in interviews with the following persons:

1. A candidate for Congress.
2. A new journalism instructor on the faculty.
3. The newly elected captain of the football team.
4. The police chief on crime trends in the city.
5. A local car dealer on forecasts for sales, new car models.

Class Discussion

Fly-Participant

In the usual reporter-source relationship the source is aware of the reporter's presence, and the reporter is an uninvolved observer. Walter Lippmann characterizes the reporter as a "fly on the wall," present but not the center of observation.

There are two other forms of reportorial work: unobtrusive observation and participant observation. The unobtrusive observer looks on while the source is unaware of his or her presence. The participant observer becomes involved in the event—an education reporter who sits in a sixth-grade class and takes part, a sports reporter who scrimmages with the Chicago Bears or who boxes with a Golden Gloves champion.

In your reading, find examples of these types, and be prepared to discuss the advantages and disadvantages of the techniques.

Joseph Reyes, Office of the Mayor

The mayor makes news.

Introduction

The reporter's task in covering events based on the spoken word is to select from the welter of words those that best summarize the heart of the event. These key quotes are usually paraphrased in the lead and then directly quoted high in the story. The nature of the event is conveyed through spoken words; therefore, the story will consist mostly of quotations of the speaker(s). For meetings, panel discussions and symposia, the story theme usually is the consensus reached, although sharp disagreement can form the lead, too. Audience reaction, if significant, should be part of the story. Location and sponsor are secondary.

Speeches

Exercises I

A. Award

On the opposite page is a news release from Colby College about a prestigious journalism award to be presented to Bill Kovach. Rewrite the material for a newspaper or broadcast station in Atlanta.

B. Kovach

Here are excerpts from an address by Bill Kovach on his being honored with the 48th Elijah Lovejoy Award for journalism at Colby College in Waterville, Me. In 1837, Lovejoy was murdered in Alton, Ill., by a pro-slavery mob that objected to his anti-slavery editorials. The mob destroyed his press as well. A graduate of Colby, Lovejoy is considered America's first martyr to freedom of the press.

Kovach worked for *The New York Times, The Washington Post* and the *Atlanta Journal-Constitution* before becoming the curator of the Nieman Foundation at Harvard. After 11 years in that post, he became chairman of the Committee of Concerned Journalists.

Write 350 words.

> Elijah Parish Lovejoy was born in Albion, Maine, on November 9, 1802, 198 years ago this day.
> Five slugs from a double barrel shotgun ended his life in Alton, Illinois, in 1837. He was buried on what would have been his 35th birthday.
> They killed Lovejoy because he believed in the promise of democracy, in human freedom and dignity. After he saw a slave burned at the stake, he said so, persistently and forcefully. . . .
> Journalism does more than inform us. Journalism engages us and allows us to moderate those forces, which shape our lives. Lovejoy used a cast-iron, hand-cranked flat bed press to try to shape and moderate the forces, which distorted the life in slaveholding America. It was a crude instrument, limited in production and distribution, for such an important task.
> Journalists today are equipped with a communications technology, which has the power to recapture Plato's sense of the best path to the truth by recreating person-to-person communication between the eyewitness of an event or the originator of an idea in a venue that allows challenges and questions.
> Journalists today routinely interact with their readers or their viewers around the world as I did several days ago by e-mail recently after an appearance on Jim Lehrer's News Hour. Doubters could challenge my views and I had the opportunity to sharpen or modify my own ideas.

Colby News

Office of Communications   Colby College   Waterville, Maine   04901 207-872-3276

For Immediate Release   Contact: Alicia MacLeay 207.872.3220

Bill Kovach To Receive Lovejoy Journalism Award, Nov. 9 at Colby

On Thursday, November 9, Bill Kovach, who has been called "a newsroom hero" for his unwavering principles as an editor, will receive the 48th Elijah Parish Lovejoy Award for journalism at Colby College in Waterville. Kovach will receive an honorary doctor of laws degree at 8 P.M. in Lorimer Chapel before delivering an address. The convocation is open to the public.

Colby established the award in 1952 for an editor, reporter or publisher who has contributed to the nation's journalistic achievement. Lovejoy was a Colby graduate who became America's first martyr to freedom of the press when he was killed Nov. 7, 1837, defending his abolitionist newspaper from a pro-slavery mob.

Kovach, the son of Albanian immigrants who settled in Tennessee, rose to editorial positions at *The New York Times*, the *Atlanta Journal-Constitution* and *The Washington Post*. For 11 years, until last June, he led the Nieman Foundation at Harvard University, which strives to elevate journalism standards through publications, seminars, conferences and fellowships. He currently is chairman of the Committee of Concerned Journalists, whose mission is to uphold the best practices of journalism.

The Lovejoy fellow is chosen by a committee of distinguished newspaper editors chaired by Matthew Storin, editor of *The Boston Globe* and including William Hilliard, former executive editor of *The Oregonian*; Ann Marie Lipinski, managing editor of *The Chicago Tribune*; Rena Pederson, editorial page editor of the *Dallas Morning News*; Colby President William D. Adams and the chair of Colby's Board of Trustees.

At 1:30 p.m. on Thursday, November 9, government professor Tony Corrado, Lipinski and Storin will discuss "The Role of the Media in Elections: Campaign Coverage 2000" in a panel discussion. The event will be in the Robins Room on the second floor of Roberts building (above the college bookstore). It is free and open to the public, and refreshments will be provided.

But for all that the means of journalism have changed since Lovejoy's time its purpose has remained constant, if not always well served. For all that the speed and the techniques and the character of news delivery have changed, there is a clear theory and philosophy of journalism which Lovejoy knew and which flows out of the function of news and it is this: the primary purpose of journalism is to provide citizens with the information they need to be free and self governing.

We entered the 21st century with a communications web with over 200 million people connected by the Internet worldwide. It is abundantly clear that the technology permits the creation of endless communities of interests.

Yet despite the potential it is far from clear whether the communications revolution will fully realize the possibilities of the democratizing power that it has made available.

This is so, in part, because of a coincidence of three events: the end of the cold war; the opening of the Internet; and the globalization of commerce. In combination these forces dramatically change the political and economic forces that shape today's press. Beginning as early as Lyndon Johnson's great society and continuing at an accelerated pace after the end of the cold war, political power has significantly shifted from the federal to the state government level.

But the organization of the press as a tool for democratic engagement has not shifted accordingly. The national focus of the most powerful news media—the national newspaper and broadcast television—keep the American people much better informed about the activities of their federal government than of state governments. Local television, in fact, does not even cover state government on a daily basis in most states.

Globalization places news organizations inside conglomerates without borders for whom the notion of citizenship and traditional community is obsolete. For these market-driven organizations their news division are valued for their ability to attract a mass audience; for the sale of the corporation's other products such as nuclear power generators or entertainment; and for the political access and influence they can command. They are among the richest and most active special interest groups, which lobby government at all levels in the United States. Their power became starkly apparent when their lobby in Washington shaped the Telecommunications Act of 1996, the first major revision of the laws since 1934, and essentially turned over control of the public air waves to private forces for an international competition which favors monopoly power.

We are seeing for the first time the rise of a market-based journalism divorced from the idea of civic responsibility. Consider the words of Rupert Murdoch talking about his company winning television rights in Singapore.

"Singapore is not liberal, but it's clean and free of drug addicts. Not so long ago it was an impoverished, exploited colony with famines, diseases and other problems. Now people find themselves in three-room apartments with jobs and clean sheets. Material incentives create business and the free market economy. If politicians try it the other way around with Democracy first, the Russian model is the result. Ninety percent of the Chinese are interested more in a better material life than in the right to vote."

These words by a modern publisher advocating capitalism without democracy have no meaningful precedent in American journalism history. Yet there is a growing list of examples of ownership subordinating journalism to commercial interests. The day *Time* magazine was acquired by America Online, Time-Warner chairman Gerald Levin called the move "a natural fit." The fact that one company had a journalistic mission and the other had none, or that the journalists at *Time* magazine, CNN or *Fortune* might now have conflicting loyalties when trying to cover the Internet, cable and a host of other areas of commercial activity, all seemed incidental.

Similarly, Michael Eisner, head of a media empire, which includes ABC News, says he does not think it appropriate that "Disney cover Disney." In the mind of the man who runs the conglomerate ABC News has not only lost its distinctive identity but now has to struggle with whether and how it can cover its parent $23 billion corporation whose global operations range from sports teams and theme parks to cable channels and Internet portals.

Thus private interest is elevated above public interest. These forces may gradually shape the First Amendment as less the protector of the citizen's right of free speech than as a private economic right.

Michael Sandel, a professor of philosophy at Harvard University has wondered if, "there should be a nagging voice in us all asking: is democracy going to be bought up too?" . . .

These uses of the technology not only change the universe with which the institutions are concerned; they also change the content the companies provide. You can see this impact most dramatically on entertainment companies as they utilize the power of computers to produce more dramatic and violent action movies—movies that need no translation and generate worldwide sales and income.

In community after community, cable systems have opened local government action to the public in a way never possible before, "creating a novel kind of television news [bringing] events directly to the people, 'gavel-to-gavel' without editing or interpretation. The audiences are small . . . but they are huge compared to the numbers who actually show up at a city council meeting or a house debate."

The key, then, lies not with the technology but with how the technology is organized. The Internet is a powerful tool for mobilizing people who are already motivated to seek out specific information. This power was clearly demonstrated by the rise of a new generation of protestors who showed up in Seattle to attack the policies of the World Trade Organization, and the international monetary fund, and other "anonymous institutions of economic power." It was seen in the ability of a woman named Jody Williams and an assortment of non-government organizations to force reluctant national governments around the world to accept an international treaty to ban the use of land mines in warfare.

Toward the end of the last century Larry Grossman, former president of the public television system and NBC television, looked ahead to the impact of the new technology on the democratic process and sounded this warning:

"As we go about the complicated task of reshaping representative government and redistributing political power in the electronic republic, we must retain the delicate constitutional balance between local and national, between private interests and the public good, and between minority freedom and majority rule. Those will not be easy tasks. But we cannot afford to miss the opportunity to use these new means of communication for the public benefit."

To accomplish that, the theory of journalism that we have inherited from Elijah Parish Lovejoy must inform the basis of journalism for a new century—a journalism of sense making based on synthesis, verification, and a fierce independence. These are the values that hold the only protection against the forces that threaten to subsume journalism inside a world of commercialized speech.

History has taught us by bloody experience what happens to a society in which the citizens act on the basis of self-interested information, whether that be the propaganda of a despotic state or the edicts of a sybaritic leisure class substituting bread and circus for sovereignty. . . .

News decisions based on the same goal of mass appeal tend to filter out important complex social and political stories, which might draw only limited audiences.

So we've come to this: after struggling for centuries to remain free of government control and censorship public interest journalism now finds itself struggling with similar pressures from private ownership. Independent journalism may in the end be dissolved in the solvent of commercial communication and synergistic self-promotion. The real meaning of the First Amendment—that a free press means an independent press—is threatened for the first time in our history even without government meddling. . . .

Civilization has produced one idea more powerful than any other, the notion that people can govern themselves. And it has created a largely unarticulated theory of information to sustain that idea called journalism. The two rise and fall together.

Our freedom in a digital century depends upon not forgetting the past, or the theory of news it produced, in a surge of faith in technological and corporate rebirth.

For, in the end, if the life and death of Elijah Parish Lovejoy teaches us anything, it teaches us that freedom and democracy do not depend upon technology or organization so much as they depend upon individuals who invest themselves in a belief in freedom and human dignity.

C. Mediocrity

Here are excerpts from the remarks of Ted Koppel, anchorman of ABC News' "Nightline," made last night at a meeting of the International Radio & Television Society, which gave him its "Broadcaster of the Year" award. Write 300 to 400 words.

Koppel has been with ABC News since 1967 and was named anchorman of "Nightline" in 1980. From 1971 to 1980, he was the network's chief diplomatic correspondent. He joined ABC News at the age of 23 after working for a New York station, WMCA, as a desk assistant and off-air reporter. He was born in England and came to the United States with his parents at the age of 13.

I don't know what's happened to our standards. I fear that we in the mass media are creating such a market for mediocrity that we've diminished the incentive for excellence. We celebrate notoriety as though it were an achievement. Fame has come to mean being recognized by more people who don't know anything about you. In politics, we have encouraged the displacement of thoughtfulness by the artful cliché. In business, individual responsibility has been diffused into corporate non-accountability. In foreign affairs, the tactics of our enemies are used to justify the suspension of our own values. In medicine, the need to be healed is modified by the capacity to pay; and the cost of the cure is a function of the healer's fear of being sued. Which brings us to the law—the very underpinning of our system.

The law is supple and endlessly rich in meaning. It is also being abused as rarely before.

What Isaac Newton discovered to be true in physics is also applicable to the affairs of men: Every action has an equal and opposite reaction. I fear that unless we restore a sense of genuine value to what we do in each of our chosen professions, we will find that even the unprecedented flexibility of the American system can and will reach a breaking point. The legal profession is becoming an abomination; as often encouraging litigation purely for profits as for justice. The crimes and quarrels of the rich are endlessly litigated—until exhaustion produces a loophole or a settlement. The quarrels of the poor are settled in violence, and those crimes, in turn, are plea-bargained in courthouse corridors during a coffee break.

Our criminal justice system is becoming a playground for the rich . . . and a burial ground for the poor. It is increasingly difficult to argue that we were worse off when the rich resolved their disputes by dueling. It is even difficult, when one considers the conditions in most of our prisons, to make the case that we have progressed much beyond the brutal, but expedited justice of flogging and a day or two in the stocks.

Which brings me to my own profession; indeed, my very own job . . . and that of several of my distinguished colleagues here. Overestimated . . . overexposed . . . and by reasonable comparison with any job outside sports and entertainment . . . overpaid. I am a television news anchor . . . role model for Miss America contestants . . . and tens of thousands of university students, in search of a degree without an education. How does one live up to the admiration of those who regard the absence of an opinion as objectivity, or (even more staggering to the imagination) as courage?

How does one grapple with a state of national confusion that celebrates questions over answers? How does one explain, or perhaps more relevantly, guard against the influence of an industry which is on the verge of becoming a hallucinogenic barrage of images, whose only grammar is pacing . . . whose principal theme is energy?

We are losing our ability to manage ideas; to contemplate, to think. We are in a constant race to be first with the obvious. We are becoming a nation of electronic voyeurs, whose capacity for dialogue is a fading memory, occasionally jolted into reflective life by a one-liner: "New ideas." "Where's the beef?" "Today is the first day of the rest of your life." "Window of vulnerability." "Freeze now." "Born again." "Gag me with a spoon." "Can we talk?"

No . . . but we can relate. Six-year-olds want to be stewardesses. Eight-year-olds want to be pilots. Nineteen-year-olds want to be anchorpersons. Grown-ups want to be left alone; to interact in solitary communion with the rest of our electronic, global village.

Consider this paradox: Almost everything that is publicly said these days is recorded. Almost nothing of what is said is worth remembering. And what *do* we remember? Thoughts that were expressed hundreds or even thousands of years ago by philosophers, thinkers and prophets whose ideas and principles were so universal that they endured without videotape or film, without the illustrations of photographs or cartoons. In many instances, even without paper; and for thousands of years without the easy duplication of the printing press.

What is largely missing in American life today is a sense of context; of saying or doing anything that is intended or even expected to live beyond the moment. There is no culture in the world that is so obsessed as ours with immediacy. In our journalism, the trivial displaces the momentous because we tend to measure the importance of events by how recently they happened. We have become so obsessed with facts that we have lost all touch with truth. . . . Without context there is no substance.

It's easy to be seduced into believing that what we're doing is just fine; after all we get money . . . fame . . . and, to a certain degree, even influence. But money, fame and influence without responsibility are the assets of a courtesan. We must accept responsibility for what we do . . . and we must think occasionally of the future . . . and our impact on the next generation; or we may discover that they too have grown up . . . just like us.

D. Cecil

You are covering a talk given by John R. Hunt, the Cobalt bureau manager for the *North Bay* (Canada) *Nugget.* Hunt has been with the newspaper 40 years and writes a widely read column and broadcasts a commentary for the Canadian Broadcasting Corp. Presume that the talk was given at a Freeport Kiwanis Club luncheon meeting at Clark's Cafe. Write 250 to 300 words.

My car was making a funny noise the other day, so I took it to one of those antiseptic palaces, where I described the symptoms to a nice young lady, who called in a distinguished-looking gentleman with a stethoscope around his neck and a certificate on the wall which announced that he was a doctor of motors.

My car was taken away while I sat in a luxurious waiting room, reading old magazines and wondering what the experts were doing. Eventually I was told that my car was ready. I was presented with the bill and wrote a check, then drove frantically to my bank, where I persuaded the manager to cover it, and by the time I got home the car was making the same funny noise again. So I went for a beer at the Legion, and bumped into Cecil, the retired mechanic.

Cecil is retired, most reluctantly, because he is just about 65 years old. He doesn't see too well, because he always insisted on using a cold chisel without any goggles and got a chunk of steel in one eye, and then he damaged the other eye because he insisted on using a welding torch, again, without any goggles.

But oh, how I wish Cecil, and all the other old mechanics I have known, were still in business today.

They didn't wear white coats; in fact, they were usually covered in grease from head to foot. They didn't use a stethoscope. Cecil could stick his thumb against the block, feel the vibrations and tell you if you needed new spark plugs, new points or a ring job.

Cecil was a man of very strong opinions and ran his own garage for years. In fact, he refused to work on my car for a long time because he was a dog lover, and when I was a member of the local council, I hired a dog catcher who picked up Cecil's dog. Cecil beat the dog catcher to a pulp and paid a heavy fine. But he also refused to work on my car, or any one else's car who supported dog catchers. In fact, I believe he refused to work on the town truck, with the result that our snow-removal program was paralyzed.

If you called Cecil out late at night, he took a pair of pliers and some baling wire and a hammer. If he couldn't get the car to start with minor adjustments, he would attack it with the hammer and beat it into submission.

If you visited Cecil in his garage, you didn't sit in a waiting room. If you were lucky, you found an old crate or an orange box, and generally you took some newspapers with you to spread or you would have to take your clothes to the cleaners. And, if Cecil liked you, he would direct you to the back of the shop, where you could usually find some potent antifreeze and a fairly clean tin cup.

But Cecil could take the motor out of a Chevy and put it into a Ford, welding new mounts and making new connections. He could take some beat-up jalopy that a teen-ager had paid twenty bucks for, and make it sing like a bird. And, if Cecil told you that your car was finished, you didn't argue, you had it towed to the dump.

And, when you got a bill from Cecil, you shoved it in your hip pocket and told him that you'd settle up on pay day, or maybe later, and he would only chuckle, or let rip with a few cuss words, and then crawl back into his grease pit and flail away with his hammer.

There are still a few Cecils out there. Running one-man garages, charging moderate bills and doing a good job. If you know one, cherish him, treat him gently, even buy him a drink, because as cars grow more complicated, and motorists more helpless, the Cecils of the automotive world are a precious and rare breed. But, I'd take him, covered in grease, smelling of booze and swearing like a trooper, in preference to all the white-coated doctors of motors that I know.

Meetings

Exercises II

A. Council

Write a story based on the following notes from a local city council meeting last night. Use all the facts here. The council decided:

1. To build a viaduct across railroad tracks at Lincoln Street, scene of three automobile-train accidents in the last seven months. To cost $300,000.
2. To dismiss George Q. Banks, welfare director. Successor not appointed. Banks criticized last month for "irregularities in finances of department," that the city manager found in an audit.
3. To add new inspector in department of sanitation. Appointed David Lowe. He has been assistant bacteriologist at Fairlawn Hospital.
4. To hold referendum at next election (May). Citizens to vote on $1,000,000 bond issue for replacement of sewers throughout downtown area. Present system in use since 1884. Leakage into groundwater supply; system inadequate for load.

Sewer construction is the first part of the 10-year City Core Regeneration Plan. Traffic rerouting next; then the downtown mall.

B. Boards

During the past week, stringers from nearby towns have been calling in with stories about meetings of their boards of education. You have written briefly about some of these meetings. Your editor now wants you to round up all of these for use in a Sunday story. Here is the material:

Selkirk: Board adopted $625,000 budget. Will hire three additional teachers, one speech therapist. Salaries up 2 percent. Turned down $175,000 request for bond issue to expand library. Property tax increased from $17 to $18/$100 in assessed valuation.

Wrigley: Board adopted budget almost same as last year, $890,000. No salary increases, no new teachers. The property tax kept at $24/$100.

Dease Lake: Board turned down request for $1 million bond issue. Bonds to be used for physical expansion of Dease Lake Junior High. Vote 5–0 after four-hour meeting at which members of Dease Lake Improvement Association asked for bond issue, but individuals said classes not overcrowded. Adopted $1,260,000 budget. Flat teacher-pay raise of $100. Tax rate continued at $28/$100.

Keno Hill: Acrimonious debate at board meeting over request by Keno Teachers Association to add 12 teachers and to increase salaries across the board by 12 percent. Association said, "Schools overcrowded," "teachers' average salary of $25,000 disgraceful." Board voted 3-2 against request. Teachers say won't sign contracts to teach next year. Board adopted $2,350,000 budget. Minor increases in most categories; 3 percent teacher salary increase. Keno Hill Real Estate Association told board property taxes now "prohibitive." Mill levy of $26/$100 retained.

Rockford: Ralph Robards, chairman of the Rockford Board of Education, said the board voted to "hold the line" in expenditures for the next school year. Robards said the board voted four to one to approve a school budget of $2,220,000.

This is an increase of $275,000 over last year. Robards said a 6 percent salary increase was voted for teachers; four new elementary school teachers will be hired; and major repairs made in the Rockford High School gymnasium.

"We managed to hold the line on our taxes, retaining the rate of $29/$100 because we anticipate new construction will enlarge the tax base," he said.

In other actions, the board turned down a request from the Rockford Committee of Concerned Citizens for $75,000 to be put into the budget for a pilot program to bus sixth-grade students from low-income areas to the recently constructed Albert Parker elementary school on Duane Street. It hired Dr. Selwyn C. Mann as principal of the Parker School. Dr. Mann is a native of Albuquerque, Arizona, and recently was granted Ph.D. at the University of Minnesota.

C. Legacy

The Black Student Group at St. Mary's College sponsored a discussion tonight, "The Legacy of Malcolm X." The speakers were Vincent Bivins, professor of political science at the college and faculty adviser to the BSG, and Judith Cramer, a member of the Freeport Human Rights Commission.

About 50 students attended the discussion on the campus. Half were black, half white. N. Francis Simms, college president, attended and said after the discussion, "This is the kind of opening up we must engage in so that we can understand each other. Discussion, debate, questions and answers do much more than confrontation."

Here are excerpts from Cramer's talk:

The legacy of Malcolm X derives from his appeal based on a strong belief in black pride and black identity, and his penetrating critique of racial inequality in this country.

In contrast to Martin Luther King, Malcolm X was the voice of the angry, dispossessed people of the northern ghettoes.

That's a section of society that's growing rapidly right now. As long as their problems exist, Malcolm X will continue to be relevant.

He was an inspirational figure who made a lot of us look in the mirror, so to speak, and be proud of who we were as black people and people of African descent.

A lot of what Malcolm dreamed is coming to pass, in some small ways.

We have to remember that Malcolm did not live to carry out the enormous changes he was in the process of making. He was murdered after he broke with Elijah Muhammad and the Nation of Islam. In 1964, after a dozen years of talking of the evil of the "white devil," he was moving to what Michael Eric Dyson, professor of African-American studies at Brown University, describes as "a broader philosophy of human community. We may conclude with certainty that Malcolm X had rejected the whites-are-devils pronouncements that helped to focus his earlier life and brought him to the attention and vilification of a nation."

But, as Professor Dyson says, "He simply did not live long enough to fulfill his promise. We are brought up short when trying to deal definitively with the universal humanitarianism of his latter days."

Here are excerpts from Bivins' talk:

It's a multifaceted struggle—it wasn't Malcolm X, it wasn't Martin Luther King. Human struggles are much more complicated than any particular person.

Malcolm functioned as a spokesman for a movement. He was an outspoken critic of America's racial situation.

But we may be paying too much attention to one or two heroes while ignoring many others who were just as important.

Clearly, Malcolm was an important figure. But I don't think he was the only person on the block. Emphasizing these one or two figures gives us a skewed view of history.

We have to understand that Malcolm never registered anyone to vote. He never led a march against segregation. He never broke down any racial barriers himself.

Given time, this could have changed. In the last year of Malcolm's life, he dropped the racist rhetoric of the Nation of Islam, thus earning him the enmity of people like Louis X, who is now Louis Farrakhan, head of the Nation of Islam. And in 1966, Martin Luther King began to move toward emphasizing black pride and the need for black economic health. We might have had a convergence of these two great figures.

Studies of Malcolm must continue to be made. We have to foresake the uncritical endorsements and attacks and examine the man and his work.

Write 300 to 400 words about the discussion for tomorrow morning's newspaper, or write a long piece for tonight's local radio news.

Assignment

Clubs

Many civic organizations—Rotary, Kiwanis, Lions—have regular luncheon meetings at which invited guests give short talks. Sometimes these talks are newsworthy. Club officials often welcome student guests. A class could ask permission to attend for practice in speech coverage.

A number of other organizations usually hold regular meetings at which there are lectures or talks. The Audubon Society, the American Association of University Women, the League of Women Voters, the Sierra Club and many other national groups have local chapters. At times, the guests are men and women of some prominence.

Attend one of these meetings and write a story of 300 to 350 words.

News Conferences

Exercises III

A. Reject

An organization known as the Concerned Parents Association two weeks ago presented a petition to the Freeport School Board asking for the removal of several books from the public schools. The association, which includes members of the three major religious groups and various racial and ethnic groups, has in past years confined its activities to submitting material, much of it used to encourage brotherhood studies in the schools. The books it asks to be removed are, according to the list of the group, *Manchild in the Promised Land,* by Claude Brown; *Laughing Boy,* by Oliver LaFarge; *The Fixer,* by Bernard Malamud; *The Adventures of Huckleberry Finn,* by Mark Twain; *Portnoy's Complaint,* by Philip Roth; and *Down These Mean Streets,* by Piri Thomas.

Five of the seven members of the city school board today issued the following statement at a news conference. The five are Albert Swimmer, Helen Epstein, Charles Thorne, Jean Silver and Salvatore Vincent. The other two board members are Edwin Minteer and John T. Voboril. Thorne, the president of the board, reads this statement:

> We intend to vote against the request when the board discusses the petition by the Concerned Parents Association next Monday. We have been holding meetings with teachers, parents and students, individually, as we promised two weeks ago when the matter was presented to the board.
>
> Several members of the association have been speaking to us, and although we believe we have heard ample evidence for the association's point of view, we certainly do not intend to prohibit them from speaking at Monday's meeting. It is possible that new arguments will be presented at that time.
>
> However, we have heard the supporters, read the books, spoken to many of those involved. The argument of the association and its supporters is best summed up by the statement of Mrs. Richard Farrington, who asks, "Why do they have to tell it the way it is? Some of these books print downright filth. As for Jim, in *Huck Finn,* he is portrayed as simple, superstitious, childlike, no role model for young blacks."
>
> We agree that some of these books are realistic. Claude Brown's book does use street language, and it goes into detail about heroin use. *Huck Finn* is a subversive book; it does subvert the values of a society Twain disliked.
>
> We respect the intention of these concerned citizens. But some arguments are as silly as the parents in a California school who asked that *The Red Badge of Courage* be removed from schools because they thought it was about a Russian war decoration.
>
> We are also concerned that should we act as we are requested we would violate the law. The courts have said that a school board violates First Amendment guarantees if it removes books already on the library shelves. One federal court said:
>
>> Here, we are concerned with the right of students to receive information which their teachers desire them to have. . . .
>>
>> A library is like a storehouse of knowledge. When created for a public school, it is an important privilege created by the state for the benefit of the students in the school. That privilege is not subject to being withdrawn by succeeding school boards whose members might desire to winnow the library for books the content of which occasioned their displeasure or disapproval.

In answer to a question, Swimmer, who is black, says:

> These books do denigrate certain groups. But that is only their superficial message. Each of them is written with a passionate regard for the dignity of mankind.
>
> But what happens when books are censored? Well, the immediate reaction here is that the popularity of these books has increased, school officials tell us. But for precisely the wrong reasons. In the long run, censorship is disastrous, for once censorship begins, it will not stop.

Epstein is asked if the charge that *The Fixer* has anti-Semitic stereotypes has some validity. She answers:

> I leafed through the book the other day after a few years, and I can see how someone would object, just as I would understand reactions to *The Merchant of Venice* and *Oliver Twist.*
>
> Clearly, Shylock and Fagin are anti-Semitic stereotypes. There is some debate about Shylock, who at times is a sympathetic character. But there is none about Fagin. Yet what good is served by censoring the books? Perhaps it is true that youngsters who cannot understand that these books reflect certain periods and feeling should not be asked to read them.
>
> I'd agree that small children have no business reading *Manchild,* but I read *Huckleberry Finn* to my 12-year-old daughter and she thought Jim was a wonderful human being.

She is asked about *Portnoy's Complaint:* Would you want your daughter to read it?

> Well, I wouldn't want her to have Portnoy for a boyfriend when she grows up. At her age—she's 12—she should not be exposed to that kind of book. But I see nothing wrong with having it on the shelves of the high school library and using it in the class for seniors.

Write a column of copy and a shorter version for www.freenews.com.

B. Minors

The mayor's office distributes the following press release and says he will discuss it tomorrow at his 11 a.m. news conference. Write a precede.

The City of Freeport	*Office of the Mayor*
For Immediate Release	*Statement by Mayor Sam Parnass on the Sale of Tobacco to Minors*

I am asking the chief of police and our city inspectors to step up their surveillance of the vendors of tobacco products. It has come to my attention that increasing numbers of teen-agers are smoking, despite the health risks, and I have had reports that some merchants are selling to underage buyers.

Tobacco takes the greatest toll on health of any substance that we are able to control. It is well established that at least a thousand deaths a day can be traced to tobacco. Recently, we have learned that there is even a toll on the unborn and the newly born. Researchers at the University of Massachusetts and at Brigham and Women's Hospital in Boston found that smoking mothers have 115,000 miscarriages a year and that 5,600 of their babies die each year. Also, they give birth to 53,000 low-weight infants and 22,000 who require intensive care at birth.

The financial toll is estimated at $43.8 billion a year in federal costs through Medicare, Medicaid and other federal entitlements.

The time to attack this problem is when potential smokers are young. We must do everything we can to prevent teen-agers from succumbing to tobacco addiction. The city will do its part through stepped-up law enforcement. I intend to ask the city council for more stringent punishments for offenders. I want their retail licenses suspended for the first offense and revoked for the second.

C. Cheating (2)

Here are excerpts from a news conference called by Stanley Stiga, provost of St. Mary's College in Freeport. The event occurred this morning and your editor wants 300 words for the 1 p.m. local broadcast news or the afternoon newspaper.

Studies show that despite public opinion that our young people are more prone to cheating, actually there is no more today than there was 30 years ago.

The differences, are that today students tend to justify their cheating and that they do it more often and engage in more serious forms of cheating, much of this made possible by the Internet. These are connected items. Because students 30 years ago knew what they were doing was wrong, their cheating was relatively minor. Today's students justify what they are doing. Their justifications include: "Everyone is doing it in society; without my doing it, I cannot make it through school, which is imposing impossible demands on me; these are just shortcuts taken for work I don't think is that important; since everyone else is doing it, unless I do it, too, I'll be shortchanged."

At St. Mary's, faculty members are worried that unless the institution acts, a cheating culture will be established. Therefore, I am taking the following steps:

1. I am asking all members of the faculty to make clear at the outset of class the penalties for cheating—course failure to expulsion.
2. The Student Council will be asked to set up an Honor Court of seven students who will:
   (a) Recommend specific methods to keep cheating under control.
   (b) Sit as an appeals court for students who are failed for cheating. They will make recommendations to me and I will make the final decision, from upholding the failing grade to expulsion.
   (c) Develop during the next year an Honor Code for Students.

Studies show that two of three students admit they have cheated at least once during the year. Our task is to establish a campus culture that will significantly reduce this number. The benefits will be considerable, to society as well as to the individual student.

You ask the provost, "Have you any figures on cheating on the St. Mary's campus?" He replies, "A member of the sociology department made a study last year, and his estimate, based on random sampling, is consistent with national figures, no better, nor worse—about 70 percent of the students admitted to having cheated at least once—on an exam, with a paper."

Panel Discussions and Symposia

Exercises IV

Teaching

The school of education at St. Mary's University held a symposium on "Teaching: What's Ahead?" The speakers are Sidney H. Ganch, York University, a visiting professor of English literature; Frederick L. Lynn, associate professor of English at the host school and moderator of the symposium; Herbert Gilkeyson, superintendent of the local school system. The symposium was held at 3 p.m. in the school's auditorium. Write about 250 words for tomorrow's paper from the following remarks:

Gilkeyson: The emphasis will be, I believe, on grade school education where the basic study habits are inculcated and educational values formed. We have overemphasized higher education, and the result has been a deficiency of resources allocated to the elementary schools. . . .

We all know the problems that students in college have cannot be remedied without massively expensive remedial aid. We must put that money into the lower grades.

At the same time, there must be rededication to teaching by the teacher. A sense of professionalism will have to reinvigorate teaching or nothing positive will result. . . .

The teacher who used to take papers home to read now wants to have preparation periods in the school to read them. Taxpayers won't pay for this, and so homework is not given with the frequency of past years. Consequently, students spend less time learning. . . .

I am confident the teacher is the key to a new spirit of learning in the future. . .

Lynn: I would agree that teachers must re-examine themselves, but so must everyone else. Teachers are no different from doctors and ditchdiggers. They reflect the society at large, and it is society we must look to that establishes values that we all accede to.

Ganch: Students must be taught how to reason, how to learn. John Dewey recommended strong teaching, not the chaos we see in the curricula today with its permissive teachers. Samuel Johnson blessed the teachers who applied the birch rod to him. Teachers must put demands on students. . . .

Campus Projects

A. Altruism

The former president of Harvard, Derek Bok, made these remarks in a commencement address:

During most of the 20th century, first artists and intellectuals, then broader segments of the society, challenged every convention, every prohibition, every regulation that cramped the human spirit or blocked its appetites and ambitions. Today, a reaction has set in, born of a recognition that the public needs common standards to hold a diverse society together, to prevent ecological disaster, to maintain confidence in government, to conserve scarce resources, to escape disease, to avoid the inhumane applications of technology. . . .

As people everywhere worry about our ethical standards, universities are bound to come under scrutiny. Almost every public servant, business executive, attorney, physician—indeed virtually all leaders in every walk of life—enter our colleges and professional schools and remain there for several formative years. . . .

In these circumstances, universities . . . need to think hard about what they can do in the face of what many perceive as a widespread decline in ethical standards.

Such evidence as we have about the values of college students only heightens these concerns. Several studies have found that undergraduates are growing less altruistic and more preoccupied with self-serving goals. In polls of entering freshmen over the past 15 to 20 years, the values that have risen most are the desire to be "very well off financially," to gain personal recognition and to have "administrative responsibility for the work of others." The goal that has plummeted furthest is the desire to find a "meaningful philosophy of life," while other values that have fallen include the desire to keep up-to-date in political affairs, to participate in community action programs and to help clean up the environment. Further studies suggest that the number of college students who admit to having cheated in class has risen appreciably over the past 30 years.

. . . what *can* universities do and what *should* they do to help students to achieve higher ethical standards?

What has your university done or is it planning anything to answer Bok's question? Check professional schools and departments to find the answer. Interview faculty members as well as the heads of departments about what has been done and how effective the action has been. Interview students to see whether they consider the action (lectures, reading, required courses) effective.

B. Social Scene

The campus scene, reports *The New York Times,* consists of:

> Socializing in unpartnered packs.
> Binge drinking.
> Unplanned and unprotected sex.

A survey by the president of Teachers College at Columbia University in New York found that students prefer "casual sexual liaisons to emotional intimacy and commitment," the *Times* reports. The newspaper quotes the president, Arthur Levine, "When students talked about relationships, the majority said they'd never seen a successful adult romantic relationship in their lives. They're scared of relationships, of deep involvement, and that doesn't happen. Sex does happen. One way you overcome the fear of a relationship is you get loaded first, and after getting loaded, you go back to somebody's room and do it."

How does this summary compare with the dating scene on your campus? Interview students of both sexes; place these interviews alongside your observations. Write 350 to 500 words.

C. Credit Cards (2)

Make a credit-card survey on your campus that covers the following:

1. Some colleges sponsor credit cards. Does yours? Are credit card marketers allowed on the campus? Do they set up tables near the campus?
2. Some students have as many as six credit cards. How many do students carry on your campus? What is their debt on their cards?
3. Have students borrowed from the college or university to meet their debts? Do they work an unusual number of hours a week to meet their debts?
4. Does your school counsel students with large debts? Interview the appropriate administrators.

Community Projects

A. Mail

People are always complaining about how long it takes letters to arrive, and the postal service says it is constantly at work speeding up the process. Check the delivery time yourself.

Select friends and relatives at several different locations and send a letter with a self-addressed stamped envelope inside. Ask the recipient to note just when the letter was postmarked and received. A form could be used. At your end, note the date the incoming letter was postmarked and the date you received it.

Mail your letters on the same day as everyone else in your class.

B. DWI

Statistics show that drunk drivers are repeaters. In New Mexico, for example, almost half the 14,000 drivers charged in a single year with drunk driving had at least one prior conviction on the charge. Traffic Bureau records show that nearly 3,500 had three or more convictions.

Make a study of figures for your city and for your state. How many of those convicted for driving while under the influence of alcohol had a prior arrest, more than one arrest? Are there any moves to tighten up the penalties for this offense?

Home Assignment

A. Oops

Newspapers and magazines are increasingly printing material with bad grammar, misspellings, wrong usage, incorrect punctuation. These are not typographical errors, mistakes in production; they are the handiwork of the newswriters. Look at these:

> "As long as they respect my corner and I respect **their's,** there's enough to go around."—*The New York Times.*
> Newark, N.J. (AP)—Americans are the worst spellers in the English-speaking world, according to the results of an international spelling bee. . . . Gallup's spelling test . . . follows a **simmlar** multination survey. . . .
> That is just one reason to cheer the publishing of this **fulsome** biography. . . .—Book review in *Nieman Reports.*
> (**Fulsome:** gross; disgusting by excess.)

Spanish words seem to give *New York Times* reporters trouble, although the city has more than a million Spanish-speaking residents:

> "I'll eat at home," he said, turning his back on the **cucinas** and Chinese restaurant. . . . (Not **cucinas,** *cocinas.*)
>
> In a piece about the advertising business in Mexico, an account executive said he had to cope with the **"morbito,"** a colloquialism for *bribe.* (It's *mordida,* from the verb *morder,* to bite.)

For the next week, be on the lookout for errors of this sort in newspapers and other publications that you read. Do any publications have a preponderance of errors? Why?

B. Guide

The textbook sums up coverage of speeches, news conferences and panel discussions with four guides and a reminder. Apply these to any story you have written from this chapter in the *Workbook.*

Class Discussion

Indefensible

> Every journalist who is not too stupid or too full of himself to notice what is going on knows that what he does is morally indefensible. He is a kind of confidence man, preying on people's vanity, ignorance, or loneliness, gaining their trust and betraying them without remorse.

This is the beginning of Janet Malcolm's book *The Journalist and the Murderer,* a description and commentary on how journalist Joe McGinniss ingratiated himself with triple-murderer Jeffrey MacDonald and then in the book *Fatal Vision* refused to accept MacDonald's version that an intruder was the killer.

Malcolm describes the relationship between journalists and their sources and subjects as one of exploitation, "seduction and betrayal," a "Devil's pact."

What do you think of Malcolm's assessment of journalistic morality?

Hunches, Feelings and Stereotypes

Ken Elkins, *The Anniston* (Ala.) *Star*

Feelings can lead to good stories.

Introduction

Hunches and intuition can lead reporters to good stories. These insights do not come out of the blue. They are the result of large and varied background knowledge and an understanding of the behavior of people. The ill-prepared reporter does not have hunches. Feelings and emotions can distort observations and influence writing. But they also can lead reporters to uncover abuses and illegalities. Reporters monitor their feelings and opinions, and they make sure to avoid stereotypes in their reporting and writing. The reporter with fixed pictures in mind of people and groups produces distorted reporting.

Exercises

A. Burger

You check into the office one morning and find the nightside reporter has left some notes for you about what seems to be a routine police report. As the police reporter, it is your job to handle the story. You go to headquarters and look at the report.

The report by Patrolman Fred Galzo (all quotes are from his report) states that while two officers were chatting in the parking lot of the Burger King at 4700 Airport Road, a 1987 white Dodge pulled in at "a fast rate of speed." Galzo asked the operator for license and registration and, his report continues, "checked vehicle and found it unsafe and informed Officer (Paul) Burns to inform headquarters that a tow truck was wanted for an impoundment of motor vehicle." Galzo then issued two summonses to the operator, George Post, 18, of 25 Domino Road. Vehicle was registered to the passenger, Thomas Polk, 18, of 10 Topeka St.

"After said vehicle was taken, the above two in question were standing in the lot and informed me that they are not going to leave and began to get loud and abusive." At this time, two other officers arrived and Galzo told them he needed help. "Who the fuck do you think you are taking our car?" one of the youths said.

"Both men were using indecent language with the indecent word (fuck) in their conversation. I informed both that they were under arrest, and the officers assisted me in arresting the accused. At this time, both men refused to get in the patrol car and became violent while we attempted to place same in the rear seat of the police vehicle.

"After the necessary amount of force was used and the arrest was completed they were transported to headquarters and booked." The two continued to make "comments about the police and our headquarters, and Post went on to say that they should burn this shit down and that he could build better shit than this and was taking out our cards from the rack and making comments about same. I asked this person several times to keep quiet and to stand at the other end of the room.

"Not replying to my request which I made several times I got up from my chair and extended my left hand outward to escort him to far side of room. He was stepping backward and tripped over Officer Gerber's chair and fell to the ground. At this time he got up and stated that his arm was broken and to send him to the doctor's. The lieutenant called the ambulance, which transported him to Community Hospital.

"Both men were charged with using loud and abusive language and failing to obey an officer's orders."

On the notes the nightside reporter left is the notation, "Released $25 bail each pending hearing tomorrow night. Post said he had fractured left wrist."

You have 15 minutes to deadline. What do you do?

B. Politico

You cover the statehouse in a state with a large Spanish-speaking population. The primary elections are coming up and the incumbent attorney general, Ralph Martinez, a Democrat, has indicated he plans to run for governor. You hear that this annoys the leadership of the Democratic Party because Martinez—a popular, crusading official—might win the party nomination. In the general election, the Democratic Party leaders believe, the Republicans would have a decided advantage if they presented a non-Spanish-speaking candidate.

You have been around state politics long enough to know that there is some logic to this thinking. Some people vote along ethnic lines, and your study of county returns has proved to you that although the state has had a Democratic governor for the past 12 years, there might be some trouble for a Democratic candidate with a Spanish surname.

You check with your sources and contacts to get the lay of the land. There is no question that the party leadership is worried by Martinez. He could lose the gubernatorial race—thus eliminating thousands of patronage jobs, inside information on contracts and the various spoils of office—and even if he were to win, his political independence is not liked by the party regulars. Some of his assistants in the attorney general's office are known to be Republicans.

One of your sources, Charles DuParte, a former reporter who is secretary to the governor, says the Democratic leadership has been meeting to discuss the situation. The last meeting was at the home of the state party chairman. Walter Kegel. The governor, John Mabee, who is retiring from politics at the expiration of his term, sat in the meeting but said nothing. He is taking a hands-off position. "It's too incendiary," DuParte says, "for him to get involved. He wants to go out smiling, and the Hispanic thing has got everybody tense."

No, you cannot quote him on any of this. You know he is truthful, and you ask him whether you can use the information without his name. He says he doesn't care so long as you keep the governor out of the scene. It's yours exclusively, he says.

At this point, you can write an interpretative story if you wish to. Make it about 250 words.

You continue to report. A county chairman of the Democratic Party, Alberto Gonzales, is in the state capital and you run into him. He says he was chatting with Don Sanchez, a state corporation commissioner, and Sanchez "was making sounds like a candidate." A candidate for what? Gonzales motions you over to a side corridor. "For governor," he whispers.

You know that Sanchez won his last race by a whisker and has had a bland career in his job as a commissioner. As a candidate for governor, he makes no sense. You tell Gonzales this, and he smiles knowingly. With a bit of condescension in his voice, he says, "Well, I thought you knew politics. Strange things happen, don't they? Especially when the right people get together."

What right people? Has Sanchez been meeting with anyone? Did he see Kegel lately? You shoot the questions at Gonzales, but all he does is smile. You decide to see Sanchez.

After the usual chitchat, you ask him what he thinks of Martinez as a candidate for governor "Oh," says Sanchez, "I didn't know he's running." So that's to be his game, you think, and you take a risk:

"I heard that's what you and Walter talked about at that meeting the other night."

Sanchez is an old hand at politics, and you watch him carefully. He won't fall out of his chair, perhaps not even blink if you hit home. He does start, and he begins to finger some papers on his desk. You've hit home. You press on.

"I heard that the fellows think you would make a good candidate." Appeal to his vanity. "They say that Martinez is not really popular up north, where you have always done well."

Sanchez melts a bit. "Yes, they liked my campaigning up there," he says. "But I'm not sure I'll run. I said that. I told them I couldn't be sure. I have two more years in this job, you know, and there are many things I want to finish up."

You know that the best thing to do now is to keep him talking, and you tell him you think that one area he could look into is the interstate trucking situation involving independent truckers, a subject he has spoken about. He warms to that. You let him talk, and then you mention that such a record would look good in a gubernatorial campaign—a candidate who has tried to bring down fees for truckers so that food and other material they bring in won't cost so much.

"Yes, I'd have something to say, all right," he says.

Of course, you tell him, he would be head-and-head with Martinez should the attorney general run, and you know what that would mean. (You are not really sure what he will take that to mean. It's an open-ended probe that he could interpret as meaning a tough campaign up north for both of them since Martinez is popular there, too. Or it could mean his candidacy would clear the way for a non-Spanish-speaking candidate to win because the Spanish-speaking electorate would split its vote.)

"What would it mean?" he asks you suspiciously.

"What everyone is saying," you answer. "That you would be a stalking horse."

"Nobody's saying that," he says testily. "Tell me who says I'm out to kill off Martinez and I'll call him a liar. Just print that, you hear. Print that when I make my decision, I'll be a candidate. I'll run and run hard and all those who make those accusations will be outside when I'm up there in the governor's office." He points to the floor above him, the governor's suite.

"Are you a candidate?" you persist.

"I'll make up my mind next week. I'm seriously thinking of it. You can say that."

You call Kegel from your office in the statehouse and try to bluff him. It doesn't work. Finally, you ask, "Are you going to tell me that Sanchez is a liar, that he is trying to commit you to something that's all a dream? That's going to look good, Walter."

He replies, "I will say that I will neither confirm nor deny that Mr. Sanchez met with the party central committee the other day. You know we cannot support a candidate. That's illegal as hell. He may have been in there to chat. He's a loyal Democrat and he has good ideas about party matters and state government. Don's one of our best state servants."

You have heard enough. You call the city editor and tell him you are ready to write an interpretative piece about the possibility of a stalking horse in the Democratic gubernatorial primary election. He tells you to give it 400 words.

Assignments

A. Documents

1. Examine wills filed for probate with the county clerk or in probate court within the last week or month for a newsworthy filing.
2. Tax-exempt organizations must file a Form 990 with the Internal Revenue Service. Organizations also are required to show the form to those requesting a copy. Obtain one from any local charity and write a story.
3. Some cities, most states and the federal government require public officials to file public disclosure forms that list their assets. Locate a form for a city, state or federal elected official and write a story based on the filing.
4. Check the real estate holdings of a local official by examining deeds, mortgages, loans, real estate transfers.

B. Pattern

Examine the latest edition of the FBI's Uniform Crime Report. Make a list of the 10 states with the highest crime rates for violent crimes—murder, non-negligent manslaughter, rape, robbery, aggravated assault—or for one of these crimes. Make a list of the 10 states with the lowest crime rates. Can you see any patterns? Write a story based on your conclusions.

C. Gifts

Each year, alumni donate billions of dollars to their alma maters. At one time, the giving was unrestricted; the donors allowed their schools to use the money as the schools saw fit. But unrestricted giving has declined. "There are more gifts with strings attached," says Peter Buchanan, president of the Council for Advancement and Support, an organization serving university administrators in the areas of alumni relations, communications and fund raising.

Some schools are unhappy with such gifts; others find input from donors positive. But there are limits. Most schools will not allow donors to dictate the professors they hire or the students they must accept. Lee Bass donated $20 million to Yale with the provision he would have a say in the appointment of professors. The gift was refused.

What is the situation on your campus? How many gifts are unrestricted, how many restricted? What is the nature of some of the restrictions?

Campus Projects

A. Ratings

Schools and departments of colleges and universities are accredited by various agencies. Accreditation reports often cite areas for improvement and occasionally deny accreditation.

Also, independent organizations and individuals rank professional schools, and several publications rank entire colleges and universities.

Dig out these accreditation reports, ratings and assessments for your college or university and its various schools and departments. A computer search will be helpful. Cite positive and negative comments and interview students, deans and department heads, faculty members and others for comments.

B. Remedial

About 30 percent of all college students take at least one remedial course. The costs are high, and in an era of budget cutting, some universities want out of the remedial business. They would have remedial teaching done by the community colleges.

California's 20 campuses have seen a rise in remedial students. In 1989, 23 percent of entering freshmen needed help in mathematics, 36 percent in English. By 1993–94, 42 percent needed remedial instruction in mathematics, 43 percent in English. The most recent figures show a continued increase. What is the situation on your campus, in your state?

Community Projects

A. Purchase

How much does it cost the city to buy school supplies, such as paper, cleaning fluids, pencils; police department supplies and equipment, such as patrol cars; street department materials, such as highway paint and signs?

Compare these costs with those in a city of comparable size in your state. Were there bids for your city's purchases, or were they negotiated? What is the state law on purchases that require competitive bidding?

B. Kids

More than half a million abused and neglected children are under state supervision. This is twice as many as 10 years ago. The child welfare system, say experts, is in chaos: Children drift from foster homes to group homes and back as the courts and state agencies try to cope.

These drifting children often become homeless, unemployed, drug-using adults.

What's the situation in your community and state? Ask authorities on campus and in the community for their opinions. Interview those in the courts and law enforcement agencies for their experiences.

C. Klan

During the 1920s, the Ku Klux Klan, which preached white supremacy and was violently anti-Catholic and anti-Semitic, had a following of several million. The Klan elected governors in Oklahoma and Oregon and "practically took over Indiana," writes the historian Samuel Eliot Morison.

Governors, state legislators and members of school boards adhered to the Klan philosophy. In Greybull, Wyo., the Klan-dominated school board told the school superintendent he had a choice: Divorce his wife or resign. The reason: His wife was Catholic.

Denver Public Library, Western History Dept.

Colorado Klan Rally

In many communities, white-robed Klan members held rallies at which they burned crosses and paraded. The photograph on the preceding page shows a portion of the 2,500 Klansmen who gathered in a canyon outside Boulder, Colo., in 1922. In the ceremony, the Boulder Klan was presented with a charter as 500 of the local members participated.

Colorado Klan members—reportedly 40,000 strong—elected a governor and five other state officials who had sought Klan support. At the University of Colorado in Boulder, the president, George Norlin, was told that the university would have its annual appropriation approved—if it cooperated with the Klan. Norlin said later:

> The Governor assured me that the University could have what it wanted in the way of appropriations provided the University would play the game with the Ku Klux Klan; that is, definitely provided the University would dismiss from its staff all Catholics and all Jews. I stated flatly to the Governor that if we had to pay such a price for the support of the Legislature, we preferred to do without that support. And we did without it.

The State Senate cut the university appropriation in half, and the House removed it entirely.

Check local and state history for a feature about the existence of the Klan in your area. In some localities, the Klan still meets and burns crosses.

Home Assignment

A. Develop

What would you do to develop stories from the following information?

1. The mayor is reported to have decided to run for governor but will not say anything himself.
2. A union is thinking of organizing the university work force: groundskeepers, librarians, secretaries, cleaning personnel.
3. An unexpected increase in strep throat has struck the city.
4. A national organization is quietly buying up property outside the city limits for construction of a large industrial park.
5. You hear through the police grapevine that soon a new police chief may be appointed and the current chief fired.

B. Self-Audit

The textbook lists several questions reporters should ask themselves every so often as a check on their emotions and feelings. Discuss the utility of some of these questions for yourself.

Class Discussion

A. Seeing

> We need intellectual vigilance now more than barricade journalism, and particularly the gift of seeing, and seeing in time, trends that may affect the life of the world.
> —James Reston

The kind of vigilant journalism Reston called for is described by some journalists as "anticipatory journalism." It depends upon the journalist's sense of the world around him or her and upon the journalist's ability to pattern events.

In your reading, see whether you can find examples of articles in newspapers or magazines that anticipate developments or trends.

B. Passive

What do you think of the prediction of Frank Deford, a sportswriter and television and radio commentator?

> I think we're almost reaching a point where we were centuries ago: A certain small percentage of the population reads, and nobody else does. It used to be just a question of literacy and illiteracy, but now we're moving toward what is essentially going to be a two-tiered population—one that reads, and one that simply watches television.
>
> I'm not a believer in "visual literacy." I find it awfully hard to believe that the written word can be replaced by the ability to play Nintendo well. You can perhaps be entertained more, but I think your intellect can only be advanced so far by visual images. At a certain point it just breaks down—it's just not sophisticated.
>
> Aldous Huxley in *Brave New World* was right. Orwell thought we were all going to be watched, oppressed from outside, but it is the other way around: We'll be doing the watching. We'll be our own oppressors. Eisenhower warned us of the military-industrial complex, but we needn't worry about that anymore. It is the entertainment-amusement complex that threatens us—benignly.

Skill Drill: Auditing Your Emotions

Reporters, like everyone else, have feelings that influence the way they see the world. Sometimes these emotional responses obstruct observation. You might audit your feelings by checking the boxes that follow and then matching your responses with those of other students.

	Positive	Neutral	Negative
Arabs	❏	❏	❏
Bill of Rights	❏	❏	❏
Bird watchers	❏	❏	❏
Black Muslims	❏	❏	❏
Capitalism	❏	❏	❏
Catholics	❏	❏	❏
China	❏	❏	❏
Conservatives	❏	❏	❏
Democrats	❏	❏	❏
Gays and lesbians	❏	❏	❏
Housewives	❏	❏	❏
Jews	❏	❏	❏
Ku Klux Klan	❏	❏	❏
Liberals	❏	❏	❏
Muslims	❏	❏	❏
Nation of Islam	❏	❏	❏
New Yorkers	❏	❏	❏
Radicals	❏	❏	❏
Rap singers	❏	❏	❏
Republicans	❏	❏	❏
The Rotary Club	❏	❏	❏
Scandinavians	❏	❏	❏
Sierra Club	❏	❏	❏
Socialism	❏	❏	❏
Southerners	❏	❏	❏
Texans	❏	❏	❏
Unitarians	❏	❏	❏
The United Nations	❏	❏	❏
Wall Street	❏	❏	❏
Zionism	❏	❏	❏

To some, college sororities provide congenial living arrangements and the members engage in campus service. To others, they foster exclusivity and frivolity. Emotions can run high on the issue.

PART FIVE

From Accidents to Education

 Accidents and Disasters

Frank Robertson, *Argus Leader*
Disaster scene—a tornado's levelling force.

Introduction

Motor vehicle accidents and fires are among the most common events a reporter covers. Accuracy is essential, which means double-checking official reports of the names and addresses of those involved, avoiding giving the cause of the accident or fire unless it is part of the official record. The accounts of those involved—investigating officers and victims—animate the story. The essential element of these stories is accurate information about those injured or killed. Property losses and effects on the community are important parts of disaster stories.

Accidents

Exercises I

A. Pedestrian

From the Freeport police reports: James Reynolds, 48, sign painter, 35 Palisades Ave. Struck by automobile at Georgia Avenue and Topeka Street, 4 p.m., Fairlawn Hospital. Critical injuries, including skull fracture. Car driven by Robert F. Magione, 872 Ogden St. Says pedestrian stepped into intersection suddenly. No charges. Investigation by Officer Sigmund Gerter.

A call to the hospital indicates that Reynolds is in intensive care. Write three paragraphs for the morning newspaper.

B. Three Dead

State highway patrol responds to your check with the following information: collision on Route 16, where it intersects with State Highway 65, 18 miles north of Freeport. Three dead, all in the car coming out of Route 16: Stanley Shaeffer, 68, of 45 Madison St.; Mildred Shaeffer, 65; their granddaughter, Anne Shaeffer, 17, of Chicago, who was visiting her grandparents while en route to Boston University where she was to be a freshman student. The second car was driven by Louis Kruger, of Hutchinson, Kansas. Kruger was taken to Fairlawn Hospital for treatment of leg fractures and internal injuries. Time: 11 last night.

Investigating officers, Albert Doris and Ben Sandler, said the Shaeffer car was turning into 65 and had apparently not stopped for the stop sign. Possibility Shaeffer had a stroke. Write four paragraphs for the afternoon newspaper.

C. Truck

Report from Clovia police with a fatal: Irwin Soto, 22, of Clovia, was killed instantly at noon on access road four miles west of Clovia. Police say he apparently had a flat and had stopped to change tires, propping up his pickup with a bumper jack. Somehow he got under the truck, it slipped, and he was crushed. Severe chest injuries, says Dr. Wayne L. Stapleton of Fairlawn Hospital.

He is survived by parents, Jack and Eileen Soto, of Clovia; his widow, Alice; and an infant daughter, Adeilada. Funeral services pending. Body at Heavenly Rest Chapel in Freeport. He was a local boy who played in all the high school sports and was a star sprinter. He spent two years at the University of Tennessee on a track scholarship but came home to run his father's dairy farm two years ago.

D. Speed

A Freeport patrolwoman you know tells you that there was a strange accident early this morning on Massachusetts Avenue. Several cars were struck by a teen-age driver, she says. The records and a conversation with the investigating officers, Sam Ratcliffe and Brut Kazazian, disclose the following: At 2 a.m., a car driven by George R. Dugan, 17, of 89 Georgia Ave., struck six cars on Massachusetts Avenue, southbound lane. No injuries, although Dugan's vehicle was demolished. The six cars were parked along the street when Dugan drove by.

"He just tore through town, probably at 70 or 80 and lost control, near as we can figure," Kazazian says:

> Dugan doesn't remember a thing. Not that he's hurt. We took him to Fairlawn and all he has is a headache and a black eye. But he has got a lot to worry about: driving without a license, speeding, reckless driving citations. He told us he had never driven before two days ago when his brother started to teach him to drive. He said he took the car belonging to his brother Ralph and decided to go on a "solo" trip to prove he could do it.
>
> He says he was at a party with some girls and other guys and they made fun of him because he was 17 and couldn't drive, so he took off and got the car to show them up. No alcohol or drugs present.
>
> The way he went through there his car was like a Ping-Pong ball, banging this way and that. He also smashed a lamp-post. It's lucky no one was on the street at the time.

Assignments I

A. Reports

Obtain from the police department copies of several newsworthy vehicular accident reports, and write stories based on the information presented. Explain your reasons for using the reports you selected.

B. Dangers

Examine the annual report of the traffic department of the state highway department. Usually, records are kept as to the location, day of week and time of day of fatal accidents on the state's highways. There also is usually a listing by cause. See whether you can find any patterns in these fatal accidents. To do this, set up hypotheses and check them:

> Are weekends more dangerous than weekdays?
> Are the evening hours more dangerous than daylight hours? (Do not ignore differences in traffic volume.)
> Are some parts of the state, some roads or highways more dangerous than others?
> Is speed, alcohol, snow, rain or some other factor a major cause of fatals?
> Have the authorities developed a test for drivers they suspect of driving under the influence of drugs?

Disasters

Exercises II

A. Gas Leak

A railroad tank car carrying chlorine gas has been cracked by a collision with another train on a siding four miles east of Freeport, and the gas is seeping out of the tank. The sheriff's office, which is responsible for the area outside the city limits, has ordered an evacuation of the area in which there are 15 residences with a total population of 70 persons.

The first word came at 7:20 a.m. from the Union Pacific office, the sheriff says. One trainman, Albert Funster, 25, of Redding, Calif., was overcome by fumes. He is in Fairlawn Hospital, where his condition is reported as not serious.

Your editor at www.freenews.com wants a news bulletin now. You check the railroad, and an official estimates it will take no more than a few hours to clear the track.

"We will put the families in a few motels, even if it is for a few hours," says the spokesman, Francis Praxton, of the local rail office. You have to write the online story with this information.

As you prepare your story for the final edition, the police reporter calls you and says a family of four has just been taken to Fairlawn Hospital in serious condition from chlorine inhalation. You call the hospital and learn their names: David Lewin, 35; Alice Lewin, 34; their son, Freddie, 7; and their daughter, Barbara, 3. They are listed by authorities as being in critical condition. They apparently live near the tracks. A hospital official says, "We understand there are several houses along there and that they are making a house-to-house search. I think the gas was seeping in all night."

You call back the railroad spokesman and he verifies that they believe the accident occurred during some siding activity last night. You tell him about the family in the hospital. He has no comment.

You call the sheriff's office again and ask about the search. He confirms it. All available officers have been sent to the area, and a contingent of state troopers—about a dozen—was sent out. The Red Cross emergency unit and some fire equipment are there.

As you are again ready to write, the police reporter calls and says a body, unidentified, has been removed from a house on U.S. 58 and taken to the North Funeral Home. It is a middle-aged woman. "We think there are more coming," he says.

It is midnight. You have no more time and must write. Write a story for *The Freeport News* or channel 17 or www.freenews.com.

B. Rain

You work for a wire service in Houston and are told to send out a story about a rainstorm that has struck the city. You are told to write about 200 words. The information:

1. Rain began to fall at 1 p.m. Continued for seven hours. Total fall, more than 7 1/2 inches, which some people say is total rainfall for the year in some parts of Texas.
2. Hardest hit area southeast of Houston where Texas Medical Center is located.
3. Creeks and bayous flooded out of banks and streets were flooded and motorists stranded. Still too early to tell if there are any casualties, but no word of any so far.
4. To baseball fans, this was a disaster. For first time in the history of Astrodome, built in 1965, the Houston Astros baseball team had to call off the game. Not because of wet grounds; dome covers field. But only a couple of hundred hardy fans reached the park.
5. "We couldn't have gone on anyway," says a dome official. "Half the players weren't here before the game either. The bat boy would have had to bat cleanup if we'd played."

Assignment II

Preparations

Make a study of disaster organizations in your community. Name them, give their functions and equipment and look into their history. When were they last used? Any changes in equipment, approach in recent years?

Citizens are expected to take certain precautions for an emergency, and once it strikes they are expected to know what actions to take. Include these in your story.

Campus Projects

A. Auditing the Campus

Using the material in the **Skill Drill: Auditing Your Emotions** in Chapter 17, survey students, faculty members, administrators, support staff.

Are there significant differences among these groups?

You can make subgroups as well: sex, age, race, etc.

B. Dating Violence

One of five college women reports having been the victim of abuse at least once, according to the Corporate Alliance to End Partner Violence. Drinking and drug use contribute up to 60 percent of the incidents, the organization says. The violence ranges from homicide to assault. Many of the victims continue an abusive relationship because they prefer it to being alone, or they are so inexperienced in relationships that they accept a violent one as normal, says the Alliance. The U.S. Justice Department has allocated $8.1 million to 21 colleges to study violence against women and to initiate programs on the campus.

What is the situation on your campus? Interview men and women about incidents they may have been involved in or have witnessed. What has been the result of some abusive relationships? In many states, dating relationship violence is not covered by domestic violence laws.

Community Projects

A. Feedback (1)

The Gannett newspapers use extensive polling and conduct focus groups to find out what readers want in their newspapers. Some of the findings include "more positive news, more human interest stories. Readers complain about too much negative news and news that's 'immoral,' " a Gannett columnist wrote. They complained about the coverage of "gays and AIDS."

A Gannett guidebook for its 93 newspapers suggests covering "shopping trends and sales, new products and restaurants" and reducing the coverage "that is institutionally driven," such as the coverage of city hall and the local planning commission. Some of the areas recommended for coverage are health, fitness and local entertainment.

Do a study of your own among residents. What do people want from their local newspaper?

B. Environment

Two out of five Americans live in areas where the air is unhealthy, reports the Environmental Protection Agency. Also, 40 percent of the nation's rivers and lakes are unfit for drinking, swimming or fishing.

"We should celebrate progress," says Fred Krupp, the executive director of the Environmental Defense Fund. "We have made a lot of progress in this country—even if it's also true that we've got a long way to go."

Among the problems is controlling the runoff of fertilizers, silt and pesticides from farms and cities. The runoff affects aquatic life. One of the consequences is that 362 species of fish have been extinguished or endangered. Some experts say that the fate of the American landscape and waters and the creatures who live there is the major domestic environmental problem the country is not coping with.

The National Biological Service reports that natural ecosystems amounting to at least half the area of the 48 contiguous states have declined to the endangerment point.

More than 5 percent of the native plant species are lost or in peril in Delaware, Maine, Vermont, Rhode Island, New York, Pennsylvania, New Jersey and Maryland. In Ohio, Indiana, Iowa, Missouri and Kansas, 3 to 5 percent are endangered.

Most states have improved the quality of their air. New Mexico, Virginia, New Jersey and New Hampshire had a decrease in air pollution of more than 50 percent. But the percentage change in emissions of hazardous air pollutants increased in five states: Nevada, Alaska, Montana, North and South Dakota.

Freshwater fish species are imperiled in the streams of every state. Those with 10 or more imperiled species are Oregon, California, Nevada, Utah, Arizona, New Mexico, Texas, Oklahoma, Missouri, Arkansas, Louisiana, Mississippi, Alabama, Georgia, Florida, Tennessee, Kentucky, North Carolina, Virginia and New York. Heading the list, according to the National Biological Service, are California, 42; Alabama, 30; Texas, 23; Arizona, 22; Virginia and North Carolina, 21; and New Mexico and Georgia, 20.

Make an environmental study of your state. Where does it rank in cleansing its air and water and in protecting wildlife and plant species?

Home Assignment

Readable

Clip from a newspaper stories that demonstrate these principles of good writing:

- Show, don't tell.
- Place quotations high in the story that reflect the thrust of the event.
- Personalize the event through human interest anecdotes high in the story.

Class Discussion

Feedback (2)

Discuss your findings in the Community Project A. Feedback (1) in this chapter. Do the suggestions of local people include the watchdog function of the press, the obligation of newspapers to ferret out significant information, whether readers enjoy reading about it or not?

Does the study show that what Gannett recommends in the area of writing—shorter, snappier stories—leads to an informed community? That is, do people want their newspaper primarily to entertain them? Or do they recognize that the newspaper has a dual function that includes explaining complex matters so that they, the public, can make informed decisions on important matters?

Susan Kirkman, *Akron Beacon Journal*
The eulogy may have news value.

Introduction

The obituary section is one of the most thoroughly read parts of the newspaper. The obituary is a summation of the person's life, a record that becomes part of the community's history. The obituary focuses on the accomplishments of the deceased and includes the cause, time and place of death. Survivors and burial plans are also included. Sometimes, survivors ask that certain information be withheld from the obituary. Usually, such requests are turned down.

Exercise

Swimmer

You are a new reporter on the Freeport newspaper and are on general assignment, and this morning you are handling obits. The Prewitt Mortuary has dropped off a notice of the death of Albert F. Swimmer, and as you look it over, one of the older hands remarks that Swimmer was an interesting character.

You get his file out of the library and glance through it before going up to the city editor to ask him how much he wants on Swimmer.

He tells you that Swimmer was a "controversial character" and that his obituary is worth at least 1,000 words.

"Don't write one of these deadly death notices," he tells you. "Give me a good story. I want to use some art with it."

Prewitt Mortuary
840 Stanford Avenue

Name:	Albert F. Swimmer.
Birth Date:	Jan. 25, 1915, Birmingham, Alabama.
Address:	1405 Sunset Drive.
Cause of death:	Cirrhosis of the liver.
Where died:	Fairlawn Hospital.
Time:	5:45 a.m.
Organizations:	Legion Post No. 156, VFW Post 22, Optimist Club, NAACP, Urban League, Phi Beta Kappa.
Church:	Freeport First Baptist.
Survivors:	Wife, Ada Ruth Johnson Swimmer, second wife; son, Sam; daughter, Linda, by his first wife, Mrs. Martha Lupton, deceased; sister, Mrs. Dodge Henry, Birmingham; three nieces and six nephews.

* * * * *

Morgue clip, June 29, 1933

Arthur Monde and Albert F. Swimmer shared scholastic honors last night at the Freeport High School graduation. Monde, the son of Mr. and Mrs. Philip C. Monde, of 1145 High St., was the valedictorian and Swimmer was the salutatorian. Swimmer is the son of Mr. and Mrs. Temple Swimmer, of 303 Manley St.

Morgue clip, July 16, 1933

* * * * *

BERKELEY, Calif.—The University of California announced today it has granted the Thomas E. Roselle scholarship to Albert F. Swimmer, of Freeport. The scholarship was established by Mr. Roselle, a graduate of the University who practiced law in Freeport for 42 years prior to his death in 1920. It is awarded to a Negro high school graduate who intends to pursue pre-law courses.

* * * * *

Morgue clip, Aug. 3, 1933

Word was received here today of the arrest in Alamogordo, New Mexico, of Albert F. Swimmer of this city on a charge of disturbing the peace.

Swimmer, 18, apparently was on his way to California to enroll in the University of California. His parents said he left here 10 days ago for the coast with limited funds. He had received a scholarship to the University of California.

* * * * *

Morgue clip, Aug. 6, 1933

Albert F. Swimmer, son of Mr. and Mrs. Temple Swimmer of this city, was sentenced to 10 days in county jail in Alamogordo, New Mex., for disturbing the peace.

His parents said he was on the way to the University of California where he was to have enrolled next week. Mr. Swimmer said his son told him there was an altercation in a local restaurant. Swimmer had pleaded not guilty.

* * * * *

Morgue clip, Dec. 13, 1936

BERKELEY, Calif.—(API)—A talented California fullback and a tough line combined to upset highly favored Stanford 7–0 today.

The game's only score came on a 101-yard runback of the kickoff opening the second half. Al Swimmer, big fullback for the University of California, scampered the length of the field.

But the lead was in peril all during the remainder of the second half. The California line had to hold off repeated thrusts of the Stanford team which managed to get down to the California 20 with ease but could never penetrate beyond the 17-yard line.

Stanford was a two touchdown favorite.

Albert Swimmer is the son of Mr. and Mrs. Temple Swimmer, 303 Manley St., and is attending the University of California on a scholarship. He was a well-known football player at Freeport High and graduated second in his class with an A-average.

The senior Swimmer is employed by Houk's Barber Shop. Mrs. Swimmer is a teacher in the G.W. Carver Grade School. They will visit their son this Christmas as the result of a gift to the Swimmers by the Freeport Junior Chamber of Commerce.

* * * * *

Morgue clip, June 6, 1937

The University of California student newspaper yesterday reported the marriage of Albert Swimmer, a graduate of Freeport High School who is attending the California institution, to Miss Martha Stratton.

The newspaper reported Miss Stratton and Mr. Swimmer eloped. She is the daughter of Robert Stratton, a former governor of the State of Washington. The couple was married in Arizona. California has a law against interracial marriages.

Swimmer is the son of Mr. and Mrs. Temple Swimmer, of 303 Manley St. Swimmer will graduate next week. During his last three years at the University he was the starting fullback. He was the second leading ground gainer in the school's history and averaged 4.5 yards a carry.

His father said his son has been offered a contract by the Chicago Bears but may attend law school instead.

The elder Swimmer said his son, who was initiated into Phi Beta Kappa, an honorary scholastic fraternity, has a fellowship from a national organization to the law school at the University of Iowa.

* * * * *

Morgue clip, March 13, 1940

Albert F. Swimmer, of 140 California Ave., and F. T. Macdonald, of 32 Brighton Ave., were among the 235 persons who passed the state bar examination.

* * * * *

Morgue clip, Sept. 15, 1941

Albert F. Swimmer was the main speaker at the Freeport Kiwanis Club at noon today. He spoke on "An Untapped Human Resource, the Negro Worker."

Swimmer said that "discrimination and racial bigotry" keep Negroes in low-paying jobs. He said federal figures reveal that Negroes have an average income of about half the average white worker's. Swimmer recently passed the state bar examination and is in practice with State Sen. Robert Wright.

* * * * *

Morgue clip, Nov. 7, 1941

Mr. and Mrs. Albert Swimmer, of 140 California Ave., today announced the birth of their first child, Linda. Mrs. Swimmer is the former Martha Stratton. Mr. Swimmer, a local attorney, enlisted in the U.S. Navy last month and is a recruit at the Bainbridge Naval Training Station in Maryland.

* * * * *

Morgue clip, April 16, 1943

HONOLULU—Steward Second Class Albert Swimmer of Freeport has been awarded the Navy Cross for heroism while on duty aboard the U.S.S. Covington, the Navy News Service reported this week.

Swimmer was the only man on an anti-aircraft detail who survived an enemy airplane attack. Despite serious leg wounds, Swimmer directed a makeshift crew which destroyed one attacking aircraft and damaged another. His commanding officer, Commander Frank C. Barnes, said Swimmer stayed at his post for six hours while the Covington was under attack.

Swimmer is in a base hospital at Pearl Harbor.

Swimmer is the husband of Mrs. Martha Swimmer, of 140 California Ave., and was on his third tour of duty with the Covington.

* * * * *

U.S. Navy

Morgue clip, April 18, 1946

Albert F. Swimmer became the first Negro to serve on the city council in Freeport's history. He led the successful Veterans Group in a sweep of the five council seats.

Swimmer defeated Morgan B. Simms 2,345 to 2,088 in a bitterly contested campaign in the Second District. Swimmer had accused Simms, the incumbent, of "complete inability to react to the times." At one time he referred to Simms as "our Stone Age councilman."

The Second District is a residential area, long considered Freeport's finest. Swimmer was the target of some resentment when he moved into the district last year. But a bi-racial citizens group was formed and the opposition died down.

The other successful candidates . . .

* * * * *

Morgue clip, May 19, 1950

The author of several unsuccessful bills to eliminate discrimination in public places in the city, Councilman Albert F. Swimmer said in an interview today his faith remains strong in the "essential goodness" of Freeport residents.

Swimmer, the only Negro ever to serve on the council, said that with summer weather near he hopes to have the council adopt an ordinance that would prohibit local swimming pools from keeping Negroes from using their facilities.

"When I was a child I used to stand outside the gates on hot August days and watch kids from my school splashing in the pool," he said. "I don't want any more youngsters to suffer as I did, and I think my fellow councilmen will . . ."

* * * * *

Morgue clip, Oct. 3, 1952

Albert Swimmer, long active in the Democratic Party, announced his support of Dwight D. Eisenhower, at a luncheon of the Freeport Democrats for Eisenhower today.

Swimmer said he based his decision on "the inability of the Democratic Party to cope with the paramount issue of our times, civil rights."

Swimmer has been elected to the city council four times as an independent but has been closely connected with Democratic party affairs. Last year, he was unsuccessful in an attempt to push through the council an ordinance prohibiting discrimination in hotels, restaurants and other establishments offering their services to the public. At the time, he said his proposal was defeated because "local Democrats who had promised assistance refused to take a stand when the going got rough." At the luncheon, Chairman Robert F. Rockford, said . . .

* * * * *

Morgue clip, Aug. 3, 1954

A car driven by City Councilman Albert F. Swimmer of 69 Harvey St. struck a telephone pole and overturned last night on U.S. 43 north of Freeport.

Swimmer suffered head injuries and was reported in good condition in the Fairlawn Hospital. A passenger, Ruth Humphrey, of 42 Broad St., was treated for cuts and released.

Freeport police cited Swimmer for reckless driving.

* * * * *

Morgue clip, Oct. 26, 1954

Magistrate Ann Rogers today dismissed reckless driving charges against City Councilman Albert F. Swimmer, 69 Harvey St., on motion of District Attorney Thomas Chambers.

* * * * *

Morgue clip, May 15, 1955

City Councilman Albert F. Swimmer today was appointed to the city board of education by Mayor Sam Weale. He is the first Negro to serve on the board. . . .

* * * * *

Morgue clip, Sept. 7, 1956

A family squabble that began with a glass of spilled milk ended with pistol shots and the hospitalization with chest wounds of City Councilman Albert F. Swimmer, 69 Harvey St.

Police said Swimmer was found unconscious in the kitchen, his sobbing wife at his side. Police said Mrs. Swimmer told them that her husband had come home late last night and had asked her to get out of bed and prepare his dinner.

When she handed him a glass of milk, it slipped from his hand. He became angry and beat her, police said Mrs. Swimmer told them. Swimmer then took a pistol from his pocket and waved it at her. When she struggled with him the gun went off and a bullet struck him in the chest.

Police said Swimmer had been drinking heavily at a meeting at the George Washington Carver Club before he left for home.

* * * * *

Morgue clip, Nov. 10, 1957

District Court today granted an uncontested divorce to Mrs. Albert Swimmer, 69 Harvey St.

Mrs. Swimmer had accused her husband of "habitual drinking, mental cruelty and behavior that embarrassed the family."

* * * * *

Morgue clip, April 15, 1958

The George Washington Carver Club today presented its annual Good Citizen award to Albert Swimmer, 1405 Sunset Drive. Swimmer was honored for his "constant work in behalf of better understanding between the races."

Dr. Frederick Y. Herbert, who made the award, said that Swimmer had been chosen because he represented the "new generation which is striving for equality of opportunity for Negroes so that they can move out of their poverty into the sunlight and share in the wealth of this country."

Swimmer is serving his seventh consecutive term in the City Council.

* * * * *

Morgue clip, March 1, 1960

This is a campaign biography of Swimmer, a candidate for re-election to the City Council for his eighth term on the Fusion ticket:

Swimmer, 45, is an active attorney in Freeport. He is a member of the Veterans of Foreign Wars, American Legion and many civic clubs. In the service of his country he lost his right leg. He won a Navy Cross in World War II. He is the father of Linda, 18, a freshman at the state university, and Sam, 14. A star football player on the high school team, he was graduated from the University of California, where he also played football, and the School of Law at the University of Iowa.

* * * * *

Morgue clip, April 17, 1960

The Fusion party retained its control of city hall by easily winning four of the five district races.

Its only defeat came in the Second District where Martin Gabel trounced Albert Swimmer, 7,503 to 4,654. The campaign in the district was described as the most bitter in the memory of local politicians.

Gabel had accused Swimmer of being "incapable of sober judgment." In turn, Swimmer had charged Gabel with "turning his back on the real problems of Freeport."

Swimmer, a veteran of local politics, had served seven consecutive terms on the city council. In his last term he had often constituted a minority of one in council votes. He had urged higher taxes and city-financed projects to stop what he described as the "growing decay of the city core."

In his campaign, he accused Gabel of "representing the lily whites of suburbia whose interests are barbecue pits, golf and bridge."

In the other district races . . .

* * * * *

Morgue clip, Dec. 15, 1965

The George Washington Carver Club today announced it will send four Freeport youngsters to Disneyland in California.

Albert F. Swimmer, the Club president, said the children, ages 8–12, were picked by teachers in the public schools. Their entire expenses will be borne by the Club.

"Most of these children have never been out of Freeport in their lives," he said. . . .

* * * * *

Morgue clip, July 5, 1969

Albert F. Swimmer, a local attorney, told members of the American Legion Post 156 last night that the "patriotism that is confined to flag saluting but not to patriotic acts is anti-American."

His remarks were made at the annual July 4 ceremonies at the Legion Hall. Swimmer, a decorated World War II hero, defined patriotic acts as . . .

* * * * *

Morgue clip, Sept. 21, 1971

Gov. William Buckley announced today he will appoint Albert F. Swimmer to the State Board of Education. Buckley said the board needs "new perspectives, new ways of looking at some of our persistent problems." Swimmer would be the first black to serve on the board . . .

* * * * *

Morgue clip, Nov. 25, 1975

A local attorney paid a return visit to the Freeport Kiwanis Club today after an absence of 35 years, and his speech touched off a harsh debate.

Albert Swimmer, former city councilman, political activist and decorated war hero, bluntly told the club members the day is not far off when "a huge social, economic and political revolution will take place.

"I'm talking about a revolution that will be caused by the unemployed, the poor and the oppressed who are now without a voice but won't be long finding one."

Swimmer recalled he had spoken in 1941 to the club about the failure of U.S. industry to use blacks.

"I reread that speech the other day and I found that the same things I said then could be said now. The only difference is that there are more than only black people involved, there is an entire group of abused, underused and forgotten people who will not stand for much more."

In the question period, Swimmer was asked to set a date for "the revolution." He replied:

"That kind of idiotic question indicates the attitude you men have toward this problem. Either you cannot or you will not take this matter seriously.

"Well, gentlemen, it's your turn now. But it won't be for very long."

* * * * *

Morgue clip, May 3, 1976

Albert F. Swimmer, a local attorney and long a maverick within the Democratic party locally, today urged his fellow party members to support Jimmy Carter for the Democratic presidential nomination.

"He's a winner," Swimmer said in telegrams sent to members of the Democratic State Central Committee, of which he is a member. "We must get aboard the victory train now or be left behind when our needs must be considered," he wired. . . .

* * * * *

Morgue clip, Nov. 1, 1978

Albert F. Swimmer, a local attorney and former city councilman, said he will fly to New Jersey tomorrow to spend the last days of the campaign working for Bill Bradley, a former basketball player who is the Democratic candidate for United States Senator.

Swimmer said he intends to campaign "among the people Bradley can help most, the minority groups." He said he met Bradley several years ago on a business trip to New York City when Bradley was playing for the New York Knicks.

* * * * *

Morgue clip, Dec. 12, 1983

Albert F. Swimmer, a local attorney, said today he will open headquarters here for the presidential campaign of Walter F. Mondale, the vice president under President Jimmy Carter.

Asked why he had decided to support Mondale, Swimmer replied, "The country has seen enough of Ronald Reagan and his utter disregard for the poor and the afflicted. We need a man of understanding and compassion back in the White House."

He added that he hoped that "my old friend, Bill Bradley of New Jersey, will be Mondale's running mate." Bradley was elected to the U.S. Senate on the Democratic ticket in 1978. Swimmer went to New Jersey to campaign for Bradley.

* * * * *

Morgue clip, Jan. 14, 1987

Albert F. Swimmer, former city council member and long a Democratic Party local leader, said he is considering running for the city council.

He said local government "needs someone who will try to stop the almighty dollar from being the dominant voice in city hall." He said he referred specifically to the "steady pressure on the elderly and the working people that is forcing them out of their homes."

Swimmer was a member of the city council for . . .

* * * * *

Morgue clip, Feb. 18, 1987

Albert F. Swimmer today took himself out of the race for city council.

Swimmer, 72, said that he saw little chance that "Freeport would support a person who sees race and class as destructive." In an interview, Swimmer, the city's first black councilman, said his election in 1946 "was a sign of hope, an indication the people wanted to solve these persistent problems.

"But now, some 40 years later, those hopes are gone. I am leaving the campaign more in sadness than in anger. . . ."

* * * * *

Morgue clip, Feb. 9, 1988

Local Democratic leaders appear to favor the presidential candidacy of Michael S. Dukakis over his leading opponents.

An informal poll of political opinion shows that Dukakis has at least half of the city's party leadership behind him with several others indicating their support will soon be announced.

Among the 20 Democratic leaders interviewed, Dukakis had 10 definite supporters, four probables and two swinging his way. Sen. Albert Gore had three behind him and Jesse Jackson trailed with one, Albert F. Swimmer.

Swimmer was the most outspoken of those interviewed.

"Of course, I'm the only one in the party establishment who will come out and say Jackson is the only candidate fit for the presidency," Swimmer said. "Everyone in the establishment is scared silly that a black man at the top of the ticket will wreck the party.

"Also, they know that Jackson is not going to play ball with them because he is tuned in to those who have never had power before. . . ."

Note in file from Bob Phelps, reporter. 3/18/88

Swimmer tells me he is under a lot of pressure to stay with Jesse Jackson but figures Jackson "will never get the nomination." "Why chase a rainbow?" he said. Keep in touch with him.

* * * * *

Morgue clip, Nov. 24, 1989

Martha Lupton, 69 Harvey St., died last night at her home after a long illness. She was 72 years old and had been hospitalized for cancer of the liver until a week ago when she returned home.

Mrs. Lupton was the former wife of Arthur F. Swimmer, and two years after their divorce in 1957 she married Arthur Lupton, a retired executive with the B. C. Krebs Manufacturing Co. . . .

* * * * *

Morgue clip, Jan. 25, 1990

Freeport politicians and citizens turned out last night to pay tribute to Albert F. Swimmer on the 75th birthday of the civic leader and civil rights pioneer.

Mayor Sam Parnass described Swimmer as a "local treasure of national stature." More than 250 people dined on chicken kiev at the $150 a plate dinner at the Regis Hotel ballroom. Proceeds were donated to local child care centers at Swimmer's request.

Swimmer, still vigorous and outspoken, warned his listeners: "We still have enormous work to do in eradicating that seemingly permanent stain on the American character, racism. The question before us is whether it is indelible. I grow less optimistic with the years. . . ."

* * * * *

Morgue clip, Oct. 5, 1992

Democratic presidential candidate Bill Clinton will campaign in Freeport Oct. 25 after he completes a California tour.

Albert F. Swimmer, head of the local Clinton headquarters, said Clinton had agreed to make the unscheduled stop in response to a personal plea Swimmer made.

"I told him that Freeport is a model of great achievements in racial harmony and in the enormous work that remains to be done," Swimmer said, "and that it is a symbol of what Clinton can do with his message of healing. . . ."

* * * * *

Morgue clip, Jan. 25, 1993

Albert F. Swimmer, former city councilman and major local Democratic leader, today said President Bill Clinton has promised to return to Freeport later this year.

Swimmer, Clinton's guest at the inauguration in Washington, said Clinton was grateful for the large vote he received locally and in the state. . . .

* * * * *

Morgue clip, May 10, 1995

Long-time Democratic Party leader Albert F. Swimmer said yesterday his party "might have to foresake President Clinton for renomination."

In a luncheon talk at the Kiwanis Club, Swimmer said the party "needs a stronger voice to oppose the heartless, greed-driven opposition." But Swimmer left the door open for Clinton: "If the president returns to the populism that marked his run for the presidency in 1992, and that he reaffirmed in his visit to Freeport the following year, then we will have a fighter for the principles the Democratic Party has always stood for."

* * * * *

Morgue Clip Dec. 23, 1998

Albert F. Swimmer, the local Democratic Party's senior statesman, today called on party leaders to "begin now the hunt for a national leader who will embrace traditional Democratic policies."

Speaking at a fund-raising dinner, Swimmer said, "We see in the people a hunger for good education for their children, safety for social security, a thriving economy and fair play for all members of society. This is what we call a liberal political policy."

He said that too many people cannot afford good health care and that the gap between the rich and the poor is growing.

"The Democratic Party has been drifting toward the middle of the spectrum," Swimmer said. "We have forgotten our heritage of populism and the New and Fair Deals."

In an interview following his talk to the $100-a-plate diners, Swimmer would not endorse a specific candidate. . . .

* * * * *

Morgue clip, Feb. 14, 1999

Albert F. Swimmer, long-time local Democratic leader, said today the "nation now must unite behind its leaders in the White House and Congress."

He described the impeachment and trial of President Clinton in a news release as "our partisan nightmare." Swimmer said, "The nation can give thanks sanity prevailed."

* * * * *

Morgue clip, April 6, 2002

Albert F. Swimmer, Freeport's elder political statesman, is turning his back on politics.

"I've had it," he said in a lengthy interview at his home. "I just cannot become engaged any longer. What I see, what I read and what I hear is too depressing," the 87-year-old patriarch of Freeport Democratic politics said.

"We are witnessing the complete takeover by the special interests. Where is the anger? Where is the political will to speak out against those who would despoil our land, air and water? How can we rest easy when so many children are born into poverty, so many families have no health coverage? . . ."

In search of anecdotes and some background material you call the president of the George Washington Carver Club, Matthew Bennington Rogers, who tells you:

Al used to have a wonderful sense of humor, but in the last few years he was more and more worried. You fellows didn't cover a talk he gave here three months ago, but none of us who heard it will forget a few of the things he said. Wait a minute, I think I jotted it down and put it in a drawer. Yes, here it is: He told us that he was in despair that blacks were the victims of racism that infects the entire society.

Incidentally, not many people know this—and your people refused to carry it when we sent in an announcement two years ago—but Al set up a $1,000 college scholarship award to the best black student in town. Said it was a repayment of a sort for his scholarship. He told me it was his move toward "compensatory payments" that he hoped would catch on. Guess it didn't. We're cooperating with the First Baptist Church tomorrow at 11 a.m. services. He will be buried in our cemetery, Carver Cemetery, at 2 p.m. that afternoon. By the way, in your story last month about the Black Parents Association wanting the schools to ban several books, you remember that Al voted against the association. He got a lot of criticism from blacks for that. He was a man of principle.

You call Gabel, Swimmer's 1960 election opponent, who says:

Al Swimmer was an unprincipled character, I'm sorry to say. I don't like to speak ill of the dead, but he drank too much, was intemperate and had regard only for himself. You notice how well he lived? Check the cost of his place—he paid $60,000 when a dollar was worth something. You notice the Cadillac he drove around? Did you know that he was earning twice as much as most lawyers in town with that colored practice? He bled in public for blacks, but in private he bled them. Sure, it's sad he had to go like he did. But he knew what he was doing and could have stopped any time. Say, don't quote me on any of this. Just say that Freeport has lost a sincere and beloved public servant.

Assignments

A. Advance

Your editor tells you she wants you to prepare background material for the files on the following persons, to be used at the time of their deaths. Write the story so that only the lead and one or more paragraphs need be placed at the top of your copy. Funeral and burial arrangements can be put at the end. You should try to interview your subjects.

President: The president of your college or university.
Mayor: The mayor of the city in which you live.
Governor: The governor of the state.
Professor: The senior member of the English Department (or any prominent member of the faculty).
Chief: The chief of police.
Operator: The switchboard operator at a large local business, law firm or educational institution.
Senior: The senior member of a local law firm.

Publisher: The publisher of the daily newspaper in the city.
Chef: The head cook at the leading restaurant in town.
Head: The head of the city board of education.
Merchant: A prominent local businessman or businesswoman.
Prelate: The highest ranking prelate of the Roman Catholic Church in the city.
Rabbi: The head of a local synagogue.
Doctor: The medical chief of a local hospital.
Athlete: A well-known former athlete living in town.

Look for human interest as well as the vital statistics of birth, birthplace, education, work history and relatives.

B. Classmate

Interview a classmate for background material for an obituary. Use any cause of death. Then write a 250-word obituary.

Campus Projects

A. Wages

The janitors, kitchen workers, security guards, yard workers on campuses are the lowest-paid employees on the campus, paid from $7 to $11 an hour. Their annual earnings usually put them at or beneath the poverty level if they are supporting a family. Find out what these workers are paid on your campus and how they manage to cope with the cost of living. Has anything been done on their behalf? (Some students have formed committees to speak for these workers.)

B. Country Music

"What often passes for country now, particularly on radio stations playing that tightly controlled format, is a bland blend of tried-and-true formulas, with every edge smoothed by waves of hit-making experience. It has strayed from its hillbilly and country-and-western roots. . . . It's all generic style, with no character or substances," says Anthony DeCurtis, a contributing editor at *Rolling Stone* magazine. He praises Johnny Cash, George Jones, Willie Nelson, and he says that Dolly Parton, Delbert McClinton and Rodney Crowell have returned to "country's roots." Others, he concludes, have cut themselves "free from that source, the heart of the heart of country" and thus "the music has insured its own irrelevance."

What country musicians are students listening to these days? What do they think of this assessment of country music?

Community Project

Costs

What does it cost to be buried? Consult funeral homes for the costs of casket, cremation, use of the funeral home and services, the cemetery. Some cities have funeral societies that offer low-cost burials. Does yours?

Home Assignment

Application

Examine the obituaries in your local newspaper and apply some of the necessities described in the textbook chapter on obituaries. How does your newspaper fare? Are the obituaries routinely written? Is there reporting done to obtain interesting and relevant background?

Some newspapers charge to print obituaries. Does yours? Is this a sound practice?

The Police Beat

Introduction

Stories of crime, detection and arrest are avidly read. Most of these stories are culled from the reports and records kept by the police department which the reporter checks on his or her rounds. Names and addresses are always double-checked for accuracy. Given time, the reporter will follow up some of these reports with interviews of the victims and, when possible, of the investigating and arresting officers. These interviews provide the human interest details lacking in the reports. Police reporters also write general stories, such as the effectiveness of the police department in crime prevention and in solving crime.

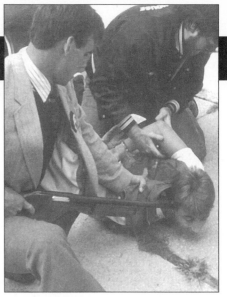

Michael Rafferty, *Asbury Park* (N.J.) *Press*
Young murder suspect captured.

Exercises

A. Drugs

Your editor hands you this story and tells you he wants a more dramatic lead, even if you have to neglect the today angle. Rewrite the story.

A Freeport youth is scheduled to be arraigned in district court here today on charges of possession of a narcotic and resisting arrest.

Police said that the youth, Mark Reib, 17, 338 Topeka St., was arrested yesterday after a downtown footrace between Reib and two sheriff's officers.

Police said Reib tried to obtain narcotics from the Stuben Drug Store on Massachusetts Avenue by giving false information over the phone.

The caller claimed to be a physician and said the prescription would be picked up shortly. The store clerk became suspicious and notified local police, who were waiting for the pickup to be made.

The chase occurred after Reib left the drugstore, police said.

Reib was freed on $5,000 bail, pending arraignment.

B. Arrested

The Freeport police announce the arrest of Carl Morton on a charge of murder. He was sought for six days in the slaying of Mildred Miller, 47, a pianist who lived at an inexpensive hotel, The Plaza, where Morton also had a room. The police announced at the time of her slaying that she had been raped and strangled. The slayer also had set her bed afire and taken a television set and radio.

Det. Sgt. Richard Raskover said that Morton, an unemployed truck driver, had been sought because Mrs. Miller's radio was found in his room. His girlfriend, who was not identified by the police, said Morton had left the night of the slaying after depositing the radio in their room and telling her he had just sold a television set and was going out to buy some food.

When she asked Morton where he had obtained the radio and television set, Raskover said, he told her not to tell anyone about them.

Morton was picked up at another downtown hotel this morning. Police would not disclose how they learned of his whereabouts. But it is a well-known police procedure to question hotel clerks about new guests.

Raskover says that Morton will be questioned about several other deaths in The Plaza. Four other women died there within the past six months under strange circumstances. All were past 60.

He did not resist arrest. No bail is set on capital charges.

You ask if Morton has a record and Raskover suggests you obtain that information elsewhere. Through a contact, you learn Morton is 37 years old, was arrested in 1988 on a robbery charge and sentenced to 2 1/2 to 5 years in the state penitentiary. Three years later, he was sentenced to 90 days on a misdemeanor, loitering, after his arrest for drug possession, a felony. In 1993, he again benefitted from plea bargaining, being sentenced to 90 days for attempted theft following his arrest for robbery in the second degree and criminal possession of stolen property, both felonies. In 1996, he was sentenced to two years for burglary.

Write a 300-word story.

C. Cookies

Your editor likes short features—she calls them "brights"—from the police beat, and the following information from a crime report sounds like a good "bright":

> The day-care center of the Freeport School District holds its classes in the basement of the United Methodist Church, 850 Brighton Ave. During the evening, a basement window on the north side of the building was broken and the basement entered. Margaret Reeder, the director of the center, said all that appeared taken was a carton containing four boxes of chocolate cookies. She says the cookies were so stale the children wouldn't eat them and the center was planning to return them.

D. Crime Reports

Total crimes, Precinct No. 2.

	Last Year	**Previous Year**
Total crimes reported	1,844	1,753
Auto thefts	262	202
Theft from motor vehicles	556	468
Burglaries	673	610
Purse snatching	55	55
Robbery	265	378
Murder	6	6
Rape and attempted rape	16	18
Possession of dangerous drugs	11	16

The Freeport police department released citywide totals on crimes reported for last year which your newspaper ran yesterday. You go to Precinct No. 2, in which St. Mary's University is located, in order to write a piece on crime in that area because it was the subject of intensive police action after a record number of crimes, 3,299, were reported in the precinct three years ago. The year following the transfer of additional officers to the precinct, the number of crimes dropped to 1,753. Last year, the number inched upward.

Police Captain Stanley Solomon tells you that the situation in the precinct is "steady," that the figures "reflect a citywide trend over the past two years of more property thefts in middle- and upper-income areas. We have always been a prime area for auto thefts. These foreign cars are attractive for some reason. Also, people around here tend to be absent-minded, and there are always the newcomers who think they're back home where they never locked their car doors. Anyone with a stereo or a camera in full view inside a car is asking for trouble."

Precinct No. 2 covers eastern Freeport. In the immediate area around the university, described as Police Post No. 3, total crimes reported went from 148 two years ago to 220 last year, the largest increase in the precinct. Most of the crimes involved thefts from motor vehicles (81) and burglaries (103). Write 300 words for *The Freeport News*. Then write the first four paragraphs of a story for the campus newspaper.

E. Bite

In making routine checks of major Freeport hospitals, you are told at 2 p.m. that a police officer has been admitted with a severe dog bite. The admitting clerk at Community Hospital identifies the officer as William Trevor, age 39. His condition is good. His injury is a dog bite to the right wrist. He was brought to the hospital by ambulance at 1:15 a.m. (today) after being picked up at his home. That is all the information she can give you.

Next you reach the public relations office at the hospital and ask for additional information. In response to questions, and after checking with others at the hospital, Beverly Collins, the director of public information, tells you that Officer Trevor has been treated with antibiotics to ward off infection from inch-deep bites to the bottom and top of his wrist. The bites reached the bone. He has been given a sedative and is resting quietly. He is expected to be released from the hospital tomorrow. He is not to take shots to prevent rabies, because the city's standard dog-bite form, which was completed by ambulance attendant K. L. Ross, indicates that the dog has been seized by an animal control officer and is being held for observation in the city dog pound. You are told that the officer is asleep and cannot be disturbed by a telephone call.

You go to the police records room, where you learn there is a written report of the incident. It was prepared by Patrolmen B. J. Kirby and A. M. Dunning. It is headed "Attempt Burglary." It says that at approximately 12:45 a.m. (today), an attempt was made to burglarize Apartment 205, the home of William Trevor. The body of the report reads as follows:

> Victim states that he was in the bedroom when he heard the balcony door open. Door is sliding type and was unlocked. Victim got out of bed, turned on light situated on bedside table and obtained service revolver, .38 Police Special, from holster in chair. On entering living room victim spotted white male, age approx. 30, in room. Victim stated, "Hold it right there," and suspect turned and ran out of sliding door. Victim aimed revolver to fire, but as he was about to fire victim's dog became excited and bit victim. Victim taken to Community Hospital with dog bites to right wrist.

The report describes the suspect as wearing a Mickey Mouse T-shirt and blue jeans but no shoes.

You check with the personnel department of the police department and are told there is no William Trevor on the local police force. You recheck the offense report and note that Trevor's business address is listed as "Clovia P.D." You call the police department in Clovia and reach the police chief, Irving Scillicide. He confirms that William Trevor is a member of his police force. He is assigned to the K-9, or dog unit. You ask Scillicide if he knows what happened. He tells you, "It's my understanding Bill surprised a burglar in his apartment and struggled with him, and Rusty bit Bill instead of the burglar. It's a damn shame when a police dog bites the wrong person."

Write 150 words for www.freenews.com.

F. Chen Arrest

Police reported the arrest of Dong Lu Chen, 51, 1658 Broadway, a janitor with the B.C. Krebs Co. He was arrested last night in connection with the death of his wife, Gian Wan Chen, 40, last night.

A police spokesman said the woman suffered a number of blows to the head from a hammer. Her death followed a domestic quarrel, police said.

His wife and two children, a son, 18, and a daughter, 16, have been living in Freeport since 1988 when they and Chen came to this country from China. He was unable to find work then and moved to Maryland. But six months ago he moved back to Freeport. Write 150 words.

Assignments

A. Age

Obtain latest local arrest figures for the following categories and write a story based on a comparison of data for preceding periods: murder, rape, assault, robbery, burglary, auto theft, drunk driving. Check the ages of those arrested.

B. Arrest Report

Go to the local police station or a nearby precinct and ask to see some of the arrest reports turned in over the last 12 hours. Select one you consider newsworthy and do a story based on it. Include the suspect's criminal record if it is available and it is legal to use it.

Community Projects

A. Car Theft

More than 1.5 million vehicles are stolen annually. Their value is estimated at $7.5 billion. The recovery rate for stolen vehicles is around 60 percent nationally and much lower in metropolitan areas. The national motor vehicle theft rate is 605 per 100,000 people, broken down as 721 in metropolitan areas, 224 in cities outside these areas and 110 in rural counties. An average of 1 of every 125 registered vehicles is stolen each year.

California has the highest state rate of motor vehicle thefts. Washington, D.C., has the highest city rate with New York and Los Angeles close behind.

Talk to police officers, garage mechanics and others about the local car theft rate and car insurance rates. Find out the best way to protect cars against theft: alarms, steering wheel immobilizers, the Lojack, ignition cutoff systems.

B. Efficiency

One measure of police efficiency is the comparison of arrests to citizen complaints. Take the numbers of each in the categories of burglary and robbery. In large urban areas, the ratio is about one arrest for every five reported burglaries and robberies.

You might extend this to all categories of crime, and if the community has precincts, you can make a precinct-by-precinct analysis.

C. Crimes

Take any 1- or 2-hour period or more over the past 24 hours, and do a total of crimes reported by category. For this story, you will have to obtain the dispatcher's record or the records of the police officer who takes all incoming calls on crimes. Some of these calls may not be serious, but record them anyway. This will be a narrow peek at a period in a day of the life of a police department.

D. Police

Interview a police officer who walks a beat or is assigned to a patrol car. Try to accompany the officer on his or her rounds or ask for a description of a typical day. Include the strong opinions the officer may have of the people he or she deals with, and ask what the officer thinks of the court system.

E. Investigation

Interview a police officer who was instrumental in solving a recent crime. How was the case broken?

F. Prevention

Unique methods have been adopted in some cities to prevent crime. One of the most common is the computerized study of high-crime areas and periods and the assignment of officers to these areas in town during the specified times. What methods are being used in your city?

G. Complaints

Is there a bureau or department in the city that handles complaints against the police? Do a story on the kinds of complaints registered and the way they are handled. Have any officers been suspended or fired as a result?

H. Con Artists

Interview local law enforcement authorities to find out what kinds of illegal activities have been used to fleece residents. One of the more lucrative schemes is fraudulent telemarketing, which is aimed mostly at the elderly. Law agencies estimate that telemarketing scams cost gullible people about $40 billion a year over the last few years. There have been more than 800 arrests of these con artists who promise to deliver goods and don't or get people to enter sweepstakes in which no one actually wins.

Another scam involves credit card fraud. Con artists manage to obtain the social security numbers of an individual and apply for a card under his or her name. Local credit agencies will have information on this activity.

Campus Projects
A. Crime Count

Studies of crime indicate that many more crimes are committed than reported. Make a survey of students and determine how many have been victims of a crime within the past year on campus. Did they report the crime to campus or local police?

Failure to report is especially high among victims of sex crimes. You might want to make a separate category for this crime and investigate the situation in depth.

B. Policy

Campus newspapers have gone to court to open campus police records, and the courts have agreed that the public has access to these records. Disciplinary records, however, are closed to the press because the courts have ruled that they fall under the protection students have from the so-called Buckley Amendment.

What is the situation on your campus? Are reporters allowed to examine campus police records? If so, does the campus newspaper and/or local newspaper examine these records on a regular basis?

C. Hate

The number of hate crimes has been increasing in some states. The data are kept by law enforcement officials and reported to the Federal Bureau of Investigation. Track the number and rate of such crimes in your state over the past years for which such data have been reported to the FBI. Do you see any trends? What is being done to avoid such crimes? Have authorities profiled those who commit these crimes? Write 350 words.

Here are some recent figures for this crime:

Rank	State	Number	Percent of Total in U.S.A.	Rank	State	Rate per 100,000 Population
1.	California	1,949	24.7	1.	Kansas	12.3
2.	New Jersey	617	7.8	2.	Massachusetts	8.2
3.	New York	590	7.5	3.	New Jersey	7.6
4.	Massachusetts	443	5.6	4.	California	5.9
5.	Michigan	407	5.2	5.	Arizona	5.6

Home Assignment

Process

Describe the process from arrest to arraignment that the police reporter covers. Follow the process for a high-profile crime that the local media have covered. Use newspaper clippings to illustrate.

Class Discussion

Banner

Oswald Garrison Villard, 1872–1949, was the editor-owner of *The Nation,* an outstanding liberal political weekly, until 1932. In a commentary on journalism, he wrote:

> It must ask last of all what were the returns of the counting room but must first inquire what ideals a given journal upheld, what moral aims it pursued, what national and international policies it championed, what was the spirit of fair play and justice which activated it, and above all on whose side and under whose banner it fought.

Select a newspaper or magazine you read regularly and use Villard's tests. What do you conclude?

Skill Drill: Police Vocabulary

Beginning reporters on most news staffs are expected to handle stories originating in or involving the police department. Accidents, reports of crimes, arrests, searches, investigations, administrative activities, corruption and other newsworthy activities require reporters to deal with the police and with material from the police. There is simply too much news for the police reporter to handle alone. This list includes terms every reporter should know and a handful with which only the police reporter might be familiar. Define:

1. ADW
2. APB
3. Arrest warrant
4. Bail
5. Booking
6. Burglary
7. Citation
8. Crime report
9. Decoy
10. Detention
11. Entrapment
12. Felony
13. Grand larceny
14. Homicide bureau
15. Interrogation
16. Miranda card
17. Misdemeanor
18. On the pad
19. Pigeon drop
20. Robbery

21 The Courts

Mary Beth Meehan, *Providence*
Lawyer and judge confer.

Introduction

The courts are a source of important and often dramatic stories, from coverage of Supreme Court decisions that affect many aspects of our lives to decisions by local courts that determine which criminal defendants will be sent to prison and whether damages will be paid in a civil suit. The two basic systems are the federal and state courts, and within these systems civil and criminal cases are heard. In civil cases, actions are initiated by an individual, usually suing another for damages. In criminal law, the government takes action for violation of the criminal statutes. Most of these cases, civil and criminal, are settled to avoid trial.

Exercises

A. Slay

A Freeport man, Hosie Gene Jones, 60, of 1347 Oklahoma Ave., a handyman, ex-convict and drug addict, has been convicted of murder after a two-week trial. Jones said he was not at the scene of the crime. He was charged with stabbing a 24-year-old advertising copywriter to death, Dorothy F. Roberts of 242 Madison St., in the hallway of her four-story building. When Jones tried to take her purse, she resisted and he stabbed her and fled. When he was captured a few blocks away, police found a sales slip addressed to Roberts rolled between $7 in bills tucked in Jones' pocket.

After three hours of deliberation, Jones was found guilty of second degree murder and was sentenced to life in prison without parole by District Judge Samuel A. McMillan. In sentencing Jones, McMillan said:

> This was a deliberate murder for gain, and although the gain was slight, a few dollars, this man was willing to kill for it. He took the life of a young woman with most of her life ahead of her. He is the lowest order of human we can imagine.
> It is clear from crimes of this sort that the state legislature must reinstitute the death penalty for murder committed while engaging in a felony, such as was the case here.

Present law allows the death penalty only for killing a police officer or other law enforcement agent. Write a story about the sentencing.

B. Conviction

In Chapter 12 of the textbook, the arrest of Calvin Jackson in connection with a series of murders is described. It is now some 18 months later and Jackson has been on trial for nine murders. The case went to the jury today, and after four hours and 11 minutes of deliberations, a guilty verdict was returned.

Jackson was convicted of killing nine women. He faces life in prison with a mandatory minimum of 25 to 30 years. Sentencing will be two weeks from today. District Court Judge Aloysius J. Melia, who presided over the six-week trial, will do the sentencing next month.

Jackson's defense was insanity. But a three-hour tape-recorded confession he made to the police, which was played to the jury, was full of details of the various crimes, and jurors said, after the trial, this convinced them he was sane at the time of the slayings. Write a story about the verdict.

C. Chen Indict

Dong Lu Chen, 51, of 1658 Broadway, who was arrested 10 days ago in connection with the death of his wife, Gian Wan Chen, was indicted today by a grand jury. (See Chapter 20, **Exercises, F. Chen Arrest**)

He was charged with second-degree murder. He has been held without bail and was returned to jail pending felony arraignment on the charge.

D. Chen Sentence

District Court Judge Marvin Hurley held a nonjury trial for Dong Lu Chen, 51, who was charged with second-degree murder in the death of his wife, Gian Wan Chen, 40.

Chen spent 18 months in jail pending trial, which began five days ago.

Judge Hurley reached a decision yesterday of second-degree manslaughter. Two hours later, he sentenced Chen to probation of five years.

During the trial, testimony showed that while Chen was in Maryland and his wife and children were in Freeport, his wife took a lover. The children testified that their mother taunted Chen about her affair.

After an argument that the children overheard, Chen knocked his wife down on the bed and hit the slight, 99-pound woman at least eight times with a hammer.

A second-degree manslaughter conviction carries a penalty of 5 to 15 years. But Hurley said that he imposed probation because of the "cultural aspects" of the case. Hurley cited "the effect of his wife's behavior on someone who is essentially born in China, raised in China and took all his Chinese customs with him to the United States."

One of Chen's witnesses was Nicholas Trowbridge, chairman of the psychology department at Mallory College, who said that marriage in China is sacred and that a husband could be expected to become enraged on learning of his wife's infidelity. The defense attorney, said, "The basis of this defense is not that it's acceptable to kill your wife as a result of her infidelity. The basis is the special high place the family holds in the Chinese community. This act of adultery would bring great shame and humiliation his entire life."

He said that because of Chen's mental state there could be no intent, and intent is essential to second-degree murder or first-degree manslaughter.

You have not covered this trial and so you will have to recapitulate much of the testimony. Your editor tells you to obtain a statement on the judge's sentence from the district attorney, Paul Robinson, who states, "Anyone who comes to this country must be prepared to live by and obey our laws. Anything less than the maximum sentence suggests that women's lives, minority women's lives are not valued."

He added, "There should be one standard of justice, not one that depends on the cultural background of a defendant."

E. Chen React

The day after Chen was sentenced, Mayor Sam Parnass issued the following statement for immediate release:

The City of Freeport   *Office of the Mayor*

For Release: Immediate

Statement

I am shocked and dismayed by District Court Judge Marvin Hurley's decision to impose a sentence of probation on a man who killed his wife with a hammer.

Judge Hurley's explanation of his nonjail sentence in the case of Dong Lu Chen was that the defendant's Chinese "cultural background made him susceptible to cracking under the circumstances" and that he was unlikely to kill again. Accordingly, the judge refused to impose a prison sentence.

This reasoning is both an affront to those of Chinese heritage and inconsistent with the philosophy that sentences for crimes should punish the offender, deter the individual from a repetition of such conduct and serve to deter others from engaging in similar conduct. Additionally, sentences for criminal conduct should communicate a message about societal values that the laws seek to promote, uphold and protect.

If Judge Hurley's reasoning were accepted, it would be used to argue mitigation for those who commit crimes against persons because of the offender's objection to the cultural, racial, sexual, religious or other characteristics of the victim. A judge in Texas recently applied this irrational philosophy when he accepted a killer's distaste for a homosexual lifestyle as an explanation for his murders and gave him a reduced sentence.

I reject stereotyping and bias based on cultural, ethnic, racial, sexual, religious or other such grounds and I urge everyone to reject it. While cultural, ethnic and other diversity are important ingredients of a heterogeneous society, diversity should not be used to excuse or justify conduct that is contrary to accepted societal norms.

F. Chen Judge

Two days after you wrote about the conviction of Dong Lu Chen (**D. Chen Sentence**) and the day after you wrote about the mayor's reaction (**E. Chen React),** the judge who sentenced him speaks out in defense of his sentence. Here are excerpts from his statement to you in an interview. Write 300 words.

> If a judge made a ruling on a cultural background it would be wrong. It wasn't that it was a defense, but it totally affected this man.
> He's not a loose cannon. That's the point. He never displayed psychopathic tendencies.
> This guy is not going to do it again, and he has suffered. There's no question he's going to suffer every day of his life.
> If you kill someone you should face some jail time. I don't find any violence acceptable . . . but in this case it wasn't that his cultural background excused him. It just made him more susceptible to cracking under the circumstances. I don't think this man would have killed her under any other circumstances.
> If he went to jail at some point he might come out a real time bomb. Under my mandate, he is under intense supervision.
> This is just a terrible tragedy all around. If you could just see this broken and dejected man and his poor family . . . this guy is not going to do this again and there's no question he's going to suffer every day for the rest of his life.

Hurley said Chen had been isolated in jail because he speaks a rare Chinese dialect and had been beaten by other inmates. He said the children asked that their father be given probation, not jail, and that Chen had suffered remorse.

Also, the National Organization for Women said it intends to file a complaint with the State Commission on Judicial Conduct.

Assignments

A. Rural

Rural prosecutors infrequently have the heavy case load of violent crime that burdens the urban prosecutor. Interview a rural prosecutor about his or her cases. Has there been any change in their nature? Also, what are the prosecutor's personal ambitions? Many rural prosecutors see the job as a stepping stone to higher political office. Most are paid little, and the job can be held in association with a private practice. Are these generalities true of your interviewee?

B. Urban

Accompany an urban prosecutor through a day in court. Keep precise track of what he or she faces by singling out some cases and following them. This is best done at arraignment, where the bulk of plea bargaining occurs. What is the prosecutor's case load? What does he or she see as the solution to the case load?

C. Legal Aid

In most large cities, the court appoints lawyers for defendants unable to hire defense attorneys. The task is usually filled by the overworked local legal aid organization. Interview a legal aid lawyer and follow the lawyer through a day's work on specific cases. Try to have the lawyer explain how he or she balances the case load. What are the lawyer's ambitions? Go into his or her background.

D. Bankrupt

If there is a federal courthouse in your area, it will have a bankruptcy court, which you can visit. Find out the total individual and total business bankruptcies for the last full year and the preceding year. Why the increase or decrease?

How are bankruptcies handled? Give specific examples of cases and the settlements reached. (See *Workbook,* Chapter 23, **Community Project, A. Broke.)**

E. Selection

Sit in on a jury selection at a trial. Try to determine the type of juror the prosecutor and the defense attorney want to seat. At a recess or adjournment, interview each and try to draw portraits of the prosecutor's and the district attorney's views of the perfect juror for this case.

F. Arraign

Visit arraignment court. In large cities, an arraignment is a confusing and inaudible proceeding. You will have to make arrangements with the court clerk and, if possible, with the presiding judge for permission to sit close to the bench. In some communities, judges are allowed to have guests sit with them on the bench. Try to follow the main course of action and, when possible, examine one or two typical cases in detail to buttress your major conclusions about the process.

G. Indict

Determine what process of indictment your state uses: grand jury action or the information. Then follow a case through this process—through indictment or the handing up of an information.

H. Reduce

Obtain data of the number of felony arrests, felony indictments, sentences on felony pleas and trials in your city. This will give your reader an idea of the extent of plea bargaining.

I. Trial

Courthouse reporters with a heavy load will only cover the high points of a trial: introductory statements of attorneys, a key witness's testimony, summaries of the attorneys, jury verdict or sentencing. Through reading of the daily newspaper, you may be able to learn when such events will occur in an interesting trial. Verify with the court clerk to avoid a wasted trip. Put the day's activities in context.

J. Youthful

Do a background story on family court or juvenile court. How many cases are on the docket each month? How does this compare with previous years? What kinds of offenses are most frequent? Make a table that shows the frequency of certain offenses.

K. Indigents

In most large cities, 60 percent or more of those arrested are unable to hire attorneys. How does your community, state or bar association handle this problem? Invite a representative of the system to speak to the class about it. Then do some reporting to find out whether the system is satisfactory to defendants, local attorneys, the bar association, judges, law professors.

L. Bail

What is the bail policy of the local court where defendants are arraigned? Some criminal courts release defendants on their own recognizance if they have jobs or a family. Others set bail, depending on the severity of the crime. There have been charges that some courts have bail policies that discriminate against members of minority groups. Make a study of actual cases over the past week.

M. Bondsman

Interview a local bail bondsman. What does this person do? How much does he or she charge? What happens when a person skips bail? In the last 10 years, how has the business changed, and why?

N. Crowding

In a number of cities and states, the courts have ordered that prisoners be given decent conditions in which to serve their sentences. The costs involved have led to early releases, and some see it as the beginning of the decriminalization of some crimes. Check the local situation. Are such crimes as marijuana possession and shoplifting decriminalized?

O. Execution

More than 3,000 inmates are on death row in state and federal prisons. Most are in prisons in California and Texas (almost 400 each) and in Florida (more than 300). All but 13 states and the District of Columbia have the death penalty.

The death penalty has been the subject of political debate. Supporters say it acts as a deterrent to violent crime. Opponents say the government has no moral right to take a life, and other opponents say it unfairly singles out members of minority groups.

Forty percent of those on death row are black; blacks constitute 12 percent of the U.S. population. The white rate of death sentences is a fifth that of the black rate.

Select the following and write 350 words after doing the research:

1. What is the maximum penalty in your state for first-degree murder, and has there been any effort to change the penalty?
2. If your state has the death penalty, how many inmates are on death row; how many have been executed in the past 20 years; what was the average length of stay on death row for those executed last year; 10, 20 years ago?
3. Make a racial and ethnic breakdown of those on death row in your state.

Campus Project

Campus Crime

Obtain data for the last few years on crimes committed on campus. Have there been major fluctuations in the nature of the most frequent crimes, or is there a pattern? Write 300 words.

Community Projects

A. White Collar

Sentence inequities have been demonstrated by journalists in a number of cities: light treatment of white-collar crime committed by middle-class managerial types, heavy sentences for low-income and minority defendants accused of theft or larceny. Obtain court documents and interview lawyers, judges, probation workers, court clerks. Can you find any pattern in sentencing?

B. Plea Bargain

Most cities encourage defendants to plead guilty in return for lesser charges. The arrangement is known as plea bargaining and affects 70 to 85 percent of all criminal cases in large cities. The arrangement is the result of the increase in criminal cases and the effect on the criminal justice system.

Without plea bargaining, say some legal experts, the system would be overwhelmed. But critics say it puts criminals back on the streets too soon. One district attorney decided to eliminate plea bargaining and in doing so voiced a belief held by police and many in the public. Plea bargaining, he said, "means that society has ceded control to those it has accused of violating its laws. And it means that our system is running us and not the other way around."

In reply, a criminal court judge said, "Plea negotiations are as vital to the system as breathing and eating and sleeping are for human survival. You have a limited number of tax dollars. You can't build a courthouse as big as the Triborough Bridge, manned by half the population of the Bronx to try the other half of the Bronx."

A civil rights lawyer said the elimination of plea bargaining has been considered by many cities and states but is in effect in few jurisdictions. Plea bargains, he continued, are "the aspect of the judicial system which most undermines confidence in it. People feel that their representative, the public prosecutor, has given in and the defendant has gotten a good deal."

Examine the situation in your city. What percentage of cases are plea bargained? Interview judges, police officers, lawyers and others for an article on how the system works locally and what its effects are.

Home Assignment

Graffiti

On the next page is a court document. Write a 300-word story.

Class Discussion

A. Family Court

What are the pros and cons of opening family or juvenile court to the public, which includes the press? Some proposals call for open court but a prohibition on using the names of juvenile offenders. The courts have ruled that the press can use the names of juvenile offenders if reporters can obtain them, but most courts are closed and deal harshly with those who disclose names of juvenile offenders. Most newspapers will refuse to use the names but make exceptions in unusual cases or when a competitor has disclosed an identity.

You might invite to class a juvenile court judge, a social worker or an attorney who handles such cases.

DISTRICT COURT OF FREEPORT

The City of Freeport
    —Plaintiff
    —against—
Paul Godfrey and Claudine Godfrey
    —Defendants

Complaint: 416-CH

Plaintiff, by its attorney, Paul Robinson of the City of Freeport, respectfully alleges upon information and belief:

1. Plaintiff City of Freeport is a municipal corporation organized and existing under state laws.
2. Defendant Paul Godfrey resides at 870 Blue Ridge Rd., Freeport.
3. Defendant Claudine Godfrey is the mother of defendant Paul Godfrey, and resides at the same address.
4. The City owns a part of the city overpass at U.S. 81 and State Highway 166.
5. The City is responsible for maintaining the highways within its boundaries, including the overpass. In fulfillment of that responsibility, the City, acting through its Department of Transportation, removes graffiti from the retaining walls of the overpass.
6. On or about the night of July 6, defendant Paul Godfrey willfully, maliciously, and unlawfully damaged the walls of the overpass by spray-painting his nickname, or "tag," consisting of the name "REAL," on those walls.
7. By reason of the foregoing acts of trespass, plaintiff has sustained damages for the costs of materials, supplies, and labor expended by plaintiff to remove the graffiti from the overpass.

First Cause of Action

8. The acts of defendant Paul Godfrey constitute a trespass, and Paul Godfrey is liable to the City for the damages to City property resulting from those actions.
9. Because the actions of defendant Paul Godfrey were unlawful, willful, and wanton, and were undertaken with the intention of damaging public property, Godfrey is liable for punitive damages in addition to whatever compensatory damages may be awarded.

Second Cause of Action

10. The foregoing acts subject defendant Paul Godfrey to the penalties of State Highway Law § 320, which provides that "[w]hoever shall injure any highway or bridge maintained at the public expense . . . shall for every such offense forfeit treble damages."

Third Cause of Action

11. Paul Godfrey is a minor over the age of ten and under the age of eighteen, and lives in the custody of his mother, defendant Claudine Godfrey.
12. Under State General Municipal Law § 78-a, defendant Claudine Godfrey is liable for up to $2,500 of the damages caused by defendant Paul Godfrey.

WHEREFORE the plaintiff demands judgment against the defendants as follows:

a) On the first cause of action, against Paul Godfrey, compensatory and punitive damages resulting from trespass, or, in the alternative, restitution;

b) On the second cause of action, against Paul Godfrey, treble damages for injuries to the highway;

c) On the third cause of action, against Claudine Godfrey, damages up to $2,500, or, in the alternative, restitution, for damages to City property;

Together with the costs and disbursements of this action and such further relief as is just and proper.

Dated: August 4

Paul Robinson
District Attorney,
The City of Freeport,
Attorney for the Plaintiff

(**Note**—Paul Godfrey is 16 years old.)

B. Harassment

You receive the following press release from the office of Mayor Sam Parnass:

Mayor Sam Parnass and the Human Rights Commission Director, Stanley Downey, announced today the settlement of a sexual harassment case involving a young Freeport proofreader who worked for the Freeport Press Corporation.

In the settlement, the corporation agreed to pay the complainant "Jane Doe" a total of $44,200.

In a complaint filed in August, a woman in her teens charged that from her first day of employment at Freeport Press, three male employees—Anthony Blount, Donald Trump and Henry Morton—sexually harassed her. The harassment allegedly included obscene jokes and sexist remarks about her and other female employees. The complainant specifically charged that Blount, a typesetter and assistant supervisor, fondled her, touched her hair with his face and brushed against her.

Mayor Parnass said, "There is no such thing as an 'okay' amount of sexual harassment or discrimination. It is incumbent on employers to keep their workplaces free of these egregious behaviors and to treat their employees' concerns about them seriously.

"Unwarranted sexual advances, sexist statements and derogatory comments based on one's gender are simply unacceptable. If employers lack the resolve to prohibit these practices from the workplace or to respond vigorously when they appear, the city will step in, as we have in this instance, to make sure the proper protections are afforded to Freeport workers."

Human Rights Commission Director Downey said, "Many women who find themselves subjected to sexist remarks and lewd behavior at work are unsure of what to do for fear of losing their jobs. This courageous woman took action and brought her case to the Commission on Human Rights. While I'm sure no amount of money would make up for this reprehensible and illegal sexual harassment, this settlement from this company sends a message to employers that they must not discriminate and that they are responsible for the behavior of their supervisors and employees."

The complainant also alleged that her own efforts to address the situation through her supervisor led to public ridicule by the male management. A requested transfer to another shift and a formal complaint filed with the Special Project and Art Composition Room Manager were unsuccessful. Finally, after a conflict with her supervisor, the complainant became emotionally upset and went home sick. The next day she was terminated.

Freeport Press has agreed to adopt and distribute a sexual harassment policy to all employees and conspicuously place posters outlining the new procedures for handling sexual harassment complaints. The company agreed to conduct special sensitivity training programs for all its supervisors and employees. Additionally, the firm agreed that the supervisory personnel responsible for enforcing the policy would have to attend an initial training session and be reviewed regularly.

Joseph Finnegan was the prosecutor for the Commission's Law Enforcement Bureau, and Pamela Bell represented the complainant.

You dig into this case, the first sexual harassment settlement in Freeport, and you learn that the "Jane Doe" is Sandra Begley, 17-year-old daughter of the city clerk.

1. Do you use her name in the story?
2. Do you use the names of the three employees who are named in the press release?
3. How much space or time would you give this story, and where in the newspaper or on a local news broadcast would you place this item?

Skill Drill: Court Terms

Define or explain the following terms:

1. Appellant
2. Arraignment
3. Bail bondsman
4. Character witness
5. Felony
6. Cross-examination
7. Directed verdict
8. Dismissal for cause (of a juror)
9. Dissenting opinion
10. Indeterminate sentence
11. Indictment
12. Mistrial
13. Peremptory challenge (of a juror)
14. Plaintiff
15. Plea bargaining
16. Preliminary injunction
17. Probation
18. Rebuttal
19. True bill
20. Waiver of immunity

Sports

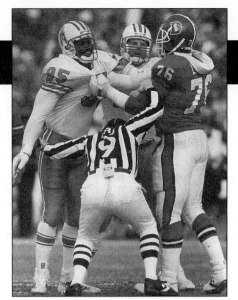

Dave Einsel, *Houston Chronicle*
Man in the middle.

Introduction

The largest single department on most newspapers is the sports department and one of the fastest-growing broadcast stations is the all-sports, all-day radio station, a reflection of interest in spectator sports. The growth of big-time sports—collegiate as well as professional—has created an audience in almost every city for intense coverage of basketball, football and baseball. Even hockey has expanded to areas that have never seen an ice-covered pond. Sports coverage is best when it is objective, when the reporter is not a home-team rooter. As television game coverage expands, newspaper accounts increasingly emphasize the game's turning points, strategy and after-the-game comments over a running account of scoring.

Exercises

A. Runner

Here are some notes from an interview with Arthur Baron, a biology major, who is a member of the Mallory College cross-country team that returned two days ago from finishing fourth at the NCAA Division III meet at Franklin Park in Boston. Baron finished 11th—considered a good finish—and this is the second time he has been in the top 25 in the annual meet. The newspaper has run a story on the meet. You are to do an interview. Here are your notes:

Baron is 5′ 11″, weighs 150, has brown hair, wears glasses.

Runs 20 miles a day—twice what most run—seven days a week in summer, lifts weights and swims as part of his training. In winter, runs at least 10 miles a day unless snowbound. Yesterday, the day after returning from Boston, he did seven miles of road work at a minus 20 degree temperature.

Baron says his coach, Steve Helmer, tries to develop internal motivation among the runners:

"It's unlike high school where everything has a rigid schedule. Steve is more oriented to the athlete than the program. You're given credit for being able to think."

"At other schools, win-oriented coaches burn out their athletes. At some schools, the runners put in twice as much road work, but there is a point of diminishing returns."

"We have no athletic scholarships here, and there is no physical education major. None of us who ran in Boston came here to be athletes. We're here for the academic program. The coach knows that the Big Ten and other big conferences attract athletes. But running, the coach says, 'is for intrinsic reasons, not money.'"

Asked about the success of the team despite the small size of the school and its lack of scholarships, Baron says the team uses a tactic called "pack running." Instead of each running his race, the four stay together until the last mile. The effect on other teams is demoralizing, particularly when the four run in front, as they try to do.

"I could possibly run faster times away from the pack on my own, but there is a mental strain to running in front all alone. Also, the feeling of running with your team can cause you to beat a better runner."

Baron is thinking of studying medicine. The other three are going into science-related fields, physics, chemistry and biology.

A call to Helmer turns up the following information:

Cross-country runners are highly disciplined and demand top performance of themselves. If there is a problem, it is that they train to excess. They are very demanding.

Cross-country runners in this country tend to come from the middle and upper classes and are good students, whereas the sprinters often are from less affluent homes. The situation in Egypt, where I spent a year, is reversed. There the military officers are the sprinters; the laboring class provides the long-distance runners.

Write 400 to 450 words.

B. Trade

Willie Suarez, an outfielder with the local professional baseball team, the Red Sox, has been complaining about playing in the northern climate and has asked to be traded. He has played three seasons in Philadelphia and one season in windswept Candlestick Park in San Francisco. He is 28 and from Puerto Rico.

"Last season, my first season here, I felt the weather bad," he said in an interview last week. However, he batted .310 and drove in 101 runs. This year, after 50 games, almost one-third of the season, he has 20 runs batted in and is hitting .274.

This afternoon, you have a call from the Sox front office. The management decided to trade Suarez to the Braves in Atlanta. They received in return Dave Martin, a utility infielder batting .246, and a reserve outfielder, George White, batting .265.

You say you don't think the team received very much.

"Well, you might say we weren't getting very much from Willie either, and since he wouldn't play in cool areas, there wasn't much bidding for him. He's got great potential, but he'll kill his career with this kind of attitude."

Your ball club source says he can't be quoted by name but you can use the fact that it came from a person "close to the club."

The team is in fourth place, 12 games out of first.

Write 200 to 250 words, preferably with a delayed lead and a feature touch.

C. Reds-Braves

Here are the lineups and an inning-by-inning account of a baseball game between the Reds and the Braves. The Braves were ahead of the Reds by two games for the division leadership before the game. Lemon is a left-hander, Katz a right-hander. Katz, 7–4, has lost two games to the Braves this year. Lemon, 11–3, has never faced the Reds. It is midseason. There is no need to identify the teams any further or to place them in any league.

This is an evening game played in the Reds' hometown, your town.

Lineups

Braves	Reds
Bumiller, Ernie cf	Eddings, Bobby ss
Vorobil, Maury ss	Manoff, Stan lf
Weiner, Tommy rf	Douge, Harry 3b
Wallis, Mike lf	Cruz, Al 1b
Hand, Denny 3b	Marwell, Chuck c
Sherman, Gene 1b	Gougeon, John cf
Day, Karl c	Kelso, Jack 2b
Weir, Rick 2b	Barrett, Eddie rf
Lemon, Carl p	Katz, Art p

Play by Play

1st inning

Braves: Bumiller walks on five pitches. Vorobil hits a 3–1 count to center-field wall; Gougeon makes putout. Weiner hits first pitch to center field for single. Bumiller goes to third. Wallis hits into double play, Eddings-Kelso-Cruz.

Reds: Eddings grounds out, Lemon to Sherman. Manoff looks at third strike. Douge flies out to Wallis.

2nd inning

Braves: Hand takes first when Kelso bobbles grounder. Sherman strikes out. Day singles to center, Hand going to third. Weir pops to Cruz. Lemon swings at and misses three pitches.

Reds: Cruz grounds out, Weir to Sherman. Marwell flies out to Weiner. Gougeon grounds out, Hand-Sherman.

3rd inning

Braves: Bumiller flies to Manoff. Vorobil singles to center. On one-one count to Weiner, Vorobil out trying to steal second. Weiner pops to Cruz.

Reds: Kelso fouls out to Day. Barrett hits 3–0 pitch to center-field wall for double. Katz grounds out, Sherman unassisted, Barrett taking third. Eddings flies to Weiner.

4th inning

Braves: Wallis grounds to deep short and is safe on close play. Reds Manager Frank Bordewich argues to no avail. Hand bunts Wallis to second, Douge throwing Hand out at first. Sherman grounds out, Kelso to Cruz. Wallis takes third. Day strikes out on four pitches.

Reds: Manoff hits first pitch into left-field stands for a home run, his 15th of the season, his 76th RBI. Douge grounds out, Vorobil to Sherman. Cruz pops to Hand. Marwell flies out to Wallis.

5th inning

Braves: Weir singles on ground over second. Lemon sacrifice bunts Weir to second, Cruz to Kelso covering first. Bumiller tops pitch that dribbles toward third, and everyone is safe, Weir on third, Bumiller on first. Vorobil hits first pitch to deep center, Gougeon making catch. Throw to plate too late to catch Weir. Weiner grounds out, Eddings to Cruz.

Reds: Gougeon hit on ankle by pitch, takes first. Kelso, trying to bunt, pops to pitcher who doubles Gougeon off first. Barrett flies to Weiner.

6th inning

Braves: Wallis walks and steals second on 2–1 pitch to Hand, who then pops to Eddings. Sherman grounds out Kelso to Cruz. Day hits grounder past first, Barrett throwing Wallis out at plate on close call that Wallis protests vehemently. He is warned by plate umpire.

Reds: Katz grounds to Sherman unassisted. Eddings flies out to Hand in foul territory. Manoff grounds out Weir to Sherman.

7th inning

Braves: Weir grounds out Eddings to Cruz. Lemon strikes out. Bumiller singles to left. Vorobil forces Bumiller, Eddings to Kelso.

Reds: Douge walks on five pitches. Cruz singles to left, Douge going to second. Marwell hits into double play, Vorobil-Weir-Sherman, Douge taking third. Gougeon pops into center, the ball dropping in front of Bumiller, Douge scoring on the single. Kelso forces Gougeon, Weir stepping on second unassisted.

8th inning

Braves: Weiner flies to Barrett. Wallis doubles down first-base line. Hand grounds out Douge to Cruz, Wallis remaining on second. Count goes to 3–0 on Sherman, and Marwell goes out to talk to Katz. Calls trainer who examines Katz's hand. Blister is developing. But Katz says he is OK. (He has not pitched a complete game this year.) Sherman walks. Day grounds to third, Douge stepping on bag, forcing Wallis.

Reds: Barrett flies out to Bumiller. Katz looks at three strikes, never lifting bat off shoulder, apparently unwilling to put stress on pitching finger with blister. Eddings flies out to Weiner.

9th inning

Braves: Weir hits 3–2 pitch into center for a single. Ahearn pinch hits for Lemon; infield expects him to bunt. Ahearn swings at first pitch and it narrowly misses being fair past first. Infield drops back. Ahearn then bunts toward third and beats throw to first. Reds manager goes out for mound conference, leaves Katz in. Bumiller hits line drive to Kelso, who makes sideways leaping catch. Runners stay put. Vorobil hits into game-ending double play around the horn, Douge throwing to Kelso for the out at second and on to first.

The game took two hours and four minutes, and the attendance was 16,069 paid.

Write an online story immediately following the game. Then write one for the next morning's newspaper. Devise a box score.

D. Loser

You cover the local team, the Red Sox, and it has just lost 2–0 to the Twins in an afternoon game. The winning pitcher was Randy Jones, the loser Bob Pierce. The Sox got six hits, the Twins 10 off Pierce. The winning runs were scored in the fourth on a base on balls to Marty Balzer and successive doubles by Gene Mica and Tom Kemper.

You interview Ted Schmidt, the Sox leading hitter, after the game, who went nothing for four and struck out twice.

"I can't recall striking out twice in a game in my life in this league," he says. "But I did." He kicks his locker. "If I were a pitcher I'd be embarrassed to go to the mound with the kind of stuff Jones has. A nothing pitcher. Nothing."

You then talk to the Sox manager, Danny Appel, and you ask him about Jones. "A helluva pitcher. He's won 12 games and the season's one-third old. A lot of the guys say he's a nothing pitcher, but what you need to stay alive in this league is control and pinpoint pitching. The guys who have a lot of stuff but can't get it over the plate bomb out fast."

"Just between us, Schmidt had a bad day and was bitching. Heck, I'd give anyone on my team for Jones. The guy's worth a sure pennant to any contending team."

Jones is now 12–2 and Pierce is 6–5. The leading team in the league, the Athletics, lost a game in the standings to the Twins by losing 5–3 to the Rangers and the Twins now trail the Athletics by two games.

Write a game story with a feature lead for a morning newspaper.

Assignments

A. Links

Go to the local golf course and chat with players and the people running the golf shop. Who are the best golfers in town, the man, the woman and the youngster? Try to interview one of them for a profile. Is the person a Sunday golfer or a regular player? How did the golfer start to play? How much of a handicap do competitors have to be given?

B. Bowler

Make the rounds of the local bowling lanes and find a league in which there are some good bowlers. Then go out one night when one of the good teams is bowling. Do a story on the players, personalizing the match if possible.

C. Minor

Many high school and college sports do not have the spectator appeal of basketball and football, but the participants enjoy them and there are vociferous and steady fans. Do a profile of one of these sports by interviewing the coach, players and fans: tennis, crew, swimming, cross country, field events (track), wrestling, fencing, soccer, golf, field hockey, rugby, lacrosse, squash, ice hockey.

D. Ambition

Interview one of the prominent players on the local college or university team about his or her ambitions; continued amateur play or professional status; the driving force behind his or her desire to play; the help of coaches; the relationship of athletics and studies.

E. Spectator

Are most students spectators, or do they work out regularly? Are students exercising sufficiently for good health? Have they embarked on exercises and sports that will engage them for their active lives, or are they playing sports that they will have to drop after they graduate?

F. Memorabilia

Sports fans collect all sorts of paraphernalia to celebrate their interest in the sport. Baseball fans save baseball cards of favorite players, bats and balls, score cards and ticket stubs. The lucky hockey fan has a puck from a game or buys a Wayne Gretzky stick. Autographs are very big with fans. In fact, the collectors have made a large and profitable market in memorabilia, so large that an industry has developed in faking these mementoes.

Locate some collectors and interview them about their collections and ask how they know their material is authentic.

World Series: 1929

This stub from a ticket to the fourth game of the 1929 World Series was found in the papers of a former sports editor. His widow says it has sentimental value. But has it any monetary value? What do collectors say about rain checks from a World Series more than 70 years ago?

The game was between the Chicago Cubs and the Philadelphia Athletics in a series that the Athletics won four games to one. Bleacher seats in those days cost less than a dollar. But for the Series, the price went up to $1 a seat.

G. Injuries

The Centers for Disease Control and Prevention reports that sports-related injuries send 2.6 million children and young adults to emergency hospital departments each year at a cost of $500 million. The most frequent injuries are associated with basketball and cycling, almost 900,000 a year, says the CDC. Other totals:

Football	250,000
Ice and roller hockey and skateboarding	150,000
Gymnastics and cheerleading	145,000
Playground	137,000
Water and snow sports	100,000

Localize this material by:

1. Obtaining figures from local hospitals on emergency department visits for sports-related injuries.
2. Checking to see whether the city has helmet laws and other safety precautions.

Write 350 words either for a Sunday feature in your local newspaper or for a radio documentary.

H. Best

Michael Jordan is regarded as the best basketball player who ever played. There is less agreement about other sports:

Baseball: Ty Cobb, Rogers Hornsby, Ted Williams, Joe DiMaggio.
Pro Football: Jim Brown, Paul Hornung, Johnny Unitas, Joe Montana, Walter Payton, Jerry Rice.
Boxing: Joe Louis, Sugar Ray Robinson, Muhammad Ali, Jack Dempsey.
Tennis: Margaret Smith, Billie, Jean King, Chris Evert, Fred Perry, Roy Emerson, Bjorn Borg.
Ice Hockey: Wayne Gretzky, Gordie Howe, Bobby Hull, Maurice Richard.
Track and Field: Jesse Owens, Harrison Dillard, Carl Lewis, Paavo Nurmi, Babe Didrikson, Gail Devers, Marion Jones.

Select a sport and nominate a player for a 300-word column that cites supporting data and the comments and observations of sports authorities.

Campus Projects

A. Coverage

Cover a game or a meet on campus. Give yourself 90 minutes to write the story after the game. If no game is available, cover one on television.

B. Professionals

Some universities are known to send athletes to professional teams. Southern California, Notre Dame and Miami, for example, have sent more than 100 of their football players to the National Football League, and Georgetown, Kentucky and North Carolina graduates have starred for the National Basketball Association.

Write a feature of 300 words about some of your school's athletes who have gone on to professional sports careers.

Community Projects

A. Fitness

Is the community aware of the need to provide facilities for residents who want to stay fit? Some communities have paths for walkers and bicyclists. Some have jogging areas, and some have set aside an area with equipment for aerobic exercises. Make a check of what is available and its use. Interview local doctors about what they consider the fitness level of local residents.

B. Prayers

Many teams hold prayer meetings before and after games. The federal courts have ruled against such public displays by tax-supported schools. Nevertheless, some schools continue the practice, especially high schools. In any games you attended or covered, if you noticed such activity write a feature story about the practice.

C. Referees

Thousands of referees of high school and youth sports activities have quit, reports the National Association of Sports Officials. The reason: misbehavior by parents and spectators, which some define as "sideline rage." The association says adult spectators yell, jeer, sometimes spit and brawl.

The result: Referees are quitting; new rules and regulations are in force. In Cleveland, coaches and parents are prohibited from yelling inappropriately during soccer games in a girls' league. In El Paso, before children can play in a city-sponsored youth program, parents must take a three and one-half hour class on appropriate fan behavior. Twenty-five state legislatures have considered bills that toughen penalties for attacks on referees.

The National Alliance for Youth Sports reports that 15 percent of youth games involve verbal or physical abuse from coaches or parents, a two-fold increase from five years before.

Despite free assault insurance to members of the Sports Officials organization, the association says many are quitting and there are areas in which the shortage of referees has caused problems in putting on games.

What is the situation in your community? Write 300 words.

Home Assignment

Background (2)

Identify the following:

1.   Manassa Mauler
2.   Michael Jordan
3.   Hank Aaron
4.   Ernie Davis
5.   Jackie Robinson
6.   Dizzy Dean
7.   Red Smith
8.   Branch Rickey
9.   Ted Williams
10. Robbie Davis

Class Discussion

Reds and Howard

Three of the most influential sports journalists of the last 50 years were Red Barber, Red Smith and Howard Cosell. Barber was an announcer for baseball teams around the country, and Smith was a sports writer for New York City newspapers. Cosell was a broadcaster best known for "Monday Night Football." Examine the files through a database search or through reference works for background on the three and prepare a summary of their attributes that modern sports writers might want to emulate.

They were noted for their fairness and integrity. Barber left his job as announcer for Dodger games when the team moved from Brooklyn to Los Angeles and the team owner urged Barber to lend vocal support to the team in his announcing. Later, when he was broadcasting Yankee games, he reported that the last place team had drawn a total of 413 fans for a game. The owners fired him for this embarrassing truth.

Smith always warned young sports writers never to root for the teams they covered, and he was a firm believer in keeping superlatives out of his copy. Cosell "entered sports broadcasting in the mid-1950s, when the predominant style was unabashed adulation," *The New York Times* said in its obituary of Cosell. "Mr. Cosell offered a brassy counterpoint that was first ridiculed, then copied until it became a dominant note of sports broadcasting."

None of these journalists exalted the sports they covered. "Sports is the toy department of human life," Cosell said.

Listen to local sports announcers, read local sports writers. Do they observe the rules Cosell, Red Smith and Red Barber followed in their work? Are these rules old-fashioned?

Skill Drill: Sports Vocabulary

Briefly define, describe, identify the following:

A. Baseball

1.   MVP
2.   Pinch runner
3.   Sacrifice fly

4. Save
5. Scratch hit
6. Texas leaguer

B. Basketball

1. Dunk shot
2. Give and go
3. NIT
4. Top of the key
5. Trailer
6. Zone defense

C. Football

1. Flanker
2. Flare out
3. Blitz
4. Sack
5. Tight end
6. Run and shoot

D. Golf

1. Eagle
2. PGA
3. Par-four hole
4. Slice

E. Hockey

1. Face off
2. High sticking
3. Icing
4. Red line
5. Sudden death

F. Soccer

1. Direct kick
2. Indirect kick
3. Goal kick
4. Yellow card
5. Trap

G. Tennis

1. Ace
2. Double fault
3. Mixed doubles
4. Passing shot

H. Thoroughbred Horse Racing

1. Claimer
2. Fractions
3. Maiden race
4. Stretch runner
5. Turf race

23 | Business Reporting

Local business is given major coverage.

Introduction

Business stories have become popular reading. Most people have a bank account, and many have a mortgage and debts to a bank and credit card company, own stocks and bonds, take part in a pension fund and either run or work for a business. Because of this wide audience, business coverage is now written in everyday language. Business reporters know how to translate the complexities of finances and economics into their consequences for the livelihood of working people. Because of the private nature of most business, reporters cultivate insiders for information for their stories.

Exercises

A. Stocks

You are to do a feature story on a club in Freeport that buys stocks. The members, 10 women who have been investing together for seven years, include four homemakers, two teachers, the manager of a local drugstore, a hairdresser and two secretaries. The club has invested about $100,000 to date, and its stocks have a market value of $162,000. All dividends have been put back into stock purchases. The women say their plan is to sell all the stock and divide the revenue in three years. Each member puts up $1,500 a year.

"This was a 10-year plan," says Mrs. Arlene Robbins, who acts as secretary of the group. "We've lost on some stocks and done well on others. We meet monthly at one of the member's homes and make a decision on buying and selling. The next meeting is Thursday at my place." You go to 65 Bismark St. to attend the meeting.

Seven of the women are there. One is ill and two are working late. The discussion is about whether to sell 1,000 shares of Goodyear and whether to buy 100 shares of Motorola, 100 shares of Gannett, 1,000 of J.C. Penney, and 100 of Texas Instruments.

The club makes its own decisions on buying and selling. Five of the women were assigned to study the stocks considered for purchase and the two others were asked to examine the merits of selling Goodyear and to report next month.

"We are doing well this year," says Mrs. Robbins. "But I am not so sure that we shouldn't consider looking at bonds as well as stocks. Let's think about that."

Mildred Bannister, 15 Hawthorne Drive, says that had the group gone into the bond market several years ago it would have done well. "The bonds were paying high interest rates to attract capital in a high-interest market situation," she said.

Alice Thomas, 56 Western Ave., cautions the women doing the checking on buying and selling to watch the yield- and price-to-earnings ratio and to report on them. She adds, "I wonder if the survivors of the dot-com shakeout are worth investigating."

You tell the city editor what you have and he suggests that you do some checking yourself so that you can give the current closing prices of the stocks they discussed. He adds, "Make sure you explain all the terms they used. Let's make this an educational feature. Add background about the clubs. I understand there are thousands of them in the country."

He tells you to write 350 to 500 words.

B. Occupancy

The Freeport Chamber of Commerce secretary, Fred Graham, tells you that the hotel occupancy rate is down. Last month, he says, 64 percent of all hotel rooms in the metropolitan area were occupied, compared with 67 percent a year ago and 82 percent three years ago, the best tourist year in the past decade.

Last month 50,300 rooms were filled. That's up slightly from last year's 49,100 but, because of the increase in the number of units available as the result of new construction, the percentage is down.

"Clearly, the people who are in the hotel business are not discouraged," Graham says. "A new hotel is going up downtown and another is in the planning stage."

You ask why present occupancy is so far down from the 82 percent. "First place, tourists aren't coming in the numbers they used to," he answers. "Also, the economy was better. Firms were out looking for business, and salesmen were on the go. Also, the area attracted a number of large conventions and annual meetings. Now, companies are not sending out the waves of salespeople they used to, and conventions are being held closer to the home office, or there are regional meetings." He adds, "We are optimistic. I predict that next year our occupancy rate will be in the 70s. You watch for it."

Write 150 words.

C. Reorganized

Atlas Equipment Associates of Freeport filed for bankruptcy a year ago. Today, it released a statement saying its board has given approval to a reorganization plan. Creditors have tentatively accepted the plan.

Under the plan, the company will be recapitalized with 45 percent of new stock going to National Corporation, which lent the company $1.5 million 10 months ago. The company has applied for a favorable tax ruling, and the plan depends on such a ruling. Other stock will be distributed: 5 percent to existing common shareholders, 7.5 percent to existing preferred stockholders, and 42.5 percent to the creditors. Atlas manufactures road-building equipment.

Write 125 words.

D. Layoff

The Exton Electric Co., a Freeport commercial cabinet manufacturing concern, says it is laying off 150 workers the first of next month. "Poor conditions in the housing market necessitate our cutting back," said Alexander Sanchez, president. "With housing starts in this area down 15 percent from last year, which was a bad year to begin with, we have fewer purchasers for our products." Exton had previously laid off 750 employees this year. Its total work force is 3,000. "I cannot say that this is the end of the layoffs," Sanchez said. "If the market picks up, we'll hire. Otherwise, we will be forced to continue to lay off workers."

Write 125 words.

E. Annual

The Baldwin Protection Systems Co., a Freeport industry that manufactures burglar alarms for vehicles, homes and industry, announced its earnings for last year:

	Last Year	Previous Year
Revenue	$4,073,421.00	$3,467,656.00
Net income	282,382.00	137,935.00
Share earns	.83	.34
Shares outstanding	340,422	400,070

Company president Felix Parrington—who founded the company 10 years ago after tinkering with alarms in his garage with a borrowed set of tools—said that the increase in income was the result of "a new sales force that is expanding our contacts with retail outlets." Baldwin products are sold over a four-state area. Parrington, who lives at 76 Roth Road, said he plans to have his alarm system sold nationally "within three years."

You check with local brokers and find that the stock is traded in the over-the-counter market and that the price per share has been around $10. The company has been conservative in its policies and has put most of its earnings back into the business. Last year, it paid a 20-cent dividend. The previous year, it was 10 cents. The broker said that the "increase in crime has been good for Baldwin. Parrington has some excellent patents, and the company clearly is a growth operation."

Write 200 words.

F. Digital

The Digital Equipment Corporation of Freeport issued its earnings report for the first fiscal quarter of the year. You know that there has been increased competition in the computer industry, which could explain the decline in Digital's earnings. You ask for some comments from business analysts and they say they think Digital did better than they had expected. "We were expecting a per-share income of 90 cents to $1 a share," said Paul Olsen, office equipment analyst at Burns & Allen Investment, Inc. Digital is the world's leading manufacturer of networked computer systems, those that can communicate with each other and share workloads and common databases. Write 150 words.

	This Year	Last Year
Revenue	$1,323,927,000	1,515,263,000
Net income	72,325,000	144,216,000
Share earns	1.20	2.45
Shares outstanding	63,927,102	59,164,197

Assignments

A. Imports

Interview dealers in domestic automobiles to see how imports have affected their business over the past year compared with the competition in previous years. Support the interview with data from automobile registrations by manufacturer, making annual comparisons for the last few years.

B. Pulse

Take the pulse and blood pressure of a variety of local businesses. Make a list of the points of measurement (gross revenues, net revenues, etc.) and use these as the vital signs of health or illness. Ascertain what elements have caused each business to be robust or ailing (location, competition, changes in taste, etc.).

C. Inventory

Make an inventory of government agencies—city, county, regional and federal—that are concerned with local business activities. Make a thumbnail sketch of the activities and powers of these agencies.

D. Authorities

Compile a list of the names of sources who can provide background for business news stories. For each authority, give the individual's credentials: position, background, area of competence.

E. Labor

How strong is organized labor in the community? Would you classify your community as pro-labor or anti-labor? First, devise ways of making this determination. One technique would be to see whether local industries have been organized by the major unions, whether industries have closed or open shops. The comments of labor leaders and local officials would be useful as well.

F. Market

Interview securities dealers to see how many people in your city invest in the stock market occasionally and how many buy and sell on a frequent basis. Try to interview individuals in each category. Why do they invest in stocks? How well have they done lately? What are some of their successful investments; some losers? If there is a local investment club, do a story on how it has fared.

G. Index

Three yardsticks of the economy are issued monthly by the government: consumer price index, wholesale price index and the index of leading economic indicators. Go to the reference library to obtain material for a story that traces the fluctuations in these indices over the past year. Do you discern some kind of trend or pattern? Can you link it to any major economic or political events?

H. Nonprofit

Do a profile of a nonprofit organization in the community. Examine the forms that it is required to file with the government and interview some of the organization's officials.

I. Open-Closed

Locate an open shop and a closed shop among the businesses in the city and compare them in terms of:

1. Reasons for status.
2. Salaries.
3. Worker satisfaction with the plan.
4. Owner's view of the situation.

J. Survey

Find out the going loan interest rates for home mortgages, automobiles, home improvement and for personal and business purchases. Compare these to the prime rate. Locate someone who has decided to take out a loan or not to borrow because of the rate, and personalize the piece.

K. Sharing

If there is a profit-sharing business or cooperative in town, do a historical profile of it. Find out who founded the business and why. How has the business fared? What do workers and management think of the arrangement?

L. Rent

Do a housing rental survey of the community. If you prefer to limit it to student rentals, fine. Find out about availability of rental units, going rental charges, quality of housing.

M. New Business

Interview the owner of a newly opened business. In your story, balance the financial aspect of the investment with the human interest detail that will personalize it. How much was borrowed? At what interest rate? How much of the person's savings were involved? What are the anticipated earnings? What does the owner's family think of the new business? Has the owner had any experience in the field? Does the business have any novel approaches? Remember, this is not a publicity puff but a careful examination of the facets of a new business.

N. Promotion

Locate a company official who recently has been promoted and write a profile, blending the person's business life with his or her personal background.

O. Execs

How many women are in executive positions in the city's major industries and businesses? Women constitute what percentage of the total number of executive positions? How recently have they been hired or promoted? What do they think of the status of women in business?

P. Construction

Obtain information on building permits over the last quarter, half year or year and compare it with previous periods. Interview people connected with the building trades. What is the overall situation?

Q. Prime

Localize the latest prime rate. Talk to bankers, officials of savings and loan associations, builders, automobile dealers and others to ascertain the local consequences. Put this latest figure in the context of the past several months and look for a trend.

R. Shares

Find a local company that has issued stock that is traded. It may not be listed on the New York Stock Exchange or other exchanges in your newspaper, but local brokers may trade it in the over-the-counter market. Trace the history of the stock: its price fluctuations, earnings, dividends, major stockholders. Interview company officials to determine whether they plan any new offerings or are trying to buy back stock.

S. Finance

How do local people or companies raise money to start a business? Ask some local business leaders, bankers, securities dealers.

T. Handouts

Many newspapers carry public relations releases in their food, business, fashion, real estate and travel sections. Does yours?

U. Broker

Many people invest in mutual funds offered by large investment companies. These funds are sold by brokers, who receive a commission on the funds they sell. A study has shown that brokers will push hardest the funds that give them the highest commission, regardless of the performance of the fund. Investigate this situation by interviewing local brokers and consulting sources of background material such as *Consumer Reports* and others that offer information to consumers about best buys.

V. History

Gather information for a feature on the history of business in your community. Some cities were created by the coming of the railroad, some by their natural or man-made harbors. Others were service centers to ranch and agricultural areas. In the photograph on the next page, an immigrant family does piece work for the garment trades, which centered in New York, that took advantage of newly arrived immigrants with few skills. The garment factories dispersed following World War II, and many are in the South now.

This photograph is by Lewis Hine, the great documentary photographer, who took photographs for the National Child Labor Committee from 1906 to 1918. Photos like this one in which a girl is shown helping her parents with the work led to a federal child labor law in 1916.

Campus Project

Market Basket

Do a market basket survey of groceries and supermarkets that students patronize. This list contains 39 items. You may want to add some. Reach general conclusions on the basis of your survey.

Item	Store A	Store B	Store C
Wonder Bread, 22 oz. package	_____	_____	_____
Kellogg's Corn Flakes, 12 oz. box	_____	_____	_____
Carolina Long Grain Rice, 3 lbs.	_____	_____	_____
Ronzoni Spaghetti, 1 lb., No. 8 strand	_____	_____	_____
Gold Medal Flour, 5 lbs. (bleached)	_____	_____	_____
Domino Sugar, 5 lb. package	_____	_____	_____
Nabisco Chocolate Chip Cookies, 19 oz. bag	_____	_____	_____

continued

An immigrant family in the garment trade

Item	Store A	Store B	Store C
Minute Maid Frozen Orange Juice, 12 oz. can	_____	_____	_____
Del Monte Canned Fruit Cocktail, 1 lb., 1 oz	_____	_____	_____
Birdseye Frozen Green Beans, 9 oz.	_____	_____	_____
Green Giant Canned Green Peas, 1 lb., 1 oz. package	_____	_____	_____
Campbell's Canned Vegetable Beef Stock Soup, 10 3/4 oz.	_____	_____	_____
Mazola brand Corn Oil, cooking oil, 24 oz.	_____	_____	_____
Del Monte Canned Corn, 1 lb., 1 oz.	_____	_____	_____
London Broil, 1 lb.	_____	_____	_____
Hamburger—ground round, 1 lb.	_____	_____	_____
Bacon—store brand, per lb.	_____	_____	_____

continued

Item	Store A	Store B	Store C
Oscar Mayer Bacon, 8 oz.	_____	_____	_____
Pork Chops, center cut, 1 lb.	_____	_____	_____
Perdue Whole Roasting Chicken, 1 lb.	_____	_____	_____
Frying chicken, cut up, no spec. brand, 1 lb.	_____	_____	_____
Chicken of the Sea Tuna in oil, chunk, 6 1/2 oz.	_____	_____	_____
Eggs, grade A large, 1 doz.	_____	_____	_____
Fleischman's Stick Margarine, 1 lb.	_____	_____	_____
Land O'Lakes Butter, stick, 1 lb.	_____	_____	_____
Whole milk, homogenized, 1 qt., list brand	_____	_____	_____
Skim milk, 1 qt., list brand	_____	_____	_____
Maxwell House Coffee, 13 oz. can	_____	_____	_____
Pepsi Cola, 6 pack, 12 oz. cans	_____	_____	_____
Taster's Choice instant regular coffee, 8 oz.	_____	_____	_____
Miller Beer, 6 pack, regular cans	_____	_____	_____
Tetley Tea, 48-bag package	_____	_____	_____
Red delicious apples, per lb.	_____	_____	_____
McIntosh apples, per lb.	_____	_____	_____
Bananas, medium size, 1 lb.	_____	_____	_____
Carrots, packaged, medium bunch	_____	_____	_____
Iceberg lettuce, per head	_____	_____	_____
Yellow onions, per lb.	_____	_____	_____
Potatoes, per lb. (Idaho, Maine, Long Island specified)	_____	_____	_____

Community Project

A. Broke

Visit the federal bankruptcy court and examine the filings. Select one that you think will make an interesting feature story. Interview the person who filed the report.

B. Savings

The business staff of your newspaper/broadcast station is planning a weekly feature, "Money Matters." For the first feature, your editor wants a piece on what various types of investments are paying in interest:

1. Bank savings accounts.
2. Certificates of deposit.
3. U.S. savings bonds.
4. Insured money market accounts.

He says he recently read an article that stated there is more than $1 trillion invested in the traditional passbook bank savings accounts, which are the lowest among safe investments.

Collect the various offerings of banks and savings and loan institutions and indicate their relative safety and the interest they pay.

C. Low Cost

At the turn of the century, many immigrants from Europe engaged in home labor. They were paid little and labored far into the night. Today, immigrants form another low-cost labor pool. Some care for lawns and gardens. Some, like those 100 years ago, work for the garment industry or labor in the fields. Is there a low-cost labor pool in your community? What is its makeup, what do the workers do, how much are they paid?

Home Assignment

A. Stocks

Check the performance so far this year of media stocks. Select a particular stock and consult the listings in today's newspaper for its current price and the year's high and low, dividend, yield and any other information the stock tables list. Make a study of the company's historical performance by examining evaluations of its earnings and other indexes of performance in a stock-rating publication such as *Value Line*.

Generally, newspaper stock prices were depressed in the early 1990s because of a falloff in advertising income and then made a comeback by the mid-1990s, only to fall again into 2002.

Write a 350-word piece on your stock.

B. Reading

List the publications a business reporter should read and some of the reference material the reporter should be familiar with.

Class Discussion

Puff

A store has an anniversary sale. A car dealership has been sold. A clothing store adds a new line of merchandise. Where is the line between free advertising and legitimate news? Draw some guidelines and apply them to the following summaries of press releases from local sources:

1. Jack A. Serge, manager of the Kmart Eastview store, today announced the opening of an expanded apparel section.
2. The Metropolitan Transit Authority today contracted to buy 25 specially designed buses from General Motors at a cost of $5 million.
3. The XYZ Repair Shop has opened in a new shopping center outside town and is having a lottery to give away a laptop computer tomorrow.
4. Wayne Miller, an employee of the Amidon Photo Exchange, is retiring after 35 years with the store.

5. Stacy Backman is being honored by the Allstate Insurance office in town for 25 years' service. She will be given a diamond pin at a dinner Friday night.

6. Robert Salmi, cashier at the First National Bank, has been promoted to assistant vice president in charge of credit.

7. Freeport Auto Repair announces new ownership. The business, located at 1273 Santa Fe St., has been purchased by the Morgantown Repairmen, a national car repair organization that has 15 other car repair shops in the state. The new owners plan to enlarge the shop and have purchased adjoining lots on each side of the current shop. The firm will have a work force of 19 mechanics when the new shop is built. Currently, 10 mechanics work for the auto repair shop.

8. The Gap Clothiers of Freeport announces its Fall sale. All clothing must be off the shelves by the end of the month. Reductions range from 25 to 75 percent on men's and women's clothing. Shoes are all 50 percent off.

The specials include 50 percent off on women's sweaters, including a line of cashmere sweaters that normally sell for $250. Also included in the 50 percent reduction are men's jackets and wool sweaters.

During the week-long sale that starts today, the store will remain open from 8 a.m. to 9 p.m.

All major credit cards are accepted, but an additional 10 percent deduction will be given for cash purchases. All purchases are final. There will be no returns accepted.

Skill Drill: Business and Labor Terms

Define these terms:

1. Bear
2. Board of directors
3. Bond
4. Chairman(-woman) of the board
5. Closed shop
6. Common stock
7. Insolvent
8. Liquidation
9. Municipal bond
10. Open shop
11. Prime rate
12. Proxy
13. Public/private company
14. Receiver
15. Stock split

24 Local Government and Education

Leslie Jean-Bart

'No new spending'—candidate's pledge.

Introduction

Cities are the custodians of public health, welfare and education. They collect our trash, regulate our traffic, tell us where we may and may not park and build and maintain our streets, schools and bridges. Reporters regularly check our caretakers to see what they are doing and how well they are doing it. A central indicator of the city's priorities is the budget, which establishes the ways the city collects and spends taxes and fees. Budgets are made in an arena in which competing interests vie for favor. Journalists cover the entire process, not just the final stage of budget adoption.

Exercises

A. Budget Talk

Last night you attended a city council meeting at which the city manager, Harold Born, submitted an idea for financing long-range construction that would avoid the issuance of bonds. Born also submitted three sets of tables regarding his proposed budget:

1. The total budget proposed for next year and the current year's budget (Table **A**).
2. A breakdown of the general operating fund, much of which is used for salaries of employees in the city's offices (Table **B**).
3. Itemization of the ad valorem tax (property tax) requirements that are included in the proposed budget. The total $821,175, will have to be raised from the tax levied on owners of real estate in Freeport through a mill levy (Table **C**).

You show the city editor your notes from the portion of the meeting that was concerned with the budget. Here are your notes:

Council members: Albert Fuentes, Bernard Garner, Fred E. Smith, Martin Davis and Marcia Gold.

Fuentes: "I think we owe thanks to Harold for the splendid job. I know he's spent considerable time working with department heads over the past few months, adjusting their needs to our realities."

Garner: "Right. This looks like a hold-tight budget, and I think we all like it. Except for one item, the one that says General Improvement in Lieu of Bonds."

Born: "Let me explain that. We need to put away money for what I project as a needed expansion of the sewage treatment plant and water lines. Also, we will have to lay out some new roads to the subdivision south sooner or later. I don't see anything immediate but I want to start building up a fund. That way we won't have to borrow and pay interest. Right now interest rates are way up and we are bonded close to our limit. Also, our debt service is high."

Smith: "But it adds to taxes, doesn't it?"

Born: "Yes, a few mills."

Davis: "So the taxpayer has to shoulder the burden."

Born: "Less, actually, than if you had to sell bonds."

(Excerpts continued on page 171.)

Table A

Current Year Expenditures	Funds	Proposed Expenditures
$ 576,945.00	General operating fund	$ 626,715.00
15,000.00	Cemetery	15,000.00
32,000.00	Improvements	24,207.00
500.00	Band	500.00
47,725.00	Library	53,210.00
15,000.00	Hospital	13,500.00
19,500.00	Firefighters' pension	19,500.00
16,500.00	Police officers' pension	16,500.00
2,500.00	Bindweed	2,500.00
20,560.00	Social Security	21,750.00
415,083.00	Debt service	497,648.00
0.00	General improvement (in lieu of bonds)	95,396.00
$1,161,313.00		$1,386,426.00

Current year mill levy: **$20,920**

Tangible assessed value of real property: **$31,798,794.** (Assessed valuation is 50% of market value. Average home has market value of **$90,000.**)

Funds raised from ad valorem taxes are supplemented by fees, licenses, fines, etc., and the total makes up the total expenditure.

Total indebtedness January: **$6,611,372.**

Current year property tax revenue: **$665,200.**

Table B

	Current Year	Proposed
City council	$ 3,815.00	$ 1,660.00
City manager	10,760.00	11,890.00
Planning and research	7,335.00	15,160.00
City clerk	10,375.00	10,170.00
Elections	10,150.00	2,595.00
City treas.–purch. agent	4,135.00	3,685.00
Building inspector	9,035.00	11,565.00
Buildings and grounds	34,445.00	26,055.00
Legal	7,650.00	8,350.00
Police court	3,675.00	3,875.00
Engineering	37,845.00	45,360.00
General overhead	8,295.00	14,400.00
Police department	122,400.00	125,665.00
Animal control	3,600.00	3,600.00
Parking meter	13,520.00	0.00
Fire department	123,350.00	133,995.00
Street department	107,250.00	103,350.00
Forestry	6,000.00	10,000.00
Street lights	18,200.00	19,480.00
Park department	23,510.00	39,700.00
Airport maintenance	2,100.00	6,160.00
Health department	9,500.00	10,000.00
Contingency appropriation	0.00	20,000.00
	$576,945.00	$626,715.00

Table C

Funds	Ad Valorem Tax Requirements
General operating	$330,275.00
Cemetery	7,545.00
General improvement	24,278.00
Band	448.00
Library	48,499.00
Hospital	11,730.00
Firefighters' pension	6,747.00
Police officers' pension	4,778.00
Bindweed	2,079.00
Social Security	4,288.00
Bond and interest	285,112.00
General improvement (in lieu of bonds)	95,396.00
Totals	$821,175.00

Gold: "Of course we all want to save money, but isn't there also a principle involved, of making the people who benefit from the services pay for them? I mean, why should present taxpayers pay for future benefits? Bonds are a much fairer way of assessing costs."

Davis: "I have a feeling that all of us are a bit gun-shy of that item, Harold."

Smith: "Yes, we can't add to taxes now. The home owner is absolutely strapped, with this and the school tax going up."

Garner: "Suppose we cut it out. How much do we save on the mill levy, Harold?"

Born: "I can figure that out in a few . . ."

Davis: "Don't bother now. Bring it in in two weeks when I think we're just going to go through the motions of adopting your budget without that item. Agreed?"

(Various nods and grunts of approval of Davis' statement.)

After reading these excerpts, the city editor says it seems certain the council will adopt the budget at the next meeting, after striking out the item for General improvement in lieu of bonds. He says that it appears to him that you can figure out the budget yourself because all the figures are available. You look at him, trying not to appear too perplexed. He senses your trouble and volunteers to take you step-by-step through the figures and to the story, which he says you should then be able to write by yourself.

First, he says, look at Table **A** and strike the item General improvement in lieu of bonds. Then refigure the proposed expenditures. He suggests you do that on your own and return with the total proposed budget for next year.

You go to your seat and do the figuring. No problem, really:

$$\begin{array}{r} \$1,386,426 \\ -95,396 \\ \hline \$1,291,030 \end{array}$$

As you are about to return to the editor, something strikes you. If you subtracted the same $95,396 figure from the total on Table **C** you would get the total ad valorem tax requirement. You know that this is the amount of money to be raised from the property tax.

So, on your own, you do that:

$$\begin{array}{r} \$821,175 \\ -95,396 \\ \hline \$725,779 \end{array}$$

That is a key figure. It is going to be the basis of the mill levy, you know. But you cannot recall how the levy is figured. You ask the city editor to tell you.

He says that if you multiply the total assessed valuation by the mill levy, you will get the funds raised from the property tax, also known as the mill levy.

This, you see, makes the following equation:

$$\text{Mill levy} \times \text{assessed valuation} = \text{total raised from the property tax}$$

You pick up the assessed valuation of the city's real estate from Table A and from Table C you take the total taxes needed from the property tax or mill levy:

$$\text{Mill levy} \times \$31,798,794 = \$725,779$$

Or, to put it in easy form for figuring out:

$$\text{Mill levy} = \frac{\$725,779}{\$31,798,794}$$

$$\text{Mill levy} = \$.0228241$$

That is 2.282 cents on the dollar, and because your city uses a mill levy on $1,000 assessed valuation, the tax levy on property is $22.82/$1,000 in assessed valuation.

You show this to your editor and he congratulates you and suggests you check it with the city manager. Born verifies your figures and confirms your feeling that the budget will be adopted at the next meeting without his item, which would have added three mills, or $3/$1,000 in property tax, he tells you.

Write a story of 750 or more words, quoting from the commission meeting.

B. School Board

The Pennsbury School Board met last night and adopted next year's budget by a vote of 5–1. The board had discussed the budget during the spring. This meeting took 10 minutes. Three board members were absent. You are to write 500 to 750 words from the following information:

The expenditures will total $21,743,000 as compared with $20,617,000 last year. The new budget will require a property tax of 108.5 mills, compared with 102.5 last year. When the school district first presented the budget to the board last spring, a 13.5 mill increase would have been necessary. Over the past several weeks, the board cut various items from the budget on its own and after public hearings.

Board member Francis Martin, the lone dissenter, said, "I'd like to save the taxpayer money. I'd like to see the athletic account back to where it was last year. I'd like to see more money taken out of the budget reserve to decrease the millage." He said the savings could be half a mill off the school tax.

Raymond Wiese, vice president of the board, opposed the suggestion. "I think if we did that we'd be cutting it pretty close. There are a number of factors that may hit us, like a wrong guess on heating and lighting costs. There's the unknown impact of children leaving nonpublic schools and the cost of transportation into New Jersey, especially if some of these schools start holding Saturday sessions."

Those voting to adopt the budget were Morris Feldman, president of the board; Wiese; William Gummere; George Littleton and Robert McKelvie.

Presume this is June 27, and next year's budget will take effect in the school year beginning in September. Tables **D, E** and **F** and Figures **1** and **2** are sheets from the budget you must consult for background for your story.

The average home in the Pennsbury School District is assessed at $30,000, but many people live in homes assessed at half that. Use both figures in your estimates of what the home owner will pay.

Of the total $21,743,000 budget, $15,140,421 will be raised through the property tax.

Table D
Proposed Budget for Next Year
Summary of Receipts

1. Anticipated balance (end of this year)	$ 540,000.00
2. Current taxes	15,571,421.00
3. Delinquent taxes	125,000.00
4. Other local sources	378,000.00
5. State sources	5,128,579.00
	$21,743,000.00

Table E
Budget Comparisons Pennsbury School District

	Actual Last Year	Actual Current Year	Anticipated Next Year
Classrooms	591	591	591
Schools	18	18	18
Students	13,292	*13,025	12,880
Classroom teachers	673	670	650
Specialists	32	30	30
Administrators	34	36	36
Guidance	28	28	28
Curriculum coordinators	9	10	10
Nurses	20	20	20
Total professional	**796**	**794**	**774**
Secretaries, clerks and supervisors	93½	89½	86
Bus drivers and bus maintenance	71	73	72
Custodians, whse., etc.	144½	144½	142
Cafeteria	141	141	139
Maintenance	28	30	29
Paraprofessionals			
Teacher aides	23	37	38
Transportation aides	10	10	9
Management assistants	4	4	4
Total noninstructional	**515**	**529**	**519**
Total employees	**1,311**	**1,323**	**1,293**
Students/classroom teacher	20.0	19.4	19.8
Students/noninstructional employee	26.2	24.6	24.8
Students/professional employee	16.9	16.4	16.7
Students/total employee	10.3	9.8	10.0

*Actual student enrollment as of March 1 this year.

Table F
Budget Comparisons Pennsbury School District

	Budget Current Year	Tentative Budget Next Year
Total budget	$20,617,000.00	$21,743,000.00
Number of students	*13,025	12,880
Decrease in students	†–(2.01)%	–(1.11)%
Increase in budget over last year's budget	9.28%	5.46%
Cost per student	$1,582.88	$1,688.11
Number of employees	1,323	1,293
Decrease or increase in employees	.91%	–(2.27)%
Total salaries	$14,166,733.68	$15,080,849.47
Increase in salaries	8.36%	6.45%
All other expenses	$6,450,266.32	$6,662,150.53
All other increases	14.53%	3.28%
Salaries cost per student	$1,087.66	$1,170.87
All other costs per student	$495.22	$517.24

*Actual student enrollment as of March 1 this year.

†Decrease from June last year average daily membership as of March 1 this year.

New Positions—Next Year

Account Number	Classification	Number
0218	Security Guard	1
0513	Mechanic	1

Figure 1

Source of Revenue

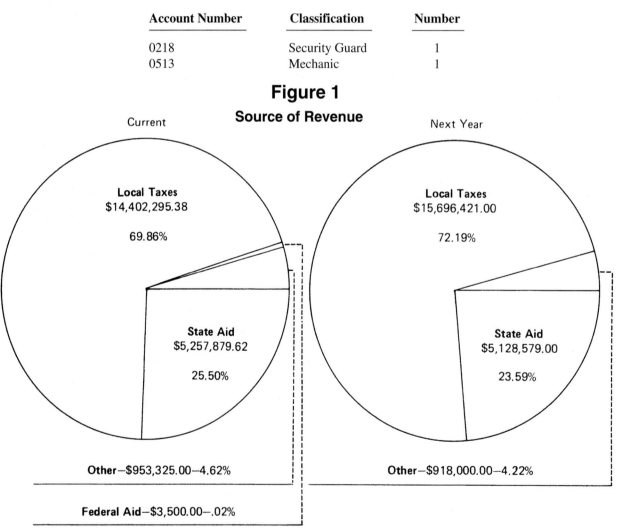

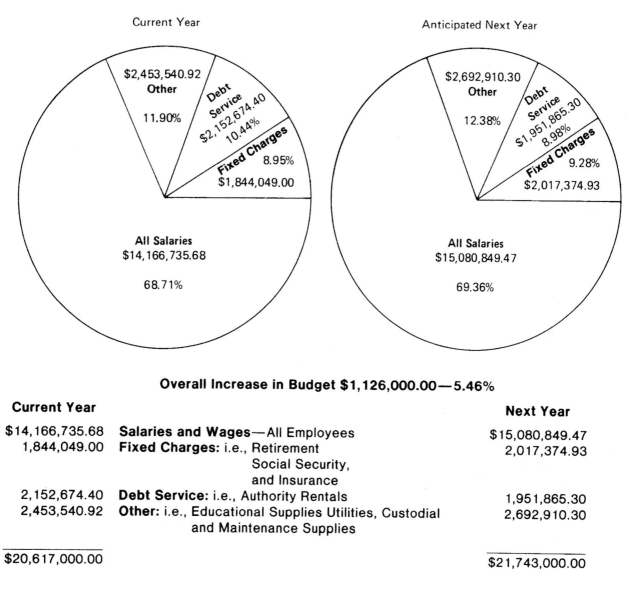

Figure 2
Distribution of Expenditures

Current Year

$2,453,540.92
Other
11.90%

Debt Service
$2,152,674.40
10.44%

Fixed Charges
8.95%
$1,844,049.00

All Salaries
$14,166,735.68

68.71%

Anticipated Next Year

$2,692,910.30
Other
12.38%

Debt Service
$1,951,865.30
8.98%

Fixed Charges
9.28%
$2,017,374.93

All Salaries
$15,080,849.47

69.36%

Overall Increase in Budget $1,126,000.00 — 5.46%

Current Year		Next Year
$14,166,735.68	**Salaries and Wages**—All Employees	$15,080,849.47
1,844,049.00	**Fixed Charges:** i.e., Retirement Social Security, and Insurance	2,017,374.93
2,152,674.40	**Debt Service:** i.e., Authority Rentals	1,951,865.30
2,453,540.92	**Other:** i.e., Educational Supplies Utilities, Custodial and Maintenance Supplies	2,692,910.30
$20,617,000.00		$21,743,000.00

C. Proposed

It is now April of the year following the budget adopted in **B. School Board.** The district superintendent of the Pennsbury School District, Ernest H. Mueller, last night submitted the school budget to the Pennsbury School Board for the coming year.

The proposed budget totals $24,168,000. A total of $18,413,449 will be raised from the property tax toward the total budget. This will necessitate a property tax of 130 mills, or $130/$1,000 in assessed valuation. You have the current year's budget totals (See **Exercises, B. School Board**) and you can compare the two.

From these comparisons and the pages taken from the proposed budget (Tables G, H and I and Figures 2, 3a, 3b and 4), write a 400- to 500-word story.

Memo

To: Pennsbury School Board
Fr: Ernest H. Mueller, District Superintendent

I hereby transmit to you the Pennsbury School District's tentative budget proposed for the next school year.

This document is the result of many hours of deliberation on the part of individual building staffs and central administration. Only through the cooperation and input of everyone concerned with the budget has it been possible to prioritize the district's needs and produce a budget that will provide those basic needs and still not overburden the tax-paying community.

We are fully aware of what burdens these fiscally difficult times placed upon the taxpayers, yet they, too, must be aware that the same inflationary escalations that affect their family and business budgets also seriously affect a school budget. Holding the total tentative budget increase to only 11.15% has required maximum efforts in all departments to make the necessary revisions and deletions without downgrading the quality of education in Pennsbury.

Since State Aid provided 23.59% of the revenue for the current budget but will provide only 18.45% for next year's budget, anyone can realize that an 11.15% increase is modest indeed. An uncontrollable fact is that the amount of receipts required from local sources has increased a full 10% in two years.

This next year 4.8 mills of the 21.5 mills required for the budget increase are a direct result of the decrease in state aid. Of the remaining 16.7 mills, 14.4 mills are required for Debt Service, Fixed Expenses and All Salaries. Only 2.28 mills of the increase go for educational supplies, utilities and custodial and maintenance supplies. This is a surprisingly low increase when one examines the real inflationary costs that affect all consumers today.

Accompanying this year's budget is the board's adopted Goals and Objectives for next year, including the financial impact that it has on the proposed budget; therefore, it is possible for the board and the community to observe that any increases, no matter how slight, are a direct result of educational commitments on the part of the board, administration, staff and community.

Since the administration and the staff, through many meetings and deliberations, have been able to effect a $418,638 (almost three full mills) reduction in the budget as it was originally drawn up, there remains little opportunity for further reductions. My staff and I, however, will stand ready to exert maximum effort to comply with the board's wishes. What we ask is that we be permitted to continue offering the kind and quality of education that the Pennsbury community needs and desires.

Table G
Proposed Budget Next Year
Summary of Receipts

1. Anticipated balance July 1	$ 356,000.00
2. Current taxes	18,785,449.00
3. Delinquent taxes	200,000.00
4. Other local sources	367,000.00
5. State sources	4,459,551.00
	$24,168,000.00

Table H
Budget Comparisons Pennsbury School District

	Actual Last Year	Actual This Year	Tentative Next Year
Classrooms	591	591	591
Schools	18	18	18
Students	13,025	*12,777	12,500
Classroom teachers	670	655	656
Specialists	30	30	31
Administrators	36	36	35
Guidance	28	28	28
Curriculum coordinators	10	10	9
Nurses	20	20	20
Total professional	**794**	**779**	**779**
Secretaries, clerks and supervisors	89½	86	88
Bus drivers and bus maintenance	73	72	72
Custodians, whse., etc.	144½	142	143
Cafeteria	141	140	140
Maintenance	30	29	32
Paraprofessionals			
Teacher aides	37	38	39
Transportation aides	10	9	9
Management asst's.	4	4	4
Total noninstructional	**529**	**520**	**527**
Total employees	**1,323**	**1,299**	**1,306**
Students/classroom teacher	19.4	19.5	19.1
Students/noninstructional employee	24.4	24.5	23.7
Students/professional employee	16.4	16.4	16.0
Students/total employee	9.8	9.8	9.6

*Actual student enrollment as of March 1 this year.

Table I
Budget Comparisons Pennsbury School District

	Budget Current Year	Tentative Budget Next Year
Total budget	$21,743,000.00	$24,168,000.00
Number of students	*12,777	12,500
Decrease in students	†–(1.41)%	–(2.17)%
Increase in budget over last year's budget	5.46%	11.15%
Cost per student	$1,701.73	$1,933.44
Number of employees	1,299	1,306
Decrease or increase in employees	–(1.81)%	.54%
Total salaries	$15,080,849.47	$16,053,305.16
Increase in salaries	6.45%	6.45%
All other expenses	$6,662,150.53	$8,114,694.84
All other increases	3.28%	21.80%
Salaries cost per student	$1,180.31	$1,284.26
All other costs per student	$521.42	$649.18

*Actual student enrollment as of March 1 this year.
†Decrease from June last year to March 1 this year.

Figure 3(a)

Source of Revenue

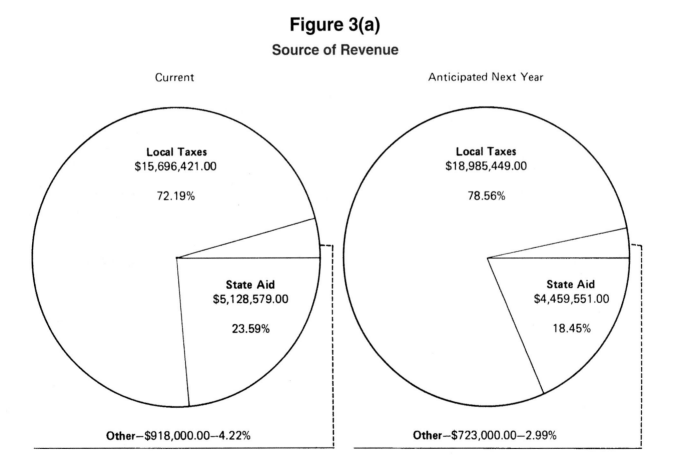

178

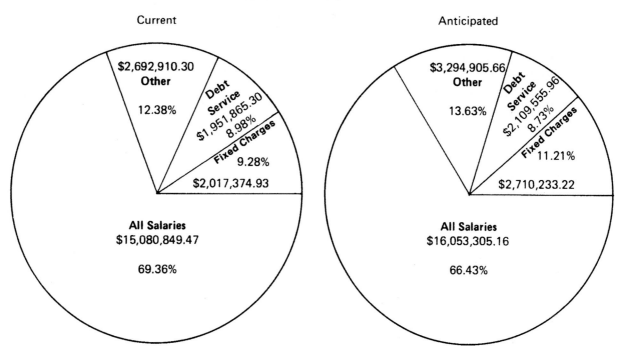

Figure 3(b)

Distribution of Expenditures

Current

$2,692,910.30
Other

12.38%

Debt Service
$1,951,865.30
8.98%

Fixed Charges
9.28%
$2,017,374.93

All Salaries
$15,080,849.47

69.36%

Anticipated

$3,294,905.66
Other

13.63%

Debt Service
$2,109,555.96
8.73%

Fixed Charges
11.21%
$2,710,233.22

All Salaries
$16,053,305.16

66.43%

Figure 4
Overall Increase in Budget $2,425,000.00—11.15%

Current Year		Next Year
$15,080,849.47	**Salaries and Wages—All Employees**	$16,053,305.16
2,017,374.93	**Fixed Charges:** i.e., Retirement, Social Security, and Insurance	2,710,233.22
1,951,865.30	**Debt Service:** i.e., Authority Rentals	2,109,555.96
2,692,910.30	**Other:** i.e., Educational Supplies, Utilities, Custodial, and Maintenance Supplies	3,294,905.66
$21,743,000.00		$24,168,000.00

Assignments

A. Constituencies

There are five major sources of news on local government finances. The organizations in these groupings have varied interests in how much the city spends and where the expenditures are directed, and they are concerned about how revenues are gathered. The groups are:

1. **Government:** the various departments, agencies, bureaus, their directors and employees.
2. **Money-providing constituencies:** the chamber of commerce, local real estate groups, property-owners associations, taxpayer and merchant groups, banks, state and federal governments.
3. **Service-demanding groups:** organized groups seeking such city services as welfare, health care, police and fire protection.
4. **Organized bureaucracies:** public employees, municipal unions, retirement fund manager.
5. **Independent groups:** League of Women Voters, various municipal information organizations.

List the people you would seek out for information about their groups' reactions to the present budget. Interview these sources about their priorities in the budget.

B. Bonds

Cities, counties, school districts and special assessment districts finance major construction by selling bonds. Examine the bonding situation of one of these governmental units and discover:

1. The plans, if any, for new construction; the anticipated interest rate; the value of the bonds.
2. The interest rate on the last bond issue sold.
3. The rating of the unit's borrowing health by one of the rating services (Moody's Investors Service Inc., Standard & Poor's Corp. and Fitch Investors Service Inc.)
4. Taxpayer reaction to issuance of bonds in the past.

C. Schools

At what level in the budget-making process is the local school district? Write a story on what has been accomplished and what remains to be done. Keep an eye on actual or anticipated major changes from the current budget.

D. Record Keeping

Go to the office of the city clerk (or the county clerk, if appropriate) and ask for the previous month's (or quarter's or year's) records for the following: marriage licenses, births, divorces, deaths, building permits, trust deeds, real estate transfers. Write a story comparing them with a comparable period one year earlier and five years earlier.

E. Business

Business conditions directly affect the city's finances. Look into a new business. One way to check on new businesses in the community is through the telephone company, which often makes available new business telephone listings. Interview the owner of a new business about plans, number of people to be hired, reason the business opened, the services to be offered, the owner's background. What are the owner's reactions to the local tax structure?

F. Data

Some journalists have done stories that show a correlation between income and employment and such factors as crime, delinquency, truancy and poor health. Where income and employment are low, deviant behavior is above average for the city, these stories indicate.

If your city has clearly identifiable income areas and you can isolate data for other factors in these areas, you can do similar stories. If the data clearly indicate relationships, you should check your findings with local officials and with authorities on the subjects on the campus and elsewhere. These sources may assist you in interpreting your findings.

Some of the basic data you will need follow:

1. **Unemployment:** Unemployment by age group, race, ethnic background.
2. **Health:** Fetal deaths, infant mortality, early infancy diseases, tuberculosis, drug-related deaths, suicide.
3. **Crime:** Rates and totals for homicide, rape, assault, robbery.
4. **Education:** Absences, truancies, percentage of students graduating from high school, percentage going to college.

The Census Bureau has material on population density, housing quality and the racial and ethnic composition of the areas under study.

G. Process

Here is a story that appeared in a local newspaper. Write a similar story for your community, or select a stage in the current budget and emphasize that in your story.

City Budget to Start

The first of many steps in compiling data for next year's city budget will start next week, City Manager Eric Turner said today. But the process of financing next year's city operations will not be finished until late in the summer.

"Next week, we will give budget request forms to all our city department heads," Turner said. "They then will have until about June 15 to compile all the programs they wish included in their operations, along with a 'narrative' telling why the programs are justified."

Past Budgets Studied

The department heads must look at last year's budget, the current budget, amounts spent during the first four months of this year and numerous other figures in order to arrive at next year's needs.

"We also have to re-evaluate the remainder of the current year's budget, in light of expenditures during the first four months," Turner pointed out. He explained that some departments may have had an expense in one phase of their operations that was greater than anticipated. But since the budget is fixed, other operations must be curtailed, or costs cut elsewhere, so that the year's total expenses will remain within the allowable total.

"On about June 15, I'll begin meeting with the department heads to work out the various details of the budget and to put all the requests into one balanced program," Turner said. "We won't take any phase of the budget to the city commission for approval until all proposals are laid out in detail."

Figures Translated

From July 1–15, Turner must translate the budget "figures" into "words," he said. He will compile a "narrative," or word explanation, of each number and need of the overall budget. This narrative will accompany budget requests submitted to the commission.

"I hope to get the narrative finished and to the commission by July 16. But this really is rushing things," he added. The complete budget is about 100 pages long. The commissioners then will have until approximately the end of July to study the proposals.

Moving on into the next phase of the operation, the city commission will meet in a lengthy session and go through all the proposals an item at a time. From this they will arrive at a final budget figure for each operation.

Following a public hearing, at which various items can be lowered but not raised, the commissioners will pass an ordinance levying the taxes to finance next year's city operations.

Budget Figures

Last year, the commission budgeted $2,621,315, of which $1,441,723 was to be raised from property taxes. These taxes, based on the assessed valuation of property, were based on a 19.89 mill levy, or $19.89 for each $1,000 property valuation. The total assessed valuation was $72,500,000.

Turner said that for the last several months, the various department heads have been listing ideas of how to increase their particular budget or to introduce new department programs at a minimum increase in expenditures.

"If they have a new program they feel is justified, they are asked to translate the money needs into a narrative. Additional equipment often can lessen one particular department cost and eventually reduce the overall department expenditures," Turner said.

He pointed out how one new machine may release manpower to be used elsewhere, where it actually is needed more. This makes it possible for a department to avoid hiring more manpower and the new machine "pays for itself within a short time because of this."

H. Records

Make a list of the following over the past 24 hours: fire calls, crime reports, arrests, hospital admissions and discharges, motor vehicle accident reports, births, deaths, marriage licenses issued, business licenses issued, property sales and transfers.

1. Indicate where and from whom such information is available.
2. Include enough information to help an editor decide which items are newsworthy. Indicate why items are worth stories.
3. Select one newsworthy item and write a story.

I. Assessments

Interview the county assessor and obtain a breakdown of assessed valuation of real and personal property for the current year. Any overall changes from the past year? Any changes in assessments of major property? Ask for the property tax rate; has that changed? Has there been an unusual number of complaints about assessments or has it been a quiet year? Obtain figures on tax-exempt property and list them if you think they might be interesting.

J. Licensing

State licensing boards decide who can practice medicine, cut hair, build and sell houses, bury the dead. Every state has such boards, some as many as 40, some as few as 10. Their purpose is to establish and enforce standards of professional competence and ethics, but many are criticized as self-serving. Write 300 to 400 words on one state licensing board. Cover the following areas:

1. How are the members appointed? Who recommends, clears, makes the appointments? How powerful is the influence in the appointment process of the trade or professional group that is being regulated?
2. What are some of the board's most recent actions?
3. Has the board been accused of practicing restrictive and exclusionary practices to cater to special interest groups?
4. How does one become licensed by the board to practice? Does it give tests, interviews? How many applicants were there for licenses and how many licenses were granted?

K. Assistance

Using a map of the city divided into districts, chart the changes in the number of people receiving welfare assistance. Gather data for the last year for which figures are available and for the previous 5 and 10 years. Are there any factors that led to the changes in numbers on welfare rolls? Have there been problems in cutting off people?

L. Vigilant

> I think we should be walking through the jungle listening for odd noises and reporting exactly what we see and hear—and be wary and vigilant.
> —Mary McGrory (on the job of the reporter covering public affairs)

Select an office, department, bureau or agency of local government and obtain answers from officials and townspeople to these questions and others you may devise:

1. What is the function of the office? What is its budget allocation, number of employees, current major projects?
2. Is the function necessary to meet public demands and needs?
3. Is the office functioning at optimum level in the opinion of its head or director, the second-in-command, some of the career employees and the newer employees?

Write a story of about 600 words based on your findings.

M. Education

Here are some assignments on education:

Majors: Survey a group of high school seniors or incoming college freshmen to see what subjects they intend to major in. One of the fastest-growing majors is business, going from about 10 percent of incoming freshmen in the 1970s to 24 percent 25 years later. Language majors dropped to 1 percent, history to 1.8 percent. Compare these national figures with your findings.

Z. Air

The I
"unhealth:

Denver
Las Vegas
Los Angel
New York
Phoenix
Portland, (
Salt Lake
Seattle

Find (
major citie
Write

Campu:

A. Right-

On a :
shocked to
of campus
Are th
and report

B. Grade

A deba
Alan Wolfe

. .
among
during (
Colleag

Devise
grade inflat

Commu

A. Status

The bu
groups, resi
those invol\
priate peopl
city official
ber of comr

1. Is the
   taxes to I
   a. A
      an
   b. A
2. What
3. Will a

Textbooks: Bias, prejudice and discrimination have been found in high school textbooks. Make a check of textbooks in various fields: U.S. history—how Native Americans are treated, whether attention is paid to black and Hispanic contributions, adequate treatment of women; biology—adequate treatment of evolution, inclusion of women scientists, adequate discussion of venereal diseases; world history—adequate treatment of Holocaust, Judaism, and other religions, suffrage, imperialism and the slave trade, Latin America, Africa and Asia. Any attacks on textbooks in use or proposed?

Movement: Are job and educational opportunities luring high school and college graduates to other states?

Accountability: How well are schoolchildren taught, and how well do they perform? Can you and your colleagues make a list of criteria to be used as the basis for reporting the effectiveness of the educational system?

One measure is how well students do on national tests such as the Scholastic Aptitude Test. For grade school children, there are standardized tests, such as the National Assessment of Educational Progress (NAEP) examinations. Another measure could be the percentage of freshman students who graduate from high school or the percentage of graduating seniors who go on to college.

Homework: Another way of looking at educational effectiveness is to examine what is being done in the classroom. How much homework is assigned daily? Give some examples of the homework assigned in English, history and arithmetic classes. What are students assigned to read in junior and senior high school English classes? How many compositions, essays, reports are they asked to write?

Do students think they have enough, too much, too little homework? What do their parents think?

Curriculum: Interview teachers about their suggestions for basic changes in the curriculum. How do their opinions differ from those held by principals and the schools' superintendent?

Math: A fourth of the students in the country could not multiply 671 by 402 and get the correct answer, 269,742. Of all 13-year-olds, a third could not do the multiplication. Fewer than half of all the teen-agers tested could figure out the area of a square given the length of one side. Draw a mathematical profile of students in local high schools. Look at the SAT scores for mathematics over the last few years and compare them to SAT figures for 10 and 15 years ago. Interview mathematics teachers and high school students.

Bright: Examine the college yearbook of 10 years ago and read news stories about graduation. Select three to five of the students considered the brightest. Where are they now? Interview them, friends, associates.

N. Comparison

Here are data that an education reporter gathered for an article comparing two adjacent cities in terms of the quality of education. List the questions you would ask at each school for a story.

	Spencer	Ruston
Per-capita income	$26,660	$45,051
Residents 25 or over with 4 years or more of college	12.5%	45.7%
Graduates attending college	50%	78%
Average SAT score	871	1,021
Percentage taking test	48%	80%
Percentage of teachers with master's degrees	21.6%	84%
Per-pupil spending	$3,848	$5,691
Median teacher's salary	$26,160	$43,820
Enrollment	993	2,362
Student/teacher ratio	13.8:1	11:1

O. Zoning

Attend a meeting of the planning and zoning body and cover a single request that seems to you to be worth following up with interviews. Use this as an example of the problems the community faces in planning.

P. Land Use

Develop a feature story on the land use design for the city and surrounding areas. What are the latest developments? Anything unforeseen when the plan was made? Any people opposing its development?

Q. Developers

Interview real estate developers and others to obtain some sense of where they think the next major moves of residential and commercial development will occur.

The New York Times v. Sullivan
Rosenbloom v. Metromedia
Wolston v. Reader's Digest

Privacy

Time, Inc. v. Hill

Search

Zurcher v. Stanford Daily

D. Yearbook

In 1995, two students at Kentucky State University, Charles Kincaid and Capri Coffer, sued the university for refusing to distribute the 1993–94 yearbook, *The Thorobred*. A vice president, Betty Gibson, had decided that the yearbook contents were unsuitable, that as a university publication it did not properly portray KSU.

The students contended that their First Amendment rights had been violated and that the university had broken its contract with students since their $80 activity fee covered the yearbook.

In 1997, a federal district court ruled in favor of the university administration. Under the *Hazelwood* decision, the judge found, yearbooks cannot be considered public or limited public forums, which do have First Amendment protection. The case is *Kincaid v. Gibson.*

The students appealed. One of their contentions was that *Hazelwood* applied only to high schools. The university replied that the yearbook "is not a forum held open to the public—or even the student body—for 'communicating thoughts' or 'discussing public questions.' "

A panel of three appellate judges in the Sixth Circuit heard the appeal in 1999, and the full court reached a decision in 2001. Pick up the case at the appellate level by examining these decisions and write a 300- to 450-word story as though the final decision were reached today.

> 191 F3d 719 (1999)
> 197 F3d 828 (1999)
> 236 F3d 342 (2001)

E. Ad Policy

Since 1991, a Holocaust denial organization headed by Bradley Smith has been placing ads in college newspapers. It gave up trying to place them in commercial newspapers, but it has had success with the college press. Within the last few years, the *Daily Aztec* at San Diego State University, the *Spectator* at Valdosta State University in Georgia and the *University Chronicle* at St. Cloud State University in Minnesota, among others, have run the Holocaust denial advertisements. In a recent year, 90 college newspapers accepted Smith's money to run his ads.

Some newspapers also carry liquor and tobacco ads.

What is the policy on advertising adopted by your campus newspaper? For background on advertising policies consult the Student Press Law Center, www.splc.org.

Has the newspaper had any complaints about its advertising, made any changes in its policies?

Write 250 to 350 words.

Campus Project

Suppression?

How free are your campus publications—the yearbook, the student newspaper, student pamphlets? Does the adviser to student publications exercise a strong hand in content? Have there been any incidents in which student expression was curtailed?

Community Projects

A. Teeth

Many schools have made financial arrangements with soft drink companies to install soda machines in the schools. School administrators say this arrangement provides much-needed money, but some parents object to the implicit encouragement their children are given to drink sodas. Some children drink six to eight cans a day, parent groups have determined.

What is the situation in your community? Has the local dental association or the American Dental Association taken a position on the situation?

B. Tracking

Ask members of your congressional delegation about a bill one of them has introduced in this session. during the semester, and at specific intervals write about it. You might want to select a controversial piece that you can obtain comments about it from constituents and officials.

Home Assignment

Plus and Minus

The textbook lists the wide-ranging freedoms for the media and the limitations the law imposes on journalists. List that you consider most important to the working journalist.

Class Discussion

A. Con Artist

You are covering the federal district court and drop in to talk to Herbert N. Kaplan, an assistant U.S. attorney. He tells you about a case involving John DeLuria, 68, last known address in New York City:

> DeLuria was born in Portugal and has a criminal record going back to 1944, when he was arrested for shoplifting in Philadelphia. He got off on that one and from most of the other charges, which include larceny, vagrancy, taking money under false pretenses, concealing leased property, fraud by wire, conspiracy. His latest caper was to convince businessmen to invest in a portfolio of stock that supposedly included blue-chip securities. Some men went in for as much as $200,000. The stock was offered through a New York firm known as Kimberly Beers Ltd., which DeLuria and his associates claimed was affiliated with DeBeers Consolidated Mines Ltd., of Kimberly, South Africa, the big diamond concern.
>
> At least 40 victims were involved, and $750,000 in losses have been accounted for, but more losses are suspected. DeLuria was granted U.S. citizenship in 1959 despite government efforts to deport him. His record shows he served a two-year sentence in Lewisburg, Pa., beginning in 1970 for fraud and since then was sent to prison four times for various offenses.
>
> DeLuria has had some interesting accomplices, one of whom served a brief prison term for participating in a $20 million religious fraud in the early 1970s. This was the Baptist Foundation of America caper.
>
> DeLuria is an old hand at taking money from people, a typical white-collar criminal with a smooth line who steals from those who have a little larceny in their hearts themselves. We know how he operates. He claims to have inside contacts, especially with a couple of local politicians, including the congressman from this district. Maybe he does. When he got citizenship in 1959, the congressman in office then wrote letters for DeLuria to the immigration people. You want to know how he operates, talk to Benjamin Fields, owner of the North Funeral Home, who invested and lost $185,000. We're looking into Fields' income taxes, for that matter.

What would you do with this information under each of the following circumstances?

1. DeLuria was arrested last night on charges of securities violations in connection with the Kimberly Beers Ltd. stock sales.
2. DeLuria has been found guilty of securities violations in connection with Kimberly and is awaiting sentence.
3. DeLuria has been sentenced to 10 years in prison by Federal Judge Charles E. Stuart.
4. A warrant has been issued for DeLuria's arrest for securities violations.

B. Names

Presume that your state legislature is considering a bill that would make it a crime to publicize the name of a rape victim. The present law prohibits the police or other public officials from disclosing the names of rape victims, but the law contains no sanctions against news organizations that do so.

The proposed law would punish journalists with a jail sentence of up to six months and a fine of $1,000 for identifying a rape victim without the victim's permission.

The bill has aroused a debate between those who support it on the basis of protecting the victim's privacy and those who say it would compromise press freedom. The sponsor concedes that "it is a tough issue, but the victim's right to privacy overrides the right to a free press.

"Freedom to publish is often the only thing that stands between freedom and tyranny. But there is a right to privacy that was upheld in *Roe vs. Wade*. Simply because a person is raped doesn't mean that right is surrendered."

He cited the case of William Kennedy Smith, a nephew of Sen. Edward M. Kennedy, who was accused of raping a woman. The alleged victim was first identified by tabloid newspapers and then by NBC News. The day after NBC made the identification, *The New York Times* and other newspapers also identified her.

as wrong," the sponsor said. "A survey shows that women say their fear of being humiliated by having the fact /aped becoming known is second only to the fear of contracting AIDS."

onents of the bill say that it is unnecessary because the present law is sufficient. The state press association stated, / an infringement on our First Amendment rights and as such is unconstitutional. As a matter of practice, virtually all /apers voluntarily shield the identities of rape victims." The Washington State Supreme Court held unconstitutional a / law that prohibited the disclosure of the identity of child victims of sexual assault.

Take a position and support it with background material you obtain from the library through a database search or other search.

Skill Drill: Libel and Privacy

How would you handle the following material? Give reasons for your decisions:

1. An out-of-state congressman who is campaigning for the Democratic candidate for Congress in your district says at a local campaign rally that the Republican candidate is "a failed businessman, unable to make a living, looking for the soft cushion."

2. A witness in a murder trial says the police beat her when they arrived at the scene of a killing. She says in her testimony that one of the two policemen was black. (The record of the incident contains the names of the two patrolmen. You know them. They are white.)

3. A city councilman states at a council meeting that he has been offered a bribe by a local contractor, Jeff Chang, owner of Chang & Sons.

4. A state legislator's monthly newsletter carries an article by the legislator stating that an architect, Bernard McDonnell, hired as a consultant for expansion of the state Supreme Court Building, is a gross incompetent and barely passed his state licensing examination.

5. The district attorney tells you he will file charges tomorrow against a teacher who, a student asserts, sexually molested her.

6. A grand jury reports that four local attorneys are part of an interstate baby-for-sale operation that nets $1 million a year. The four attorneys are named.

7. You have conducted a lengthy interview with a famous rock star who is in town for a concert. You have heard rumors that recently he was released from an expensive German clinic that specializes in narcotic rehabilitation. He refuses to comment on it, but you know he was out of circulation for three months, and a national publication made a veiled reference to his cocaine addiction.

8. The attorney general tells you that a candidate for the state supreme court fathered an illegitimate daughter 30 years ago and supported her for 21 years until her marriage. You cannot quote him, but it is in the candidate's files the local bar association has, he says.

9. A man testifying before a state legislative committee in favor of medical payments to indigent women seeking abortions, you learn, served 30 days in jail for "reckless endangerment" in connection with an abortion that he supposedly helped perform 15 years ago.

10. A man, accused of possession of a large amount of heroin, is being defended by a lawyer whose clients include men accused and convicted of drug possession and sales, vice operations and gambling in a tri-state area and worthless securities sales. He is known among lawyers around the state as "the Mafia's man." Can you identify him this way in a story?

The Library of Congress

Too strong for a black history feature?

Introduction

What constitutes acceptable language and subject matter for the journalist cannot be precisely defined. What was taboo yesterday has become commonplace today. Definitions of acceptability vary with the nature of the medium, the audience and the status of the individuals involved. National magazines feel free to explore the limits of acceptable taste, whereas newspapers and commercial broadcasting are more susceptible to pressures from organized groups. Television is regulated by the Federal Communications Commission, which sets standards.

Exercises

A. Questionable

Your instructor will make available to you material from events that included frank language and explicit detail on sexual matters. You are to write news stories for:

1. A newspaper of 15,000 circulation in a Kansas agricultural community.
2. A radio station in Chicago.
3. A metropolitan daily newspaper.

B. Demographics

You receive a release from the mayor's office that includes data based on studies made by various city agencies. Your editor has examined the material and tells you to do a story that "makes some logical sense out of these figures." He says the mayor's statement should be helpful.

The statement says in part:

> The figures on income and unemployment indicate trouble spots for our community. Clearly, we have to do something about these factors because the consequences can be chilling for community life.
>
> In our country, problems of race and class are serious. We can see that they have come to Freeport.

You call around and learn that one of the "consequences" has been a record crime increase in districts 4 and 5, with felonies last year rising 18 percent in district 4 and 22 percent in district 5.

You check with the mayor's office and are told by an aide, "Mayor Sam Parnass says that increased crime in districts 4 and 5 is one of the consequences he was referring to."

You have no time to check further. (A map of the city districts is on the next page. A demographic profile of Freeport is on page 197.)

Write a 350- to 500-word story based on the data and the mayor's statement.

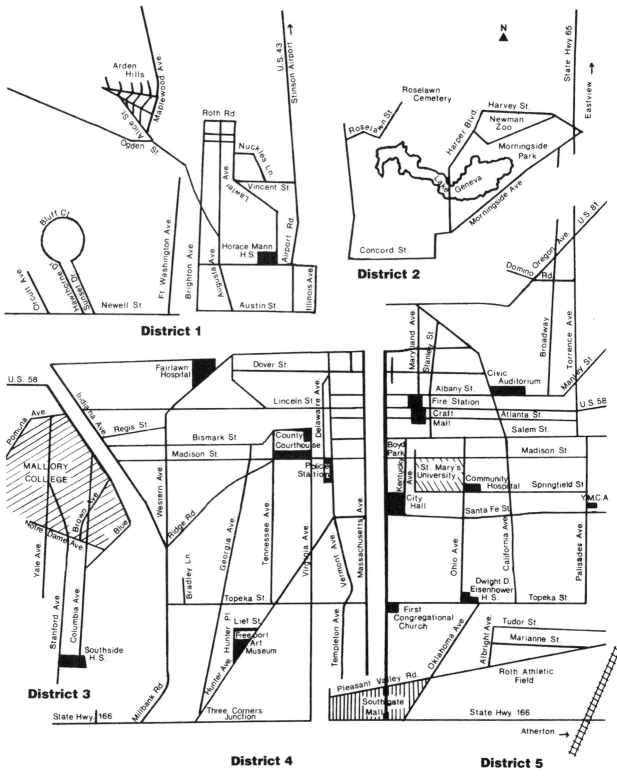

Freeport Districts

Freeport Demographic Profile

District	Percent of Total Families with Female Householders, No Husband Present	Percent with 12 Years or More of Schooling	Mean Household Income	Percent of Total Population in the District That Is Minority	Percent of Total Labor Force Unemployed
1	14.7	53.3	$36,842	18.5	6.3
2	10.8	88.8	$59,113	12.4	4.1
3	11.5	64.5	$47,406	21.7	4.9
4	31.6	43.6	$16,327	37.6	13.4
5	41.2	41.4	$11,669	56.3	17.8
City	19.4	53.5	$24,895	26.6	8.4

District	No. of Reported Felonies	Homicide Rate	Robbery Rate	Burglary Rate	Rape Rate
1	1,922	16.8	117.1	1,566.9	6.9
2	2,612	3.0	142.6	1,485.3	20.8
3	2,533	20.2	224.8	1,333.8	16.7
4	2,956	38.3	244.9	1,876.2	133.5
5	3,297	45.7	276.9	2,002.8	78.3
City	13,320	20.9	258.6	1,592.3	38.7

Assignment

Chitchat

Handle this assignment with the technique of unobtrusive observation. (See Chapter 11 in the textbook for a definition and examples.) Visit a high school cafeteria or a luncheonette where students eat or visit a student hangout. Report verbatim what students are talking about, what subjects occupy them. Write the story precisely as you heard it. Discuss in class whether you can use some of the language and subject matter for the local newspaper or radio station.

Campus Project

Kit

A number of colleges present college freshmen with an orientation kit. At some schools, the kit consists of pamphlets and booklets. Others are more generous, or more imaginative:

    Loyola Marymount University, Los Angeles—A beeper.
    Reed College—A copy of Homer's *The Iliad,* which they are expected to read at once.
    Oberlin College—A CD-ROM of the college's art museum; a 10-minute long distance phone card; a coupon for a pint of Ben and Jerry's ice cream.
    Hampshire College—Packets on good eating, healthy living and safe sex, with a condom.
    Loyola University, Chicago—An invitation to buy for $5 a goldfish, tank, food and gravel. "It's nice for them to have something to take care of," says an administrator.

What does your school give freshmen? What would they like? Interview freshmen, sophomores, juniors and seniors.

Community Project

Sex Education

Teen-age pregnancies are at all-time highs in some cities, and the incidence of AIDS and sexually transmitted diseases is increasing among young men and women. Two-thirds of sexually active adolescents have had two or more sexual partners, up from 39 percent 20 years before.

Of sexually active women under 20, a third have had four or more sexual partners, and 5 percent reported 10 or more partners.

The Alan Guttmacher Institute reports that there is a steady trend "toward multiple sexual partners." Its study said this "means we need to be facing the reality of the risks of sexually transmitted diseases. We need to be concerned not only about preventing unintended pregnancy, but about guarding against sexually transmitted diseases such as HIV and chlamydia and gonorrhea, which can cause infertility."

Dr. Jacqueline Darroch Forrest, author of the study, said younger women are growing up in "an era of relaxed sexual mores," and this increases their vulnerability.

What is the status of sex education and education on AIDS and other sexually transmitted diseases in your junior and senior high schools? Is there counseling on birth control, distribution of condoms? Classes in sex education?

Interview students, teachers, parents. What do they think schools should do in this area?

Home Assignment

A. Policy

The editor of the local newspaper (50,000 circulation in a county seat in Illinois) has asked you to draw up for her a policy statement on taste that she will consider for adoption by her staff. Write about 500 words as a "position paper" and include some general suggestions and your reasons for them. Cite actual cases and the comments and experiences of reporters and editors.

B. Epithet

The textbook describes an epithet George W. Bush directed at a *New York Times* reporter and the ways the media handled the epithet. What would you have done if:

1. You were covering the event for the *Times*.
2. You reported for a major television network.
3. You read the epithet on the AP wire story and edited the story for your newspaper of 25,000 circulation in Texas.
4. You edited the story for a metropolitan newspaper.

Class Discussion

A. Guidelines

Where do you draw the line?

When Col. Oliver North testified before Congress that Rep. Ron Dellums of California should not be on the House Intelligence Committee because he opposed the Vietnam War, Rep. Pete Stark, another Democrat from California, said to North, "Frankly, Colonel, you are full of shit."

The actress Regina Taylor recalled that in the early 1970s she was among the first group of blacks to integrate a junior high school in Oklahoma. The first day in class she was seated next to a white girl who told the teacher, "I do not want to sit next to this nigger."

In the lyrics of a rap song by 2 Live Crew, the group recites, "I'll break ya down and dick ya long/Bust your pussy then break your backbone."

Earl Butz, a member of President Ford's cabinet, said in the hearing of a reporter," . . . coloreds only want three things: first, a tight pussy; second, loose shoes; and third, a warm place to shit. That's all."

Madonna at a Live Aid concert refused to take off her blazer. "I'm not taking shit off."

For a profile, Clint Eastwood told the interviewer he could not accept the notion of a wrathful god—"some great villain who would come down and beat the shit out of you if you sinned."

What would you do with this language and with any other words and situations you have come across in your reading and experience? Can you suggest guidelines?

B. Johns

You receive this press release from the mayor's office:

Mayor Sam Parnass today announced that the Mayor's Office of Midtown Enforcement and the City Police Department last night closed three houses of prostitution on Torrence Avenue. Also last night, the Public Morals Division of the Police Department arrested 29 prostitutes and eight of their clients and confiscated three automobiles at 10 locations along Torrence Avenue.

Mayor Parnass said, "Last month, after consultation with District Attorney Paul Robinson, I directed my Office of Midtown Enforcement to assist the Police in their efforts to address the growing prostitution problem. As a result, six illegal brothels were closed last week and three more were closed last night.

"These achievements bode well for the success of interagency cooperation and I am confident that with city agencies working together with the support of the District Attorney's office, the quality of life will improve for our citizens."

The three illegal businesses—located at 6310, 6522, and 6770 Torrence Ave.—were closed last night pursuant to the City's Nuisance Abatement Law, which provides for the immediate closure of establishments that have a history of prostitution arrests during the previous year. Midtown Enforcement attorneys initiated the three lawsuits based on numerous prostitution arrests made by the Police Department's Public Morals Division. The closing orders were signed by District Judge Mary Farrell.

Also, we are confiscating cars belonging to men who cruise looking for prostitutes. We will not have our neighborhoods used for illicit purposes.

You check the arrest records and obtain the names of seven of those arrested. The officer in charge suggests that you check the ownership of the three confiscated automobiles, and you do so with the motor vehicle department. You learn one of the automobiles is registered in the name of Herbert Blitzer, dean of the school of journalism; the other two are registered to two of the seven arrested.

You ask who the eighth person was and the police tell you they are holding his name because he is a minor. Through sources, you learn he is Donald Blitzer, the 16-year-old son of the dean.

How would you handle the story?

1. Would you use the names of the prostitutes, some of whom have local addresses?
2. Would you use the names of the local men?
3. Would you use Donald Blitzer's name? (The law does not prohibit publication of the names of minors; it penalizes those who disclose them.)

C. Lynching

This chapter opens with a photograph of a lynching that was taken in Florida in 1929 by a traveling salesman. The handcuffs on the man indicate he was in police custody when he was abducted and murdered by a lynch mob. His identity is unknown.

Would you use this to illustrate your feature to run during Black History Month?

D. Survival

You will be covering a speech next week by the head of the International Human Rights Foundation, Theodore Girsang. The title of his talk is "Gender Inequality."

You receive a press release and an accompanying photograph from the Foundation. The material describes the photo: "Although this mother was assured she had breast milk sufficient for her baby girl and boy, she chose to breast-feed only the boy. UNICEF workers tried to save the baby girl's life, but she died shortly after the photograph was taken of malnutrition."

The press release:

Theodore Girsang, president of the International Human Rights Foundation, has recently returned from a trip that took him to Europe, the Middle East, the Indian subcontinent and Asia. He reports that in contrast to the situation in Europe, countries with gender inequality like Pakistan and China have a high ratio of female to male mortality.

This is true in these countries despite the fact that female children generally have a substantial survival advantage at birth.

The reasons are complex, and Mr. Girsang will discuss them in his talk. These factors include the economics of the country or region, its cultural heritage, male-dominated property rights, religious beliefs.

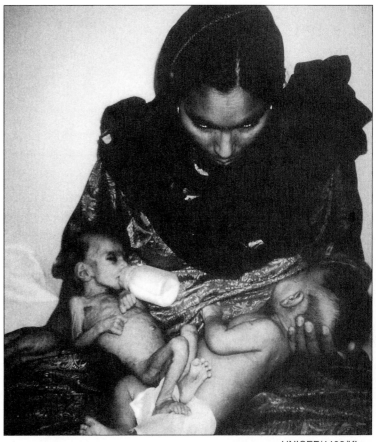

UNICEF/4402/Khan

1. Write a 100-word precede.
2. Discuss whether you would use the accompanying photo with the precede or with his talk, or with neither.

E. Indiscretion

You learn that a congressman from your area who is a major figure in his party had an extramarital affair 35 years ago. The congressman often spoke about the need for public officials to maintain a high ethical standard. Do you use the material for a story?

27 The Morality of Journalism

Stephen Gross, *The Anniston* (Ala.) *Star*

Journalists give voice to all in the community.

Introduction

Journalism is a moral enterprise. Journalists recognize their obligation to check on power as the reason they are given First Amendment protection. They understand they are the conscience of the community, that they not only transcribe the community's formal activities but also actively seek out information that helps all of those in the community to lead happy, fruitful lives. Journalists subscribe to a code of ethics and a personal credo that make public service journalism's major obligation. Journalists are expected to be impartial in their reporting and free of conflicts of interest.

Exercises

A. Quit

You are covering Washington for your newspaper and a congressman from a district in which your newspaper circulates calls you in to announce he has managed to keep a post office building in your city. The Postal Service had intended to consolidate it with a post office in the nearby city of New Plains as an economy move. The service, he said, has canceled its plan. The congressman, William Hartwell, has served six terms in the House. He is a Democrat. He has been a good source for years.

You chat with him about the criticism of Congress as a contentious, even capricious body, beset by partisan considerations, unable to act decisively. He agrees that there is merit in the criticism, and then goes on:

I am having second thoughts about staying in Congress. An office holder has to ask himself if he is serving the public interest to the best of his ability. It really has to be a passion. I have gradually become aware that my enthusiasm for public service has been waning under the weight of my frustrated hopes, others' unreasonable pressures and the job's persistent demands.

People want you to act for their interests, and often this is against the public interest. But how can you build a political base without catering to local demands? Yet it is the increasing narrowness, the declining public spirit that you see locally that you can't really cater to.

The years have eroded my tolerance, stamina and patience. I am tiring of the criticism and the demands of my constituents. I am not sure I can continue to live with Jefferson's dictum, "When a man assumes a public trust, he should consider himself public property."

It is difficult for a public servant to live in an atmosphere of suspicion and distrust. It may be that the ineffectiveness of Congress is the result of these pulls and tugs.

The other night, I was working past midnight when I spotted a letter from a constituent that complained I should not have voted for a pay raise, that I did not deserve one because I don't work hard enough. Here it was, 1:30 in the morning and I was starting to write to her. Then I thought, "Do I have to take this?"

People are cynical about politicians. They shoot you down first and then ask questions. Let's be realistic. Most of us are not in this for the money. We get some sort of ego satisfaction in serving; some like the opportunity of moving up to something higher. But the grind is too great. I've had 69 days of vacation since I've been in Congress, and my marriage broke up because I could not afford to have my wife and four children in Washington, and we were separated for long periods.

Maybe my time is running out anyway. I may be too liberal for my constituents. I've supported programs for the poor, and these are becoming less and less popular in my district. Also, I hate the prospect of having to raise so much money for the campaign. . . .

You are taking careful notes as he speaks, and he suddenly stops to ask, "You're not going to use that are you?" You say that you intend to, and he says he was not speaking for the record. You ask if he intends to run for re-election or is only thinking about running or not running, and he answers that he has definitely made up his mind to go home, to quit. All the more reason, you say, you want to use the story. He owes it to his constituents to tell them he is not going to seek re-election.

No, he answers. Not now. You remind him of your understanding with your sources: no retroactive off-the-record remarks. He says he understands that, but he hopes you will hold off a while.

1. What do you do?
2. Presume you will write a story and write 300 words.

B. Death

You decide to follow up on the demographic material that you wrote about a few weeks ago. (See Chapter 26, **Exercises, B. Demographics.**)

You visit the city health department and obtain data from last year on causes of death. The mayor had mentioned "poor health" as a consequence of the data he had released then.

You look at the figures, and it is evident that the mayor was on the right track. You show the data to your editor and he tells you he wants 500 words on the subject. (A map of health districts is on the next page.)

"I want you to make clear correlations between these figures and social and economic factors," he tells you.

Freeport

District	Percent of Total Families with Female Householders, No Husband Present	Percent with 12 Years or More of Schooling	Mean Household Income	Percent of Total Population in the District Who Belong to Minority Group	Percent of Total Labor Force Unemployed
1	14.7	53.3	$36,842	18.5	6.3
2	10.8	88.8	$59,113	12.4	4.1
3	11.5	64.5	$47,406	21.7	4.9
4	31.6	43.6	$16,327	37.6	13.4
5	41.2	41.4	$11,669	56.3	17.8
City	19.4	53.5	$24,895	26.6	8.4

Death Rates

District	All Causes	Infant Mortality	Heart Disease	Cancer	Flu and Pneumonia	Cirrhosis of Liver	AIDS	Drug Dependence	Homicide	Accident	Suicide
1	10.1	11.8	489.2	179.3	45.6	14.9	14.0	8.5	16.8	13.6	7.7
2	10.9	5.1	520.7	236.0	39.5	15.6	9.4	6.5	3.0	1.8	10.1
3	11.1	7.6	572.8	202.3	44.2	16.9	8.8	5.2	20.2	16.5	4.4
4	7.1	13.8	182.1	147.9	67.7	22.0	57.2	53.2	38.3	14.5	8.7
5	11.2	16.5	338.1	318.9	63.3	40.9	66.5	36.9	45.7	14.4	12.6
City	10.8	11.0	401.5	196.1	46.2	15.9	37.5	10.8	20.9	7.7	7.1

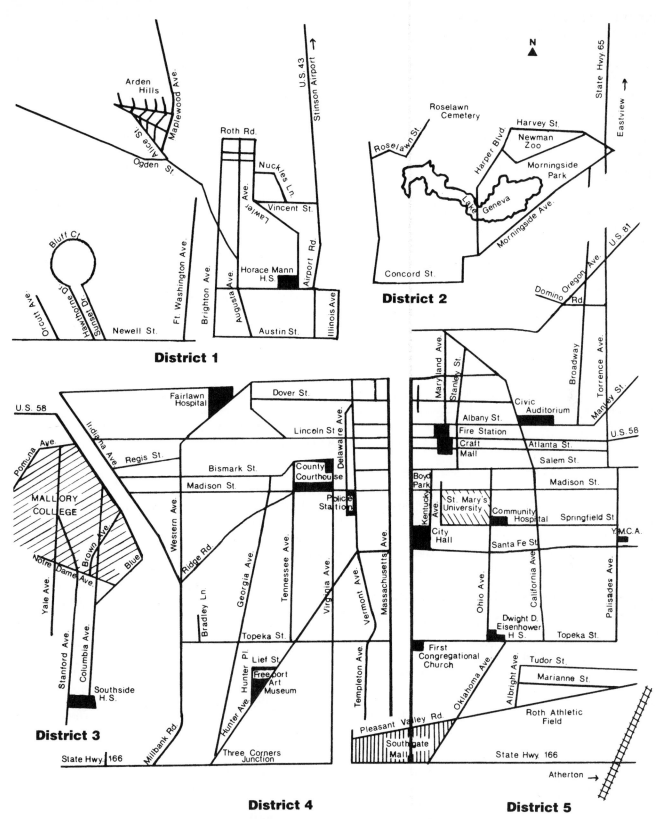

Freeport Health Districts

Assignments

A. Pose

Reporter teams have posed as couples needing loans and as the owners of malfunctioning automobiles. The textbook describes the differing views of the morality of using disguises in reporting. Interview a local editor about his or her views.

B. Problems

Interview a reporter or editor of a local newspaper or broadcast station about an event or a story that posed ethical problems. What was the issue and how was it resolved? In class, discuss any generalities that can be drawn from the variety of experiences the interviews turn up.

Campus and Community Project

Omission

Interview students on the campus and residents in the community: Are there activities, events, personalities, problems that the campus or community newspapers or broadcast stations are not covering?

Or is your criticism broader, that the media that local people read, listen to and watch are primarily bulletin boards, offering only news of overt events and matters of record, not digging into problems, not initiating or enterprising coverage? Is there an excess of gossip columns and the news of the activities of people in the field of entertainment?

Campus Project

Segregated

Campus ethnic groups have successfully sought separate housing and dining facilities on many campuses since the 1960s. In recent years, the concept has come under attack. Kenneth B. Clark, professor emeritus at the City College of New York and a major figure in the Supreme Court's desegregation of public schools, argued that black, Native American and Latino dormitories violate the 1964 Federal Civil Rights Act, which forbids federal financial support to institutions that permit racially segregated facilities.

Clark compared such segregation and its defense by some institutions such as Cornell University as akin to the "rationalizations that guardians of the Old South offered in defense of their racist traditions."

In commenting on the resistance of Cornell to desegregate, Clark and Michael Meyers, the executive director of the New York Civil Rights Coalition, wrote:

"In accommodating the mindlessness of race-based campus housing in Ithaca and accepting the alibis for separatism, Cornell and the Board of Regents are accessories to a functional repeal of the Supreme Court's *Brown v. Board of Education* pronouncement that separate education is inherently unequal."

What is the situation on your campus? Is there racially separate housing and are other facilities separated? Has there been a drive for such? Obtain the comments on this subject from a variety of perspectives: black, Native American and Latino students; university administrators; members of the faculty.

Home Assignment

A. Contribution

Here is a list of men and women who have made a contribution to journalism. Select an individual and write a short profile for www.freenews.com. about his or her role in journalism. You may want to write about someone of your own choosing.

Paul Y. Anderson	John Knight	Lillian Ross
Nellie Bly	Walter Lippmann	Edward W. Scripps
O.K. Bovard	Henry Luce	Hazel Brannon Smith
Edna Buchanan	Ralph McGill	Lincoln Steffens
Hodding Carter	Rupert Murdoch	I. F. Stone
Janet Cooke	Edward R. Murrow	Ida M. Tarbell
Elmer Davis	Al Neuharth	Oswald Garrison Villard
Frederick Douglass	Drew Pearson	Ida B. Wells
Bernard Kilgore	Ernie Pyle	Walter Winchell

B. Heroes

> I guess I grew up in a different era, with people with moral courage around me who spoke out against injustice, who made such issues central in their lives. . . . I have learned that my students don't have living moral heroes.
> —Susannah Heschel, professor of religion, Case Western Reserve University

Have you a hero in journalism? Perhaps one of those listed in the preceding assignment would meet the criterion Heschel sets. Select a journalist who has "moral courage" and discuss his or her attributes and accomplishments.

C. Prisoner

The textbook discusses the dilemma of reporter Kevin Krajick about using material about a man serving a life sentence in a New York penitentiary. Do you agree or disagree with Krajick's decision? Why?

Class Discussion

A. Agenda

George Orwell said a strong motive in his writing was to right wrongs. Some journalists agree. They say they have an agenda for their communities and that they practice an activist journalism.

On the other hand, some believe the press should not lead, not take an activist position.

"It is not the role of the press to fix the problems of society," said Katherine Graham, chairman of the board of *The Washington Post.* "We need to broaden our coverage, to show the problem and how it's being fought. We can't and shouldn't lead in that sense (as advocate). What we can do is to report it better. . . ."

". . . newspapers are information bringers, not advocates. . . . when you get into being a leader in a campaign, you screw up your news. . . ."

Here is the view of Eugene Patterson, former editor of the *St. Petersburg Times:*

> The press is not anointed to set the public's agenda for it. However, it is situated, and in the best sense obligated, to be the listener and messenger that hears and conveys the people's own agenda to the public arena. . . .
>
> . . . reporters are beginning to turn where they should, back to the people, to hear their definitions of the real issues that touch their lives. By giving those concerns sharper voice in the politician's press conferences, the press is starting to interrupt the political vaudeville of past campaigns and ask the legitimate questions, those of the public. . . .

Yet many of the great achievements in journalism—see the work of the muckrakers—were those of advocates.

What is your position in this debate over the role of the journalist? Should the journalist have an agenda? Should he or she be active in digging out news relevant to items on the agenda? Is it advocacy when a reporter who finds a high rate of infant mortality in the community bases his or her journalism on lowering the rate?

B. Dumb-Down

Newspaper advertising was down. Circulation was failing to keep up with population growth. Newspapers had lost 5.5 million subscribers. Studies showed that the precise audience, the men and women ages 25–43, who are big buyers of the products newspapers advertise, were not reading newspapers. The media critic of *The Washington Post* wrote, "The smell of death permeates the newspaper business."

In a massive self-analysis, publishers, editors and reporters have tried to find a formula that would bring back the newspaper reader. Here are excerpts from one response to some of the remedies. It is by David Nyhen, columnist for *The Boston Globe:*

> Newspapers have been fighting off the TV monster for so long, we've turned our newspapers into black-and-white-and-color replications of television—in print.
>
> Our editors now think in terms of television. You can't really blame them. They watched this gunk seven hours a day, like most everyone else, and their brains were turned to jellied eel. . . .

> [We are] dulling [newspapers] down. Dumbing them down, "Safing" them down, by reducing friction with local advertisers, interest groups or loud-mouthed lobbies. . . . Newspaper proprietors, a notoriously timid bunch, weighed their various alternative strategies for the Nineties, and came to the near-unanimous conclusion: time to hunker down. Boat-rocking is definitely out. Pulling in your journalistic horns is definitely in. . . .

What do you think would be a good newspaper strategy for the 21st century?

C. Background

The police report that an explosion in a local residence has resulted in the death of a man. Your check of the files determines that the dead man had served time in the state penitentiary for armed robbery. Do you include his conviction in the story about the death?

D. Advocacy

Katherine Graham, publisher of *The Washington Post:* ". . . newspapers are information bringers, not advocates. . . . When you get into being a leader in a campaign, you screw up your news."

The textbook contains many examples in Chapter 27 of advocacy by newspapers.

On which side of the division do you stand?

Skill Drill: Ethical

Discuss the journalistic ethics involved in the following situations:

1. Your editor has told you to get a story on a local golf club that is discussing the protests of women who say they are discriminated against. The meeting is closed, but an adjoining room is vacant and you can hear the discussion. Should you listen in?
2. You are a sports reporter and the manager of a local bowling alley that is on your beat offers to buy you a drink on your rounds, buy you lunch. Do you accept?
3. You are a consumer reporter doing a check on local auto repair shops. Upon completion, you ask a local association of automobile dealers for a comment, and the executive director says that he will advise his members to pull their advertising if you print the story. What do you do?
4. An executive session is being held by the local Independent Party to select a candidate for mayor. You can hear the closed-door discussions across an air shaft; you can hear them better if you toss a small microphone on a long cable over the air shaft to a window sill and record the discussion. Do you listen in?
5. A good source has told you that he can obtain a document about candidates for the job of city manager, including their personal records. Do you ask him to slip you the material?
6. You cover city hall. A local wrestling promoter has asked the sports editor to recommend someone who can write weekly news releases on the wrestling matches in the two-state area the promoter covers, and the editor gives him your name. He offers you the job. Do you take it?
7. A source inside the police department who has given you considerable information not otherwise available was transferred from the vice squad to a low-level desk job for an infraction. He indicates that if you run a story about him you have lost him as a source. Do you write it?
8. You cover the state legislature and develop some personal friends among legislators and lobbyists. They have a friendly weekly poker game and invite you to join them as a regular. Do you?
9. You are going over data on homicides and other violent crimes for the past year, and you notice that race and ethnic origin are included in the homicide figures but not in the rape data. You ask for the data and the police chief says that the department keeps it but has not distributed it because it is "volatile." You obtain the material and understand what he means. Almost 80 percent of the rape arrests involve members of minority groups. As in the case of homicides, the bulk of the victims were of the same race or ethnic origin as the alleged perpetrators. The chief warns you about using the rape data. "Murder is one thing. People can accept it. But rape. . . ." Do you use all the figures?
10. You cover business and finance. A local banker suggests you buy stock in his parent bank because of an expansion program yet unannounced. Do you buy?
11. Your newspaper, you learn from a confidential source, hired a CIA agent in the 1970s and gave him cover as a reporter. Do you write a story?
12. The local chapter of a medical organization is willing to finance your way to the annual convention of the American Medical Association because of the splendid way you have handled medical news over the past year. Your newspaper would like you to go but cannot afford the $1,500 in costs, the editor says. He tells you to use your judgment about accepting the offer. Do you go?
13. A reporter is asked out for an evening—dinner and the theater—by a source. The evening is a social engagement; it is not related to any story the reporter is covering. The reporter is attracted to the source. Should the reporter accept?

14. A source involved in a federal government contract tells you that he has been involved in an illegal scheme to inflate costs. He names two other company officials, who deny the allegations. Your source gives you some documents that allude to the scheme but do not prove it. It is his word against theirs, and you believe him on the basis of long acquaintance. You know that if you run the story he will be fired.

15. You learn that the newspaper plant (or broadcast station property) is vastly underassessed. You plan to include this in a story about evaluation of downtown property. The editor sends the story upstairs, and mention of the newspaper (or station) is edited out. What do you do?

16. Two basketball players make anti-Semitic remarks in passing during an interview. Do you include the remarks in your story?

17. A reporter for a weekly student newspaper at Dartmouth College attended a meeting of the Gay Students Association at the college and secretly taped the session. She wrote an article that contained excerpts of people describing their sexual experiences and she named two gay leaders. The moderator had read an oath of confidentiality at the start of the meeting. What do you think of the reporter's use of a secret tape recorder? Do you consider this an invasion of the privacy of members of the group?

18. The textbook gives opposing views on whether the press should examine the sexual lives of presidential candidates. Do you think it is morally correct to investigate the sex lives of candidates? Was the technique *The Miami Herald* used— staking out Gary Hart's home—ethical? Was the coverage of a woman's allegations of a lengthy sexual liaison with Bill Clinton ethical? Was the press too preoccupied with the Monica Lewinsky–Bill Clinton relationship?

19. Many travel writers are guests of the hotels, cruise lines, tourist attractions that they write about. A number of articles have appeared that question the ethics of accepting these favors. Is the practice of your area newspapers to accept subsidies for coverage?

20. A standard January 1 story is about the first baby born in the new year. In Peoria, Ill., two local television stations, WMBD and WEEK, led their listeners to believe that Brooke Rochelle Hamby was the first. She wasn't. Actually, 45 minutes before, a 14-year-old unmarried black girl who hadn't known she was pregnant gave birth in an ambulance. The stations had decided to ignore the birth.

    "We've got to have pictures, video," said a TV reporter in defense of the decision. The hospital said it did not have permission to give out the mother's name and that her family did not want the story done.

    The director of the Peoria Planned Parenthood office said, "I don't think the public is ever served by withholding such information. We have, as many communities do, teens giving birth. We'd all like to see something done about the problem, but we can't act as if it doesn't happen."

    What would you have done if you were the manager of one of the television stations?

21. For a few years, several sportswriters knew that Arthur Ashe had AIDS. The world-famous tennis player, who had devoted his time after his playing days to teaching inner-city youngsters the game, had asked that journalists respect his privacy. But *USA Today* revealed that he had the disease. The reporter said the story was known too widely to suppress.

22. When Woody Hayes was coaching the Ohio State University football team, a crucial game was nearing the end and his team was behind. An opposing player intercepted an Ohio State pass, and as the player who had made the interception passed Hayes, the enraged coach punched him. ABC-TV, which was televising the game, did not show a replay of the incident, and its announcers did not discuss Hayes' reaction. Should ABC have shown and discussed Hayes' violence?

23. A columnist for the *New York Post* quoted in his column an anti-Semitic epithet that a New York Yankee baseball player directed at him. Does a journalist use personal experiences in his or her work?

24. Newspapers, magazines and television are charged with overemphasizing athletes and celebrities, with the result that younger readers have aspirations that rarely match their abilities and society's needs. What do you think of the media coverage in your area?

25. Have you discussed in class or found in your reading sufficient information to reach some decisions on a set of personal guidelines regarding the coverage of the personal lives of public figures, the acceptance of favors, taking a second job, using poses and disguises, engaging in an activist journalism, community agenda-setting?

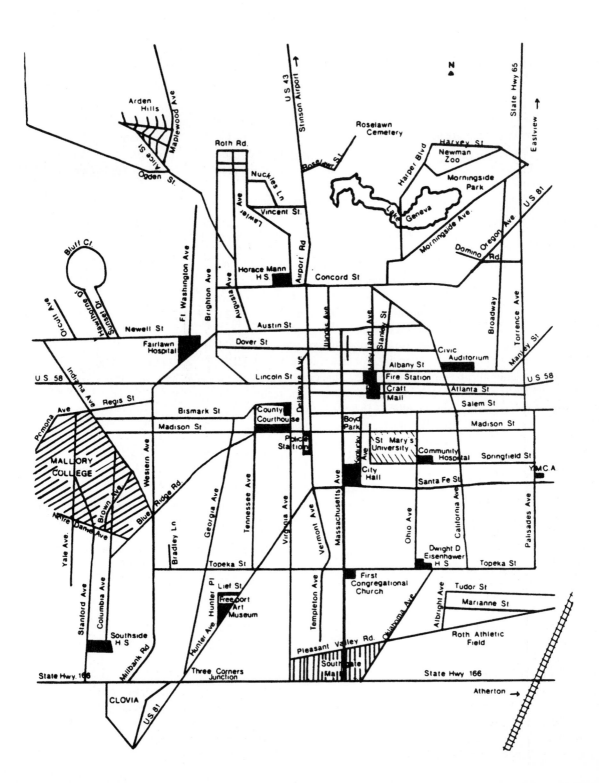

Note: Unless designated otherwise—Av, Rd, Dr—addresses are for streets.

A-1 Shopping Center   77 Notre Dame Av
Abele Forrest L   Atherton
Abromovitch Sterling   2633 Springfield
Addison Rodney   424 Nuckles Ln
Adler Margot   728 Augusta
Alcohol Control Center   570 Western Av
Allen Hotel   212 Albany
Allstate Insurance Co   65 Atlanta
Aluko Sharon   2487 Oregon Av
American Cancer Society   10 Dover
Amidon Photo Exchange   70 Dover
Anders Sparky   18 Tudor
Antonow, Jack   146 Alice
Appel Alan   1133 Madison
Applegate William   3 Hunter Pl
Arnold Alfred MD
  Ofc   10 Dover
  Res   1280 Lawler Av
Ashkinaze Thomas   61 California
Ashkinaze's Men's Styles   742 Springfield
Atlas Equipment Associates   97 Albany

B & D Butchers   742 Springfield
Backman Stacy   548 Atlanta
Baldwin Protection Systems Co   65 Lincoln
Banks George Q   928 Springfield
Bannister Mildred   15 Hawthorne Dr
Barber Billy Jo   56 Roth Rd
Barnes Jake   675 Stanford Av
Bartles Adele   431 Topeka
Barton Hotel   26 Vermont Av
Battle Richard   258 Topeka
Baylor Ulysses   3950 Broadway
Begley Vivian   1280 Madison
Bell Pamela E   606 Vincent
Belmont Motel   7989 Airport Rd
Bennett Elizabeth   88 Columbia Av
Berents Bernzar   76 Newell
Berlin John F   176 Tudor
Berry Lawrence   3468 Salem
Big Jo Lumber Yard   Clovia
Bishop Barney Advg
  Ofc   370 Massachusetts Av
  Res   12 Roth Rd
Bivins Vincent   479 Springfield
Blitzer Herbert   124 Georgia Av
Blount Anthony E   32 Oregon
Bob's Electrical Supply   Southgate Mall

Bokum Baths Inc   5200 Hunter Av
Born Harold   876 Palisades Av
Borns Claude   624 Dover
Borns Robert   438 Oklahoma Av
Bradford Hugh J   Atherton
Braverman C L   529 Palisades Av
Brezen Stanley   17 Tudor
Brown's Auto Supply   3355 Oregon Av
Brown Plumbing and Heating   Clovia
Burger King   4700 Airport Rd
Burgess-Stevens Architects   650 Massachusetts Av
Burns & Allen Investment Inc   370 Massachusetts Av
Burns Paul   Clovia

Cahan Daniel   515 Pleasant Valley Rd
Cahan Mildred   15 Lincoln
Camuto Philip   1338 Tennessee Av
Carruthers Helen   39 Lincoln
Carter Bart   190 Blue Ridge Rd
Carver Cemetery   2222 Salem
Catton Marianne   51 Vermont Av
Chaffee Frank   1440 Springfield
Chamberlain Thomas   88 Austin
Chang Jeff   316 Ogden
Chang & Sons Construction   9 Ft Washington Av
Channel 7   250 Kentucky Av
Chavez Daniel   479 Springfield
Chen Dong Lu   1658 Broadway
City Hall   800 Massachusetts Av
Civic Auditorium   3600 Albany
Clark's Cafe   3769 Oregon Av
Cohen Cory   479 Springfield
Collins Beverly   159 Orcutt Av
Community Hospital   200 Ohio Av
County Courthouse   700 Virginia Av
Cramer Judith   33 Springfield
Crane Ronald K   2063 Ohio Av
Croft Ronald C   865 Indiana Av
Crosson Cafe   127 Lincoln
Crosson Ralph   15 Blue Ridge Rd
Crossroads Grocery   8005 Hunter Ave

Daisy's Pet Shop   1270 California Av
Daly William H   402 Stanford Av
Dantzic Mervin   481 Springfield
David Ross   524 Springfield
Davis Martin   52 Lawler Av
Dean Jerry   479 Springfield

Delta, Delta, Delta House   186 Blue Ridge Rd
Deluxe Adult Videos and Books   4062 Airport Rd
Diamond Alvin   596 Austin
Digital Equipment Corp   18 Concord
Dimmesdale Arthur Rev
  Ofc   4700 Massachusetts Av
  Res   5587 Salem
Donne Harold   190 Blue Ridge Rd
Downey Anne   165 Vincent
Downey Stanley   165 Vincent
Dufur James   225 Ohio Av
Dugan Harold   89 Georgia Av
Dunning Arthur M   9868 Highway 166
Dwight D Eisenhower High School   216 Topeka

Earl Lloyd   1492 Brighton Av
Eighty-One Groceries   6730 Hunter Av
Eisenhower Dwight D High School   216 Topeka
Elman Richard   3732 Palisades Av
Elston Aaron   Arden Hills
Epstein Helen   864 Madison
Erlanger Donald   45 Domino Rd
Evans Charlotte DDS   66 Bluff Ct
Everingham Thomas   373 Vermont Av
Exton Electric Co   777 Atlanta

Fairlawn Hospital   570 Western Av
Falcione Marshall Atty
  Ofc   370 Massachusetts Av
  Res   666 Western Av
Farrell Mary   86 Bradley Ln
Farrington Richard   332 Bismark
Feeney Raymond   167 Kentucky Av
Felson Charles   565 Concord
Feron Gerald   75 Hunter Pl
Fields Benjamin   1272 Broadway
Figuera Robert   97 Maryland Av
Finnegan Joseph   228 Vermont Av
Fire Station   100 Lincoln
First Baptist Church   1730 Atlanta
First Congregational Church   4700 Massachusetts Av
First National Bank   55 Massachusetts Av
Flagg Arnold   571 Broadway
Flynn Clark   9 Roth Rd
Folger Betty   190 Blue Ridge Rd
Forde Betty   896 Santa Fe
Fox Daniel   833 Santa Fe
Frank's Deli   740 Springfield
Fraser James   76 Albright Av
Freedman Martin   537 Dover
Freeport Auto Repair   1273 Santa Fe
Freeport Chamber of Commerce
    22 Massachusetts Av
Freeport Dodge Inc   2121 Broadway
Freeport Golf Course   952 Airport Rd
Freeport Kiwanis Club   326 Albany

Freeport Motor Lodge   2485 Oregon Av
Freeport News, The   7620 Torrence Av
Freeport Press Corp   7620 Torrence Av
Freeport Rotary Club   6993 Lincoln
Fuentes Albert   720 Georgia Av
Fulton Robert Elementary School   1109 Santa Fe

Gabel Martin   1325 Morningside Av
Galzo Frederick   435 Albany
Gamm William Atty
  Ofc   34 Massachusetts Av
  Res   583 Millbank Rd
Gap Clothiers The   1770 Broadway
Garner Bernard   72 Albright Av
George Packer Elementary School   66 Maryland Av
George Washington Carver Club   3030 Airport Rd
Gerber Phil   348 Millbank Rd
Gerter Sigmund   55 Templeton Av
Gilkeyson Herbert   1643 Newell
Glasser Sara F   555 Blue Ridge Rd
Godfrey Claudine   870 Blue Ridge Rd
Gold Marcia   831 Brighton Av
Golden Years Club   110 Newell
Gonzales George   1523 Ogden
Graham Fred
  Ofc   22 Massachusetts Av
  Res   71 Hunter Pl
Greek Orthodox Cathedral   1015 Indiana Av
Green David   104 Springfield
Green Richard MD
  Ofc   16 Dover
  Res   84 Maryland Av
Gregory James   91 Bluff Ct
Grimes EW Co   1560 Broadway
Grubbs Oscar   Smith Farms
Gruner Donald   280 Lawler Av
Gulf Drive-Up   4950 Oregon Av
Guth George T   626 Manley
Guzman Clifford   16 Brighton Av

Halpern William   479 Atlanta
Halpert Wesley Atty
  Ofc   370 Massachusetts Av
  Res   18 Marianne
Harris Arthur B   123 Western Av
Hastings Abner   576 Atlanta
Hay Peter   5 Nuckles Ln
Heavenly Rest Chapel   1485 Tennessee Av
Hecht's Fine Furniture   715 Vermont Av
Hedberg Milton   9843 California Av
Hedberg-Smith Stkbrkrs   690 Massachusetts Av
Heffner Albert   1842 Salem
Held Dennis   630 Orcutt Av
Helmer Steve   63 Lincoln
Helmet Steven   533 Yale Av
Hess James   867 Brighton Av

Hilliard's Body Shop   6584 Hunter Av
Himmelstein Dale L   42 Ft Washington Av
Ho Robert T F   763 Airport Rd
Hoch Arthur   474 Tudor
Holing John OD   53 Bluff Ct
Holy Trinity Church   300 Madison
Hoover Ralph   190 Blue Ridge Rd
Horace Mann H.S.   370 Concord
Hosmer James   91 Tudor
Huff Martin   202 Blue Ridge Rd
Hulbert George W   69 Topeka
Hunscher David   1515 Salem
Hurley Marvin   1060 Columbia Av
Hurst Fanny MD   590 Brighton Av

IGA   135 Kentucky Av
Isaac Peter   190 Blue Ridge Rd

Jack's Mobile Serve   6481 Hunter Av
Jacobs Anne   702 Bismark
Jacobson J   44 Austin
Jenkins Stephen C   89 Manley
Jones Hosie Gene   1347 Oklahoma Av
Jopper Frank   622 Broadway
Joseph Barney G   1625 Tennessee Av
Joseph Pharmacy   450 Stanley
Joshua Baptist Church   8724 Torrence Av
Joyce Coleman   44 Broadway

Kaplan Herbert N   897 Madison
Katzen Arthur   12 Ft Washington Av
Kay's Diner   128 Atlanta
Kazazian Brut   515 Santa Fe
Keenan Kenneth   918 Blue Ridge Rd
Kempe Harry   7 Manley
Kilafar Dianne MD   324 Indiana Av
Kinney Fay   8280 Lincoln
Kirby B J   122 Oklahoma Av
Kliff Paul A   29 Tudor
Kmart Eastview   4339 Oregon Av
Knudson Jerry PhD   562 Bismark
Konner John   333 Austin
Kragler Bertha   2260 Bismark
Kramer John   164 Albright Av
Krane Katherine   190 Blue Ridge Rd
Krane Ray   1215 Albany
Krebs B C Manufacturing Co   10 Concord
Kroeger B   88 Augusta Av

Lane Sarah   540 Regis
Leek's Cafe   15 Lincoln
Lemieux Jacques   225 Augusta Av
Lentz Robin   484 Springfield
Levine Leonard   264 Ogden
Levy Richard   54 Maplewood Av
Lewin David   8440 Lincoln

Logan Ann   2960 Salem
Longo Frank   465 Lief
Loran Anley   98 Western Av
Love Harry   190 Blue Ridge Rd
Lowe David   19 Millbank Rd
Lucky 7 Grocery   1384 Santa Fe
Lynn Frederick L   18 Madison
Lyon P   77 Dover

Magione Robert F   872 Ogden
Mallory College   500 Indiana Av
Marple Jane   6 Millbank Rd
Martinez Reginaldo   190 Blue Ridge Rd
Marvello Rosario   4143 Torrence Av
Mayfair Fabrics   740 Springfield
McCoy Frank   320 Manley
McMillan Samuel A   48 Orcutt Av
Melia Aloysius J   653 Madison
Menton Sigmund   194 Blue Ridge Rd
Metro Transit Authority   9643 Highway 166
Meyers Bernard A   3320 Madison
Miller Wayne   614 Albany
Minteer Edwin   8456 Lincoln
Mitchell & Co   889 Newell
Mohawk Brush Building   1620 Blue Ridge Rd
Mom's Maternity Fashion   91 Broadway
Morgan Robert   2255 California Av
Morton Henry   687 Pleasant Valley Rd

NCR Corporation   266 Atlanta
National Car Rental   6901 Airport Rd
National Kidney Foundation   729 Albany
Nelley Margaret   96 Albright Av
Newton Fred   190 Blue Ridge Rd
Nicholson Philip   18 Marianne
North Funeral Home   1620 Tennessee Av
Norton Ralph   6522 Torrence Av
No-Tell Motel   3969 Broadway

Oh Herbert   190 Blue Ridge Rd
Olsen Paul   863 Morningside Av
Opal Alice   190 Blue Ridge Rd
Oregon Groceteria   5333 Oregon Av
O'Reilly Sandy   459 Brighton Av
Oshiro Mary   1360 California Av
Overton Ted   190 Blue Ridge Rd

Packer George Elementary School   66 Maryland Av
Palmer Thomas   568 Madison
Pardee Francis   1874 Ogden
Parker Bayard   1618 Brighton Av
Parnass Sam   716 Broadway
Parrington Felix   76 Roth Rd
Pearl Mildred   175 Virginia Av
Peat Marshall   84 Notre Dame Av
People's Bus Line Inc   1320 Torrence Av

Perkins William F   1105 Madison
Petrie Donald   386 Brighton Av
Phealan Ronald   526 Albany
Pietro Peter   824 Vincent
Plaza Hotel The   912 California Av
Podhoretz Hobart Bayward   82 Bluff Ct
Police Station   900 Vermont Av
Polk George   10 Topeka
Pop's Cleaners   249 Austin
Popvich Robert   81 Millbank Rd
Pork Parlor   405 Regis
Post Theodore   25 Domino Rd
Potts L P   52 Bradley Ln
Praxton Francis   1160 Broadway
Prewitt Mortuary   840 Stanford Av
Purdue Jack   726 California Av

Quick Stop Laundry   39 Millbank Rd
Quire Karl   38 Concord

Ramsgate Charles   265 Virginia Av
Raskover Richard   766 Augusta
Ratcliffe Sam   5 Hunter Pl
Reeder M   82 Hunter Pl
Regis Hotel   88 Dover
Reib Rachel   338 Topeka
Renaldi Ruth P   22 Columbia Av
Reynolds James   35 Palisades Av
Richards Donald L   94 Hawthorne Dr
Rieder's Trading Post   7935 Hunter Av
Robbins Edward   65 Bismark
Robert Matthew B   569 Blue Ridge Rd
Roberts Dorothy F   242 Madison
Robinson Paul   730 Georgia Av
Rogers M B   935 Millbank Rd
Roper Leon   6 Bradley Ln
Ross David   2920 Madison
Ross K L   323 Lief
Rothkrug Russell   37 Bluff Ct
Rubens Merle   648 Austin
Ruiz Alfredo   190 Blue Ridge Rd
Russ's Market   929 Indiana Av
Ryan Scott   1580 Oklahoma Av

St. Mary's University   290 Madison
Salmi Robert   1280 Blue Ridge Rd
Sanchez Alexander   86 Santa Fe
Sanchez Luis   54 Millbank Rd
Sandler Ross   355 Pleasant Valley Rd
Scarpino Joan   539 Columbia Av
Schneider Burton   269 Topeka
Schneider Stella   4 Hawthorne Dr
Schwartz Harry   768 Albany
Scillicide Irving   Clovia
Scott Building   2000 Torrence Av
Seaver Dorothy   1120 Brighton Av

Seaver Vincent   333 Millbank Rd
Serge Jack A   640 Columbia Av
Serpa Kelly   46 Topeka
Shaeffer Stanley   45 Madison
Shalom Moving & Storage   6432 Newell
Sharman William   522 Virginia Av
Sharon's Used Goods   65 Virginia Av
Shelly's Laundromat   402 Newell
Shelton O M   666 Stanley
Sherman Albert   266 Maplewood
Silver Isadore   88 Virginia Av
Silver Jean   88 Virginia Av
Simms N Francis   290 Madison
Simpson Motors Co   1880 Palisades Av
Sinclair Margaret   161 Albany
Skinner Vernon   9690 California Av
Slinkard Thomas   4 Bluff Ct
Smith Frances   132 Alice
Smith Fred E   66 Templeton Av
Smith Harvey   145 Nuckles Ln
Smith Walter   926 Columbia Av
Snead Daniel   481 Yale Av
Solomon Stanley   47 Palisades Av
Soto Irwin   Clovia
Soto Jack   Clovia
Southside High School   1370 Stanford Av
Stapleton Wayne L MD
    Ofc   10 Dover
    Res   2620 Morningside Av
Steinberg Alfred   145 Columbia Av
Stern Franklin W   9529 Millbank Rd
Stiga Stanley   909 Lawler Av
Stinson Airport   8900 Airport Rd
Stranger's Department Store   25 Massachusetts Av
Stroh Bruce   1215 Millbank Rd
Stuben Drug Store   472 Massachusetts Av
Sunoco Service   5431 Hunter Av
Sutherland Karl   368 Atlanta
Swimmer Albert F   1405 Sunset Dr

Taylor Alan   349 Santa Fe
Temple B'nai Shalom   1282 Airport Rd
Temple Emmanuel   457 Oregon Av
Terada Winifred   294 Broadway
Texaco Fuel Stop   4266 Oregon Av
Thames Arthur Atty   416 Pleasant Valley Rd
Thomas Jules   56 Western Av
Thorne Charles   1855 Atlanta
Three Corners Cafe   4700 Hunter Av
Tobin Barry   112 Bismark
Trenzier William   460 Lincoln
Trevor William   Clovia
Trimbel Department Store   17 Vermont Av
Trowbridge Nicholas   90 Austin
Trump Donald   418 Palisades Av
Tsouprake Demetrios A   560 Tudor

Tucek Cyrus   1280 Bismark
Turner Eric   441 Georgia Av

United Methodist Church   850 Brighton Av
Unruh Joseph   190 Blue Ridge Rd

Verzon Jewelry   Southgate Mall
Vincent Salvatore   44 Concord
Voboril John T   1496 Blue Ridge Rd

Walker Damon   67 Roth Rd
Walnut J C and Co   850 Albany
Walnut, James C   215 Manley
Walnut Theodore   1018 Millbank Rd
Walters Tess   843 Columbia Av
Ward Samuel   47 Harper Blvd
Wigglesworth James   349 Springfield
Williams Adam   1423 Harper Blvd

Williams Margaret   7 Bradley Ln
Williams Mildred C   1423 Harper Blvd
Williams Milton   496 Brighton Av
Wilson's Rest Stop   6631 Hunter Av
Wolfe T   6 Stanford Av
Woodcock Joseph C   748 Lincoln
Wright Beulah   26 Domino Rd
Wrightston Industries Inc   3640 Broadway
Wrightston James   4716 Airport Rd

X Francis T   677 Palisades Av
XYZ Typewriter Repair   345 Concord

York Alfred   15 Templeton Av
Young William   42 Broadway

Ziegler Alfred   444 Bismark
Zimmerman Martha   340 Lincoln

Freeport Cross Directory

The cross directory is also known as the *reverse directory*.

Airport Rd

763	Ho Robert T F
952	Freeport Golf Course
1282	Temple B'nai Shalom
3030	George Washington Carver Club
4062	Deluxe Adult Videos and Books
4700	Burger King
4716	Wrightston James
6901	National Car Rental
7989	Belmont Motel
8900	Stinson Airport

Albany

97	Atlas Equipment Associates
161	Sinclair Margaret
212	Allen Hotel
326	Freeport Kiwanis Club
435	Galzo Frederick
526	Phealan Ronald
614	Miller Wayne
729	National Kidney Foundation
768	Schwartz Harry
850	Walnut JC and Co
1215	Krane Ray
3600	Civic Auditorium

Albright Av

72	Garner Bernard
76	Fraser James
96	Nelley Margaret
164	Kramer John

Alice

132	Smith Frances
146	Antonow Jack

Arden Hills

	Elston Aaron

Atherton

	Abele Forrest L
	Bradford Hugh J

Atlanta

65	Allstate Insurance Co
128	Kay's Diner
266	NCR Corporation
368	Sutherland Karl
479	Halpern William
548	Backman Stacy
777	Exton Electric Co
1730	First Baptist Church
1855	Thorne Charles

Augusta Av

88	Kroeger B
225	Lemieux Jacques
576	Hastings Abner
728	Adler Margot
766	Raskover Richard

Austin

44	Jacobson J
88	Chamberlain Thomas
90	Trowbridge Nicholas
249	Pop's Cleaners
333	Konner John
596	Diamond Alvin
648	Rubens Merle

Bismark

65	Robbins Edward
112	Tobin Barry
332	Farrington Richard
444	Ziegler Alfred
562	Knudson Jerry PhD
702	Jacobs Anne
1280	Tucek Cyrus
2260	Kragler Bertha

Blue Ridge Rd

15	Crosson Ralph
186	Delta, Delta, Delta House
190	Carter Bart
	Donne Harold
	Folger Betty
	Hoover Ralph
	Isaac Peter
	Krane Katherine
	Love Harry
	Martinez Reginaldo
	Newton Fred
	Opal Alice
	Overton Ted
	Oh Herbert
	Ruiz Alfredo
	Unruh Joseph
194	Menton Sigmund
202	Huff Martin
555	Glasser Sara F
569	Robert Matthew B
870	Godfrey Claudine
918	Keenan Kenneth
1280	Salmi Robert
1496	Voboril John T
1620	Mohawk Brush Building

Bluff Ct

4	Slinkard Thomas
37	Rothkrug Russell
53	Holding John OD
66	Evans Charlotte DDS
82	Podhoretz Hobart Bayward
91	Gregory James

Bradley Ln

6	Roper Leon
7	Williams Margaret
52	Potts L P
86	Farrell Mary

Brighton Av

16	Guzman Clifford
386	Petrie Donald
459	O'Reilly Sandy
496	Williams Milton
590	Hurst Fanny MD
831	Gold Marcia
850	United Methodist Church
867	Hess James
1120	Seaver Dorothy
1492	Lloyd Earl
1618	Parker Bayard

Broadway

42	Young William
44	Joyce Coleman
191	Mom's Maternity Fashion
294	Terada Winifred
571	Flagg Arnold
622	Jopper Frank
716	Parnass Sam
1160	Praxton Francis
1272	Fields Benjamin
1560	E W Grimes Co
1658	Chen Dong Lu
1770	Gap Clothiers The
2121	Freeport Dodge Inc
3640	Wrightson Industries Inc
3950	Baylor Ulysses
3969	No-Tell Motel

California Av

61	Ashkinaze Thomas
726	Purdue Jack
912	Plaza Hotel The
1270	Daisy's Pet Shop
1360	Oshiro Mary
2255	Morgan Robert
9690	Skinner Vernon
9843	Hedberg Milton

Clovia

	Big Jo Lumber Yard
	Brown Plumbing and Heating
	Burns Paul
	Scillicide Irving
	Soto Irwin
	Soto Jack
	Trevor William

Columbia Av

22	Renaldi Ruth P
88	Bennett Elizabeth
145	Steinberg Alfred
539	Scarpino Joan
646	Serge Jack A
843	Walters Tess
926	Smith Walter
1060	Hurley Marvin

Concord

10	Krebs B C Manufacturing Co
18	Digital Equipment Corp
38	Quire Karl
345	XYZ Typewriter Repair
370	Horace Mann High School
444	Vincent Salvatore
565	Felson Charles

Domino Rd

25	Post Theodore
26	Wright Beulah
45	Erlanger Donald

Dover

10	American Cancer Society
10	Arnold Alfred MD Ofc
10	Stapleton Wayne L Ofc
16	Green Richard MD Ofc
70	Amidon Photo Exchange
77	Lyon P
88	Regis Hotel
537	Friedman Martin
624	Borns Claude

Ft Washington Av

9	Chang & Sons Construction
12	Katzen Arthur
42	Himmelstein Dale L

Georgia Av

89	Dugan Harold
124	Blitzer Herbert
441	Turner Eric
720	Fuentes Albert
730	Robinson Paul

Harper Blvd

47	Ward Samuel
1423	Williams Adam
1423	Williams Mildred C

Hawthorne Dr

4	Schneider Stella
15	Bannister Mildred
94	Richards Donald L

Highway 166

9643	Metro Transit Authority
9868	Dunning Arthur M

Hunter Pl

3	Applegate William
5	Ratcliffe Sam
71	Graham Fred Res
75	Feron Gerald
82	Reeder M

Hunter Av

4700	Three Corners Cafe
5200	Bokum Baths Inc
5431	Sunoco Service
6481	Jack's Mobil Serve
6584	Hilliard's Body Shop
6631	Wilson's Rest Stop
6730	Eighty-One Groceries
7935	Rieder's Trading Post
8005	Crossroads Grocery

Indiana Av

324	Kilafar Dianne MD
500	Mallory College
865	Croft Ronald C
929	Russ's Market
1015	Greek Orthodox Cathedral

Kentucky Av

135	IGA
167	Feeney Raymond
250	Channel 7

Lawler Av

52	Davis Martin
280	Gruner Donald

909	Stiga Stanley
1280	Arnold Alfred MD Res

Lief

323	Ross K L
465	Longo Frank

Lincoln

15	Cahan Mildred
15	Leek's Cafe
39	Carruthers Helen
63	Helmer Steve
65	Baldwin Protection Systems
100	Fire Station
127	Crosson Cafe
340	Zimmerman Martha
460	Trenzier William
784	Woodcock Joseph C
6993	Freeport Rotary Club
8280	Kinney Fay
8440	Lewin Daivd
8456	Minteer Edwin

Madison

18	Lynn Frederick L
45	Shaeffer Stanley
242	Roberts Dorothy
290	St. Mary's University
290	Simms N Francis
300	Holy Trinity Church
568	Palmer Thomas
653	Melia Aloysius J
864	Epstein Helen
897	Kaplan Herbert N
1105	Perkins William F
1133	Appel Alan
1280	Begley Vivian
2920	Ross David
3320	Meyers Bernard A

Manley

7	Kempe Harry
89	Jenkins Stephen C
215	Walnut James C
320	McCoy Frank
626	Guth George T

Maplewood Av

54	Levy Richard
266	Sherman Albert

Marianne

18	Halpert Wesley Atty Res
18	Nicholson Philip

Maryland Av

66	George Packer Elementary School
84	Green Richard MD Res
97	Figuera Robert

Massachusetts Av

22	Freeport Chamber of Commerce
22	Graham Fred Ofc
25	Stranger's Department Store
34	Gamm William
55	First National Bank
370	Bishop Barney Advertising Ofc
370	Burns & Allen Investment Inc
370	Falcione Marshall Atty Ofc
370	Halpert Wesley Atty Ofc
472	Stuben Drug Store
650	Burgess-Stevens Architects
690	Hedberg-Smith Stkbrkrs
800	City Hall
4700	Dimmesdale Arthur Rev Ofc
4700	First Congregational Church

Millbank Rd

6	Marple Jane
19	Lowe David
39	Quick Stop Laundry
54	Sanchez Luis
81	Popvich Robert
333	Seaver Vincent
348	Gerber Phil
583	Gamm William
935	Rogers M B
1018	Walnut Theodore
1215	Stroh Bruce
9529	Stern Franklin W

Morningside Av

863	Olsen Paul
1325	Gabel Martin
2620	Stapleton Wayne L Res

Newell

76	Berents Bernzar
110	Golden Years Club
402	Shelly's Laundromat
889	Mitchell & Co
1643	Gilkeyson Herbert
6432	Shalom Moving & Storage

Notre Dame Av

77	A-1 Shopping Center
84	Peat Marshall

Nuckles Ln

5	Hay Peter
145	Smith Harvey
424	Addison Rodney

Ogden

264	Levine Leonard
316	Chang Jeff
872	Magione Robert F
1523	Gonzales George
1874	Pardee Francis

Ohio

200	Community Hospital
225	Dufur James
2063	Crane Ronald K

Oklahoma Av

122	Kirby BJ
438	Borns Robert
1347	Jones Hosie Gene
1580	Ryan Scott

Orcutt Av

48	McMillan Samuel A
159	Collins Beverly
630	Held Dennis

Oregon Av

322	Blount Anthony E
457	Temple Emmanuel
2485	Freeport Motor Lodge
2487	Aluko Sharon
3355	Brown's Auto Supply
3769	Clark's Cafe

4266	Texaco Fuel Stop	1273	Freeport Auto Repair	**Tennessee Av**	
4339	Kmart Eastview	1384	Lucky 7 Grocery		
4950	Gulf Drive-Up			1338	Camuto Philip
5333	Oregon Groceteria	**Smith Farms**		1485	Heavenly Rest Chapel
				1620	North Funeral Home
Palisades Av			Grubbs Oscar	1625	Joseph Barney G

Palisades Av

35	Reynolds James
47	Solomon Stanley
418	Trump Donald
529	Braverman C L
876	Born Harold
1880	Simpson Motor Co
3732	Elman Richard
5677	X Francis T

Smith Farms

Grubbs Oscar

Southgate Mall

Bob's Electrical Supply
Venzon Jewelry

Springfield

33	Cramer Judith
104	Green David
349	Wigglesworth James
479	Bivins Vincent
479	Chavez Daniel
479	Cohen Cory
479	Dean Jerry
481	Dantzic Mervin
484	Lentz Robin
524	David Ross
740	Frank's Deli
740	Mayfair Fabrics
742	Ashkinaze's Men's Styles
742	B & D Butchers
928	Banks George Q
1440	Chaffee Frank
2633	Abromovitch Sterling

Pleasant Valley Rd

355	Sandler Ross
415	Thames Arthur Atty
515	Cahan David
687	Morton Henry

Regis

405	Pork Parlor
540	Lane Sarah

Roth Rd

9	Flynn Clark
12	Bishop Barney Advertising Res
56	Barber Billy Jo
67	Walker Damon
76	Parrington Felix

Stanford Av

6	Wolfe T
402	Daly William H
675	Barnes Jake
840	Prewitt Mortuary
1370	Southside High School

Salem

1515	Hunscher David
1842	Heffner Albert
2222	Carver Cemetery
2960	Logan Ann
3468	Berry Lawrence
5587	Dimmesdale Arthur Reverend Res

Stanley

450	Joseph Pharmacy
666	Shelton O M

Sunset Dr

1405	Swimmer Albert F

Santa Fe

86	Sanchez Alexander
349	Taylor Ann
515	Kazazian Brut
833	Fox Daniel
896	Forde Betty
1109	Fulton Robert Elementary School

Templeton Av

15	York Alfred
55	Gerter Sigmund
66	Smith Fred E

Tennessee Av

1338	Camuto Philip
1485	Heavenly Rest Chapel
1620	North Funeral Home
1625	Joseph Barney G

Topeka

10	Polk George
46	Serpa Kelly
69	Hulbert George W
216	Dwight D Eisenhower High School
258	Battle Richard
269	Schneider Burton
338	Reib Rachel
431	Bartles Adele

Torrence Av

1320	People's Bus Line Inc
2000	Scott Building
4143	Marvello Rosario
6522	Norton Ralph
7620	Freeport Press Corp
7620	The Freeport News
8724	Joshua Baptist Church

Tudor

17	Brezen Stanley
18	Anders Sparky
29	Kliff Paul A
91	Hosmer James
176	Berlin John F
474	Hoch Arthur
560	Tsouprake Demetrios A

Vermont Av

17	Trimbel Department Store
26	Barton Hotel
51	Catton Marianne
228	Finnegan Joseph
373	Everingham Thomas
715	Hecht's Fine Furniture
900	Police Station

Vincent

165	Downey Anne
165	Downey Stanley
606	Bell Pamela E
824	Pietro Peter

Virginia Av

65	Sharon's Used Goods
88	Silver Isadore
88	Silver Jean
175	Pearl Mildred
265	Ramsgate Charles
522	Sharman WIlliam
700	County Courthouse

Western Av

56	Thomas Jules
98	Loran Anley
123	Harris Arthur B
570	Alcohol Control Center
570	Fairlawn Hospital
666	Falcione Marshall Atty Res

Yale Av

481	Snead Daniel
533	Helmer Steven

Freeport City Officials

Airport manager	Marshall Peat
Budget director	Albert Heffner
Building inspector, chief	Barry Tobin
City clerk	Vivian Begley
City Council members	Albert Fuentes
	Bernard Garner
	Fred E. Smith
	Martin Davis
	Marcia Gold
City engineer	O. M. Shelton
City forester	John T. Voboril
City manager	Harold Born
City treasurer	Daniel Cahan
Computer and data communications services agency	Sterling Abromovitch
County manager	David Hunscher
Fire chief	Mervin Dantzic
Health Department director	Jane Jacobson
Health and Hospital Corp. director	Mildred Pearl
Housing Authority director	Charles Ramsgate
Human Rights Commission director	Stanley Downey
Human Rights Commission member	Judith Cramer
Land use board director	Matthew B. Robert
Latino affairs director	Marlene Figuera
Mayor	Sam Parnass
Deputy Mayor	Stanley Brezen
Parks Department director	Thomas Chamberlain
Planning board chairman	Philip Nicholson
Planning board secretary	Betty Forde
Police chief	Lloyd Earl
Press Secretary to the Mayor	Leon Roper
Public Works Dept. director	Robin Lentz
Deputy director	Ralph Norton
Sanitation commissioner	William Applegate
Social Services director	Cory Cohen
Voluntary Action Center director	Martha Zimmerman
Water Dept. superintendent	L. P. Potts
Welfare director	George Q. Banks
Zoning and Planning Board member	Harry Kempe
Zoo director	Cyrus Tucek
Zoo asst. director	Bayard Parker

Freeport Court Officials

Clerk of Court	Abner Hastings
Civil Court judge	John Kramer
City Court administrative officer	William Halpern

District attorney
   Chief asst. D.A.
   Asst. D.A.
District court administrative judge
District judge
District judge
District judge
District judge
District judge

Paul Robinson
Robert Morgan
Joseph C. Woodcock Jr.
Ross David
Mary Farrell
Marvin Hurley
Samuel A. McMillan
Aloysius J. Melia
Harvey Smith

Freeport School Officials

Board of education chairman
Board of education president
Board of education members

Rodney Addison
Charles Thorne
Albert Swimmer
Helen Epstein
Jean Silver
Salvatore Vincent
Edwin Minteer
John T. Voboril

Superintendent
English coordinator, high schools
Dwight D. Eisenhower H.S. principal
Horace Mann H.S. principal
Horace Mann asst. principal
Atherton school board chairman

Herbert Gilkeyson
F. W. Stern
Bernard A. Meyers
Richard Battle
Daniel Fox
Forrest L. Abele

Mallory College

Adviser, student paper
Afro-American Studies dept. chair
Arts & Sciences dean
Basketball coach
Committee on Academic Standing, member
Dean of Students
   Associate dean
Education dept. chair.
English dept. chair.
Journalism dean
Library science dean
Physics professor
President
Provost
Psychology dept. chair.
Sociology dept. chair.
Track coach
Trustee

Robert Figuera
James Gregory
Hobart Bayward Podhoretz
George Gonzales
Walter Smith
William Sharman
Claudine Godfrey
Alfred Steinberg
Samuel Ward
Herbert Blitzer
Donald L. Richards
Albert Sherman
Ruth Pitts Renaldi
Thomas Palmer
Nicholas Trowbridge
Margot Adler
Steve Helmer
Karl Quire

St. Mary's College

English assoc. prof.
Financial aid director
Political Science prof.

Frederick L. Lynn
C. L. Braverman
Vincent Bivins

President   N. Francis Simms
Provost   Stanley Stiga
Trustee   Dorothy M. Seaver

Civic and Service Groups

American Civil Liberties Union local chapter president	Sara F. Glasser
Elks (Benevolent and Protective Order of Elks or B.P.O.E.) Secretary	Peter Hay
Freeport Chamber of Commerce	
President	Clifford Guzman
Secretary	Fred Graham
Public relations director	Thomas Everingham
Freeport Civic Society president	Lawrence Berry
Good Citizens League head	Alvin Diamond
Jewish Community Council director	Arthur Hoch
Kiwanis Club manager	John F. Berlin
League of Women Voters local chairwoman	Mildred Cahan

Hospital Officials

Community Hospital	
Director	Vincent Seaver
Medical services director	Stanley Downey
Medical staff director	Alfred Arnold
Public information director	Beverly Collins
Fairlawn Hospital	
Alcohol control center head	Charles Felson
Director	Milton Williams
Medical resources director	Dianne Kilafar

State Officials

Attorney General	Alfred Steinberg
Deputy Attorney General	Michael Canzian
State assemblyman	Peter Pietro
Commissioner of Aeronautics	William Sullivan
Comptroller	Thomas Wolfe
Public Utilities Commission chairman	Michael McKirdy
Press officer	Jack Nagel
State senator	Joseph Margeretta
Governor	Janet Kocieniewski
Lieut. Governor	Harry Lee Waterfield
Ombudsman for state prisoners	Bruce Stroh

Federal Officials

U.S. Attorney	Stephen C. Jenkins
Asst. U.S. Attorney	Herbert N. Kaplan
Congressman	William Trenzier
Senators	Janice Cooper
	James Dufur

Business Executives

Baldwin Protection Systems president	Felix Parrington
Exton Electric president	Alexander Sanchez
National Security Bank, Freeport branch, president	Elizabeth Bennett
People's Bus Line, Inc., owner	George W. Hulbert

Union Officials

City Trade Union Fed. director	Daniel Chavez
Hotel and Restaurant Workers union head, state	Bert Gentle
Nat'l Federation of Teachers, local head	Helen Carruthers

Illustration Credits

Chapter 1

Opener: Wayne Miller; **p. 10:** Ladies Professional Golf Association.

Chapter 2

Opener: Mike Roemer.

Chapter 3

Opener: Mike Roemer.

Chapter 4

Opener: Jean Pierre Rivest, *The Gazette.*

Chapter 5

Opener: Jon Shearer.

Chapter 6

Opener: Michel du Cille; **p. 49:** Rodger Mallison, *Fort Worth Star Telegram;* **p. 51:** Jeff W. Henderson.

Chapter 7

Opener: Mike Roemer.

Chapter 8

Opener: Cindy Shultz, *Times Union;* **p. 65:** The Library of Congress; **p. 66:** Bharati Sadasivam.

Chapter 9

Opener: Judith Siewert; **p. 73:** Betty Tichich, *Houston Chronicle.*

Chapter 11

Opener: Spencer Tullis, *The Leader Herald,* Gloversville, N.Y.

Chapter 12

Opener: Mary Beth Meehan, *Providence Journal-Bulletin.*

Chapter 13

Opener: Jack Rendulich, *Duluth News-Tribune;* **p. 95:** Bob Thayer, *The Journal-Bulletin;* **p. 96:** The Library of Congress.

Chapter 14

Opener: CNET.

Chapter 15

Opener: Roy Karten, *City and State;* **p. 108:** Vern Herschberger, *Waco Tribune-Herald.*

Chapter 16

Opener: Joseph Reyes, Office of the Mayor.

Chapter 17

Opener: Ken Elkins, *The Anniston* (Ala.) *Star;* **p. 125:** Denver Public Library, Western History Department.

Chapter 18

Opener: Frank Robertson, *Argus Leader.*

Chapter 19

Opener: Susan Kirkman, *Akron Beacon Journal;* **p. 135:** U.S. Navy.

Chapter 20

Opener: Michael Rafferty, *Asbury Park* (N.J.) *Press.*

Chapter 21

Opener: Mary Beth Meehan, *Providence Journal-Bulletin.*

Chapter 22

Opener: Dave Einsel, *Houston Chronicle.*

Chapter 23

p. 165: The Library of Congress.

Chapter 24

Opener: Leslie Jean-Bart.

Chapter 25

Opener: Lois Bernstein, *The Sacramento Bee.*

Chapter 26

Opener: The Library of Congress; **p. 199:** UNICEF/4402/Khan.

Chapter 27

Opener: Stephen Gross, *The Anniston* (Ala.) *Star.*

Index

Exercises and Assignments

Campus Projects

Community Projects

Home Assignments